"In the Company Secretary's Office of BP, we owe a great deal of debt to Dr. Carver, and, in our opinion, his ideas on how boards should work are without equal."

—**Rodney L. Insall,** vice president of corporate governance,
British Petroleum, London

"As Mexico enters a new era, modern governance principles should be thoroughly analyzed and implemented in different areas of the government and the private sector. Dr. Carver's anthology is a convenient resource and important reference work which offers a visionary, yet practical approach to governance design."

—**Adalberto Palma Gomez,** member, board of directors, Institute for the
Protection of Bank Savings, Mexico City

"Dr. Carver is the best known and most highly regarded scholar and practitioner in the field of not-for-profit corporate governance and the leading exponent, throughout the world, of the value and necessity of improving the governance of these organizations. Indeed, he is the father of contemporary governance practices in the extremely large not-for-profit sector."

—**James M. Gillies,** professor emeritus, York University Schulich School of
Business, Toronto; author of *Boardroom Renaissance, Facing Reality,* and
Where Business Fails

"Dr. John Carver is internationally recognized as the leader in improving the governance of nonprofit organizations. His Policy Governance model has been adopted by numerous organizations on five continents. Widely considered the leading pioneer in reconceptualization of the board-executive partnership, Dr. Carver offers a visionary yet practical approach to governance design that is truly transforming, powerful, and attainable."

—**The University of Georgia Institute for Nonprofit Organizations,**
Athens, Georgia

"John is not only refreshingly revolutionary in his thinking, but he matches his bold thinking with the ability to communicate with both passion and precision. Add to these qualities his thorough professionalism and you have an individual who towers over others in the field."

—**Jerry Cianciolo,** editor, *Contributions*

"This book—bringing together material hitherto scattered throughout a myriad of different publications—is a treasure chest of inspiration and practical guidance for everyone involved with the job of governing."

> —**Caroline Oliver,** board chair, The International Policy Governance® Association

"Dr. Carver's governance model has been the key in empowering the State Bar of California Board of Governors to focus on policy that would help our judicial system and the 180,000 lawyers in California, while increasing our effectiveness and efficiency."

> —**Andrew J. Guilford,** 1999–2000 president, State Bar of California

"John Carver is the new guru of nonprofits."

> —**Books for Business,** Toronto

JOHN CARVER

ON BOARD
LEADERSHIP

JOHN CARVER
ON BOARD LEADERSHIP

SELECTED WRITINGS FROM
THE CREATOR OF THE WORLD'S
MOST PROVOCATIVE AND
SYSTEMATIC GOVERNANCE MODEL

JOHN CARVER

FOREWORD BY SIR ADRIAN CADBURY

JOSSEY-BASS
A Wiley Company
www.josseybass.com

Published by

JOSSEY-BASS
A Wiley Company
989 Market Street
San Francisco, CA 94103-1741

www.josseybass.com

Jossey-Bass books and products are available through most bookstores. To contact Jossey-Bass directly, call (888) 378–2537, fax to (800) 605–2665, or visit our website at www.josseybass.com. Substantial discounts on bulk quantities of Jossey-Bass books are available to corporations, professional associations, and other organizations. For details and discount information, contact the special sales department at Jossey-Bass.

We at Jossey-Bass strive to use the most environmentally sensitive paper stocks available to us. Our publications are printed on acid-free recycled stock whenever possible, and our paper always meets or exceeds minimum GPO and EPA requirements.

Policy Governance® is the registered service mark of John Carver.

Credits appear on p. 665.

Library of Congress Cataloging-in-Publication Data

Carver, John.
    John Carver on board leadership: selected writings from the creator of the world's most provocative and systematic governance model / John Carver; foreword by Sir Adrian Cadbury.
        p. cm.—(The Jossey-Bass nonprofit and public management series)
    Includes bibliographical references and index.
        ISBN 0–7879–5844–1
    1. Boards of directors. 2. Corporate governance. I. Title: On board leadership. II. Title: Selected writings from the creator of the world's most provocative and systematic governance model. III. Title. IV. Series.
HD2745 .C3723 2002
658.4'22—dc21   2001003770

HB Printing   10 9 8 7 6 5 4 3 2   FIRST EDITION

The Jossey-Bass
Nonprofit and Public Management Series

Contents

Frequently Asked Questions Guide   xv

Foreword   xxix
Sir Adrian Cadbury

Introduction   xxxi

About the Author   xlv

1 A Theory of Governance: The Search for Universal Principles   1

A Theory of Governing the Public's Business: Redesigning the Jobs
  of Boards, Councils, and Commissions 3

Is Policy Governance the *One* Best Way? 25

Rethinking Governance Research 29

Watch Out for Misleading Interpretations of Governance Research 35

Why Is Conceptual Wholeness So Difficult for Boards? 38

Are Boards Searching for the Holy Grail? 42

Can Things Go Horribly Wrong for Boards That Use Policy Governance? 47

2 The Moral Basis of Board Authority: Where the Chain of Command Begins   53

Ownership 55

Understanding the Special Board-Ownership Relationship 57

Determining Who Your Owners Are 66

Connecting with the Ownership 68

What to Do If You Find a Consumer on Your Board 76

Achieving Meaningful Diversity in the Boardroom 79

Making Hierarchy Work: Exercising Appropriate Board Authority in the
   Service of Mission 84

Elected Boards: Meeting Their Special Governance Challenge 89

Your Board's Market Surrogate Obligation 94

Leading, Following, and the Wisdom to Know the Difference 99

Families of Boards, Part One: Federations 104

Families of Boards, Part Two: Holding Companies 113

When Owners Are Customers: The Confusion of Dual Board Hats 121

3 Creating the Board's Single Voice: Appropriate Roles of Committees, Officers, and Individual Members   129

Creating a Single Voice: The Prerequisite to Board Leadership 131

Boards Should Have Their Own Voice 136

Protecting Board Integrity from the Renegade Board Member 142

When the Founding Parent Stays on the Board 146

The Executive Committee: Turning a Governance Liability into an Asset 150

A Team of Equals 156

Policies Я Us 160

Recruiting Leaders: What to Look for in New Board Members 164

Should Your CEO Be a Board Member? 169

What If the Committee Chair Just Wants to Know? 172

Reining In a Runaway Chair 177

Does Your Board Drive Away Its Most Promising Members? 181

A Few Tips for the Chairperson 185

Sometimes You Have to Fire Your Chair 188

What to Do with Your Board's Philosophy, Values, and Beliefs 191

Crafting the Board Job Description 196

Planning the Board's Conduct 202

4 Linking Governance to Operations: The Board-Management Connection 209

To Tell or Not to Tell: One CEO Learns the Right Way to Inform Her Board 211

Governing in the Shadow of a Founder-CEO 214

If You Want It Done Right, *Delegate It!* 218

What to Do When Staff Take Complaints Directly to Board Members 224

When Board Members Are the Only Staff in Sight 227

The CEO's Objectives Are Not Proper Board Business 231

Why Only the CEO Can Interpret the Board's Ends and Executive Limitations Policies 234

Getting It Right from the Start: The CEO's Job Description 237

Do You Really Have a CEO? 240

Does Policy Governance Give Too Much Authority to the CEO? 243

5 Putting Purpose First: Deciding, Delegating, and Demanding Organizational "Ends" 249

Boards Lead Best When Services, Programs, and Curricula Are Transparent 251

A Community Board Struggles with the Cost of Its Results 255

Beware the "Quality" Fetish 260

First Things First 263

Evaluating the Mission Statement 268

The Board of a Trade Association Establishes Ends Policies 274

A Public School Board Establishes Ends Policies 281

A City Council Creates Ends Policies 288

A Hospital Board Creates Ends Policies 293

6 Safely Avoiding Micromanagement: Staff Freedom Within Defined Limits 299

Free Your Board and Staff Through Executive Limitations 301

Making Informed Fiscal Policy 305

Running Afoul of Governance 308

Crafting Policy to Safeguard Your Organization's Actual Fiscal Condition 311

Crafting Policy to Guide Your Organization's Budget 316

Fiduciary Responsibility 327

Redefining the Board's Role in Fiscal Planning 330

7 What the Board's Words Mean: Harnessing Interpretation for Control and Empowerment 345

The "Any Reasonable Interpretation" Rule: Leap of Faith or Sine Qua Non of Delegation? 347

Boards Should Be Not the Final Authority but the Initial Authority 353

Abstracting Up: Discovering the Big Issues Among the Trivia 357

Who's in Charge? Is Your Organization Too Staff-Driven? Too Volunteer-Driven? 361

Never Cast in Stone: Flexible Policy Supports Management and Saves Board Time 368

Policy Governance Is Not a "Hands Off" Model 371

8 When the Board Meets: Products, Process, Discipline, and Costs 377

Is Your Board in a Rut? Shake Up Your Routine! 379

Why Not Set Your Quorum Requirement at 100 Percent? 382

Owning Your Agenda: A Long-Term View Is the Key to Taking Charge 387

Calculating the Real Costs of Governance 390

The Consent Agenda and Responsible Rubber-Stamping 393

9 Assuring Board and Management Performance: Measurement, Evaluation, and Discipline 397

Painful Lessons: Learning from the United Way Misfortune 399

One Board Fails to Follow Its Own Monitoring Policy—and Courts Fiscal Disaster 405

The Misguided Focus on Administrative Cost 408

A Simple Matter of Comparison: Monitoring Fiscal Management in Your Organization 413

Board Approvals and Monitoring Are Very Different Actions 419

Giving Measurement Its Due in Policy Governance 424

Honey, I Shrunk the Policies 427

The Mechanics of Direct Inspection Monitoring 429

Redefining Board Self-Evaluation: The Key to Keeping on Track 434

Living Up to Your Own Expectations: Implementing Self-Evaluation to Make a Difference in Your Organization 437

The Importance of Trust in the Board-CEO Relationship 444

Evaluating the CEO: An Effective Approach to Ensure Future Organizational Success 448

Putting CEO Evaluation in Perspective 450

Off Limits: What Not to Do in Your CEO Evaluation 460

A CEO Self-Evaluation Checklist 462

10 Safeguarding Governance Viability for the Long Term 465

What to Do When All Your Policies Are in Place 467

Nine Steps to Implementing Policy Governance 472

Shaping Up Your Bylaws 479

What Happens to Conventional Documents Under Policy Governance? 486

How You Can Tell When Your Board Is Not Using Policy Governance 492

CEOs! Guiding Your Board Toward Better Governance 496

Policy Governance Won't Work Because . . . 500

Protecting Governance from Law, Funders, and Accreditors 504

11 When Governing Boards Perform Nongoverning Roles 509

When Board Members Act as Staff Advisors 511

Tips for Creating Advisory Boards and Committees 516

Giving, Getting, and Governing: Finding a Place for Fundraising Among the Responsibilities of Leadership 519

Girl Scout Council Learns What Kind of Help Counts the Most 523

Board Members as Amateur CEOs 526

12 Policy Governance for Specific Audiences   529

Remaking Governance 531

Toward Coherent Governance 540

Partnership for Public Service 548

Governing Parks and Recreation 560

Education Accountability and Legislative Oversight 565

New Means to an End 576

Reinventing Governance 579

To Focus on Shaping the Future, Many Hospital Boards Might Require a
    Radical Overhaul 589

Corporate Governance Model from an Unexpected Source—Nonprofits 595

A Theory of Corporate Governance: Finding a New Balance for Boards and
    Their CEOs 602

The Opportunity for Reinventing Corporate Governance in
    Joint Venture Companies 614

What Use Is Business Experience on a Nonprofit or Governmental Board? 625

Seizing the Governance Opportunity for Central European NGOs 634

Building an Infrastructure of Governance in Eastern Europe 638

References   645

Index   653

Frequently Asked Questions
GUIDE

**What Is Wrong with Established Governance Practices,
and What Should a Model of Governance Do?**

What should a model of governance do? ➥ SEE PAGES **26, 46**

Why is governance necessary? ➥ SEE PAGES **8, 31**

What are the essential characteristics of boards? ➥ SEE PAGE **43**

What are the elements of governance effectiveness? ➥ SEE PAGE **33**

What do elected boards and nonprofit boards have in common? ➥ SEE PAGE **89**

Is it important for the board to know whether it is governing a federation or a
holding company? ➥ SEE PAGE **104**

How is governance different from management? ➥ SEE PAGE **156**

In what respects is corporate governance an inappropriate role model for nonprofit
governance? ➥ SEE PAGE **171**

What do elected boards have in common? ➥ SEE PAGE **288**

What is the weakest link in public education? ➥ SEE PAGE **565**

What is wrong with traditional governance? ➥ SEE PAGE **580**

Is there a fundamental difference between governance and management?
➥ SEE PAGE **581**

What should government funders require of nonprofit governance? ➥ SEE PAGE 556

What is missing from corporate governance? ➥ SEE PAGE 596

What is the difference between nonprofit or public boards and business boards?
➥ SEE PAGES 95, 628

What does nonprofit governance have to do with democracy? ➥ SEE PAGES 634, 636, 639

What does a nonprofit have to do with the civil society? ➥ SEE PAGES 636, 641

How can state departments of education help improve local governance?
➥ SEE PAGE 572

What Is the Policy Governance Model?

How does traditional representational governance fit with Policy Governance?
➥ SEE PAGE 60

Is there a philosophical basis for Policy Governance? ➥ SEE PAGE 10

How was the Policy Governance model developed? ➥ SEE PAGE 338

Has research shown that Policy Governance is better than other approaches?
➥ SEE PAGES 30, 35

How can Policy Governance be the "one size" that "fits all"? ➥ SEE PAGE 43

What other governance models are available? ➥ SEE PAGE 4

Isn't the hierarchical nature of Policy Governance out of step with modern
participative organizational styles? ➥ SEE PAGE 84

Why doesn't Policy Governance encourage boards to have a vision statement?
➥ SEE PAGE 194

Under Policy Governance, do ends always justify means? ➥ SEE PAGE 631

Why doesn't Policy Governance use standard terms like *goals* and *objectives*?
➥ SEE PAGE 15

How does Policy Governance differentiate between what the board says and what
staff says? ➥ SEE PAGE 138

Does Policy Governance work for a board with no staff? ➥ SEE PAGE 227

To Whom Is the Board Accountable?

What does *ownership* mean? ➥ SEE PAGE 590

What is the role of an advocacy group in effective governance? ➥ SEE PAGE 6

To whom is a board accountable? ➡ SEE PAGE 58

Where does the board get its authority? ➡ SEE PAGE 58

Is *owner* just another name for *stakeholder*? ➡ SEE PAGE 59

What if the customers and owners are the same people? ➡ SEE PAGES 62, 121, 274

Is it possible to have more than one group of owners? ➡ SEE PAGE 67

Can the diversity of the ownership be represented by the diversity of the board members? ➡ SEE PAGE 80

How can a board be sure that it truly represents its ownership? ➡ SEE PAGE 81

How does the CEO deal with members-as-owners in a federation? ➡ SEE PAGE 109

What is the line of authority in a holding company? ➡ SEE PAGE 116

Why does the board's acting as "final authority" damage delegation? ➡ SEE PAGE 353

What is the appropriate way for owners to exercise their authority? ➡ SEE PAGE 362

What Is Board Holism?

If board members disagree, how can they possibly speak with one voice?
➡ SEE PAGES 82, 157, 501

How can a board ensure that it speaks as a whole? ➡ SEE PAGE 133

How does the Policy Governance model prevent unacceptable behavior of individual board members? ➡ SEE PAGE 143

How can a board effectively use individual expertise to develop policy?
➡ SEE PAGE 306

What Is the Role of Committees in Board Governance?

Why does the Policy Governance model see board committees in such an unfavorable light? ➡ SEE PAGES 22, 150, 583

Under Policy Governance, what happens to considerations of having an executive committee? ➡ SEE PAGE 154

Is there any appropriate role for a finance committee under Policy Governance?
➡ SEE PAGE 173

Should a board create committees to help the CEO? ➡ SEE PAGE 220

Why shouldn't the accountant, personnel professional, and marketing expert on the board chair the finance, human resources, and marketing committees, respectively? ➡ SEE PAGE 512

What conditions force a board to authorize an executive committee to make board decisions between board meetings? ➡ SEE PAGE 152

What Are Organizational Ends?

What exactly is meant by *ends*? ➡ SEE PAGE 551

What are a board's *products*? ➡ SEE PAGE 373

How can a board really know what the products of their organization are worth? ➡ SEE PAGE 96

What could ends for a federation look like? ➡ SEE PAGE 110

What if a board doesn't have enough resources to meet the needs in the community? ➡ SEE PAGE 521

Under Policy Governance, why do an organization's statements of vision, values, and philosophy need to be reworked? ➡ SEE PAGE 191

Are the board's ends policies the same as the CEO's goals? ➡ SEE PAGE 232

Can you really separate ends from means? ➡ SEE PAGE 252

Shouldn't a board determine its ends "one program at a time?" ➡ SEE PAGE 253

Since it's difficult to determine the ultimate purpose of an organization, how can a board jump-start its thinking about ends? ➡ SEE PAGE 265

Are organizational ends always stable? ➡ SEE PAGE 467

What is meant by the term *mega-ends*? ➡ SEE PAGE 256

Does a board need to frame its mega-ends statement in such a way that results can be measured? ➡ SEE PAGE 276

What is the relationship between an organization's mission and the board's ends? ➡ SEE PAGE 269

What guidelines will help our board draft effective ends? ➡ SEE PAGE 275

What is the difference between strategic plans and ends? ➡ SEE PAGE 488

How does the board ensure that the organization has a customer focus? ➡ SEE PAGE 63

How does the board deal with customer concerns? ➡ SEE PAGE 71

What Is the Role of Board Policies?

How do Policy Governance policies differentiate board values from staff values? ➡ SEE PAGE 163

How does a board develop board policies? ➡ SEE PAGE 16

What is the logical containment principle? ➡ SEE PAGES 17, 599

How do Policy Governance policies differ from conventional board policies? ➡ SEE PAGE 20

How can an organization's statements of vision, values, and philosophy be integrated into Policy Governance policy? ➡ SEE PAGE 192

How much information does a board need to develop effective ends policies? ➡ SEE PAGE 287

Does the level of detail developed in ends policies determine their value and power? ➡ SEE PAGE 284

How should a board word its mega-ends policies? ➡ SEE PAGE 289

Is it important for the level of detail in every ends policy to be consistent? ➡ SEE PAGE 297

Doesn't writing board policies in the negative set a bad tone? ➡ SEE PAGE 303

How can relatively few board policies possibly cover everything? ➡ SEE PAGES 15, 358

Why is it best to develop policy "from the largest to the smallest"? ➡ SEE PAGE 359

If a policy does not cover an unforeseen situation—like a one-time expense—should the board simply make an exception? ➡ SEE PAGE 368

Does Policy Governance provide for one-time exceptions in policy? ➡ SEE PAGE 369

How can policies cover a broad range of eventualities without becoming mired in details? ➡ SEE PAGE 369

What's the relationship between the board's policies and my organization's bylaws? ➡ SEE PAGE 479

When a board adopts Policy Governance, what happens to its previous policies? ➡ SEE PAGE 562

What's wrong with traditional policy? ➡ SEE PAGE 591

What Should the Board Look Like and Who Should Serve?

When board members are elected or appointed, how can the board ensure getting members with qualities that contribute to the board's success? ➡ SEE PAGE 165

Shouldn't board members be chosen for their management expertise? ➡ SEE PAGE 23

What are some criteria for choosing board members? ➡ SEE PAGE 102

Who are the best candidates for Policy Governance board membership?
    ➡ SEE PAGE 166

How can desirable board member characteristics be codified in policy and practice?
    ➡ SEE PAGE 168

Can businesspeople bring special skills to nonprofit and governmental boards?
    ➡ SEE PAGE 630

Is it ever appropriate to deter people from serving on the board? ➡ SEE PAGE 181

What board characteristics are unattractive to promising leaders? ➡ SEE PAGE 182

Won't a larger board mean there is greater diversity in governance? ➡ SEE PAGE 81

What is wrong with the traditional board member job descriptions?
    ➡ SEE PAGE 197

Are boards only as strong as their members? ➡ SEE PAGE 569

What is the effect of frequent turnover in board members? ➡ SEE PAGE 48

What Is the Board's Job?

How can a board use hierarchy appropriately? ➡ SEE PAGE 87

How can the chair lead the board effectively? ➡ SEE PAGE 185

How should a board gather input from its ownership? ➡ SEE PAGE 71

How can the board practice active listening? ➡ SEE PAGE 100

How can federation board members ensure they look beyond their own
    organization's point of view? ➡ SEE PAGE 107

How does a board member deal with constituency expectations? ➡ SEE PAGES 18,
    77, 99, 538

How can a school board be accountable for the performance of a school district
    without becoming involved in the details of its management? ➡ SEE PAGE 535

Do the boards of nonprofit and for-profit organizations have different jobs?
    ➡ SEE PAGE 94

Why shouldn't the chairperson supervise the CEO? ➡ SEE PAGES 178, 241

What is the relationship between the board chair and the CEO? ➡ SEE PAGE 593

What does the board need to know about an organization in order to govern it effectively? ➡ SEE PAGE 102

On what subjects should a board officially speak? ➡ SEE PAGE 140

What if board members just want to know about some aspect of operations? ➡ SEE PAGE 174

What can be done about an intimidating board member who assumes executive authority? ➡ SEE PAGE 147

Shouldn't a board be concerned with the quality of the services the organization provides? ➡ SEE PAGE 260

Under Policy Governance, what duties should *not* concern the board? ➡ SEE PAGE 375

Should a board be held accountable for *all* staff behavior? ➡ SEE PAGE 400

How can a board lead an organization, instead of being carried along by events? ➡ SEE PAGE 553

Isn't the board's job to run the organization? ➡ SEE PAGE 561

With whom should the board communicate most frequently? ➡ SEE PAGE 573

Is the board's primary relationship with the CEO? ➡ SEE PAGE 582

Does the board have any role in means decisions? ➡ SEE PAGE 591

Who determines the board's means? ➡ SEE PAGE 599

Who is responsible for the board getting its job done? ➡ SEE PAGE 635

Shouldn't a board be involved in an organization? Isn't it the board's job to know what's going on? ➡ SEE PAGE 629

What is wrong with a board's approving CEO recommendations and reports? ➡ SEE PAGE 583

In Policy Governance, why does the board not approve staff plans such as personnel policies? ➡ SEE PAGE 420

Should a board ever determine or approve staff means? ➡ SEE PAGE 302

How does a board keep a CEO from abusing personality-based power? ➡ SEE PAGE 216

How does the board ensure that the founder's dream lasts? ➡ SEE PAGE 217

What if a board member has seen or been told about something wrong going on? ➡ SEE PAGE 225

What Is the Nature of Board Delegation to the Staff?

How can the board control operational decisions without making them?
➝ SEE PAGE 599

Since operational decisions are delegated to the CEO, how does the board deal with important, expensive, or politically charged decisions? ➝ SEE PAGE 212

Can the board of a self-governing profession delegate professional discipline to the CEO? ➝ SEE PAGES 219, 221

How do staff members understand the new relationship between the board and CEO under Policy Governance? ➝ SEE PAGE 226

What is the "any reasonable interpretation" rule? ➝ SEE PAGE 235

How much authority should be given to the CEO? ➝ SEE PAGE 238

Are executive limitations a set of minimal requirements? ➝ SEE PAGE 308

How can a board keep executive limitations from becoming a policing function?
➝ SEE PAGE 310

What happens when the "reasonable interpretation rule" isn't followed?
➝ SEE PAGE 349

Doesn't the Policy Governance model require too much confidence in the CEO?
➝ SEE PAGE 350

How specific should a board get in limiting interpretation? ➝ SEE PAGE 351

With so few policies, isn't the board giving over too much control to the CEO?
➝ SEE PAGE 427

How can a board ensure there is a high level of trust in the board-CEO relationship?
➝ SEE PAGE 445

Aren't the board and staff partners? ➝ SEE PAGE 86

Can board members instruct staff below the CEO under Policy Governance?
➝ SEE PAGE 583

Who interprets board policies on ends and executive limitations? ➝ SEE PAGE 592

How can a board assure it hears what it would like to know, without micromanaging? ➝ SEE PAGE 175

How can boards keep from meddling with staff means? ➝ SEE PAGE 163

What is the purpose of having broadly stated limitations on staff means?
➝ SEE PAGE 303

What if an employee bypasses the CEO and makes an end run to a board member?
➤ SEE PAGE 225

What are the proper chair and CEO roles in business? ➤ SEE PAGE 611

Should Board Members Advise Staff or Volunteer?

Should the CEO ever ask individual board members for advice? ➤ SEE PAGE 304

How can staff know that board advice is not actually veiled instruction?
➤ SEE PAGE 518

Who should create board-to-staff advisory bodies? ➤ SEE PAGE 517

If board members feel that they have useful advice for staff, should they offer it
directly? ➤ SEE PAGE 514

Can staff safely ignore advice and instructions from individual school board
trustees? ➤ SEE PAGE 534

What is the proper role for volunteers? ➤ SEE PAGE 361

Can board members also volunteer their time in the organization? ➤ SEE PAGE 525

We can't expect a CEO to know everything, so why shouldn't volunteers help?
➤ SEE PAGE 365

Is it appropriate for volunteers to report to paid staff? Shouldn't volunteers report
directly to the board? ➤ SEE PAGE 366

Why shouldn't the board help its staff manage? ➤ SEE PAGE 526

What Is the Staff's Job?

What are *staff means*? ➤ SEE PAGE 302

What are the advantages of having a CEO? ➤ SEE PAGE 241

What should a CEO job description look like? ➤ SEE PAGE 238

How does the CEO inform the board of significant operational decisions or
changes? ➤ SEE PAGE 213

What is the CEO's role in support of the board speaking with one voice?
➤ SEE PAGE 134

Is there any difference between an executive director (general manager, president,
etc.) and a CEO? ➤ SEE PAGE 206

Whom does the school superintendent work for—the board or the public? → SEE PAGE 544

Why does the school superintendent's job exist? → SEE PAGE 546

What are the expectations of the school superintendent under Policy Governance? → SEE PAGE 543

Is it fair to blame poor school performance on the school superintendent? → SEE PAGE 533

Whose job is it to run schools and the school system? → SEE PAGE 541

Under Policy Governance, what can a CEO do about board members who abuse their position? → SEE PAGE 179

What can the CEO do to support better governance? → SEE PAGE 463

Is the CEO responsible for board performance? → SEE PAGE 582

How can CEOs encourage boards to better define their role? → SEE PAGE 584

Can the CEO lead the board in adopting policy governance? → SEE PAGE 496

As CEO, what should I start doing to reinforce Policy Governance? → SEE PAGE 498

Can staff members help the board determine the organization's ends? → SEE PAGE 265

What is the staff's role in creating the board's policies? → SEE PAGE 577

Are CEOs better off with Policy Governance? → SEE PAGE 578

How can the CEO avoid dragging the board into managerial details? → SEE PAGE 213

What Should Board Meetings and Agendas Look Like?

Should boards hear monitoring reports about executive limitations at meetings? → SEE PAGE 310

What can a board do if it is losing good board members simply because its meetings are boring? → SEE PAGE 380

What would a school board meeting look like under Policy Governance? → SEE PAGE 537

We have trouble getting good attendance at board meetings because emergencies always seem to come up. What can we do? → SEE PAGE 385

How can we deal with board members who repeatedly fail to show up for board meetings? → SEE PAGE 386

Why is it important to have good attendance at board meetings? ➡ SEE PAGE 385

Isn't it important, for consistency, to have a board meeting every month, in the same place, with a similar agenda? ➡ SEE PAGE 379

Should the CEO put together the board's agenda? ➡ SEE PAGE 387

What role should a chair have in determining the board's agenda? ➡ SEE PAGE 388

How Should a Board Conduct Self-Evaluation?

How does the Policy Governance approach to board evaluation differ from more traditional approaches? ➡ SEE PAGE 438

What criteria should a board use to evaluate its own performance? ➡ SEE PAGE 435

How often should the board do a self-evaluation? ➡ SEE PAGE 436

Are there some guidelines a board can follow in doing a self-evaluation?
➡ SEE PAGE 438

How does a board ensure the integrity of its own conduct? ➡ SEE PAGE 203

How Should a Board Monitor and Evaluate CEO Performance?

How does CEO evaluation fit into the overall system of Policy Governance?
➡ SEE PAGE 456

How does a board handle concerns about CEO competence? ➡ SEE PAGE 242

How can a board evaluate the CEO's performance without evaluating achievement of operational objectives? ➡ SEE PAGE 233

Who sets the criteria for CEO performance—the board or the CEO? ➡ SEE PAGE 232

What information does a board need in order to monitor the CEO? ➡ SEE PAGE 406

What is the difference between direct inspection monitoring and traditional approval? ➡ SEE PAGE 431

What should the board do if a direct inspection uncovers noncompliance?
➡ SEE PAGE 432

What criteria should the board use for CEO evaluation? ➡ SEE PAGE 451

How can the board determine when it is ready to proceed with the ongoing process of evaluating the CEO? ➡ SEE PAGE 454

How can the board ensure that its process for evaluating the CEO is fair?
➤ SEE PAGE 457

When evaluating a CEO, is there ever a time when it is appropriate to seek input from staff, clients, or the public? ➤ SEE PAGE 461

How does the board assess CEO and organizational performance? ➤ SEE PAGE 593

How does a board cope with the inherent imprecision of measuring certain ends?
➤ SEE PAGE 629

What does the board do if the CEO violates its policies? ➤ SEE PAGE 453

How can the board protect against the CEO being too powerful? ➤ SEE PAGE 245

What Is the Board's Fiduciary Responsibility with Regard to Finances, Fundraising, and Budgets?

What is the board's role in fundraising? ➤ SEE PAGE 520

Why should the budget and "actual" fiscal condition be treated independently?
➤ SEE PAGE 312

What fiscal conditions should concern the board? ➤ SEE PAGE 313

What is the board's role in budgeting? ➤ SEE PAGE 414

What aspects of the budget are of legitimate concern to the board? ➤ SEE PAGE 341

Do budget numbers have governance value? ➤ SEE PAGES 321, 334

What must the board do before the CEO can develop a budget? ➤ SEE PAGE 315

What is the relationship between ends and budget? ➤ SEE PAGE 323

What is wrong with board approval of budgets? ➤ SEE PAGE 331

Why is budget approval a poor way to demonstrate fiduciary responsibility?
➤ SEE PAGE 316

How do traditional financial approval practices disempower boards and management? ➤ SEE PAGE 328

What is the best way to monitor actual performance? ➤ SEE PAGE 414

Does using a finance committee to examine the budget improve governance?
➤ SEE PAGE 320

How can fiduciary responsibility be achieved without a treasurer or finance committee? ➤ SEE PAGE 328

Is it OK to let a financial expert on the board advise the board on whether to accept financial reports? ➡ SEE PAGE **305**

What constitutes monitoring information? ➡ SEE PAGE **416**

How does the board get monitoring information? ➡ SEE PAGES **416, 429**

How can nonaccountant board members be assured they understand the monitoring data? ➡ SEE PAGE **417**

What does *bottom line* mean in a government or nonprofit organization? ➡ SEE PAGE **628**

Does the Policy Governance model really require boards to forget about numbers and measurement? ➡ SEE PAGE **425**

How can a board effectively represent its ownership when it is under more immediate pressure from an accrediting organization? ➡ SEE PAGE **505**

How can the public be sure that its money is well spent? ➡ SEE PAGE **551**

Doesn't tying costs to results entangle a board in fiscal management? ➡ SEE PAGE **255**

What types of costs should a board be concerned about? ➡ SEE PAGES **257, 392, 410**

What are the "hidden costs" of governance? ➡ SEE PAGE **391**

How can a board cost an outcome without determining the cost of all the activities producing it? ➡ SEE PAGES **258, 261**

What Are the Most Common Problems in Implementing and Sustaining Policy Governance?

How can the board ensure the maintenance of Policy Governance? ➡ SEE PAGE **435**

What are the most common obstacles to the implementation of Policy Governance? ➡ SEE PAGE **40**

Does the Policy Governance model cure all board problems? ➡ SEE PAGE **48**

Are certain corporate circumstances particularly conducive to Policy Governance acceptance? ➡ SEE PAGE **616**

If, by law, the board must approve personnel actions, purchases, or budgets, can it still use Policy Governance? ➡ SEE PAGES **140, 395**

Is it all right if we gradually ease ourselves into adopting Policy Governance? ➡ SEE PAGE **472**

How many members of a board need to agree before Policy Governance can be adopted? ➞ SEE PAGE **474**

Once we've adopted Policy Governance, do we shed our previous policies and procedures? ➞ SEE PAGE **486**

Can a board improve its leadership by applying only portions of the Policy Governance model? ➞ SEE PAGE **493**

What are the greatest challenges that a large public organization will face in implementing the Policy Governance model? ➞ SEE PAGE **557**

Isn't it risky for a public institution to adopt Policy Governance? ➞ SEE PAGE **559**

If a board's commitment to Policy Governance has waned, what steps can the board take to recommit to excellence? ➞ SEE PAGE **189**

How can a board overcome serious governance flaws without unreasonable time commitments? ➞ SEE PAGE **404**

What happens when there is ambiguity about whether an organization is a federation or a holding company? ➞ SEE PAGE **114**

What special challenges do federation boards face? ➞ SEE PAGE **106**

Does the Policy Governance model cure all board problems? ➞ SEE PAGE **48**

Foreword

THE IMPORTANCE of John Carver's writings in relation to governance is that they fill a crucial gap in our approach to determining the true purpose, and method of working, of boards of all kinds. The present worldwide focus on governance has nudged boards toward a clearer understanding of what they should and—equally relevant—what they should not be doing. The drawback of the spate of governance initiatives of recent years, however, is that they have lacked an agreed starting point. What has been missing is an agreement on what boards are for, whom they should be serving, and what distinguishes governance from management. Such an understanding is the essential building block on which advice on governance needs to be based if it is to be consistent and self-reinforcing.

What I value about John Carver's thinking is that it provides a logical and coherent base from which to evaluate any form of board. In that sense it is a unifying theory of governance that covers both the corporate and the voluntary sectors. We have tended to treat governance issues as individual instances to be resolved on their own merits and in their own particular context. John Carver has shown how such issues can be analyzed and treated on a universal and consistent basis in accordance with an integrated theory of governance.

This is not only intellectually satisfying but it will ensure, where his thinking is followed, that governance counseling and training will be consistent and will assist board members to become more effective in their role. In the absence of an integrated theory of governance, the risk is that board counseling and training will be inconsistent and therefore often misdirected.

John Carver has given the task of raising levels of board effectiveness a much-needed sense of direction. His Policy Governance model positions the board as the bridge between those to whom the board is accountable and those who are accountable to the board. The board primarily looks outward to those whose aims it is there to serve. Its job is to design policies that will ensure that those aims are met. Boards are in place to govern, not to manage. Governance involves setting the ends for which an organization exists and the boundaries within which it must work in achieving them. Management is concerned with how those aims are to be met within the system of values that the board has adopted.

John Carver's distinction between ends and means is all embracing; it can be applied to any type of board or organization. It provides a universal definition of the difference between governance and management rather than the more usual approach of attempting to allocate functions between them. His theory of governance has positive and practical applications in all manner of institutions and situations. In one of his essays, he appositely quotes Kurt Lewin's conclusion that "there is nothing so practical as a good theory." This book proves that point.

This collection of John Carver's writings, not all of which have been easily accessible before, brings home the intellectual rigor of his thinking and the coherence of his approach to governance, which is summarized in the Policy Governance model. It is a volume that will be warmly welcomed by everyone with a stake in the improved governance of our institutions, and it will provide a rich mine of ideas for practitioners and researchers alike to quarry.

Knowle, Solihull, West Midlands, U.K.   Sir Adrian Cadbury
August 2001

Note: Sir Adrian Cadbury was chairman of the Committee on Financial Aspects of Corporate Governance in the U.K. (The "Cadbury Report"), author of *The Company Chairman*, director of the Bank of England, chairman of Cadbury-Schweppes, Chancellor of Aston University, and Honorary Fellow, King's College, Cambridge.

Introduction

If we do not concern ourselves with how we can rule organizations, the organizations will rule us.

J. K. Louden, *The Effective Director in Action,* p. 117

A S YOU READ this introduction and, indeed, as I write it, competence beyond my understanding is at work in the world's organizations. Thanks to the organizations I've served as consultant, I'm acquainted with a small part of that amazing spectrum of competence: A nuclear engineer hourly calculates the cooling requirements of an operating atomic power plant. A classroom teacher conveys an idea, steering skillfully around a student's learning disability. A technician repairs the electronics of a hospital's MRI. An analyst working in a pension fund assesses risks inherent in a stock purchase. A journalist creates a carefully crafted layout of educational content in a trade association magazine. A police officer risks her own life to balance enforcement and courtesy. A research scientist struggles to produce new knowledge in the cellular biology of cancer. A dedicated worker, using an obscure language, brings well-digging technology to an underdeveloped country. A psychotherapist exercises dazzling insight to free a troubled soul from social dysfunction and mental anguish. A physicist adjusts a cyclotron producing a radioactive medical product.

The list goes on as far as the human talent it represents—and I have been honored to observe some of it in action. The world is at work. And a substantial amount of this work is governed by boards.

Most of my experience, however, isn't really with these impressive skills, for they are found inside the organizations whose missions embrace them. My experience is largely with the boards that govern these organizations. Boards of business corporations. Boards of nonprofit agencies and associations. Boards of cities and other political entities. A board ordinarily does not do the work of an organization, it governs what that work will be. *Govern*—the word bespeaks authority, the highest authority in an organization. When the world works as it should, the word also bespeaks accountability, the greatest measure of accountability in the organization to be commensurate with the greatest authority. Yet when I first became a student of governance, it became obvious that something was—and today still is—amiss with the accountability of boards.

Typically, all workers in an organization are clearer about their jobs than is the board that governs their work. The accountant, the nurse, the janitor, the airline pilot—they know the objectives, the appropriate conduct, the reporting relationships, the required skills, and the discipline attendant to their jobs. Boards are typically confused and deficient in all these areas. It is not that board members are less intelligent or less dedicated. In fact, sometimes boards are composed of just the kind of skilled, committed, experienced persons whose day jobs I've just extolled. The problem is that the governing role is "one of the least studied in the entire spectrum of industrial activities" (Juran and Louden, 1966, p. 7) and that boards are "often little more than high-powered, well-intentioned people engaged in low-level activities" (Chait, Holland, and Taylor, 1996, p. 1).

My personal experience confirms these assessments and often underscores the grievous human cost of traditional board processes. I have seen CEOs destroyed by the gut-wrenching dynamics that occur when boards judge on criteria they've never stated. Where CEOs have fought back after capricious dismissals, I have seen donors' hard-earned contributions wasted by boards defending resultant suits. I have seen boards that take no responsibility for the illegitimately intrusive behavior of renegade members, thus sacrificing the organization to a few board members' need to treat organizations as their personal toys. I have also seen boards manipulated and stage-managed by their CEOs, sometimes even frankly misled, while their boards default on their obligations to lead. I have seen organizations that are not compelled to find ever better ways to produce results for their consumers because their boards reward activity, not results. I have seen organizations whose stewardship of the donated wealth of contributors or the forced "donations" of taxpayers is next to nonexistent, even though all the accounting is in order. I have seen board members whose political or personal self-interest makes servant-leadership seem like a naive ideal. I have seen well-intended, intelligent board members whose potential contribution is thwarted by the mediocre activities they continue to be taught is the proper substance of governance. I have been amazed when board members say system improvement isn't warranted because "everything is going well now"—the same board members who in their market-tested business would never accept today's effectiveness to be sufficient for tomorrow's challenges. I have been amazed to hear a respected faculty member of a top university say that nonprofit boards are pretty good the way they are.

I am not alone in my unflattering observations about boards ("largely irrelevant," Gillies, 1992; "ornaments," Mace, 1971; and, most picturesquely, "ants on a log in turbulent water who think they are steering the log," quoted from an unnamed source by Leighton and Thain, 1997). Of course, the most famous damnation was Drucker's "they do not function" (1974). As my interest grew in boards in the mid-1970s, the attention of others was also turning to board roles, responsibilities, and effectiveness. Over the intervening years, discussion of boards has risen to a crescendo in business, nonprofit, and governmental arenas. Writers, such as myself, turned out exhortations at an increasing pace. Researchers took notice. If research can resolve the most effective cardiovascular training, treatment for schizophrenia, and auto emission control, can it not find the route to board effectiveness?

Board Effectiveness—The Muddled Debate

Let's get the stark truth out right away: No approach to governance by a governing board has been shown by credible, replicated research to be most effective.

In view of the extreme authority wielded by boards, their long history, and the two decades of steadily growing interest in them, the lack of research is incredible. Graduate schools, by and large, have not flocked to the issue. Business schools have ignored corporate boards. Schools of public administration, social work, health administration, and others have been slow to focus on anything higher than management. But negligible research does not mean no research. The number of published articles and books on the topic has grown. But we still have no definitive research on board effectiveness. Why?

I believe the reason is that we haven't figured out what we want governance to accomplish. That is, we don't agree on what boards are for. And it is impossible to research whether one or another method is more effective when we haven't gotten together on what they should be effective at! If a board is to raise funds, we can find what methods are more effective. If a board is to advise staff, we can find what produces the most useful advice. If a board is to find glitches in financial reports, we can find how that can best be done. But in each case, we must start with the purpose first or research on effectiveness is meaningless.

There appears to be little agreement on what boards are for, at least judging from actions people take. For some, the purpose of a board is to fulfill what the law or regulators require of boards. For others, the purpose of a board is to satisfy the managers; or to satisfy people who come to watch board meetings; or to satisfy a large contributor or major shareholder; or to satisfy board members with meaningful involvement; or to satisfy current clients, students, or patients, or other customers. These reference groups yield very different tests of board effectiveness.

So discovering what is "most effective" requires knowing what boards should produce. Deciding upon what boards should produce depends on our framing of the matter, our sense of why governance exists. In other words, what precedes effectiveness research is governance theory—said by some corporate governance writers (Mueller, 1996; Leighton and Thain, 1997, p. 29) not to exist! So it was that I determined some years ago, despite my own doctoral training in human behavior research, that the primary missing link in the governance quandary was not research but credible theory.

The Policy Governance model, which I developed beginning a quarter century ago, is often criticized for not being founded in research. Of course it isn't. It could not have been. Research is good at testing what is, but it is less inspiring at creating what isn't. The Policy Governance model was a leap of insight, a philosophical endeavor, not a research finding. The Policy Governance model was not discovered; it was invented.

Producing a Theory of Governance— Reaching for the Universal

The Policy Governance model became the first—and, arguably, still the only—theory of governance in the world. Theory it is, but not without a great deal of concrete experience behind its inception. I had been a chief executive working for boards for ten years, had created and chaired a national organization, and had served on numerous local boards. I had walked the walk, but was appalled at the conceptual fragmentation of what I was doing.

Why should the conduct of governance not be as impeccable as we expect school bus maintenance, surgery, accounting, and roof repair to be? Why should boards exhibit less responsibility than they require of the people who work for them? Why should the parts of an organization make more sense than the whole? Why must the most powerful organizational unit be the least studied, least developed, and least rational? Why should boards be excused from taking responsibility for their own jobs, a default viewed as acceptable by Herman and Heimovics (1991) and even by Drucker (1990)? Must mediocrity be acceptable just because it is the norm?

Holland chided prescriptive governance modeling as "idealized, even romanticized" (1991, p. 26). Herman (1989b) dismissed an appeal like mine for being a "heroic" board model. Admittedly, the competence and leadership I call for in the governance role, if compared to today's standards, may well seem idealized and romanticized. That is the burden of introducing a new order of things. But, given the massive accountabilities and powers of boards, why should we not expect heroic performance? Do we have any right to accept less?

Consider employees whose pension fund board controls billions of dollars of their retirement savings. Consider a school board whose actions affect the future of thousands of young people. Consider literally trillions of dollars of the world's wealth and millions of lives all to a considerable degree under the control of boards. How exactly are we to excuse anything less than heroic? Yet virtually without question we countenance far less competence in boards than we demand in pilots, surgeons, and cosmetologists. Must we really shoot so low?

Historically, however, we've not been short on using heroic words. Commonly accepted platitudes about boards being visionary leaders that deal with policy and delegate clearly have been unmasked as hollow rhetoric by recent writers. But why must that embarrassing revelation induce us to settle for a less heroic role, rather than to rally 'round the challenge to fulfill it. Having found that boards had feet of clay, governance writers were quick to adopt clay as a proper building material. If there is any chance that boards might fulfill the high hopes of servant-leadership (Greenleaf, 1991), is it not incumbent on us to try before throwing in the towel? Must we give up so easily when we haven't even tried the approach of better theory? And if there is no governance theory, I reasoned in the mid-1970s, why not create one?

Governance *theory*, of course, implies a degree of universality. A theory that fits only one board isn't very helpful. Can theory fit just mental health boards or trade associations? How about a theory that works for all nonprofits? But why stop there? Indeed, is it possible to find a universal theory that is truly universal—one that offers a paradigm for governing boards of any endeavor and in any land? A universal theory must cover all instances of board governance, yet have no more parts than necessary. Einstein's wisdom to "make everything as simple as possible, but not simpler" would certainly have to apply.

It is only right that justification is required of extraordinary claims. But when we start to examine the actual functioning of boards, the claims of Policy Governance begin to lose their air of radicalism, and might better be described as organized common sense. For example, all observers of boards would agree that a board should know its role as distinguished from other roles (such as the CEO's). They would undoubtedly agree that governing boards are accountable for the organizations they govern. They'd agree that the clearer a board is with delegatees about what it wants, the more likely it is that the board will actually get what it wants. They might even agree that employees function more creatively when the board gives them as much room to do things their own way as possible.

These statements and others upon which widespread agreement is possible constitute a body of characteristics that comprise a generic snapshot of good governance in any kind of organization at any stage of development. By itself, a list, however well constructed, is not sufficiently coherent and whole to be called a *model*, but it does establish that there are characteristics of good governance that are true across all cases. At this very low level of abstraction, it is not only possible that there be universally applicable truths about governance, *it is almost impossible that there not be!* Having reached that conclusion, the challenge was to construct a comprehensive, coherent framework of concepts and principles into an internally consistent paradigm. To the extent that internal congruity with external utility is accomplished, the higher-integrity meaning of the word *model* will have been achieved. It should not be surprising that the Policy Governance model is generically applicable, for it was intentionally constructed with only those elements that can claim universality.

The reaction to Policy Governance has been curiously mixed. Interest in it has spread to many countries and it is probably unrivaled in its influence on governance thinking, but the model has not come to be universally *practiced*. That in itself is not disturbing, for there is a great burden of tradition-blessed mediocrity to overcome and, for many boards, little incentive to make the effort. But the lack of informed criticism is disturbing. Whereas most book reviews have commented favorably on Policy Governance (usually while reviewing *Boards That Make a Difference* [Carver, 1990a, 1997]), some critics have spoken out against the model's stringency or practicality.

I would argue that these criticisms are based on fundamental misunderstandings. One critic has claimed, in effect, that the model is susceptible to human bungling—a charge so generic as to apply to anything: It is not valid criticism of improved auto safety devices to say that driver error can nullify their utility. A more common criticism is that Policy Governance is a "one size fits all" model—the erroneous suggestion here is that universal applicability is a dangerous fantasy: Because as individuals we are all unique does not prevent physicians from learning how the liver functions as though we are all the same. Some have charged that the model will fail if it is not applied in its entirety—as if it were possible for any coherent system to work when it is only partially applied: All the fine craft required to make my watch comes to naught by removing but one of the little wheels. Another criticism has made much of a limited study that suggests that board members were no more "satisfied" with Policy Governance than with any other model. The authors later conceded that they had been unable to discern whether, in fact, the boards had really been using Policy Governance when they made their study. I'd argue further that personal satisfaction of board members (particularly members chosen under existing expectations about board work) has no necessary connection to effective governance.

Many of the major organizations who would normally be expected to take the lead in governance improvement have largely been bystanders to Policy Governance—even as the model was spreading internationally and enjoying widespread esteem. The reasons that these organizations have practiced this disregard are almost certainly complicated; but in all cases, I believe that it is evidence of steadfast adherence to tradition-blessed wisdom. Ultimately, I believe this disregard is evidence of a reluctance to face new and innovative solutions to serious governance problems. If I am wrong about that—if, indeed, these organizations frankly think Policy Governance is ill-conceived or misguided—they have neglected to present a careful and scholarly criticism to their members and to the public. This is unfortunate, but the model has slowly been making inroads in these quarters; and it may simply be that change of the magnitude represented by Policy Governance will require even more time to take hold than I expected.

It should be no surprise that paradigm shifts encounter greater difficulty than, as Thomas Kuhn (1996) put it, "development-by-accumulation" (p. 2). Although we usually think of science as advancing smoothly and with unbiased commitment to new knowledge, Kuhn argues a compelling case for the resistance in science to enlightenment beyond the paradigms of the day. As to the social and psychological aspects of human existence, however, both Kuhn and Edward O. Wilson (1998) observe that impediments to paradigm shifts are far greater than in science. The process of a board as it goes about its business is, of course, more a matter of interpersonal interaction than physics. Overcoming tradition-blessed methods and mentality in governance should not be expected to move quickly.

The larger story of the Policy Governance model, however, has been its widespread success. It has been recognized by the Australian Institute Company Directors, and adopted by the Association of Community College Trustees, the Association of Junior Leagues International, British Petroleum, the United Nations Credit Union, and an international list that has grown far beyond any ability to enumerate. The list extends across a number of countries and is sufficient to give Policy Governance (or in some quarters, the "Carver model") arguably the greatest name identification of any approach to board work and to make *Boards That Make a Difference* (Carver, 1990a, 1997) a Jossey-Bass best-seller. Still, there is far to go. In bringing governance into the twenty-first century, the Policy Governance model may have been the spark that started the forest fire, but that fire still burns spottily, and in many strongholds of conventional wisdom the strong pronouncements of the model are easier to ignore than to confront.

The Policy Governance Model—An Instrument of Servant-Leadership in the Boardroom

The Policy Governance model is a carefully crafted framework, designed to enable intelligent, well-intended board members to govern as well as it is possible to do. That is, it channels the wisdom of board members, links them and their work to important constituencies, focuses them on the large long-term issues, and makes possible the optimal empowerment and fair judgment of management. These things require a powerful tool, indeed. But they also require that powerful tool to be precisely used. And although I have great feelings about the model, the model itself is a cold, even rigid instrument. The board chairperson of a well-known American nonprofit said that she welcomes a model that is itself passionless, because it provides a neutral receptacle into which she can confidently invest her own passion. My word processor is a passionless mechanism, indifferent to the ardor my words might hold for me; my automobile is only cold engineering, though it provides an emotional experience as well as transportation. For that matter, most games consist of a rigid set of rules, within which we are able to play, emote, and interpret excellence. In like manner, Policy Governance is an emotionless, rigid set of rules in the service of purpose, passion, and the emotional intensity that drives us to organize, to join our commitments and our efforts. My passion has been to press the conceptual integrity of this tool to the limit. But Policy Governance cannot make an uncommitted board committed, a sloppy board careful, or an unintelligent board intelligent. In the end, the personal virtues of board members as servant-leaders will determine whether the tool is used to their distinction or doomed to irrelevancy.

This Introduction is not the place to explain the specifics of the Policy Governance model, for the collection of publications to follow do just that, along with three books and fourteen monographs not represented here (Carver, 1990a, 1997; Carver and Mayhew, 1994; Carver and Carver, 1997; Carver and Carver, 1996–1997). But a brief summary may set the stage for the articles included in this collection, articles originally published in a variety of publications between 1990 and 2001.

First, it is important that Policy Governance is not a prescribed structure. It is a set of concepts and principles. Those principles often influence structure, but so do other factors peculiar to each organization.

Second, Policy Governance is not a management discipline but a governance discipline. That is, it is not a repackaging of management at a step higher than the real managers. It is, instead, a focusing of the owner-representative role one step below the real owners. In short, the board doesn't exist to determine so much what the organization *does* as what it is *for.* It views governance not as management one step up, but ownership one step down.

Third, the board is a locus of decision making in the owner-to-operator sequence of authority, not merely an overseer of management actions. The board is not an approver, but a generator, an active link in the chain of command.

Fourth, Policy Governance is not simply a compilation of all the old bromides about boards: Boards should make policy, boards should deal with vision and the long term, boards should avoid trivia, boards shouldn't meddle and micromanage, all board members should come prepared and participate, and so forth. These exhortations may be good ones, but they are elementary in the extreme—more fitting for Polonius than for a theorist. At any rate, it is embarrassing that they are the level addressed by many of the efforts to improve modern governance. Policy Governance goes much, much further.

Fifth, Policy Governance is not simply what happens when boards conscientiously conduct themselves up to the standards of the prevalent ideal, for it is the long-standing ideal itself that is flawed. Indeed, the model's precepts indict as obsolete the governance practices still promoted by many prominent organizations, and a host of other sources of tradition-blessed, business-as-usual governance instruction.

Sixth, the model is an operational description of Greenleaf's servant-leadership (Carver, 1999b) as it applies to a governing board. The board's primary relationship is with the legitimacy base or constituency that either legally or morally "owns" the organization; its secondary relationship is with the staff. I have described elsewhere the philosophical foundations of the model in servant-leadership and in Rousseau's social contract philosophy (Carver, 1999a, 1999b).

Let me explain what the model does not cover. The model does not dictate matters of structure, such as a specific set of committees, a certain board size, list of officers, or that there be a chief executive officer. Also, it doesn't deal directly with group dynamics, methods of needs assessment, basic problem solving, interpersonal relationships, fund raising, or the management of change. These are important topics but are well-addressed by other theorists and practitioners. None of them are exclusively governance topics, though they provide skills or insights that any decision maker can profitably use—including boards. What Policy Governance does provide is the *framework* in which the board views its job, therefore the framework within which these other skills can be applied. A Policy Governance board would be well-advised to make use of any skills that can enhance its performance—but what constitutes desired performance is itself a function of the governance model.

Policy Governance, then, was not born from notions of what a board should do, but an examination of what a board is for. When our idea about the purpose of governance shifts, many ramifications arise about what a board should do, what it should talk about, to whom it should relate and in what way, and other, even more concrete matters. Because the model begins by reconceptualizing the most fundamental aspects of boards, it operates at a level that applies to all boards. The reader of this book, for example, can be sure that the principles found here will apply to whatever governing board on which he or she sits. For example, even a board that has no staff at all—though it does not have as much need for advanced governance concepts—can find its work improved by conceiving of the two separate "hats" it wears when, first, it debates and decides purpose (as a board) then, second, goes out itself to get various aspects of the work done (as if it were its own staff).

I do not maintain that Policy Governance is the only generic, universal model of governance possible. Someday it will be seen as merely the earliest of a growing number of alternatives. But there is no doubt that Policy Governance is the most thoroughly thought-through, conceptually coherent and complete theory of governance in the world today. If it is still so in twenty years, however, I shall be flattered but profoundly disappointed.

The Personal Story—Successes and Failures

When my interest in governance began in the mid-1970s, my single motivation was to learn about a process that had thus far escaped my understanding. To put a finer point on it, I felt not only unenlightened, but ignorant. I had been by that time chief executive officer (CEO) in two mental health organizations and on several boards—one a national trade association—sometimes as chair. At a superficial level, boards were not a mystery to me, but I had the uncomfortable feeling of being part of a process that didn't fully make sense. Driven by my disquieting illiteracy, I read everything on boards I could find and went to countless conference seminars on board roles and responsibilities. The result of my fretting and studying was an even more troubling discovery that the state of the governance art was primitive, indeed. Governance practice was not (and is largely still not) built from the application of sound theory. It was and is a hodge-podge of bits and pieces that added up to trivia-beset agendas, inadequate forethought and planning, faulty delegation, inappropriate adaptation of management tools, unnecessary interpersonal struggle, default, role confusion, damaged people, and lost opportunity.

That so little discipline and design could characterize the most powerful position in organizations seemed inconceivable but was disappointingly true. So I set out to think the matter through, at least to make sense of the board role for myself. I could never have dreamed of what came to pass over the next quarter-century.

By the year 2000, twenty-five years later, I had done consulting work in Mexico, Canada, the United Kingdom (including Northern Ireland), Australia, Turkey, Ethiopia, Kenya, Tanzania, Switzerland, Austria, Germany, Belgium, The Netherlands, Denmark, Nepal, India, Argentina, and the United States. I'd worked with boards whose accountability was for up to $52 billion in assets and $50 billion annual revenues. My name had become associated with governance in many parts of the world, in some sectors more by far than any other name identified with the topic. Organizations in which I'd consulted included ones engaged in all manner of enterprise: nuclear power, telecommunications, petroleum, national defense, local and state public education, universities, colleges, private schools, hospitals, credit unions, fraternities, trade associations, lotteries, professional societies, voluntary health agencies, pension funds, social services, and more. But of all these experiences, let me cite a couple of examples out of the legion of instances of change induced by and enabled by the model—the first an international development agency, the second a national defense establishment.

The board of the development agency met quarterly to spend three days approving new development grants for recipients in Third World countries. The staff prepared briefing papers on scores of individual grants, complete with descriptions and even little inset maps of the affected sites. The board would listen to long explanations of a project, ask a few questions, then vote to approve. Failure to approve a project was a very rare event. The board, while happy to have such a competent staff, couldn't help feeling a bit like a rubber stamp. So to overcome that uncomfortable feeling, board members would ask even more questions than necessary and would occasionally resort to tinkering with project details in order to exert some influence. Policy Governance brought an entirely different view of governing the international development carried out by staff, one that resulted in entirely different board meeting agendas. The new board behavior was to spend time hearing from experts on needs in the Third World, debating the big-value choices, and deciding what outcomes would be sought in what populations and at what cost or priority. (An example of a big-value choice is whether the focus should be on the poorest of the poor or on the slightly more fortunate with whom larger life changes could be wrought for the same money.) The staff was free to devise projects without going through the charade that the board needed to help them do work for which they were hired. Board meetings became far more high-level, more philosophically satisfying to everyone, and the board's feelings of rubber stamping evaporated.

The national defense establishment, committed to using the Balanced Scorecard (Kaplan and Norton, 1996) (designed specifically for "mapping" management strategy), was also attracted to the delegation philosophy of Policy Governance, designed specifically for boards. It is interesting that this national organization has no governing boards at all but values ideas from any source in its commitment to improved defense *management*. Policy Governance is designed to optimize the balance of control and freedom. Control is necessary for accountability and for certainty that a system will perform as expected. Freedom is necessary to get the most out of human creativity, innovation, and sparks of ingenuity. The Policy Governance mantra of *control all you must, not all you can*, along with the model's differential control of means versus control of ends, enable maximum empowerment of subordinates without "giving away the shop." The defense establishment decided to use the ends-means differential in documents beginning as high as the minister of defense and extending down through the chiefs of army, air force, and navy, thence to their subordinates. The result of their integration of technologies from two separate domains was clearer jobs (therefore, clearer tracing of accountability and less ambiguity among jobs), but without the artificiality and rigidity of detailed prescription (therefore, freedom from procedure-strangulation).

In addition to direct work with thousands of boards, by the new century my wife (consulting colleague and author, Miriam Mayhew Carver) and I had trained 150 consultants and other leaders from five countries in an intensive five-day course of theory and application (called the Policy Governance Academy and ordinarily held in Atlanta). Some of these enthusiasts recently formed the International Policy Governance Association in order to begin to take over responsibility for further spread of the model worldwide. Although I had failed to reach the goal set twenty years earlier of transforming governance by the new millennium, the effects were gratifyingly far-reaching.

Back in the 1980s, efforts to find a publisher for my first book met with a number of rejections. Lynn Luckow, an editor at Jossey-Bass, was the first to find potential publishing merit in my work. As Lynn was promoted to CEO, Alan Shrader, at that time with Jossey-Bass, shepherded me gently through the production of *Boards That Make a Difference* (first published in 1990, then after ten printings, issued in a second edition in 1997). My wife, Miriam, and I wrote *A New Vision of Board Leadership* (Carver and Mayhew, 1994), *The CarverGuide Series* of monographs (Carver and Carver, 1996–1997), and then *Reinventing Your Board* (Carver and Carver, 1997). By the turn of the century, I had authored (or coauthored with Miriam) the three books, fourteen monographs, and over 160 separate articles, published in four countries. My publications had appeared widely, including in *The Times* (of London), *Trustee, Solicitors' Journal, Economic Development Review, Practice of Ministry in Canada, Voices of Ser-*

vant-Leadership Series, Association Management, Association, National Association of Corporate Directors Monograph Series, Chronicle of Philanthropy, The School Administrator, The National School Board Journal, The Corporate Board, Corporate Governance—An International Review, Gouvernance: Revue Internationale, Contributions, and *Nonprofit World,* as well as my Jossey-Bass bimonthly of over eight years running, *Board Leadership.*

How to Use This Book

The purpose of this book is to bring together in an easily accessible place many of the articles of this oeuvre otherwise scattered across many periodicals. Most of these articles have been unavailable to board members and their chief executives. A selection among the articles yielded the contents of this book. Nothing is included from the easily available books *Boards That Make a Difference, Reinventing Your Board,* and *A New Vision of Board Leadership,* or the twelve *CarverGuide Series* monographs.

This collection of articles is intended for a wide audience. Foremost, of course, it is for board members in any setting, along with the management staff who directly serve them. Boards and their staffs are in an important partnership, but the nature of that partnership can be more or less conducive to good governance and good management. Though boards must accept full responsibility for their own jobs, boards and their staffs would do well to study governance together. The book is also intended for consultants, researchers, funders, and other students of governance. The fact that Policy Governance did not grow out of research does not mean that research should not be used to test it. Raising governance dialogue to a new level may well generate new governance theory, perhaps theory that will displace Policy Governance from its current position in that arena. If so, my model will have made its greatest contribution.

This book is meant to be a reference work. There is no need to read it straight through, as with my (and our) previous books. We have done our best to organize it in a useful way, but the very nature of publishing in many organs, often covering more than one facet of the Policy Governance model, makes a cleanly distinct organization impossible. My hope is that the articles published here can be used for general reading of governance enthusiasts, can provide articles for board or academic discussion, and can be used as an occasional source for commentary on specific Policy Governance applications.

Acknowledgments

My foremost appreciation must be expressed to the publications that have graciously allowed the republication of these articles. I am greatly in their debt.

I owe enormous gratitude to Sir Adrian Cadbury for his support of my work and his gracious willingness to contribute the Foreword to this book. Long a respected leader in company boards, Sir Adrian became virtually an icon, his name known in corporate governance worldwide, following release in 1992 of Britain's famed "Cadbury Report"—still the best-known critique of corporate boards.

Ocean Howell and Dorothy Hearst of Jossey-Bass saw the value to readers in such a book and were supportive and most indulgent with my whims, schedules, and intentions. Ocean, as lead editor, mastered massive amounts of material and contributed insights that were consistently helpful.

I am indebted to the graduates of the Policy Governance Academy who helped in assembling the frequently asked questions (FAQs): Barbara Hanna, Carol Gabanna, Linda Stier, Margaret Keip, Jannice Moore, Judi Osborne, Anne Dalton, Catherine Raso, Michael Conduff, Linda Dawson, and Randy Quinn.

Ivan Benson, faithful and patient executive assistant, keeps all the logistics of my consulting practice ordered so I can think about ideas and how to present them. Without his stewardship of my work life, many of my words would not find their way to paper.

As always, Miriam Carver, has been my most model-knowledgeable supporter, knowing at times more than I do myself what I intend for the intellectual soundness of Policy Governance. As to Policy Governance integrity, Miriam fulfills this astute definition of a friend: someone who knows the words of your song and sings them back when you forget. No one knows Policy Governance better than she.

Thanks to everyone who has given me the opportunity, however inadequately I may have performed, to change the world just a little bit.

Atlanta, Georgia   John Carver
August 2001

About the Author

WITH UNRIVALED name recognition in nonprofit and public governance worldwide, John Carver's contribution to board theory and practice is without equal. Although less well known among business boards, his Policy Governance model is drawing increasing attention there as well. His redesign of the governing board task is constructed as a universally applicable paradigm—the world's first theory of governance.

A native of Chattanooga, Tennessee, he served in the U.S. Air Force Electronic Security Command. He earned a B.S. degree in business and economics (1964) and M.Ed. degree in educational psychology (1965) at the University of Tennessee at Chattanooga and a Ph.D. degree in clinical psychology (1968) at Emory University, Atlanta, and was inducted into the honorary scientific research society, Sigma Xi.

He was a licensed psychologist in Tennessee, Texas, and Indiana; for fifteen years, he served as chief executive in public mental health and developmental disabilities agencies in these states before becoming a full-time consultant. In the early 1970s, he incorporated and served as first board chairperson of the National Council of Community Mental Health Centers. On several occasions, he testified before committees of state legislatures and the U.S. Congress. As consultant, he has worked with governance issues in North and South America, Europe, Africa, and Asia.

Carver is author of *Boards That Make a Difference: A New Design for Leadership in Nonprofit and Public Organizations* (Jossey-Bass, 1997) and—with Miriam Carver—*A New Vision of Board Leadership: Governing the Community College* (Association of

Community College Trustees, 1994) and *Reinventing Your Board: A Step-by-Step Guide to Implementing Policy Governance* (Jossey-Bass, 1997). His published monographs include *The Unique Double Servant-Leadership Role of the Board Chairperson* (1999) for the Greenleaf Center for Servant-Leadership and *Business Leadership on Nonprofit Boards* for the National Association of Corporate Directors (1980). He has written a regular question-and-answer column for *Contributions* since 1997 and has written and edited the bimonthly *Board Leadership,* published by Jossey-Bass, since 1992.

Currently, Carver is adjunct professor in the University of Georgia Institute for Nonprofit Organizations. He has held positions as adjunct or visiting faculty at the University of Tennessee Space Institute, the University of Texas School of Public Health, the University of Minnesota Program in Hospital and Healthcare Administration, and the Tulane University School of Public Health and Tropical Medicine.

John Carver and his wife, Miriam Carver, work with individual boards, teach seminars, and train consultants internationally from their Atlanta base. Carver operates as Carver Governance Design, Inc. (Web site: www.carvergovernance.com; e-mail: johncarver@carvergovernance.com). The Carvers live in Atlanta with two very spoiled cats, Bonnie and Clyde.

JOHN CARVER

ON BOARD

LEADERSHIP

Chapter One

A Theory of Governance

The Search for Universal Principles

Conventional wisdom in governance did not develop out of credible theory, but from trial and error, tradition-blessed familiarity, and the dominance of either managers or management mentality. Policy Governance, a total system of thought designed specifically for governing by a group of peers, borrows from—but does not mimic—management. It is a paradigm of concepts and principles applicable to any governing board, whether profit, nonprofit, or governmental, and whether appointed or elected. That there should be universal principles of governance is no more surprising than that there are universal principles of molecular biology for a variety of organisms.

1

A Theory of Governing the Public's Business: Redesigning the Jobs of Boards, Councils, and Commissions

Public Management Review, Volume 3, Issue 1, Mar. 2001

THE MOST VEXING element of public management is that which links *public* and *management.* Municipal councils, utility commissions, school boards, hospital trustees, college and university governors, and many more public bodies—all of which I will refer to as *boards*—are charged with connecting the public to public enterprise. That dynamic connection, which I will refer to as *governance,* has long been beset with meager theory development and discomfiting pragmatics. While management of the public's business has become continually more sophisticated, much of public governance ranges from the merely ineffective to the frankly embarrassing.

Although these boards' pivotal role in society is founded in political philosophy, their customs and conduct are normally not rooted in the profound, but in a hodge-podge of tradition-blessed practices and individual personalities. Most scholarly attention and most practical study of public management continues to be just that, a focus on *management.* Despite its authoritative oversight role, governance remains the most understudied, undeveloped, least rational element in enterprise.

> Despite its authoritative oversight role, governance remains the most understudied, undeveloped, least rational element in enterprise.

The job confronting a public board is staggering. Is it even possible to design a part-time leadership role with any hope of addressing the massive burden of accountability thrust upon it? How can a board do more than rubber-stamp the rapid flow of choices when there is no time for relaxed deliberation? How can boards fully exercise their authority without intruding into CEO prerogatives, thereby damaging the executive force crucial to success? In the case of elected bodies, can independently elected officials be expected to coalesce into a responsible group? How can a board know what it needs to know without being overwhelmed with data? How can a public board get

FAQ ➡
What other governance models are available?

its arms around the organization while keeping its fingers out? The conventional wisdom provides insufficient guidance for these issues. The problem is not simply that traditional *practices* are inadequate—existing *concepts* of governance are not up to the task. The need seems obvious for governance theory capable of rationally framing the myriad issues that confront governing boards.

To my knowledge, other than the Policy Governance model described in this article, there is no complete or conceptually coherent theory of governance in existence. Mueller claimed "that there is no accepted theory of governance" (1996, p. 11). Indeed, not everyone agrees that such a framework is possible. Leighton and Thain, for example, observe not only that "there is no existing generally-agreed description, theory, or model of the board system" (1997, p. 29), but

> Other than the Policy Governance model described in this article, there is no complete or conceptually coherent theory of governance in existence.

also express a belief that it is "impossible to frame a statement of board system rules that would be universally valid" (p. 64). I have challenged this position (Carver 1997, 1998, 1999a) and proposed the Policy Governance model as first—and so far the only—candidate for the thus-far missing theory.

Public Governance and Social Contract Philosophy

Any public organization—that is to say, any enterprise "owned" by the public at large—is a microcosm of the state. Social contract philosophy saw the state as a creation of the general public—an incorporeal construct existing merely because real persons will it to exist. Rousseau calls that crucial fiction the "sovereign," but then goes on to clothe it with a tangible legislature to divine and define the public's will. Although this article is not concerned with the nature and administration of whole countries, every public organization can reasonably be considered a creation of the general public. To that extent, the nature of public organizations can be enlightened by social contract philosophy. Hence, when Rousseau ([1762] 1999b) describes the totality of the "sovereign" and its relationship to the general will, we are justified in relating his comments to, say, a city council, though the council is limited to a domain (city government) enclosed within the larger entity (the sovereign state). In other words, within limits a single public organization can be constituted with as broad a portfolio as the public wishes. Therefore, by adjusting for recognition of partial rather than total domain, social contract philosophy can be applied to public boards.

Board as Owner-Representative

One might refer to the public as the *ownership* of public enterprise. The relationship of the public to the public organization is one of ownership in that both the state and the public organization are creatures of the public and wholly subject to its dominion. (The concept of ownership applies, of course, to nonpublic entities as well. For equity corporations, ownership is represented by shares. For some nonprofit organizations, ownership is represented by membership—as in professional societies or trade associations. For nonprofit organizations of a more quasi-public nature, such as public hospitals or charities, ownership may be more akin to the "moral" ownership of social contract than it is to a legal kind of ownership.) I will use the term *ownership* to refer to the legitimacy base formed by the general public. I will use *owners* when referring to members of the ownership but in their individual capacities. Borrowing further from Rousseau, I will refer to the aggregate desire of the ownership, as does Rousseau, as the *general will.*

Determining the general will is so formidable a task that Wolfe (1996, p. 97) hints that it may be impossible. However, I will assume that the existence of a public organization is itself proof that some manner of general will, however imprecisely interpreted, underlay its formation. Certainly, the size of the population of owners and the breadth of an organization's charge will contribute to the difficulty in determining the general will. Hence, discerning the general will is harder for a city of one million than for a village of five hundred. Similarly, the general will of a population with respect to a city government will be more difficult to make out than the general will with respect to a community library. In a joint venture company with only two parent corporations, the directors will more easily know what owners want than in a publicly traded company with a million shareholders.

Having conceived of an ownership, we must next contend with giving that disembodied entity presence and voice. Except for very small populations, the ownership is easy to envision but hard to find. People-as-a-whole makes an inspiring anthem but an ambiguous ruler. It is necessary to attach to the ownership—possessed as it is with compelling moral authority but encumbered with an incapacitating indistinctness— a function intended to borrow its moral authority but to lend it back explicit articulation. For Rousseau, the embodiment of this role is the legislature; for this article, it is the board.

Of course, the ownership can make its will known through town meetings and elections, but these devices hardly work for larger groups, more complex issues, or where decisions are more numerous. Hume saw the ability of a population actually to know its best interest as problematic:

> Were all men possessed of so perfect an understanding, as always to know their own interests, no form of government had ever been submitted to, but what was established on consent, and was fully canvassed by every member of society. But this state of perfection, is likewise much superior to human nature. (Hume, 1817, p. 469)

A smaller, more focused body has the possibility of minimizing both social complexity and human imperfection.

Because a smaller, more focused body has the possibility of minimizing both social complexity and human imperfection, Hume, Mill (1867), and the conventional wisdom all lead us toward representative forums in which the voice of ownership is expressed largely through small groups speaking on the ownership's behalf. This *owner-representative* role of the board is the source of both board authority and board obligation for servant-leadership (Greenleaf, 1991; Carver, 1999b).

For the owner-representative to know what the ownership wants is a daunting task. It is perplexing to determine what a heterogeneous population wishes, particularly on contentious and controversial issues. Public board members who form their ideas of a general will based on a few phone calls, random interactions with constituents, or even public meetings (due to the non-randomness of their self-selected participants) would disappoint Rousseau, who maintained that the general will "must be

FAQ ➡

What is the role of an advocacy group in effective governance?

clearly distinguished from the particular will, beginning with that of the individual self" ([1758] 1999a, p. 10). Just as in the familiar ink-blot exercise, interpreting that which is obscure invites projection of the perceiver's own needs into the "reality" thus perceived. For individual board members, this projection is a seductive and powerful impediment to properly assessing the general will.

The board member is to take care not only to prevent his or her personal wishes from diluting or contaminating calculation of the general will, but also to prevent the cacophony of splinter groups from causing the same perversion. Rousseau would deter boards from the easy path of pleasing advocacy groups, political parties, or other such subgrouping of an otherwise amorphous and perplexingly diverse ownership.

These groups, each of which must deal with its own internal diversity in order to present a united front to influence the board, act to mask the board's task by appearing to assume part of the difficulty. That is, when the board contents itself with the more attainable goal of appeasing interest groups, it disenfranchises owners who are not members of these groups or perhaps not members of the more effective groups.

So while relating to groups of influence eases the board's burden, it does so by diminishing the integrity of governance. As Wolfe interpreted Rousseau, "When 'interest groups' form, and people vote for the interest of their particular group, then there is no reason to believe that the general will would emerge from the process of voting" (Wolfe, 1996, p. 91). That is, a board will more likely fail in its fidelity to the public when influenced by lobbyists, citizen groups, and other ownership segments, for a collection of interest groups is unlikely to illuminate the general will. Rousseau ([1762] 1999b, p. 67) argues that it would be better if there were no "partial societies," for the number of owners, in effect, becomes the number of associations rather than the number of persons. But if partial associations cannot be prevented, the ability of a board to discern the general will is greater if there are more rather than fewer associations and less rather than more inequality among them. In any event, this seductively appealing shortcut is not an acceptable tool for governance but an abdication of board responsibility.

> When the board contents itself with appeasing interest groups, it disenfranchises owners who are not members of these groups.

A theory of governance must address the integrity of a board's relationship with the ownership, including strategies to overcome the snares inherent in exercising group responsibility, discerning the general will, and rising above personal agendas.

Board as Governor

Even a masterful job of defining the general will is for naught unless that will propels action toward its satisfaction. "Freedom can not produce its best effects and often breaks down altogether, unless means can be found of combining it with trained and skilled administration" (Mill, 1867, p. 129). The public board must interact with an executive function in a way most likely to ensure realization of the general will the board has painstakingly defined. Consequently, the measure of accountability for any public board is the *fulfillment* of public will—the

> Even a masterful job of defining the general will is for naught unless that will propels action toward its satisfaction.

product of two separate functions: first determining that will, then ensuring its execution. This is an unremarkable conclusion, albeit one that requires adroit handling of the governance-management relationship—the first quandary of which is to properly conceive the difference in these roles.

FAQ ➡

Why is governance necessary?

Mill ("there is a radical difference between controlling the business of government and actually doing it" [1867, p. 100]) and Rousseau ("It is not good that the person who makes laws should execute them, nor that the body of the people should turn its attention from general considerations towards particular matters" [(1762) 1999b, p. 101]) both recognized a substantive difference between governance and management. They clearly argued for the separation of three distinct roles: the ownership as seat of legitimacy; board as translator or definer of the general will; administration for actual accomplishment of that will as it is defined by the board. But Mill and Rousseau contributed little to understanding the form a board's expressions should take to optimize its Janus-like role—a subject to which I shall return in describing the Policy Governance model of board leadership.

They did, however, recognize that delegation to management is fraught with pitfalls. Mill warns that boards should not "dictate in detail to those who have the charge of administration," for "the interference is almost always injurious. Every branch of public administration is a skilled business, which has its own peculiar principles" (1867, p. 103). With reference apparently to board review of managerial acts, he refers to the board tendency toward "inexperience sitting in judgment on experience, ignorance on knowledge" (1867, p. 104). With further insight into the foibles of public boards, Mill also points out that boards "may give power by wholesale, and take it back in detail, by multiplied single acts of interference in the business of administration" (1867, p. 121). These phenomena are known to public administrators all too well.

Enlightened delegation is more than pulling the strings of puppets.

Crafting an effective relationship between the board and those who administer must honor the separation of these roles. The board cannot be timid about being in charge (lest the general will be weakly expressed), but must at the same time delegate powerfully to maximize the managerial product (lest the general will be weakly executed). Enlightened delegation is more than pulling the strings of puppets. The public's business deserves the full engagement of professional, scientific, or other competence even while it is being controlled in a larger sense by the board's translation of the general will.

The phenomenon is not unlike one I might have with my solicitor. He or she must be free to use the full range of training and experience, yet always toward ends that I control. My intelligence must go toward clear enunciation of my needs; my solicitor's intelligence must go toward how best to satisfy them. There is a legitimacy in the roles of both principal and agent. In other words, a board would be wise to stick to its own knitting, rather than to meddle in the proper roles of its subordinates.

Just what the board's "knitting" should be and how it is best carried out are, of course, the central questions for a theory of governance. Ironically, an important part of the answer is found in the argument of Plato's antagonist in a fictional account by Hospers:

> It is reasonable to consult an expert on what means we should adopt once the end is specified, but the situation is not the same with regard to the ends at which the governmental policies should aim ... But whether the end aimed at is itself a good thing—whether the ideology in question is really an evil one—is a moral question which is not the special prerogative of the expert. . . . It requires men of great vision and understanding, with the *assistance* of experts who can inform them of countless details that they cannot possibly know, to rule the state. I gladly leave the means to experts—that is what they are trained for; but I do not willingly leave the choice of ends to them. The freedom to choose ends must be left, ultimately, to the people themselves. (Hospers, 1970, p. 370)

A theory of governance must address the integrity of a board's relationship with management, including strategies for empowerment, fairness, and accountability. The result of that relationship should be that the board is rigorously in control and, simultaneously, management is optimally empowered. Practices popularly labeled "micromanaging," "meddling," as well as "rubber-stamping" have no place in such a theory.

> A theory of governance must address the integrity of a board's relationship with management, including strategies for empowerment, fairness, and accountability.

The Policy Governance Model

The profound intimacy between a board and the ownership should both precede and dominate the relationship between a board and management. The board is foremost a voice from ownership to management and only secondarily a link in the other direction. The board's rightful fidelity is to the ownership, not to management. The pertinent consanguinity is board-ownership, not board-administration. Therefore, *the governance function is a derivative of ownership rather than of management.* A theory of governance does not begin with considerations of the needs and language of management, then, but considerations of the needs and language of ownership.

This point of departure flies in the face of common practice, in which boards are counseled that the deluge of managerial material, formats, and concepts is precisely what they should master. Because governance is less developed than management, boards have accepted managerial concepts as the *lingua franca* of the boardroom.

The board is foremost a voice from ownership to management and only secondarily a link in the other direction.

Boards have construed their job as looking over the shoulders of managers, reviewing the same reports, confronting the same questions, operating with the same time horizons, and trudging through the same details. Governance, in other words, has been treated as a subcategory of management rather than as a distinct function with its own principles and concepts. It is no wonder that distinguishing governance from management—board and CEO roles—has been perennially difficult. Indeed, some contend an adversary relationship to be inevitable.

To the extent a theory of governance is conceptually coherent and complete, it creates a framework in which a host of familiar, concrete issues can be resolved. These include all the questions that come up around CEO evaluation, board role in planning, fiduciary responsibility, constituent relationships, board training, agenda control, role of the chairperson, committee assignments, and many others. Since public boards so commonly exhibit a great deal of indecision, confusion, inconsistency, and even outright incompetence in the face of these familiar issues, there is reason to question the adequacy of underlying assumptions about governance and, I maintain, reason to strive for a more effective paradigm upon which boards can operate.

FAQ ➡️

Is there a philosophical basis for Policy Governance?

The Policy Governance model is a complete theory of governance built from social contract philosophy, from Greenleaf's concept of servant-leadership, and from modern management. Rather than a theory of execution, it is a theory of ownership and the expression of ownership in the organizational context. It positions the board as a completely separate function facing the ownership in the primary direction and the executive organization in the other—quite different from seeing governance as an extension or subdiscipline of management. It requires board members to be servant-leaders rather than either demagogues or administrators.

What follows is an explication of major themes of the Policy Governance model, a theory of governance. As a shift in the very paradigm by which we conceive of the board role, it cannot be properly understood as a set of tips or incremental improvements in board life. One must approach it as a whole, never as separable parts to be evaluated on their own merits. (Indeed, a single segment of even a superb paradigm might, if taken alone, cause more harm than good.) Further, as a generic model, Policy Governance addresses the needs of governance in all settings. It was not constructed to solve specific problems but to leap beyond problems to a new ideal. So while it can be used to resolve problems, it is not a reaction to the flaws peculiar to a specific board. Consequently, its various prescriptions should not be used to address problems *qua* problems but to *redesign the logic of board leadership.*

To set the stage for this logic, let me emphasize that the board is not seen here as "running" the organization it governs. The municipal council is not running city government and the hospital board is not running the hospital. (American corporate law still has outdated language which speaks of the board "managing" the company.) Put another way, the board does not exist to help management manage—its purpose is not to advise but to govern. The literature and practice in quasi-public nonprofits and in public organizations commonly present the board as augmenting management and concerning itself with the specifics of managing. The Policy Governance model, in concert with Mill and Rousseau, conceives of the board as a body having its arms firmly around public purpose rather than its fingers in the execution of that purpose. To be consistent with this peculiar role, differentiating among the complex aspects of the public's business requires concepts and language different from those of management.

> The Policy Governance model conceives of the board as a body having its arms firmly around public purpose rather than its fingers in the execution of that purpose.

Customizing the Distinctions of Governance

Even a superficial inspection of an organization finds an impressive array of people in action. These people are deciding, acting, moving, planning, and doing. Newcomers to the boardroom as well as to the executive office are confronted with a bewildering set of facts, issues, and personalities. One issue or another attracts attention; one wheel squeaks louder than others. Boards must make their way through these distractions. If a board is to lead, it must not only keep up with the dazzling array, but also get in front of it.

Of course, no organization is an undefined, diffuse mass of activity. There are distinguishing characteristics that allow us to make sense of it. Certain expenditures are for operations, some for capital items. Some activity addresses the design of a service while other activity seeks to influence public perception of that service. Personnel are divided into salaried and hourly. Some intentions are goals, others are objectives, still others are long-range strategy. Each of these and many other *distinctions* are utilized to enable understanding and control. Moreover, different advisors are advocates for different distinctions: measurable departmental and individual objectives for one; reduction of variation and continual improvement for another; degree of leverage for yet another. We live and affect life through the defining and handling of these distinctions.

In management, as would be expected, the distinctions enable better *management*. If governance were simply management writ large, perhaps boards might use the same distinctions productively. But governance, as Mill pointed out, is not an enterprise of action, but of talk. He claimed not to know:

> how a representative assembly can more usefully employ itself than in talk, when the subject of talk is the great public interests of the country . . . talking and discussion are their proper business, while *doing,* as the result of discussion, is the task not of a miscellaneous body, but of individuals specially trained to it. (Mill, 1867, p. 117)

The principles governing the politics of talk and the creation of group vision differ from those that guide division of labor and administrative specificity. Hence, effectively distinguishing segments and aspects of governance calls for distinctions designed for governance rather than borrowed from management. The Policy Governance model embraces a small number of unique but powerful distinctions peculiarly instructive for the board's otherwise indistinct role. These begin with distinctions among organizational values pertinent to governance and the structure of their articulation.

Governing by Values

I mean nothing esoteric by the word *values* in this context. In fact, *values and perspectives* is likely more accurate, inasmuch as I mean to include not only judgments about what is worth what (values), but in what ways we choose to look at various aspects of organizational life (perspectives). We may have certain values about liquidity and certain perspectives about proper CEO performance monitoring. For brevity's sake, I will use the word *values* to cover both concepts.

Everything we do is a function of our values as they encounter various environmental conditions. A choice, an action, an activity, a decision, an intention . . . these all are behavioral manifestations of the values that we bring to the existing circumstances. I may have little control over the environment, but my values are mine and are therefore subject to philosophical molding and conscious intentions. Although the organization embodies uncountable decisions, activities, goals, and circumstances, this mass of action occurs as the result of values held by persons at all levels.

Rousseau recognized that the amount of detail under a board's purview would be overwhelming, but that some salvation lay in "the spirit of the law which must guide decisions in cases which it has been impossible to foresee" ([1758] 1999a, pp. 12–13). Just what constitutes the "spirit" of a law has always been a source of difficulty. A straightforward resolution is for boards to speak in terms of the spirit to begin with. In other words, boards would focus on making clear the values underlying decisions rather than making the decisions themselves.

The variety of organizational levels at which choices are made, the variety of points in time when choices are made, and the variety of subject matter within which choices are made yield an infinite set of decisions and practices. But these uncountable decisions are based on a more manageable number of values. Mastering organizational values offers an economical way to get a handle on the organization in all its complexity. That is, it would if values themselves were not a relatively undifferentiated mass. To illustrate, we have values about filing systems, carpet cleanliness, and machinery repair as well as about markets, supervisory techniques, and acceptable variation in productive processes. We have values about family life, about tariff protection and free trade, and about glass ceilings for women executives. If organizational values offer a route for boards to translate the general will into organizational reality, just which values are relevant and how must they be articulated?

> Which values are relevant and how must they be articulated?

Distinguishing Ends from Means

Consider a simple distinction that divides all organizational values into two sets: values about *ends* and values about *means*. The definitions are more developed than those voiced by Hospers but are consistent with his expressed intent.

> Consider a simple distinction that divides all organizational values into two sets: values about *ends* and values about *means*.

Values about organizational ends. The organization causes the world to be different. First, the world is different in that something of worth is produced. Hungry people have food. The homeless have shelter. Children acquire literacy. Municipal residents have safety. The organization creates results for consumers or other beneficiary groups. All possible results compete for scarce resources. Designation of which results are to be produced is a value choice.

Second, those results make a difference for some recipients and not others. Persons of a certain family income may be chosen for certain benefits. Residents on one side of town may have sewerage before others. Children with special needs might receive particular benefits. All of these possible recipients compete for scarce resources. Designation of beneficiaries is a value choice.

Third, results for certain recipients have a certain worth. That worth might be expressed in coin of the realm or in priority among results. In any event, there are an infinite number of choices about what is worth what. Designations of cost or priority of results is a value choice.

To borrow the terminology of Argenti (1993), ends deal with what the organization is *for,* not what it *does.* It is in its ends that the economic worth of an organization is demonstrated. The ends concept in Policy Governance comprises the designation of consumer results, designation of recipients, and designation of the worth of those results. Ends are not concerned with designation of activities, methods, ways of doing business or any choices that do not meet the strict ends definition. It is obvious that what results a public organization has, for whom it produces those results, and what quantity of results are produced for the funds spent are all legitimized by the general will.

Values about organizational means. With its point of departure on ends values, the Policy Governance model simply classifies all other values as means. Whatever the desired ends, there are innumerable points of view on how to achieve them. We bring our values to these "how to" questions as well as to the "why." How should the table of organization be arranged? Should we own our fleet or lease? How much liquidity must be maintained? Is an executive incentive plan justified? Should we self-insure? There is an unending stream of means issues in organizational life.

As important as means issues are, they do not embody why the organization exists, but how it can best function in the service of its ends. Dividing all organizational issues into these two general categories, the board now has available a very simple, yet powerful principle:

> *The ends-means principle:* Prescribe organizational ends and the
> board's own means, but stay out of executive means except to
> declare that which is unacceptable.

The board attends to both ends and means, but dealing with executive means exclusively in a negative or limiting manner leaves far more room for managerial innovation. The board does not tell management how to do its job but how *not* to do it. The effect is to give managers wide latitude on means (which pleases Hospers' concern), but within board-controlled boundaries.

The familiar management terms, *goals* and *objectives,* are not used here because they do not observe the ends-means distinction. (Managers regularly establish both goals and objectives for both ends and means.) A board using the Policy Governance model uses the distinctions most powerful for purposes of governance and allows management to employ whatever tools serve its purposes best.

← **FAQ**

Why doesn't Policy Governance use standard terms like *goals* and *objectives*?

Distinguishing Values of Differing Sizes

Dealing only proscriptively with executive means reduces the amount of board work inasmuch as the board is not drawn into planning or problem solving about managerial issues. Managers know that as long as they stay within the boundaries (ordinarily ones of prudence and ethics), they are authorized to select any means they wish.

← **FAQ**

How can relatively few board policies possibly cover everything?

Because the board need not become involved in specific acts, the time available for more profound debate is increased. But even though values about ends and unacceptable means are fewer than the managerial decisions that subsequently flow from those values, there are still far too many organizational values to enable careful board attention to each. To our great fortune, however, *values come in sizes.* There are large values about ends and small ones. There are large values about means and small ones. Decisions upon larger value issues act to contain the possible range of subsidiary or smaller, related values.

Choosing to produce shelter for the poor encompasses many "lower" decisions, for example, about which poor will have top priority during the next strategic period or what degree of shelter is intended. Taking advantage of this "nesting" of smaller value choices within larger ones, the board first resolves the largest value choice within each category of board values before attending to smaller ones. The board thus defines a field within which all narrower value choices must lie. Therefore, with regard to both ends and means values, the board indirectly controls all levels of organizational values by dealing directly only with the larger ones.

> Because the board need not become involved in specific acts, the time available for more profound debate is increased.

I will call the resultant board statements which set forth the board's values *policies,* though principles, guidelines, or other such label would serve as well. It is important to remember that policy is thereby defined as *the value or perspective that underlies action.* The policy categories—within each of which the nesting phenomenon is possible—will be referred to here as ends policies, executive limitations policies (inasmuch as they are constraints on executive means), governance process policies, and board-staff linkage policies (these last two are the board's own means). Extensive instruction in writing policies in this way, along with numerous examples, can be found in Carver and Carver (1997b).

> The board thus defines a field within which all narrower value choices must lie.

The first policy in each category, then, is a statement of the largest or broadest value in that category. The broadest level of such policies might take a brief and summative form like the following examples. *Governance process policy:* "The board as a whole will govern on behalf of the people of Jefferson by dictating the largest organizational ends and precluding unacceptable management means, especially those of long-term significance." *Board-staff linkage policy:* "The board will connect governance and management through a single chief executive officer, to whom all executive authority is delegated and upon whom all organizational accountability devolves." *Ends policy:* "Children will have the skills and understandings necessary for a successful life for a cost not to exceed that of comparable systems." *Executive limitations policy:* "The CEO shall not cause or allow any action or practice which is unlawful, unethical, or in violation of commonly accepted business practice and probity."

> **FAQ** ➡
>
> How does a board develop board policies?

If the board is willing to accept *any reasonable interpretation by the CEO* of its broad ends and executive limitations policies, then it need say no more. Invariably, however, policy at so great a breadth leaves a wider range of interpretation than the board can accept. Consequently, the board addresses the next lower (narrower) level of value and so on until the board majority is willing to accept any reasonable interpretation of the policy language thus narrowed. For example, the proscription against violating commonly accepted business practice and probity can be taken to the detail of specifying lower limits for liquidity or protection of assets. This logic yields a pivotal principle for policy development:

> Invariably, however, policy at so great a breadth leaves a wider range of interpretation than the board can accept.

The logical containment principle: The board declares organizational values in a sequence from broadest toward narrower, but stops at the level of detail at which any reasonable interpretation of its words would be acceptable.

While this principle is simple, it requires more verbal discipline than groups can achieve without studied attention. Issues are not allowed to come up for discussion simply because they are of interest to someone or because they arise from wheels that squeak. Moreover, board pronouncements must be articulated one "level" at a time, each level being subjected to the "any reasonable interpretation" test before going into more detail. Resulting board documents encompass a variety of value "breadths" and will have emerged from a disciplined *level-by-level* discovery and enunciation of board values.

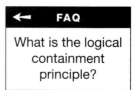

FAQ

What is the logical containment principle?

The nature of the board's role can be stated concisely: The purpose of a governing board is to ensure, on behalf of some ownership, that an organization achieves what it should and avoids that which is unacceptable. That is, the board is accountable for all practices, achievements, and failures of the organization, both of ends and means and both large and small. Yet it

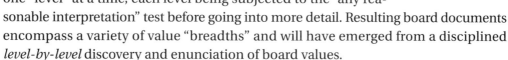

Issues are not allowed to come up for discussion simply because they are of interest to someone or because they arise from wheels that squeak.

can fulfill this pan-accountability while still preserving an empowered, innovative, and creative management. It is through judiciously employing the ends-means and logical containment principles that the board fulfills its accountability for organizational details without being entrapped in them. Board policies tend to be few, brief, and seamless when carefully crafted according to the foregoing principles.

Implications of the New Governance

Implications of this paradigm shift extend to all facets of board operation and the board's relationship with the CEO, constituents, and other entities. While far

The purpose of a governing board is to ensure, on behalf of some ownership, that an organization achieves what it should and avoids that which is unacceptable.

more complete explications of the Policy Governance model appear elsewhere in the literature (among them, Royer, 1996; Carver, 1997; Carver and Carver, 1997a; Oliver, 1999), these brief illustrations will suffice for making the point here. Consider the

> Board policies tend to be few, brief, and seamless when carefully crafted according to the foregoing principles.

major changes in the practices of public boards caused by these practical implications of the model.

Board Connection to the Public

Social contract philosophy and common wisdom indicate that the link between ownership and board is tantamount to the relationship between principal and agent. Yet most public boards have little exposure to the public at large, though they hold meetings to which members of the public may come if they choose. What results is a tradition of open meetings to which a negligible segment of the public comes if, indeed, anyone does at all. Moreover, the segment is self-selected due to personal interest in the organization's service or purchases—vendors and disgruntled customers. At any rate, public boards spend most of their time relating to staff and staff issues rather than to pursuing ever-better methods to connect with the ownership. This leaves them vulnerable, as Rousseau warned, to lobbyists, pressure groups, splinter delegations, and others who represent themselves but hardly represent the public.

FAQ ➡

How does a board member deal with constituency expectations?

Public Input

In some jurisdictions, particularly with elected boards, there is an ethic referred to as "citizen participation." It is considered democratic for the board to engage constituents in the workings of government. A consequence of the contemporary failure to distinguish governance and management properly is that the participation engages citizens with managerial rather than with governance activity. Curiously, at the same time that the board fails to engage extensive public input into governance, it foists a lesser kind of input into the execution domain. In the United States, it is common for a city council to delegate to a parks board authority that conflicts with that granted to the city manager. The city manager delegates running of the parks to a parks director, who is faced with how to deal with the council-empowered parks board. The council can tout its commitment to citizen participation, when actually it has only granted a few citizens meddling rights at the expense of municipal effectiveness for the many.

> Most public boards have little exposure to the public at large, though they hold meetings to which members of the public may come if they choose.

Wolfe's interpretation of Rousseau is that "it would be absurd to organize this task democratically, in the sense of involving universal participation" (1996, p. 88). In the Policy Governance model, the board reaches out with extensive mechanisms to tap into the general will but leaves the CEO to his or her own devices as to public involvement in managerial prerogatives. In other words, public input at the true governance level is more extensive and of more effect due to engaging the public in determination of the general will, not in the technology of execution. Carefully designed interplay with the public should go far to address the failure of boards to engender, in Greenleaf's terms, a "*mechanism of consensus,* a way of making up our collective minds" (1991, p. 34).

An additional outcome of greater board interaction with the public in this way is that traditional expectations by the public for board involvement in administrative detail can be lessened. Boards often use public expectations as their excuse for inappropriate board activity but disregard that the public has been educated to these expectations by long years of inappropriate board engagements.

Delegation to the CEO

CEO authority begins where the board has chosen to stop descending into greater detail in its ends and executive limitations policies. All further decisions in these domains belong to the CEO without any need for obtaining board or committee approval. By stating its values ahead of time, the board has, in effect, already given the CEO all the criteria to define what is approvable. Moreover, the CEO is only obliged to use a reasonable interpretation of what the board has prescribed

> By stating its values ahead of time, the board has, in effect, already given the CEO all the criteria to define what is approvable.

and proscribed, not the particular interpretation the board might have had in mind and certainly not the interpretation favored by specific board members, regardless of their personal power or persistence. In other words, the CEO operates in an environment wherein board words can be trusted. In turn, the CEO is able to delegate to others more confidently because he or she need not worry that board intrusions will frequently "undelegate" specific decisions.

Delegation to the Chairperson

Chairperson authority begins where the board has chosen to stop speaking in its governance process policies and board-staff linkage policies. All further decisions in these domains belong to the chairperson. The only exception is when the board elects to delegate some specified portion of these areas to another officer or to a committee. That is, all decisions about how the board does its own job—after being defined by the board to whatever detail it wishes—automatically belong to the chairperson, absent a contrary decision by the board.

Policy Making

Because policy has been defined to include all possible pronouncements within a carefully crafted arrangement, the compendium of board policies is at the same time exhaustive and brief. It is the single, central repository of written board wisdom, rather than one of several board products. Replacing reams of previous board documents, these documents often number fewer than fifty pages—board members can actually master all of them, using them as working documents and making frequent amendments. Moreover, board policies are truly *the board's* policies, having been generated from board deliberation, not parroted from management recommendations. Explicit, comprehensive governing values of the organization enable new board members to find quickly what the board stands for. The chairperson and CEO have an unambiguous source for knowing board expectations of their roles. To find what the board has said, there is no need to search through years of minutes and document approvals, along with all the chancy inferences needed in such a process, or to listen to single board members' versions.

FAQ ➡

How do Policy Governance policies differ from conventional board policies?

Board Approvals

The familiar process of board approval of management documents in their exhaustive detail is unnecessary, awkward, trivializing to appropriate boardroom mentality, and frequently demeaning to management (when board members choose to chase small points or grill managers on inconsequential issues). As to plans carefully constructed by administrators, Mill lamented that the House of Commons "will not forego the precious privilege of tinkering it [*sic*] with their clumsy hands" (1867, p. 110).

> Explicit, comprehensive governing values of the organization enable new board members to find quickly what the board stands for.

The approval process offers only the appearance of probity. Board members can be seen asking sagacious questions, demonstrating their scrutiny of administrative actions, and posturing for political gain—all of which elected boards in particular enjoy demonstrating. But this is only the appearance of leadership, for the board has neglected to create with one voice explicit criteria, the rigorous monitoring of which would have made this hit-and-miss show unnecessary. The approval process constitutes tinkering more than governing—a phenomenon painfully obvious when boards approve budgets. The peculiarly proactive approach in Policy Governance, by causing the board to set its criteria out in carefully crafted form at the outset, both empowers and constrains budgets, long-range plans, personnel packages, and the like. The board's need to be reassured of organizational fidelity on a regular basis can be done more succinctly and with less pretense simply by receiving monitoring data that disclose whether the policy-based criteria have been met.

Monitoring Performance

Board approvals are suspect as a monitoring device largely because they usually occur in the absence of prestated criteria upon which the approval-disapproval decision will be made. Should criteria be in place, other monitoring approaches are far more efficient and have fewer deleterious effects. Since the board will have stated all its expectations in ends and executive limitations policies, it has thereby established criteria for CEO performance. To monitor, the board demands to receive data that disclose the degree of performance on these criteria, and to do so at whatever

> The approval process constitutes tinkering more than governing—a phenomenon painfully obvious when boards approve budgets.

frequency the board wishes. Discrepancies between policy expectations and monitoring data may signal a failure in CEO performance or a need to change the board's policies. It is not appropriate to judge the CEO on other, unstated criteria (which commonly happens in approvals).

Board Holism

The board is a legitimate owner-representative only as a group. Holism does not require unanimous votes but does call for agreement that a passed vote defines what the board has said. To preserve its ability to be a responsible governor, the board must clearly state that the operating organization need never heed the wishes of a board member or even a group of members. The CEO's obligation must be to the board speaking as a whole rather than to board members. This board position saves management from board members—but its primary effect is to preserve the integrity of governance.

Elected board members often arrive at the table with more investment in voicing their individual opinions than in helping generate a collective group voice. Governance theory will not change that, but it can guide boards to a process that only recognizes decisions made by the group. When board members come with the intent of individually controlling the organization and even, in some cases, hindering its performance, the governance rule that the board speaks authoritatively with a group voice or none at all can overcome the deleterious effects this political reality frequently causes.

FAQ ➡️

Why does the Policy Governance model see board committees in such an unfavorable light?

Committees

Wholeness is damaged when dominance over specific turfs is bestowed on board committees. It is best that board committees should (1) engage only in helping the board with its work, never the CEO, and (2) never instruct the CEO. Audit committees, as an example, pass the first test. They can easily fail the second, however, if they go beyond monitoring performance and impose expectations of their own. The CEO would thereby become accountable for committee criteria, not board criteria. Executive committees, for all their ubiquity, serve chiefly to concentrate power in a few or to make up for a board, which due to size, commitment, or other factor, is too awkward to do its job.

Agenda Control

Board meetings should be the board's meetings, not management's meetings for the board. As long as boards fill their time with the examination of managerial material and as long as they allow management to move ahead only after detailed approvals, board agendas will necessarily be filled to overflowing with management matters. Managers, of course, know these matters better than anyone, so come to be masters of their masters' agendas—a formula for

---

Wholeness is damaged when dominance over specific turfs is bestowed on board committees.

---

poor governance. The board can own its own agenda simply by attending to the policy concepts already discussed. It merely looks several years into the future and plans its own job of clarifying values. There is no need to exclude the CEO from this process; indeed, to do so would be wasteful of the board's greatest resource. But the CEO can be helpful as the board does its job rather than by his or her assuming ownership of the board's job. Regardless how pure the CEO's motives, taking more responsibility for governance than do the governors cannot create good governance but only its superficial appearance. As Wolfe contended:

> Who . . . sets the agenda? This is not a trivial question. Often the most powerful person is not the one who decides yes or no, but the person who puts the questions in the first

place. Participatory politics becomes far less appealing if the agenda is to be set by appointed officials. (1996, p. 101)

Board Members as Advisors

Board members as individuals have traditionally been a support-ive or, at least, usefully critical resource to management. Among nonprofits more board seats have been filled as if to provide pan-els of advisors than bodies of authoritative leadership. But with the board role construed as the voice of ownership, the board's pri-mary function is not to counsel and advise, but to *own the busi-ness*. It is best that the board as a whole only govern (never advise), while individual board members advise if they wish (but never gov-

> ← FAQ
>
> Shouldn't board members be chosen for their management expertise?

ern). In other words, the CEO can use board members as advisors *when the CEO chooses to do so* and only as individuals, never as a body. Since the CEO does not work for board members, but for the board, it is possible with sufficient discipline to keep the respective hats separate. Greenleaf warns, however, that despite due care, board members who cross over even on an individual basis into administration "compromise the objectivity that trustees need" (1991, p. 10). Advice from the convenient pool of experienced board members should never be allowed to jeopardize the integrity of either governance or management, even if certainty on this matter calls for sacrificing the advisory role.

Interaction Among Boards

A public or quasi-public board works on behalf of an ownership that also "owns" other public and quasi-public boards. Considered as an array of servants of the same ownership, these boards cannot per-form optimally in ignorance of each other. Moreover, one aspect of a board's connect-

> Public boards should have a far greater investment of time in their communications and joint reasoning with each other than is now the case.

ing with the ownership might be connecting with other organs of the same ownership. Public boards should have a far greater investment of time in their communications and joint reasoning with each other than is now the case. The two major topics on which these public servants might work together are their ends policies and the governance function itself. The former focus is due to the fact that the aggregate product of all pub-lic and quasi-public organizations makes up much of what affects people, particularly in a given community. The latter focus is due to the fact that problems of governance tend to be generic, so that learning is transferable across dissimilar organizations (for example, city councils, hospital trustees, social service boards).

Conclusion

The public board's job is political science that partakes of management and management that partakes of political science. But it is not informed enough by either field to attain the sophistication demanded by modern circumstances. Exercising authority over complex and technical organizations by a group of peers demands concepts and principles sufficient to assure the public voice as well as to delegate powerfully to professional management.

> The public board's job is political science that partakes of management and management that partakes of political science.

An assessment of governance possibilities, if circumscribed by today's reality, would suggest some aspects of the Policy Governance model to be impractical, arrested by the grip of conventional wisdom. Clearly, current law and tradition in most jurisdictions are in conflict with responsible governance reform, for statutes and public expectations were forged under the very misconceptions that good theory attempts to escape. The future of governance has little to gain, however, from imagination impoverished by the bounds of today's limitations as if they were universal constants. If good theory must wait for the absence of such impediments, there will never be good theory with which to overcome the impediments.

Nevertheless, uncomplicated implementation of the ideas presented here is thwarted in certain kinds of public organizations. In those cases the task in the short run requires a creative effort to devise lawful and publicly acceptable ways to govern well. (One such tactic is liberal use of the "consent agenda" for legally required but conceptually unwarranted board actions.) The challenge in the long run is to educate public understanding, modernize laws, and create new traditions.

> Transforming today's governance of the public's business calls for a conceptually compelling logic around which forces for improvement can coalesce.

Transforming today's governance of the public's business calls for a conceptually compelling logic around which forces for improvement can coalesce. A full-fledged theory of governance, offering a coherent framework with which to rationalize complex leadership issues, provides that logic. But realizing its potential depends on our ability to look beyond time-blessed methods, existing legal requirements, and the ubiquitous bad habits of public governance.

Is Policy Governance the *One* Best Way?

BOARD LEADERSHIP, NUMBER 37, MAY-JUNE 1998

THIS QUESTION was raised at a recent workshop. It reminds me of an article with that question as a title published a few years ago in a prominent Canadian journal. Unfortunately, the author's failure to understand Policy Governance rendered his commentary of little value. But it is a legitimate question, though sometimes I hear it asked with an undertone of "surely you can't be saying this is the only way for boards to operate!" So, is Policy Governance the one best way?

We are all offended by extreme claims. However, in order to engage in a truly honest inquiry, we must neutralize our natural suspicion of absolutes and even of presumptuousness. If Policy Governance is not the best way, then claiming it to be is not just presumptuous, but wrong. On the other hand, if Policy Governance is the best way, then saying it is constitutes not presumptuousness but accuracy. One nice feature of an extreme claim is that it is likely to be either a true breakthrough or a mad raving—there isn't much in between. The most startling breakthroughs in the long human story must have seemed strange when first they were voiced. But the same could be said for the most bizarre ideas.

In other words, bombast aside, the proof is still in the pudding. Is it the best way or not? Even if it is not, it may still be a *good* way, of course, but let me explore the question in its extreme form. Is it the *best* way? The first problem with a straight answer is obvious to any student of Policy Governance: This is a judging action, an evaluation. Evaluations are always done against criteria (unfortunately, often unspoken ones), but done best against explicit ones. So what criteria are to be used to decide what is "best" in this case? That is, what would one want a governance scheme to do? Only with this clearly in mind can we evaluate any scheme and, by extension, evaluate whether the Policy Governance model is even acceptable, much less superior.

In order to take a stab at coming up with criteria, let me say what I want a governance approach to do. (While it might be ideal to start with what board members would like from a governance approach, I know of no research that shows what a cross section of board members want one to do.) For example, I want an approach to be conceptually coherent enough that it goes beyond being an "approach" or a "scheme" or a "plan" and can truly be called a "model" in the scientific sense. That is, I want a view of governance to wrap up all relevant aspects in a sensible whole; a set of tips won't be good enough. I won't be satisfied with a mosaic with only a few nice stones. I want one that gives me the whole picture. So, to return to the question, what should a governance model do? It would

FAQ ➡

What should a model of governance do?

- Guide board wisdom to the most important issues (large ones, long-term ones, the most cogent ones), particularly the explication of *values*

- Facilitate and encourage real board leadership rather than rubber stamping or ritual roles

- Enable board control without meddling, that is, full exercise of authority without unnecessary intrusion into managerial prerogatives

- Offer a logical way to construe the interrelationships of roles

- Provide a clear basis for knowing whether roles have been fulfilled, that is, that acceptable performance has occurred

- Allow managers as much room as possible while still assuring board accountability for the total

- Use board and management time efficiently

- Connect the board to its constituencies

- Be generic, applicable across all or a wide variety of organizations because of its focus on underlying truths rather than superficial and situation-specific features

Notice that I've formed these desires at an overview level in order to leave as much possibility for discovery as possible. For example, "Clarify the role of the third vice president" doesn't show up on the list, for there might not need to be a third vice president.

Let's assume that other people agree that the actions proposed in this list represent important criteria. Then let me pose a question in response to the initial question: Can an approach to governance be found that fulfills these requirements as well as Policy Governance does? Of course, we don't know what approaches are yet to be invented. And we might not know of approaches currently unpublished or otherwise unheralded. To my knowledge, however, there is no other approach known that even comes close. But isn't that what you'd expect the creator of a model to say? As intellectually honest as I might try to be, I do still have a vested interest in the matter.

Keep in mind that the Policy Governance model has within it many areas of flexibility and possibilities for "tweaking" that allow tailoring to specific circumstances. For example, Policy Governance doesn't require a small board, a CEO, a board's relinquishing all control over "means," or board decision making about only the very broadest of issues—as many apparently think it does. Similarly, it doesn't prohibit committees, board members as operational volunteers, an executive committee, a treasurer, or board fund raising—as many apparently think it does.

> The Policy Governance model has within it many areas of flexibility and possibilities for "tweaking" that allow tailoring to specific circumstances.

Finding the flexibility in Policy Governance to embrace many varied circumstances is not outside the model's applicability, but clearly within it.

To be sure, there are situations in which using Policy Governance principles is quite difficult. For example, lawmakers often design bizarre arrangements of boards and executives. When they do so, it is hard then to devise *any* process that makes managerial sense, including Policy Governance. I don't count such instances as ones in which the model fails to apply. I count them as ones in which the statutory authority (often a legislature) has simply made good governance almost impossible. In other words, the model is consistently appropriate, but often faced with legally prescribed, impossible circumstances, ones that doom any governance to mediocrity.

In the final analysis, the answer to the question must be an empirical one. For example, what opinion would emerge from a group of unbiased "judges" as thoroughly familiar with Policy Governance as with other, more traditional governance approaches? Even more to the point, the real test would result from research on the effectiveness of organizations whose boards use different governance arrangements. This kind of research has not, to my knowledge, occurred anywhere. A few studies have been published, but in each case researchers either were incapable of distinguishing when a board was using Policy Governance and when it was not or were unable to find research subjects using the model well enough and long enough to affect organizational outputs. How to interpret research about boards that *claim* to be using Policy Governance is puzzling at best; most boards that say they are using it are not anywhere close. This is not an easy research topic.

I would welcome research of this sort as well as research about what attributes would be considered crucial in a governance approach. Until that time, while experience and impression are the only guides, I've no hesitation in answering that yes, given the distressingly primitive state of the governance art, Policy Governance for the time being is the best way.

Rethinking Governance Research

UNPUBLISHED ARTICLE IN THE COLLECTION OF THE UNIVERSITY OF GEORGIA INSTITUTE OF NONPROFIT ORGANIZATIONS, ATHENS, APR. 10, 2001

WORK WITH BOARDS is predicated on the supposed importance of governance to organizational performance. Certainly, governance participants, consultants, and writers seem to think so. There is, of course, a widespread suspicion that governance is rather irrelevant to organizational effectiveness, though this belief is normally uttered *sotto voce*. Although we commonly ascribe "ultimate accountability" to governing boards with rhetorical flourish, we just as commonly let boards off the hook when criticizing the organizations they govern. School boards and public education are an instructive example.

Still, the ultimate test of a governance method is generally thought to be whether an organization actually performs better. Let me introduce, if not an outright rejection of that point of view, a strong caution about taking it too seriously.

Considering the role I have enjoyed in the advancement of governance theory, that statement may seem an odd one. But I believe any inspection of the relationship between governance and organizational performance is prone to a deadly trap.

> Any inspection of the relationship between governance and organizational performance is prone to a deadly trap.

First of all, people have a firmer hold on what they mean by organizational effectiveness than by governance effectiveness. About organizations, we assume there to be relative agreement about the value (and, to a great extent, the definitions) of efficiency, productivity, climate, and financial performance. When people speak of whether governance improvements enhance organizational effectiveness, these are the indices of organizational effectiveness they typically mean.

But when outside observers or researchers look at effectiveness indicators, will they decide upon the specific definitions of effectiveness that the organization's board chooses? Will the board's choice of types of results, the balance among various results, the targeting of those results among competing potential consumers, and the costs of those results be the same as observers'? Will a board's values about the ethics of the workplace be the same as outsiders'? There is no reason to believe so.

> **FAQ** ➡
>
> Has research shown that Policy Governance is better than other approaches?

A governance system is designed to enable a board to govern. If "to govern" means less than determining the organizational outputs and its place in the world, it doesn't mean enough to dwell on. A governance system is simply a process by which a board explores, expresses, and achieves its intentions about that which it governs. A governance system does not exist so that observers' intentions are achieved, nor even that commonly accepted wisdom concerning what should be achieved is achieved.

The test of a governance system *per se,* then, cannot be whether outside definitions of effectiveness are realized, but whether the board is able to determine, enunciate, then control its own definitions. Will a school system with a good governance system be a better school system than one with a poor governance system? The answer is not so readily apparent as we would like. It is perfectly possible that a board unable to determine, enunciate, and control those definitions is blessed with an operational organization that is excellent in the eyes of the rest of the world. It is also possible that a board of exceptional capability justifiably

> It seems perverse somehow to divorce one's assessment of governance from its effects.

chooses and sees to the achievement of definitions which the rest of us find not only ineffective but reprehensible.

When we make informal, off-the-cuff evaluations of organizations and their boards—as we constantly do, especially of public, highly visible organizations like schools and municipal governments—we typically confound the issues of governance and management effectiveness. Perhaps in our offhand remarks we need not hold ourselves to a high standard of rigor. But when we set out to find a serious answer to the serious question of governance effectiveness, rigor is mandatory. Can excellence in governance be considered apart from independently judged excellence of the organization governed? Even with the argument I've just made in that direction, it seems perverse somehow to divorce one's assessment of governance from its effects.

To be sure, governance does not exist for itself. There is little value in having a carefully crafted governance system if it is of no effect on organizational behavior, thus on organizational performance. And yet, as I have shown, to test whether the organization meets some generally agreed upon (by outside observers) definition of effectiveness is not a proper test of governance. Where are we to go with this dilemma? Good governance can be associated with ineffective organizations and bad governance can be associated with effective organizations . . . as these judgments are made by outsiders.

> Good governance can be associated with ineffective organizations and bad governance can be associated with effective organizations.

Consider this purpose of governance: *Governance exists in order to translate the wishes of an organization's owners into organizational performance.* That simple statement is not simple to carry out. In fact, measured against this *raison d'être* for governing boards, I'd argue that most boards are mediocre at best. In other words, typical governance systems are ineffective whether or not their organizations are performing well according to commonly accepted expectations for that performance. Their ineffectiveness lies in their inability to know, translate, then assure the organizational performance the owners desire.

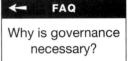

← FAQ

Why is governance necessary?

Let me explain my repeated reference to "owners." Shareholders of an equity corporation are owners in a very direct and concrete way. Nonprofit corporations and governmental entities ordinarily have no such owners. But clearly all boards operate on someone's behalf rather than simply their own. Boards of membership associations, for example, operate on behalf of members in much the same way as though those members were owners in a legal sense. City councils operate on behalf of municipal residents just as though they are shareholders. So the ownership function exists in a moral sense in organizations where it does not exist in a purely legal sense of holding title. A local hospital board, for example, might act as though its owners are the local community. Moreover, this ownership concept exists separately from concepts of customers, clients, students, or other consumers, though conceivably persons can be more than one.

> Governance exists in order to translate the wishes of an organization's owners into organizational performance.

Assume a board operates with complete fidelity to an ownership that desires organizational performance thought by outside observers to be inadequate. These observers would judge the organization to be ineffective. But the board performed its function well. Assume, however, an organization whose performance pleases outsiders, but whose board has no fidelity to owners or fails to hold staff accountable. In these scenarios, good governance is paired with poor organizational performance and poor governance with good organizational performance. The conundrum arises in having spoken of "good organizational performance" apart from achieving what owners want, that is, in allowing an outside viewpoint to be the arbiter of what good organizational performance is. The presumptuousness of this proposition is obvious.

> Is translation of the wishes of owners into organizational performance not the heart of servant-leadership?

So it is that governance research must confront the unhappy predicament that the seemingly sensible relationship between better governance and better organizational performance is not as straightforward as it would appear. We can escape the enigma only if we have the audacity to elevate outside notions of organizational performance above a board's fidelity to the ownership. Is translation of the wishes of owners into organizational performance not the heart of servant-leadership? With what will we replace that fidelity if we, in effect, grant outside observers the right to define the organizational effectiveness that owners *should* want?

Paradoxical and counterintuitive as it might be, my argument is that governance systems must be evaluated in their own right, apart from organizational effectiveness as it is commonly construed. Does organizational effectiveness matter? Of course it does. But the test of organizational effectiveness is not whether it meets the expectations of some outside source of wisdom. The test is whether it meets the expectations of those who own the enterprise.

This implies that organizational effectiveness is not a meaningful concept without having first made governance a meaningful concept. Unless the owners have spoken, we cannot judge the fulfillment of their wishes. The board is owner-representative and, as such, is the authoritative and only channel of owner expression as far as the staff organization is concerned. Unless the board plays its role with fealty and accuracy, there can be no rational judgment of organizational effectiveness.

This argument, then, establishes governance as the independent variable and management as the dependent variable, rather than the reverse as most governance research conversations would have it. Simply put, we cannot back into discovery of governance effectiveness by using commonly accepted definitions of organizational effectiveness as our point of departure. We cannot rationally discuss the models, forms, and complexions of management until we first know the expectations for management that emanate from a board practicing good governance. The relevant research question, therefore, is not what processes of governance best contribute to organizational performance (as some separately existing phenomenon), but *what processes of governance best enable a board to ensure that its definition of effectiveness is achieved, that is, that organizational performance translates board values into actual accomplishment.* Organizational performance is thus the board's tool for fulfilling board accountability. Given any meaningful definition of governance, organizational performance has no meaning outside this context.

Research inquiry must begin, in other words, with considerations of governance, not of management. To do so means conceiving of governance—reinventing governance, if you will—*without any reference whatsoever* to the tools, practices, documents, and language of management, lest once again we find ourselves conceptually chasing our own tails. And, while we need not regress so profoundly as did Descartes to find a substantive starting point, make no mistake—giving new birth to governance is a task of philosophical proportion.

The task, however, is not so daunting as at first it might appear. The beginning point is with the ownership—one person perhaps, but more likely a collection of persons with at least some purpose in common or largely in common. The common purpose might be explicitly stated (as members of a trade association can do) or implied (as the "community" in "community mental health center" can rarely do). Residents of a jurisdiction wish the benefits of public education or of medical intervention in disease and trauma. Practitioners of a trade wish the benefits of interchange and information. Holders of capital wish a financial return. Determining who is the legitimate ownership of a nonprofit enterprise can be easy or difficult, but it is never irrelevant.

Then what are the elements of governance effectiveness— each independent from *a priori* indices of organizational effectiveness—that cry out for research inquiry? At the outset, they would seem to include at least these factors: First, to what extent does a governance paradigm take the true owners into serious account at all? Second, to what extent are the board's proceedings driven by fidelity to that ownership? Third, to what extent is

> ← **FAQ**
>
> What are the elements of governance effectiveness?

the board, in expression of its owner-representative role, capable of demanding its desired organizational performance? Fourth, to what extent is the board able to craft those demands in a way that optimizes the potential of the performing organization (avoiding the bull-in-a-china-shop shortsightedness of command style)? Fifth, to what extent is the board able to forge an accountability link between itself and its organization that assures the performance it has specified? Sixth, to what extent is a board able to discipline its conduct, marshal its wisdom, inform its deliberations, stimulate its vision, and summon its assertiveness in this servant-leadership role? No doubt, as the history of all research has repeatedly taught us, these beginning questions will be enhanced, surpassed, and even later appear simplistic and amateurish as we learn not only how better to answer, but also how more wisely to question.

That the scientific investigation of governance should begin somewhere other than with organizational realities (the seemingly obvious place) may seem counterintuitive but really should not surprise us. How we even look at governance and management arises from our paradigms about these things. Then what can be seen through our paradigms becomes to us the concrete reality—more real than the ideas that made them possible. It may be easy to accept, as the eminent biologist Edward O. Wilson observed, that nothing in either science or life makes sense without theory. But it is harder for research scientists to integrate Wilson's further observation that scientific theory is itself a product of imagination. Certainly Einstein did not pursue the mysteries of light by staring at the sun or by turning his lamp on and off. He relentlessly pursued the integrity of his own thoughts.

If we are to consider the servant-leadership work of Robert Greenleaf with more than passing interest, is it even a stretch to anchor our governance search in questions that precede and are independent from all the intricacies of organization—to whom is a board servant and on whose behalf does it exercise leadership? If the board role is imbued with an accountability susceptible to description and analysis, these "first cause" questions—with our knowledge of organizations carefully held in abeyance—are the ones that both inform and compel serious inquiry into the nature of governance and the duties requisite to its fulfillment.

Watch Out for Misleading Interpretations of Governance Research

BOARD LEADERSHIP, NUMBER 40, NOV.-DEC. 1998

EVER SINCE Policy Governance attained a measure of popularity, it has been clear that a board's claim to be using the model has little to do with whether it really is using it. Policy Governance requires considerable discipline of process and clarity in written values (policies), characteristics that are desired more often than achieved. For years, most calls that I've gotten from boards that say they are using the model are not doing anything I'd recognize as Policy Governance.

> A board's claim to be using the model has little to do with whether it really is using it.

That fact, so obvious to anyone who fully understands the model, is not obvious to persons who know the model less well. Research published by Vic Murray and Jeff Brudney (1997) put a great deal of stock in self-reported use of the model. The authors reported the response of 851 Canadian nonprofit leaders (92 percent of them CEOs) to several questions, including, with respect to "changes in your board's functioning," "in the past three years, . . . did it matter whether you used board models (such as John Carver's well-known model)?"

← FAQ

Has research shown that Policy Governance is better than other approaches?

Their research showed that boards that used a "model" (I suppose that means "some identifiable approach") were more satisfied with their changes than boards that did not. But they also found that "Carver users were no more satisfied than users of any other model or combination of models." Even though the authors do note that "Carver insists that his approach will work best only when adopted in its entirety," at that time they did not correct for or even note that Policy Governance may not have been adopted in its entirety or even substantially. So a "Carver user" is defined in their study as any board whose CEO says that the Policy Governance model was used in the change effort.

This research does yield information but is open to erroneous interpretation by virtually anyone who is unaware of the large gap between Policy Governance lip service and reality. Already, writers are misconstruing the research, despite the researchers' subsequent disclaimer: "We intended no implication that the Carver model was proven to be no better than others. We fully agree that such an inference is not possible based on the data reported" (Murray and Brudney, 1998b). In a later publication of the same research (Murray and Brudney, 1998a), the authors were more careful to point out that their findings could have been due to several reasons, including that "some models were applied ineptly" (p. 343).

Ruth Armstrong (1998a), arguing the side against Policy Governance, states that the Murray-Brudney study found that "Carver users were no more satisfied with their board changes than the users of any other model or combination of models. This leads me to challenge Carver's insistence that his model will work best only when it is adopted in its entirety" (p. 14). Not only has Armstrong announced a finding not supported by the research, but she has built in a non sequitur as well. If the model had been shown to be unremarkable, the very possibility that it was not used fully is enough to explain the results. The findings do not "lead to" challenging the insistence that the model be used fully but may even suggest the opposite.

No one would expect a sophisticated navigation instrument to work if one "sort of" uses it.

Moreover, with no explanation that the term "Carver user" might be completely misleading, Armstrong (1998b) again claimed that the Murray-Brudney study shows that "Carver users were no more satisfied with their board changes than the users of any other model or combination of models" and concludes that "using a model of governance is useful; however, the type of model should fit the organization's characteristics." Apparently, the final comment is an argument against the possibility of a generic model.

There are two major problems with the interpretations being made of the Murray-Brudney study. First, as already explained, I would expect any Policy Governance benefits that might otherwise be shown to exist would be washed out when the "Carver user" group includes everyone who simply claims to use Policy Governance. Second, whether a board is "satisfied," useful as that information might be, may have little to do with assessing the effectiveness of governance methods. (For example, one might be more satisfied by attainment of mediocre goals than by falling short of more ambitious goals.)

The Policy Governance model is a technology of governance that fulfills its promise only with precise use and consistent application. No one would expect a sophisticated navigation instrument to work if one "sort of" uses it. I fully agree that the extensive claims for Policy Governance cry out for research. If research indeed finds that faithful application of the model produces no better governance, integrity is served. But research that fails to distinguish when it is or isn't in use can provide no data on its effectiveness. Neither can unwarranted interpretations of existing studies.

Why Is Conceptual Wholeness So Difficult for Boards?

BOARD LEADERSHIP, NUMBER 39, SEPT.-OCT. 1998

ONE OF THE CONSTANT impediments to board leadership is the difficulty boards have in maintaining consistency. Our expectations of boards with regard to conceptual wholeness have been so low for so long, boards themselves seem not to notice the most glaring inconsistencies in their approach to governance.

Perhaps an analogy will help make the point. The airline industry makes a great deal of fuss about ensuring that counterfeit parts not be used when maintaining and repairing airplanes. With lives at stake, the appropriate bolts, fasteners, cables, and other components of an aircraft must be used to ensure that the total system operates properly. It is not simply a matter of high standards for individual parts (though that is important) but rather one of guaranteeing the right fit in a total system. Similarly, boards must ensure that what they do fits into the total system of organizational leadership.

> **Boards must ensure that what they do fits into the total system of organizational leadership.**

However, most boards use a governance approach cobbled together from bits and pieces of each board member's experience and opinions, rather than a carefully constructed, integrated system of governance thinking—more of a hodgepodge than a pattern. One board member prefers a certain way of conducting meetings. Another has a strong opinion about what policy should look like. Still another wants budgets to be in a certain format.

It is folly for any board to resolve such issues (and hundreds of others) without beginning first with a model or framework of governance in mind. The folly is so common, unfortunately, that it is the rule rather than the exception. But commonplace or not, that approach is just as unfruitful as trying to construct a clock by putting together whatever separate cogged wheels strike each member's fancy. I am continually astonished at the primitive states of governance I encounter, in which the idea of a system is still an alien concept.

> I am continually astonished at the primitive states of governance I encounter, in which the idea of a system is still an alien concept.

Policy Governance is a *system* of governance, a complete paradigm or conceptual framework. Rather than a collection of separate opinions, even good ones, it presumes to build from basic beliefs (for example, that the board is accountable for the whole) a set of generic principles of governing. (I'd argue that only from thoughtfully constructing such a "theory of governance" can we transcend the current fragmented state of board leadership.) But implementation of Policy Governance requires boards to value conceptual wholeness and the consistency that goes with it in ways most boards have never even discussed, much less approached. This feature may be the single greatest impediment to full Policy Governance implementation.

This problem would be true no matter what paradigm a board sought to follow. Boards seem to have difficulty being committed to, true to, and disciplined to any single paradigm. Yet board members, individually, are disciplined, responsible, intelligent persons. Undoubtedly, they are quite committed to consistency in their individual pursuits. Physicians, pilots, educators, farmers, and persons in almost any walk of life commonly operate from a framework of concepts and principles that make sense as a whole. People don't go to school to become board members; we've fallen into regarding board service as something any reasonably competent person can do.

> People don't go to school to become board members; we've fallen into regarding board service as something any reasonably competent person can do.

Closer to home, good parenting rests on one's philosophy about learning, confidence, moral and intellectual growth, self-concept, and other aspects of healthy development. To be sure, as parents we tend not to act consistently with these factors, but without them inconsistency is the rule instead of the frequent exception. So why is the idea so hard for boards? I do not presume to know the full answer to this perplexing question. But I do think the following characteristics figure in the problem. To the extent that they do, any board seeking to ensure its own leadership must come to terms with these tendencies, finding strategies to deal with them.

FAQ ➡

What are the most common obstacles to the implementation of Policy Governance?

Allure of eclecticism. Everyone, it seems, wants to be eclectic. No one wants to "swallow whole" someone else's way of doing things. This is quite understandable and even commendable. Besides, there is something attractively democratic about each person (or each board) blazing its own unique trail through the wilderness. The problem with eclecticism when designing systems (of thought or of machinery), however, is that all the parts must work together for the benefit of the whole. One wouldn't switch the little wheels from various watches in the name of eclecticism and expect the devices still to tell accurate time.

Self-affirmation of previous successes. Board members, just like managers, are full of "how we did it where I used to be" stories, particularly when their approach was associated with success (in reality or merely in their own minds). Even if every idea adopted by a board has previously been proved by the hard-won experience of the several board members, combining them could result in disaster. The point is not that experience is worthless as a teacher but that when truths learned in one paradigm are tried in another setting, they must prove themselves all over again.

Worship of compromise. Life demands compromises, board life perhaps more than most other areas. One cannot conceive of a group of assertive people being able to function without compromise. In democratic societies, the art of compromise lies at the foundation of all politics. Surely compromise will be necessary as a board makes choices, but compromise has a downside that should give any board pause. The compromise between choice A and choice B may be worse than either A or B. Nowhere is this phenomenon more threatening than in choosing whole systems.

> Life demands compromises, board life perhaps more than most other areas.

Fear of having all the eggs in one basket. Choosing a formal, fixed framework and going all out with it intentionally shuts out other choices. Maintaining as many options as long as possible has its value, to be sure. But at some point, commitment to a single course is the only path to a worthy result. That doesn't mean that boards should make premature decisions and not consider alternatives. But there comes a time when, as Tom Peters has said, the most effective plan is "ready, fire, aim."

> But at some point, commitment to a single course is the only path to a worthy result.

Easy mosaic of best practices. The term *best practices* has become popular—it refers to a more studied version of the "self-affirmation" trap already discussed. Imitating what others have done well makes sense. But best practices taken one at a time about various aspects of the board job may become the poorest practices when combined. A good system is not made from parts. Good parts are made from systems.

Mental laziness. Board members, although disciplined individuals, often welcome the unstructured way in which board dynamics allow members to talk about or engage in virtually whatever they please. What will a board talk about? The all-too-frequent

> A good system is not made from parts. Good parts are made from systems.

answer is, anything someone brings up. Conceptual wholeness requires that board behavior, not just board documents, be consistent with an overall scheme of governance. Board discussion that splinters across different issues simultaneously and also across several levels of each issue may be a natural phenomenon, but it dashes any chance for a disciplined process. In my coaching role with boards, getting the group to stick to the issue at hand until it is settled is frequently the hardest challenge I face.

Unfamiliarity of conceptual wholeness in governance. Board members, staff, and funding organizations are not accustomed to conceptual coherence in governance. Governance has so long been a collection of practices workable here and there that few analysts even notice how conceptually fragmented the topic is. Before engineering and physics had aerodynamics and other scientific paradigms, they were incapable of making much progress in

> What will a board talk about? The all-too-frequent answer is, anything someone brings up.

flight. It is not that what they previously knew was false. But reliance on trial and error rendered the striking advances of modern aeronautics impossible. Nothing is as practical, Kurt Lewin said, as a good theory.

Are Boards Searching for the Holy Grail?

ASSOCIATION, VOLUME 16, ISSUE 1, DEC. 1998–JAN. 1999

ASSOCIATIONS VARY one from another: traditions, histories and personalities are different. Chambers of commerce, professional societies, and advocacy groups live in almost different worlds. Surely no single model structure applies to them all. Moreover, circumstances in Canada are different from those in the United Kingdom or United States. Certain committees or board sizes that work in one setting will not necessarily work in another. Organizations today differ from what they were yesterday and what they will be tomorrow. Can one solution apply to all stages and permutations? Is the answer to the question "How is it best to govern?" always destined to be "It depends"?

While we might discuss what is best for one specific association, is it not folly to talk about what is best for them all? Perhaps. But if it is possible to isolate widely applicable principles of governance, boards everywhere can gain a profitable foundation for their task. If there are principles and concepts that can take us beyond the anecdotal wisdom that insular experience offers, each board will be able to struggle with its own peculiar situation rather than with the underlying nature of governance. Without a model, a hospital board must contend not only with issues of health care, but with the nature of the board job itself. Without a model, an association board must grapple not only with the realities of its trade or profession, but with the character of governance as well.

Western medicine made scant advances as long as it depended on the anecdotal wisdom of experience. It only began to leap ahead when it could be built on models of biochemistry, microbiology, and other technologies. As individuals, each of us is different in so many ways, but the physician who treats us must begin with a basic model of how the human body works. Individual application is important, to be sure, but without the generic, there is nothing to apply.

The challenge for association boards—as, indeed, for any other organization—is to find what is universally true about governance, then apply it to their particular circumstances. But is *anything* universally true about governance? Is there anything we can say that would apply to *any* board that governs *any* organization? Let me offer a few simple characteristics that are least likely to encounter dissent:

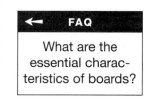

← FAQ

What are the essential characteristics of boards?

- Any governing board is the initial authority in any organization—barring the role played by members, shareholders, or their equivalent.

- Because the board has initial and therefore dominant authority, other roles in an operating organization can only obtain the authority that the board chooses to grant.

- The board's wishes will more likely be achieved by those to whom the board has granted authority if it holds them accountable for satisfying its expectations and if it is clear about these expectations.

> The challenge for association boards is to find what is universally true about governance, then apply it to their particular circumstances.

This simple list easily illustrates universally desirable characteristics of governing boards that are totally unaffected by the size, type, or age of the organization governed, just as they are unrelated to whether the board is large, small, elected, appointed, paid, or voluntary.

But even with universal applicability, the most extensive list of piecemeal characteristics would not constitute a model in the more scientific sense of the word. So would it be feasible to devise a universal or near-universal *model* of governance? Indeed, can there even be agreement on just what a universal model of governance—if one is possible—should do for associations or other organizations? And what can associations expect from a governance model? Quite a lot, actually.

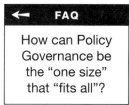

← FAQ

How can Policy Governance be the "one size" that "fits all"?

However, seeking a universal governance model can easily be discredited as a search for the "right way" to do something in a field where alleged right answers are immediately suspect. Yet throughout history, many advances have resulted from a quest for the correct way to, for example, prevent polio, send messages over long distances, or harness the power of steam. The "right way," of course, is not synonymous with the "only way," and surely there can be more than one equally right way. But the best method at a given point in time and capability can reasonably be considered "the right way" at that moment. As applied to governance, the search for a model is therefore a reasonable quest for conceptual integrity greater than other alternatives and "right" only until a better way comes along.

Even the very idea of a "model" can be either elusive or offensive. The word suggests applicability across many distinct situations, insulting to our investment in uniqueness. But without this generic quality no model can justify our attention and we are then faced with an idiosyncratic "model" for every organization. The search for a model is the search for common denominators within complexity and diversity. It is the creation of a theory of governance. "There is nothing as practical," Kurt Lewin said, "as a good theory."

> The search for a model is the search for common denominators within complexity and diversity.

Let me emphasize that my use of the word *model* does not refer to a structure or even an arrangement of currently popular "best practices." Sound theory must run much deeper than mere structural ideas and arrangements of practices: A given conceptual model may be manifest in various structural arrangements. Assigned a more bedrock definition, a model is a collection of principles and concepts that make sense as a conceptually integrated whole, is internally consistent with external utility, and is crafted from elements logically derived from postulates.

For association boards, what is the use of a model with the broadest possible applicability? Why not just work out something specific to associations (or for each type of association)? The scientific mindset answered this question long ago. For uncharted time, common knowledge provided familiarity with motion, gravity, and other physical phenomena. Isaac Newton discovered principles at work underlying observable phenomena that could be applied far beyond everyday experience.

> A governance model conceptually elegant enough to be universal today will be replaced as more sophisticated models come along.

Celestial orbits became more understandable and the calculation of longitude more accurate. Then Albert Einstein demonstrated that Newton's laws were not generic enough. Through his theories of relativity, Einstein took humankind to a far more generic level of understanding of the universe. Minor variations in orbital mechanics that frustrated Newtonian physics now fit neatly into Einsteinian physics.

But the story doesn't end there. Modern work with string theory, worm holes, the hoped-for "theory of everything," and even the "consilience" of Edward O. Wilson (1998), continue the grand human challenge of discovery. Similarly, a governance model conceptually elegant enough to be universal today will be replaced as more sophisticated models come along. If there is a "right" fundamental model of governance, it will not be the best answer for long.

> Responsible board members are compelled to become students of governance quite as much as experts in their fields.

What does this code for association boards today? It means that the opportunity for professionalization of association governance is greater to the extent that generic concepts can be found upon which specialized association applications can be built. It means that the first step in advancing association governance lies in looking outside association governance to governance in general. It means that responsible board members are compelled to become students of governance quite as much as experts in their fields.

Looking to a generic governance model as the proper point of departure for organizing a given association's governance calls for great care. First, it is essential to choose a conceptually coherent, rigorously rational model at the outset. I know of no governance approach worldwide that either claims such universality or is widely regarded as generic other than my own Policy Governance model—a presumptuous claim, to be sure, and one that

> The legitimate need for tailoring should not become a masquerade for conceptual sloppiness.

cries out for knowledgeable research. Second, care must be taken to apply the model so that its conceptual wholeness is preserved. The legitimate need for tailoring should not become a masquerade for conceptual sloppiness. Clockworks don't work if only some of the wheels are used.

For students of governance, settling for the "everybody's different" approach is either a truism or a dumbing-down of the search. As a truism, it adds nothing and, if anything, opts for seat-of-the-pants governance. It is no revelation that every organization is different; who can possibly argue otherwise? As a dumbing-down, it obstructs and demeans the imperative taken on by every trustee: the obligation to pursue ever greater integrity in our conception of board leadership.

What Associations Should Expect a Governance Model to Be

FAQ ➡

What should
a model of
governance do?

- Generic—applicable across all or a wide variety of organizations because of its focus on underlying truths rather than superficial or situation-specific features

- Conceptually coherent enough to go beyond simply an "approach" or even a compendium of brilliant tips—and be a *model* in the scientific sense, embracing all relevant aspects of governance in a sensible whole

- A connection between the board and its constituencies, particularly those whom the board represents

- A focus on the most important issues facing the board (large ones, long-term ones and the most cogent ones), particularly the assurance of probity and explication of *values*

- A mode to enable substantive board leadership, along with elimination of rubber stamping and purely ritualistic behavior

- A mechanism to establish control without meddling, that is, undiluted exercise of board authority with minimal intrusion into prerogatives more productively left to others

- A means to allow delegatees as much latitude for decisions, creativity, and performance as possible while still assuring board accountability for the total

Can Things Go Horribly Wrong for Boards That Use Policy Governance?

BOARD LEADERSHIP, NUMBER 56, JULY-AUG. 2001

CAN THINGS GO horribly wrong for boards that use policy governance? Yes. But first let me be clear that I am referring to boards that are *really* using Policy Governance. Boards that merely pretend to be using Policy Governance routinely encounter failures ranging from unpleasant to disastrous. But in twenty-five years of practice, I have never heard of a board that is sticking to the discipline of Policy Governance getting into the kind of trouble that a better governance framework could have prevented.

So in answer to the question "Can things go wrong for a board that is *partially* implementing the model?" the answer is a resounding yes, just as partially using the controls in your automobile can produce unintended effects, some of them catastrophic. But what about a board that has followed all of the rules? It is that kind of board that I want to talk about in this article.

> Can things go wrong for a board that is *partially* implementing the model? The answer is a resounding yes.

Let's review what such a board has done (and is doing). The board has created policies in all four categories, carefully following the principles with respect to descending breadths and proscriptive boundaries on staff means. The board is receiving and absorbing routine monitoring reports that disclose the organization's performance compared to the relevant policies. I'll assume the board has established a CEO role to make the governance-operations linkage easier. If so, all executive delegation and accountability is routed through the CEO. Board committees help the board do its job but never interfere with, overlap, or even help the staff with their jobs. These are ways of doing business that Policy Governance boards observe religiously.

So far, so good. This board already sounds like it is better than 95 percent of the governing boards in the world. Can things still go horribly wrong?

Yes.

Why? This board is using the Policy Governance model and using it correctly. Isn't that supposed to be the magic cure for what ails the boards of the world? Actually, no. The model establishes a framework of thought and action that enables a responsible, intelligent group of people to govern with excellence.

> **FAQ** ↵➡
>
> Does the Policy Governance model cure all board problems?

Without the model, we get what the average board does—confusing governing with managing, speaking with multiple voices, confounding delegation, monitoring the wrong things, leaving ends unspecified, mixing up beneficiaries and owners, and on and on. But even with the model, there can still be crucial failings. Let's look at some of them.

Focusing on the short term. Even if a board is rigorous about driving the organization toward an adequate magnitude of results in the lives of the right persons for the money spent, it may be projecting its vision over too short a time period. In other words, board members might limit themselves to thinking only about ends that could be achieved, for example, in the next six months, rather than thinking creatively about ends that could only be achieved given a longer period of time. We must remember that boards and their staffs have traditionally been more focused on annual budgets than long-term plans. (Many organizations have no credible long-range planning, but rarely do you find one without an annual budget.) Moreover, boards and their staffs have been accustomed to board meetings that deal more with last month than with the next decade. The history of near-term preoccupation can easily infect the way boards think, even after they've made the big switch to Policy Governance. Here are a couple of specific influences that encourage short-term thinking.

> **FAQ** ➡
>
> What is the effect of frequent turnover in board members?

■ Short *terms* encourage the short *term.* Frequent turnover in board seats biases members against a long-term view. Board members like to see the difference they can make in the time they serve. If that is a short period, say, two years, the board can forever be locked into thinking short-term. It is hard to think in terms of results that can only be achieved over longer time periods, yet frequently the results that really make a difference in the world require that kind of time line. Why is it common to have such a high board member turnover rate? For some organizations— for example, associations—there is more interest in passing the honor around than

> The history of near-term preoccupation can easily infect the way boards think, even after they've made the big switch to Policy Governance.

in having good governance. High turnover makes substantive governance development extremely difficult and unlikely. There is a very high price to pay for rapid turnover in both time horizon shortening and in general governance competence.

■ Measurement anxiety tempts toward the short term. How boards approach monitoring often leads to short-term thinking. Board members worry that if they set expectations that only bear fruit over a multiyear period, they will be at a loss to monitor

organizational performance in the short term. "How can we wait five years to see if things turned out right?" they might ask. "Given longer-term ends, how can we know we are getting there?" I would remind them that they don't know *now*. But easy monitoring (which is hard with

> High turnover makes substantive governance development extremely difficult and unlikely.

longer-term aims) is only one tool the board has to enforce its expectations. Another is incessant, obsessive focus on the ends it has decreed, even if measurement is difficult or impossible in the short run. This is much better than not setting the longer-term expectations at all.

Narrow vision and limited ambition when determining ends. Short-term thinking is not the only way boards can limit themselves when establishing ends. To get started creating ends policies, many boards simply convert the *current* results, recipients, and costs into ends policies. In other words, they "jump-start" the process by accepting present performance as sufficient. If this approach prevents a board from putting off the difficult process interminably, then it is justified. But it is very easy for the board to get stuck in this mode, thereby establishing a practice of allowing the present to determine the future. A community college board I know, working on its ends, was able to avoid getting stuck by going beyond the usual listing of student skills to the unexplored region of setting the college's sight on a community with high average educational attainments (compared with national averages). This bold stroke means that the college cannot succeed simply by doing well with the students it has; it must influence the whole community's attitude toward education, the performance of the local public schools, and other difficult tasks for which it is not now organized and for which it does not now have the competence. Can it possibly succeed? Will this bold ends expectation set the college up for failure? Perhaps; perhaps not. But if our organizations are not swinging for the fences, why aren't they? The purpose of inspired ends work is to envision the future, not to memorialize yesterday's achievements.

Not adequately considering constraints on staff means. Some boards are so determined not to get into detail that they fail to do enough "what if" thinking. Consequently, they leave far too much latitude for the non-ends organizational behaviors and situations (staff means), allowing dangerous financial or other sensitive circumstances to jeopardize the institution, even though the CEO is staying within the inadequate policies the board does have. I remember one very persuasive board member who thought that any policy over a couple of sentences constituted "micromanaging." He convinced his board to leave the policies excessively broad. The proof that the breadth was excessive is that the members of this board found later that they were quite displeased with the CEO's performance even though the CEO was using a reasonable interpretation of their words. They were disciplined enough to stick to the model—that is, to recognize the problem was in their words, not in the CEO's performance. Despite how much some board member thinks the board is micromanaging, the board *must* go into as much detail in policy setting as it will later go into in monitoring; otherwise, it is misleading the CEO and shortchanging its own accountability.

> The purpose of inspired ends work is to envision the future, not to memorialize yesterday's achievements.

Not monitoring often enough. The frequency of monitoring is a board decision based on the jeopardy posed by various conditions and actions. Most persons would think that monitoring financial condition once every five years is too infrequent—that is obvious. But how many other policy violations could become serious threats within the board-established monitoring cycle? And is such a critical matter settled once and for all, or should a board not revisit its monitoring frequency routinely? To illustrate, consider an executive limitations policy that at its global level prohibits the CEO from allowing "development of fiscal jeopardy or a material deviation of actual expenditures from board priorities established in ends policies." Assume—as is fairly common among Policy Governance boards—that there is a substatement under this broad heading that says the CEO shall not "allow tax payments or other government-ordered

payments or filings to be overdue or inaccurately filed." Knowing how disastrous it
is to fail to submit withheld taxes, prudence might dictate that monitoring this
policy provision once a year is too lax.

The Policy Governance model does
not guarantee wise governance;
it *enables* wise governance

It is easy to see the thread through these sources of misadventure—all facing
boards that are following all the rules in Policy Governance—and that thread is *responsible care and judgment exercised by servant-leaders*. The mechanics of the model are
important; they have been designed as carefully as the works of a watch. But the board
that uses the model must also concern itself with using it wisely. The model provides
the vessel; only probity, care, and wisdom provide the wine. The Policy Governance
model does not guarantee wise governance; it *enables* wise governance.

Chapter Two

The Moral Basis of Board Authority

Where the Chain of Command Begins

Standing between owners and operators, the board is an active and decisive link in the chain of authority. Conceptualizing, defining, and connecting to the owners—difficult though that might be—constitute the point of departure for responsible governance. The reason for the board's existence is not to be managers' advisors, helpers, adversaries, or even supporters. Its *raison d'être* is, as owner-representative, to define and demand success.

Ownership

BOARD LEADERSHIP, NUMBER 18, MAR.-APR. 1995

OWNERSHIP is one of the concepts of Policy Governance that has been difficult for many people to understand. Board members know that they serve on behalf of someone else; they know that they do not wield their corporate authority for only themselves. Indeed, board members frequently refer to such terms as *constituency, public, membership, clients,* and *stakeholders.* These terms are useful and have important referents. However, while these words somewhat relate to the idea of ownership, they are as likely to obscure the concept as to illuminate it.

The Policy Governance model finely details this important aspect of board accountability. I place this unusual emphasis on the concept of ownership, as distinct from the broader stakeholder phenomenon, simply because boards, except in rare instances, do not possess their authority by virtue of themselves alone. Their authority comes from somewhere. And defining board leadership is dependent on this source of board authority, for all board authority must spring from the *initial base of legitimacy.*

Ownership is not a complicated idea. We deal with it routinely in our personal and business lives. For boards of business corporations, stockholders clearly own these companies (regardless of how well corporate boards honor that entitlement). Community

---

Note: In each of *Board Leadership*'s first two subscription years, one expanded issue was devoted to a single theme. The first five articles in this chapter are taken from a special issue that focused on the concept of *ownership.*

boards usually view their owners to be the community. Association boards rightfully see their members as the legitimate owners.

At first glance, then, the concept of ownership seems too apparent to deserve special treatment. After all, it's obvious that an organization is owned by someone or, more accurately, by a number of people. Certainly the board is accountable to the owners of the organization, whether they hold title in a legal or only a moral sense. It is generally accepted that boards have obligations of trusteeship or—to use a more recent term that downplays the formal, legal meaning of trust—*civic trusteeship*. Simply put, the board governs on behalf of persons who are not seated at the board table.

> The board governs on behalf of persons who are not seated at the board table.

Identifying ownership merits more critical examination than our customarily casual treatment of it suggests. After all, to make sense of board effectiveness, we must ask, effectiveness *on whose behalf?* To put it another way, as the CEO is accountable to the board, to whom is the board accountable?

To stimulate your board's discussion of its ownership, this issue is divided into four articles, the first three of which are intended to be read in order. The first, "Understanding the Special Board-Ownership Relationship," explains how this relationship lies at the heart of board authority. In this article I draw distinctions between owners and stakeholders and, further, between owners and customers. The second, "Determining Who Your Owners Are," addresses the job of determining who the ownership consists of—for some organizations this task is not nearly as easy as it seems. In the next article, "Connecting with the Ownership," I discuss the board's obligation, and available methods, for spending more governance energy linking with its "boss" than most boards currently practice. The final article, "What to Do If You Find a Consumer on Your Board," deals with what boards should do when, by accident or design, a consumer has membership on the board.

> Engage your board in discussion and resolution about who owns your organization.

I encourage you to engage your board in discussion and resolution about who owns your organization. Some of this process might be uncomfortable, perhaps even politically incorrect, but your organization will be on a stronger footing by doing so.

Understanding the Special Board-Ownership Relationship

Board Leadership, Number 18, Mar.-April 1995

Nonprofit—and sometimes public—boards are often like employees in search of a boss. Where does their authority come from? When we speak of board effectiveness, on whose behalf is this effectiveness attained? When public and quasi-public boards are referred to as *civic trustees,* whose trust do they serve? Of course boards should be accountable, but to whom are they to be accountable?

At the outset, ownership appears to be a simple idea. It is comparable to the notion of stockholders but is a narrower concept than *stakeholders,* a term that includes all parties who have an interest in the organization. Staff members and suppliers certainly have a stake in the organization, but neither of these groups is the ownership. Before jobs are created that require a staff and suppliers, a reason for operating must exist. That is, some preeminent process must intend some outcome for somebody. Despite the initiator of such a process (legislators, founders, incorporators, or appointing authorities), the burden of continuing that process eventually rests with a governing board. If the governing body is given authority to choose which beneficiaries will be served and with what benefits, it will make that choice on someone's behalf.

The board-ownership relationship is the essential, defining relationship of an organization. Board members stand in for the ownership, operating on its behalf. The board can be seen as a microcosm of the ownership, a workable subpart of an awkwardly large group. The board's primary relationship is to the ownership, not to the staff. The board owes its authority to the ownership, not to the staff. Hence, the nature and identity of that ownership are critical to the development of board leadership.

FAQ →

To whom is
a board
accountable?

Let me narrow this topic. One could correctly say that a board is accountable to the law, or to community standards, or even to Western civilization. Such accountabilities exist but are not what I will deal with here. Certainly, these accountabilities are true even in a business corporation, yet we all have a more focused meaning for *accountability* when we speak of stockholders. If I open a retail store with my own money, the store would be accountable to the law and so forth, but I'd accept absolutely no dilution of the fact that in terms of ownership, the store is accountable to me. I own it.

My employees, suppliers, neighbors, and creditors have a legitimate stake in my store. They are critical stakeholders, and their interests merit respect. But not one of these obligations changes the fact that the store belongs to me. I would not only tolerate but also desire that employees have a sense of emotional ownership in the business. I'd even try to manage so that they could control their own jobs as much as possible and share in the store's profitability, perhaps through profit-sharing. None of these considerations, however, changes the fact that the store belongs to me.

> The board can be seen as a microcosm of the ownership, a workable subpart of an awkwardly large group.

So when the Policy Governance model addresses the issue of ownership, it is defining this narrowly focused view of ownership. Nothing in the concept denies the importance of other interests. It simply recognizes that this particular meaning of ownership is imbued with a special significance that other meanings do not have.

Owners Are Not Always Obvious

FAQ →

Where does
the board get
its authority?

In some instances, who the owners are is clear. Most people would agree, I think, that the source of legitimacy for a school board's decisions is the population of its district, even though the school board as an institution is a creature of state or provincial legislation. The source of legitimacy for a city council is the citizenry of the municipality, despite the fact that the city is incorporated by virtue of higher governmental action. The source of authority for a membership organization is the membership. The source for many nonprofits is often an amorphous general public.

It is important to recognize that even though owners are equivalent to stockholders, they are often not legal owners. Members in an association and citizens in a city, just like stockholders, are legal owners. But for the many nonprofits that are quasi-public in their intent, their general public ownerships are not legally linked as owners. Because the ownership concept does not have to be legal in nature to have its effect, I often use the term *moral ownership* to describe those who own the organization, for in many cases their ownership exists only in a moral sense, not in a legal one.

In addition, corporate "memberships" are common under not-for-profit statutes. This membership has real meaning in membership associations. In quasi-public organizations (for example, social service agencies and hospitals), the membership is more a legal ritual than a truly meaningful group. Its utility may lie more in being a fundraising base or a public relations gimmick, but in such cases it bears little relationship to the broad-based ownership I've defined here. Consequently, it would be inaccurate to think of a legally required membership as the ownership without careful scrutiny.

The Stakeholder Confusion

Let's return to a frequent source of confusion: the concept of stakeholder. If we go back to the retail store example above, the reason an owner is not the same as a stakeholder becomes apparent. As demonstrated, *stakeholder* is a more inclusive concept than *owner.* All owners are stakeholders, but not all stakeholders are owners. Figuring out who the stakeholders are is fairly easy—they include everyone who has a stake in the organization. To begin to disentangle the concepts, let's look more closely at stakeholders.

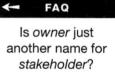

← FAQ

Is *owner* just another name for *stakeholder*?

The term *stakeholder* has gained great currency among nonprofits over the past few years, probably because it has played a role in corporate boards' acquiring a wider sensitivity. In the corporate world, the concept stretched minds that occasionally placed stockholder interests above environmental protection and even basic ethical conduct. For nonprofit boards, however, the stockholder-equivalent never fully developed

> All owners are stakeholders, but not all stakeholders are owners.

to begin with, so there has been little myopia about owners to mend. Consequently, nonprofits' push to recognize an array of interested parties—stakeholders—in effect constitutes embellishment upon a hollow core.

Stakeholders are indeed an important assemblage. A typical stakeholder list for nonprofit and public organizations includes consumers (clients, patients, students, customers), corporate members (under some nonprofit statutes), the general public, funders, employees, consultants, suppliers, regulators, volunteers, user organizations (to public schools, for example, colleges and employers are user organizations), trainees, neighbors, researchers, professional societies, trade associations, and board members themselves.

To conceive of such a disparate grouping as stakeholders is a useful idea, even beyond its utility in expanding the consciousness of business leaders, so I've no argument with the concept of stakeholders. *But it is not the same concept as owners.* The board's primary accountability is to the owners. Owners form the vital legitimacy base, the fundamental reference group for a governing board. Stakeholders, by contrast, are the wider group to whom the board owes obligations of all possible descriptions.

All of which is to say that a governing board's first obligation is not to consumers, nor to the staff. The foremost debt of fealty is to the ownership. I know this statement sounds like heresy, especially in view of recent history, in which confounding the various roles has become politically correct. Colleges and universities in some jurisdictions have been forced into a cogovernance situation with a senate or other designated faculty group having as much power as the board of governors. Staff members of various organizations are given board membership so that there is "staff representation." Clients, patients, or students are given board seats in order to "represent" consumers. By mistaking stakeholders for owners, a whole host of consumers, advocacy groups, funders, staffs, unions, and other groupings are included as though they are equal partners in owning the organization. These actions reduce the effectiveness of governance by splitting the board's attention away from the real owners.

> **FAQ** ➡
>
> How does traditional representational governance fit with Policy Governance?

This distraction is particularly insidious in that other admittedly important groups are more visible and more present to most boards than is the ownership. When the elusive ownership role is not well defined and made an explicit object of board attention, it is natural for these other groups to acquire de facto ownership status. Of course, they move into the vacuum with their own agendas. Not uncommonly, this phenomenon of counterfeit owners leads a public service organization (for example, a mental health center, school system, counseling service, or branch of government) to operate as much for the benefit of its staff as for the public. Staffs have been known to choose what the public (or membership or stockholders) wants more than the public does.

Staffs have been known to choose what the public (or membership or stockholders) wants more than the public does.

So it is that citizens of a city, *not* city employees, own municipal government—and the city council had better speak for the citizen-owners. Citizens, *not* educators, own the public school system—and the school board is duty bound to represent them. Members of an association, *not* the staff, own the association—and the board had better govern putting members' interests first. Are staff members still important? Of course they are. Are they the owners? By no means—at least not in their role as the staff. Are the staff part of an amorphous group called stakeholders? Yes, they are, right along with

> Members of an association, *not* the staff, own the association.

the owners. And that is why we need a special category for owners, one not adulterated with other groups, no matter how important these other groups may be.

Keep in mind that defining an ownership in these terms does not suggest that a board should ignore nonowner stakeholders. The board should listen to anyone who can increase its wisdom. The difference is that the board *works for* the ownership, just as the CEO works for the board. This obligation to the ownership is not simply the board's primary obligation in the sense of its greatest obligation. It is the "point of departure" obligation, the one that frames all other obligations and within which obligations to other stakeholders are conceived and weighed.

The Consumer Confusion

Just as prevalent as is the flaw of allowing the staff to become the de facto owners by default, the most difficult confusion for boards lies in understanding why consumers should not be treated as the owners. After all, the business world has been inundated with the need to be "customer focused." This entreaty has been taken to heart by non-profit and public organizations—and it should be. So why shouldn't the board's first obligation be to consumers?

Owners and consumers are both important groups of people. They have different relationships to the organization and are entitled to their respective prerogatives. But problems arise when the board does not recognize the difference, a particularly tricky task when consumers and owners are the same people. I'll explore this situation with you, but let us first examine how acting as a consumer is different from acting as an owner.

Consumers have the prerogative to demand good and courteous treatment. They have the right to be dealt with in a humane and civil way. They have the right to complain to whomever they wish, with no obligation to respect chains of command or the needs of other consumers. If you purchase a product at a retail outlet, you will exercise all these prerogatives if you feel the need. You'll demand your money back or replacement of the purchase if you receive shoddy goods. You'll write a nasty letter to the salesperson, president, or board chairperson if you want to. You don't have to worry about the needs of other consumers or the organization's need to be fiscally sound.

Owners have the prerogative to have a say in what the organization exists for, what business it is in, and how much return it should earn (for nonprofits and government, return translates into how much good is done per dollar—an ends issue). Owners must respect the chain of command, and they can only be heard along with other owners, for they don't have the individual rights that consumers have. After all, an individual owner is really only a joint owner with others.

To illustrate, I can go into a sportswear store and order a pizza. But as a customer I have no right whatsoever to tell the company that it should produce pizzas. I do have the right to demand good value and courteous treatment if I want to buy running shoes. No one would claim that consumers have the right to decide what will be produced. Only owners have that prerogative.

> A board of directors is established to gather the desires of multiple owners and to translate these competing wishes into strategic direction.

Now, let us complicate the matter a bit. Let's say I buy stock in the corporation that operates the sportswear store. Now I am an owner as well as a customer. Everyone understands that a majority of owners can, in fact, decree that their stores will henceforth be in the pizza market as well as in sportswear. But no one would expect that one stockholder (unless my stock is the majority!) could make such a command. Because even if I owned all the stock, I would never give an instruction to a single store employee.

FAQ ➡
What if the customers and owners are the same people?

A board of directors is established to gather the desires of multiple owners and to translate these competing wishes (for short-term versus long-term gain, for example, or for emerging markets versus historically proven ones) into strategic direction. The board of directors is not a body established to represent consumers, nor does it need to be. (Which consumers would they be representing anyway? Yesterday's, today's, tomorrow's, or all potential consumers?) The board's job is to gather and process input from the owners.

Now, consider situations in which consumers and owners are the same people. A city council is a board that represents *city residents as owners*. It governs an organization that produces benefits for *city residents as consumers*. Its owners and consumers are not totally identical (visitors to a city will be consumers, but not owners), but are similar enough for me to make my point. If as a citizen I have views on how much taxation is worth how much protection from burglars, I am thinking as an owner. If as a citizen, I am upset at having been haughtily treated by a city employee or am happy that a police officer was courteous and helpful, I am thinking as a consumer.

But consider your city council or school board meetings wherein citizens complain or otherwise attempt to influence the council. Much if not most of what these officials hear is consumer input! Yet these boards hear little that could truly be called owner input. And when they do, it is not a representative sampling of all owners. Remember that as one owner I have no right to affect the sportswear store. As two stockholders, you and I together have no right to do so. Only a majority of owners has that right. So the city councils and school boards face a quandary: First, they hear only a small amount of owner input out of the many hours of citizen input they endure. Second, the owner input they do hear is from a self-selected, extremely small proportion of the ownership. (Indeed, most city councils and school boards can actually name the handful of persons they repeatedly hear from!)

This matter is not as clear-cut for quasi-public, nonprofit boards, though the same phenomenon exists for them. Almost no boards, with the possible exception of association boards, get the kind of ownership input that would enable the board to be a true organ of ownership. Even then, association boards tend to hear the consumer viewpoints of their members more than they receive ownership input.

Before sounding even more heretical than I intend, let me insert that the CEO's and operating organization's first priority is to the consumers, *once they have been defined*. Once it is clear, for example, what a social service organization is to accomplish and for which populations, the CEO must see to it that the identified consumers get what they should from the organization. For a public school board, once it is clear what the public investment is intended to produce (for example, literacy or democratic participation skills) and with which group of children (gifted, mainstream, developmentally disabled, or physically challenged), the CEO must ensure that these consumers benefit as they should from the system.

> ← **FAQ**
>
> How does the board ensure that the organization has a customer focus?

With what legitimacy or on whose behalf did the respective boards make these ends judgments? If they had the right to define what benefits and which consumers, *they must have had that right before the consumers were defined*. The authority of the board must derive from another, preexisting source. And the source of one's authority has first claim on how the authority is used. In other words, the board derives its

> In nonprofit and public organizations, consumer focus is ordinarily more rhetoric than reality.

moral legitimacy from a base larger than itself, yet not tied to any particular consumer group.

Despite its initial sound, this concept is far from a repudiation of the consumer focus that has become a buzzword in organization development. Traditional board operation, overburdened and distracted by an endless stream of means issues, has neither the time nor the discipline to delineate ends criteria. We cannot expect organizations to have a powerful consumer focus when consumers and the satisfaction of their needs have been poorly defined. Consequently, in nonprofit and public organizations, consumer focus is ordinarily more rhetoric than reality. Social service agencies or city governments trying to implement a consumer focus is like someone with no concept of the multiplication table trying to use calculus. The staff can and should be more pointedly oriented to consumer satisfaction, but this orientation requires the board to determine who the consumers are to be and what is to be changed in their lives. The truth is that the staff can be more aggressively consumer focused if the board is obsessively owner focused.

> The truth is that the staff can be more aggressively consumer focused if the board is obsessively owner focused.

Ironically, using this approach, a school board will spend far more time talking about student benefits than does the traditional school board. But its interest in what to accomplish for kids is informed by and, in the end, governed by those who own the system. The board is an organ of ownership. It is not an organ of staff, nor is it even an organ of consumers. But out of its obligation to owners, it is interested in both staff and consumers and realizes that defining and achieving something for appropriately chosen consumers is the only justification for continuing the organization.

> The board is an organ of ownership. It is not an organ of staff, nor is it even an organ of consumers.

In other words, causing the board to relate primarily to the ownership rather than to consumers can lead to *more* pointed delineation of consumers than is the case with traditional board operation. After all, the board itself does not serve consumers; its staff does. The board, in a manner of speaking, serves the owners; it serves them by defining consumers, consumer benefits, and economical production on their behalf.

In summary, the ownership concept is critical in establishing the nature of governance, particularly in tracing board authority and accountability to their source. Consequently, the concept has far more than academic significance, but rather, in a more practical sense, fuels the planning of board job and agenda.

The ownership concept is critical in establishing the nature of governance, particularly in tracing board authority and accountability to their source.

Defining Ownerships

Defining some ownerships is easy . . .

> Halton Region Board of Education—*the residents of Halton Region.*
>
> Association of Community College Trustees—*community college trustees who are members of ACCT.*
>
> Metropolitan Indianapolis Board of Realtors—*realtors who are MIBOR members.*
>
> City Government of Plano—*citizens of Plano.*

. . . and defining some ownerships is more difficult

> Public radio station KQED—*donors, general public in the listening area, talk radio show advocates?*
>
> American Red Cross—*official members (volunteers) of the Red Cross or all Americans?*
>
> National Endowment for the Arts—*the general public, the government, artists, writers?*
>
> Girl Scouts of the USA—*girls, parents, society at large?*

Determining Who Your Owners Are

BOARD LEADERSHIP, NUMBER 18, MAR.-APR. 1995

O NCE A BOARD understands the importance of connecting with its ownership, its next question is almost always, "Well, who is our ownership anyway?" It's shocking but true that most boards don't have a clear understanding of who their ownership is, a confusion that too often leads boards to undermine their own authority and subvert the governance process by listening too carefully to the wrong voices while ignoring the group to which they are legitimately obliged.

To begin this inquiry, first get a clear picture of who the owners *aren't.*

Determining ownership isn't always easy, but it's an absolute necessity for boards who wish to get in touch with the true source of their authority—and their own true governing power. But before you can contact your owners and hear their voices, you have to have a clear idea of who they are. To begin this inquiry, first get a clear picture of who the owners *aren't.* They are not the funders, the consumers, the regulators, or the staff. True, there are cases where, for example, funders and owners may turn out to be the same people, or where staff members are part of a larger ownership group.

See if the ownership question has already been settled for you. If your organization is created by a law, the legislation may clarify the matter or merely confuse it. A state board might find that its ownership consists of the general public, the legislature, or the governor, but just as likely lawmakers have left the point unclear. Membership associations are usually an obvious case of members-as-owners. Be careful in this latter situation, for members are also customers and in this inquiry you are only interested in members' ownership role.

It is not necessary that your owners know that they are owners. Indeed, for most nonprofit organizations operating as quasi-public agencies, most owners will have no idea that you exist. (Elected political boards will be better known.) It is not even important at this stage whether the ownership will be difficult or even impossible to reach for input. The task at this point is merely to establish who they are.

If you find that two or more distinct groups seem to be your owners, look harder to see whether you are being rigorous enough in definition. Is it really just one of the groups, though the other also deserves your ear? For example, is it general public *and* donors?; or all citizens of our county *and* people who've signed up as corporate "members"? Or is there a higher-order grouping that would resolve the matter? For example, for a public radio station, two seemingly separate groups, donors and classical buffs for instance, might be reframed as "all persons committed to a presence of classical music in everyday life." It is possible to have a "this and that" ownership, but don't accept dualities before investigating to see if more creativity or rigor is needed in the defining process.

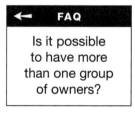

Some boards will find that defining the ownership is quite easy, but for others it will be very difficult. Since a great deal of board energy in Policy Governance is put into interaction with the ownership, it is rather fundamental to have a carefully reasoned definition of who these important people are.

If you find that two or more distinct groups seem to be your owners, look harder.

Connecting with the Ownership

BOARD LEADERSHIP, NUMBER 18, MAR.-APR. 1995

Having determined who the owners are, a board is then faced with how to establish contact with them. The contact is intended to allow owners' values and wishes to be represented in board debate, largely about ends. The contact is not intended for public relations purposes, though these may be a side benefit. Open meetings will not suffice. Only a handful of owners attend, scarcely representative of the total ownership. Most owners are unaware that they are owners, particularly in the case of quasi-public nonprofit agencies. Rather than waiting passively for the ownership to contact the board, the board should take the initiative to develop more affirmative actions, going out to the ownership in innovative ways.

> Most owners are unaware that they are owners, particularly in the case of quasi-public nonprofit agencies.

Formalize the Board-Ownership Relationship

The first step toward connecting with the ownership is to codify the commitment by creating policy that describes the board-ownership relationship. Remember that in Policy Governance, *all* board values are committed to writing, including board values about the initial accountability link and how the board will fulfill it. This policy belongs, of course, in the governance process category.

The point of departure for such a policy is a description of the ownership as you understand it. (All policies are created in outline form so that the larger issues are resolved first and smaller ones addressed in turn.) The preamble, or broadest statement, might say something like this: "The board provides the legitimate link between the owners of Elveden Community College, residents of Elveden County, and the operating organization. Staff members, faculty, students, and others who meet this definition of owners will be accorded the rights of owners, but not disproportionately to their numbers in the ownership." In subpoints, this policy might go on to describe the ownership more exactly, if needed, along with methods to be used for establishing the linkage.

Distinguishing Between Owner Input and Consumer Input

Before a board sets out for owner input, it must first be able to distinguish owner input from other commentary. For example, owner input is that which relates to owning an organization, rather than input that relates to being served by the organization. The treatment of a particular consumer is consumer input, though how the organization will treat consumers in general is owner input. This distinction, rarely recognized by boards, is critical to obtaining the appropriate ownership linkage.

The biggest confusion is that some owners might also be consumers. The pressure to comment as a consumer is ordinarily greater than the pressure to comment as an owner. Take a city council, for example. People who go to city council meetings to have their say are both consumers and owners of city government. This situation is one of those in which both roles are played by the same people. So when Jorge or Monique Q. Public speaks to the city council, is the council hearing from an owner or a consumer? It could be hearing from either, but a quick survey of what citizens say to their city councils will reveal that most comments relate to consumer issues of city services rather than owner issues.

If I complain to my city council that potholes haven't been repaired on my street or that the drainage ditch is overflowing, these are customer complaints. However, if my comments deal with how much smooth roadbed is worth how much taxation, I am speaking as an owner. In the latter case, I am adding my voice to those of others in order to influence the council's ends decisions (what benefits, for whom, and at what cost). In the former case, such global decisions have ostensibly been made; I am merely fighting for my personal piece of the benefits.

As you can see, city councils that patiently listen to a great deal of citizen input are not necessarily getting the ownership input they need to govern. They are unable to tell the difference between consumer and owner comments, partly because it is common to obscure the difference by referring to both groups as "constituents," an undifferentiated term. This condition is also largely true for school boards, for whom there is only a partial overlap of owners and consumers.

This problem is very real in any organization where the consumers and owners are the same people. For example, in membership associations the board works for the members as owners, yet governs an organization intended to benefit the members as consumers. Such boards should engage members in a continual dialogue about what they want their organization to be, what it should accomplish, and what these benefits are worth in dues charged to members. This type of interaction would be a true ownership dialogue. Instead, they hear more often from members as disgruntled consumers and, mistakenly, think they have therefore done their job to connect with the membership. The board should connect with members as owners, and define consumers and benefits out of that dialogue. Then the staff would connect with members in their roles as consumers. Members would exercise *no* owner prerogatives directly to staff members and would need to exercise *no* consumer prerogatives to the board.

> City councils that listen to a great deal of citizen input are not necessarily getting the ownership input they need to govern.

Perhaps a couple of everyday examples will highlight the difference between owner concerns and consumer concerns when the same people wear both hats. As owners, we want safety rules and adequate enforcement of highway driving. As consumers, we want to know where traffic radar is so that we can speed; we'll follow trucks closely if it seems they know where the cops are. As owners, we want an effective government revenue service. As consumers, we may skirt the rules, even to the point of borderline cheating.

> As owners, we want safety rules and enforcement. As consumers, we want to know where traffic radar is so that we can speed.

Owner input influences the organization's never-ending struggle with its justifications for existence: what difference is to be made for whom and at what cost. Consumer input addresses the success or failure of a benefit that the consumer feels is deserved.

Consumers need an avenue of expression, and the board should insist that management provide such a path. The path of consumer expression should not typically be to the board. Operating systems should be able to resolve consumer issues. In fact, when consumers must grieve to the board to get legitimate complaints dealt with, it is symptomatic of an unacceptable system. The board should look beyond the consumer grievance at hand and ask the CEO why such matters ever get to the board. Is there no way that consumer problems are to be systemically responded to? Why not? Is there no ombudsperson or, at least, sympathetic ear available to consumers?

> Operating systems should be able to resolve consumer issues.

Dealing with Input from Nonowners

Nonowners (or the consumer aspect of persons who are both owners and consumers) can be insistent, however, so board members need to know how to deal with them. Perhaps the most useful way for the board to deal with the input of nonowners is to resolve *not* to deal with it on a case-by-case basis. To do so drags the board into operational matters. If the board deals with nonowner input at all, it should deal with it on an aggregate basis as part of monitoring executive performance (if and only if the board has already set performance criteria). There might be occasions when the board legitimately contacts consumers to be sure that they are, in fact, getting what the board has decreed for them. This effort, however, is at the board's behest

FAQ ← How does the board deal with customer concerns?

as part of a total monitoring scheme. It is not intended to hear complaints and certainly not meant to resolve them. The intent, should this approach be used, is merely to monitor one or more aspects of CEO performance. Like other monitoring, it should not be scatter-gun in nature but targeted to specific, policy-stated criteria.

> Perhaps the most useful way for the board to deal with the input of nonowners is to resolve *not* to deal with it on a case-by-case basis.

It is easy to see how school board and city council meetings would change if they were not strangled with direct board-consumer interactions. There would be time for ownership concerns. These concerns tend to be longer term and intently focused on what outputs are worth what costs—the very long-term ends issues that boards currently overlook so consistently.

Measures Toward Connecting with the Full Ownership

The key to the board-ownership linkage is the active endeavor of a committed board to contact and heed its true ownership. With this in mind, I often recommend that boards include in their policy language text along these lines: "The board will pursue ownership input on an affirmative basis, not waiting for input to be initiated

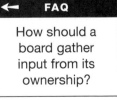

FAQ ← How should a board gather input from its ownership?

by owners." If boards don't go out after the input, they will likely receive either (1) virtually no owner input, (2) occasional owner input, but so outweighed by consumer input that the owner input is not useful, or (3) disproportionately weighted owner input due to some owners having better access, more fervor, or greater verbal ability than others.

For boards of public, quasi-public, and large membership associations, the ownership is too large a group to reach easily. Consequently, the board will not be able to hear directly from more than a fraction of the owners. Moreover, most owners will not think of themselves as owners with owner prerogatives. In this case, it is all too easy to allow the few owners who are heard to wield far more influence than their numbers warrant. Too often boards will make decisions based on the few owners who happen to have contacted board members.

> The key to the board-ownership linkage is the active endeavor of a committed board to contact and heed its true ownership.

Consequently, a board must work diligently to design input processes to overcome these impediments, committing their methods to policy, making them part of the board's prescribed governance activity. The aim is not to reach every owner—which would be impossible for large groups—but to reach whatever sampling would be a reasonably representative input. Focus groups and surveys with these persons can be useful. But due to our perennial distortion and negligence of this broad ownership input, it would be healthy to look at each method with a critical eye. Let's look at a few methods of connecting with the ownership. Some methods may not apply to your board, though all will apply to some boards. Boards fully committed to leadership will invent far more than I can list and, indeed, far more than I know.

> Too often boards will make decisions based on the few owners who happen to have contacted board members.

■ Recruitment or appointment of new board members can take into account a candidate's ability to identify with and connect to the ownership. This need not mean a slavish formula of board member demographics that turns into a bizarre casting call. So while individually representing a small segment of the ownership is not recommended, firsthand experience with the ownership will help the board member keep focused on ownership issues.

■ Whatever its composition, a board can link at least abstractly by attending formally and explicitly to its linkage responsibility. This includes talking about the obligation, discussing the interests consequently to receive front-burner consideration, and finding ways to disentangle nonowner input from the real thing.

■ The board can enhance its linkage ability by gathering statistical data, particularly demographics and values assessment, that relate to the specific ownership as defined. The challenge is getting data about the ownership rather than some other grouping, even though other sources may be less expensive and easier to obtain.

■ The board can listen to vocal and assertive subparts of the ownership when these subparts request a hearing, but the board shouldn't assume that these smaller groups represent the total ownership. Try to get such groups to say not only what the organization should do more of, but

> Invite groups that push you in opposite directions to debate the matter between themselves in your presence.

also what it should in consequence do less of. Invite groups that push you in opposite directions to debate the matter between themselves in your presence.

■ Owners can be educated as much as possible, and boards should at least make sure that they don't miseducate them. Public boards continually teach the public inappropriate behaviors by the way board meetings and public input are structured. It is as if the public is enticed into missing the point of ownership. While educating the ownership might be a tricky undertaking, in some situations (for example, trade associations) it is quite achievable.

■ Written or oral questioning can be used to survey the ownership. Be sure you get a representative sampling, using stratification and randomness as appropriate. Remember that you are seeking input about what benefits for whom have what relative and absolute worth. You are not seeking input about means.

■ Focus groups can sample owners' values and wishes in depth. Notice that the more of these data a public board has, the better it can deal with splinter groups that claim themselves as representatives of the public. You need not shut them out, but with no ill intent you will drown them out with more extensive data about ownership wishes than they can ever claim.

■ Broadcast communication with the ownership is possible, for example, through the commercial press. Report results and delineate ends quandaries. One client of mine bought advertising space in a daily newspaper for a quarterly report to the public. Note that this communication is not for the purpose of selling the organization or making it popular—in short, it is not for public relations in the usual sense—but for reporting to the board's "boss." Take great care in the design, since such a report can be terribly boring to owners not nearly as excited about their role as you are.

■ Boards can lead the press rather than being led or intimidated by them. The press will consistently confuse the owner-consumer distinction and the ends-means distinction. How the press presents public ownership has a massive effect, though thus far not a very helpful one.

Connecting with Other Boards

It is likely that the board is only one of several boards that work for the same ownership. A hospital board may have the same ownership as the school system, mental health center, and city council. These boards could be seen as employees working for the same boss. Just as in a management situation, they must communicate productively with each other in order to serve that boss well.

One tactic in approximating the ownership connection is to link with other organs of that ownership: other boards. Boards should talk with boards—a valuable activity almost completely overlooked in current governance patterns. The commitment to do so is first thought through and put into the board policy I mentioned earlier. One board added this: "Other boards will be chosen based on their having (1) similar or overlapping ownership or (2) similar mission. Those boards most capable of communicating about ends and governance process will be given priority."

> Boards should talk with boards—a valuable activity almost completely overlooked in current governance patterns.

Another added this phasing intention: "Board-to-board communication will be a minor board activity for one year from adoption of this policy, but will grow to a significant engagement after three years." More specific language might go on to describe just which boards will be focused on and what the objectives of the interaction will be. Because this policy is part of the governance process category, unless the board designates another person or committee to make further decisions, the board chair is given the right to use any reasonable interpretation in carrying the board's words to fulfillment.

When boards get together, what should they talk about? I think the most productive topics are ends and governance itself. In a community setting, the ends of all community organizations (political and otherwise) taken together largely define the effect the community has for people. While boards may not agree with each other about the aggregate of these separate visions, it is folly for them to be operating in ignorance of it, yet we do it routinely. Governance is a natural topic; boards can help each other find better ways to govern, including more creative ways to link with their ownerships.

> When boards get together, what should they talk about? I think the most productive topics are ends and governance itself.

Now, a disconcerting dash of reality: At this point in the history of governance development, it is likely that other boards will not be able to match your own board's ability to have a productive dialogue. They are too mired in staff work instead of board work. So your board will either wait a very long time to engage in such an advanced dialogue or—here is my challenge—your board can work for a revolution in governance in your community!

There's Such a Thing as Being Responsible Owners, Too!

AS A PEOPLE, we have a hard time being responsible owners of our public and nonprofit organizations. We have difficulty (1) knowing what to expect of the boards that represent us and (2) treating those boards appropriately once they are operating. Here are a few tips to association members, community members, city residents, and other owners (enough to include us all!).

1. Expect the board to consider a wide range of opinion rather than to short circuit that diversity based on board members' biases or on disproportionate input by a few vocal subparts of the ownership.

2. Recognize that we as owners do not agree with each other, so the board cannot make everyone happy. It should be expected to use a well-designed, fair process and deserves support as long as it does its task with integrity. The board needs—and deserves—our encouragement most when the opinions it is balancing are most diverse or most passionately held, that is, when we are even more likely to be unhappy with its decisions!

3. Understand that the staff is obligated to fulfill the board's interpretation of what we the ownership wants. The staff is not obligated to fulfill your or my interpretation, so don't judge the CEO based on our individual criteria.

4. Demand good leadership, but give leaders a chance to lead!

What to Do If You Find a Consumer on Your Board

Board Leadership, Number 18, Mar.-Apr. 1995

I F A BOARD IS required by law or other pressure to have consumers on the board, what should it do? Of course, it must obey rightful authorities. But strict obedience aside, the board is obligated to its ownership to protect the integrity of governance however it lawfully can. That integrity is best served if the consumer member sees himself or herself as equal to other board members. In other words, the client, patient, or student on the board should set out to represent the public just as much as anyone else. He or she should represent the full ownership as a full-fledged board member—not as a token or a representative of consumers.

I'd apply the same rule to all board members who could be described as "constituency" board members. (This term is often used to refer to board members who are identified with and derive their seats from a category other than owners at large.) This would mean that the board member from the local business community would not "represent" business, nor would the clergyperson represent clerics or churches, nor would the faculty member on a college board represent the faculty, nor would the staff member represent the staff. Such requirements arise out of regulators', funders', and lawmakers' muddled governance concepts. But as long as such requirements must be tolerated, boards can try their best to minimize the antiownership effects by construing all board members, regardless of where they individually come from, as trustees for the ownership as a whole, a legitimacy base that often includes but is never dominated by the special constituencies.

The board can help these constituency members by capturing the sentiment just outlined in policy (in the governance process category) and trying to educate all constituencies about this more holistic, owner-focused way of seeing the trusteeship obligation. The trick may be for individual members of the board to see themselves as "from" a constituency, but not "representing" it. After all, everyone is from somewhere. And a collection of the individuals' origins in a board small enough to be workable is insufficient to ensure that the entire ownership is represented. So even if tokenism is rampant, the board is just as obligated to reach out for an extensive amount of ownership input as it would have been without constituency members.

FAQ

How does a board member deal with constituency expectations?

When there are consumers on the board, a board would do well to frequently examine how well the conflicting hats are kept separate. Making sure that consumer board members know where to take their concerns *as* consumers will help. Board meetings are the wrong place, though meetings are the right place for all board members to take concerns *about* consumers. The most effective safeguard, however, will be provided by a full board schedule that continually structures genuine owner input. Inappropriate consumer input can thereby be flooded out, for boards often stray into the wrong issues simply because they are not consumed by the right ones.

> Boards often stray into the wrong issues simply because they are not consumed by the right ones.

Part of the answer lies in a board constantly disciplining all discussions according to rules in its governance process policies. Such a board tests every agenda item or discussion topic as to whether it is a legitimate board issue. The raising of inappropriate consumer matters is not singled out but encounters the same scrutiny met by other proposed topics.

Funding agencies, accrediting agencies, political authorities, and others who make demands on nonprofit boards could help a great deal by putting a stop to their well-intended, but misguided pressure to have consumers on boards. Now that it has become politically correct to do so, however, a rational correction of this trend may be slow in coming. Failing such a stalwart action on the part of authorities, nonprofit

---

Bid this consumer-become-governor to be as bold and powerful a voice of owners as any nonconsumer on the board.

---

boards must obey. But they should not take the requirement seriously. It is simply one of many existing impediments to governance integrity.

So what do you do if you find (or, under pressure, put) a consumer on your board? You help him or her to understand the trusteeship in board leadership, the intimate and compelling identity with owners, and the proper way for consumer needs and concerns to be expressed. Then bid this consumer-become-governor to be as bold and powerful a voice of owners as any nonconsumer on the board. His or her portfolio as owner representative is one of sweeping importance.

Achieving Meaningful Diversity in the Boardroom

BOARD LEADERSHIP, NUMBER 8, JULY-AUG. 1993

MUCH IS MADE OF diversity these days. *Board Leadership* is not the forum for weighing the social and moral dimensions of this important topic, but there are a number of governance implications that I would like to examine with you.

Recent social pressures have caused many boards to reexamine their commitment to diversity. This is right and just. Boards naturally inherit this obligation; the people they represent—the *ownership,* as I call them—have the right to demand it of them. But what does diversity actually mean in the governance context? Just what kind of diversity should boards pursue? In this article I want to share a rationale for the need and nature of diversity around the board table.

> Very few nonprofit or public boards govern on their own behalf.

Obligation to the Ownership

Very few nonprofit or public boards govern on their own behalf. Ordinarily, boards exercise their authority as a kind of stewardship on behalf of others. In other words, there is some population that, at least in a moral sense if not a legal one, "owns" the organization.

The concept of ownership is narrower than *stakeholder.* Stakeholders can be staff, vendors, neighbors, service recipients, and others, as well as those I am calling owners.

Owners stand in relation to the organization just as stockholders do in an equity corporation. They constitute—even if unorganized, unrecognized, and often undefined—the primary object of board allegiance and often its source of moral authority. Hence, a school board governs on behalf of citizens of the school district; a trade association board governs on behalf of the association members; a community hospital board governs on behalf of the local public.

Representing the ownership requires that a board represent the diversity within the ownership.

Because the ownership is made up of individuals (or individual organizations, in the case of federations) there are bound to be differences. Human beings come in different colors, temperaments, philosophies, appetites, genders, and versions of reality. Representing the ownership requires that a board represent the diversity within the ownership. The moral imperative for diversity in board life derives, then, not from some abstract commitment to humanity, but from the simple fact that responsible action is impossible unless the diversity present in the ownership is integrated into governance.

This obligation requires the board first to be sure just who its ownership is and, second, to arrange for that diversity to express itself in the boardroom.

Meaningful Diversity in the Boardroom

FAQ ➡

Can the diversity of the ownership be represented by the diversity of the board members?

For the array of humankind and human opinion in the ownership to find its way into governance, the most obvious mechanism is to constitute the board to be a reflection of the ownership. Gender, racial, religious, and geographic diversity in the ownership can, within limits, be paralleled in board membership. Expectations for quasi-public boards to be representative in this demographic way have increased greatly in the past couple of decades. Having women, blacks, Hispanics, disabled people, teens, consumers, or environmentalists on the board can indeed enhance true diversity if they enrich board sensitivity to the needs of its ownership.

Gender, racial, religious, and geographic diversity in the ownership can, within limits, be paralleled in board membership.

But the tendency toward tokenism often burdens these "special" board members with the daunting task of representing everyone with whom they share whatever characteristic identifies them. Excluding anyone from board membership because of identification with a certain group would be reprehensible. But in a twist of irony tokenism often imparts, having a carefully chosen "representative" membership can seduce a board into slackness about actually gathering input from such groups. Boards can miss the opportunity to find true diversity by settling for what amounts to a cosmetic solution.

> Having a carefully chosen "representative" membership can seduce a board into slackness about actually gathering input from such groups.

In fact, there is no way that a board can be constituted so that it represents all diversity present in the ownership. The entire range of diversity can be accommodated only by swelling the board to unmanageable size. Consider the extreme: A public or nonprofit board might represent a community of, say, 150,000. *Absolute* representation of the diversity in such a population would call for putting 150,000 on the board. Boardrooms aren't

> ← FAQ
> Won't a larger board mean there is greater diversity in governance?

made that large, so let's consider reducing the board size to 15,000 persons, a 10:1 ratio. To be even more practical, let's cut the board to 1,500 or 500 or fifty. By the time we've dropped to these numbers, any ability of this board to embody the full diversity of its community has been lost several digits ago. Yet the board's ability to be assertive, to be agile, to deliberate, and to speak powerfully on the ownership's behalf increases dramatically as the numbers are reduced. A board of ten is far more able to take charge of its own leadership obligations than one of fifty—or even twenty.

> There is no way that a board can be constituted so that it represents all diversity present in the ownership.

How often I have seen boards grow to twenty or forty members in the name of diversity, only to gain awkwardness and ineffectiveness in exchange for a mere semblance of diversity. After making even Herculean efforts to honor diversity in board composition, diversity *in board members* can never pay sufficient homage to diversity *in the ownership*. That is why it is not good enough for a board to represent diversity in itself. It has the far higher calling to become *the channel through which ownership diversity is expressed*.

Positive Steps for Change

Actually assimilating an appropriate amount and array of diversity in the board's deliberations requires deliberate, planned steps. Let's look at a few elements that the board should consider.

> ← FAQ
> How can a board be sure that it truly represents its ownership?

The true ownership is usually not the funding source.

1. Define your ownership. For some boards (city councils, professional societies, churches, trade associations), there is an easily identified owner group. For others (social service agencies, community hospitals, advocacy associations), the task may be more difficult. For boards in the latter situation, geographic locale or like-mindedness may be the identifying factor. The true ownership is usually *not* the funding source, as many organizations that are dependent on grants or government contracts might at first think.

2. With the ownership defined, the board then must adopt a frame of mind of acting on the ownership's behalf. School board members, if the general public is deemed to be the ownership, would deliberate and vote their best judgment of what is best primarily for the general public, not for parents. This does not mean that the school board is not interested in children or parents, but that their interest is *on behalf of* the public at large. Community hospital board members would form their opinions with respect primarily to what is best for the community at large, not what is best for physicians or administrative staff.

The board's tough task at this point is to avoid being distracted by other voices. It is easy for boards to become captured by one interest group or another. The power elite, the staff, a fiscal officer, or a particularly vociferous customer group can assume control by effectively usurping it from the ownership at large. These other parties are to be heard, of course, and they certainly have their own importance. But they are not to be heard as owners, lest the true owners be cheated. The board is responsible that such corruptions of its obligation to ownership diversity not occur. Therefore, while the diverse ideas that nonowners bring can be enlightening, stimulating, and perhaps even necessary, hearing them will not satisfy the board's obligation to govern from the ownership's diversity. Fulfilling this kind of civic trusteeship for those who morally own the organization is an acid test of board integrity.

Fulfilling this kind of civic trusteeship for those who morally own the organization is an acid test of board integrity.

FAQ →

If board members disagree, how can they possibly speak with one voice?

3. The board must cultivate an accepting atmosphere about dissent in the boardroom. For diversity to flourish, it must be socially acceptable to examine all ideas, regardless of origin. Otherwise, the rich variety of opinion can become either so squelched or so strident as to become ineffective. It is easy for a board to

become so enamored with presenting a united front that it seeks to play down any disagreements. Such a board has forgotten that its real strength is that it is able to make single-minded decisions from a diverse base. Diversity assures a broad base of wisdom. The vote assures that diversity does not deteriorate into a kind of group fibrillation and consequent lack of resolute action.

> It is easy for a board to become so enamored with presenting a united front that it seeks to play down any disagreements.

In addition to encouraging dissent before a board decision, the board should also clarify how dissent is to be expressed after the vote. For example, a board may choose not to shackle dissent even then, but to demand that members pair any public dissenting remarks with a recognition that the board's single voice (the vote) must and should prevail. That is, they support the legitimacy of the process even while disagreeing about a decision.

4. The board should gather data in a way that reflects all aspects of the ownership. The statistical base from which the board operates will be rooted in the full expanse of the ownership. The various tides of opinion, the heat and passion with which they are held, and the underlying social issues will be demonstrated in the data assembled for deliberation.

Further, the board should seek diverse opinions from persons outside the board membership itself. Proponents of opposing points of view would be invited to present and even to debate. The board will meet with, gather input from, and otherwise interact with the broad base of own-

> Getting direct input from the ownership usually requires going after it.

ership. For example, board members might hold focus groups, attend functions, and interview people in the ownership. Getting direct input from the ownership usually requires going after it. Boards that wait for constituents to take the initiative receive a lot of customer complaints but little ownership input.

Ownership input—in all its diversity—is the only morally defensible foundation for board decisions. Seeking and attending to the diversity of ownership input plus careful integration of other sources of wisdom are the foundation of legitimacy in board decisions.

Making Hierarchy Work: Exercising Appropriate Board Authority in the Service of Mission

BOARD LEADERSHIP, NUMBER 12, MAR.-APR. 1994

S OME PEOPLE have difficulty with what they perceive to be the hierarchical nature of the Policy Governance model: The board is clearly dominant, the CEO is not an equal partner with the board, the staff is not an equal partner with the CEO. Such hierarchy is not only off-putting to them, but also borders on being regressive, rigid, militaristic, and, for some, antifeminist. These critics often speak of the "partnership" of board and staff as if there were no differences in authority.

FAQ ➡

Isn't the hierarchical nature of Policy Governance out of step with modern participative organizational styles?

In recent years, autocratic management has fallen into disfavor as more participative styles have emerged. There has been a trend away from "vertical" and toward "horizontal" organization. Unfortunately, it has become more a symbol of political correctness than of accuracy to confuse *fewer* levels of organization with *no* levels, to misconstrue humanely administered authority as *no* superior authority. Being wedded to current fashion accounts, perhaps, for making it an article of faith to pretend that board and staff have the same level of responsibility and authority.

Without a doubt, hierarchy has often served as a mechanism for the denial of representation, the squelching of human potential, and even outright abuse. Hierarchy, like any other method of distributing power, warrants careful scrutiny, especially with respect to fairness and the balancing of authority and responsibility. In the larger world, beyond management, a great deal of political and social thought has struggled with this issue.

I make no case that hierarchy is morally beneficial or nonbeneficial. Hierarchy *is*. (Even the most egalitarian person expresses hierarchy when unilaterally deciding to employ or retain a plumber, hairdresser, or lawyer.) Consequently, Policy Governance seeks to ameliorate the potentially negative effects of hierarchy; it does not seek to deny the existence or justifiability of whatever natural hierarchy exists.

> I make no case that hierarchy is morally beneficial or nonbeneficial. Hierarchy *is*.

Perhaps I'd better explain *natural hierarchy*. I have an automobile. It seems that, by the nature of things, I have greater authority over my car than does a casual passerby or the mechanic I've hired to repair the car. Then, with respect to any actions taken concerning my car, I "outrank" the mechanic. I am higher in the car-things hierarchy than the mechanic.

Similarly, the rider to whom I regularly give a lift to work has an interest in my car, as does the person who sells me gasoline. They, too, rank lower in this hierarchy than I, though each has a stake in what is done with my car. In no way does our hierarchical relationship make me a better or smarter person than the mechanic, rider, or gas station manager. So let's establish right away that no matter what hierarchy contributes to understanding, it doesn't help at all in judging personal worth.

Owning Up to Ownership

For any organization, there are groups with some stake in its existence, its operation, its success, and perhaps even its failure. These stakeholders are staff members, board members, advisers, suppliers, neighbors, customers, owners, labor unions, protagonists, antagonists, and even people with similar beliefs. However, owners—whoever they may be—have a special role of a different order from other stakeholders. Surely there is a distinct difference between the other stakeholders in my car and me.

The biggest difference is that I own the car. In fact, is that not what *ownership* ordinarily means—first priority on use, disposition, and treatment? It doesn't mean that no one else has a stake, nor does it mean that I am therefore somehow better than them.

For most nonprofit organizations and all public organizations, the legitimate owners are a population of people beyond the board and staff. The citizens of a city own their municipal government. The members of a trade association own their association. These persons are not better, not smarter, and perhaps not even more caring about the organization than other stakeholders, but *they are the owners*. And that warrants their being at the top of the hierarchy.

To pretend that anyone else is their equal on this measure is

FAQ ➡
Aren't the board and staff partners?

just that—a pretense. It would be ludicrous for city employees—no matter how much laudable personal investment they have in government—to maintain that their ownership of city government supersedes or even equals that of citizens as a group. The same observation could be made of public school teachers and the public, trade association staffs and trade association members, church staffs and congregations. Is that hierarchy? You bet it is . . . and without apology.

Recognizing Hierarchy

A governing board is a microcosm of the owners, fulfilling what has been called a *civic trusteeship* role on the owners' behalf. It is as if the owners are the principal and the board its agent. The board exercises its stewardship role with a legitimacy unmatched by the staff or other stakeholders. Hence, the initial point of hierarchy—the ownership—passes to the second level of hierarchy—the governing board.

In seeing to the execution of its decisions, the board charges a CEO with the accountability of performance. Doing so requires that the CEO be granted commensurate authority. At this point, no one else is held accountable to the board but the CEO; therefore, no one else need be granted authority. The hierarchy continues.

The principle of what one might call *sequentially linked authority* connects these elements of enterprise from owner on through to filing clerk. At what point in the chain would we interrupt it in order to terminate the "downward" extension of its inherent hierarchy? And how would we justify disempowering whoever we have left as the last in the chain? He, she, or they would be charged with an accountability from above with no commensurate authority to perform upon it. Indeed, what is the reason for interrupting this seemingly natural linkage in the first place, other than some belief that there should be no hierarchy?

> To *recognize* natural hierarchy is no excuse for accepting its potentially destructive features.

Yet to *recognize* natural hierarchy is no excuse for accepting its potentially destructive features. An important challenge in the design of human systems—including governance and management systems—is to imbue structures of power with a human face, thereby marshaling both power *and* humanity in the service of mission.

Harnessing Hierarchy

Policy Governance, then, seeks not to deny hierarchy but to harness it and ameliorate its untoward effects. Harnessing consists chiefly of making it impossible for elements of hierarchy—most pointedly the board and CEO—to escape recognition of their accountability. Amelioration consists of two aspects of decision making and control.

> ← **FAQ**
>
> How can a board use hierarchy appropriately?

First, those higher on the ladder can make better decisions and, at the same time, reduce ill effects by soliciting participation in their decisions from those on lower rungs. Anything that contributes to better decisions benefits everyone in the long run. In Policy Governance, the CEO gathers multiple, divergent staff input for board decisions rather than disregarding that diversity in order to submit a single CEO recommendation. Within staff operations, a similar tack would benefit the CEO for his or her own decisions.

Second, those on a higher rung can best "control" the next rung down with minimal rather than extensive restraints. In Policy Governance, control by the board is embodied in ends policies and executive limitations policies. In each case, the operating rule is that the board be no more detailed in its policy requirements than necessary, stopping its detail at whatever point it can accept *any* reasonable interpretation of a stated expectation. The effect of such control is to fulfill the board's accountability, but in a way

> The virtually universal failing of boards to use power appropriately has done more damage to organizational effectiveness than antihierarchy advocates ever have.

that minimizes the controlling effect on staff. Although Policy Governance does not address internal management, I strongly suggest that the same principle be followed at each supervisory level.

As you can see, I do not support the antihierarchical attitude that demands greater authority for lower positions in the chain than is commensurate with their burden of accountability. In nonprofit and public organizations, it is likely staff members who complain about hierarchy would place their own desired authority higher than the authority of persons charged with the ownership's proxy. This is not power to the people, but power usurped from the people. It is true, of course, that a board may not exercise its proxy responsibly, but why should we believe that pretenders to the crown will do it better?

I do not, however, support unnecessary and thoughtless use of the power that hierarchy can encourage. And the virtually universal failing of boards to use power appropriately has done more damage to organizational effectiveness than antihierarchy advocates ever have. The problem has not been that hierarchy in itself has done harm, but that failing to fulfill the obligations attendant to hierarchical position has allowed brute force—or, more commonly, brute negligence—to cause or allow conditions that are ineffective at best, inhumane and oppressive at worst.

Hierarchy is obligated to be—and should be held accountable to be—thoughtful, humane, and even gentle with power, but need never apologize for existing.

Political Boards and Councils Have Consistently Failed to Live Up to Their Potential

Elected Boards: Meeting Their Special Governance Challenge

BOARD LEADERSHIP, NUMBER 15, SEPT.-OCT. 1994

Boards of our bodies politic have a tough time with governance. No nonprofit board should ever look to city councils, county commissions or boards of supervisors, legislatures, port authorities, school boards, water districts, parliaments, or congresses for pointers on how to govern. These bodies are best used as examples of what board leadership should *not* look like.

And yet, in a democratic society, elected boards are the backbone of public policy, the prime channel through which people design their laws, their society, and their economies. It would seem that the sheer importance of elected bodies and their crucial role in our increasingly complicated world would compel them to be exemplars of governing leadership. But not so. If any group is utterly seized by the ghost of governance-past, it is the forum elected to conduct the public's business. Why are elected bodies perhaps more prone to micromanagement, trivia, short-term thinking, and empty rituals than their nonprofit cousins?

The similarities between the fundamental tasks of elected boards and nonprofit governance are striking and, I believe, far more extensive than elected officials would like to think. Consider municipal government. In common with all organizations, each city government is an enterprise with purpose and policies, with governance and management functions to be differentiated and optimized, with resources to be carefully allocated. In common

← FAQ

What do elected boards and non-profit boards have in common?

The similarities between the fundamental tasks of elected boards and nonprofit governance are striking.

with trade associations and professional societies, municipal government's owners and customers are confusingly the same people. In common with hospitals and relief agencies, municipal government deals with intractable problems of the greater society. In common with business, it produces products and services for a demanding and discriminating public.

Not Like Other Boards

Despite the generic similarities of various types of governance, let's recognize that a city council or legislature is, indeed, different from a nonprofit board. One difference is that some elected bodies are imbued with what political scientists call "police power." In addition to being able to tell their employees what to do, these elected bodies have the socially legitimized authority to tell the rest of us what to do as well. That is, they have law-making authority.

These bodies' right to enforce their will on others lends a certain gravity to their task. Accordingly, extraordinary safeguards against caprice and mischief are warranted. More than usual public exposure of deliberations and decisions is warranted. Because their actions so directly affect the conduct of others, they encounter massive tides of public opinion at every turn. Even small decisions stimulate petitions, complaints, and criticism.

Further, individually elected officials have a very personal connection to the electorate. They are hired and fired by the voters. They answer to voters, not to their peers. Hence, development of group action, the cultivation of group responsibility, and the crucial establishment of a healthy wholeness in the governing body are difficult. Elected officials can consequently act like prima donnas. When a group mentality does emerge, it is as likely to be by party affiliation as by membership in the same elected forum.

City and county governments are hampered in their flexibility by laws that regulate them to the point of paralysis.

City and county governments are hampered in their flexibility to deal with their daunting task because of laws that regulate them to the point of paralysis. They are the political equivalents of companies whose efficiency is mired in a procedural quagmire. Agendas reflect much that is trivial and little of the stuff of true leadership. School boards by law must themselves take action on the hiring of every teacher, a board activity as ludicrous as it is ritualistic. Do we really think the school system isn't competent to hire teachers without help from board members? If the system isn't competent to operate a personnel system without board involvement, how can we possibly trust it to educate our children?

Elected bodies' access to power inhibits change, since change alters relationships that feed on reflections of that power.

But even if legislators had not created the tangle of laws that, in effect, *require* our elected forums to govern poorly, the iron grip of tradition would do so anyway. Old rules and old ways persist tenaciously. Congressional methods of operating—including officious micromanagement by committee—predate ideas of modern management. Consequently, the familiar committee system, detailed oversight, and lack of group discipline prevail in a body that can blame no higher authority for its rules.

When individual elected officials try to change these circumstances, the power patterns quickly become obvious. Just as in a nonprofit board, if having a personnel committee makes no governance sense, the committee may be allowed to live on simply because the committee

Before we blame elected officials for everything, let's admit that *we* elect them.

chair will fight to retain his or her bully pulpit. Elected bodies exist in order to exercise massive power that belongs to the electorate. That very access to power inhibits change, since change alters relationships that feed on reflections of that power.

Politicians Aren't the Real Problem

Before we blame elected officials for everything, let's admit that *we* elect them. They must be doing what it takes to get elected and to stay in office. It isn't just that officials are mismanaging governance, but that we, the electorate, tolerate and even demand that mismanagement.

Citizens who complain to school boards, for example, are far more likely to drag those boards into the micromanagement of bus routes and classroom practices than to spur them toward strategic leadership. Citizens write their legislators to influence a specific choice rather than to chide them toward better governance. Each of us operates much more as a customer of government than as a joint owner, even though it is the latter role that offers long-term improvement.

Each of us operates much more as a customer of government than as a joint owner, even though it is the latter role that offers long-term improvement.

Because of what it takes to please us, the very visibility to which publicly elected boards are exposed is itself a big impediment to good governance. City council members, for example, are as busy posturing as producing. We the public respond to the "old politics" skills of behind-the-scenes maneuvering and lining up votes with a wink (if not with admiration), much as a slack parent would call a misbehaving child cute. Posturing even goes so far as seating arrangements. Look at the physical seating typical for county commissions, city councils, and school boards. It is invariably arranged not for the give and take struggle of constructing public policy, *but for a performance!*

> We the public are as happy as the officials are to let the hard questions slide.

Wouldn't it be refreshing to hear a city council say, "We really have no idea how to deal with the deteriorating infrastructure without massive tax increases. Let's be sure we get all the facts about the matter. We'll provide public education and carefully structured, systematic citizen input (and not just depend on whoever happens to show up for a public hearing). Then, armed with a legitimate sampling of how the public feels about this dilemma, we have no choice but to make hard decisions about long-term municipal viability."

> Public boards, councils, and commissions have the opportunity to be exemplars of governance instead of its most visible negative examples.

But we the public are as happy as the officials are to let the hard questions slide. "The council a few years from now can deal with this hot potato" is a municipal equivalent of Neville Chamberlain's infamous statement of political procrastination, "Peace for our time." No wonder that with the crucial need for exceptional public governance, we are more likely to get obfuscation, empty political correctness, and demagoguery. Statespersonship by individual elected officials is a rare and precious quality. Statespersonship by boards, councils, and commissions of elected officials is practically unknown.

Raising Our Expectations for Governance

Despite the unique circumstances of elected boards and the long tradition of dysfunctional practice, it is possible not only to improve, but also literally to transform governance in our elected forums. In fact, the challenge to elected boards goes beyond their own excellence: Public boards, councils, and commissions have the opportunity to be exemplars of governance—teaching the rest of us how to do it—instead of its most visible negative examples.

The long-term solution to the problems of governance—whether of elected bodies or not—lies in a general public that must be more sophisticated about what to expect from our elected forums and other boards. After all, the boards that everyone sees are city and county bodies, legislatures, and school boards. They are the forums from which we learn, and, so far, what we can learn best from them is how *not* to govern. (Can you think of a worse way for students to learn governance than to watch the typical school board?) But to teach governance by example means that elected boards must first overcome their own barriers.

When elected bodies govern in a respectable fashion, individual members of city councils will have neither the time nor the right to meddle in the public works, parks, or police departments. Senators won't be able to interfere with bank examinations or federal housing grants. Committees of legislatures will no longer make virtually unilateral decisions about regulations in mental health or education. School boards will no longer hire school principals.

But to adopt Policy Governance, school boards and city councils must bring their constituencies along with them on their governance journey. Elected bodies would only be asking for trouble if they were to embark on such a radical shift—regardless of its benefits—without ensuring that the general public, press, unions, every pressure group, and all funding and regulating bodies understand the effort. (Boards of large membership associations are faced with a similar challenge.) This adds to the cost of making the change, but it is a cost that is inescapable under the circumstances and is, in any event, less than the cost that conventional governance currently imposes.

How will Policy Governance look in those vaulted chambers? City councils would continually weigh exactly what municipal outcomes for citizens are worth how much taxation. Should our city government produce safe streets, civic attractiveness, and potable water? If so, how much of each is worth how much taxation? What of the other municipal products? School boards would struggle with and determine exactly what skills and insights for tomorrow's adult citizens are worth what part of the education dollar. How will the resources be apportioned among mainstream kids and ones with special difficulties or special gifts?

Instead of tinkering with management, these bodies would be the electorate's hired thinkers in the business of crafting tomorrow's political reality. Perhaps it is too much to expect elected boards, councils, and commissions to be our moral beacons. But rather than being among society's most calcified elements, they should at least be the visionaries of our bodies politic.

Your Board's Market Surrogate Obligation

BOARD LEADERSHIP, NUMBER 30, MAR.-APR. 1997

ECAUSE POLICY GOVERNANCE applies to governing boards of any type, I am often asked what I see as the salient difference between nonprofit and profit governance. Is there a difference between the board task in governing a social service agency, for example, and a widget manufacturer? The question is usually rhetorical, for virtually everyone believes there are massive differences.

And I do, too. But the differences I see are usually unlike the differences others emphasize. People ordinarily believe the most striking difference between a profit and a nonprofit organization is that one is organized for profit and one is not. Certainly this is the distinction most of us have chosen to focus on simply by referring to organizations as profit and nonprofit. Others express a more value-laden judgment of the same thing: One organization is for people, the other for money. Nonprofit organizations sometimes take this expression to some pretty self-righteous extremes. A less loaded distinction is that profit organizations distribute a monetary return to investors, and nonprofits do not.

> **FAQ** →
>
> Do the boards of nonprofit and for-profit organizations have different jobs?

I don't think any of these differences have a substantial effect on the nature of governance. The job of the board is the same in all cases—to see to it, on behalf of some "ownership," that its organization (1) achieves what it should and (2) avoids what is unacceptable. With no difficulty at all, one can apply this board job description to business corporations just as well as to school boards, chambers of commerce, city councils, and community action agencies. So, if there is a significant difference, just what is it?

One difference appears to lie in the nature of ownership. Let's look at the nonprofit and governmental circumstance first. Owners are either persons (or organizations) that freely associate themselves with the owned organization, or they are persons who can move into and out of the ownership for reasons largely unrelated to the ownership role itself. The former is illustrated by a trade association or professional society. The latter is illustrated by a city or other jurisdiction. In business, owners can move in and out as well but do so by purchase and sale of stock.

In either case, the board might be working for a shifting ownership and must take into account commensurate shifts in what best represents ownership interests and wishes. But whether the owners are stockholders or citizens or members, the nature of the governance task is unaffected.

The crucial difference, I believe, lies in the market circumstances faced by profit organizations and by nonprofit or governmental organizations. Businesses ordinarily compete in a relatively free market—that is, a market in which potential consumers decide whether to pay the full cost of production (plus profit) for some perceived benefit. If enough consumers choose to do so, the organization is said to have produced something worth its cost. The aggregate consumer judgment is directly reflected in sales and therefore can be seen in black and white in an income (profit and loss) statement.

← FAQ

What is the difference between nonprofit or public boards and business boards?

Examine what happens in most nonprofit and governmental organizations. They produce something of value too, and also at some cost. A school board "produces" the ability to read by expending certain resources. A trade association may "produce" a favorable public image for its members, but at some cost in dues. A city council "produces" safe traffic flow at the cost of some tax burden and some loss of drivers' freedom (to drive as they please). The productive process is similar.

But look at the market judgment. For nonprofits and governmental organizations, there is no automatic test of product worth by consumers paying the full cost of production. If consumers pay some reduced amount (such as the "sliding fee scale" used by social service agencies or tuition by state universities), their choice tells us only that what they are receiving is worth the amount they pay, not whether it is worth what it cost to produce. In fact, nonprofit and governmental organizations are often established intentionally to separate consumer benefit from consumer payment. They are established to address unacceptable conditions that a true market would allow (such as starvation, homelessness, or illiteracy). True, cities and others often impose

> The lack of a clear market voice is the difference that really matters.

"user fees," which may or may not represent the full cost of production, but this is the exception, not the rule. The result is that the market voice is nonexistent or, at most, substantially muted. Thus, organizations that operate in this muted market have no way to know what their products are worth!

And that—the lack of a clear market voice—is the difference that really matters. If you don't know what your products are worth, how can you know if you've produced them efficiently? Keep in mind that the products I'm referring to are not services, programs, curricula, or any other organizational activities. The real products are the changes, benefits, or effects in consumers' lives; otherwise, we are only attending to our well-intentioned busyness rather than truly to our desired organizational results.

FAQ ➡

How can a board really know what the products of their organization are worth?

We know what a pair of shoes is worth. We know what a crowned tooth is worth. We know what an automobile water pump is worth. We know what a Madonna CD is worth. The market tells us in unmistakable terms. We may or may not like it, but the market speaks with the behavioral choices of thousands or millions of persons who could have spent their money another way but chose not to. *Vox populi, vox Dei* ("the voice of the people is the voice of God").

What is it worth for a dysfunctional family to be functional? What is it worth for a child to read at the seventh-grade level rather than the sixth? What is it worth for a homeless person to have shelter? What is it worth for a real estate agent to have timely, accurate data on property for sale? What is it worth for the infant mortality rate to be 1 percent lower? Why don't nonprofit and public boards routinely debate these things? If deliberating priorities isn't about choices among competing benefits and their costs, what is it about?

> If deliberating priorities isn't about choices among competing benefits and their costs, what is it about?

Keep in mind that *cost* or *worth,* as I am using the terms here, can be denominated in any number of ways. The economists' term *opportunity cost* comes the closest to my meaning. Opportunity cost is anything of value given up in order to have some commodity, experience, or other benefit. In other words, when a hospital ponders whether to provide relief from the full range of burn traumas, it does so at some cost. The cost might be stated as a $2.5 million capital outlay and an estimated level of new risk. But it may also be stated as forgoing the production of a competing benefit, for example, respite and recovery for psychiatric disorders. Further, the cost of results can be seen in terms of the relationships among various results or recipients. For example, just stating relative priorities among results or recipients is a statement of their relative worth. Less immediately tangible but just as real, the cost of producing a certain result or of producing it for a certain population might be a decline in public image or a loss of specific donors. The concept that benefit bears a cost is a simple one. The application can be difficult.

Obviously, it takes a board focus on ends (not means) to even get started on such a quest. Traditional governance cannot even get into this game, much less hope to play it well, for it rarely deals directly with the ends concept at all. Traditional boards are quite content to compare the costs of activities (programs, services, curricula) rather than having to struggle with the results and their worth. The real challenge to nonprofit and public governing boards is not just to have a focus on results as compelled by Policy Governance but also to make decisions about *which results are worth what cost,* choices that Policy Governance both allows and obliges them to make. It allows them to make the choice by providing a rational conceptual framework in which to do so. It obliges them to make the choice because only when the board has specified results, recipients, and the cost or worth of those results has it completed its ends work. This is not easy work, but a Policy Governance board is committed to grappling with this task in perpetuity.

> The real challenge to nonprofit and public governing boards is to make decisions about *which results are worth what cost.*

In other words, the nonprofit or governmental board must stand in for a market that cannot speak clearly for itself, to be, in effect, a *market surrogate.* There is no necessity for such a role in business corporations, which are engaged in meeting a market that speaks quite clearly as to the worth of what is produced. Businesses have to second-guess, survive, and, if fortunate, thrive in a market, but they never have to speak for it.

Moreover, the nonprofit or governmental board is acting on behalf of an ownership that is likely far larger than the board membership (as is usually the case with business boards as well). The board carries out its market surrogate function on behalf of that far-flung ownership,

> The nonprofit or governmental board must stand in for a market that cannot speak clearly for itself, to be, in effect, a *market surrogate.*

which means that the board must be in touch with elusive ownership values in order to determine the worth of different results in various consumer populations—a task

Fulfilling the market surrogate obligation responsibly is the most difficult challenge to nonprofit and governmental board leadership.

sufficiently demanding that no respectable board has time for the wasteful and trivial agendas typical of nonprofit and governmental boards today.

Fulfilling the market surrogate obligation responsibly is the most difficult challenge to nonprofit and governmental board leadership. The product of its fulfillment is that wise, ownership-driven choices can be made about what is required of the organization in terms of what results for which recipients at what cost or relative worth.

Leading, Following, and the Wisdom to Know the Difference

Board Leadership, Number 36, Mar.-Apr. 1998

T HIS ARTICLE IS INSPIRED BY a board member's recent question during a seminar. A bit wary that I was recommending a "board-as-poll-taker" approach, he asked, "Does the board just listen to what owners want, then vote to have it done?" My zeal in underscoring the importance of boards listening to the ownership had mistakenly painted for him a picture in which the board is merely a slave to surveys.

His watchful sensitivity pinpointed a topic of great difficulty, perhaps the toughest quandary in the exercise of board judgment. The dilemma is this: The board represents some base of legitimacy outside itself (in Policy Governance, this reference group is referred to simply as the ownership) and must, therefore, speak on its behalf. To do that, the board must have a clear understanding of what owners want. However, the board is oblig-

> **◄ FAQ**
>
> How does a board member deal with constituency expectations?

ated to focus on and learn about the topic at hand in order to be, in effect, the ownership's policy experts on the matter. Surely, for example, the ownership of a school board—the general public—has a right to expect the board to know far more than the average citizen about the future of, challenges to, and possibilities in education.

Can a board—as my questioner feared I was advocating—simply do what owners want done, even though board members have more insight and experience about the board's subject matter than do most owners? Is the board not obligated to *lead*, rather than just to follow the polls? Yet leading by forging ahead, by ignoring or omitting

> The board's path to wisdom is to listen, to learn, and to judge.

input, will be criticized as being out of touch or elitist. Every legislator and board member faces this lead-follow uncertainty.

I do not to know how to make this dilemma easy to resolve, but in this article I recommend a way to think about it. The board's path to wisdom is to listen, to learn, and to judge.

Attentive Listening

Since the board's job is founded in its owner-representative role, awareness of owners' wishes, values, and opinions is of paramount importance. No amount of input from staff, other providers, or even of current consumers can substitute for the relationship between, as it were, principal and agent. (For an extensive discussion of distinguishing owners from other groups, see the first four articles in this chapter.) This phase of board leadership may not look like leading, but without it subsequent leading is robbed of authenticity.

FAQ ➡
How can the board practice active listening?

So how does a board listen to the ownership? A board needs a strategy for listening, partly because owners are not ordinarily knocking down the doors to be heard. Some owners don't even know they are owners. For example, I know some organizations in my own community (school, city, hospital authority, community college) that could legitimately consider me part of their ownership, but I am undoubtedly unaware of most of them. Another reason strategy is needed is that nonowner groups that can be confused with ownership are crowding in to be heard. The most likely such groups are staff, current consumers (or more likely, subgroups of consumers), funders, and sometimes vendors. Owners, who may be amorphous and aren't usually angry at the moment, can easily be left out.

> A board needs a strategy for listening, partly because owners are not ordinarily knocking down the doors to be heard.

For example, city councils should arrange to hear from citizens about what they find various levels of city benefits worth in taxation. That differs from the widespread practice of listening to disgruntled city customers about potholes or stop sign placement. Association boards should schedule focus groups with members to see how much potential association benefits are worth in dues. These meetings are not, by the way, meant as evaluation of current operations but as wisdom-building for the council or board as it considers the ends (results, recipients, and worth of those results) of the future. And while such listening will do wonders for a board's image, these arrangements are not for public relations. The purpose of these meetings is for boards to listen, not to talk or explain themselves.

These are just examples. Such listening can take many forms. Focus groups, surveys, town meetings, and other mechanisms should all be tried, as appropriate. The listening phase tends to make board members more like the owners. If it is good to construe boards as servant-leaders, as I believe, the servant mode dominates in the act of listening.

> The listening phase tends to make board members more like the owners.

Studious Learning

Good listening will acquaint a board with what owners know. But owners do not know enough to govern. That is why a board exists to begin with. Owners have a right to demand that their representatives listen to them, but just as surely they are entitled to representatives who know more than they do. So this phase of leadership consists of board members searching out special knowledge relevant to their task—scholarship and erudition are the aim. The board might say, as a legislator once did, that it votes the way its owners would vote if they knew what it does. This phase tends to make board members *unlike* the owners.

Boards must learn what is necessary to govern, not to manage. While that understanding includes a sense of what dangers to avoid (in order to establish wise policies of executive limitations), the toughest knowledge to be acquired is that which prepares the board for the judicious choice of ends.

> Owners have a right to demand that their representatives listen to them, but they are entitled to representatives who know more than they do.

What prepares a board to make ends choices? One obvious necessity is knowledge about the variety and extent of human needs. The board needs to know the current state as well as what the situation will likely become in the absence of its organization. Another useful understanding comes from exposure to differing, even radical, points of view about the nature and causation of relevant aspects of the human condition. A third type of learning is knowledge of what others have been able to accomplish and at what cost (the equivalent of *industry averages* in business). Notice that none of the necessary knowledge is about how to run programs or design services. The proper learning is not so much about the organization being governed but about the world in which the organization is an instrument.

FAQ ➡

What does the board need to know about an organization in order to govern it effectively?

The only exception to this external focus is this: The board needs to know what is more and less possible with the organization it has today. That is, the board will need to know something about its "instrument" in order to choose intelligently among possible ends. But this knowledge is about its capabilities and incapabilities rather than its operational workings per se. For example, if a board considers focusing its organization on needs of children rather than adults, it is important to know that the organization currently has no expertise about children, though it is not important for the board to know how to run programs for children. Choosing to reorient the organization toward children can still be done, but this choice carries a higher initial cost as the organization regears.

Therefore, a community action agency board would become proficient in the nature and causes of poverty. A school board would become expert in the skills and understandings needed for thriving in a world several decades hence. A trade association board would be knowledgeable about the threats and opportunities its trade is likely to encounter a number of years out.

Sound Judgment

FAQ ➡

What are some criteria for choosing board members?

Listening conscientiously to the ownership and becoming absolutely erudite about the applicable topics will still not lead to wise governance unless the third element can be added. After all, board members are—or should be—chosen for discernment, probity, common sense, perspicacity, and discretion. In short, the board, with its grasp of ownership values and concerns and its understanding of a body of knowledge, must then apply its good judgment.

As much as the exercise of good judgment is a personal quality gained from years of experience and competence-building, it is also the product of care and procedure. A board can affect the process by which it transforms individual judgment into group judgment. The board needs an approach to decision making that guarantees that all facets of an argument are heard. Because the compelling power of group-think can overwhelm almost anything in its path, an ironclad rule of procedure can help. For example, does the board require that even points of view not represented at the table be given a voice? Because the board cannot be large enough to include all diversity present in the ownership, even successfully encouraging all board members to speak up is not enough. Board members can be selected to argue for points of view not their own or, better still, outside spokespersons for unpopular views can be included in board debate.

Moreover, the board can institutionalize the questioning of its own positions. Has it heard from the bold, the radical, the unthinkable—whatever opinion challenges the wisdom of the day? Is the board being too safe, too restrained on one hand, or, on the other hand, too bold or unrealistic? Are the ends under consideration too ambitious or not far-reaching enough? What vested interests in this decision must the board take into account? Boards should ask themselves this: If some organization, sometime, will blaze the trail to a breakthrough, why will it not be us?

> Boards should ask themselves this: If some organization, sometime, will blaze the trail to a breakthrough, why will it not be us?

Some boards might institutionalize these and other questions in their process. Some might work best by using a modified adversarial system with teams of board members arrayed against each other. Other boards will find that a cooperative, team-of-the-whole approach might, in the popular skunk-works fashion, energize the audacious thinking that allows ordinary people to do the extraordinary.

> A board should strive for a wisdom that is not driven by safety or ordinariness, even though it is planted firmly in reality.

A board should strive for a wisdom that is not driven by safety or ordinariness, even though it is planted firmly in reality. Boards without a meaningful connection to their legitimacy base (the ownership) or without a masterful grasp of realities (the knowledge) will not have the grounding to pull this kind of leadership off even if they have the basic ability and the inclination. For, while creative board leadership might often appear unbridled and free, it should not be merely the enthusiastic sharing of ignorance. However, a degree of informed dreaming is necessary. Indeed, true leadership demands that a board abandon its role as overseer of operations. It must embrace a new role—that of the think tank that creatively and vigorously drives and informs policy, creating a dynamism of its own.

Families of Boards, Part One: Federations

Board Leadership, Number 25, May-June 1996

Most of the examples used in *Board Leadership* have dealt with single governing boards of independent organizations. But Policy Governance applies as well to "families" of boards. By families of boards I mean federations, in which multiple organizations own a single organization, and parent-subsidiary arrangements, also called *holding companies,* in which a single organization owns one or more other organizations. I have had the pleasure of working with many such families of boards.

The two types of families have much in common. For example, in both types each board in the family governs a separate corporation. Each board in the family is truly a governing board in its own right even though it may be owned by another organization. Board members in each type still have a responsibility to exercise leadership, though on whose behalf they do so deserves discussion. There is a striking difference, however: structurally, holding companies and federations are upside-down versions of each other (see Figure 2.1).

Among nonprofit organizations, the federation form is the most common type of family. International, national, and regional associations are often federations, although there are

> Each board in the family is truly a governing board in its own right even though it may be owned by another organization.

FAQ ➡

Is it important for the board to know whether it is governing a federation or a holding company?

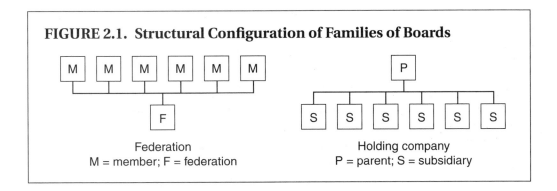

FIGURE 2.1. Structural Configuration of Families of Boards

instances of the parent-subsidiary model. Disturbingly, nonprofit families of boards are frequently confused attempts to be both models at once. For example, if you can't tell clearly whether the national organization is owned by the locals or vice versa, a dysfunctional confounding of the two distinct types exists. Thousands of local, national, and international federations struggle with governance problems caused by lack of role clarity.

In this article, I will present major challenges federations face as they try to implement good governance and explore ways to meet the challenges. In the next article, I will deal with the parent-subsidiary form of board family.

Federations, often called associations, are formed when two or more existing organizations want to accomplish something beyond what any one of them can do alone. Hospitals band together (federate) in order to upgrade their shared image or to influence government funding. Downtown merchants create a federation to stimulate downtown shopping or to convince the municipal council to improve public transportation. The organizations that own the federation are commonly called *members.*

> Federations are formed when organizations want to accomplish something beyond what any one of them can do alone.

The word *federation* itself can be confusing. In its limited sense it refers to the second-order, jointly created entity itself. In its inclusive sense, it refers to the whole family of organizations, including the members themselves as well as the federation proper. Naturally, the word *association* can be confusing for the same reason. To avoid confusion here I'll say *federation* when I mean the single organization created and owned by members, and I'll say *federation family* when I mean the entire family of boards. Therefore, the National School Boards Association (NSBA) in Washington is a federation, but the NSBA plus all its local member school boards constitute a federation family.

FAQ →

What special challenges do federation boards face?
In large part boards of federations have the same challenges that all boards have. In this article, however, I want to address five topics in which federation boards are confronted with an unusual amount of difficulty. These hurdles are not entirely peculiar to federations but do seem to be exacerbated by federation circumstances. Much of the special difficulty arises from the facts that (1) federation memberships are owners and customers simultaneously and (2) issues inherent in the customer role are more concretely evident than issues in the owner role. I'll begin with that basic dilemma.

The Owner-Customer Confusion

All boards should recognize the important differences between owners and customers, but for federation boards the task is unusually difficult. Federations exist, for the most part, to make life better for their members. That is, their members are not only the federation's owners but their customers as well. (For more on the dilemma that occurs when customers and owners are the same people, see the article, "Ownership," at the beginning of this chapter.) However, the role of a *governing board*—including the federation board—is to be an organ of ownership, not an organ of customership. Concerns of customers are important, of course, but direct dealing with them is a management task, not the job of the board.

From day to day the bulk of a member organization's dealings with the federation is around the customer relationship rather than the ownership relationship. Customer interactions include requests for publications, specific services, and information retrieval. Owner interactions pertain to decisions about the products of the federation; for example, how much, in dues, is it worth to add something of value to member organizations? In an organization that is both owner and customer, customer concerns tend to be more immediate and concrete than the often ambiguous owner issues of what is best for the whole. Federation boards are virtually always composed of persons associated with member organizations. Consequently, a federation board member is likely to arrive at a federation board meeting having most recently been relating to the federation in a customer role, not an owner role.

When federation board members misconstrue themselves as customers, they inappropriately drag into their board service the concerns and issues of customers. Federation board members who act like customers do grave damage to the holistic task of speaking with one voice on behalf of the disparate wishes of owners. The danger is that boards will drift toward being groups of privileged customers rather than governors who act on behalf of the membership at large. When this happens, staff give special attention to board members' organizations, putting their needs ahead of other member organizations that do not have a person on the board. Staff's cater-

> The danger is that boards will drift toward being groups of privileged customers rather than governors who act on behalf of the membership at large.

ing to board members constitutes a clear loss of integrity in the federation's obligation to the whole membership.

In a productive setting, customers must be pleased one at a time, while owners must be pleased as a group. Once owners as a group have determined what will be produced for customers (the group takes a vote), then customers *as individuals* have rights and expectations (no vote needed) that we ordinarily associate with consumers; for example, to be given honest product information, to be given full measure. Concern of governors *about* customers and designation of which customers will receive which benefits are appropriate topics for a governing board. Concerns of governors *as* customers are not.

Fidelity to an Entire Membership

Except in very small federation families, there are fewer federation board members than federation members (organizations). Each board member, then, may represent many members, not just the member with which he or she is directly associated. Failure to do so shows a lack of fidelity to the task of governing on behalf of the entire membership. But fidelity to the whole can be difficult for federation board members.

Even after eliminating customer issues in favor of owner issues, each board member will naturally be more conscious of and invested in his or her own organization's point of view than in the opinions of other member organizations. This distraction can be minimized by a clear code of conduct for federation board members and by institutionalizing rigorous, continual linkage between the federation board and *all* federation members. Fig-

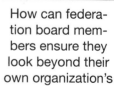

← FAQ

How can federation board members ensure they look beyond their own organization's point of view?

ure 2.2 illustrates one aspect of such resolve, committed to written form in a governance process policy. The board is in place to represent the entire membership (as owners) and cannot do so responsibly if board members represent their own organizations.

FIGURE 2.2. The Organizational Chain of Relationships

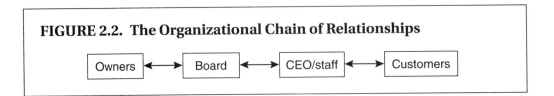

Policy Type: Governance Process
Policy Title: Board as Owner-Representative

The board as a group represents the members' ownership interest in the federation.

I. Although board members are drawn from member organizations, which are customers of the federation as well as its owners, board members must distinguish and serve those interests that are incident to the role of owners, not that of customers.

   A. Members as owners have the right to determine and delegate the purpose and dues cost of the federation.

   B. Members as customers are of direct relevance to governance only in that the board must (1) decide what benefits are to be provided to members and (2) ascertain that members receive those benefits. Both actions are done on behalf of members-as-owners.

   C. It is inappropriate for board members to bring into board meetings their home organization's customer relationship with the federation, except when part of a general board monitoring of CEO compliance with board policies about customer benefits or treatment.

II. Board members' ethical obligation is to represent the entire ownership, not specifically the home organizations from which they are selected.

   A. Appropriate broad-based input from members must be sought and assimilated.

   B. The full range of members' views as to purpose and cost of the federation must be incorporated into board deliberations, not just those points of view held personally by board members.

Interface Between Owners and Operators

The federation board is situated between members-as-owners and the federation staff. Federation staff is situated between the federation board and members-as-customers (see Figure 2.2). The federation CEO should certainly be accountable to the federation board. But the federation CEO should not be accountable to or necessarily have any official relationship with members-as-owners. He or she and the staff would, of course, have official contact with members-as-customers.

Members-as-owners have the right to determine what the federation is for (which is expressed through the owners' representatives, the federation board). Members-as-customers do not; they have the right to receive the benefits the board has determined. Kellogg customers do not have a right to decide that Kellogg will sell automobiles. Kellogg stockholders (owners) have the right not only to decide what business to be in, but whether in fact to liquidate the company and be in no business at all. Owners and consumers are both critical to the enterprise and due their own respective homage, but the prerogatives attendant to each role are vastly different.

> ← **FAQ**
>
> How does the CEO deal with members-as-owners in a federation?

How should a board guard against the deterioration or blurring of these clear relationships? Simply stated, the board should (1) declare and carry out its role in being an accessible and effective channel for owners' expression, and (2) declare and meticulously observe that the CEO answers to the board and to the board alone. I have worked with quite a few federations that were in trouble simply because of their failure to act in this way. Many federation CEOs have been ground painfully between forces out of control because boards defaulted on their primary role. Frankly, the reason federation CEOs get entangled in an inappropriate ownership connection is that their boards have failed to govern appropriately.

Ends Appropriate to a Federation

The ends of a federation are usually, though not exclusively, focused on benefits for members. Because members pay dues, one format for a mega-ends statement would be that "certain results for members are worth a certain dues burden." Hence, a board of Realtors might decide that its mega-end is "favorable conditions for success in real estate by member Realtors for annual dues of X." Like all mega-ends statements, of course, this one begs to be further defined.

Members of a federation must understand that they give up some part of their resources or autonomy in joining the federation. Payment of dues is the most obvious

> Members of a federation must understand that they give up some part of their resources or autonomy in joining the federation.

FAQ ➡

What could ends for a federation look like?

example, but a member might have to agree further to maintain a certain public image or standard in order to belong to the federation. In the federation family Planned Parenthood Federation of America, for example, affiliates (local agencies) must meet certain criteria in order to use the service mark "Planned Parenthood" in their names.

The ends established by a federation board should be ends for the federation, not for the federation family. A common flaw in federations is to state the ends in terms of what the entire family of federation members produces. This is a case of the federation standing on the backs of its members, for it amounts to a claim that the federation in its purview is to be credited with results that are really the work of the members.

Consider two examples. An association of provincial mental health centers doesn't bring about mentally healthy communities, though its members might produce

> Federation ends should address only what the federation itself brings to the party.

that. A state association of community colleges doesn't produce employable graduates, though we hope its member colleges do. Yet federations such as these typically describe their results as if they were the whole federation family instead of simply the federation portion of it. As depicted in

Figure 2.3, federation ends should address only what the federation itself brings to the party: A federation's (B) ends are not identical to the total ends of the family (C), but they may be derived from the family's hoped-for collective product of members (A) and the federation itself.

Hence, in the examples just used, the ends of the association of mental health centers might include an informed legislature, a province-wide database of salaries, and a favorable public image for member organizations. Ends of the association of community colleges might include a menu of governance approaches (for college boards' use), a database of statewide costs for various student results, and member awareness of impending legislative issues. Notice that in each case, the federation is producing value of its own, not piggy-backing on the production of its member organizations.

To be sure, one could speak of the ends of the entire family taken in the aggregate (see Figure 2.3). The desired effect of the entire family is not the effect of the federation, though it might be the driving force that causes the federation board to choose

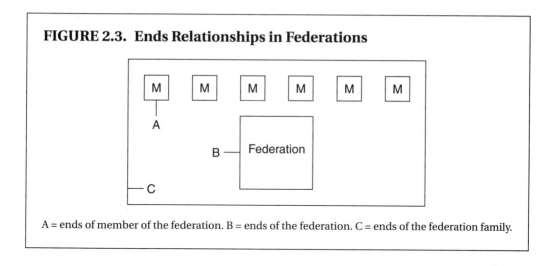

FIGURE 2.3. Ends Relationships in Federations

A = ends of member of the federation. B = ends of the federation. C = ends of the federation family.

certain ends for itself. In this case, if the federation achieves certain ends and the members achieve certain other ends, the federation family will produce a desired collective effect.

For example, local school boards may produce literate young people while the National School Boards Association produces an informed Congress, school financing options, or a well-researched menu of approaches to school governance. Hence, federation members and the federation itself have different but complementary products. As a result the federation family as a whole produces a nation that—with respect to public education—legislates, funds, governs, and operates better than would otherwise have been possible.

Members as Responsible Owners

One of the toughest challenges for federation members is to be responsible owners. It is easy for a member to get into an adversarial relationship with its own creation. A member-as-customer might demand something from the federation that the federation board (on behalf of all members-as-owners) has not established as a product. For example, the federation board, given the press of higher priorities, might have decided that supervisory skills

> One of the toughest challenges for federation members is to be responsible owners.

for members will not be a product of the federation. Yet a single member-as-customer might clamor for just that. As mature adults, members-as-owners should understand that the federation cannot be all things to all people; it cannot produce whatever any member-as-customer wants at any time. Moreover, it would be unfair of the member-as-customer to deride the federation staff for not providing that benefit. Federation staff are often sacrificed on the altar of members' misplaced anger or disappointment.

Members-as-owners have to compromise on their diverse notions of what the federation should produce. Often, in my experience with federations, such maturity has been lost along the way. I frequently see federation families in which the owner organizations treat the federation as the enemy rather than as a product of their own code-termination with other owners. This adversarial relationship often focuses on the federation's CEO, who comes to embody "the evil empire" to the very people who own it!

Thus do members-as-customers often attack the federation staff, as if the problem is of the staff's making. If members' ire should be directed anywhere, it should be directed at the federation board, not the staff. Then the question should be whether the federation board is doing a good job in weighing and choosing among the diverse wishes of owners. If it is not, some reform of board behavior is in order. If it is, some growing up for members is in order. Next, is the federation board exercising its oversight role in demanding that the CEO perform upon the board's expectations? If it is not, reform of board behavior is in order. If it is, members simply need to grow up.

I don't want to leave the impression that federation staffs never attempt to take over prerogatives to which they are not entitled. Sometimes they do. It is possible for a federation, like any other organization, to become staff-driven in a way that is unhealthy. But being inappropriately staff-driven cannot occur except in the absence of proper board leadership.

Federations confront the usual challenges of governing plus a few added difficulties peculiar to their unique design. In the next article, I will address the special challenges that face the other form of board family, the holding company, as it relates to subsidiaries.

Families of Boards, Part Two: Holding Companies

Board Leadership, Number 27, Sept.-Oct. 1996

IN THE PREVIOUS ARTICLE, I introduced the Policy Governance treatment of *families* of boards. By that term, I mean arrangements wherein organizations are owned by other organizations. Hence, governing boards—which, by definition, are the top of their organizations—find themselves beholden to other boards. In the previous article, I showed how Policy Governance helps federations clear up potentially confusing governance issues. In this article, I will show how Policy Governance applies to strengthening the governance system of holding companies.

In the parent-subsidiary arrangement one organization owns—or "holds"—one or more others. Structurally, they are an inverted version of federations. In business, it is common for a single corporation to purchase other corporations. Holding companies are common; federations are infrequent. In government, a peculiar version of a holding company is found quite frequently, though stock ownership is not normally the way that ownership is evidenced. For example, city councils "own" a plethora of boards and commissions (parks, hospitals, airports, and other municipally related functions). Crown corporations (in the United Kingdom or Canada) and their U.S. version (for example, the U.S. Postal Service or state teachers' retirement fund) could be considered subsidiary organizations that have a unit of government as parent. In the nonprofit world, corporations sometimes spawn one or more subsidiaries to carry out functions best performed at arm's length from the original entity.

113

For this article, I'll define my terms this way: *parent* will mean the holding company itself, so I might speak of the parent board or the parent CEO or merely the parent. If I simply say parent, that will refer to the holding company as a unit without distinguishing between its board or staff. *Subsidiary* will mean a corporate body owned by a parent. Subsidiaries are separate corporations in their own right; otherwise they are merely divisions, departments, or chapters of the parent. *Parent-subsidiary family* or *holding company family* will mean the entire family of corporations in this arrangement. Now, let's examine peculiarities relevant to applying the principles of Policy Governance that I have found in parent-subsidiary families.

Confounding the Federation and the Parent-Subsidiary Forms

FAQ ➡

What happens when there is ambiguity about whether an organization is a federation or a holding company?

There are enough differences between the parent-subsidiary family and the federation that it would seem the two could never be confused. But I have dealt with many families of boards that have confounded the two forms in striking ways.

For example, a national organization I worked with had spawned regional chapters that were, for various reasons, incorporated in their home states. Chapters had been created initially as part of carrying out the purposes of the national organization. Because each regional chapter was a corporation in its own right, each had a governing board of directors. Historically, it was clear that the arrangement was of the parent-subsidiary variety.

Enter the ambiguity: Each chapter had staff. Each staff wanted to see its chapter free of the constraints of the national organization. This point of view was flattering to regional board members, so in little ways there developed an enmity between the regional and national organizations. Because national board members were also active in chapters (sometimes on their boards as well), it could be mistakenly assumed that the chapters were the owners of the national organization. Pretty soon some of the family's practices made it seem as though it was a federation family (chapters own the national) and some as though it were a parent-subsidiary family (national owns the chapters). The flurry of mixed messages threw everyone into a great deal of wasteful interactions, hurtful interpersonal transactions, and general organizational ineffectiveness.

This organization could function as a federation or as a holding company with subsidiaries. But it could not have it both ways without serious dysfunction of the people and the mission. The core problem (aside from the political one) is really a question of ownership. Organizationally, who or what owns whom or what?

Ownership

While the owners of this specific national organization are the thousands of individuals nationwide, the owner of the state groups is the national organization. This is one salient characteristic of the holding company family: The parent organization is the unambiguous owner.

If we were discussing business corporations, shares of stock would be the currency of ownership. When there is no stock, ownership is less concretely symbolized. So I am willing to accept softer evidence of ownership. If a nonprofit is created such that another organization is named as its single corporate member, that member is parent. For example, a hospital might create a foundation for which the hospital itself is the sole corporate member—hence able to choose the foundation's board and issue it directives. If the board of a governmental unit is created by, totally answerable to, and its board membership appointed by a larger or more inclusive unit of government, I would consider the authorizing, appointing authority to be parent. For example, a city council might be parent to a library or airport authority.

> This is one salient characteristic of the holding company family: The parent organization is the unambiguous owner.

In these cases, the owner has the prerogative to direct the subsidiary board to act as though some other group were the owner. For example, a city council might instruct an airport authority that for considerations except tax rate implications it should act as though the population of some defined jurisdiction were the owner rather than the city council itself. Unfortunately, city councils along with many other parent corporations rarely make such matters clear to their subsidiaries or even to themselves. That leads us to another item to be cleared up: accountability.

Overlap in Lines of Delegation

I've already referred to an arrangement similar to a holding company commonly found in municipal governments. City councils create commissions, airport authorities, or other entities subservient to the city council yet operating at arm's length. The intent is the same as that of a holding company: to retain essential control over a function yet at the same time consign it to a separate organization. Even though the subsidiaries are ordinarily not incorporated (not strictly fulfilling the independent corporation requirement), their relationship to the city council is similar to that of subsidiary to parent.

City councils are not very careful about separating what they delegate to subsidiary boards and what they delegate to their city manager

City councils are not very careful about separating what they delegate to subsidiary boards and what they delegate to their city manager (CEO). I commonly find that there is disturbing overlap and, at best, great lack of clarity about delegation. For example, a parks board may think it is accountable for—and has authority over—parks and recreation functions, while the city manager understandably thinks that he or she is in that position.

Cutting Subsidiary Boards Out of the Loop

FAQ ➡

What is the line of authority in a holding company?

When a parent owns a subsidiary, the line of authority from parent to subsidiary should be from parent to the subsidiary board, not to the subsidiary CEO. Yet parent corporations regularly connect directly with subsidiary CEOs, bypassing the subsidiary boards and rendering them largely ineffective (see Figure 2.4).

Several of my Catholic hospital system clients wondered why subsidiary boards were not as responsible as they'd like. Upon inspection, the parent was communicating with, delegating to, evaluating, and often even hiring and firing the subsidiaries' CEOs!

State and provincial governments issue instructions directly to the CEOs of funded agencies, thus bypassing the agencies' boards. This common practice is made to seem

---

FIGURE 2.4. Parent Corporation Inappropriately Linking Directly with CEO of Subsidiary Corporations

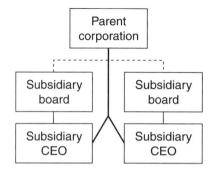

Note: For this illustration, the parent company is drawn without distinguishing parent board from parent CEO.

more reasonable inasmuch as governments communicate about so many items of managerial detail that bypassing local boards is an act of mercy. But communication on that level of triviality is necessary only because the governments haven't done their own jobs to begin with—stating expected ends and proscribing certain means. *Institutionalized entanglement in subordinates' means leads to circumventing the very boards governments rely on to oversee subsidiary performance.*

Institutionalized entanglement in subordinates' means leads to circumventing the very boards governments rely on to oversee subsidiary performance.

The parent should delegate to the subsidiary board and the subsidiary board only, not to the subsidiary CEO (see Figure 2.5). It should hold the subsidiary board accountable for playing the governing role well or else replace the members of that board. There should never be any question that the subsidiary CEO works for the subsidiary board and for no one at the parent corporation.

Empowerment Within Boundaries

Nonprofit and governmental organizations tend toward piecemeal authorization. That is, someone requests authority to do this or that, then a superior authority decides whether to grant the request. "May I do this?" is followed by "You are (or are not) authorized to do that" in a costly, continual grown-up version of the children's game "Mother, may I?"

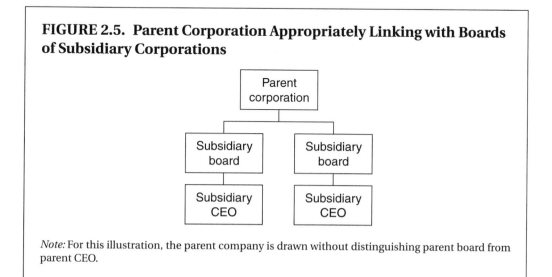

FIGURE 2.5. Parent Corporation Appropriately Linking with Boards of Subsidiary Corporations

Note: For this illustration, the parent company is drawn without distinguishing parent board from parent CEO.

Piecemeal authorization turns subordinates into supplicants, a demeaning situation for those one should be helping toward decision making and professionalism. Policy Governance, by contrast, approaches authorization in a way that enhances the authority of subordinates while freeing superiors from the unending involvement in decisions more appropriately made at subordinates' levels. It does this by granting blanket authorization with associated boundaries: "Within domain A, you are granted complete authority, except that you cannot do X, Y, or Z." This Policy Governance approach to board-to-CEO delegation works just as well for a parent-to-subsidiary format. Subordinates (subsidiaries) know their decision latitude, so they can plan and problem solve accordingly. Their relationship with the manager (parent) is no longer based on "May I do this?" Those in the manager (parent) position are not repeatedly drawn into the subordinate (subsidiary) job and, therefore, away from their own.

> Policy Governance enhances the authority of subordinates while freeing superiors from involvement in decisions more appropriately made at subordinates' levels.

Establishing a Stockholder Representative

Assume that the holding company connects itself appropriately to the subsidiary board, not to the subsidiary CEO. If the lower end of the chain of command attaches to the subsidiary board, where does the upper end attach—just who at the holding company exercises the connection?

The parent board could itself be—as a group—the point of connection. If so, the parent board would be delegating directly to a subsidiary board just as it delegates directly to the parent CEO. Or the parent board could form a committee that would be empowered to "supervise" the subsidiary board. Or the parent board could instruct an officer—perhaps the chairperson—to carry out that task. Figure 2.6 illustrates the options.

Keep in mind that the attachment point is not merely an honorary or ritual position, nor is it merely for passing information. That group or person must be held accountable by the parent board for subsidiary performance. After all, he, she, or they will be in the direct line of authority and, therefore, the direct line of accountability. This is a serious matter, so the person or group must be chosen for the ability to exercise that role successfully.

Again, municipal government provides us with a good example of poor practice. City councils traditionally appoint a "liaison" to subsidiary boards—a member of the council who attends subsidiary board meetings and personally forms the link between council and subsidiary. For example, one council member would be named "airport

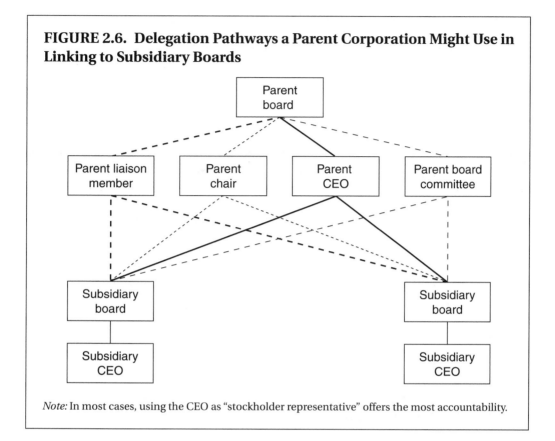

FIGURE 2.6. Delegation Pathways a Parent Corporation Might Use in Linking to Subsidiary Boards

Note: In most cases, using the CEO as "stockholder representative" offers the most accountability.

authority liaison." This common practice cheats the integrity of governance. It is a poor practice, first because individual council members typically do not represent the council as a whole but their own individual views. Second, they can easily run roughshod over the rightful authority to the subsidiary board by interfering with its authorized prerogatives—with nothing the subsidiary board can do about the encroachment that isn't politically risky. Insertion of such personal power severely handicaps proper board process. Third, the city council will not hold the liaison accountable for the subsidiary board's performance (and the liaison would likely not accept it); therefore, the liaison exercises authority with scant accountability.

Of course, a parent board could choose its chairperson as the liaison, but the chair is afflicted with the same complications that befall an individual liaison member. A committee could play the linking role, but committees are notably difficult to hold accountable for operational performance. Besides, we would now have inserted a "miniboard" between two real boards. With any of these choices, the parent CEO cannot be held

---

The most reliable pathway through which the parent board can exercise its ownership of subsidiary organizations is the parent CEO.

---

accountable for subsidiary performance, thus rendering the board's most secure solution for total system accountability unavailable.

Consequently, the most reliable pathway through which the parent board can exercise its ownership of subsidiary organizations is the parent CEO. He or she can therefore be held accountable by the parent board not only for the parent corporation itself but also for the performance of the entire system. Who is better situated and motivated to accomplish that than the parent CEO?

In keeping with this view, the board of a very large insurance holding company client of mine appointed its CEO as "stockholder representative" to carry out the ownership connection. The stockholder representative appoints subsidiary board members, gives subsidiary boards their charge, and replaces subsidiary board members when necessary. With this sobering authority, the CEO was then legitimately held accountable by the parent board for the performance of the entire system of almost one hundred corporations.

Families of boards, whether parent-subsidiary or federation, are just instances of governance with a few extra parts. The principles of Policy Governance not only apply just as well as they do for single boards, but even more so—the more complex the system, the more benefit is to be gained from a powerful organizational framework.

When Owners Are Customers: The Confusion of Dual Board Hats

NONPROFIT WORLD, VOLUME 10, ISSUE 4, JULY-AUG. 1992

OWNERS AND CUSTOMERS are distinct enough in business. Those who hold stock and those who purchase the product or service can be kept clearly separate even when someone on occasion plays both roles.

For many nonprofit undertakings, however, these separate concepts become confounded. Note that a nonprofit's *customers* are its beneficiaries—clients, patients, students, etc. A nonprofit's *owners*—equivalent to a corporation's stockholders—might be members (for a professional association), citizens of a jurisdiction (for a public school system or city government), or local organizations (for a national association or federation).

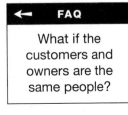

← FAQ

What if the customers and owners are the same people?

The most common error occurs when, perhaps for its rhetorical value, a nonprofit board proclaims that its first obligation is to its customers. More truthfully, its primary obligation is to its owners, on whose behalf and with whose empowerment the board *then* determines which customers will command the staff's obligation. There are *no* customers until the board decides who they will be by establishing the organization's priorities among service populations.

Another example of confounding occurs when either fashionable inclination or

> There are *no* customers until the board decides who they will be by establishing the organization's priorities among service populations.

funder requirement insists that a customer be on the board. Services should certainly be more customer-focused, but if this necessitates either tokenism (one person to "represent" the customer point of view) or distorting the meaning of ownership (disproportionate representation by customers compared with non-customer owners), then the organizational flaw is deeper than a perfunctory board membership will correct.

If the board has clearly decided who customers will be (what populations will be served), then the organization should pointedly listen to those customer groups in order to serve them more effectively. If the staff organization is so fundamentally askew that it is not doing this, adding a customer to the board addresses the wrong problem.

> Having a funder representative on the board is a role conflict to be avoided.

Funding bodies will sometimes be represented on a grantee board. The conflict of interest is but thinly veiled, but more relevant here is the further confounding of owners and customers. For most nonprofits, it is far healthier to see funders as bulk customers than as owners. Bulk customers, however much homage must be paid them for fiscal sustenance, are entities with which the organization makes a deal. Having a funder representative on the board is a role conflict to be avoided.

> Since ownership is an important element of enterprise, its indeterminate status leaves a conceptual vacuum.

The ownership dilemma is typically left undefined by nonprofit boards. For some, it is easy enough to identify owners. For example, the ownership of a professional association board is its membership. For many others, it is not so apparent. By ignoring the issue, the board leaves the group to which it is accountable forever unspecified. Since ownership is an important element of enterprise, its indeterminate status leaves a conceptual vacuum upon which other, more definitive groups encroach.

One such group is the staff. Staff can become owners without portfolio, simply because the board does not posit a more compelling case for a legitimate ownership. It is not that the board has decreed that its staff is its ownership. It is that, by failing to identify the true owners, the organization acts *as though* it exists to serve staff prerogatives.

Another definitive group is that of the organization's customers, who, because they are identifiable and sometimes vocal, can also move into the ownership vacuum. Vocal customers often do not represent customers as a whole, so that bogus ownership is expressed by a splinter group of customers. Such groups can whip board loyalties around as though it is they who should command primary board attention. City councils, county commissioners, and public school boards are examples. In countless open meetings, the board is buffeted about by these legitimate albeit mislabeled interests. The consequent

> Vocal customers often do not represent customers as a whole, so that bogus ownership is expressed by a splinter group of customers.

rolling and swaying illustrate the need for a stable underpinning of legitimacy, a foundation the true ownership concept can provide.

I have dealt elsewhere with the rewards of keeping the owner and customer concepts separate, honoring each in different ways (see, for example, Carver, 1997). It is difficult to conceive of excellence in governance when these two groups are not kept distinct. Community social-service agencies may be morally owned by an entire community, but they exist to serve subpopulations beset by particular life difficulties. The community as a whole (owners) may, for example, own an effort to make normal life more possible for retarded people (customers). The board, representing this broad ownership, should as a body keep the concepts apart even when individual board members must strain to do so, as when a trustee has a retarded child in the program.

Organizations in which *all* board members are also customers present special challenges. Individual tendencies are not then so easily balanced by other members, for all members are in the same situation. Not only are they all customers, but they attained their board seats at the behest of other customers and, consequently, can legitimately see themselves as representing other customers. Trade or professional associations, interest groups, and organizational federations are examples.

Unlike social-service and health agencies, such organizations *exist primarily to serve their ownerships.* Their basic organizational design is—with no denigration intended—self-serving. Hence, the board of the Embroiderers Guild of America is both owned and designed to benefit people who enjoy embroidery. The board of Realtors is owned by and exists to make commerce better for its membership, individual Realtors. The American Hospital Association is owned by and exists for the success of its member organizations. (Often such federations also exist to attain broader goals than their constituent members can achieve acting as individual organizations. Success is construed here to include the attaining of members' more expansive ideals.)

The overlap of customers and owners, common but inconsequential in most community service organizations, is total and even integral to the purpose of such self-serving organizations. Are we to conclude in such cases that the owner-customer distinction has disintegrated? Not at all, as we shall see in our next section.

Maintaining the Distinction

Even in the organization which exists solely to serve its own ownership, governance will be more effective by observing the owner-customer distinction *as rigorously as if owners and customers were not the same people.* This is particularly cogent for individual board members as they seek to play their respective roles with integrity. A brief sketch of the board's role as governing body is necessary before outlining the appropriate board member mentality in this challenging situation.

The board governs as a single body, not as a collection of individuals. Although individual board members have no authority over the organization, the board as a whole has total authority. The board does not exist to help the staff but to own the business, even if in trust. The staff works for the board, not vice versa, though the volunteer mentality often obscures the compelling accountability this employment implies. If the board chooses to use a chief executive officer (CEO) to span governance and operations, then the board expresses its requirements only to the CEO, not to individual staff members. The board should evaluate its CEO only against criteria which have been set forth by the board as a whole at the outset. The evaluative relationship is never to be a capricious one.

While these characteristics are generally accepted as ingredients of good governance, they are seldom true in reality. In fact, the typical strategies of governance as we currently know it conspire *against* these ideals. But for this discussion, we need merely observe that the qualities of trusteeship, board holism, board hegemony, board-CEO linkage integrity, and board discipline are critical for effective governance.

> The qualities of trusteeship, board holism, board hegemony, board-CEO linkage integrity, and board discipline are critical for effective governance.

Unlike the ownership role, the customer role focuses on specific transactions between a customer or customer group and the organization. It deals with single supplier-consumer transactions specifically to maximize customer payoff. The customer need not consider long-range corporate well-being, planning processes, policies, procedures, delegation patterns, owners' wishes, *or even other customers.*

Individuals who serve on boards of owner-serving organizations partake of both worlds. They find themselves thinking as owners and as customers intermittently, often simultaneously, and always confusedly. As a customer, one expects to benefit from the organization's service or product. As an ownership representative, one expects a voice in what that service or product is to be. To make sense of this duality, board members must understand the following role differences.

Individual versus group authority. Even when extraordinary authority is vested in speaking as a customer (due to volume of business or size of constituency), it is expressed as an individual: *I* want this or that. However, an owner can give direction only when speaking with other board members as a group. The board has authority only as a body, not as a collection of individual voices. The *I* can only transact with the organization as a *we*.

Speaking for self versus speaking for others. As a customer, you speak for yourself. You may even speak for a number of customers similarly situated in order to have a greater voice. But you are not *obligated* to speak for others as you are when being an owner representative. Speaking for others must be done with fidelity. Thus, as an owner representative, you must reach out to hear the needs and desires of others. You are obligated to know what owners want.

Judging staff specifically versus judging staff universally. As a customer, your pleasure with the organization comes from staff who "represent" the organization to you, the personal contacts through whom your needs are satisfied or frustrated. As a board member, you judge the chief executive (the accountable embodiment of the whole organization), not individual staff members.

Speaking to anyone versus speaking only to the CEO. As a customer, you can and doubtlessly will speak to anyone whose ear you can command or who can satisfy your need. As a board member, though you can converse with anyone, your only authoritative path is to the CEO—and then only if it is not you but the board doing the speaking.

Pursuing the moment's need versus playing by the rules. As a customer, you can act out of your current needs. As an owner representative, responding out of the moment is likely to jerk the organization around in a dysfunctional and myopic way. Your board obligation, therefore, is to constancy of purpose rather than satisfaction of immediate needs.

Freedom to confront single-event issues versus obligation to "abstract up." Issues between customer and organization ordinarily present themselves as specific events while conducting business. But issues between board and organization require "abstracting up" to a higher, broader, or more inclusive level. As a customer, for example, you might complain that parking places are too narrow or that the shower in your hotel room does not work. As a board member, you can more effectively communicate your concern in terms of customer comfort or impeccability of guest rooms.

Potential adversary of the organization versus creator of the organization. The organization is whatever the board continues to create and empower. Consequently, a board which governs cannot have an adversarial relationship with its organization in the sense of standing outside and judging, as if the board has nothing to do with the situation. The board is leader of the team rather than extraneous observer. It has the authority to change whatever is unacceptable.

Customers, however, can easily take issue with the organization. Therefore, as a customer, you might be in an adversarial relationship with the organization, though as a board member you cannot be. A board member may well be at odds with other members about what should characterize the organization, but since the organization must be what the board as a body wishes, dissident members only have an issue with their colleagues.

Little required discipline versus extensive discipline. Customers do not need the discipline required of owner representatives to balance all the issues and to act responsibly. Owner representatives, however, must use vigilant discipline lest wholeness in the board process disintegrate.

Natural versus unnatural role. Clearly the customer role is a more natural one, more integrally related to our daily life, than playing owner representative. As an independent agent, you make economic transactions in your best interest. As a board member, you are an unseverable part of a group transaction with the chief executive. So acting only through a group dynamic takes an extra measure of devotion and thought.

Systematic Support in the Struggle

For board members of owner-serving organizations, the conflict of roles presents perpetual difficulty. The solution is threefold:

1. *Adopt an adequate governance philosophy.* Any approach to governance which does not respect the owner-customer distinction will *contribute* to the role confusion, rather than resolve it. Further, any model which fails to provide a practical design for the governance role will offer insufficient rules of discipline, thereby allowing proper governance to erode.

All forms of conventional governance wisdom fail in these ways. Accepted practice, including the bulk of available litera-

> Any approach to governance which does not respect the owner-customer distinction will *contribute* to the role confusion, rather than resolve it.

ture, is overdue for fundamental conceptual change. My model for boards is intended (among other improvements in governance) to enable boards to deal more effectively with both owners and customers (see Carver, 1997).

2. *Support one another.* Trustees assume a challenging task, which calls for rigor and commitment. "Hard" devices, such as budgets, plans, committees, and reports, are necessary. But the "soft" mechanism of mutual support is also crucial.

Mutual support means helping each other stay true to a carefully designed discipline for board operation. It means recognizing that commitment to good process often fades in the face of conflict; therefore, *designed* discipline is necessary. It means not allowing politeness and tolerance for straying to become counterfeits of real support.

We must encourage dissent without being held hostage by dissenters. We must support each other in order to pursue excellence, not to excuse inaction.

3. *Develop responsible ownership.* Owners (such as a membership) can make their boards *less* effective, a phenomenon strikingly visible in large federations and in political jurisdictions. Parents assail school boards for trivial matters rather than lobbying for better student outcomes. Citizens urge Congress for favors rather than for more responsible government systems.

In each case, board members (or elected officials) can become advocates for specific customers, thus defaulting on their commitment to represent all owners. As long as owners (*citizens* in the case of political jurisdictions) reward such demagoguery, we will never have quality governance. Boards—exemplified by school boards and city councils—will continue to excuse themselves as victims of unschooled owners.

Boards are not usually well positioned to bring about more responsible owner behavior. A federation board's telling the membership to shape up might meet with the same favor as a school board admonishing the public. But there is a leadership opportunity for boards to teach, persuade, and set examples of disciplined owner behavior. Such leadership is akin to teaching your boss to be a better boss. It works best when the subordinate (in this case, the board) has the integrity to advocate improved process, rather than manipulating toward a particular outcome.

Federation boards at membership conferences might schedule workshops and discussions on the membership-board linkage and on governance itself. Political boards and councils can rearrange board meetings to involve citizens in strategic leadership. They need not teach by example that board meetings are for administrative detail and organizational housekeeping.

Chapter Three

Creating the Board's Single Voice

Appropriate Roles of Committees, Officers, and Individual Members

The group voice is the only expression of board authority. Maintenance of group responsibility and holism requires careful treatment of the segments into which boards are commonly partitioned: officers, committees, and individual board members. When group authority is fragmented, governance can suffer from manipulation, power cliques, and group-think. Although unanimity is not required, unless the board speaks with one voice, it cannot authoritatively speak at all.

Creating a Single Voice: The Prerequisite to Board Leadership

BOARD LEADERSHIP, NUMBER 2, JULY-AUG. 1992

IF YOUR BOARD is to make authoritative decisions—if it is to lead—then on a given issue it must have a single voice. The strength of this single voice arises from the diversity of viewpoints and intentions you and other board members bring to the board, as well as from the way the board focuses this multiplicity into unity. In this article, I'll explain how to do this.

Let's begin with an obvious point. Terry, Sara, Juanita, and Lindsey—or whatever your board members are named—are just themselves until they speak as a group. When they do this, something occurs that's both magic and commonplace: It is not these individuals who have spoken, but the city council, school board, hospital board, or board of regents on which they sit. In other words, your governing board—as opposed to any other group of individuals—exists only because of *corporate* reality. Invisibly, the corporate organization shapes the several individuals into a single, artificial organism.

Threats to Unity

Often the legitimate group voice is usurped, however. You have seen boards whose chairperson or loudest member somehow presumes individual ownership of the board's voice. You have probably also encountered a committee of the board that wields power as if it were the full group. You might have seen board members individually instructing staff. Sometimes the individuals are officers, such as the treasurer, and sometimes the committees are officers as a group, such as the executive committee. It is quite common for executive committees to acquire for themselves virtual board authority, though finance, program, or planning committees often do so as well.

The original simplicity has been lost—the principle that the board speaks only as a group—and with it the basis for effectiveness and leadership. Something has gone awry. Now, it seems the board has several voices. If you were the chief executive, whom would you listen to: to the chairperson? to the executive committee? to the finance committee? to the personnel committee? to the treasurer? to the program committee? to the chairpersons of these committees? to the individual board members who, due to intellect, decibels, or persistence, have the strongest influence on others? or to the board as a whole—*though how would you know what that is?*

If you have any political savvy at all, you will listen to every one of them. But you will learn to assess where the real power lies and give that source particular attention. Power centers change, so you will have to be watchful and ready to shift your attention and your loyalties. It's a high-stakes game, for as chief executive you can ill afford to miscall the next shift in power. If you are really slick, you will "guide" the various groups and individuals so that, taken as a whole, they establish fewer conflicting

> Power centers change, so you will have to be watchful and ready to shift your attention and your loyalties. It's a high-stakes game.

expectations. You will learn to do your guiding carefully so that your behavior is not recognized as the benevolent manipulation that it is.

Oh-oh. I have just described what most nonprofit and public chief executives would recognize as ordinary. It goes with the territory. Most board members *believe* that the board should speak with one voice but have come to accept a state of affairs in which the *pluribus* has a more commanding presence than the *unum*.

And by the way, did you notice how fatiguing and distracting that list of CEO quandaries can be? Have you ever calculated the cost in CEO leadership lost while playing that kind of board-induced game? When the board table is merely a pulpit for articulating individual desires and judg-

> When the board table is merely a pulpit for articulating individual desires and judgments, a board has evaded its responsibility.

ments, a board has evaded its responsibility to work *as a board*. Much of the CEO's energy must take up the slack—an expensive and unhealthy undertaking, indeed. Remember, too, that multiple sources of instruction are always accompanied by multiple sources of judgment. The CEO and staff are subjected to shifting and often contradictory standards of performance.

Voice of Unity and Leadership

Unless a board masters the art of speaking as a group, it has little power to lead. A board speaks with one voice . . . or it doesn't speak at all. Yet most nonprofit and public boards in my experience fail to speak with an unambiguous, single voice.

The problem is, though much talk goes on, groups have a very hard time speaking! As individuals, we communicate all the time. I can usually tell what you are saying, just as you can usually tell what I am saying. But how can you tell what a *group* is saying?

Creating a Single Voice

You could, of course, try to identify a group voice by listening to the interchange among board members. Indeed, individual board members and the CEO regularly form impressions of their colleagues' positions this way. But these idiosyncratic impressions are a risky way to interpret board will. Moreover, the group deserves to control its own expression rather than to be "interpreted." Fortunately, it is an easy matter for a group to state its will simply by taking a vote. Voting imparts a voice to the group that is different from a collection of individual voices.

Recognizing this single group voice by no means presupposes unanimity among the individual voices. They need not agree. In fact, if board members continually agree, they are not all needed. Their obligation to bring multiple views to the table is so great that polite agreement can be an abuse of responsibility. Individual dissenting board members must, however, support the proposition that staff are to follow the group voice rather than their own.

Of course, individuals can still speak, just as they did before. Nothing inherent in the board situation keeps them from exercising their previous freedom. But when individuals speak as individuals, they speak in a capacity they had prior to and irrespective of the board, which is to say, with no organizational power at all.

Your board as a body, then, is obligated to protect its staff from board members as individuals. The mechanics to realize the appropriate wholeness are simple:

1. The board says in writing that the CEO is responsible to the board *only* for decisions it has made as a body.

2. The board resolves that the CEO is bound to honor only *written* board expectations. In the Policy Governance model, these expectations are in the form of ends policies and executive limitations policies.

3. The board permits no fragmentation of its voice. For example, its various committees do not speak *for* the board, but *to* the board.

> ← FAQ
>
> How can a board
> ensure that
> it speaks as
> a whole?

No chairperson, executive committee, or other interpreter can "cover" for the board's failure to speak.

4. In evaluating its CEO, the board *never* makes a judgment on any criterion the board as a full body did not explicitly set.

Under these conditions, individual members can readily give advice, because no one will confuse advice with instruction. By the same token, meddling can be safely deflected by staff, for the board itself will have confirmed that anything less than the board's voice is simply the voice of individuals.

Some Final Tips on Avoiding Trouble

Neither governance nor management can be excellent when the staff works for a boardroom full of bosses. Speaking with one voice will prevent that. But the upshot is that nothing now lets your board off the hook for saying what it needs to say. No chairperson, executive committee, or other interpreter can "cover" for the board's failure to speak.

> **FAQ** ➡
>
> What is the CEO's role in support of the board speaking with one voice?

The CEO has a responsibility to be supportive of the board's new resolve. At the least, the CEO should not sabotage the board's beginning efforts to speak with one voice. For example, the chief executive must take the risk that the board truly means what it says and that he or she will not be held accountable for remarks or expectations voiced—however loudly or pointedly—by individual board members. The CEO *must* stop trying to please individual members and committees, focusing instead on pleasing only the board's mandates. Acting otherwise seduces the board back into old ways.

Further, the chief executive must instruct staff that board members are owed only courtesy and are given no special voice in the organization. That will not be easy at first for the municipal department head who is phoned by a member of council. Nor will it be easy for the nonprofit agency finance director who is approached by an accountant who sits on the board. It is the CEO's task to instruct and support staff members in the new relationship with board members.

But while the chief executive and staff should not make the board's task more difficult, they do *not* bear responsibility for the board's discipline. That responsibility must be owned by the board itself, or else board leadership is oxymoronic. Having accepted that obligation, your board's most useful tactic is to instruct the chief executive to be deaf to all board utterances except those expressed by a successful vote.

For Board Discussion

- Do your board members ever instruct staff or interpret what the board "really meant"? Is the chief executive ever expected to respond to a board member's "I think we need a report on . . ." statement?

- Does your board ever hold the CEO accountable for something the board never took a vote on?

- Are staff members held accountable to please board committees (without the board having "budgeted" some amount of staff support for such committees)? Is your board irritated by the idea of formality (taking a vote) in expressing its voice? Ask your chief executive if he or she is ever confused about just what the board's one voice is.

Boards Should Have Their Own Voice

BOARD LEADERSHIP, NUMBER 33, SEPT.-OCT. 1997

ONE OF THE MAJOR weaknesses in how most boards operate is that they fail to communicate strongly and clearly their intentions and expectations to all those who need to hear them. Of course, most boards think that they are doing a lot of communicating. Don't they have minutes as a record of what they've stated? Doesn't a motion that receives a passing vote prove that the board has a perfectly obvious way of speaking for itself and communicating its decisions in a nice, public way for all to see? In fact, these statements are correct as far as they go. But let's examine exactly what the board is communicating in these usual kinds of communication.

> If you look at the minutes of most board meetings, you will easily find what the board has to say about things on which the board has no need to speak.

If you look at the minutes of most board meetings, you will easily find what the board has to say about things on which the board has no need to speak—for example, trading in a vehicle, giving a staff member a raise, or approving the CEO's staff development plan. However, it is unlikely that in many boards' minutes you would find much about the things on which I believe a board is obliged to speak—such as, "In five years population X will replace population Y as our primary beneficiary." Even though the board may be speaking a lot, on crucial matters we may still be unclear what the board has to say.

For a board to be effective, for it to truly lead and guide an organization, it needs to know when it should speak, and on what topics, and how to do so with clarity and purpose. A board must find its voice and use it well. This is where Policy Governance comes in. Policy Governance forces boards to discipline themselves about where they speak and where they don't, as well as how to frame their speaking. The model is invaluable in helping boards find their proper voice.

> A board must find its voice and use it well.

To help you see how this can happen, I offer in the following paragraphs descriptions of three areas in which how the board speaks can pose a problem. In each example, I explain how the Policy Governance approach would avert these problems.

Approving Staff Plans

Traditionally, the staff brings to the board a recommended course of action, usually embodied in a plan. Common examples are budgets, program plans, and personnel policies. These documents say a lot, much of it in great detail. The board will study the matter, sometimes assigning a committee for preliminary study, and will eventually approve the plan. This is seen as very crucial board work, particularly in the case of budgets, though most often approval is predictable after some minor tinkering.

> How can we tell the difference between staff decisions the board merely blessed and decisions that were truly decisions of the board itself?

Now, here is a quandary. On an official level, whatever is in a board-approved plan can be said to be what the board has to say on the matter. Hence, in a $5 million budget, the board has decided that reupholstering office furniture deserves $45,000 of the scarce funds and that newsprint needed for stand-up easels is worth $750. But everyone knows that the board likely had no opinion at all on these and hundreds of similar items. Yet the board's approval of the budget suggests that the board, in fact, decrees these numbers. We all know that the staff made those determinations, so it is actually clearer what the staff had to say than what the board had to say. Yet are there no aspects of that budget (or other plan) that we can ascribe to the board? Does the board not have a discernible voice other than merely saying "ditto" to the staff's voice? If so, where is it to be found? How can we tell the difference between staff decisions the board merely blessed and decisions that were truly decisions of the board itself?

Even though the board has clearly approved the budget and looked it over in detail, as observers we don't know what the board has said. More important, the board members themselves have no idea what the board has said. There has been a lot of talk, but there has been no clear board voice.

FAQ ➡️

How does Policy Governance differentiate between what the board says and what staff says?

Policy Governance avoids this confounding of board and staff voices by having the board proactively address the fundamental values of finances, budgeting, personnel, and so forth. That is, what the board has to say about these and other high-level policy matters is clearly distinct from what staff is allowed to decide. The policies of Policy Governance (ends, executive limitations, board-staff linkage, and governance process) are exclusively board documents with no staff components at all. *Fundamental values* are those that underlie the myriad of specific decisions that could be made within each topic. For example, revenue and expense totals would be limited by an underlying value of balance. In debating and deciding these values, the board can listen to staff just as it can listen to various other sources of wisdom. But the decisions are made by the board and, therefore, the documents are generated by the board, not just approved by it. There need never be any confusion about what the board itself has decided to say.

Approving or Accepting Staff Performance Reports

Traditionally, the staff brings to the board an accounting of staff actions or achievement, usually referred to as a *report,* whether oral or written. Common examples are balance sheets, income statements, lists of disbursements, and program or staff activity reports. The reports may be a recounting of event-by-event occurrences (as in a list of payments) or a summary (as in most financial statements). Boards ordinarily receive these reports on a regular basis and either approve or *accept* them in a formal board meeting.

The policies of Policy Governance are exclusively board documents with no staff components at all.

And here we have another quandary. By approving the report, the board has officially said that the report is acceptable; the performance it recounts pleases the board. It would seem that the board has certainly said something in this case. Yet reports about the past, like plans about the future, can be rendered in any amount of detail. Just what about a report made it acceptable? What about the report didn't matter at all because the board frankly didn't care about that feature? For each specific item in the approved report, we can surely say that the board found that reported action, balance, ratio, or decision acceptable (if the board cared at all). But we have no idea what other variations of that same action, balance, ratio, or decision would also have been acceptable.

Even though the board has approved or accepted the report, even though the board might have discussed the report in great detail, we still don't know what the board used as criteria of acceptability. We don't know why the report was pleasing or what would have made it displeasing. As to the criteria of acceptable staff performance, even though we have an approved report of that performance, as observers we have precious little idea what the board has said. But as before, what is far more important is that the board members have no idea what the board has said. There has been a lot of talk, but there has been no clear board voice.

> In Policy Governance, reports of staff cannot confuse the board's own voice, for the voice has already made itself heard.

The Policy Governance model avoids this lack of clarity in how staff reports are handled. First of all, reports of staff activity and achievements are distinguished one from another by whether they are (1) monitoring reports or (2) reports of information that the board will find interesting. The information presented in monitoring reports, for example, shows only how performance measures up against the criteria the board has set forth in written policies about ends and executive limitations. There is nothing to approve and the criteria are already known. In the case of merely incidental information, board members don't even have to read the reports unless they want to.

In Policy Governance, reports of staff cannot confuse the board's own voice, for the voice has already made itself heard. The board does not, by its reaction to monitoring reports, create or even imply new criteria. By taking the reports seriously, the board merely reinforces criteria already established.

Deciding Issues Below the Proper Board Level

Often it is completely clear what the board has said. The obscuring just described that occurs in approving plans or reports can be avoided if the board acts upon a single decision for which the CEO has not submitted a recommendation. For example, the board decides to seed the lawn instead of using sod. Or perhaps the board decides the width of parking spaces in the lot. In each event it is easy to see what the board has said. Its voice is clear and is distinct from the voice of its staff. From a governance perspective, however, there has been a clear voice, but on something that doesn't matter!

FAQ ➡

If, by law, the board must approve personnel actions, purchases, or budgets, can it still use Policy Governance?

In Policy Governance, the board simply does not make decisions below its proper level of decision making. The single exception is when certain decisions are required by law or other authority to be made by the board itself. In this case, the board makes the decision as a matter of form, but does not treat the decision as one of substance. The way to do this is to use a *consent agenda* in which the board officially performs a ritual approval of actions for which it has already assigned authority to the CEO. Thus, the outside authority is obeyed, but governance and management are not compromised.

What a Board Itself Needs to Say

If a board is in control of its bylaws, then the appropriate content of bylaws should be said by the board, certainly not the staff. If a board is not in control of its bylaws, some identifiable membership is. A central feature of bylaws is that they establish the conditions under which the board can be considered to have said anything. (For example, the board has spoken only when a certain percentage of a group of a certain size, appointed or elected in a certain way, meeting together after a certain kind of notice, consent to a properly recognized proposition.) This article is concerned only with what the board has to say when it does officially speak. Within the paradigm of Policy Governance, the board has only four types of things to say.

> A central feature of bylaws is that they establish the conditions under which the board can be considered to have said anything.

FAQ ➡

On what subjects should a board officially speak?

Results, recipients, worth. The board must say what is to be different for persons outside the operating organization (consumers or other populations), which persons those are, and what those results are worth. The board's distinct voice on these matters can be found in ends policies. The policies address the broadest levels of description, leaving more detailed description to any reasonable interpretation the CEO chooses.

Unacceptable situations and activities. The board must set the boundaries on acceptable staff endeavors and circumstances. It need not tell the staff how to accomplish the desired results-recipients-worth, but it must put limits on what would otherwise be unbounded authority for the CEO. The board's distinct voice on these matters is found in executive limitations policies. As in ends policies, these policies address the broadest levels of description, leaving more detailed description to any reasonable interpretation the CEO chooses.

The board's own job. About its own job, the board must set forth its philosophy, accountability, outputs, process, and rules of discipline. The board's distinct voice about these matters is captured in governance process policies. They describe the broadest levels of the applicable issues, leaving details to any reasonable interpretation of the chairperson.

The governance-management interface. The board must say how it connects itself to the operational organization, that is, how it relates to its staff. For example, a board with a CEO would proclaim a single official junction, the CEO. (While nothing need stop informal communication between board members and staff, the board would never instruct or judge anyone but the CEO.) The board has its say on this topic in board-staff linkage policies. These policies describe the broadest levels of linkage decisions, leaving details to any reasonable interpretation of the chairperson.

Beyond these matters, there is nothing more a board legitimately has to say. But omitting any one of these or expressing too little about them produces a voiceless board, no matter how long its meetings, how tedious its minutes, or how comprehensive the documents it approves.

Protecting Board Integrity from the Renegade Board Member

BOARD LEADERSHIP, NUMBER 13, MAY-JUNE 1994

EVERY BOARD MEMBER or CEO with a few years' experience has had to deal with a renegade board member. By *renegade* I don't mean the board member who stimulates new thoughts, spurs the board on to better leadership, or even vehemently dissents. I mean the board member who acts in conflict with the board's group discipline in a way that jeopardizes the integrity of governance.

A renegade might, for example, unilaterally instruct the CEO or another staff member, assume an unauthorized prerogative to speak publicly for the board, or use the close confines of a board committee to work his or her personal agenda. Sometimes the renegade appears to have appointed himself or herself to be an unofficial, intermittent CEO. Boards also endure renegades whose behavior is not aimed at staff so much as at the public or—in membership associations—the members. But I'll limit this article to the member whose unacceptable behavior involves dealings with staff. The renegade behavior to be discussed here consequently threatens or destroys the board's integrity either in establishing expectations for the CEO or in the board's integrity in assessing organizational performance.

> For CEOs and their staffs, renegade board members can make life quite difficult, as they contradict or illegitimately add to what the board itself has said.

For CEOs and their staffs, renegade board members can make life quite difficult, as they contradict or illegitimately add to what the board itself has said. Sometimes the renegade is not without influence among board members, so the staff finds itself in a politically ticklish position. Rather than risk offending the renegade—fearing retribution from a board that he or she unduly influences—staff members dance around the matter, sometimes pretending to follow the renegade's wishes and sometimes giving up and doing as they are told. The staff simply doesn't trust the board to protect it from this untenable situation. The board demands staff discipline, but may well not come to terms with its own.

> What can a board do to avoid or correct the problem of loose cannons? Foremost, the board should not wait until the problem arises.

Of course, the opposite manipulation can occur as well. Staff members who do not want to follow the board's instructions can side with a renegade who believes as they do. In this case, the renegade still thwarts the board's resolve, but does so with the instigation of staff confederates. In both situations, the integrity of governance is severely damaged and the effectiveness of the staff is reduced.

What can a board do to avoid or correct the problem of loose cannons? Foremost, the board should not wait until the problem arises. Indeed, the board as a body may not know that the problem exists! Renegades may be open and loud about their actions, but just as likely they may not. Consequently, the board has no idea of what is going on, and the staff is reluctant to be seen as tattling. Sometimes I'm asked how boards can be more aware of such renegades. Fortunately, there is not much need to improve the board's awareness, for the solution ordinarily does not require knowing about renegade behavior, but rather requires constructing governance so that renegadism is neutralized.

Prevention is the best solution. If a board waits until it is aware of a problem, any solution will seem like a personal attack. Consequently, steps to prevention are relevant to every board—*your* board—not just to boards that perceive they have a renegade afoot. The Policy Governance model, if used thoroughly, prevents or at least defuses the renegade. So the steps to prevention are integral aspects of the model itself.

← FAQ

How does the Policy Governance model prevent unacceptable behavior of individual board members?

Establish written policy—including guidelines for individual board member conduct—clearly stating that no board member has any authority over the CEO. The CEO, it might be said, works for no *one!* Almost everyone agrees that this should be the case, but it is normal for boards to omit committing this philosophy to paper. Hence, the belief is implemented in a spotty fashion, leaving enough holes in the board's resolve for renegade behavior to thrive. In various issues of *Board Leadership,* I have argued the importance of the board's speaking with one voice: The board speaks with one voice or it doesn't speak at all. (That doesn't mean a pretense of unanimity, just that the vote determines subsequent direction.) Disciplined board leadership is *group* leadership, though certainly individual board members play a critical role in generating group integrity. But it is common for boards to violate this principle routinely by allowing officers and committees to establish expectations for one or another staff function.

> Disciplined board leadership is *group* leadership, though certainly individual board members play a critical role in generating group integrity.

To be best equipped to deal with idiosyncratic renegades, a board must first have eliminated its *structural* renegades. The board needs to rid itself of the customary official renegadism built into the chairperson's job (wherein the chairperson is allowed to instruct or interpret board wishes to the ostensible CEO), the treasurer's role (wherein a board officer is allowed to render judgments of staff performance on criteria the board never set), and comparable committee practices. Personnel, finance, and program committees (board committees that are highly questionable when viewed from the Policy Governance perspective) are traditional offenders in this regard.

> Allowing an individual to make a personal plaything out of an important organization is simply not good stewardship on the board's part.

Renegade-minded board members will still exist—the leopard's spots are not changed by simple decree. But such board members are now incapable of causing a great deal of trouble for staff. The CEO is confident that he or she can instruct staff that the offending board member is to be treated courteously, but given no special status. That is, no one has to pay any attention to the person. This is not done to be kind to staff, though it has that effect; it is done to prevent a single board member from unilaterally destroying what careful effort an entire board has put together. The board as a body knows that allowing an individual so disposed to make a personal plaything out of an important organization is simply not good stewardship on the board's part.

Allow assessments of CEO performance only against criteria that the board as a body has established, never those held forth by individual members or committees. Board members all have opinions about what good administration is and isn't, what good programming is and isn't, and what is achievable, allowable, and reprehensible. In fact, if board members did not have differing ideas about these things, there would be no reason to have a board. An individual could govern quite as well and far more efficiently. Policy Governance requires board members to put their differences up front, however, not after staff actions have been taken or detailed plans have been formulated. The board, in effect, need not be the final authority as we have so long proclaimed, but should instead be the *initial* authority.

In keeping with this strategy, board members pool their differences in the act of determining the CEO's criteria of performance. Because the chief executive is truly a CEO rather than simply the top staff person, the performance of the *total operational organization* (you can't hold the CEO accountable for board performance) is the measure of his or her performance. It would be dysfunctional to give the CEO these expectations and then allow him or

> Policy Governance requires board members to put their differences up front.

her to be judged on expectations that the group did not give. In other words, individual board members *do not have the right* to judge the CEO or staff on the basis of criteria they could not convince their colleagues to impose. Doing so is unacceptable, renegade behavior—for the right to make a judgment based on one's personal criteria has the same effect as, in fact, setting those criteria. In other words, renegadism in unilaterally judging the staff is the same as renegadism in instructing the staff.

Exercise "courteous disregard" with a renegade who persists; then, only as a last resort, employ outright censure. The most effective protection for the integrity of governance and for the board-CEO link is having a proper board-CEO relationship to begin with. With that in place, neither staff nor board need attack or even stoutly defend against the renegade. When the renegade is exhibiting renegade behavior (not at other times), he or she is simply disregarded. Only when the behavior becomes sufficiently obnoxious or disruptive does the board need to resort first to private, then to public censure. Private censure might be a meeting between the board chairperson and the renegade or, going further, it might consist of a closed session for only board members in which the renegade is confronted by all his or her colleagues. Public censure might incorporate a press release, published statement, or other broadcast reprimand. Clearly, these more extreme measures are best avoided. Even private confrontation is difficult for everyone concerned, so much so that boards will often tolerate egregious behavior before resorting to it. Under these strained conditions, having relevant board policies already in place can be quite comforting. Happily, if the board integrity is first intact, these more extreme solutions are rarely called for.

When the Founding Parent Stays on the Board

BOARD LEADERSHIP, NUMBER 31, MAY-JUNE 1997

B OARD SERVICE is, by its very nature, an instance of group leadership—typically a difficult challenge. The difficulty can be significantly greater when one board member is the person whose hard work and zeal created the organization in the first place. When the efforts of a crusader call for establishing a corporate vehicle, a governing board is required. But founders are reluctant to hand over their baby to a group, no matter how carefully chosen. The new board's ability to become an effective group can be thwarted by its understandable homage to the founder. If the founder is not only a member of the board but also its chair, the dilemma is even greater.

> Boards with a founder-member are just as accountable for assertive governance conduct as they would be in the absence of a founder on the board.

Founding fathers and mothers deserve our respect. Often their insights and drive inspire us. Compared with founders who have spent tears and years often struggling alone, new board members are latecomers. Out of respect and esteem, it is hard for the board not to defer to the founder's wishes, even though formally the founder is now just another board member. Yet boards with a founder-member are just as accountable for assertive governance conduct as they would be in the absence of a founder on the board.

Since founders are often more skilled at initiating than governing, they will often bypass their board's rightful prerogatives in their relationship with the public and with the staff, leaving the board with only two options, both unpleasant: directly confronting the founder or meekly disregarding the founder's inappropriate, controlling behavior. Direct confrontation is a delicate matter, for even thoughtful questioning can be perceived as disrespect for the founder's years of hard work. What is the board to do? How can it continue to value and even revere the founder without failing in its own responsibility? And is it really possible for the board to censure or even expel its founder?

> How can the board continue to value and even revere the founder without failing in its own responsibility?

Let me give an example of a community organization that faced this kind of problem. I had no consulting relationship with this organization, so I could not help with resolving the problem. The organization had been established largely through the commitment and efforts of a single dynamo. She gathered a group of prominent persons around her to form the first board. Because of her indefatigable work and relentless fundraising, her election as chair encountered no opposition. An executive director and staff were hired, and the organization became not just a reality but a financially secure one.

← FAQ

What can be done about an intimidating board member who assumes executive authority?

But there were flaws in the otherwise happy situation. The board was unwilling to confront the founder, so she was allowed to impose one-woman rule. Board members did what they were told. The executive director found that he did not really report to a board so much as to the board chair. In fact, instructions came directly from the board chair without any board involvement. Even with board involvement, the board exercised little judgment of its own apart from pleasing the chair.

To complicate matters further, the chair would make commitments to staff members without either board or CEO involvement. For example, on one of her frequent and influential visits, she stopped a staff member in the hall and told him that he would get a raise in salary for his good work. The CEO had no part in that promise and was not only miffed that a CEO prerogative had been stolen but was baffled about how to deal with other deserving staff members whom the chair had not singled out.

Clearly, both board and CEO effectiveness were greatly hampered by this person. While well-intentioned, she was severely damaging the very organization to which she'd given birth. Her personality or her misguided idea of what a board chair should do simply would not allow her to let go or to recognize that anything was outside her scope of personal authority. To further illustrate the stranglehold this person had over the organization, even after her term as chair expired, her behavior remained both unchanged and unchallenged.

Some boards, aware of the dilemma but paralyzed by it, merely wait for the founder to retire or move on to other challenges. Besides the obvious costs to the organization, there is a less evident downside to letting time substitute for courage. The board develops a culture of nonassertiveness that is not easily or quickly repaired. Moreover, as the years pass, the better members tend to drop out and the more timid ones to predominate. The corporate world contains many examples of this dysfunctional plight, the most visible being Alfred P. Sloan's prolonged dominance of the General Motors board, a dominance that did not build a strong board. Withdrawal of a powerful parent figure, of course, exposes a board's inadequacy, removing any doubt that the board desperately needs the strong founder to maintain control!

> Some boards merely wait for the founder to retire or move on to other challenges.

Uncomfortable as it may be, the most effective course of action for members of a board with a dominating founder is to take responsibility for changing the situation, not to turn a blind eye and wait the situation out. To do little or nothing is to suggest that the organization's mission is worth little or nothing—a suggestion I'm sure board members do not want to make. But what would taking responsibility in this way mean?

> To do little or nothing is to suggest that the organization's mission is worth little or nothing.

First, board members must grasp their responsibility for the problem as a group. They must see the matter as a flaw in the integrity of governance, *their* governance. It is best if they discard the idea that the matter is a problem of the founder. Unless the founder is threatening them with deadly force, the board members still have the authority to do as they wish. The founder has only one vote. If board members refuse to use their authority, they cannot blame the founder for their own faintheartedness. Moreover, board members must never, never leave the problem for the CEO to work out. In the story I just told, the board had left the CEO at the mercy of a chair's inappropriate behavior. Board weakness in protecting the CEO from any renegade board member, chair or not, could be seen as an ethics failure.

Because the best antidote to the negative effects of personalities is a good system, you must carefully define the separate jobs of board and CEO as well as the jobs of board and chair. Those definitions will be best if they follow Policy Governance principles. Here are some of the more relevant ones:

> If board members refuse to use their authority, they cannot blame the founder for their own faintheartedness.

- The CEO is obliged to follow board directions in ends and executive limitations policies but is not required to heed an individual board member's instructions, even the founder's or the chair's.

- The CEO is within his or her rights to instruct all staff members that they work for the CEO, not for the board or board members. Directions and promises issued inappropriately by a board member are to be disregarded.

- An individual board member's authority is circumscribed by the board's policies about governance process and board-staff linkage. The chair has some leeway (he or she can use any reasonable interpretation of these policy categories) but is bound nonetheless.

In summary, the surest cure for the founding parent syndrome is for board members to do what they should do in any event—govern with integrity. One or more strong members need not damage the honor of governance; their visionary or gadfly roles need not be sacrificed but

> The surest cure for the founding parent syndrome is for board members to do what they should do in any event—govern with integrity.

must be made part of an appropriate process. Unfortunately, traditional concepts of the board-management partnership not only leave boards unnecessarily vulnerable to the painful predicaments wrought by personality issues but also allow us to think that the personalities are the problem. Even more unfortunately, it is common for the integrity of governance, rather than the autonomy of the founding parent, to be sacrificed. Although this may be the most comfortable immediate resolution for board and founder alike, it makes a mockery of accountability and endangers the hearty governance needed to sustain the dream and pass it on to future guardians. The solution to the founder-chair dilemma is proper governance.

The Executive Committee: Turning a Governance Liability into an Asset

Board Leadership, Number 14, July-Aug. 1994

IN EVERY SEMINAR, without fail, I am asked about the proper role of an executive committee. Among workshop participants, I commonly find a discomfort with executive committees along with a sense that they are necessary. Board members tend to feel that an executive committee is needed to keep the board's work in order and, at the same time, that there is something disempowering about having a miniboard within the board.

In this article, I will look at the executive committee from the perspective of my Policy Governance model. I believe there is widespread overuse of the executive committee concept and, further, that a strong executive committee is more likely to jeopardize board leadership than support it. Before commenting on the executive committee itself, however, let me review a few principles about board committees in general.

FAQ ➡

Why does the Policy Governance model see board committees in such an unfavorable light?

The board job must be described before committee jobs can be described. It makes no sense to design parts of the whole before the whole itself is clearly in mind, though this circumstance seems to be the norm. Therefore, the board should not assume a need for *any* committees when adopting a new system of governance. Because the board is rethinking all aspects of its operation, even committees that have been critically useful may be unnecessary and even detrimental under the new paradigm.

The board should minimize committees, creating them sparingly, only as needed. A board with many committees is like a machine with too many parts. It breaks down more and is harder to repair when it does break down. Moreover, committee work tends to fragment board members' sense of the whole because it focuses them on particular segments or aspects of the organization. When boards complain that they have so much work to do that committees are necessary, it is usually the case that the board is doing staff work—not board work—with its committees.

> A strong executive committee is more likely to jeopardize board leadership than support it.

The board may create committees to help with its own job, but never to help with staff jobs. If the staff wants committees, it may freely create them. The board is in control of its own job, however, so it must create whatever mechanisms are needed to get its job done.

> A board with many committees is like a machine with too many parts. It breaks down more and is harder to repair.

These simple principles would render personnel committees, most finance committees, and most program committees out of order. Why? Because they are knee-deep in staff work, not board work. They are delving into staff means, either giving thinly veiled orders about them or advising about them. Such committees embody institutionalized meddling.

The Committee That's More Equal Than the Rest

But what of that very special committee, the executive? The executive committee differs from other committees in that boards typically give their executive committee the power to make board decisions between board meetings. In short, boards empower their executive committees to *be* the board when the board is not in session. Technically, the executive committee is the board far more of the time than the board is.

Some executive committees utilize this power more than others. I have seen executive committees that virtually never use their special authority. I have also seen executive committees that act on every item that will later appear on the board's agenda—or perhaps on agendas that never make it to the full board. There are executive committees whose extensive involvement makes other board members wonder why they bother coming to board meetings.

There are executive committees whose extensive involvement makes other board members wonder why they bother coming to board meetings.

Granting an executive committee authority is often justified by the fact that the board must subsequently ratify executive committee actions. But if an action is not official until ratification, it can wait until the next board meeting anyway. If it is official before subsequent board action, then the ratification is ritual, and the committee is actually wielding board authority, despite the pro forma requirement of ratification.

Although board members may feel upstaged by their executive committee, they ordinarily keep it because they fear that a board decision really might need to be made between board meetings. Since not everything can be predicted ahead of time, there is always the risk that a board action will be needed quickly. A quorum of the full board may be difficult to call together; a committee is easier to assemble. So the board members' love-hate relationship with the executive committee continues.

Let me assert a strong proposition:

FAQ ➡

What conditions force a board to authorize an executive committee to make board decisions between board meetings?

The only excuse for a board to authorize an executive committee to make board decisions between board meetings is if the board is too awkward to do its own job.

My implication, of course, is that if the board were to perform its governing job appropriately, there would be no need to establish what is, in effect, a board within the board. But let's take a look at the matter of awkwardness: it can arise from board size, cost of meetings, or poor process.

Awkwardness due to size. Large boards have a hard time resolving issues unless stage-managed. Even arranging meeting times so that everyone can attend is difficult, much less scheduling special meetings for special circumstances. Large boards, more than small ones, have difficulty grappling with issues and being decisive. If size is the source of awkwardness, I recommend that the board downsize if at all possible. How can it do this? Downsizing won't always be painless, but enabling real board leadership is worth going through some hoops. My impression is that more and more large boards are finding the courage to reduce their size. If reducing is socially or politically impossible in the short run, try building in a gradual reduction over some more palatable period. For example, resistance to reduction can sometimes be avoided by introducing just enough gradualism so that current board members are not affected!

Awkwardness due to cost. Assembling a nationwide board is an expensive proposition, so organizations conscientiously try to keep costs down by having less frequent board meetings, filling in with cheaper, more frequent executive committee meetings. Geography-based awkwardness is hard to cure, though I have encountered organizations where a number of unnecessary committees (beyond the executive) were eliminated, making it possible to have, say, four board meetings a year instead of three. At four meetings a year, the awkwardness is reduced sufficiently so that

> Large boards, more than small ones, have difficulty grappling with issues and being decisive. Downsize if at all possible.

good governance practices enable the board to govern without an executive committee or, at least, with one empowered only for emergency decisions.

Awkwardness due to poor process. I won't spend any time on this one, for you know what I'll say: The poor process can be largely taken care of by implementing Policy Governance!

Executive Committees—Why Not?

In any event, granting an executive committee the authority of the board comes at some expense. Imagine a standard organizational chart with the board on top and a single CEO just below it, followed by a span of managers. An executive committee with power finds itself between the board and CEO, in effect putting a new box on the chart. The only way to supply the executive committee with authority is to diminish the authority of either the board or the CEO—or both. Similar to fluid dynamics,

> The only way to supply the executive committee with authority is to diminish the authority of either the board or the CEO—or both.

authority at this level can come from nowhere else. In short, empowered executive committees disempower at least one other position in the line of authority.

When an executive committee acts as the preboard board, board members not on the executive committee sometimes lose their sense of vigilance and full participation. Even though the board—the full board—is legally and morally accountable for the organization, board members tend to let the executive committee carry the burden and run the show. Board members often forget that the executive committee works for the board, not the other way around.

When the executive committee is empowered to make board decisions, the idea evolves that the CEO works for the committee, often more clearly than that he or she works for the board. A wise CEO can quickly size up whom to keep happy. When the committee comes to be seen as supervising the CEO, the danger has clearly set in. In these cases, the simple though crucial line of authority between a board and its CEO has been seriously damaged.

Because an executive committee is smaller and more agile, it tends to get into more issues than the full board can. Consequently, meddling is more likely, with the CEO participating in the dysfunction by taking more items to the committee than he or she would take to the board. I have seen cases where the executive committee became the de facto CEO because it was extensively involved in what would otherwise have been CEO prerogatives.

Rethinking the Executive Committee

So let me assume that the board has downsized as much as it can, that it is not possible to settle the geography issue, and that the board has adopted the Policy Governance model. With whatever still remains of the awkwardness, governance must go on. If the board holds to the principles in Policy Governance, here is what will happen with considerations of having an executive committee:

FAQ ➡
Under Policy Governance, what happens to considerations of having an executive committee?

1. The board will first consider whether it has delegated to its CEO all the authority it possibly can, short of jeopardizing the board's own accountability for organizational performance and conduct. One way of doing this is to create the ends and executive limitations policies as if there were not going to be an executive committee. This perspective will push rigorous delegation to its limit. When decisions that are considered board decisions must frequently be made between board meetings, it could be a sign that meetings are too infrequent. More often, however, it's a sign that the board has not delegated enough decision-making authority to its CEO. In other words, the need for an executive committee is ordinarily due to insufficient delegation.

2. The board will examine whether further honing of the governance process is possible so that the board, even under awkward circumstances, can get its job done

better. A nationwide board might reconsider that one more board meeting per
year—though costly—is worth the cost in
terms of the improved governance it
offers. Or a board might pull back from
optional activities to get its central job

> The need for an executive committee is ordinarily due to insufficient delegation.

done as a full board. For example, instead of using board committees to gather options
for impending board decisions, the staff could be given this job (though staff members
should not make the board choices).

3. If the board still fears that crucial board decisions might arise between meetings and has determined that these decisions should not fall into the CEO's purview,
then an empowered executive committee can be considered. But instead of granting
a blanket authority to the committee, the board should carefully craft a policy delineating exactly what decisions could be made and within what constraints. Such a policy would be one of the governance process policies.

4. Periodically, the board will reexamine this emergency delegation to see that the
guidelines are still needed and still appropriate. Such system-patching solutions often
outlive the problems they were intended to solve, and so must stand rejustification
periodically.

5. Even if no authority for independent action is given, an executive committee can still perform a useful function.
For example, it can be commissioned to
oversee the board's own process, flow and
balance of work, and perhaps even the

> Executive committees are not decreed in the natural order of things—they are entirely optional.

level of board member preparedness. These tasks would not produce a board-within-
the-board dynamic, though they would detract from what would otherwise be delegated to the chairperson. Another nonexecutive function for an executive committee
would be to do all preparatory work for board debate on policies in the governance
process and board-staff linkage categories. Since executive committees are ordinarily composed of elected officers, overseeing the board's own process seems to be a
natural assignment.

In summary, executive committees are not decreed in the natural order of things—
they are entirely optional. Further, giving an executive committee the authority commonly given either the board or the CEO reflects important flaws in the existing
governance or, in fact, causes them.

A Team of Equals

BOARD LEADERSHIP, NUMBER 19, MAY-JUNE 1995

A BOARD MEMBER asked me to help him explore why he found being a board member so difficult. This board member (let's call him Sam), an excellent manager in his own career, sits on the chamber of commerce board and the local arts council. Like many good managers sitting on nonprofit and public boards, Sam tried valiantly to contribute by applying his hard-won managerial skills. Board members with managerial experience find many of the difficulties in governance to be familiar managerial dilemmas. I asked Sam to look at the aspects of governance that might actually put good managers at a disadvantage. In a few instructive respects, governance is management upside down!

Management Is Deductive

> **FAQ** ➡️
>
> How is governance different from management?

As a manager, Sam takes a challenging goal and divides it into tasks. Long ago he learned to analyze and assign the parts of a whole so that his team could work together to accomplish that whole. In a retail business, Sam is able to break a major sales campaign into its components of display, advertising, merchandise buying, and personnel.

Deciding on divisions of labor is always a gamble because breaking a whole into parts has many pitfalls. Delegated parts must be commensurate with individual staff members' strengths. Delegated parts must also integrate both freedom and control in order to make use of the competence and caring of delegatees. And delegated parts must be designed so that subparts of the organization do not war with each other, maximizing individual situations but ill-serving the whole.

These matters are not easy to balance. And when they are well balanced, it would be folly for any manager to expect them to remain so. Managers keep a constant vigil over such things, continually adjusting and correcting them.

Governance Is Inductive

While management takes a large idea and breaks it into discrete parts, the challenge to governance is ordinarily the reverse. While management consists of an individual delegating to a group, the challenge to governance goes the other way. Sam knows that his arts council and chamber board are teams by their very nature, not just by choice. While managers have the commendable *option* of using a team approach, responsible board leadership offers no option not to.

The most obvious reversal is that governance consists of a group delegating to an individual rather than an individual delegating to a group, as is the case in management. Delegating to a CEO is easier for two reasons. The first is that there is only one person to instruct and only one person's performance to evaluate. The second is that the board has no need to subdivide the task. That is, the board does not need to worry about how to break its instruction into doable parts and does not need to calculate to whom it will delegate the various tasks. It is not uncommon, however, for a board to lose this advantage by assuming the responsibility of deciding which staff member or department should take on a task, whether a staff member is too busy or a department is understaffed, and other considerations best left to the CEO. In other words, boards have a tendency to delegate department by department, even when having a CEO makes this practice not only unnecessary but also intrusive. School boards delegate in this way routinely. Many boards do it by establishing a de facto reporting relationship with their chief financial officer.

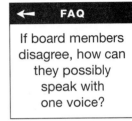

← FAQ

If board members disagree, how can they possibly speak with one voice?

Another upside-down characteristic of governance is that ideas and values begin with a number of individuals, each with different viewpoints that must be melded into a single position. The dialogue proceeds from disparate parts to a conceptual whole. Particularly on the arts council, Sam has seen almost unresolvable diversity among board members about what should be the organization's pursuits for the next few years. The scenario is more complicated than putting a picture puzzle together, for the parts (board members' disagreements) do not fit into some grand design of a whole. The best the board can hope for is to devise the most correct picture that can be approximated from parts that don't fit! In this way, the board arrives at official policies of the body that are the best amalgam of individualistic board members.

Herein lies another reason for why board policies—with all the difficulty involved—should be hammered out by a full board, not inherited from various committees. At least by full board authorship, the eventual whole picture represents the aggregation of values of the same set of persons. Traditionally, boards sidestep this important governance function by granting far too much de facto authority to committees (for example, for personnel, finance, or public relations, or for program functions). The effect is a set of separate miniboards, each controlling or unduly influencing a single aspect of the organization.

The governance function must consistently translate the trivial into the profound.

Governance should proceed from conceptual parts toward a whole without the subsequent need to break the whole into its several performable parts. In a parallel way, a board confronted with specific worries or concerns about discrete staff actions has the task of going back to the higher plane before reacting. For example, when the arts council was faced with how to react to a reported incident wherein a theatergoer received poor treatment, Sam was able to press the council to explore the true governance issue within the reported act. The result of this deliberation went far beyond mere reaction to the specific event; it clarified council values for the executive director, values that were able to influence many more events than the one that brought the matter to the board's attention. To keep governors from slipping into managers' roles, the governance function must consistently translate the trivial into the profound, that is, move from the concrete instances of implementation to the more abstract aspects that characterize the whole.

The group must honor its "teamness."

Finally, the boards that Sam sits on each consist of a team of equals by their very nature. In each case, board authority at the top of an organization originates not in Sam or any other individual, but in the group. The group must honor its "teamness." It is not acceptable for some members to control the group or for individual members to "own" specific aspects of the organization, such as when an accountant on a board owns the problem of fiscal governance, or a PR expert on a board owns the governance of public image. In these cases, some board members are necessarily left behind, thereby defaulting on their obligation to govern on behalf of the ownership, for they are as fully accountable as board members who steal the reins. But despite having no responsible choice but to be a team, boards often do default to an individual (in the case of Sam's chamber board, the controlling individual had been the prior chairperson) in what might be called the "heroic leader" error.

Managers on boards, including good managers like Sam, can become frustrated with the pace and repeated inanity of group decision making. After all, group decisions take more interaction, are typically less incisive, and tend toward timidity and the lowest common denominator. (History has given us many great individuals, as one workshop participant remarked to me, but few if any great boards.) Managers frustrated with group process cannot help but feel a tug toward that which they know best: managerial behavior.

> Managers frustrated with group process cannot help but feel a tug toward that which they know best: managerial behavior.

Sam now has a better grasp of the vast differences—even upside-downness!—between governance and management. By understanding more aspects of these differences, he will be better equipped to help his boards in replacing poor governance with good governance rather than replacing poor governance with misplaced management.

Policies Я Us

BOARD LEADERSHIP, NUMBER 20, JULY-AUG. 1995

B OARD POLICIES should be the expression of a board's soul. Policies created under the Policy Governance model embody the board's beliefs, commitments, values, and vision. If governance doesn't have a flavor of the spiritual or metaphysical, it is probably not sufficiently soul-searching. After all, board leadership is a continual struggle with what is important.

Board Leadership readers are well aware of the four policy categories of Policy Governance; I want to direct your attention in this article to the philosophical more than the nuts-and-bolts aspects of the model. Think of the four policy categories as first stimulating, then capturing the board's *heart* on these matters:

Governance process. Who are we as a board? From what group do we derive our authority? Should we reflect or should we inspire their values . . . or both? With what beliefs and philosophies do we engage in our task? What self-discipline is required of those who would be stewards?

> Board leadership is a continual struggle with what is important.

Ends. What vision of the human condition forms our mission? What difference will we make in the world; for whom; how soon? In delimiting our mission, which ills of humanity will we consciously choose *not* to aid? Indeed, which pain will we be prepared to *cause* (for example, taxation and expenditure are measures of other human satisfactions we have agreed to forego).

Board-staff linkage. How should our power be shared? How much? Are our global values to be reflected in our dealings with staff? How can we empower and inspire the creativity of these persons while not defaulting on our own accountability?

Executive limitations. What are the limits to actions and circumstances that can be countenanced in our name? What constitutes unacceptable treatment of human beings and material assets? What are our worries about staff activity and conduct? Which are important enough to control and which can we responsibly allow to vary?

These issues are philosophical quandaries about the nature of enterprise, the relationship of human beings in enterprise, and the obligations of stewardship. Some are unabashedly existential questions worthy of struggle and debate. But to leave them at a philosophical level would be to trade governance that is shallow for governance that is rhetorically profound but pragmatically inconsequential. Good policymaking begins with what seem to be philosophical musings but moves straightaway to practical documents that form the foundation of managerial respectability.

Philosophy Central to Policy

Board members' collective philosophy, then, should be central to board policy. But traditional policymaking is more likely to be driven by forces outside the board. Often, even the policy language is formulated externally. It is common, for example, for the CEO to recommend a board policy on this or that; or for committees to work out all the pros and cons of an issue, then recommend a full-blown (read "predigested") policy to the board. It is even common for a funder or government to require a board to have a certain policy, sometimes to the point of dictating the wording! Although it may be normal, this kind of policymaking is a travesty, a counterfeit of board leadership.

In Policy Governance, the board's struggle with values leads to policies that are not the product of the staff, of the CEO, or even of the board chairperson. Moreover, they are not the product of any committee, including the executive committee. These policies are not devised by someone else, then brought to the board for approval (how often I've wished I could ban the word "approval" from board members' language!). From the stage of musing to the stage of black-on-white documents, in the practice of Policy Governance, these policies are the product of the board itself.

Not only should the board decide for itself what its policy provisions will be, it should also decide what to have policies *about* and what level of prescriptive or proscriptive

---

> Proper policymaking is about values.

---

detail the policies will go into. It is critical to the integrity of board leadership that the board and the board alone control these documents. Let me use a personal example to underscore the close relationship that exists between a board and its policies when governance is at its best.

As an individual, I seek a philosophy of life. How do I develop one? I will listen to or read many points of view. I might even ally myself with a guru or mentor to assist me in my own path. But it is my inquiry, my quandary, my search for relevant and helpful input, my struggle for wholeness.

What I will not do is hire someone to develop a philosophy of life for my approval!

Proper policymaking—as opposed to that which conventionally passes for policymaking—is about values. Most of us would be loathe to hire someone to tell us what our values are.

Confusing Board and Staff Values

We have complicated the matter by allowing the work of boards to become indistinct from the work of staff. Consequently, boards are saddled with agenda items that should be left to staff members and their values. And they could be if the *board's* values were clear enough that staff judgment could be turned loose within the broader limits of those values.

> Boards spend precious time applying their values to staff issues—the wrong issues—a practice that undervalues both board and staff.

Thus, boards spend precious time applying their values to staff issues—the wrong issues—a practice that undervalues both board and staff. And this is tedious work inasmuch as the board is less in touch with the practicalities of staff work. Applying board values to staff issues is a time-consuming and often amateurish undertaking. Completing the unfortunate circle, the more time this misguided process consumes, the less time is available for arguing and deciding the very board values that, if made explicit, would make such involvement unnecessary! Traditional boards fail to clarify true board values, while not allowing staff the freedom to tap fully into their own.

Taken to the extreme, the scenario describes what is often called meddling, for meddling seems necessary only when a board has failed to do its own job. The opposite, *rubber stamping,* occurs when a board defaults upon its own values in favor of letting the staff have free rein. The board might in fact pass policies, but its words come prefabricated from the staff. In either event, we get less from the wisdom of both groups than we otherwise would. Ironically, no matter how opposite meddling and rubber stamping appear, they both spring from leaving values important to board members unexpressed. Neither board nor staff is all it can be; thus is wasted the most precious resource available to any organization—its people.

> Meddling seems necessary only when a board has failed to do its own job.

The Policy Governance Solution

The Policy Governance solution is for the board to tend to its own job, to be the author of its own policies, the creator of its own creed. The organization must cease using documents that obscure just whose values are being represented. Board-approved budgets are good examples of this. After the board's approval, one cannot tell which values about fiscal planning were being controlled by the board. The board, by exercising its approval prerogative, controls every jot and tittle, even though most budgetary items are essentially based on staff values and would have been passed by the board even if they had been vastly different. For example, if out-of-state travel is budgeted as twice as valuable as furniture replacement, is that the board's value or the CEO's?

> ← **FAQ**
> How do Policy Governance policies differentiate board values from staff values?

> ← **FAQ**
> How can boards keep from meddling with staff means?

With the new kind of board decision making proposed in Policy Governance, decisions of the board truly belong to the board and must unmistakably represent the board's values on behalf of the ownership, not the values of staff or other experts. Though others can be employed to inform the board's wisdom, they may not substitute for it.

Board policies under Policy Governance, *generated* by the board, not parroted or approved by it, get at the very soul of governance. If the board's wisdom is not reflected in these policies, a central

> The Policy Governance solution is for the board to tend to its own job, to be the author of its own policies, the creator of its own creed.

feature of real board leadership has been missed. It may not be that everything a board is or stands for can be found in properly executed policies, but everything about which *one can be certain* the board is and stands for can be.

When policymaking is properly construed, the board *is* its policies.

Recruiting Leaders: What to Look for in New Board Members

Board Leadership, Number 23, Jan.–Feb. 1996

A T ALMOST EVERY SEMINAR I conduct, someone asks what boards should look for as they search for new members. Whom shall we recruit? What persons will make the best board members?

I have often emphasized that the problem of governance is not the people, but the outmoded, poorly designed process boards typically employ. But I want to address board member selection in this article, for once the faulty process is corrected, it is important to find the best people.

> It has become politically correct to maintain that everyone is equally capable of discharging board responsibilities, but that is simply not true.

First, I'd like to commend boards that put considerable thought into answering this recruitment question. Some people are better fitted to the work of governance than others. It has become politically correct to maintain that everyone is equally capable of discharging board responsibilities, but that is simply not true. It is not a matter of individual worth; not everyone is cut out to be a plumber, mathematician, or board member. In twenty years' experience working closely with boards, my impression is that we are pretty sloppy about filling board seats, often putting people on boards for all the wrong reasons.

Let's face it. The reasons board members are selected often come down to who has time, who fits some preset demographic description, or—in the case of politically appointed boards—who is owed a favor. Sometimes the only requirement is that a potential board member care about the organizational mission. Often the persons chosen are very accomplished in their fields but skilled in ways that may have little to do with proper board behavior.

Most boards would fire their CEOs for filling staff positions as haphazardly as the board recruits for board positions. Selecting board members is much like choosing a finance officer, dentist, or auto mechanic. Determining job requirements must precede establishing board member requirements. Commonly, boards have little regard for matching candidates' abilities to job requirements. To begin with, using the term *job requirements* with a board suggests that a board has a real job to do. If the board is only window-dressing, or merely a supportive body that occasionally peers over managers' shoulders, then determining leadership skills isn't terribly important. But if a board is to lead, it must inquire into the abilities necessary to do the job well. While gender, color, and ethnicity have a role to play in selection of members, choosing the "best" people has less to do with our ways of dividing up the human race than with the skills, personality, and life experience that qualify a person for board leadership. To determine who will be the best people for the task, then, we must understand governance as a productive part of the organization.

> Selecting board members is much like choosing a finance officer, dentist, or auto mechanic.

Outlining the process necessary to be successful in that role can lead us to the board member characteristics that would make the process successful. As the nature of governance evolves toward the Policy Governance model, the set of qualities constituting a good board member evolves along with it. Policy Governance represents a substantial evolution in how board leadership is expressed, both in the *products* and the *process* of the governing board.

Before current boards reach out to fill their vacancies, they had best give considerable thought to the leadership qualities they ought to seek. In cases where the board doesn't control its membership (for example, when there is an outside appointing authority or an election by an association membership), boards should influence the authorities or educate their memberships to make the appointments consistent with the leadership characteristics needed. (I support influencing for requisite characteristics, not manipulating for certain individuals.)

← FAQ

When board members are elected or appointed, how can the board ensure getting members with qualities that contribute to the board's success?

So what characteristics make a person a good board member? What should boards look for in recruiting new members for their social service board? What should we tell appointing authorities to keep in mind as they make appointments to the health board or airport authority? What should electors think about when casting their votes for trade association board, city council, or school board? I will assume that the intent in each case is to create a board capable of ambitious board leadership. What is needed in board members, then, to create the ideal board?

My recommendations, in whatever priority is applicable to the specific board circumstance, are that you look for board members who

FAQ ➡

Who are the best candidates for Policy Governance board membership?

Are visionary, able to create alternate futures. I don't mean that they have their heads in the clouds, but that they are bold enough to see what can be quite as readily as what is. Some people have more ability and take more joy in creating the future than others. People who are not strong in this quality can make valuable contributions in roles other than being on a governing board. The inclination and capability to work with long-term issues reside in persons who can forego the comfort of shorter-term concreteness.

Are conceptual thinkers. There are two aspects to this characteristic. First, board members need to go beyond making single-event decisions. They need to be able to examine, debate, and decide on the values that form the basis for such decisions—in short, to make policy. Second, leadership is most potent when people recast ideas, think in new ways, and remain conceptually flexible. People whose inclination is to think only in concrete terms or who have difficulty thinking outside their customary boxes may find their contributions are more valuable at a lower organizational level.

Grasp the big picture. Probably related to the first two qualities, this characteristic is the ability to see the whole as more than the accumulation of parts. Some people are better than others at putting small considerations into a perspective guided by a larger view.

Are connected to the ownership. The board is an organ of ownership, so board members owe their primary allegiance to those who morally own the organization. To fulfill that obligation, persons should be as connected with that population as possible. Being connected means, among other things, sharing similar personal or demographic characteristics, caring about data and input from or about the ownership, identifying with the whole ownership (rather than the segment from which one personally comes), and having structured contact with owners (as in focus groups or invited discussions).

Demonstrate moral courage. Group dynamics offer easy refuge for those wishing to avoid taking a stand. Members of a group are tempted to act far less responsibly than they would as individuals. Moral cowardice takes many forms. I've seen boards intimidated by vocal splinter groups default on their obligation to work for the greater good of the majority. (Elected bodies are prone to this weakness.) I've seen boards of well-meaning, good people allow heartless and even brutal treatment of staff or others to go unchecked, timidly giving in to an out-of-control process. Board members must be able to raise uncomfortable issues and recognize when the emperor is wearing no clothes.

> Board members must be able to raise uncomfortable issues and recognize when the emperor is wearing no clothes.

Can work as a group. Board activity is a matter of group responsibility, it's not just the sum of individual responsibilities. Thus, board members must be able to support each other in airing competing viewpoints while also taking personal responsibility for the discipline of the whole. If governance is to escape being scattered and undisciplined, group responsibility is required, and each member should take responsibility for the performance and discipline of the group. As with a football team, a board's success is not determined by how well the members like each other.

> As with a football team, a board's success is not determined by how well the members like each other.

Accept and use authority. Not everyone is comfortable with power. Responsible use of authority begins with "owning" it, that is, accepting that one has it. Some persons on boards tend to shrink from their own newfound authority. Reluctance to use one's authority works no kindness, but actually causes or allows damage.

Can allow others to lead. It is only when the board has fully accepted the comprehensiveness of its authority that it is able to exercise that authority effectively—by giving most of it away. Empowering the CEO, who can then delegate to staff, is a key to top performance as long as the criteria for judging performance are made clear. Board members must understand how to lead leaders.

In certain cases, have fundraising or other skills peculiar to a specific organizational need. Some boards will add special output requirements to their fundamental job description. Beyond maintaining a link with the ownership, providing written policies, and assuring executive performance (functions basic to all boards), a given board might decide to acquire donor funds, effect legislative change, or create some other job product. If so, board members need to contribute the special skill or understanding called for or be capable of acquiring it.

FAQ ➡

How can desirable board member characteristics be codified in policy and practice?

These desired characteristics—or any others a board decides upon—should be put into a policy, succinctly, and filed in the governance process category. The chair is authorized to interpret and act on the intentions expressed in this category unless the board assigns that right to someone else. The someone else might be another officer but could be a board committee charged with recruitment. One creative board I know established what they called a board development committee, giving it the recruitment role as well as making it responsible for board self-evaluation, board education, and new member orientation. In any event, the delegation—whether it be to the chairperson, to another board member, or to a committee—should ensure there will be a reliable path from the carefully stated board recruitment criteria to their realization.

Another more immediate benefit of a board's setting forth such a list, however, is the effect that doing so has on *current* board members. Whatever the desired characteristics of future board members, the same are propitious characteristics for current board members to bring forth in their own board service. Codifying the desired characteristics of new members serves, then, to guide existing members in their own personal contribution to board leadership.

Should Your CEO Be a Board Member?

BOARD LEADERSHIP, NUMBER 26, JULY-AUG. 1996

STRICTLY SPEAKING, whether the CEO is a member of the board is not relevant to either the principles or the mechanics of CEO evaluation. But the issue potentially has a strong effect on the psychology of CEO evaluation.

First of all, let me define the CEO as a member of the board if he or she has a vote as a board member. In some organizations, the CEO is given board membership without a vote. I am never quite sure what that status is, but I'll treat it as synonymous with not being a board member. So when I refer to having board membership, I mean membership with a vote.

Elsewhere I've discussed that the board represents the ownership in instructing the CEO, its single employee. Further, the CEO's performance or, rather, the CEO's success in getting the organization to perform, must be pointedly monitored and reacted to by the board. In this scenario, there is no room in board leadership for conflict, shyness, unassertiveness, or other reticence in playing out this board role with rigor.

> Having the CEO on the board *must eventually damage governance in some way.*

Yet having the CEO be a member of the very board that instructs and assesses him or her is by its very nature a conflict of interest. That conflict may cause only a small problem or can be a major impediment to the integrity of governance. But having the CEO on the board *must eventually damage governance in some way.*

Let's assume a situation in which a CEO is a member of the board. When that person speaks in a board meeting, what role is he or she assuming, board member or CEO? The two roles are different, even if played by the same person. Does the CEO know which role he or she is playing in each situation? Further, it isn't enough that the CEO know, but everyone else must be clear as well. Are they? To be sure, every utterance of the CEO should be explicitly labeled as being, on the one hand, from a board member who happens to be the CEO or, on the other hand, from the CEO who happens to be a board member.

Moreover, when other board members speak to the CEO, do they indicate clearly whether they are speaking to the CEO in his or her capacity as CEO or as board member? The problem is not limited to board meetings. The CEO–board member continues to be both when outside the board meeting as well. So even talking with that person in his or her CEO office cannot in itself be a prima facie indication that he or she is now acting as the CEO.

Remember, too, that board members are obligated to act on behalf of the ownership. They do not represent the staff or even their own personal benefit. If the CEO is a board member, he or she is just as obligated to represent the ownership in that role as are other board members. Anything less is a dereliction of duty.

Board and management role confusion is a hallmark of governance as we have known it. Because the Policy Governance model is committed to clarifying these confused roles, it must radically reorder traditional concepts in order to do so well. Yet in making the CEO a board member, a board adds an unnecessary and troublesome source of role confusion.

I cannot think of a single legitimate reason for a board to include its CEO as a voting member.

The resulting ambiguity and awkwardness is so easily avoided. Not only is it easily avoided, but allowing the CEO to be on the board actually adds nothing of value that cannot be achieved another way. Consider the two reasons most boards give for awarding their CEOs a voting seat on the board.

First, some boards think that giving the CEO a board seat bestows prestige. Board membership is a perk, a reward, a vote of confidence. Some CEO-candidates see things the same way, negotiating a board seat for themselves as part of agreeing to accept employment. This way of thinking is an unfortunate comment on the way boards treat their CEOs. I'd rather a board bestow so much honor on its CEO *as CEO* that adding board membership adds little to it. A board need not give away board prerogatives or forget who works for whom in order to confer distinction and even pay a certain kind of homage to the person who holds this special position.

Second, as some boards have said to me, the CEO should be on the board because of the board's constant need of CEO input. But the CEO can be—and should be—regularly present at board meetings whether or not he or she is a voting member of the group. Consequently, the need for continual CEO counsel is irrelevant to the issue of CEO board membership because it makes the CEO no more available to the board than he or she would have been otherwise.

So the board can confer all the esteem any CEO could possibly want and it can have complete access to CEO assistance without the cost of added role confusion and built-in conflict of interest. I cannot think of a single legitimate reason for a board to include its CEO as a voting member.

But you may have noticed that it is common practice in business corporations for the CEO to be on the board and, quite often, even the chair of the board. When nonprofits rush headlong toward the supposed virtue of being "more like a business," they often slavishly mimic business's warts as well as its assets. Corporate governance is one area in which business is not a deserving role model for nonprofit and public organizations. Corporate governance is no less flawed than nonprofit and public governance. It is not uncommon for corporate boards to serve the present management more than stockholders. It is difficult to be chosen by management, compensated by management, spoon-fed by management, and stage-managed by management and still pretend to be acting with unconflicted loyalty to owners. So putting the CEO on the board is merely an illustration of the pathology of corporate governance, not a venerated practice worth emulating.

> **← FAQ**
>
> In what respects is corporate governance an inappropriate role model for nonprofit governance?

So, should the CEO be on the board? Certainly not. Can CEO evaluation proceed in a more orderly, rigorous manner if the CEO is off the board? There is no doubt.

What If the Committee Chair Just Wants to Know?

BOARD LEADERSHIP, NUMBER 29, JAN.-FEB. 1997

I HAD A CALL RECENTLY from the finance committee chair of a large membership orga-nization I'd been helping to implement Policy Governance. Two management events had come to her attention somewhat by accident. One event was a strong dis-ciplinary action taken by the CEO against a member of the fiscal staff. The other was a contract the CEO signed with an accounting firm for an in-depth study to improve management practices.

The finance committee chair wondered whether management was remiss in not informing her officially of these events. Surely the CEO ought to know that a finance committee chair should be told about such things.

This board, while making a number of changes en route to Policy Governance, had only partially dealt with its pre-Policy Governance committees. Although it had got-ten rid of some, it had condensed a long list of others into a handful of new commit-tees, each one loosely responsible for the topics covered by the older committees it now subsumed. Committees were instructed by the board to design their own jobs, but to "use Policy Governance principles."

Everyone knew that committee jobs would be different under Policy Governance, but because the board had not specified the new committees' jobs, committee chairs were understandably jittery. The chair of the finance committee, somewhat affronted by the discipline and contract issues, was jittery enough to call me.

Finance committees and their chairs are particularly vulnerable to a misplaced sense of responsibility. The general public, the membership, and even other board members somehow think the finance committee chair should be knowledgeable about every jot and tittle of financial management. Policy Governance boards learn that their job is not financial management but the governance of financial management. And from that perspective it is clear that the board has no financial management role to delegate to its officers or committees. That role has already been delegated to the CEO.

> Policy Governance boards learn that their job is not financial management but the governance of financial management.

If there is to be a finance committee at all, its role must be something other than attending to the details of financial management. For example, there might be a finance committee to help the board manage an endowment (when that role has not been delegated to the CEO). Or there might be a finance committee that is essentially an audit committee helping the board negotiate with an outside auditor—or even doing some limited fiscal auditing, itself. In the latter case, of course, the only allowable auditing would be according to criteria the board has set out in policy. Under Policy Governance, legitimate auditing (merely another word for monitoring) can never be according to committee criteria, criteria the board itself never set.

← **FAQ**

Is there any appropriate role for a finance committee under Policy Governance?

Under Policy Governance, there would be no finance committee at all, unless the board decided it needed one to help with a legitimate board responsibility. In the case under discussion, the finance committee task was as yet unclear, but the board had required that all committees be bound by the same Policy Governance principles as had been adopted by and for the full board. Here is what I advised the committee chair:

■ Because the board had, indeed, begun to treat its CEO according to Policy Governance principles, the decisions taken were clearly within the CEO's purview. There was no hint that the CEO's actions violated a board policy about conflict of interest or staff treatment.

■ In a formal sense, then, the CEO was not required to inform the board about these decisions and, by extension, was not obligated to inform the finance committee or its chair. A board committee, under Policy Governance, cannot have a job or a right that isn't first the board's job or right. The board had made it clear that the CEO could take any action that complied with a reasonable interpretation of the board's executive limitations policies. The CEO was merely exercising that authority.

FAQ ➡

What if board members just want to know about some aspect of operations?

■ Nevertheless, there is nothing wrong with the board or its individual members just wanting to know about aspects of the organization that do not qualify for monitoring according to the established criteria. Individual board members are limited (according to this particular board's board-staff linkage policies) to information that does not require a material amount of resources to produce. The board as a full body, of course, can get any question it chooses answered, regardless of the cost.

■ This board had already adopted an executive limitations policy that made it unacceptable for the CEO to keep the board in the dark on certain matters the board was curious about. It is quite acceptable to adopt such a policy, as long as the board and CEO never confuse this sharing of incidental information with monitoring. The board can put whatever it wants on the "just let us know" list but must remember not to judge CEO performance using these data and not to take board action on them.

■ This board's provisions did not cover the kind of information this finance chair sought. I suggested to her that since she obviously thought the board should be informed, she should try to convince her colleagues to amend the existing board policy.

■ The board can adjust its policies about being informed in order to correct any oversights, but it must take care not to lessen the authority of the CEO. It is important that such an occurrence be attributed to the board's oversight, not the CEO's. The CEO was simply proceeding on the belief that the board meant what it said.

> It is paramount that the board have the information it needs to determine whether ends are being achieved and unacceptable means are being avoided.

■ It is extremely important to keep information for monitoring separate from incidental information. When these different types of information are allowed to mingle, the board is sure to lose the discipline required for proper monitoring. It is paramount that the board have the information it needs to determine whether ends are being achieved and unacceptable means are being avoided. Nothing can be allowed to obscure this inquiry.

Shouldn't the CEO have known, anyway, what the committee chair would want to know? Maybe so; maybe not. Reasonable people disagree widely on what someone "should have known." Why leave this gap in communication when it is so easy for the board just to say what it wants? Keep in mind that whether the board knows what it wishes to know is a matter of means, not ends. Because the board controls staff means by limiting or proscribing, the instruction to the CEO, in its broadest form, is "don't let us be uninformed."

To illustrate actual policy wording, here is an excerpt from an executive limitations policy my clients usually title "Communication and Support to the Board." I'll show its preamble (the global prohibition) and, of its several subparts, the one that is relevant to this article:

> The CEO shall not permit the board to be uninformed or unsupported in its work.
>
> 1. He or she shall not allow the board to be unaware of (a) relevant trends, (b) anticipated adverse media coverage, (c) hiring, promotion, demotion, or firing of executive personnel, (d) substantial lawsuits against the organization, (e) unexpected or unexplained client death, (f) publicly visible external and internal changes, (g) major contracts or ones with high public visibility, (h) changes in the assumptions upon which any board policy has previously been established.

With only occasional adjustments, such a policy can assure that board members hear about what they'd like to know, yet without entangling them once again in detailed micromanagement. You can see that the wording shown here would have taken care of my caller's concern about the contract (item 1g), though not her wish to know about the disciplinary action. If her board's policy had looked like my example, she might want to convince the board to add to it an element dealing with "disciplinary action" or "disciplinary action toward staff in sensitive positions."

← FAQ
How can a board assure it hears what it would like to know, without micromanaging?

But if my caller wants the board to control (rather than just know about) such matters, then she must convince her colleagues to make such actions off-limits to the CEO by amending the part of the executive limitations policy that controls practices toward staff. (She cannot institute such changes on her own authority.) Extending executive limitations in this manner, however, would dismantle much of the delegation the board had painstakingly put into place.

This conscientious finance committee chair was dragging old governance concepts into the board's new governance environment. She thought she should be more responsible than the full board for financial detail. Apparently she thought she had an obligation and a right to know whatever financial detail she chose (quite apart from what the board had chosen). Her behavior even implied that the CEO was at fault for taking unilateral action—even though the board had empowered him to do so.

She can legitimately ask for and get the information she wants, in any case, but it does not reflect badly on the CEO that, in the absence of a board policy such as the one above, he did not read her mind.

She could also legitimately counsel the board about which financial criteria to establish or advise the board on the apparent accuracy of financial monitoring data (according to criteria already set by the full board). But as to the issues she called me about, the organization will be more effective if she just learns to relax! The only remaining, unfinished task is for this board to question seriously why it needs a finance committee at all.

A Responsible Board Is Obligated to Ensure a
Responsible Chair

Reining In a Runaway Chair

BOARD LEADERSHIP, NUMBER 38, JULY-AUG. 1998

A FRIEND OF MINE is CEO of a national voluntary health organization. She has been very successful at bringing the organization from the brink of financial disaster to fiscal health. Her board has expressed pleasure at her performance. But now she is facing a difficult situation, which threatens not only to disrupt her career but also to gravely damage the organization she runs. To eliminate the pronouns, I'll call her Maria.

The board chairperson—let's call him Ted—is having an affair with one of Maria's direct reports. The direct report—I'll call her Susan—has turned out to be an unreliable employee, one who consistently fails to satisfy the requirements of her job (requirements that are crucial to the organization's economic viability). Maria has tried everything she can to support improvement in Susan's performance, but Susan does not improve and even fudges performance data in order to cover her tracks. She seems to think that her relationship with Ted will protect her from any disciplinary action Maria might take.

And so far Susan has been correct. Ted, seemingly oblivious to his ethically vulnerable position, intervenes with Maria on Susan's behalf, preventing Maria from terminating Susan or even placing her on probation. Having been quite careful in documenting Susan's failures, Maria is certain that the organization and its mission cannot afford Susan's behavior. But the board chair's unrelenting interference has Maria stymied. On one hand, if she fires Susan against the board chair's will, his subsequent vendetta could reasonably be expected to cost Maria her own job. On the other hand, if Maria does not fire Susan, organizational performance for which Maria is accountable would suffer and, in retrospect, Maria could be seen as not having fulfilled her responsibility in the matter. Yet Maria is reluctant to take Ted on in a board meeting.

Needless to say, Maria's board does not use the Policy Governance model. If it did, this unfortunate situation could not have arisen. I don't mean, of course, that personal relationships could not exist between board members and staff members, who are, after all, human. But under proper governance such a relationship would not cause a governance or management problem.

When a board fails to have the elements of responsible governance in place, actions available to rectify a bad situation are only piecemeal at best. Maria's board isn't worse than most boards, and its members aren't less responsible than most board members. But the board's traditional governance arrangement is vulnerable to the sort of abuse of authority Ted is exhibiting.

I counseled Maria to reframe the problem. She was so frustrated and angry with Ted that it was difficult to see beyond his reprehensible behavior. I wanted Maria to understand that although the chair is indeed culpable, and certainly infuriating, it is not he who is the source of her problem. In over two decades of consulting, I've observed a consistent tendency in people to blame individuals or personalities for problems that, if not systemic in origin, are at least systemic in their solution. Maria did not at first find this line of approach satisfying, continuing to protest that the chair is meddlesome, unethical, and vengeful. It was not my contention that Maria was wrong, just that Ted's ignoble traits are a poor focus for her problem solving.

FAQ ➡
Why shouldn't the chairperson supervise the CEO?

My point? The chair has no authority that the board does not allow him to have. Under Policy Governance principles, we see that the board, by allowing the chair to have authority over Maria, has in effect said that Ted rather than Maria is the CEO (even though the board hasn't meant to say this). We also know that the board is accountable for the behavior of its subordinates, including the chair (the chair, properly construed, works for the board, not the other way around). If a board has *intentionally* given the chair authority to steer or even influence the CEO's decisions, then the ostensible CEO doesn't really work for the board but for the board chair. Maria's board, however, had certainly not given her such a message before. If in fact the board has not given the chair such authority, then Ted has been abusing his role and the board should take swift action before the organization suffers. If the board does not take that action, it is culpable.

As Maria gave me more facts, I learned that the board is not only unaware of Ted's behavior but is just as unaware of its responsibility for making the finer points of delegation clear. The very lack of clarity is what opens the door to behavior like that which the chair is displaying. But if it weren't this chair acting this way, it could easily be another chair acting another inappropriate way. In other words, focusing on the chair as the problem is only a short-term solution, which yields no systemic improvement, just a change of personalities. Maria could get swept again into a duel she can't win. The key is to focus on the *board* as the problem—as indeed it is. Maria's board is being irresponsible in allowing this situation to exist (or, more accurately, in allowing the conditions under which a situation like this can exist).

How can Maria confront her board? Because she doesn't know how responsibly her board will act, she must be careful. She knows that two or three board members are aware of the chair's behavior and are appalled. Her best approach is through these board members. She must convince them that the board is accountable for the chair's behavior and directly responsible for the restoration of integrity to the situation. If they will carry the torch, it is best for them to do so. That way, if the board obsti-

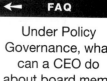

← FAQ

Under Policy Governance, what can a CEO do about board members who abuse their position?

nately refuses to shoulder the problem, the situation will not backlash onto Maria for causing an uncomfortable confrontation. It is not uncommon for boards to love their psychological comfort so much that they'll allow someone else (usually the CEO) to go down in flames in order to protect it. In other words, rather than confront each other, board members will often allow a good CEO to be hung out to dry.

What if the one or two friendly board members will not confront the board? Then Maria's best bet is to go directly to the board herself *with the systemic issue* as opposed to the specific issue. In other words, she need not bring up Ted and Susan's affair, but she must ask whether

> Rather than confront each other, board members will often allow a good CEO to be hung out to dry.

she reports truly to the board alone. That may be a daunting thing to do, but taking no action at all would be even more dangerous. The jury is still out on this continuing case, but I hope that if the issue is not resolved in a more painless way that Maria will say something like this to her board:

> I need to take a few minutes of your time to get clarification from you on a matter that is significant in the management of your association. More important, this matter is crucial to how effective I can be in serving our mission.
>
> You hired me as your CEO six years ago with the understanding that I would be held accountable for considerable improvements in the organization's achievements and in

what was at the time its dangerous fiscal situation. I asked for as free a hand as you could give me in carrying out my job. That was to protect me from having to check out every move with the board or a committee before acting. But it was also to protect you from my ever being able to hide behind board meddling as an excuse for nonperformance. We've operated that way for these six years with more success than any of us dreamed.

Over the past several months it has become apparent that, as chairperson, Ted wishes the board to operate in another way, which, of course, the board has a right to do. But Ted has begun, without the board having made a decision to reverse its initial agreement with me, to operate as if the board has already decided to involve itself directly in internal management. While I am somewhat embarrassed to be bringing such a sensitive matter to your attention, Ted's direct intervention in personnel issues and in staff supervision for the past several months represents such a major shift in my relationship with the board—and so jeopardizes my ability to manage your association—that I am forced to ask the board for clarification of my role here.

Will this approach work for Maria? At the outset, no one can tell. But it does serve to put the matter squarely in the board's lap. No responsible board will allow a problem like this to remain Maria's problem; it must be the board's problem. Under Policy Governance, the board chair could not intervene—or if he did, the board wouldn't stand for it—and Maria would feel completely safe in using her judgment (within board policy, of course) in dealing with Susan.

It is easy for boards to disavow or, at least, conveniently overlook the actions of a runaway chair. A responsible board cannot do that, for it understands that it is fully accountable for all behavior of its chair.

Does Your Board Drive Away Its Most Promising Members?

BOARD LEADERSHIP, NUMBER 35, JAN.-FEB. 1998

SOME FORTUNATE ORGANIZATIONS have no trouble filling board vacancies with talented leaders. Many others are not so blessed. Although there are a number of factors involved in describing, recruiting, and retaining capable governors, in this article I want to focus on one infrequently discussed aspect of the vacancy challenge—the way boards drive away existing or potential members and how they can avoid doing it.

First, let's admit that boards, in fact, do frequently drive away persons who could contribute much needed leadership. Sometimes these persons are already board members but eventually find the experience so unpalatable they decide to leave. Sometimes they are not board members but would contemplate board service if they thought they could tolerate it. This article considers both groups together.

Second, let's also recognize that it is perfectly all right that some persons are put off by board service. If, by the way a board operates, it makes itself unattractive to people whose interest is blatantly self-serving (for example, the insurance broker who wants a captive customer), who are intellectually incapable, or who are too busy to attend regularly, that is commendable. If a strict bylaws attendance provision automatically eliminates members who continue to miss meetings, the board process is made stronger.

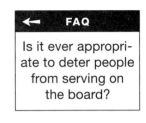

← FAQ

Is it ever appropriate to deter people from serving on the board?

FAQ ➡

What board
characteristics are
unattractive to
promising leaders?

My concern in this article is not about driving away persons in whose absence governance improves. If anything, boards need more effective ways to do that. The problem I'm discussing is that traditional governance drives away the people it most needs to enhance board leadership. Let's look at some rather typical circumstances that make board participation unattractive to the very best possible leaders.

The board really doesn't matter. This may sound like a bizarre consideration, but in the total scheme of organizational realities, many boards just don't matter! They may be paper tigers; they may be flesh-and-blood decorations for staff-driven organizations. A board like this may be a social plus for persons who need the organization more than it needs them. But the board's chances for achieving excellence are greater if it is composed of people who have no patience for wasting their time as figureheads. Leaders want to matter.

Meetings drown in details. Real leaders recognize that the details must be filled in and, in fact, are in their own way quite concerned with them. When Mies van der Rohe observed that "God is in the details," he didn't mean that as lead architect he had to saw the miter joints, but that all the details must be true to the broader principles in which he had an uncompromising personal interest. It is getting those broad principles right that most challenges a world-class architect—or governing board. To be sure, there are details of a sort that boards and architects cannot delegate—for example, for boards, the details of their governance rules. However, details dealt with at an inappropriately high level can simply be called trivia. The big-picture leaders with vision, which governing boards need, avoid serving on boards that dabble in detail inappropriate for such a lofty level of leadership.

> Real leaders recognize that the details must be filled in and, in fact, are in their own way quite concerned with them.

Personality prevails over ideas. Some boards resemble social clubs. The organization and its mission can be treated like the board members' toy rather than their solemn responsibility. As in clubs, cliques can form, turning the board meeting into a political back-scratching event rather than a forum for ideas in conflict. Leaders who enjoy the challenge of debating ideas and forging a vision are bored or even discouraged by interpersonal commerce in predilections and power.

Controversy is avoided. It is hard to find a nonprofit or governmental pursuit that is not fraught with controversy or, at least, with a host of competing public values. Yet it is common to find boards that regularly operate as if there are no big issues to be debated—as if the controversies don't exist or their existence rudely interferes with polite discourse. Such boards exact a high personal cost from leaders who bring unpopular views to the table or who demand that unpopular views, including those that they themselves disagree with, be heard. The kinds of leaders governing boards need are not invested in pretending that everything important has already been decided and in running board meetings as though they were love-ins.

Resolution is avoided. Meanwhile, some boards (like George and Martha in *Who's Afraid of Virginia Woolf?*) are constantly bickering about one thing or another, yet never settling anything. Leaders have little tolerance for such silliness, so they tend to avoid being yoked with persons who do. Such boards often see Policy Governance as flawed "because we won't be able to agree on ends, so the model can't work." To the contrary, the board can surely agree on an extremely broad mega-ends statement (tantamount to mission). At whatever subsequent level of definition the board finds it cannot agree upon, it stops. The CEO, though, can move forward, since he or she is authorized to use any reasonable interpretation of the ends statement at the level at which the board did reach a resolution. Besides, even at the mega-ends level, unanimity is not needed, only a majority vote.

Members' time is not valued. Some boards operate as if members are persons of leisure, having no other pressing claims on their time. Board meetings go on and on. Committee meetings are held to debate decisions individuals could just as well have made on their own. A few board members monopolize the group's precious time, unrestrained by any clear group decision about the use of its time. (It is amazing how grown adults will allow themselves to be held hostage by one or two people dominating a group.) Such boards slowly lose members whose time is valuable and gain members whose time evidently isn't. In one case, I saw the chairperson's job made so time-intensive that only a few persons could afford to take it on—thereby disqualifying a whole pool of potential chairs. Real leaders treat time as a nonrenewable resource, one to be marshaled with great care. They respect their time too much to treat it cavalierly.

> It is amazing how grown adults will allow themselves to be held hostage by one or two people dominating a group.

Governance is a tough job calling
for intelligence, moral courage,
and commitment. In short, it calls
for leaders.

There are few or no rules. For any important job, discipline is indispensable. When a board makes insufficient rules for itself, it cripples its crucial accountability. The board lacks the ability to recognize whether a board member's behavior is appropriate or inappropriate. How much meeting nonattendance is acceptable? Which comments on staff performance are acceptable and which are not? What can the board chairperson unilaterally decide, and what would be an abuse of the position? Does the CEO have to follow directions issued by the chairperson? Does the board "shoot from the hip" on important issues of process, or does it follow carefully agreed to methods? The leaders who can contribute best to good governance demand that an important job be organized as an important job.

The proper role of governance is not merely ceremonial or symbolic. It is not just a convenient mechanism for staff ratification. Its proper decisions are not simply endorsements of motherhood and apple pie. Governance is a tough job calling for intelligence, moral courage, and commitment. In short, it calls for leaders. Rather than driving leaders away, boards should do whatever is necessary to make leaders want to be board members.

A Few Tips for the Chairperson

BOARD LEADERSHIP, NUMBER 3, SEPT.-OCT. 1992

Hᴏᴡ ʏᴏᴜ ᴀs ᴄʜᴀɪʀᴘᴇʀsᴏɴ carry out your role has much to do with the success of the board. A weak chair often fails to move a board along and may be unable to save the board from indecisiveness and the tendency to dance around issues. Whereas strong chairs have been known to run roughly over dissent and participation, the point is not simply that you should be either retiring or strong. The point is that you should lead individuals to become a *leadership group* in which members never assume they can relax their responsibility because the chair will be responsible on their behalf. Here are a few tips for chairing more effectively:

Be the chairperson, not an intermittent CEO. Do your own job. The board has already designated the top staff officer as chief executive. Your role is to help the board do a good job, not to run the organization. If your organization is too small to have a staff CEO, you may in fact have to perform both roles. If so, just be clear yourself and communicate clearly to others which hat you are wearing at any particular time. (Generally in these tips, I'll assume your organization has assigned the role of CEO to its top staff person.)

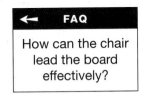

← **FAQ**

How can the chair lead the board effectively?

Lead the board, not the CEO. Your focus should be on the board, not on the staff. The CEO works for the board, not for you. Only the board has the right to tell the CEO what to do or to add to the board's criteria for judging CEO performance. An intermediary can only *detract* from crisp accountability. Consequently, don't worry about the CEO, worry about the board—that will be worry enough.

> When you enforce the rules, it will be better if you are enforcing the board's rules, not yours.

Lead the board to define its own job. Your purview is not to work your own agenda for the operating organization. Even your desire for better governance has to become the board's commitment before you can have much effect. Press the board to explore the ramifications of its moral (or sometimes legal) trusteeship and to define just what its job is. When the job is thus defined in its relatively permanent form, have the board set annual targets within segments of that job. This will help later as you set specific meeting agendas.

Lead the board to design its discipline. When you enforce the rules, it will be better if you are enforcing the board's rules, not yours. Help the board examine and plan its process—how the board will deal with dissent, with renegade members, with attendance, and with coming to meetings unprepared. Decisions about the rules the board chooses for itself should be written and adopted as board policy. Without group-determined discipline, there'll either be insufficient discipline or you will end up personally creating it.

> Because it is easy for a board to slip back into old habits, I suggest self-evaluation be done every meeting.

Lead the board to evaluate its performance. Regularly return the board to what it adopted about its own job. Has it followed through? Is it behaving the way it said it would? Be sure you stick to what the board has adopted as expectations and intentions for itself. Evaluations done apart from the job description are not as useful and may be a waste of time. Because it is easy for a board to slip back into old habits, I suggest self-evaluation be done every meeting.

Take responsibility for the agenda. This is the board's agenda, not the staff's—so don't leave the agenda to staff. The board's job is not to look over what the staff did last month or quarter, but to get its own job done. If the board doesn't know about its own job more than staff does, then recognize that as a problem and go back to "lead the board to define its own job," above. Developing agendas for specific meetings will be both easier and more board-empowering if the board as a body has engaged itself—even with a broad brush—in annual agenda planning.

Run participative but efficient meetings. Keep it open, but keep it moving! Encourage debate and differences; bring people out; make it acceptable to disagree. Create an atmosphere of respectful diversity. Yet do not allow the board to talk an issue to death. Using a simple poll—"How many have your minds made up already?"—can yield surprising and enlightening results. The informal polling technique, by the way, can be used to get quick readings from the board in many situations.

> Using a simple poll—"How many have your minds made up already?"—can yield surprising and enlightening results.

Take the long view—build capability. Efficient meetings are important, but don't put your emphasis on effective meetings per se. Focus on the long-term ability of the board to govern. You won't worry too much if a particular meeting is awkward and tedious if the board learns needed skills and insights from it . . . or grapples meaningfully with an important value issue. Set out to leave the next chair with a board more in control of itself than you found it. The board will be less vulnerable to unhappy conditions thereafter, such as having a chairperson less wonderful than you are!

Your job as chairperson comes as close to a pure instance of Robert Greenleaf's *servant-leader* as I can imagine. You are clearly the board's leader and just as surely its servant as well. You might get a philosophical boost for that challenge by reading Greenleaf's thoughts on the matter. Understand servant-leadership, understand governance, understand your board . . . then you will be ready to help your board understand itself.

Sometimes You Have to Fire Your Chair

BOARD LEADERSHIP, NUMBER 28, NOV.-DEC. 1996

EARLIER THIS YEAR I dealt with a trade association board that had made little progress over the past few years in making the governance changes we'd planned at an initial workshop. The board had originally been enthusiastic about the possibilities offered by Policy Governance. They had retained me to help them develop an entire set of executive limitations, governance process, and board-staff linkage policies. That was then, this is now. When I met with them recently, the board was unenthusiastic, a bit disgruntled, and beset with controversy about board members' and management decisions.

What on earth went wrong? At some level, they had done a lot of work and had even done some things right. Keep in mind that the board had already developed three of the four categories of board policies during the jump-start I'd helped them with. Here is what I found:

- Leadership for the governance rebirth they had wanted had come from the CEO. Board members were happy to let her carry the torch. So the CEO had devised exercises for the board, had involved board members in managerial operations for their education, and had provided whatever new-member orientation that was needed.

- The board, despite professing to use their new governance, still spoke in the same old-think language and still thought about monitoring, program design, and committees in the same traditional way. To hear them talk, you'd think they had never heard of Policy Governance principles.

- They had employed a consultant who knew nothing of Policy Governance to facilitate a goal-setting session. Predictably, the consultant ignored the principles they'd committed themselves to and, of course, so did they. The consultant was chosen by the CEO (of course!), who understandably though wrongly thought getting the board into more of management would be an interim step to their getting into governance.

- The board chair not only failed to lead the board closer to its own policies but also actively opposed Policy Governance and introduced management-based methods into the increasingly confused mix. The chair clearly wanted to have authority over the CEO, be able to instruct staff, and chair the board in the way he saw fit.

I spent a day reacquainting board members with the principles they'd already paid to learn and which they'd already put into their own tailored, but model-consistent policies. There had been a fair amount of turnover, but new board members had received no focused training in the unfamiliar governance approach the board had voted to live by. But the real problem for this board was its own commitment to be a disciplined body. Each member was a successful business person in his or her own right. Each was accustomed to discipline and perseverance. Yet as a group they seemed to think that "adopting the model" constituted being an effective board, even in the absence of any real change!

So what can make the difference for this board? It is possible, of course, that nothing can—nothing, that is, except a turnaround in their commitment to excellence. And what concrete steps would that take? I believe they are these:

Make a decision. This board should confront the age-old "fish or cut bait" question. Are we going to use a model—which implies rules based on an integrated set of principles and concepts—or continue to shoot from the hip, following the same ruts and reacting to the moment's interest?

> **← FAQ**
>
> If a board's commitment to Policy Governance has waned, what steps can the board take to recommit to excellence?

Correct any deterioration. If the board commits to the model (Policy Governance) it already ostensibly committed to, it should next "clean up" all the model-inconsistent policy insertions made in the interim, so it can restart trusting its documents. After the board with my assistance had drafted a new policy framework, the CEO had transferred previous board documents more or less as they were into the new policy manual without being rigorous in making them conform to the new principles.

Get policy-picky. The board's governance process and board-staff linkage policies (especially with a small amount of cleaning up) already form a rule book, so to speak, for the board to follow. Board members should focus on these policies, word for word, until their conduct matches their own codified ideal. The policies aren't very long, and with a little work, they are completely doable.

Fire the chair. Well, maybe not fire the chair, but give the chair a clear choice: Either chair the board in accord with board policies (which he had not been doing) or step down. Having a nonperforming chair is no excuse for the board that doesn't get its job done. It does not matter in the least whether the chair likes the board's chosen governance style. The job of the chair is what the board decides it is, not what the chair decides. It cannot be otherwise if the board is to be a responsible group. It cannot be otherwise if board members are to be true to their moral obligation to the ownership.

> The job of the chair is what the board decides it is, not what the chair decides. It cannot be otherwise if the board is to be a responsible group.

Actually, the fourth point—though clearly difficult for any board to confront—is made easier by a governance process policy that they had (and one I always recommend), which describes the chair's primary purpose as seeing to it that the board follows its own policies. If the chair has a substantive role at all—rather than merely ceremonial—this is what it is. But this chair was more interested in being part-time CEO than in being chair, more invested in doing someone else's job than his own. This board could have legitimately fired its CEO for the dereliction of duty almost proudly carried out by its chair.

Will this board make it? I honestly don't know, but I worry that they will not. As you can tell, this topic has a lot more to do with the board's overall commitment than it does about the chair's mode of leadership. When I left, some were still wondering aloud how they might keep their same committees, how to placate the chair (they haven't seriously considered changing chairs), and how to measure the results they'd never defined. I guess excellence isn't for everybody.

What to Do with Your Board's Philosophy, Values, and Beliefs

BOARD LEADERSHIP, NUMBER 34, NOV.-DEC. 1997

I FREQUENTLY ENCOUNTER boards that have laboriously produced statements of mission, vision, values, and philosophy. Unfortunately, these statements, often recommended by popular approaches to strategic planning, can remain just words on a page and never get reflected in any meaningful way in the organization. The Policy Governance model, however, is designed to make sure that the mission, vision, values, and philosophy of the organization become an integral part of the organization's life. Thus, when a board decides to implement Policy Governance, it will find that while these statements *as they are written* are no longer relevant, most of the sentiments they communicate and their implications for the organization will be more effectively expressed in Policy Governance documents.

> **← FAQ**
>
> Under Policy Governance, why do an organization's statements of vision, values, and philosophy need to be reworked?

Policy Governance is a complete model for governance. It does not augment traditional governance concepts and practices but replaces them. Mixing the concepts and practices from two distinct paradigms works about as well as mixing the rules of baseball and football and hoping to have an intelligible game. No matter how important they might be to a lineman, tips about tackling are not useful for coaching infielders. A board's documents embody not only a board's "rules of the game," but its proprietary "plays" as well. Confounding documents peculiar to one form of governance with those of another introduces a weakness, not a strength.

Policy Governance is a complete model for governance. It does not augment traditional governance concepts and practices but replaces them.

That said, aren't the sentiments to be found in a carefully worded philosophy or vision statement useful to a Policy Governance board? In most cases, the answer is yes; but if those statements are left in their pre–Policy Governance form, they will detract from the clarity of the board's new governance style. Let's look at what might be done with each type of statement.

Mission Statement

FAQ ➡

How can an organization's statements of vision, values, and philosophy be integrated into Policy Governance policy?

In Policy Governance there is a document that clearly outlines the organization's mission—the ends category of board policies. These few pages, taken all together, designate what benefits will occur for whom and at what cost. The briefest, most inclusive core of these policies is usually a statement no more than one sentence long that succinctly states how the world will be different as a result of the organization's work. I often call this statement a *mega-ends* or over-arching ends policy, but it could also be called a mission statement.

One would think, then, that a board's previous mission statement could be translated directly into the Policy Governance framework. Sadly, it rarely can because conventional mission statements rarely observe distinctions required of an ends statement, that is, to proclaim the overall difference the organization is to make in the world, in terms of both production and consumption.

Confounding documents peculiar to one form of governance with those of another introduces a weakness, not a strength.

In fact, most mission statements state no results at all, if by results we mean the benefit or change that is to accrue to consumers or other target populations. They may occasionally be rather clear about the "for whom" part of the ends concept, but without the results component and, of course, without the cost of results component, few traditional mission statements pass the test to be a Policy Governance mega-ends policy.

As a result, most pre–Policy Governance mission statements are simply discarded when Policy Governance is being implemented. At best they are briefly consulted for a hint of what results might have been implied.

Philosophy or Belief Statement

Unexamined governance is not worth leading, to paraphrase Socrates a bit. I absolutely concur with boards' examining, deliberating about, and deciding upon the philosophy that underlies their work. Under the topics of philosophy and beliefs, I am including the board's convictions, ideology, perspectives on the board role or on the world, understanding of leadership obligations, and other expressions of the board personality. These matters affect any board's choices, so they are relevant to board leadership and, because of that, it is profitable to make them explicit and visible to all.

It is important, however, that such a statement not be confused with what the board, using its philosophy and beliefs as points of departure, then chooses to direct the CEO to accomplish or to avoid. Instructions to the CEO (that is, to the organization) involve a *separate* set of board decisions. Although guided by a certain philosophy, they must take into account real-world contingencies and conditions. So while a board might well believe in a racially color-blind world and may have developed statements proclaiming this belief, it may for good practical reasons not choose to charge a CEO with producing one, but only

> Philosophy is very important, but it is philosophy only, not instruction.

with producing a community condition in which color is not a significant factor in various settings. Philosophy is very important, but it is philosophy only, not instruction.

Statements of board philosophy or belief belong in the governance process category of board policies, then, because they describe the board's mentality in doing its job or, in more colloquial parlance, where the board is "coming from."

Decisions about what is to be achieved for consumers are partially determined by a board's philosophy, but once they are made they are included as board instructions in the ends policies. Which activities and situations are deemed unacceptable will be influenced by the board's philosophy, but once they are decided upon they take the form of board instructions in the executive limitations policies. A description of the operating relationship between governance and management may flow somewhat from a board's philosophy, but the description itself is placed into the board-staff linkage policies. It is unfair to judge CEO performance using criteria other than those that are explicitly defined in ends and executive limitations policies.

Vision Statement

FAQ ➡

Why doesn't Policy Governance encourage boards to have a vision statement?

Some people find Policy Governance confusing in that it claims to afford boards the opportunity to be visionary, yet it has no identifiable statement called "vision." Yet in a sense, most of the board policies in Policy Governance are statements of vision. Governance process policies establish a vision of what accountable governance should be and—going beyond vision alone—how a board can exemplify it. As just discussed, a board's philosophy or beliefs are to be found in its governance process policies—vision statements about the board and its governance.

Another, perhaps less impressive, form of vision statement is found in the board-staff linkage policies that describe a board's commitment to empowering, accountable delegation. Even executive limitations policies are vision statements in that they delineate the prudence and ethics an organization must adhere to.

> Governance process policies establish a vision of what accountable governance should be and—going beyond vision alone—how a board can exemplify it.

But the vision most people mean is that which is codified in ends policies. These policies describe the true difference the organization is to make and thus could be regarded as the strongest possible vision statements. By creating ends policies with a long-range perspective, the board is essentially generating the vision toward which managerial plans plan. In other words, there is clearly an articulation of the board's vision in Policy Governance, but it appears in more than one place, depending on what kind of vision it is.

Values

Policy Governance divides the board's values into values about ends, values about unacceptable means, values about the governance task and process itself, and values about the sharing or delegation of authority to others. It is, in fact, *values governance* (a term I used at one time prior to settling on the term Policy Governance). Values (and vision) are so integral to Policy Governance that the system is built on distinctions between various types of values and vision. Ultimately, all policies under Policy Governance are value statements.

> Ultimately, all policies under Policy Governance are value statements.

Integrating Philosophy, Beliefs, Mission, Vision, and Values into Policy Governance

Almost all organizations that adopt Policy Governance can simply fold the previous statements into the appropriate Policy Governance policy category or, where that is not appropriate, they can take parts of the previous statements and apportion them among the proper policy categories. The previous work is rarely lost. But preserving it in its pre–Policy Governance form will definitely compromise the integrity of the policy system, for where and how the board says what it has to say makes a difference.

Crafting the Board Job Description

BOARD LEADERSHIP, NUMBER 10, NOV.-DEC. 1993

BOARD SELF-EVALUATION can only be an absurdity if the board does not know its job. In this article, I explain how to describe a job and illustrate an effective description of the board's job. Just to underscore the importance of the job description, consider that without one your next board meeting can't even have an agenda, for you'd have no idea what the board needs to do. Well, yes, there'd be one agenda item: to decide on a job description! At any rate, evaluating whether the board is getting its job done is ludicrous without having first said what that job is! So let's discuss the crafting of a job description.

The most useful job descriptions focus not on activities but rather on the outcomes of those activities.

There is nothing new about describing jobs. Job descriptions are a common organizational phenomenon. By tradition, we are accustomed to describing what a person does in a job. Indeed, if we look at a typical job description, we're likely to find a listing of job activities: type letters, review reports, administer a program, conduct training, mow lawn, wash dishes. But more sophisticated managers know that the most useful job descriptions focus not on activities but rather on the outcomes of those activities.

Knowing what to do in a job and continually improving the ability to do those things—what is often called *process improvement*—is important. But the worth of a better process lies in its contribution to getting a job done. Even monumental progress in methods is wasted if it is not aimed toward the appropriate job outputs.

No job exists to *do* anything. A job exists for the *result of the doing.*

Focusing on Outputs

By job outputs I mean the conditions or states that will be realized if the job is successfully accomplished. What will be the case in one or another domain of organizational life? For example, a therapist's job exists not to do therapy but to help dysfunctional clients become functional. A program evaluator's job does not exist to do evaluation studies but to give program managers accurate data about program effectiveness.

In other words, no job exists to *do* anything. A job exists for the *result of the doing.* It exists to make a difference in something besides itself. Clarity about the difference to be made is the essence of a powerful job description. Consequently, a far more robust description of a job is in terms of outputs rather than activities. Activities, conduct, and process are not unimportant, but their importance is largely a function of whether the job outputs are achieved. If we focus on describing the needed outputs first, appropriate activities can be designed and improvements in process pursued. However, we focus first on the process, leaving outputs unstated, we can come to treat the process as the output itself: Methods become more important than results.

Unfortunately, however, almost all published definitions of the board's job are statements of activities or methods: approve budgets, make policy, oversee finances, participate in discussion, hire the CEO, read monitoring reports, listen to input, review plans, read the mailings, learn to read financial statements, become better communicators, attend meetings, keep minutes, call on donors, and so on ad infinitum. It is not that these oft-prescribed engagements are wrong, *but using activities as the beginning point for describing the board's job actually sabotages board leadership.* They are not results in themselves but activities

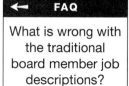

← FAQ

What is wrong with the traditional board member job descriptions?

or processes that ostensibly serve some intended results. It is possible for boards to carry out all the activities prescribed by the conventional wisdom and still fail to fulfill a useful organizational role. Hence, a major aspect of board self-evaluation is, first, the careful specification—in outcome terms—of just what the board's job *is!*

It is possible for boards to carry out all the activities prescribed by the conventional wisdom and still fail to fulfill a useful organizational role.

Defining Achievement

To define achievement, we must determine just what the board is to accomplish. Exactly what is the "value added" for which the board exists in the first place? What does the board contribute to the organization that sets it apart from the CEO and from staff members? It does no good for the board to be good at what it does, if what it does doesn't need to be done. Clear definition of just what the board is to achieve is paramount. The board's expression of mission is an example of such thinking—or should be. In this article, however, the subject is not the mission of the organization but the mission of the board's job. For example, except in very small organizations, the board's direct job is not the accomplishment of mission but *the statement of mission* in a clear and compelling way.

The deliberation that generates a board job description is soul searching, lengthy, and utterly individual. The discussion is never alike for any two boards, even though the resulting policy language may be similar. It's important to realize that with this discussion—where policy describing the board job is generated—the board takes a substantial step in establishing a system of self-evaluation, for the policy establishes the principal criteria by which that evaluation will take place.

The deliberation that generates a board job description is soul searching, lengthy, and utterly individual.

The very act of writing these policies, most boards discover, teaches them more about why they exist than they have ever known before. Before a board even begins its first formal self-evaluation, then, it already has a clearer sense of what it needs to achieve, simply because it has gone through the process of spelling out its job policy.

The boxed text depicts a finished policy from the board of the United States Cycling Federation (USCF), a U.S. Olympics Committee-affiliated membership organization located in Colorado Springs. I use this policy here to point out features in the USCF board job description and show how these ultimately relate to the ongoing process of board self-evaluation. Remember that this policy describes the board's job, not the organization's job. Of all the "gifts" that it takes to make an organization work, which ones does the board contribute? That is, in addition to staff contributions, what does the board bring to the party? Notice the disconcerting lack of verbs in most segments of the USCF policy. This unfamiliar style is simply an instance of bending over backward to be sure that the outcome condition is highlighted, not the actions required to produce it. That is, the job is not to advocate, encourage, or work toward any of the outcomes; the job is that the outcomes exist. So the USCF board is avoiding language that could let it off the hook, even at the expense of slightly curious wording.

Policy Type: Governance Process
Policy Title: Board Job Description

The job of the board is to make contributions that lead USCF toward the desired performance and assure that it occurs.

The obligations of the board shall be

I. The link between USCF and its membership.

II. Written governing policies that, at the broadest level, address

   A. Ends: products of the federation, impacts, benefits, outcomes. What good will the federation do for whose needs and at what cost?

   B. Executive limitations: prudence and ethics boundaries for executive authority, activity, and decisions.

   C. Governance process: specifications of how the board conceives, carries out, and monitors its task.

   D. Board-executive director relationship: how power is delegated and its proper use monitored.

III. The assurance of executive director performance.

The USCF board determined that the board's job purpose, most broadly stated (and, therefore, in the preamble), is whatever "contributions . . . lead . . . toward the desired (organizational) performance and ensure" that performance. While the preamble only gives a broad-brush explication of the job outputs of the board, the finer points 1 to 3 make the outputs far clearer.

1. The first point obligates the board to produce a link between the thousands of members of USCF and the operating organization. This board recognizes that it is the "bridge" between those who own USCF (its members) and the organization that they own. In the rush of organizational details, it is easy for a board to forget its pivotal role with regard to ownership linkage.

For another board, this linkage may not be with a membership per se, but with some ownership group. For example, a city council's job description under Policy Governance obligates the council to produce a linkage between city citizens and the machinery of city government. A church board would form the link between the congregation and the workings of the church organization.

Annually, the board might further define what level of thoroughness or inclusiveness is to be achieved in this linkage. That is, the board might be more definitive about the nature of that linkage. In some year to come, for example, the USCF board might expand the wording to say that linkage will mean that 20 percent of the membership will participate in focus groups or surveys about what they think their federation should produce for them. In the service of this linkage the board will devise activities, such as meeting with regional representatives, having more membership access to board members during annual conventions, or other methods of producing a more effective linkage.

It is important to note that the linkage here is with *owners,* not customers. For membership associations and city councils, owners and customers are largely the same people, so opportunities for confusion are legion. From owners, an organization learns what kind of organization it is to be, particularly what difference it will make (an ends question). From customers, the organization discovers how well it is providing that which it has decided to provide. In most cases, feedback deteriorates—as is common for city councils—into a forum for disgruntled customers. The latter is fine for monitoring staff performance but helps little in doing the board's work of deciding what the ends should be.

This policy recognizes that the integrity, completeness, unbiasedness, and timeliness of the connection between members and the organization is a board product, for which only the board is accountable. The carrying out of activities is not what is evaluated; the intended outcome (quality of linkage) is evaluated. Evaluation might take any number of forms. For example, the board can engage in a bit of soul searching about the extent of its linkage or, better still, it can ask the members.

2. The USCF board's second point states that the board policies themselves are an important job contribution of the board. The policies must cover the four categories listed. This emphasis on policymaking in the list of board products, like the emphasis on ownership linkage, reflects a key element in my approach to board leadership. For the staff to manage well, the board must govern well, and governing well involves converting the sundry opinions and values of individual board members into a consistent set of explicit values and positions. Incidentally, financial, program, and personnel matters are not on the USCF list, for they are simply among the management responsibilities that these policies control.

Further, if the board puts its enunciations into the categories of the Policy Governance model, it not only will create explicit board values and opinions but also will do so in a format that best enables management to proceed well. This kind of policymaking is not the ethereal sort that leads many people to consider policies to be removed from the real world—that is, they don't make much difference. But it is just as important to note that this kind of policymaking is not the detailed sort that ties an organization up in bureaucratic knots.

The upshot is that a board that adopts this approach will naturally spend most of its time creating, analyzing, and revising policy—activities that contribute to continual self-evaluation and lie at the core of board leadership. Again, it is not the spending of time that is evaluated but whether board policies are indeed complete.

3. USCF's third point connects board performance to CEO performance. If the CEO does not perform acceptably (as measured against the policies created in 2A and 2B), the board is therefore not performing acceptably. The board's job description not only pays homage to the board's accountability for staff effectiveness but also clearly states that if the CEO doesn't get the job done, the board cannot score well in subsequent evaluation of its own achievement.

Point 3 serves a role that some management writers have referred to as a "linking pin" that renders the performance in a superior job dependent on the performance of a subordinate job. If the chief executive—which is to say, the entire staff organization—does not perform well and continues not to perform well, the board itself is culpable. So while USCF board job product number 3 requires rigorous monitoring of organizational performance, the activity of monitoring does not itself fulfill the board's job responsibility. No, the self-evaluative question, as with each of the foregoing job products, is not whether the board carried out *activities* intended to produce the products but whether in fact the products are produced. In this case, the board will ask itself whether an acceptable level of "assurance" of executive performance exists.

Having a board job description such as USCF's in place establishes the board's expectations with respect to its actual contributions to the organization. With clarity about job outputs, every board action and every improvement can and must be justified and assessed with respect to the board's ability to perform with greater integrity on these outputs. Every part of an agenda, for example, would be in the service of some part of the intended job outputs. Putting such output job expectations in place, then, not only forms the board's central guide to all further job activities but also creates the most important part of the foundation for self-evaluation.

While it is critical for a board to determine the outputs toward which its work will be aimed, as this article has pointed out, still it cannot omit a careful crafting of its *job process,* the well-disciplined conduct required to get the job done. Discipline in governance is the subject of the next article, "Planning the Board's Conduct."

Planning the Board's Conduct

BOARD LEADERSHIP, NUMBER 10, NOV.-DEC. 1993

BOARD EVALUATION is, in part, an attempt to find the answer to the question, "Are we acting the way we should?" Since making the most of evaluation means being clear about expectations up front, the question becomes, "Are we acting the way we said we would?" In other words, is the board's conduct measuring up to its intentions? This is an evaluation not of the board's accomplishment of intended outputs but of the board's discipline in sticking to its own rules.

> The question becomes, "Are we acting the way we said we would?"

The *process* of work—that is, the way in which it is done or the conduct of the worker—is extremely important for any job. Common experience confirms that *method* makes a substantial difference in job success. Depending on the role being played, the job process might concern how we go about supervising subordinates, how we route files, how we keep records, or how we instruct preschoolers. Indeed, professional and technical training is largely about learning the "how to" of some pursuit. Many, if not most, disciplines are bodies of knowledge in method of technique.

Conduct in any job is important, of course, but board conduct requires more than usual vigilance. First, because the board is a group of individuals, questions of group conduct versus individual conduct are confounded under the best of conditions. Second, because the board is a group of peers, the board must learn to govern itself before presuming to govern others. Third, because other people depend on the board's style of operating (for example, the staff, the public, or a membership), there must be some predictability and stability.

> Because other people depend on the board's style of operating, there must be some predictability and stability.

In the Policy Governance model, the board addresses both its products and its conduct. Having established its intentions with respect to each, subsequent evaluation is simply a matter of inspecting whether the products are produced and the proper conduct followed. The preceding article, "Crafting the Board Job Description," deals with establishing board outputs. The subject

← **FAQ**

How does a board ensure the integrity of its own conduct?

of this article is the board's intended conduct or process. In Policy Governance, intentions about conduct show up in two policy categories: governance process and board-staff relationship. In the governance process policies, the board records its intended conduct with respect to its internal workings and the connection with its stockholder equivalents (the *ownership*). In the board-staff relationship policies, the board records its intended conduct with respect to staff delegation and accountability. Capturing such expectations in policy yields an important part of the foundation for self-evaluation, though, frankly, a great deal is accomplished merely by the group discussion leading to policies such as these.

Designing Discipline for the Board

Discipline must be designed for the conduct of the board's own particular role. In a general sense, this includes valuing diversity, giving full airing to points of view, giving sufficient and timely attention to big issues, being open with the ownership, requiring of itself honest dealings, keeping its word, and other such virtues.

The boxed text depicts the governing approach policy adopted by the board of the National Ballet of Canada, based in Toronto. This is only one of several policies in the governance process category. Others might deal with how the board will use committees, how it will go about recruiting new members, what the exact authority of its chairperson will be, and so on. But the policy highlighted here is one that every board should have in one form or another. It enumerates several fundamental intentions with respect to process that can be evaluated. Incidentally, while it is important that

Policy Type: Governance Process
Policy Title: Governing Approach

The board will approach its task with a commitment to emphasize outward vision rather than internal preoccupation, encouragement of diversity in viewpoints and strategic leadership more than administrative detail, clear distinction of board and staff roles, collective rather than individual decisions, future rather than past or present, and proactivity rather than reactivity.

   More specifically the board will

I.   Operate in all ways mindful of its stewardship obligation to all Canadians.

II.   Enforce on itself whatever discipline is needed to govern with excellence. Discipline will apply to matters such as attendance at board and committee meetings, policymaking principles, respect of roles, and speaking with one voice.

III.   Monitor the organization so as to be accountable to the Canadian public for competent, conscientious, and effective accomplishment of its obligations as a body. It will allow no officer, individual, or committee of the board to usurp this role or hinder this commitment.

IV.   Direct, control, and guide the organization through the careful establishment of the broadest organizational values and perspectives through written policies.

V.   Inspire through leading by example.

VI.   Be an initiator of policy, not merely a reactor to staff initiatives.

VII.   Focus chiefly on intended long-term impacts on the world outside the organization (ends) and not primarily on the administrative or programmatic means of attaining those effects.

VIII. Use the expertise of individual board members to enhance the ability of the board as a body, rather than to substitute their individual values for the group's values.

IX.   Monitor and regularly discuss the board's own process and performance. Ensure the continuity of its governance capability by retraining and development.

       A. Self-monitoring will include a frequent comparison of board activity and discipline to governance process and board-staff relationship policies.

       B. Continual development will include orientation of new members in the board's adopted governance process and periodic board discussion of improvement.

every board have such a policy, the name itself is not important. *Governance style* or *governing manner* are alternative titles for this policy often used by boards operating on the Policy Governance model.

Let's examine the kind of conduct to which the National Ballet board committed itself. In the manner of Policy Governance policies, the preamble expresses the all-encompassing thought, with policy development always proceeding from the big idea toward smaller ones. In this preamble, the board expresses what will be the general tone of its work: externality, bigness, futurity, role clarity, proactivity, and groupness.

The National Ballet's board created a preamble that sets a tone for all further board behavior. Some of these provisions would seem to be of the motherhood and apple pie variety until you notice that boards do not typically act with the kind of demeanor that these words set forth. The preamble alone signals a massive change in the typical nonprofit or public board's behavior. How would your board fare if evaluated under the provisions of this preamble?

But the National Ballet board went further in describing its carefully adopted governance approach. The numbered points seem self-explanatory, and largely they are. But they were generated after much discussion. For example, point 1 seems straightforward enough, but it grew out of an intention to have the Toronto-based ballet company think broadly of Canada as a whole, not just the Toronto area. Does your board have a comparable dilemma?

Note the "no-whining" clause of point 3. The board decided to allow itself no way out: It cannot absolve itself for poor governance just because a committee, a chairperson, or anyone else doesn't get his, her, or their job done. The buck stops at the boardroom.

Note the board wholeness declared in point 8. If there is a fiscal expert on the board or, for that matter, a ballet expert, the expert is to be used to educate the board toward competence in making governance decisions. The expert will not be used to unilaterally determine criteria that the chief executive will be held accountable to meet.

And, of course, point 9 is the board's resolution about self-evaluation. The expressions "monitor and regularly discuss," "frequent comparison," "periodic discussion of improvement," and so forth surely express commitments. The words used—as all words everywhere—are open to interpretation. The board can certainly nail these terms down in further detail at some point in the future, but they will still work for now. They will work because the board has charged its chairperson with the further interpretation of these words and the action that will make them come alive. (Elsewhere in board policy created under the Policy Governance model, the chairperson is granted the authority to interpret governance process and board-staff relationship policies.) Not only are these commitments available for formal evaluation of board behavior, but they may—and should—be pointed out at any time by any board member when he or she thinks that the board is straying.

Setting Expectations for Relations with Staff

Even if the board conducts its own task well, it must also be sure that it maintains a proper connection with its executive arm. A board might do its own visionary, policymaking job well, but if it cannot link productively with those who have the time and skills to get the organizational work done, the enterprise will falter.

Connecting with staff entails assignment, empowerment, and, finally, monitoring or evaluation of staff performance. In other words, the board must tell its staff what job is to be done. It must convey sufficient authority for effective and creative staff action. And, finally, it must keep up with whether the staff job is getting done. There are many ways in which a board's process can obscure assignment, impede empowerment, and muddle monitoring. Consequently, the board must carefully design the way in which it delegates to its staff. Much of this can be captured in the way the board charges its chief executive officer.

FAQ ➡
Is there any difference between an executive director (general manager, president, etc.) and a CEO?

The next box shows the "delegation to the city manager" policy of the city council in Plano, Texas. Again, the title is unimportant; for nonprofits, it is more common to call this policy "delegation to the executive director" or simply "delegation to the CEO." (In Plano, the city council wisely chooses to treat its city manager as a chief executive officer.) It is very important, however, that a board have such a policy, regardless of the name it finds fitting.

The Plano City Council would have enabled a measure of meaningful evaluation if it had only gone as far as the preamble in writing this policy. It would be forced to ask itself if it has truly stuck to the "broadest policies" in city government and if the council or any one of its members has interfered in the city manager's creation of "subsidiary policies."

The city council might have chosen to stop with this big idea and allow finer tuning to be done by the mayor (comparable in Plano to a board chairperson). But the evaluative questions that would have been generated by the preamble alone were not pointed enough for the city council, so it went into greater detail in describing the delegation relationship with its chief executive. So let's look at the greater definition given to the preamble by the numbered parts of this policy.

The first point commits the council to treating the city manager as the sole link between council and staff insofar as authority and accountability are concerned. This means that although members of council and staff can certainly talk with one another, the council will never instruct or judge staff below the CEO (city manager). Later, the

> ## Policy Type: Council-City Manager Relationship
> ## Policy Title: Delegation to the City Manager
>
> The city council job is generally confined to establishing the broadest policies, leaving implementation and subsidiary policy development to the city manager.
>
> 1. All council authority delegated to staff is delegated through the city manager, so that all authority and accountability of staff—as far as the Council is concerned—is considered to be the authority and accountability of the city manager.
>
> 2. Ends policies direct the city manager to achieve certain results; executive limitations policies constrain the city manager to act within acceptable boundaries of prudence and ethics. With respect to ends and executive means, the city manager is authorized to establish all further policies, make all decisions, take all actions, and develop all activities as long as they are consonant with any reasonable interpretation of the council's policies.
>
> 3. The council may change its policies, thereby shifting the boundary between council and city manager domains. Consequently, the council may change the latitude of choice given to the city manager; but so long as any particular delegation is in place, the council and its members will respect and support the city manager's choices. This does not prevent the council from obtaining information in the delegated areas.
>
> 4. No council member or officer or committee has any authority over the city manager. Information may be requested by these individuals or groups; but if such request, in the city manager's judgment, requires a material amount of staff time, it may be refused.

council can evaluate whether it has given instructions to a staff member other than the CEO or whether it has made statements assessing job performance of a staff member other than the CEO. Either of these actions would be in violation of this policy's first point.

The second point states that the board will express its instructions to the city manager in terms of ends policies and executive limitation policies. This is a strong commitment, ruling out willy-nilly, piecemeal instructions, but the next point is even more demanding: The council will allow the city manager to make all decisions that can be shown to be within "*any* reasonable interpretation" of those policies. The utility of this explicit statement in structuring later evaluation is that the council does not expect the city manager to read council members' minds in interpreting council language.

The third point goes even further to forswear the weak delegation to which many elected officials are often prone. Although the wording retains the council's right to change the policies at any time, if the council or its members taken individually make judgments about or interfere in the area of decision making granted to the city manager, the council is violating its policy. The final item hammers this point home by putting a limit on what would otherwise be an unrestricted right of single council members to commandeer city resources by demanding to have their individual queries researched regardless of cost.

Having such a policy clarifying empowerment of the CEO establishes the board's expectations with respect to its delegation to staff. Putting such an expectation in place creates an important part of the foundation not only for self-evaluation but also for meeting-by-meeting commentary on council discipline.

These two policies may be altered whenever the board's wisdom so dictates, so they are not cast in stone. But as long as they are not changed, everyone should be able to safely count on the board to act according to these intentions. Further, these policies can be augmented by other policies that would serve to further define the language. For example, the governance style policy might be amplified by others on agenda control or the annual board planning cycle.

While it is critical for a board to determine the discipline that will guide its process, as I have argued in this article, still it cannot omit a specific enumeration of its *job products,* the actual outcomes that this well-disciplined process is intended to create. These job products are the subject of the preceding chapter, "Crafting the Board Job Description."

Chapter Four

Linking Governance to Operations

The Board-Management Connection

Linking the board and operations usually calls for a chief executive officer (CEO), but in any event requires careful definition of roles. The nature of the unequal partnership between a board and its management demands rethinking the unique role of CEO, the meaning of accountability, and even the time-honored practices of staff recommendations and board approvals. Distinguishing governance from management is not so simple as dividing policy from procedure or goals from objectives, but it is both possible and necessary.

To Tell or Not to Tell: One CEO Learns the Right Way to Inform Her Board

BOARD LEADERSHIP, NUMBER 12, MAR.-APR. 1994

A FORMER CLIENT was having a bit of unexpected conflict. I received a call from the CEO, who was troubled over the unhappy turn her well-intended action had taken. Her organization operates urban parks. Its activities and controversies are quite visible to everyone.

Her board had begun using the Policy Governance model a year earlier and was implementing it successfully. The CEO had been given a large amount of authority, authority thoughtfully bounded by *ends* (policies that detailed what benefits were to be produced for which populations at what cost) and *executive limitations* (constraints on the allowable range of activities and conduct). The board was well under way in developing enough discipline to confine itself to its own job, and it had done pretty well in keeping itself out of staff means.

It so happened, however, that as the staff busied itself in finding the most effective ways to accomplish board ends without violating the limitations, it came up with a striking change in how to go about an important, highly visible segment of staff operations. Because public safety and the possibility of mischief are factors in operating public parks, guards are used to ensure protection. Whether to arm the guards is controversial to some segments of the public, though the staff had determined that this particular means—arming guards—would more reliably ensure the "safe environment" demand in the board's ends policies. There was no reason to believe that arming or not arming guards violated any of the board's executive limitations policies.

FAQ ➡

Since operational decisions are delegated to the CEO, how does the board deal with important, expensive, or politically charged decisions?

Because the CEO knew her decision would generate phone calls to board members from the public, she decided to inform the board of her decision in detail. In fact, she had no choice, for in one of the board's executive limitations policies, it had told the CEO that making significant, publicly visible organizational changes without the board's knowledge would be unacceptable. (This policy did not involve the board in the CEO's decision but made certain the board would be informed.)

So the CEO took to the board her complete plan of arming the guards, including the fine points, the phase-in schedule, the extra training planned, the kinds of weapons to be used, and the rules for their use. She took her plan to the board with the request, "I would like whatever input you might have on my plan."

The good discipline began to slip. When asked for input, people give input. So each board member began to comment on one or another aspect of the plan, including the politically hot issue of whether to arm the guards. Would arming the guards really lead to greater public safety? What is the evidence? Has the staff considered this . . . and that . . . and that? The CEO had brought one executive-level staff member with her, but the questions reached for more detail than even this person could answer easily. Neither person had expected

> Regardless of what question a board is asked, it should maintain the discipline that leadership demands of it.

that the board, with no preparation, would set out to relive the entire staff deliberation of several months in one meeting. The board's discipline and the CEO's equanimity came unglued.

When the CEO called me, she was seriously asking herself whether telling the board had been smart, whether she should have had a more detailed brief of all the staff considerations leading to her decision, and whether the Policy Governance model works in a politicized atmosphere. Professional fulfillment was not among her blessings that day.

Now, one can make a good case that regardless of what question a board is asked, it should maintain the discipline that leadership demands of it. I surely won't argue with that line of thought. Somehow, the potential heat of the issues and the virtual invitation to meddle created too strong a seduction for this board to refuse. But my caller was the CEO, so I felt I must answer her question about her own role in this. I could have a word with the board later.

I told the CEO that she did the right thing in informing the board. Even if there had not been a policy like the one I cited above, informing board members that they might get blindsided by public reaction seems a courteous thing to do, quite apart from the formalities of governance. But when she took her plan to the board, she made the wrong request. She asked the board to join her and the staff in doing staff work (providing input into the plan). I strongly recommended that in the future—should this kind of situation arise—she should approach the board with the following question: "I am prepared to demonstrate, if you wish, that everything in my plan is consistent with board policy and consistent with my authority to move on this plan under board policy. But I realize you may be in for political heat because of what I do, no matter how much you support my right to have made the decision. Given that, does anything in my plan cause you to want to change *your* policy?"

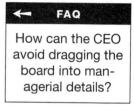

← FAQ

How does the CEO inform the board of significant operational decisions or changes?

Notice what this question does. First, it does not cloud the matter of where the to-arm-or-not-to-arm decision belongs. Under the policies then in effect, it clearly belonged to the CEO. Second, it recognizes that no matter how steadfast board members are in supporting the CEO and no matter how proper her decision, they stand to be inconvenienced by her choice and deserve some warning. Third, neither of these points should be allowed to undo governance integrity by involving the board in piecemeal participation in staff work. Fourth, the board's path to any solution is not intrusion into staff work, but *rethinking of its own work.*

← FAQ

How can the CEO avoid dragging the board into managerial details?

For example, the board might want to debate an executive limitations policy that would prohibit the use of deadly force even in the service of safety or, conversely, policy that would prohibit making unprotected targets of enforcement personnel. After this hurdle has been passed, the board might want to examine why such an obvious issue was not dealt with when board policy was initially created. It isn't possible to think of everything, but it is possible to improve systems so that fewer and fewer important issues come up at the last minute, like this one did.

Drawing boards into the wrong issues can be done with the best of intentions.

In any event, drawing boards into the wrong issues can be done with the best of intentions. Both boards and their CEOs must be vigilant about asking the right questions, for it is impossible for the board to answer the wrong question right.

Governing in the Shadow of a Founder-CEO

BOARD LEADERSHIP, NUMBER 22, NOV.-DEC. 1995

O NE PERSON'S heroic efforts can bring into being an organization that extends and outlives that person's reach. A woman I know opened a women's shelter—thanks to her crusading spirit and years of work—and became the CEO. A mission-driven physician established a medical research organization with his own funds—and became the CEO. Yet when the CEO of an organization is the person whose vision and tenacity created it, assertive governing is particularly difficult for boards.

> Should board members' first act, then, be to shackle the founder's vision—just to exercise their acquired authority?

When a founder forms a corporation to formalize his or her efforts, a board is called for. A founder-as-CEO must by necessity work for the board, but boards are often stymied by the inversion of authority that can develop.

Most of my commentary also applies to boards that have a "star" CEO, even if that CEO has not played a founding role. Certain rare CEOs wield more political power than their boards: Boards can be intimidated by politicians or other star-CEOs—not only by founding parents. When the star isn't a founder, however, there may be a sustaining organizational history of board assertiveness.

Let's begin by giving these founding fathers and mothers their due. Many areas of human endeavor are blessed by souls so insightful and driven that they inspire others of us to new levels of commitment. These leaders struggle against apathy and hardship until finally the rest of us catch up. Founding parents are gifts to the world. Their dreams enhance our lives; their commitment makes us all a little taller. By the time a founding parent

> A board with a founder-CEO is just as accountable as any other board—and must therefore govern assertively.

incorporates, he or she has already invested tears and years in a lonely vigil. Members of a newly created board are respectful latecomers. Should board members' first act, then, be to shackle the founder's vision—just to exercise their acquired authority?

A board fortunate enough to employ a founding leader is greatly blessed, but it is also presented with a dilemma. How can board members require "employee behavior" of the person whose efforts they admired enough to join the board to begin with? It is difficult to do more than rubber-stamp such a founder's wishes—or to subject them to rigorous scrutiny. The most common resolution is easy (if misguided): Members of the board see themselves as advisors rather than governors, imagining that this is how the founding parent probably construed their roles anyway. But the uncomfortable fact is that a board with a founder-CEO is just as accountable as any other board—and must therefore govern assertively.

> It takes a visionary to breathe life into an organization at its inception, but it takes an effective chief executive to keep an organization going.

Since founders are often more skilled at initiating projects than managing them, organizations in which the founder has been granted carte blanche can develop great rifts—without the board even knowing it. In these organizations even reasonable questioning of the CEO is discouraged as undeservedly harsh treatment. Prudent board oversight can be undermined by timidity masquerading as respect.

It was probably not the founder's managerial skill that attracted board members to begin with, but the founder's vision, inspiration, or dogged determination. This is ironic, because the board's failure to exercise proper oversight is largely a matter of failing to oversee the managerial effectiveness of the CEO. It takes a visionary to breathe life into an organization at its inception, but it takes an effective chief executive to be able to keep an organization going and transform good intentions into good results. Certainly a founder-CEO can be capable of both kinds of leadership, but a board takes that dual aptitude for granted at its peril.

What is the board to do? How can it continue to value and even to revere the founder without failing in its own responsibilities? And is the ultimate board control really an option: *firing* the founder? If not, is all lesser authority then moot?

Moreover, to the extent that the resolution of this dilemma can be said to revolve around the founder's personality—as a substantial part of it most certainly does—the organization and its mission are vulnerable to the unpredictable reversals that personality-related matters can undergo. A board's relationship to its founder-CEO is based on admiration, social attractiveness, esteem, even sometimes veneration—which is to say, it is not sustained and justified primarily by ongoing organizational performance. Just as when a board employs a star-CEO, it is compelling—and probably necessary—to choose a CEO based on what he or she *has* accomplished. But a board must assess and decide to keep a CEO based on what he or she *continues* to accomplish.

The best insurance against the abuse of personality-based power is a well-defined system. Satisfactory resolution of the board's dilemma requires careful attention to defining the separate jobs of board and CEO. It demands excellence in a board's governance framework, enough to protect the organization's mission and integrity despite the complexities of the founding-parent syndrome. Consider how the board can "control" its founder-CEO by creating two instructive policy categories: executive limitations and ends.

> **FAQ ➡**
>
> How does a board keep a CEO from abusing personality-based power?

Executive limitations. The policies within this category limit the range of executive action; they should be created whether or not the board thinks anything is currently out of order. That is, these policies are not primarily intended to solve existing problems or to squelch recent misdeeds. They establish boundaries around staff activity, defining and preventing potential misdeeds. These policies are driven not by the board's perceptions of current CEO behavior and capability, but by board values and beliefs about prudence and ethics. In other words, board values are not dependent on the degree the board trusts its current CEO.

> The best insurance against the abuse of personality-based power is a well-defined system.

The board would create the same executive limitations policies regardless of the presence or absence of a founder-CEO.

Ends. The breadth of board policies concerning ends, however, might differ depending on whether or not a founding parent is present. Remember that a board must prescribe the most broadly stated ends—the Policy Governance equivalent of a mission statement. If the board is unwilling to accept all reasonable interpretations the CEO might make of this mega-ends statement, then the board must further define these expected ends. Even still, the board is operating very near the broadest level, a level that leaves a great deal of latitude to CEO interpretation. As the board progressively narrows its ends definition, it will stop only at the point where it is content to give the CEO full authorization to interpret within the remaining reduced range.

> For there to be effective governance, it is not necessary that the founding parent be disempowered either as CEO or as visionary.

When there is a founding parent-CEO, the board will undoubtedly be content to stay very broad in its ends pronouncements. By doing so, it leaves maximum freedom to the founding parent to be expansive, creative, and autonomous, though always within the broad but authoritatively proclaimed board ends policies.

Ends work, even at the broadest level, constitutes a profound engagement with the organization's raison d'être. That engagement is the greatest insurance for continuity of the dream beyond the founding parent's life or tenure. Loss of a founder-CEO through relocation, disability, or death can bring even an aggressive program to its knees if there is no such vessel to assure constancy of purpose. While a board might rally to the emergency, if it hasn't exercised its power until now, the board may well be unwilling or unable to rise to the occasion. So to the extent the mission inspired initially by the founder is important, authentic board ownership—not simply board support—is a fitting investment in its survival.

Ends policies embody the organization's dream in terms of what difference the organization will make. The most significant challenge to the board is the difficulty of assuring that the founder's dream endures beyond the founder's lifetime. That hope is jeopardized if the board is not able assertively to take ownership of that dream.

← FAQ
How does the board ensure that the founder's dream lasts?

For there to be effective governance, it is not necessary that the founding parent be disempowered either as CEO or as visionary. Conversely, strong management and farsighted executive leadership need not compromise the governing board's legal and moral accountability. But traditional concepts of the board-management partnership often set board and executive strengths against each other. In these cases, it is common for the integrity of governance, rather than the autonomy of the founding parent, to be sacrificed. While this may be the most comfortable immediate resolution for board and founder alike, it makes a mockery of accountability and endangers the need for governing strength to keep the dream alive beyond the reach of the current actors. The solution to the founding-CEO dilemma is proper governance.

If You Want It Done Right, *Delegate It!*

BOARD LEADERSHIP, NUMBER 29, JAN.-FEB. 1997

WE HAVE ALL heard, "If you want it done right, do it yourself." However, managers everywhere have had to learn that "doing it yourself" is not an option when there is an overwhelming amount of work to do. Management as a field of study and practice exists to address the difficulties caused by being accountable for more than you yourself can possibly do. Let me describe and then discuss a rather specific delegation difficulty that many professional and trade associations encounter.

> Everyone involved is best served when the board does not get involved in the administration of discipline but rather governs by proper delegation.

Associations can have a potentially devastating impact on the livelihood of individual members. Nowhere is this more evident than in the disciplinary functions of a self-governing profession. It is commonly felt that professional peers are the only persons qualified to administer discipline to association members charged with misconduct. Consequently, as an association's ruling body, the board is likely to have a direct hand in adjudicating misconduct or malpractice actions.

In many ways the arrangement makes sense. You can make a case that physicians are the most competent judges of physicians and that accountants are the best judges of other accountants. But what I question is why *the board* must be directly involved.

I believe (and will argue, shortly) that everyone involved is best served when the board does not get involved in the administration of discipline but rather *governs* disciplinary action in the same way it governs other aspects of the organization, that is, by proper delegation.

Although I am here discussing professional associations' disciplinary processes, there are many situations in which, even though there is a CEO accountable to the full board for operational matters, board committees become involved in overseeing staff and even performing staff work. The reason always given for this intrusion of board members into sub-board activity is that, as professionals, they understand what is required and must therefore have a direct hand in this or that process.

> **← FAQ**
>
> Can the board of a self-governing profession delegate professional discipline to the CEO?

But allow me to expand on the disciplinary matter with a real example from a real board. The association in my example has authority to discipline its membership and, like most, had formed a disciplinary committee. The board's discipline committee would review the complaints against members, decide which should be heard, conduct the hearings, and render a disciplinary decision.

After some investigation, I found that the staff did almost all the processing. Staff arranged forms and methods for the public to register charges. Staff made sure members knew how to behave if a charge of misconduct were raised against them. Staff processed charges, dismissing those that were not within the jurisdiction of the association and forwarding for further work those that qualified. Staff studied and wrote briefs on the circumstances

Board members often inappropriately exercised board authority with respect to staff actions.

and took statements from the "litigants." Staff set times and venues for committee meetings, seeing to it that committee members had sufficient preparatory materials. Staff put all the paperwork into place after a verdict was reached by the committee.

As you might guess, the committee members were busy people. To schedule them for meetings was a horrendous affair and, of course, the staff had no control over whether the members came prepared. Regardless of how poorly board members performed, staff members could not pressure or require them to do anything. Meanwhile, board members often inappropriately exercised board authority with respect to staff actions. In other words, staff members could not restrict board members' access to administrative activity, even though they were ostensibly present for only a specific and circumscribed task.

FAQ ➡

Should a
board create
committees to
help the CEO?

When a CEO is held accountable for an outcome and given the authority to pursue it, he or she can and will aggressively set out to do so. When a CEO must share that authority with another entity whose portion of that authority and accountability is ever changing, the stage is set for role confusion and the accompanying loss of dynamic single-mindedness. An old management maxim states: If two persons are responsible for a job, nobody is.

Holding a CEO's feet to the fire to perform is relatively easy for all but the most ineffective of boards. His or her job is on the line. Holding a board committee responsible is considerably harder. It is socially difficult for board members to deal with their peers with the rigor appropriate to the delegator-delegatee relationship. Moreover, even getting good monitoring data on a committee's performance is harder. Who is to gather the data? The committee? Staff? There are simply many more sources of slippage when delegating to a committee than to the CEO.

At this point, let me remind you that in Policy Governance, instead of owning a whole function—like discipline, budget, or planning—the board "owns" the values underlying all functions. While the board is accountable for how all organizational topics in their entirety turn out, its hands-on responsibility is merely (1) to determine what the higher concerns of various endeavors shall be, that is, what values or criteria must be adhered to by delegatees, then (2) to gather monitoring data to assure that these criteria have been met. In other words, accountability for the countless functions the board can never personally touch is achieved through (1) stating expectations, (2) assigning their achievement to someone, and (3) checking to see if expectations were met. To be accountable for something in no way means the board must do it itself.

> The committee felt it had dominion over all aspects of discipline, including those carried out by staff.

In the case under discussion, the board felt that membership discipline, being a board accountability, should also be hands-on, and it conveyed that way of seeing the job to the committee. Consequently, the committee felt it had dominion over all aspects of discipline, including those carried out by staff. Worse, *individual* committee members would intrude into what the staff was perfectly able to do without help. The effect of such intrusion, quite the reverse of what is intended, is that such "help" makes it harder for staff to get the job done (like when your child "helps" you clean the kitchen).

A self-destructive tendency in nonprofit and governmental governance seems to ensure that the more important an issue is, the more we seem determined to do it

poorly. It should be no surprise that, due to confounded delegation, the disciplinary process was the least well-operated one in
the organization. So how can a board facing this sensitive task be
sure that it is done well? It should follow the rules of good governance even more fastidiously than ever. Here is the line of reasoning I have recommended to quite a few organizations:

← FAQ

Can the board of
a self-governing
profession dele-
gate professional
discipline to
the CEO?

Go to the basics of the result you want. Stop thinking of the disciplinary process and think instead of the disciplinary results you
want. In most cases, the result is that "members accused of misconduct receive strict
but fair judgment by peers." In other words, state the way you want situations of
alleged misconduct to come out rather than how that will be achieved.

Describe what you want in ends policy. Notice, of course, that the foregoing statement is an ends policy. It fits within the framework of ends decisions the board is mak-

ing about any number of issues. An
alternative ends policy might be that "the
public is served by an ethical, competent
profession, with any grievances against it
settled fairly and in a timely way." This
policy is formulated in terms of the public, not the professional.

> State the way you want situations
> of alleged misconduct to come
> out rather than how that will be
> achieved.

Expand your ends policy as needed. Obviously, like all words, the words of this policy are open to interpretation. Let's say that the board is not willing to let the CEO
interpret the meaning of "fair judgment by peers." In this case, the board could go
further to say that fair judgment means "judgment rendered by a panel of persons
aware of the nuances of the case and exposed to all relevant sides of the issue," and
that peers means "at least five persons, the majority of whom are professionals in the
subspecialty involved in the dispute."

Prohibit any unacceptable situations or actions. For example, it may be unacceptable if parties to a conflict are kept in the dark as to progress of the process, or if peer
judgment is contaminated by staff lobbying, or if complainants receive no response
within sixty days, or if charged members are even subtly treated as guilty prior to adju-
dication. Any new prohibitions would be added to an existing executive limitations
policy if possible; if not, a new policy could be created.

Allow the CEO to get to work (get out of the way!). The CEO will then set out to create the conditions necessary for achieving the ends and avoiding unacceptable means. Because the board will have required the outcome to be "fair judgment by peers," or an expanded definition of this, it behooves the CEO to create a process by which association members are tapped for service on a disciplinary panel from time to time. Peers who demonstrate that they cannot be counted on to be prepared, to show up on time, or to complete necessary paperwork will be dropped off the list. The CEO couldn't do that with a board committee, and the board itself is unlikely to do it to colleagues. The CEO will make sure such a process is in place and operating, for his or her performance is at stake.

> The CEO is accountable for ensuring the integrity and timeliness of the process that leads to the judgment.

Expect and monitor CEO success. Notice that the CEO is successful only if the board gets what it wanted in the first place, that is, judgment rendered by properly prepared but impartial peers. The CEO is not the source of the judgment itself but is accountable for ensuring the integrity and timeliness of the process that leads to the judgment.

Thus the board gets what it wants with no board members involved at all. In fact, the board gets what it wants better than if board members were involved. Moreover, the board is likely to have described what it wants with far greater clarity than boards usually do when they are delegating to themselves. In theory, board members could be among the panelists selected for discipline panel duty, but it would have to be clear to all concerned that the board member panelist is not "more equal" than the other panel members. The staff would have to be certain of this in order to carry out their responsibilities firmly. However, while in theory board member involvement is acceptable, pragmatically speaking, it is better avoided.

Now let's look at a real estate board example. Real estate boards, even ones with large staffs, often have a board committee to oversee the format, preparation, and distribution of comprehensive listings of property for sale. This board committee becomes a de facto miniboard over the applicable staff functions, often interfering in staff work and fracturing the board.

Under Policy Governance, the board would clearly describe the data it wants real estate agents to have. In fact, it might even stipulate that the desired ends should incorporate user judgment, thus: "complete, timely, and accurate listings of property for sale, easily useful to agents, for a cost not materially greater than other similar organizations in the region." As in all ends policy development, the board might choose to define what is meant by *complete, timely, useful,* and each of the other terms, rather than leaving them open to interpretation by the CEO. For example, *useful* might be defined as "found easy to interpret and convenient to carry by at

> Board leadership is not a function of doing more, but of demanding more and delegating effectively.

least 75 percent of the agents." The CEO is then held accountable for carrying out the charge and will thus be driven to periodically assemble a representative group of real estate agents (not board members) to critique the listing book and advise about it. So if a committee is created, it is the CEO's committee, not the board's.

Intuitively, most of us think we can more reliably get a job done if we do it ourselves than if we trust someone else to do it. We delegate as a necessary evil—a second-best alternative to doing things the way we'd really like. To the contrary, however, many (perhaps most) things are done better through delegation than through self-action. That is, delegation is not the alternate route, but the preferred one. Much of Policy Governance deals with the issue of delegation as it is encountered by a governing board.

My examples in this article have drawn on experience with real estate boards and professional societies in the United States, as well as law societies and regulatory colleges in Canada. But there are many other types of organizations that exercise some degree of discipline over members either because law has given them that authority or because members have voluntarily submitted to it. In any event, even in this sensitive domain, board leadership is not a function of doing more, but of demanding more and delegating effectively.

What to Do When Staff Take Complaints Directly to Board Members

BOARD LEADERSHIP, NUMBER 31, MAY-JUNE 1997

IHAVE OFTEN BEEN with boards that were in a quandary due to direct communications between board members and staff members about one or another alleged complaint. One such board governed a large hospital that had grown from a small size. Recently there had been a spate of complaints going to board members from unhappy employees.

The CEO was both miffed and worried about the practice, particularly since some board members were dealing with the complaints as if they were employee advocates. Not a passive person, and fearful of the emerging board conduct on such matters, the CEO set about to put a stop to what she saw as inappropriate employee end runs. Her actions, in turn, were seen by some staff as squelching dissent and by some board members as cutting the board off from important information.

> End runs can arise from desperation or from an intent to manipulate.

Most board members find employee end runs embarrassing. They believe that getting involved is inappropriate, but turning a deaf ear is callous and maybe even irresponsible. In contrast, a few board members relish the idea of fielding internal problems, particularly of the personnel variety. They see themselves as adjudicators and perhaps protectors of the "little guy" against the brute force of management. Or, like journalists selectively quoting unidentified sources to support their own view, there are board members who instigate end runs in order to bolster a point they want to make.

Let's be evenhanded. On the one hand, employees can be unfairly treated by CEOs or their delegatees. On the other hand, CEOs and others can be victimized by employee end runs. Let's recognize as well that while some end runs are employee-instigated, others are board member-instigated—situations that are not mutually exclusive. End runs can arise from desperation or from an intent to manipulate.

So what did I counsel this board? My recommendation was that its predicament should be acted on as quickly as possible, for the situation can deteriorate past the point of easy repair. Further, the action would have to come from the board, not from management, and it would have to appear to everyone concerned that all the dangers had been taken into consideration. For example, merely to take a hard line against any employee–board member contact would be to overlook the possibility that employees truly are being mistreated. But to open up willy-nilly to any employee who wants to complain would be to overlook the potential for egregious harm that disgruntled employees can recklessly inflict on others.

 FAQ

What if an employee bypasses the CEO and makes an end run to a board member?

Moreover, a board that values excellence knows that it must resolve issues with an eye to the future, instead of just fixing the present. In other words, even if the employees making end runs today are clearly ne'er-do-wells, the board should still not act as if its chief role in addressing the end-run issue is to discipline employ-

> A board that values excellence knows that it must resolve issues with an eye to the future, instead of just fixing the present.

ees. What if the employees are of sterling intent but are trapped in an oppressive system by a tyrant of a CEO? The board's solution should speak to the future by resolving all these possibilities at once, not just today's specific incarnation.

Here was the solution for the hospital board. It will work for all boards.

The board committed itself to the *one voice* principle. That is, the only criteria set for CEO behavior and the only judgments to be made about that behavior will be the board's group judgment, not the judgment of individuals or even of a board committee. Unless the board has established an expectation as a group, there is no expectation binding on the CEO.

FAQ

What if a board member has seen or been told about something wrong going on?

Whether the CEO has met a reasonable interpretation of the board's criteria is a board judgment, not an individual board member judgment.

The board voted on the staff situations or types of staff treatment that it would find unacceptable. These prohibitions always begin broadly but may become as detailed as the board wishes. For example, the board might prohibit unsafe working conditions, undignified treatment, or having no way to express grievances. My client called the resulting policy "Staff Treatment," filed as one of its executive limitations policies. These policy statements become the only criteria that can be used in judging CEO performance on this topic.

The board demanded monitoring data about these criteria on a routine basis. Those data can be from the CEO, from an outsider, or from a direct board inspection. The choice of method as well as the frequency of monitoring belong to the board. The only legitimate monitoring question is, "Have these criteria, interpreted by the CEO in any reasonable way, been met?"

Whether the CEO has, indeed, met a reasonable interpretation of the board's criteria is a board judgment, not an individual board member judgment. So the CEO does not at any time have to justify his or her actions to an individual. The board becomes able to handle staff complaints as it does any other alleged or possible violation of board policy—without drawing board members into continuing dialogue with aggrieved staff.

FAQ ➡

How do staff members understand the new relationship between the board and CEO under Policy Governance?

Staff members learned that the board took both its criteria-setting and its monitoring responsibilities seriously, yet they understood that the CEO would always be supported as long as the criteria had been met. (While board policy is addressed to the CEO, not the staff, and the CEO, not the staff, is granted the right to interpret board policy, the policies are not secret from the staff.) Not only did frivolous complaints become less likely, so did managerial misconduct.

The most immediate payoff was that the board had created a way to be assured that its humane obligation to staff would be continuously honored, not sporadically administered when enough unrest erupted to cause end runs. At the same time, the CEO felt protected from haphazard judgments that, at worst, could create a witch-hunt atmosphere, and at best would constitute unfair caprice. Happily, the hospital board was able to correct the deteriorating situation before personal antagonisms became irreparable.

When Board Members Are the Only Staff in Sight

BOARD LEADERSHIP, NUMBER 9, SEPT.-OCT. 1993

SOME BOARDS have paid staff. But many people also serve on less blessed boards, ones that have no staff at all or, at most, a mere handful of paid employees. Community-based advocacy groups, civic clubs, and even small trade or professional associations are likely to fit this description. For such organizations, board members compose not only the governing body but the work force as well.

Surprisingly, the governance portion of such a board's job is virtually the same as it would be if it had a thousand staff. As a governing body, the board must determine purpose and values. Exploring and deliberating about the organizational vision, for example, is still the centerpiece of board work. But the board with no staff has a much tougher job in delegating the work to be done, for it has no CEO to whom it can look for implementation.

<table>
<tr><td>←   FAQ</td></tr>
<tr><td>Does Policy Governance work for a board with no staff?</td></tr>
</table>

To whom, then, does the board delegate? It delegates to board members themselves. That is, the board with no staff delegates staff work to itself. Just as would be the case if the board had a CEO, it enables more creative work by giving wide, albeit bounded, latitude for innovative action. Consequently, the ends-versus-means distinction used in the Policy Governance model helps even when there is no staff. Similarly, delegation is better if the board addresses only the broadest issues about ends and unacceptable means so it can leave delegatees an unobstructed field in which to decide lesser issues.

To whom does the board delegate? The board with no staff delegates staff work to itself.

Three Peculiarities of the No-Staff Organization

Consider three peculiarities in the work of a board with no staff—or more specifically, with no CEO. I will briefly note two and focus chiefly on the third.

■ *It is less possible to enforce accountability for board members acting as staff than for a paid CEO.* Put this matter on the table, for it calls for frank discussion and an explicitly stated solution. It will help enormously just to deal openly with the various committee and individual tasks. Be sure committee reports deal with accomplishments, not just activities. When nonperformance has nowhere to hide, natural peer pressure can work in the group's favor.

■ *Lack of a CEO causes the board itself to be the tedious point where all the operational parts are brought together to produce the whole.* The board itself will have to see that constituent parts of the total job do indeed add up to the desired total, for the board as a group is surrogate for the missing CEO. Again, open and recurring board discussion

---

The board must always distinguish between its role as governing board and its role as work group or staff.

---

of this challenge will help. You might, of course, give CEO authority to the board chair. If so, the board should discuss how board members can help the chair with that task. Because the chair will be supervising peers, she or he will have less enforcement power than most CEOs have.

■ *The board may become enamored of its working role and become negligent about the governing portion of its task, such as making the overall vision clear and establishing basic values.* Scheduling separate time for each function will help. The most important rule is that the board must always distinguish between its role as governing board and its role as work group or staff. Hence, board members in the very small organization are likely to wear two hats: a board hat and a staff hat.

Consider the separate roles carried out by different people in a large organization. When a board has a CEO, as in Figure 4.1, board members (X) who wish to volunteer within the operational organization should be treated like any other volunteer staff members (V) working alongside paid members of the staff (S). Not only must any board member who wears both hats keep the roles separate, but everyone else (such

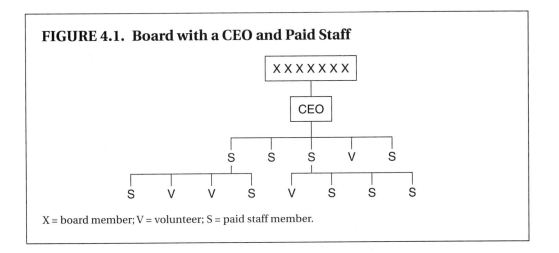

FIGURE 4.1. Board with a CEO and Paid Staff

X = board member; V = volunteer; S = paid staff member.

as other staff and board members) must perceive the difference as well. The CEO can be held accountable for operational performance because he or she has authority over how the job is carried out, even if board members are among those involved in staff work. Board members as

Board members as individuals, then, must work for the CEO, even though the CEO works for the board as a group.

individuals, then, must work for the CEO, even though the CEO works for the board as a group.

But what if the board can afford only an extremely small staff or none at all? Even if the board is able to employ a full- or part-time staff person, board members still do the bulk of the work, as shown in Figure 4.2. The staff member's job may be to ensure that meeting places are secured, the bank balance is in order, and the telephone is answered. Notice, however, that she or he is not accountable for the staff

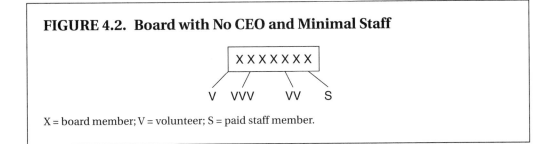

FIGURE 4.2. Board with No CEO and Minimal Staff

X = board member; V = volunteer; S = paid staff member.

work done by board members. In other words, the staff member—even if there is one—is not a CEO.

Board members engaged in staff work will show up as the V's in either figure. Which one depends solely on whether the board decides to vest CEO authority in someone. The difference is not determined by organizational size or by the top employee's salary, though these may be related issues.

Boards without a CEO are saddled with more potential role confusion, which requires of them discipline of an additional sort. Where there is no CEO, then, the more explicitly the board wears its two hats, the better it will carry out both roles.

The CEO's Objectives Are Not Proper Board Business

Board Leadership, Number 20, July-Aug. 1995

R ECENTLY, I WAS with a board that was trying to use Policy Governance but having considerable difficulty. They were departing from the model in a number of ways and wondering why it wasn't working well for them. One of several ways they went astray was in choosing to review the CEO's personal objectives.

Annually the board would ask the CEO to bring in the objectives she planned for herself in the ensuing year. The board would review these objectives and decide whether they needed to be adjusted. Ordinarily, aside from a few questions for the CEO, the board would approve the list. The intent was that at the end of the coming year, the board would have a basis for CEO evaluation.

> The CEO's own objectives are not of concern to the board as long as organizational performance fulfills the requirements of board policy.

Under traditional governance, the foregoing practice would be considered a conscientious board oversight of administrative planning. But under Policy Governance, board involvement in the CEO's objectives is not only evidence of the board's defaulting on its role but an unnecessary intrusion into management. The CEO's own objectives are not of concern to the board as long as organizational performance fulfills the requirements of board policy. Let me tell you what I recommended to this board.

FAQ ➡

Who sets the criteria for CEO performance—the board or the CEO?

In stated intent, this board had adopted the Policy Governance model. That was a good step, but the model is only theory until a board carries out real-life practice. It is not uncommon, by the way, for a board to make this first step of intention, announce that it is now using the Policy Governance model, but actually change virtually nothing! For example, if this board had completed its work on ends and executive limitations policies, the practice of reviewing the CEO's objectives would have been revealed as not only unnecessary but dysfunctional. In other words, the board needed to complete stating its expectations about (1) the organization's results, the beneficiaries of those results, and the acceptable costs of the results (together, the *ends*) and (2) the boundaries of acceptable organizational conduct and activity (*executive limitations*). That done, the board need only demand whatever monitoring data would illuminate the organization's performance on these ends and executive limitations. Objectives created by the CEO—no matter how useful to the CEO—are irrelevant to the board. If presented as relevant, they only serve to deter the board from its own task of creating the ends and executive limitations policies. This board had been able to avoid confronting its own unfinished task because it could pretend that it had obtained a legitimate basis for CEO evaluation. In this way, the avoidance not only illustrated a flaw in governance but actually helped sustain that flaw.

The objectives the CEO had faithfully presented every year were set either as organizational achievements or as her personal achievements. Let's examine the fallacies in the board's receiving and acting upon both kinds of objectives.

The Illusion of Organizational Objectives

FAQ ➡

Are the board's ends policies the same as the CEO's goals?

If the CEO's objectives are aimed at the entire organization, they are ostensibly derived from what the board has expressed as its expectations. But if the board has not expressed itself in a complete way, the CEO's objectives *substitute* for the board's desires rather than flesh them out in more detail. If the board *has* made its expectations clear (through full ends and executive limitations policies), the test of CEO performance is not whether the CEO crafts good subsidiary objectives, but whether the *board's* expectations are fulfilled.

Because the CEO must break the board's more broadly stated expectations down into doable tasks for herself and her staff, tracking performance on her personal objectives distracts the board from understanding whether its broader demands are being achieved. Successes on smaller items are the CEO's problem, and they must add up to success on the broader achievements. But it is just this indication of summative success that the board fails to assess when it gets sidetracked by an interest in subsidiary elements.

The CEO in this case had brought for board review a mixture of objectives. Some dealt with the readiness of the accounting department to take advantage of certain governmental payment systems, some with staff training intentions, some with program reorganizations. Basically, the

> If the board has not expressed itself in a complete way, the CEO's objectives *substitute* for the board's desires.

objectives included the more important (in the CEO's estimation) departmental objectives along with some objectives the CEO herself planned to achieve. It is easy to see how this list provided considerable opportunity for the board to reach deep into organizational mechanics. It invited meddling.

Now, if the board were to state its expectations at the front end and require periodic data on performance, there would be no need for it to concern itself about the more detailed objectives that grow out of the CEO's subsequent implementation. The proper test is whether board criteria are met, not whether internal objectives are pleasing.

← FAQ

How can a board evaluate the CEO's performance without evaluating achievement of operational objectives?

The Illusion of CEO Personal Objectives

If the objectives the CEO brings to the board are her personal ones separated out from the objectives she has delegated to other staff, the irrelevance is even clearer. The job of a CEO is to ensure that total organizational performance fulfills board expectations. The board does not need to know the CEO's personal contribution to the total.

The CEO's personal objectives are important nevertheless. They are what is left when sub-CEO delegations—those the CEO determines—are subtracted from the big picture. CEOs differ in which job outputs they delegate to their staff and which ones they retain for themselves. The CEO in this case had submitted a few objectives of the personal kind: One dealt with her filling an important position, one with establishing an incentive plan for direct reports, and one with obtaining strategic planning skills for herself.

What a CEO retains for his or her own job and delegates to others is immaterial to the board's judgment of CEO performance. In other words, the CEO's achievement of her personal goals should not be evaluated separately from what she *and* her subordinates attain. The proper philosophy of CEO evaluation is to assess the entire organization and pin the outcome on the CEO.

This board understood the problem and promptly changed its way of operating. It suspended the practice of reviewing and approving CEO objectives in favor of putting more diligence into completing its ends and executive limitations policies. This board is well on its way to greater board leadership.

Why Only the CEO Can Interpret the Board's Ends and Executive Limitations Policies

BOARD LEADERSHIP, NUMBER 46, NOV.-DEC. 1999

I N POLICY GOVERNANCE, the board instructs the CEO with ends policies and with executive limitations policies. These policies are ordinarily few and brief, and hence the language used by the board in these policies is of utmost importance. One aspect of Policy Governance that many boards struggle with is that after taking so much care in crafting policies, they have to grant the CEO the exclusive right to interpret their words. John Carver looks at how one board tackled this issue.

Recently, the board of a division of a national health charity was having trouble with the provision of Policy Governance that calls for boards to let the CEO—and not the board itself—act as the interpreter of the board's policies. One board member, a lawyer by trade, was of the strong opinion that the board should never give away the right to say what its words mean. Consequently, the board was considering the following wording in its "Monitoring CEO Performance" policy:

> In monitoring the organization with respect to ends and executive limitations, the standard of performance will be any reasonable interpretation by the board of the words of these policies.

Including the words "by the board" is sufficient to destroy the ability of Policy Governance to fulfill its promise of governance excellence. And yet the board member's concern certainly seems to make sense. Why would a board work so hard at choosing the right words, only to forfeit the right to ensure that they are interpreted as the board intended? The obvious answer is that this is exactly the reason they need to take great care in choosing their words—to make sure that the board's words can be properly understood by someone else.

> Why would a board work so hard at choosing the right words, only to forfeit the right to ensure that they are interpreted as the board intended?

If I demand to be the final arbiter of what my words mean, no one can trust my words. It makes sense, of course, that I be the final arbiter of what I meant to say. As the only authority on what I mean, I can correct my error if I've used words that convey something other than my meaning. But it is clearly my error to be corrected, not the receiver's. And so it is in Policy Governance. The board can, at any time, change the words of its policies so as more accurately to convey what is meant. But the opportunity for self-correction was not what this concerned board member had in mind. He wanted the board to judge the CEO's performance using the board's interpretation of its words, corrected or not. Remember that in Policy Governance, *corrected* may simply mean "further defined" by going into more detailed policy language, thereby giving the CEO more specific instructions.

The fact that the board will assess organizational performance—judge the CEO's success—based on the words of its policies makes the assignment of interpretation rights critical. If the board wants the grounds kept clean, for example, it had better describe what it means by the word *clean* if it is unwilling for the CEO to use "any reasonable interpretation" of that word. There are so many details in even a small organization, much less a large or complex one, that any alternative to allowing the CEO these interpretation rights is unmanageable. Either the CEO sends a constant stream of requests for clarification to the board, or the CEO risks being judged by the board on unstated criteria. The former is enough to clutter the board's agenda and keep it from far more important work. The latter puts the CEO back into the same dilemma he or she was in before Policy Governance.

Under Policy Governance, the communication rule from the board to the CEO is simply this: "We will take responsibility for using the words we mean, recognizing that all words are open to interpretation. We will take care to use words that define our meaning sufficiently so that we can entrust our words to you. We demand

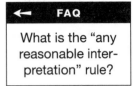

FAQ

What is the "any reasonable interpretation" rule?

only that the organization perform in a way that reflects a reasonable interpretation of our words. If that yields a performance we don't like, we'll take responsibility for our error and change our words for clarity of future understanding.

FIGURE 4.3. Organizational Performance: A Decision Pathway

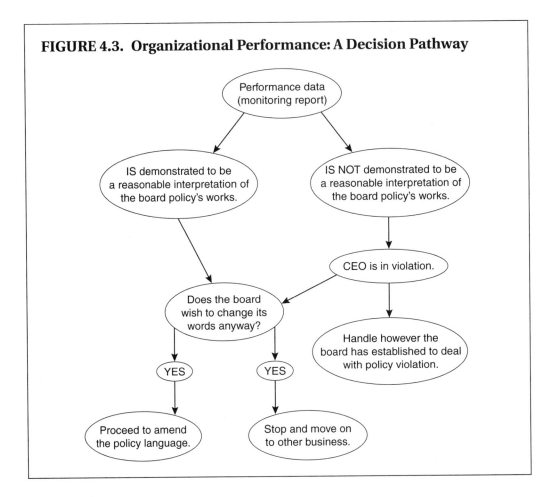

However, if you are unable to demonstrate that organizational performance is a reasonable interpretation of our words, you will be considered to have violated our policies."

The accompanying flowchart illustrates the decision pathway that a board should use when considering organizational performance (Figure 4.3). That performance is considered every time monitoring data are received. The board does not, of course, have go to through all these steps for each piece of monitoring data, but it should know what sequence to follow when applicable.

It turns out the lawyer and the charity board he sat on were ultimately satisfied with the Policy Governance rationale on this matter, so they changed the wording they had originally proposed to read as follows: "In monitoring the organization with respect to ends and executive limitations, the standard of performance will be any reasonable interpretation by the CEO of the words of these policies."

Getting It Right from the Start: The CEO's Job Description

BOARD LEADERSHIP, NUMBER 26, JULY-AUG. 1996

JOBS CAN BE DESCRIBED in various ways. The CEO's job can be described in terms of the *activities* expected to be performed or the *results* expected to be achieved. The former is more familiar; the latter is far more powerful.

A conventional CEO job description often includes items such as these:

Administers the agency

Hires and supervises staff

Evaluates staff and programs

Writes budgets and program plans

Represents the agency to local officials

Writes grant applications

Oversees care of property

Submits financial reports

I don't recommend any of these descriptions; they are a primitive way to describe a CEO job. In fact, they actually miss the point of what a CEO job is for. A board needs a CEO, but not to stay busy at various tasks, even seemingly necessary ones. A board needs a CEO to make everything come out right.

A board needs a CEO to make everything come out right.

Now, what do I mean by "everything come out right"? I simply mean that the organization achieves what the board says it should and, while doing so, avoids those situations and activities that the board feels should not occur. If that is so, then why not just describe the CEO's job that way? Here is the description I recommend:

FAQ ➡

What should a CEO job description look like?

The job of chief executive officer is to ensure the (1) achievement of a reasonable interpretation of the organizational results, beneficiaries, and costs of those results described in the board's ends policies, and (2) avoidance of a reasonable interpretation of the unacceptable conditions and actions described in the board's executive limitations policies.

That is it. There is no further job description needed except by reference, of course, to the ends and executive limitations policies mentioned.

Telling the CEO to do a list of things demeans the job.

But won't the CEO have to hire and supervise staff, write budgets, administer, and do the things listed on the rest of the original list? Of course, he or she will, and even more. But that is the point. The CEO will have to do whatever is needed to achieve ends and comply with executive limitations, whether or not the board would have thought of the entire list. Telling the CEO to do a list of things demeans the job. If *doing* certain things—rather than attaining certain things—is the job, then the board must give the CEO credit for doing these things whether or not they work!

FAQ ➡

How much authority should be given to the CEO?

But what does this job description have to say about the amount of authority given to the CEO? I have found that the nature of delegation is best built into a separate board policy, perhaps called "Delegation to the CEO." Ordinarily, wording similar to the following is used within that policy:

The CEO is empowered to make all decisions, create all policies, and authorize all engagements that he or she can demonstrate upon board request are consistent with a reasonable interpretation of the board's ends and executive limitations policies.

This statement belongs in the board-staff linkage category of board policies because it describes the basic nature of the transfer of limited authority from the board to the CEO. It defines the format, so to speak, of board-to-CEO delegation and refers to where the board's specific expectations can be found. Like all board policies, of course, it can be expanded into further detail.

Board members, establishing rigor and trustworthiness are balls in *your* court!

But even if the policy remains at the broad level just discussed, the CEO now knows the criteria upon which he or she will be judged and knows what limits exist to his or her authority. These are the *only* instructions a competent CEO needs or wants . . . as long as he or she can trust that the board really means what it says.

But what if the CEO is not competent? The same approach will enable the board to make that discovery sooner rather than later. In both cases, board members, establishing rigor and trustworthiness are balls in *your* court!

Do You Really Have a CEO?

BOARD LEADERSHIP, NUMBER 26, JULY-AUG. 1996

IT MAKES LITTLE SENSE for your board to work on CEO evaluation if, in fact, you have no CEO. This observation may seem a bit unnecessary, but I have found that nonprofit and public boards regularly have difficulty assigning a true CEO role to anyone. Many boards think they have a CEO, but don't. Giving someone the *title* CEO means nothing in itself.

What does it take to be a real CEO? The answer lies in two features of the role: authority and accountability. Whether your staff is several or many, an uncountable number of their combined actions must come together well in order to produce a successful organization. *Chief executive officer* names a function that is blessed with personal authority over all these actions and people, but burdened with personal accountability for those same actions and people.

> The CEO is like the narrow part of a venturi or the constricted waist of an egg timer.

In a way, the CEO is like the narrow part of a venturi or the constricted waist of an egg timer. *Above* the CEO is a group of people, albeit acting as one, that determines expectations for the organization's production and character. *Below* the CEO is a group of people, divided by type of labor, that pursues the attainment of those expectations. The CEO is normally the only point in the entire chain of decision making where the "flow" of authority downward and accountability upward go through a single human being. He or she is often the only person who works for a group and over a group.

The board, of course, must be responsible for "acting as one" and the CEO must be responsible for the divisions of staff labor intended to produce the desired outcomes. In another sense, while the board has its own servant-leader (the chairperson) to assist it in acting properly as one, the board chooses a CEO to

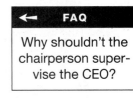

← FAQ

Why shouldn't the chairperson supervise the CEO?

worry about all the components of production. The chairperson, therefore, leads the board; the CEO leads the staff. It is important to keep that straight, even though there are ample opportunities to confound these roles.

The divisions of labor required to produce the organizational products are a tempting arena for improper board involvement. Boards like to delve into internal arrangements, such as organization charts and departmental structures. Boards even fall into delegating directly to these sub-CEO structural components (for example, giving a certain job to the public relations department or charging the accounting

> The chairperson leads the board; the CEO leads the staff.

department with a task). Further, boards like to judge the performance of sub-CEO personnel or departments. A responsible board should never indulge itself in intrusions of this nature. Does the CEO have control over these matters or not? If so, then the board should get out of his or her way. If not, then the board has only fooled itself into thinking it has granted the CEO authority.

Pity, for the CEO function is the greatest labor-saving device a board could have. With a CEO, the board never has to concern itself with what components did not get the job done, or with what arrangement of components is needed to get a future job done. If you do choose to have a CEO—and I'd recommend

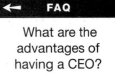

← FAQ

What are the advantages of having a CEO?

that—the board would do well to treat everything beyond the CEO as if it were invisible. It is not mandatory that a board have a CEO, for an organization can operate without one. The board's task is many times more difficult, however, in the absence of a CEO role. But you can't have it both ways: You either have a CEO or you have a weaker, less accountable role that doesn't deserve the name.

Given these considerations, let me just list a few pseudo-CEO situations I have run across over the years:

The CEO function is the greatest labor-saving device a board could have.

- A school board that regularly delegates to assistant superintendents tasks to accomplish or data to gather. The superintendent is not the CEO because the board is not delegating executive matters *exclusively* to him or her.

- A trade association board that appoints a committee of association members to join with staff in putting together a publication for members. The executive director is not the CEO because the board is not leaving operational matters to her prerogative.

- A community action agency board that fired the entire accounting staff for incompetence. The executive director is not the CEO because the board is neither content to let him manage nor willing to hold him, not the accounting department, accountable for incompetent accounting.

- A city council that allows members of the council to instruct the director of public works. The city manager is not the CEO because the council in effect goes around him to control staff actions.

Governing bodies need to learn that a CEO is not just a lead staff officer, the top position in the staffing chart. It is a position unlike any other in an organization—not quite board member and not quite staff, but the bridging interface that transforms purpose into performance. In Policy Governance, for example, board policies on ends and executive limitations are written as instructions to the CEO, not to the staff. While there can be a great deal of profitable board-staff interaction, there is no direct instruction of staff or judging of their individual performances. Those interactions are reserved for the CEO alone.

To deal most effectively with a CEO, boards should delegate in a more contemplative, blanket-like manner. That is, instead of a "do this, now do that" kind of real time, boss-like behavior, the board can issue carefully considered overview statements that establish long-term expectations and arenas of action. The CEO is then treated like a self-starting, self-disciplined professional.

FAQ ➡️

How does a board handle concerns about CEO competence?

Some boards worry that their lead staff person cannot handle this kind of focal accountability. Yet board coddling is a self-fulfilling destroyer of the CEO role. My recommendation is that your board give careful consideration to whether it really wants a CEO function. If you do, then demand CEO behavior and give your current officeholder the opportunity to bloom and grow. It's possible that you will have to monitor performance a little more frequently to quell your predictable anxiety. But don't give up on your current semi-CEO until he or she has been given a chance.

Does Policy Governance Give Too Much Authority to the CEO?

BOARD LEADERSHIP, NUMBER 55, MAY-JUNE 2001

IN NONPROFIT and governmental circles, one frequently hears concern that the Policy Governance model gives the CEO too much authority. Even boards that don't ordinarily worry about being "staff driven"—as is fairly common in associations—fear that potent delegation equals perilous abdication. To their credit, board members who are afraid of putting too much authority into staff hands are not usually against giving out some authority. It's the "too much" that bothers them. In this article, I examine what too much delegation looks like and how the Policy Governance model gives boards more effective tools to deal with this danger than do the more conventional approaches to governance.

Let me begin by saying that I fear granting too much authority to staff, too. It is a real, not an imagined, danger. And it is exceptionally easy to do. It is not uncommon for boards to be asleep at the switch, to allow organizations to do what they shouldn't do and to achieve less than they should. It is not uncommon for boards to be manipulated by their staffs and treated as a necessary but bothersome appendage to the real workers. Of course, many boards in essence beg to be manipulated and are, in fact, bothersome appendages. How well would most board meetings go if they weren't almost entirely stage-managed by staff? How much time is wasted by amateurs pretending to supervise professionals? How much unofficial delegation occurs when staffs and boards conspire to keep the board focused on trivia while the staff make all the really important decisions? The issue of delegating too much or too little can be complex when you get beyond the rhetoric in which both board and staff participate.

> Many boards in essence beg to be manipulated and are, in fact, bothersome appendages.

It is also important to remember that whatever authority a staff has, the board has granted—intentionally and consciously, or not. So we cannot look to staff for the blame, nor for the solution for over- or underdelegation. The board is in charge, whether or not it wears that mantle happily. Except for the higher authorities that precede it (such as law and ownership prerogatives), the board has at the outset *all* the organizational authority along with the right to decide how much and to whom to give away. We could discuss others to whom a board ordinarily gives a portion of its authority, such as officers and committees, but I'm confining these remarks to what is ordinarily a more voluminous delegation: to the staff. If the board has chosen to use the CEO device for centralizing accountability (which I'll assume here), then granting authority to the staff really means granting authority to the CEO.

Now, let's look at just why a board should grant *any* authority to a CEO. After all, the authority has been entrusted to the board either by law (as in a public school system), by a membership (as in associations), by holders of equity (as in business corporations), or by some other implied legitimacy base (in the way we might infer the local population to be the "moral ownership" of a community hospital). There are only two justifications for a board to voluntarily relinquish to anyone this precious authority it holds in trust. The most compelling justification—and the one that goes to the heart of having an organization in the first place—is that the board wants something to be different in the world and considers an operating organization to be the most auspicious tool for fulfilling that desire. If an organization of human beings is to achieve what the board wants, those human beings must have the authority to make decisions and take actions necessary to achieve the board's desire. The board has no choice but to grant that authority.

The most succinct and most pointed way for the board to express itself on this central matter is to put its wishes into terms that describe the difference it wants to make, the populations among whom it wishes the difference to be made, and the amount of that difference to be made in return for the resources consumed. (A closer inspection of these "ends" reveals a little more than this simplicity, but the foregoing wording conveys what I wish for now.) But if we are dealing here with anything beyond the very simplest or most unambitious ends, the board will never have the time or even the knowledge to express its wishes in all the detail life presents. The school board might say literacy will average at national grade level with no more than 5 percent of children falling below the tenth percentile, but it can never make incremental decisions of levels of literacy during the school year for each child. Teachers, however, will make these ends decisions routinely. Not only, then, must persons in the organization have the authority to hire and fire, design curriculum and field trips, they must also have the authority to determine the all-important ends at levels below which the board has addressed.

Since the staff gets the organizational work done and, in doing so, makes countless decisions every day, we could say that the board actually gives away *most* of its authority, not just some of it. And that is justified only if the organization really does achieve what the board has directed it to achieve. In Policy Governance, all those more detailed ends decisions made on staff are said to be justified if they are "reasonable interpretations" of the board's broader language. If they are not reasonable interpretations, then the

> Since the staff gets the organizational work done and makes countless decisions every day, the board actually gives away *most* of its authority.

board has lost control and its justification for granting authority just evaporated. Boards (most traditional ones, in fact) that fail even to state the broad ends expectations begin *and remain* in this illegitimate status, having negligently granted staff too much authority.

In other words, the first step to being sure the CEO has not been given too much authority is for the board do its duty with respect to ends specification to begin with. Ironically, most persons who fret that Policy Governance grants too much authority will, at the same time, see no problem with boards failing to state and demand compliance of ends rigorously!

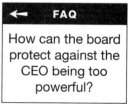

FAQ

How can the board protect against the CEO being too powerful?

But there is a second step a board must consider to be sure it is not giving the CEO too much authority. Quite apart from the need for staff to participate in ends determination (and for which, as I have pointed out, it need authority), there are innumerable decisions that must be made by staff that are not of the ends type. Policy Governance refers to *all* non-ends decisions as *means,* in this case, the staff's means. Surely, these staff means decisions offer another domain in which the board can give the CEO too much authority.

And that is correct. Staffs can be granted—again, whether intentionally or not isn't important—too much authority with respect to these means decisions. (Readers familiar with Policy Governance know that these non-ends decisions run the gamut of issues across personnel, financial, physical arrangements, planning, and countless other areas. They are truly extensive, outnumbering ends decisions many times over.) One way of handling this delegated authority is merely for the board to tell its CEO to do whatever he or she finds necessary to accomplish the ends. After all, such latitude would maximize room for creativity, innovation, agility in response to changes in circumstances, and staff comfort in making decisions. Since the board's command is to accomplish ends and since the board will subsequently monitor that accomplishment, one could contend that the board could profitably allow means delegation to be unlimited.

As far as concerns organizational effectiveness at achieving ends, that will work—there is no possibility of giving the CEO too much authority, so the board needn't worry about it. But there is another source of worry, and it is a big one. While the ends pressure will assure that means are effective, it does nothing to assure that means are ethical and prudent. If the board fails to control means, it will have negligently granted staff too much authority.

Still the most prevalent governance tactic is for boards to worry a lot about means, so much so that prescribing ends is largely neglected. Most board agenda items, most board committee assignments, indeed most recruitment strategies are built typically around means control. But by involving itself in staff means, boards interfere with the staff's unswerving marshalling of its (and its advisors') strengths to accomplish ends.

The CEO cannot be held as accountable for ends if a board personnel committee is "helping" with personnel issues or a board finance committee is inserting itself into the budgeting process. "Working with" the board (or often, in spite of the board) becomes as important as working on ends

> The board must state the ends in the detail necessary for any reasonable interpretation of them to suffice.

production. The board, thinking that there is some virtue in being "involved," feels more engaged and in touch with "what's going on," though the organization is less effective. Of course, neither board nor staff can tell that it is more effective because the ends have not been clearly stated nor rigorously monitored.

So the board that wants to be prudent about how much authority it gives its CEO is in a bind. If it gives too much, it loses control. If it gives too little, it causes the organization to be less effective and its linkage with the organization less accountable.

The solution is simple, but it is not to be found in all the years of board history until the advent of the Policy Governance model: First, the board must state the ends in the detail necessary for any reasonable interpretation of them to suffice. Second, the board must delineate the boundaries of acceptability, within which (given any reasonable interpretation by the CEO) *all* staff decisions, activities, or circumstances are acceptable. Then the board must systematically examine data that demonstrate the degree of compliance both with ends expectations and boundary observance. That's it.

Let me summarize. The board has the option in Policy Governance of defining the ends to whatever degree necessary to satisfy the board's own values, thereby assuring the CEO will aim the organization in a board-determined direction. The board has the option in Policy Governance to define the unacceptable means to whatever degree necessary to satisfy the board's own values, thereby shrinking the CEO's authority as it chooses. Policy Governance gives a board more carefully crafted control over the amount and type of authority delegated to its CEO than is available through other means. So while one might disagree with the amount of latitude a board chooses to give as it uses the model, *it is impossible for the Policy Governance model per se to give the CEO too much authority!*

Chapter Five

Putting Purpose First

Deciding, Delegating, and Demanding Organizational "Ends"

The most important feature of any organization is what it is for, as distinguished from what it does—what difference it makes in the world versus how it organizes and behaves to make that difference. Consequently, the most demanding and crucial task of governance is to define what results are to be achieved, for whom, and at what cost or priority (these constitute the *ends* concept). The *ends* focus is entirely different from attending to services, programs, curricula, markets, products, personnel, and finances—for these are all *means.* No organization is justified to exist due to its means, but only due to its ends.

Boards Lead Best When Services, Programs, and Curricula Are Transparent

BOARD LEADERSHIP, NUMBER 19, MAY-JUNE 1995

IT IS ALWAYS a bit startling to my workshop participants when I say that boards should treat services, programs, and curricula as transparent. But I mean it. Boards should see right through them to something far more important. From a proper board perspective, *they don't matter!*

Everyone professes a commitment to accountability, but until this simple lesson is learned—and it has not been thus far—accountability will remain an almost meaningless concept in most nonprofit and governmental organizations. Services, programs, and curricula have virtually no value apart from their making life better for the right people at an acceptable cost. The value is not in the entities themselves, but in what they accomplish.

Yet board and staff members alike are naturally drawn to service delivery as a process. Services, programs, and curricula have visible identities and their detailed description can be captivating. Indeed, our organizations ordinarily define themselves more by *how* they deliver a human benefit than by the benefit itself! (For example, we have family counseling centers, not healthy family centers.) Nothing may be wrong with this language per se, but something is amiss when we become more invested in our activities than in the difference these activities make in people's lives.

The End Result Is What Counts

It isn't the reading program wherein the value lies but rather in that people learn to read. It isn't the CPR program but that people live. It isn't the curriculum but the resultant knowledge. It isn't the emergency room but that trauma effects are minimal. It isn't the Multiple Listing Service book but sales agents' easy access to understandable market information. It isn't having a slick publication but that there is a well-informed readership. In other words, it isn't the tool that matters but the tool's results for people.

All this is not to say that the counseling, emergency room, CPR training, and publications aren't important. Of course, they are. Without appropriate and effective means, ends will only be pipe dreams. The means are critically important. But to recognize the critical nature of proper services, programs, and curricula is not to equate them with the ends that justify their existence. Careful determination of the ends is important. Careful design of the means is important. And they are important in that order. Ends first. Means second. If a board gets the ends it wants, it can afford to let the means vary as long as they aren't imprudent or unethical. Yet it is folly to get the means we want and miss our desired ends. And that is exactly the situation set up by a dominant focus on means.

> It isn't the reading program wherein the value lies but rather in that people learn to read.

Of course, if the board can't get a handle on whether programs, services, and curricula are producing the desired ends, all the conscientious, time-consuming attention to means rather misses the point. It is pretty easy to demonstrate that boards typically do not know whether ends are being met because they do not, except in rare cases, even know what the ends are supposed to be! In other words, this unhappy state is the norm.

> Careful determination of the ends is important. Careful design of the means is important. In that order. Ends first. Means second.

Some would complain that we have a lot of schooling but too little learning. We have poverty programs but still have a lot of people in poverty. We have policing yet are afraid of our own streets at night. We have a lot of medical treatment but too little health. We have legislatures and councils but precious little public leadership. Indeed, particularly in nonprofit and public administration, entrenched means acquire a powerful inertia of their own, quite apart from whether they work!

In every case, boards and their staffs examine, discuss, debate, and in every way continually focus on the services, programs, and curricula involved. Boards need to look past staff activity, no matter how impressive it is. Particularly when a

> Entrenched means acquire a powerful inertia of their own, quite apart from whether they work!

board governs a highly technical or professional staff, it is easy to give staff activity well-deserved admiration, without subjecting that activity to the hard test of results. A board's appreciation for its staff is not wrong, of course, but allowing that appreciation to deter the board from its responsibility is very wrong. Boards can appreciate and even pay homage to the fine design of means, but then should get back to their own jobs: defining the ends against which all means should be brutally and repeatedly tested.

I am not suggesting that the board should never know what services, programs, or curricula are conducted. This information is interesting, and knowing it may be politically useful. I am suggesting that boards should pay little official attention to these commendable staff activities and, moreover, give the CEO no credit for them. What the CEO gets credit for (and you may lavish this credit, if you wish!) is whether monitoring data show that the organization is bringing about the desired life changes in the right people for the right cost.

Beware of Targeting Specific Programs

My warning against attending to programs, services, and curricula even precludes a board from creating genuine ends one program at a time. In other words, a board should not examine a program in order to create ends for it. For example, a school board should not focus on a particular curriculum in order to prescribe the results it should achieve; a family service agency

> **← FAQ**
> Shouldn't a board determine its ends "one program at a time?"

board should not have its ends guided by staff-defined services. Not only would this situation be putting the cart before the horse, but also there is not, and need not be, a one-to-one correspondence between specific results and programs. Several programs may serve varying aspects of the same ends. Conversely, one program may simultaneously address several of the board's ends. Boards jeopardize their effectiveness by creating ends one program at a time.

For these same reasons, a Policy Governance board would have no interest in budgets created program by program ("program budgeting") rather than in total. Program budgets state the cost of program activity, a useful tool for managers who must manipulate the components of cost. From a board perspective, however, the

---

There is not, and need not be, a one-to-one correspondence between specific results and programs.

---

relevant matter is the cost of results, not the costs of methods.

To inspect, budget, or utilize means as the point of departure for board thinking is to doom the board's leadership to the creativity-confining effect of trying to lead within staff-created categories of means. Starting from existing staff methods contaminates leadership about ends—like driving a car by intently focusing on and steering with the rear view mirror. So do not discuss, debate, and decide on ends by inspecting and analyzing existing programs. To the contrary, let the staff discuss, debate, and decide on programs, being driven by the board's desired ends.

In the same vein, monitoring data on program activity, or even program existence, never fulfills the board's obligation to monitor ends. In other words, *the board never needs to assess programs per se.* The only data that address the board's assessment needs are those that directly compare the actual outcomes to board-stated expectations about results, recipients, and costs of the results. (There will be occasions when, by happenstance, a direct relationship exists between a given result and a single, specific program. This relationship presents no problem, as long as the board keeps in mind that the program's success or failure is not what the board should focus on, but rather the overall organization's success in producing the desired effects, which translates directly into the CEO's success.) Admittedly, the relevant data may be harder to get and tougher to quantify than most means data. But as always, it is better to measure the right things crudely than the wrong things precisely.

It is better to measure the right things crudely than the wrong things precisely.

In summary, services, programs, and curricula describe the consumer-related activities (means) in which your organization engages. Ends describe the difference you seek to make in the lives of clients, patients, students, members, consumers, or community. Accountability for ends has intrinsic importance; accountability for the activities intended to achieve ends is an unnecessary and distracting construct. Your organization does not exist for *anything* your staff is doing, no matter how well-intended, impressive, politically correct, or even righteous. It exists to make a difference.

A Community Board Struggles with the Cost of Its Results

BOARD LEADERSHIP, NUMBER 23, JAN.-FEB. 1996

I RECEIVED A LETTER asking me to explain how the "at what cost" element is determined when a board is establishing ends policies. The request came from a community organization that connects various types of learning and learners. In this article, I want to share my response.

First, let's recognize that cost was a human concept long before it became an accounting concept. If I let down my guard and take a nap, a tiger might eat me. Rest has a cost. If I lay aside seed for next year, I cannot eat it now. Investment in the future has a cost. If I study for the exam now, I can't hang out at the pub. I can't go to the movie and to the concert at the same time. Fore-

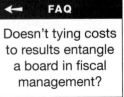

FAQ

Doesn't tying costs to results entangle a board in fiscal management?

going one is the cost of the other. If I live my values, I give up certain friends. Cost is an integral part of life and its unending choices. In fact, a choice would not be a choice if cost in its broad sense were not involved. Cost is a human issue, just the kind of human issue that boards exist to grapple with. Board members who are not accountants should not automatically defer to accountants with regard to cost. Cost is not fundamentally an accounting issue. It concerns the core of the board's ends work: What is worth what?

Nonprofit and public bodies, however, have wandered into a quagmire with respect to cost. And the most "cost-conscious" boards are the worst. Oh, they are concerned about costs all right, but they are concerned about the costs of the wrong things!

Do not automatically defer to accountants with regard to cost. Cost is not fundamentally an accounting issue.

Accountants haven't helped much, for they almost always trace the costs of activities or types of expenditures, not costs of results. Look at any budget: You'll find it easy to determine the costs to the organization for insurance, rent, salaries, renovations, vehicles, and innumerable other means. You will find it difficult or impossible to determine the costs of specific effects or results for consumers. And yet, to the world outside the organization, component costs of a desired result are unimportant, while the total cost of the result is of paramount concern. For example, the total cost of a new automobile is important to the buyer; the cost that went into reaming the cylinders is not.

> **FAQ** ➡
>
> What is meant by the term *mega-ends*?

My questioner's board had adopted a mission statement something like this: *"Individuals and organizations in our community will be linked in their pursuit of excellence in learning."* The board had gone further to define four "mission outcomes" (in their language) shown just below. These results typify the Policy Governance idea of further defining the *mega-ends* or mission statement. That is, these outcomes begin to break down the general into the more specific. They are, at the first level of detail, what the board means by people *"linked in their pursuit of excellence in learning"*:

1. A heightened understanding of issues affecting learning
2. A highly skilled, informed, connected membership
3. An appreciation of the value of learning
4. A favorable learning environment

In other words, within the broader statement of mission, the board wants the CEO to attain more specific results for particular segments of its membership (high-level skills, connectedness, favorable learning environment). Those accomplishments have worth in terms of each other (relative priorities) or in terms of dollar cost.

The overall result (people linked in learning excellence) has an effect on the world that is also worth a certain amount. It makes sense, then, that the total budget is spent on the total result as proclaimed in the mission. Stated differently, the total mission is worth the total burden on members (in terms of dues). The board is saying—even if only implicitly—that the outputs of the mission are worth the budget used to pursue it.

Let's consider a level or two of specificity within the broad level of mission—those four listed outcomes and their further definition. In whom is the heightened understanding to occur: Only in members? Also in the general public? In specific decision makers? Who is to gain appreciation of the value of learning: legislators? The general public? Graduates? Parents? These ends must be brought into sharper focus as part of the board's ends work—unless the board is willing for the CEO to make that further interpretation.

Provided that the existing level of detail is as far as the board wishes to go in specifying intended results and recipients of those results, let us now consider the question of cost. What, then, are these results worth?

> **← FAQ**
> What types of costs should a board be concerned about?

A board discussion must take place about the relative worth of the four results. At this stage, the board needn't worry about assigning precise costs. It can start in a very general way, for example, exploring whether any of the outputs is more important than any others. Does one stand out? Does one obviously bring up the rear? If the board could have only one, which would it be? Can they be ranked? One or more of these approaches will strike a chord that is meaningful to this particular board.

This discussion should allow a number of values to surface; the form of those values determines the next path to pursue. For example, extreme difficulty in ranking or prioritizing might suggest that the outputs are relatively equal in priority. Having rough cost estimates for each would be helpful. It doesn't matter that they are rough. What would it cost to produce a favorable learning environment, or at least as favorable in the chosen settings as you wish to produce? Differing degrees of accomplishment cost different amounts, of course, so you'd try to get a handle on that variation. For example, for so many dollars you can expect to have a certain population reach a certain level of understanding of the value of learning.

As difficult as this exercise may be, beware the temptation to fall back into costing activities instead of results. It is relevant to governance that reaching a certain level of awareness in a certain population would cost $250,000. But it is

The cost of a means is not automatically the cost of a result.

not relevant to governance that it would cost $250,000 to conduct a one-year media campaign intended to raise awareness. The latter will be relevant to the CEO as she weighs and manipulates various methods to attain the result. Because there is not necessarily a one-to-one correlation between specific ends and specific means, the cost of a means is not automatically the cost of a result. The media campaign (a means) may be one method you'd use to accomplish the desired end. Or to figure it in the other direction, the media campaign might be designed to bring about portions of several ends. But even if each distinct result could be linked to one identifiable means, costing the activity would still be less rigorous than costing the outcomes.

One might ask how a board can cost an outcome other than by first determining the cost of all activities intended to lead to the outcome. That would, of course, involve the board in an essentially means-focused process, comparing various courses of action against others—a task the Policy Governance model clearly assigns to staff. Let us resolve this dilemma.

> **FAQ** ➡️
>
> How can a board cost an outcome without determining the cost of all the activities producing it?

The governance task is to determine how much various results *are worth* to the board, not to "cost" them in the sense of figuring out the cost. The board can let the staff do the work of costing various means to accomplish the first iteration of board ends. Staff can manipulate, reconfigure, and rethink all the means it wishes. The board merely needs to know whether what the staff comes up with is in line with what the board thinks the results are worth.

But how would the board know the staff has come up with as good a cost as possible? It can compare what its staff can do to what has been demonstrated possible in other places (comparable to "industry averages" in business). It can compare with what its own staff has done in the past (is the staff capable of producing more per dollar each year?). In some respects, it is not as important that there be a perfect starting place as that the process begins and then is honed every year. Moreover, even if the staff is able to produce certain results at less cost than anyone else in the universe, if the board believes those results are not worth that cost, the board does not elect to pursue them.

> It is not as important that there be a perfect starting place as that the process begins and then is honed every year.

As imprecise as the process is, it will propel the organization in a desired direction far more powerfully than any amount of precision in controlling means. Many means measurements are—or seem to be—very precise (calculating current ratio or the number of column inches per public relations dollar expended). We are accustomed to abandoning meaningfulness in exchange for more easily measured statistics. It would be wonderful to be as exact in costing results as we can be in costing means, but precision is not the most important characteristic of board instruction. It is more important to cost the right thing (the desired result) than to be exact in costing the derivative thing (the activity done to achieve the desired result).

It is more important to cost the right thing than to be exact in costing the derivative thing.

Just looking at the value of outcomes virtually eliminates the rhetorical flourishes organizations hide behind. When our systems reward us for touting our fine programs instead of examining their results, it is easy for good works to take the place of doing any good. The profound exploration of discussing relative importance is enlightening to the board and membership and highly instructive to the CEO long before the board can confidently state the results for certain recipients along with respective costs—and it can take place long before all the results and costs are in.

You can see that ends work is challenging and perpetual. But don't despair. Although it is likely the board will never fully answer these questions of value, the fact that this issue forms the central conversation of governance will have a powerful effect on the board mentality, on the relationships between board and staff and between board and ownership, and on the quality of board leadership. For the CEO, board-stated ends are his or her master objectives. For the board, however, deliberating about and establishing ends—including the cost component—is a journey rather than a destination.

Beware the "Quality" Fetish

BOARD LEADERSHIP, NUMBER 37, MAY-JUNE 1998

A RECENT consulting experience with a hospital board brought to my attention once again the insidious nature of a very popular concept: quality. This article recounts what I advised the board, its medical staff, and its administrators about that omnipresent, rarely questioned ideal called quality.

Like all hospital boards, this board was concerned about its role in overseeing quality. There was a Quality Committee composed of board members, physicians, and top managers. They would receive reports from various internal committees and from the medical staff organization. These reports focused on one or more aspects of quality in medical care. The Quality Committee also reviewed the list of new physicians to be given staff privileges (permission to admit patients and to treat them in the hospital). The Quality Committee would pass its recommendations on to the full board. Quality was the watchword and a characteristic of hospital life that received a great deal of attention and discussion. Yet a number of the board members were still unsettled about their role with regard to this elusive, technical concept of medical quality.

> **FAQ** ➡
>
> Shouldn't a board be concerned with the quality of the services the organization provides?

Let me be clear: I am not against quality. I like quality in food, clothing, cars, movies, and governance. And I surely enjoy quality in medical and dental care. Quality is a useful shorthand. The fact that it means different things to different people does not disturb me; most words do. My problem with such steadfast concentration on quality by boards (not just in health care, but in education and other areas as well) is twofold. First, the word's self-serving history obscures a board's focus on the real reasons for pursuing quality in the first place. Second, if a board prescribes ends and proscribes means as Policy Governance requires, all

> If a board prescribes ends and proscribes means, all the aspects of quality important *at the governance level* will already have been addressed.

the aspects of quality important *at the governance level* will already have been addressed—and more stringently, at that.

Consider the shady history of the word. In health care and in education, to cite two very visible examples, the description of quality has been largely about providers' characteristics and providers' methods. In other words, service carried out in a certain prescribed and accepted way by persons of certain training and certification can be called quality service. The glaring omission is that quality so defined includes no reference to effectiveness. So it is that quality mental health service is unrelated to whether that

> ← **FAQ**
>
> How can a board cost an outcome without determining the cost of all the activities producing it?

service works. That is, measures of quality do not embrace measures or even estimates of consumer outcomes. I am not arguing that outcome measurement is easy or even that there aren't good reasons for quality to have acquired a meaning divorced from effectiveness. I am arguing that board members must take this omission into account.

But the more important consideration is that the ends-means format of Policy Governance covers all the governance-relevant aspects of quality anyway, plus crucial aspects that professionally defined quality has often omitted. This is the way I made the point with the hospital board: the intent of hospital service is to have certain impacts on patients' lives. The impact or benefit might be cure of disease, relief from pain, successful childbirth, restored function, ability to see to one's own health needs, or any number of outcomes. If the hospital causes the desired outcomes for the right persons (there may well be priorities among the potential patient populations) for the right cost, then the board's ends will have been achieved.

Add to this consideration that because of the necessity for management to heed executive limitations policies the board would have promulgated, the hospital board can ensure that the service provided should not, for example, cause undue hardship to patients, expose them to insensitive or unnecessarily undignified treatment, give them iatrogenic disease, subject them to procedures for which they haven't been fully informed of risk, and other such unacceptable situations and actions.

> At the board level, not only is quality service an unnecessary concern, but so is *any* kind of service.

Now, if the hospital achieves proper outcomes and avoids unacceptable situations and activities, just what does the term *quality* have to offer that adds anything to this? First, quality doesn't commonly cover the matter of outcomes sufficiently to add further to the ends concept. Second, quality does typically add other matters of prescribed methods that professions may need to control but that the board does not. In fact, at the board level, not only is quality service an unnecessary concern, but so is *any* kind of service. That is, it isn't service (an activity, a means) that should concern the board, but that certain ends are achieved and certain unacceptable means are avoided.

As you might surmise, this hospital board had worshiped quality for so long that it would have to think about these remarks for awhile. As I left them they were struggling with this new idea that if the board attends as it should to hospital ends and unacceptable hospital means, quality in its usual sense can be left to the professionals.

First Things First

BOARD LEADERSHIP, NUMBER 1, MAY-JUNE 1992

WHAT IS YOUR FONDEST hope for your organization? For most board members it would be that the organization make a difference. You want your efforts as a member of the board to amount to something, to be worthwhile. In later years, looking back, you will be able to shrug off many criticisms. But to conclude that the organization you helped lead didn't matter much will surely sting.

In this article, I am going to address the question of how your board can steer the organization toward making the kind of impact you will be proud of. But first things first: Before it takes on the world, an organization must first and foremost have a strong, clear sense of the difference it wants to make.

Good Activity or Good Effects?

It is the board's primary function to create a wisely considered and compelling vision, though this is rarely what boards spend much of their time doing. Most boards waste precious time in areas where they have little business—meddling in areas of staff responsibility, for example—to the neglect of their own crucial responsibility.

So, board member, exactly what difference is it that you want to make? Not what do you want your organization engaged in, but what difference its engagements should cause. The question is not what to be busy at, but what conditions or changes to bring to pass.

An organization must first and foremost have a strong, clear sense of the difference it wants to make.

Take care not to be fooled by the immediate attractiveness of good deeds. Well-intended organizational activity may be impressive, but under the harsh light of subsequent judgment will be hollow if results are poor. To fulfill your own good intentions—not to mention the expectations of others—your board must relentlessly probe behind good activity in search of good effects.

This is easier said than done. Most program reporting systems and accounting systems tell us far more about activity than results; you may have to blaze unfamiliar trails in finding new ways to report on that which is most important. Public education, social service, and city government, to name but three of many areas, report in ways that obscure results or, more accurately, obscure the fact that we don't know what the results are. Besides, ascertaining the results of previous activity is a monitoring question, which I will leave for another discussion. The even greater problem is that *your board may not even have said what it wants the results to be.* And that leads to the simple point of this article: Your board would do well to devote most of its time to discussing, debating, and deciding what difference it wishes to make.

Your board would do well to devote most of its time to discussing, debating, and deciding what difference it wishes to make.

Ends and Means

I refer to this difficult and largely overlooked pursuit as *ends work,* to distinguish it from work that deals with means. Means—that is, methods, activities, practices—are so inviting that a board can stay entangled in them forever, having never completed its ends work! Strange though it may seem, in nonprofit and public organizations we are ordinarily much clearer about means than we are about the ends those means ostensibly serve.

Even if a board is convinced that it should spend more time creating and maintaining a vision of the future, getting started is difficult. Ends decisions are demanding; they are the organizational equivalent of, "What is life?" or at least, "What is the good life?" This doesn't mean you have to go to the shelf for Plato, but let there be no mistake: The board's ends work is close cousin to these concerns.

Let's look at how a board might get started on putting first things first:

Prepare for simplicity. The question of what difference you want to make is simple and should be kept that way: What good will be done, for whom, and at what? Although the question is simple, the answers are not. Finding answers will take most of your available time, so getting the clutter out of board and committee meetings is necessary.

For example, your board must find a way to withdraw safely from the myriad operational issues that so insistently claim its attention. A raft of traditionally honored board actions—including budget approvals, personnel matters, and contract specifics—seduce boards into a narrow focus on means.

Tradition offers an inviting technique: Farm these matters out to a number of committees so that the board as a whole does not have to deal with them. But this practice leaves the board fragmented in its understanding of the whole and often results in your staff having to deal with several single-topic miniboards. The kind of thinking you will need in order to make a difference requires a sense of the whole, an overview, a high vantage point. Consequently, your board will have to commit itself to becoming more a think tank for vision than a reviewer of staff decisions and activities.

Imagine how the world is likely to be *without* your organization. Try starting this exciting journey with assumptions about your world rather than by attacking those daunting ends choices directly. Begin by postulating what the world might be like if your organization did not exist. *World* for you may be community, district, area of trade, or other arena of intended effect. Perhaps you can think of this as a kind of *It's a Wonderful Life* exercise in which your guardian angel shows you what the world would have been like if you had never existed.

← FAQ

Since it's difficult to determine the ultimate purpose of an organization, how can a board jump-start its thinking about ends?

Study the matter. Gather reasonable projections. Do a little "what if" conjecture. Include an array of opinions. Remember to stand outside the organization for your viewpoint. Create several alternative scenarios of the future. You need not decide that one prophesy is correct and others are not. You are devising assumptions about the future, not certainties. Be careful to keep your organization *out* of these considerations. Remember, it does not exist!

Gather information. You will have to learn new things. Intelligently arriving at a vision will take information you do not now have, so you must decide what you need to know and then get it. Arrange board education as needed. Keep it stimulating and carefully targeted. Board education about the wrong things might make you smarter, but it won't help you govern better. You may be able to use staff members in the process, but just as likely you may not. The point is not simply to learn what your staff already know; you may be misguidedly learning how

← FAQ

Can staff members help the board determine the organization's ends?

to do staff jobs better. You are working at a different level of questioning than staff are typically engaged in. With all good intent, they could derail the process. You might go to funding bodies, local experts, organizations similar to your own, or any number of sources for information. Don't shortchange this phase; in it you are building a base upon which to exercise your wisdom.

Boards of education, for example, should look to see what challenges the world of the future will present to today's students' ability to survive, thrive, and participate. What will happen to them, their communities, or their country without sufficient job skills and personal abilities, not to mention a comfort with diversity, competition, and the faster pace of change?

> The point is not simply to learn what your staff already know; you may be misguidedly learning how to do staff jobs better.

It may help to research what the world was like *before* your organization was created. Review the climate in which it came into being and the reasons for which the founders established it. Visit other locations where organizations such as yours do not exist. Beware, however, that you don't let the exercise become one that chiefly looks backward. The idea is to learn from the past, not to be determined by it. Keep your primary focus on drawing a picture of the future.

What's *wrong* in that picture? After careful study of the probable futures without your organization, you are ready to focus your values. What is unacceptable to you in those futures? In other words, what would you make different about where your part of the world appears to be going? If there is nothing of significance to change, perhaps the world could make better use of the resources your present organization consumes.

As board members confront these issues, there are likely to be lively and wide-ranging responses. Excellent. Gather them without judgment, then go back and take a more critical look. When your process has become well developed, bring more people into your struggle. It may be awkward to do so at first, but you can include others through special focus groups, natural groupings (church groups, neighborhoods), board-to-board dialogue, or any other method that works.

You can even involve staff in the fun, as long as they are not speaking from their narrowly defined, job-specific interest but as particularly informed citizens. There is no need to have a staff recommendation, for your board will be looking for diverse points of view.

Make the hard choices. The big job is yet to be done, but now you are ready to do it. Having "jumpstarted" your ends work with the assumptions approach, you must now follow through and make the hard choices: Which changes in the world should be made? What differences are to be made, for whom should they be made, and what is it worth to do so?

You must now follow through and make the hard choices: Which changes in the world should be made?

Deciding the answers will cause you to confront differences in values among your members, so you must prepare yourselves for compassionate, as well as passionate, disagreements. Even knowing your own personal values about these matters may take work; be ready for a struggle. This is not fast work. You may not produce even a paper product quickly. But immediately you will feel the difference between this kind of board interaction and that which over the years has wasted so much of your talent and wisdom.

Put into written form, your board's choices can result in a set of board policies about ends, policies that determine the destiny of the organization and how the world will be different because it exists. But the world keeps changing, as do your values and your organization's strengths. The answers are answers only for a short while. Be prepared to create, question, and re-create these answers as long as your board exists.

This is putting first things first. Boards that do this well find little need to meddle in staff work. Indeed, meddling occurs largely because boards have not done their primary job. The assumptions method of jumpstarting the process is one way to get the ball rolling. It may save your board from looking at the future through the

The answers are answers only for a short while. Be prepared to create, question, and re-create these answers as long as your board exists.

handy—but myopia-inducing—lens of the organization as it is today. But the method itself is not important; other formats may work better for your board. Use whatever methods, persuasions, and gimmicks you can find to keep first things first. Keep the "difference you want to make" up front in your agendas as well as in your heart.

Evaluating the Mission Statement

BOARD LEADERSHIP, NUMBER 5, JAN.-FEB. 1993

EVERY ORGANIZATION—indeed, every productive system—needs an aim, a direction to which its many parts and processes are dedicated. Purpose is something more meaningful than a description of the internal goings-on. It is bigger than the sum of those parts. Greater than the myriad and intricately technical activities of a hospital is the *why* of its existence. Greater than the esoteric activities of a research institute is the hope of discovery toward which the institute is directed.

> The aim or grand intent is philosophical and even intensely personal, arising as it does from what we believe the world should be.

The aim or grand intent is philosophical and even intensely personal, arising as it does from what we believe the world should be. Why do we have a public school system? What justifies the trade association, pension fund, or social service agency? It is no accident that the word *mission* has not only strategic but frankly religious overtones. What are we about? What human need compels our organization?

The answer that is short and to the point should be found in your mission state-

Note: I am indebted to the organizations that submitted mission statements in response to my requests. Thanks for bravely allowing your work to be examined according to the principles of the Policy Governance model.

ment. Its few words embody the organization's basic commission to make something happen in the world. There is nothing new, of course, about writing mission statements. Many readers have doubtlessly been involved in that chore several times. In this article, we'll take a new look at that familiar task.

Producing a mission statement under Policy Governance principles calls for more rigor than usual. The mission, if crafted as the board's master ends statement, must abide by criteria applicable to a declaration of ends. Ends are not activities but products, outputs, or other effects we will have in the lives of certain recipients (see Exhibit 5.1).

> **← FAQ**
>
> What is the relationship between an organization's mission and the board's ends?

The following critique should not be taken as harsh criticism but as a demonstration of how even good work done in traditional form can be changed under a transformed governance. My stringency is not due to an isolated, pedantic notion of how a mission ought to appear. Precision is needed because this broadest of board ends pronouncements—the *mega-ends* statement, if you will— becomes the *foundation* for all further organizational ends.

> Lutheran Social Services of Illinois [LSSI] is the social service agency of the Evangelical Lutheran Church in America's Illinois synods, serving on behalf of and in partnership with the Illinois synods and their congregations.
>
> The Gospel calls the church to serve people in the name of Christ. Through service and advocacy, the agency shall seek to bring healing, justice, and wholeness to persons and to enhance the quality of people's lives.
>
> As an agency of the church, Lutheran Social Services of Illinois shall strive for excellence in providing a wide range of social services for persons of all races, creeds, and economic classes throughout the State of Illinois.

LSSI (this and further organizational abbreviations used are mine) has tried to wrap a lot about its beliefs and methods into one statement. The result shows a lot of careful thought and does tell us something important about the organization. But we are forced to search through many words to find just what will be different in the world due to LSSI's efforts. The majority of this statement is aimed at means, not ends. What is the ends issue in this statement? We cannot be sure, for inferring ends from a means statement is always tricky. Perhaps the desired phrase embodying outcome and recipients would be, "healing, justice, and wholeness in the lives of Illinois residents." However, as stated, the commitment is not that these good works be accomplished but that LSSI will "seek to bring" them to people.

EXHIBIT 5.1. Mission Statement Checklist

How does your mission statement measure up? Use this checklist to analyze your statement.

☐ **Ends, not means.** Does your mission statement address what difference your organization will make for its beneficiaries, or does it merely describe what yur organization will be doing? Keep in mind that the mission statement (and all ends statements) must deal with *them*—the world outside the operating organization—not *you*.

☐ **Effort.** Does the language used in your mission statement elevate effort to effect? Do words such as *try, seek, influence,* or *encourage* allow your staff to organize their activities around righteous exertion rather than results?

☐ **Verbs.** Does a verb—any verb—figure prominently in your mission statement? Even when they don't equivocate like the ones just mentioned, verbs ordinarily refer to something that is to go on rather than the intended *outcome*. Beware of your verbs!

☐ **Nouns embodying activities.** Does your mission statement use nouns that signify a type of means rather than an outcome? Beware of words like *advocacy, education, program,* and *service.*

☐ **Brevity.** Is your mission statement too long? Does it ramble, making it difficult to locate the main point? Burying the mission in two or three padded paragraphs will be sure to weaken its power to guide and shape your organization.

☐ **Accuracy, not cosmetics.** Is your mission accurate? Or does it embroider or glorify your organization's intentions to make them *sound* better, loftier, more extensive, or more glamorous than they are? Don't worry if the most accurate statement has a bare-bones look—a more cosmetically pleasing statement can always be created for public consumption. Your mission statement has another function: to serve as the mega-ends statement on which al other ends policies are built.

☐ **Too broad or too narrow.** Does your mission statement project the ends of your organization too broadly? Does it contain unrealistic goals such as "to create a world that works for everyone?" Or, is it too narrow to cover the range of effects you intend? Try brainstorming about the possible effects your organization might have in the world. Rank these by "size" and then discuss their relative merits.

☐ **Net value added.** If your organization is a federation or another type of membership organization or if your board has authority over other boards, does your mission statement deal with the additional result intended *beyond what the members or subsidiaries would have produced themselves anyway?* For example, the mission for a state department of education should denote the net contribution of that organization and not merely summarize the intended output of all the local education agencies.

☐ **Relation to other boards.** How does your mission statement compare to others? Particularly in communities, it's important to consider your mission in light of other boards' missions. Without regular interboard communication, similarly situated organizations run the risk of serving a disjointed patchwork of ends. The total system may make little sense.

The mission of the Community College League of California [CCLC] is to support the local community college districts of California in providing high-quality, accessible postsecondary educational services and programs in a well-planned, effective and caring manner.

It is clear what CCLC wants its member colleges to provide. It is not so clear what CCLC itself will provide except support. Although "support" could be an output, it is more likely an activity, as in the doing of supportive things. While "well-planned, effective and caring" tells us something about CCLC's beliefs, it tells nothing about its product. To be a mega-ends mission statement, CCLC's would have to say what is to be different for community colleges or for the community college movement. Some possibilities are a favorable legislative environment, joint purchasing savings, or some broader effect that subsumes outputs like these.

Hospice of North Iowa [HNI] seeks to enhance the quality of life for dying and grieving persons and the community at large through the provision of hospice supportive care services and education.

> What typically happens is that organizations focus on and measure the activities of seeking rather than the quality of life itself.

Perhaps you spotted the verb *seeks* as a culprit that lets HNI off the hook. The quality of life does not have to be enhanced; merely seeking it will satisfy the mission as stated. What typically happens is that organizations focus on and measure the activities of seeking rather than the quality of life itself. It would be better to say more specifically what an enhanced quality of life means. It could mean that people drive newer, more luxurious cars. But that is surely not what HNI intends. Perhaps *"dignity, comfort, and peace of mind in dying"* gets closer to what HNI wants to bring about.

It may well be that the HNI board does not fully intend the "community at large" to be part of its statement, though as outsiders we cannot tell. The board may have made the more expansive statement because it reasons that if the quality of life for dying and grieving persons is made better, there will be a payoff for the entire community. But if the board does not actually intend the chief executive to mount efforts that would create that broader effect, it should not put this in the mission. If the broader payoff is simply a collateral benefit (a side effect of HNI's purpose), then its presence in the mission is more a rhetorical flourish than an expectation for staff accomplishment.

> The American Assembly of Collegiate Schools of Business [AACSB] is committed to fostering excellence in management education in colleges and universities.

What a nicely compact mission statement! AACSB is clearly committed to a high ideal, but its wording puts the act of "fostering" in center stage. Although this mission statement comes very close to the mega-ends ideal, its subsequent effect on further ends policy development will be strengthened by moving the emphasis from fostering to that which is to be fostered.

> The mission of the Indiana Association of Realtors [IAR] in partnership with effective local Boards/Associations, is to enhance the ability and opportunity of its members to achieve professional, ethical real estate services.

If members of IAR really end up with enhanced ability and opportunity, then IAR will have been successful. The statement is weakened somewhat by citing an activity (to enhance) rather than an outcome condition as the mission. This may be a minor wording problem, but it could become the source for IAR giving itself credit for the activity of enhancing.

More problematic is the "in partnership" reference. Certainly, the combined effect of a productive state association and effective local organizations is that realtors will have greater ability and opportunity. But does IAR not bring something to that partnership that is uniquely its own output? What is that? The statement fails to say, even though making IAR's specific contribution clear should be the chief function of a mission. IAR might produce materials, training course content, statewide comparative data, legislative effects, or other unique "values added." If the board could capture these in summarizing language, the new mission statement would more accurately and usefully address why IAR itself exists.

A world where women take their legitimate place as participants/designers in the global community [YWCA of Vancouver, British Columbia; YWCAV].

This statement of mission, currently being considered by YWCAV, speaks unambiguously to "what good" and "which people." It does not address cost, but that is a negligible omission at this level of discourse. Note the stark ends terminology—the statement leaves the "how" for someone else to decide. This statement may be guilty of a little overreach, but it boldly avoids any hiding place within the good intentions of programs, services, and other means. It presents a punchy, uncompromising snapshot of the legacy intended to be left by this organization. A mission statement such as this is not a grand summary of well-intended activity but a robust commitment to make a difference.

The mission of East Allen County Schools [EACS; Ft. Wayne, Indiana] is an educated and informed community of life-long learners.

Excellent! Here are no effort words to conceal nonperformance; no activities to obscure intended outcomes. Looking boldly beyond its own walls, EACS crafted a vision not just for today's students but for tomorrow's community.

In public education, the ends dialogue is often lost in the frantic pursuit of micromanagement. It is a pleasure to conclude this article with an ambitious and compelling mission by an elected school board. Just consider what could be generated in social good and tax-dollar payoff if the EACS board were to confer regularly on this vision with the library board, park board, and other community leaders!

The Board of a Trade Association Establishes Ends Policies

Board Leadership, Number 31, May-June 1997

To HELP MAKE the ends topic more concrete, this article and the next three will be about ends policies for a specific type of organization. Even if your organization is not one of those featured, you will be able to glean generally applicable principles that can be easily translated to your own organization.

This article traces the development of ends policies by the board of a trade association. Let me point out how trade associations differ from many other types of organizations. First, they govern on behalf of an ownership that is a designated membership. This task is unlike that faced by school boards or community hospitals, for example, whose ownership is a widespread, amorphous population. Second, unlike most organizations, the results of trade associations are targeted right back to the owners. That is, members are owners and are also customers—sometimes the only customers. As the board establishes ends policies on behalf of members (in their capacity as owners), it will designate particular organizational results for many or all of those same members (in their capacity as customers).

> **FAQ** ➡
>
> What if the customers and owners are the same people?

To illustrate how a trade association would establish good ends policies, let me create a fictitious federation called the National Council of Car Care Companies. The NCCCC has a membership of three hundred companies engaged in easy-access mechanical and cosmetic care of automobiles. Members' biggest competitors are car

A Brief Refresher on Ends

Because the ends concept is so crucial to responsible board leadership . . . and because boards are so accustomed to overlooking it or confusing it, every governing board should come back to the concept regularly to refresh its understanding of and commitment to the idea.

← FAQ

What guidelines will help our board draft effective ends?

It is important to remember that a decision is an ends decision if it (1) designates results in terms of some change in or benefit to a consumer recipient group, (2) designates just who those recipients are to be, or (3) establishes the cost, worth, or relative priority of the designated results for the designated recipients. A decision is *not* an ends decision simply because it is important, is required by law, is seen as a board decision, is about money, is a policy matter, or has an effect on ends. A board discussion about the following statements might help sharpen the distinction for you.

- The results component of ends describes a human need that is to be reduced or eliminated rather than any solution to that need or strategy for meeting it.

- Ends address what your organization is for, not what it does.

- Of all the various aspects of organization, only those included in the ends concept justify the organization's existence.

- The cost component of ends is almost never to be found in budgets and financial reports as we know them.

- Cost accounting, of all the methods developed by accountancy, has the greatest chance of being useful in addressing the cost component of ends.

- Strategy and strategic plans are virtually never ends issues.

- Whether to have a history curriculum in the schools or a job training program in the city are not ends issues.

If board members are to work successfully with Policy Governance, they must master the ends concept. If you find the statements here confusing in any way, you may want to go back and review the basics. Chapter Four of my book *Boards That Make a Difference* (Jossey-Bass, 1997) gives a good overview of ends.

dealerships, freestanding car washes and detailers, and small auto maintenance shops. The board is seven company owners elected by national region.

As in each category of policymaking, the first step is to decide upon the global or most inclusive statement. In the ends category, this *mega-ends* statement is the Policy Governance equivalent of a mission statement. It is not a statement of philosophy or some unattainable vision of the future, but realistic and fully intended to be achieved.

FAQ ➡

Does a board need to frame its mega-ends statement in such a way that results can be measured?

The first ends task, then, is to create as succinct and accurate a statement as possible that sums up the results, recipients, and cost that will drive this organization. There is no need to complicate the task by trying to create a slogan or other public relations device. A rhetorically beautiful statement can be prepared later by staff for brochures and other persuasive materials. Further, there is no need to complicate the matter by considerations of how results will be measured. While measurement is an important matter (see "Giving Measurement Its Due in Policy Governance" in Chapter Nine), it will only complicate the delicate process of deciding what should be the products of organizational existence.

In its initial attempt at crafting the global ends statement, the board will undoubtedly produce a number of effort terms, means, and references to subcomponents of the as yet undefined overall purpose. These must be discarded, for they depart from the rigor required of a proper mega-ends statement. (For another concrete treatment of several real organizations' global ends statements, see the preceding article.) My hypothetical NCCCC board, for example, considers and eliminates "pursue public image of members" because giving itself points for "pursuing" is tantamount to getting credit for trying. Further, the board expunges "advocacy for more favorable laws" because, much like the effort phenomenon, it focuses on means (advocacy is an activity) rather than ends. Finally, the board rejects "advertising skills for members" because, while it is a true result, it is not the inclusive or global one being sought.

After considering and discarding a number of "candidates" for this important global ends policy, the NCCCC board decides on a bare-bones, global statement of intended results, recipients, and cost. Here it is: *Conditions favorable for member success for dues no greater than in comparable associations.*

That certainly sums up what the association is for, though clearly—and intentionally—not what it does. Now the board must deal with a question it will repeat at each level of ends, namely, "Are we willing to let the CEO use any reasonable interpretation of these words, or must we go further into detail to define them ourselves?" Note that the board does *not* move from the global ends statement to how it is to be accomplished (for example, into work plans, strategies, or programs). To see what might need to be further defined about the broad statement just adopted, often a board need look no farther than the actual words of what it has expressed. Let me illustrate, referring to the specific words in the foregoing mega-ends statement.

Conditions. These could be economic conditions, regulatory conditions, skills or other characteristics in the members themselves, conditions in potential customers, conditions in the capital markets available to members, or perhaps even conditions about cars themselves (designed to be easier to wash). If economic conditions, do we mean general economy or economic considerations peculiar to local business, small business, auto cosmetic business, or car repair business? If regulatory, do we mean national, state-provincial, or local regulations? Are we setting out to affect regulations that deal with environmental issues (detergent and oil disposal), small business employment, or others? If conditions in the members themselves, do we mean business skills, car wash equipment technology, marketing, or employee relations? If conditions in potential customers, do we mean a sterling public image of members or perhaps a great desire for well-washed and maintained cars?

Further, how important are these various intentions compared with each other? Are relative priorities intended to stay constant or to shift over time? That is, might the building of consumer desire for clean cars be a greater priority in the first few years than the building of member image in consumers' eyes, but after three years the relative weight would reverse? What is the claim of each upon NCCCC resources? In all these issues, will the board decide (thereby extending its written ends policies into greater detail) or leave them to any reasonable interpretation the CEO chooses?

Favorable. Favorable in the sense of a slight improvement over the status quo or favorable in terms of making failure nearly impossible? Just how favorable is favorable to be? Will the board decide, or will the CEO be allowed to do so?

Members. As the board looks at further definitions of its global result, it will be seen that some results are really for some members more than others. Members new to the business may need certain results that established businesses do not. Members in crowded urban areas may differ in need from rural members. Large businesses may have needs very different from small ones. How are results to be apportioned among what seemed at first to be a homogeneous group? Will the board decide (thereby extending its ends policy into greater detail) or leave these questions to any reasonable interpretation the CEO chooses?

Success. It may at first appear that economic success is the obvious intention of this word. But it is possible that members want other kinds of success, such as quality of work life from being in a respected and trusted business, or quality of personal life due to being able to balance the demands of this business with other needs. Will the board decide (thereby extending ends policy into greater detail) or leave this to any reasonable interpretation the CEO chooses?

Comparable. What comparability is intended—comparable trades or trade associations of comparable size? How comparable is comparable—within a standard deviation or simply not materially deviant? Will the board decide or allow the CEO to use any reasonable interpretation?

> If the board has allowed any means to show up in the global statement, it might now be misled into defining methods instead of results, recipients, and costs.

Lest this litany become overwhelming, it is important to note that the board isn't compelled to decide any of these questions. It can always leave them to the CEO. But to be effective and fair, the board must authorize the CEO to use any reasonable interpretation of the broader decisions the board has chosen to make. At some point, however, the board will have to allow the CEO to make further decisions; it'll have no choice. The question really is, at what level does the board stop making decisions and delegate that right?

So after establishing the global ends statement "conditions favorable for member success for dues no greater than in comparable associations" the board can often merely define the words and phrases used there. This simple technique will work only if the board has obsessively avoided elements that do not strictly belong in an ends statement. For instance, if the board has allowed any means to show up in the global statement, it might now be misled into defining methods instead of results, recipients, and costs.

Here is what my hypothetical NCCCC board of directors produced after considering these finer distinctions (see the accompanying box). Remember that whatever the board has not further defined, the CEO is authorized to decide as long as his or her choice can be shown to be a reasonable interpretation of the broader element defined by the board.

There were many heated arguments before this policy was completed. One argument was about whether member skills should be self-supporting (costs covered by fees beyond dues) or a benefit of the dues-funded general fund. As you can see, the vote determined that while member skills are to be a product of NCCCC, they are not to impose a net cost on the organization. Item I.A.2 caused quite a stir because a few board members adamantly opposed stopping with "more constraining than is nec-

Ends Policies for NCCCC

The National Council of Car Care Companies exists for this purpose: Conditions favorable for member success for dues no greater than in comparable associations.

I. The emphasis on conditions for success will be on environmental factors, but with a minor focus on member skills, at a cost to the association of no more than 65 percent of all resources.

   A. Favorable regulatory conditions.

      1. The schedule of implementing regulations will not be punitive in its severity or speed.

      2. Regulations imposed on members will be no more constraining than is necessary to produce the intended environmental protection goals.

      3. Federal regulations impinging on the operation of car care companies will take precedence over state and local regulations.

   B. Favorable public image of car care companies, at a cost to the association of no more than $1.5 million per annum.

      1. The driving public considers car care companies to be friendly, careful, and competent.

      2. The driving public considers car care companies to be more trustworthy than competitive alternatives.

   C. Skilled members.

      1. Members new to the business willing to pay the full cost of skill upgrading will have adequate basic business skills for market survival and profitability.

      2. All members willing to pay the full cost of skill upgrading will have advanced technology skills and knowledge about materials and equipment.

II. Costs to members for the association's results will be comparable to dues and user fees common to other trade associations in other states.

   A. Except for the costs of skill enhancement, costs will be borne by the general dues base.

   B. Costs of skill enhancement will be borne by users and will be competitive with private providers of similar skills.

essary." They wanted to go into more detail so that the board would define this element further. But the largest debate centered on whether producing a favorable public image is worth $1.5 million when a greater share of resources should be (in the opinion of some) left available to bringing about favorable legislation and regulations.

In this ends policy, the board has obviously chosen to define some elements and leave others, at a rather high level, to the CEO. For example, the board has specified cost or relative priority in some instances and not in others. The CEO's first task is to interpret further just as the board would have had to do, knowing that he or she will be called upon later to defend the reasonableness of interpretations. Subsequent monitoring of CEO performance will thus illuminate both the CEO's interpretations and performance about those interpretations. Meanwhile, the board can periodically consider extending its policymaking into more detail or amending it in response to environmental changes or shifts in member values. Ends work never ends.

A Public School Board Establishes Ends Policies

BOARD LEADERSHIP, NUMBER 32, JULY-AUG. 1997

THIS ARTICLE is the second in a series of four, each examining ends development for a different kind of organization. Remember that ends policies are those in which the board describes the intended results of the organization, for whom those results are to be achieved, and the cost or relative worth of those results. In the preceding article, I used a trade association as an example. In this article, I'll discuss ends of an organization important to everyone—the public school system.

Public school boards face the same governance challenge all other governing bodies face. But several aspects of their situation set them apart from most boards: First, school boards are elected and, therefore, are highly visible; everything they do is open to scrutiny by persons unschooled in governance. Second, school boards are highly regulated by law with scant recognition of modern management, much less modern governance. Third, school boards engage in a business of high emotional significance—the education of our children—with all the highly charged constituencies that implies. Fourth, school boards govern an undertaking in which everyone considers himself or herself an expert; after all, we all went to school. Fifth, school boards use a lot of taxpayers' money; at local and state or provincial levels, education is a major part of the public budget.

Despite these significant distinctions, however, the core of governance is the same. School boards exist on behalf of a definable jurisdiction (of parents and nonparents alike) to see to it that the public schools achieve what they should and avoid situations and activities that are unacceptable. The "achieve what they should" part is, of course, the central focus of ends policies. What should the schools achieve? What difference should they make? In short, what are they for?

> Where would a school board begin development of its ends policies? Just as in all other policy development—at the top.

The rules of Policy Governance preclude addressing questions about what schools do, that is, what activities they are engaged in or what methods they use. The questions must be answered in terms of the results to be attained in the lives of defined populations of students for some defined cost or with defined relative priorities. Crafting answers to these questions is extremely hard work, the hard work public officials take on as their sworn assignment. Not only are the answers hard to develop, even the framing of the issues is difficult. Consequently, ten school boards that have precisely the same values, if such a thing were possible, could come up with ten ways of expressing those values. The example I give in this article will undoubtedly be quite different from ones my readers would produce, even if all their work was carefully consistent with Policy Governance principles.

So where would a school board begin development of its ends policies? Just as it does in all other policy development, it should begin at the top. It starts with the mega-ends statement, the one that embraces in broad language what the school system is to achieve, for whom, and at what cost. When most groups set out to do this, they invariably find themselves describing methods (means) or subsidiary ends (rather than the overarching ones). That is to be expected, but at this stage the board must discipline itself to avoid defining these elements and return its focus to ends policies. Let's see what a typical school board might go through.

The West York School Board finds it hard to avoid the tendency to address what the schools will be doing. For example, it begins the process by focusing on "teaching," "educating," or "preparing" students. As attractive as these ideas are, they describe what the schools will be doing rather than what ultimate impact the schools will have on students. Proper ends language is never about an organization, its activities, or its competencies but about its intended effects in the lives of consumers. The West York board found that it helps to ask "why" whenever it slips into describing activities. This technique does not always work, but often it leads the board to the effects it associates with some activity.

Thus, "to provide a quality education" is discarded, as is "to become the most effective education system in our region." Neither describes what results, which recipients, or what cost. Much like other school boards dealing with the results component of ends, West York gravitates toward a statement that sums up what it wants to be true for students as they encounter their post-schooling world. At one point in their discussion, "A successful life" is considered. But it is thrown out, since the board doesn't think it can be responsible for students' success, only for providing them with the competencies for success.

Although the "which recipients" component of ends will become harder when the board later deals with gifted, mainstream, disabled, and other groupings of children, at the mega-ends level the West York board thinks that "children of West York" will be sufficiently descriptive.

The "at what cost" component of ends is also confusing at first. On the one hand, the board wants all results to be obtained at a reasonable cost. At the broadest level of consideration, the cost per result should be in the ballpark of what other systems would require to produce the same results. In other words, the board, at first blush, is willing to accept a market rate of efficiency, even though it plans to become more discriminating about the matter in the future. The West York board does not want its standard of comparison forever tied to others' inefficiencies.

> Proper ends language is never about an organization, its activities, or its competencies but about its intended effects in the lives of consumers.

On the other hand, there is another element of cost that concerns the board. The board knows that the public will not accept an unlimited tax burden, no matter how efficient the system. That is, even if a school system is producing greater results per dollar than any other in history, citizens still will be willing to assign the schools only a certain proportion of their income. So in the case of a public organization, cost must be capped. Again, the West York board chooses to state a broad value at this point rather than set a specific tax rate or tax receipts total. Certainly the value the board determines here will be the basis for whatever tax burden is chosen year by year.

Consequently, after much debate, the West York School Board settles on the following statement as its most encompassing ends policy: *The children of West York will attain competencies for a successful life at a reasonable cost, including a tax burden no greater than in comparable communities.*

Notice that the West York ends policy speaks directly to the trade-off between cost and benefit to which the board commits the system. Now it must decide whether this broad statement will be further defined by the superintendent or whether the board itself will now proceed into greater detail, one level at a time. I've never known a school board to stop at this mega level and, if I were a school board member, I would want to go further, too. Yet let me not disparage the power of this simple ends statement standing alone with no further board elucidation. Most citizens would be ecstatic if they could be sure that their public schools would, in fact, fulfill a reasonable interpretation—*any* reasonable interpretation—of these broad terms.

> **FAQ** ➡️
>
> Does the level of detail developed in ends policies determine their value and power?

As it goes into more detail, the West York board must continually remind itself that the power of governance lies not in detailed definition of organizational aims but in a board's meaning unequivocally what it says about its broadly stated expectations. Specificity of content cannot substitute for integrity of process. Anything the board says about ends after the initial, mega-ends statement is of less consequence than an unwavering insistence that management produce. Rigorous accountability for broadly defined output beats slack accountability for highly defined output.

The West York board chooses to go into the next level of ends detail and even to add greater specificity to some of the second-level statements that emerge. The accompanying box illustrates what the West York board produced. The board struggled for a while with whether it should go into the most detail possible, perhaps using a professionally defined educational taxonomy. But the board wisely decided that its job is to be a responsible purchasing agent for the people of West York, not to rival educational researchers in the ability to break the educational product into its tiniest constituent pieces.

Rigorous accountability for broadly defined output beats slack accountability for highly defined output.

At each level of policymaking, the consideration of whether to add more detail engages the board in four kinds of arguments:

1. *Should we go into more detail at all?* For example, after the board decided on I.D (see box), there was substantial disagreement whether to add the subordinate level, items I.D.1 through I.D.4. About half the board members were quite content to leave the matter to the superintendent, as long, of course, as the superintendent would stay within the range of reasonable interpretation for I.D.

2. *How is it best to frame the next level's content?* The board had some difficulty coming up with the breakdown of "knowledge and ability for living in a multicultural, high-tech society" represented by I.A through I.D. There were other ways to organize its intentions about knowledge and ability. How to structure the issue of variable costs for variable students also presented great difficulty (III.A through III.D).

The West York School Board's Ends Policies

The children of West York will attain competencies for a successful life at a reasonable cost, including a tax burden no greater than in comparable communities.

I. Students will have the knowledge and ability for living in a multicultural, high-tech society at or above age-level expectations.

   A. Students will have the cognitive tools necessary for acquiring and using information. Priority assigned to this result is 35 percent.

      1. Literacy skills.

      2. Numeracy skills.

      3. Skills to find resources.

      4. Computer skills.

      5. Analysis, problem-solving, and decision-making skills.

   B. Students will have a core of social-political-scientific knowledge necessary to thrive in modern society at or above age level expectations. Priority assigned to this result is 25 percent.

      1. Understanding of life sciences.

      2. Understanding of geography and earth systems.

      3. Understanding of civic structure and process.

      4. Understanding of multicultural domestic and international societies.

      5. Understanding of literature.

   C. Students will have skills in social interaction and group participation at or above age-level expectations. Priority assigned to this result is 20 percent.

      1. Skills to both compete and cooperate as appropriate.

      2. Skills to make decisions in groups.

      3. Skills to seek and engage in employment.

      4. Skills to comfortably and respectfully participate in a diverse society.

      5. Skills to interact socially in polite society.

(Continued)

D. Students will have the ability to make value choices. Priority assigned to this result is 20 percent.

1. Understanding of the roles values play in perception and behavior.

2. Strong personal framework of values.

3. Ability to evaluate consequences of personal choices.

4. Moral courage and ability to stand up for beliefs.

II. Students will be all children between the ages of 5 and 18 who live in West York and young adults for whom tuition costs are recovered, without regard to gender, race, religion, or physical ability.

III. Costs to achieve the results for the heterogeneous range of students will be no more than $_____ average student cost, but no more in total than $_____.

A. Gifted children will achieve advanced results, but for no more on average than 200 percent of the average student cost.

B. Developmentally disabled students will achieve ability-appropriate results, but for no more on average than 300 percent of the average student cost.

C. Physically disadvantaged students will achieve ability-appropriate results, but for no more on average than 300 percent of the average student cost.

D. Behaviorally disordered students will achieve ability-appropriate results, but for no more on average than 300 percent of the average student cost.

3. *What shall we say about these subsidiary matters?* Now that the argument is settled about going into more detail and the tricky framing is decided, the central content question is encountered. Board members have widely different values. Is it appropriate, for example, for a gifted child to get from the public purse twice what a "normal" child gets (see III.A)? Isn't it better to cultivate the brightest of the bright? Or isn't it better to give more resources to children with greater need? After all, gifted children will achieve a great deal on their own.

4. *How much information do we need, and from what sources?*
There will never be perfect information—neither perfectly thorough, perfectly authoritative, perfectly objective, perfectly irrefutable, nor perfectly affordable. Profound choices must be made with defective, incomplete, dubious, subjective, expensive information. How much is enough?

> **← FAQ**
>
> How much information does a board need to develop effective ends policies?

To develop these statements, the West York board juggled various sources of input, the most prominent ones being citizens in general and the school staff. School staff helped the board understand what is possible and what costs are associated with various results or with various groupings of students. Citizen input helped the board learn what the community wants from its schools. There was a great deal of board deliberation and exercise of judgment, however, since such a broad range of input contains conflicting viewpoints. West York also calls upon the associations of which it is a member for help in finding out what has been achieved in other school systems. It even uses an occasional futurist or experts in other fields to help it see the future to which its vision must apply.

The board need not restrict itself to the policy levels shown in the box, of course. It may continue further, going into far more detail than this. It may do so for some parts of the outline and not for others. Remember that it isn't the level of ends detail that provides the striking power of governing in this way, but the fact that the board requires (the CEO's job is on the line) that a reasonable interpretation of these ends actually comes true. More than for most organizations one can imagine, the ends of school systems have the power to change the world.

A City Council Creates Ends Policies

Board Leadership, Number 33, Sept.-Oct. 1997

NOWHERE is governance reform more needed than in government. In this article, I continue with the third of my four-part series on creating ends policies—those policies established by the board that describe the results to be achieved by the organization, who is to receive the results, and the costs of these results. This time we will focus on the ends of municipal government. Let us examine the case of a city council with a mayor who operates chiefly as the chairperson and a city manager who is the CEO.

> **FAQ** ➡
>
> What do elected boards have in common?

City council members will point out that governing a city is quite different from governing a hospital, trade association, or social service agency. They are right, of course, though I do not believe the differences are as fundamental as they think. Let's review some of the differences. First, in common with school boards, which were the subject of my previous ends article, city councils are elected by the general population. As elected officials, they are vulnerable to the whims, short memories, and expectations of the rest of us—the electorate. To cover that vulnerability, elected officials frequently adopt a number of behaviors that curiously we both demand of them and excoriate them for (pontification, simplistic solutions, and demagoguery). These behaviors, though they may be understandable, undermine effective governance. Second, city councils are themselves governed by higher governmental prescriptions about how they must operate, prescriptions that are antiquated and antithetical to good governance. Third, city councils have authority that goes beyond the right to govern their own employees; They have a portion of the state's *police power*, that is, the right to govern the rest of us as well. This power lies in their authority to enact law (called ordinances in the United States, bylaws in Canada, and byelaws in the United Kingdom).

Nevertheless, when we get right down to the essentials, it is the city council's job, on behalf of a city population, to see to it that municipal government achieves what it should and avoids what is unacceptable—the same as any other governing board. City councils do not erect stop signs, pave roads, process building permits, put out house fires, or mow the park lawn. Their staffs do those things, ostensibly in such a way that citizens get the governmental "products" or outputs that they want, for an acceptable burden of taxes, user fees, and losses of freedom (the costs of the city's results). To best represent the interests of owners (city residents), how can a city council best use its time, best focus its discussions, best discipline its process, and best frame its decisions?

Policy Governance speaks to all those issues, of course, and in this article I want to delve a bit into how a city council might establish the ends of city government. (The ends not only instruct staff but form the point of departure for the council's subsequent creation of law. Laws force the environment to align with the vision for that environment.) So let's look at the city council's most engaging task, that of deciding ends, a task in which the council acts as purchasing agent for the public. In that endeavor, the council will describe (1) what amount of citizen cost should yield (2) what amount of results (3) for whom.

What is the broadest way the council can state the ends of city government that is still instructive and useful? To use shorthand, I will refer to this mission-level, encompassing ends policy as the *mega-ends* statement. Normally, a council entering this process will err repeatedly by falling into the age-old trap of focusing on activities instead of results. The city council of Burton began with

← FAQ
How should a board word its mega-ends policies?

a number of such missteps but had the tenacity to keep bringing itself back to the rigor of a true ends dialogue. For example, "To provide city services" was one of the opening missteps. There are no results stated; the city exists to aim its busyness (called services) at people. Services are not results; they are organized arrangements of staff activities. Services exist in order to improve citizens' lives. But in what ways are citizens' lives to be better? Specifying these is the central challenge of ends policies.

Similarly, the Burton Council considered and discarded "to protect and to serve," "to operate a world class city government," and "to minimize taxpayer burden" as potential mega-ends statements. None of these describes the results for which city government is created. After a tedious struggle, the council agreed on wording that covered all three elements of ends (results, recipients, cost): *The City of Burton exists so that residents and visitors in the municipal area have the essentials of pleasant civic life at a reasonable burden of monetary and personal costs.*

In the process of coming up with this wording , council members argued mainly about "residents and visitors," "pleasant," "civic life," and the "monetary and personal" wording. As to the "for whom" component of ends, there was debate about including visitors as a part of the designation. "After all," some councilors argued, "the city exists for its residents, not for others. To the extent that visitors benefit, that is merely a collateral effect—nice, but we wouldn't create city government for that effect." Others disagreed and won the vote, as did those who felt "residents" rather than "citizens" was the proper word.

The city council ultimately chose to state the mega-result of city government as "pleasant civic life," but "pleasant" and "civic" were arrived at only after lengthy consideration. City councils are concerned about safety, welfare, and other outputs of city government, and Burton officials finally agreed that pleasant life encompassed all such specific outputs. But councilors were unwilling to address city government to all aspects of pleasant life. For instance, individual wealth, family cohesiveness, and occupational success were not intended. So the council hit upon the modifier "civic" to narrow the scope of pleasant life. Similarly, "monetary and personal" were chosen in order to recognize that the cost of city government is not just taxation and other dollar-denominated burdens, but the restriction of individual freedom.

The resulting mega-ends statement forms the starting point for all further development of ends policies. So let's see where the Burton officials went from there. As

---

City of Burton's Ends

The City of Burton exists so that residents and visitors in the municipal area have the essentials of pleasant civic life at a reasonable burden of monetary and personal costs.

I.   The city will be a safe, orderly, attractive environment in which to conduct commerce and to enjoy personal and interpersonal life.

    A.   Persons are reasonably free from jeopardy to body and property.

1. Crimes against persons and property will be such that persons can enjoy outdoor activity without fear; safety in their homes; rights to maintain and use their property without fear of loss

2. Fire loss rate will qualify as AAA insurance risk

3. Human injury from animals is negligible

4. Flood damage probability will qualify for lowest insurance rates

5. No jeopardy from water run-off damage for other than hundred-year flood conditions

B. Environment is free from pollutants and refuse build-up.

    1. No visible accumulation of trash or garbage

    2. No toxic leakage or disposal

C. Persons can move into, out of, and within Burton safely and efficiently.

    1. Minimal intrusiveness with traffic flow consistent with safety

    2. Clearly marked egress, ingress, and through traffic

    3. Maximum safety for pedestrian and bicycle traffic

D. Public spaces will be clean and inviting.

    1. No abandoned buildings except as necessary to observe due process

    2. City and neighborhood entrances clearly and attractively demarcated

    3. Vegetation is in a controlled condition

    4. No visible junked and abandoned vehicles except as necessary to observe due process

II. Combined cost to citizens and visitors of taxes, user fees, and other impositions will be no greater than that of comparable municipalities providing essentially similar benefits.

A. Where user fees are levied, they will not be set above total, all-inclusive cost.

B. For 19xx and 19xy, property tax rate will be $0.60 per $100 valuation.

III. City benefits are intended primarily for residents and, where any priority-setting is applicable, secondarily for visitors.

was the case in previous articles in this series, the difficulty of "framing" further ends work comes up at this point. The accompanying box illustrates what came out of months of work listening to citizens, considering staff input, and gathering information from other cities (some through Burton's membership in the league of cities).

Many of the issues that seem settled by the council's eventual ends language are still hot topics among residents in Burton. Environmental groups want a greater priority to be given to sources of possible toxicity, while a number of influential civic groups want even higher levels of personal safety. Some think the city should take on challenges now being handled by the economic development commission (a separate organization in Burton) by adopting ends related to "diverse economic base" or "countercyclical business mix." Because water is provided by a separate authority, the council did not have to consider "potable water" as one of its results. In the same way, because the library is a separate organization in Burton, "cultural information base" or other values-added of a library system were not included.

Like the West York School Board cited in the previous chapter, the Burton City Council felt uncomfortable in saying (in section II) that the cost of city outputs is to be "no greater than that of comparable municipalities providing essentially similar benefits." In other words, do about as well as others. Rather than shooting to do better than others, this language ties Burton's cost-benefit to that achieved in other cities. The council intends to update this statement within the next year after further study of how to require either more achievement or lower cost.

Last in a Series of Articles on How Different Kinds of Organizations Define the Difference They Want to Make

A Hospital Board Creates Ends Policies

BOARD LEADERSHIP, NUMBER 34, NOV.-DEC. 1997

HOSPITALS literally hold the power of life and death over most of us at some point in our lives. The boards that govern these complex organizations, particularly in the United States and Canada, face staggering fiscal, political, and liability issues. In this fourth—and last—installment in a series on the development of ends policies, I illustrate the daunting task of creating ends policies as the board of a nonprofit hospital in a mid-size community might approach it.

Let's begin by recognizing the special circumstances under which the Mel P. Ractice Hospital board functions. First, the lead players in the treatment of trauma and disease are physicians. The physicians who admit patients to Mel P. Ractice are private practitioners who do not work for the hospital. In this community, there is no other hospital, so doctors have little choice about which hospital to affiliate with. Second, physicians with privilege to practice form a "medical staff organization" that wields considerable political and technical power. Third, since the hospital is in a mid-sized community and is a major employer there, its internal workings are known widely.

Still, a hospital is just like every other organization in the world: It exists for a definable purpose. There are options about just what that purpose is, and the board is accountable for the choice of options. Some hospitals are well prepared to help patients survive extensive burns or inoperable cancer; others are not. Some are capable of dealing effectively with extensive neonatal abnormalities or psychiatric disturbances; some are not. Some have greater abilities than others do to treat life-threatening physical trauma. Indeed, hospitals do differ in the types of medical results to which they are attuned and in the populations they are best adapted to serve. Some accept a broader mission to affect community health. In other words, in the terms of Policy Governance, their ends are different.

Remember that in this article I am concerned only with the creation of ends policies, not with means, such as organizational design, pension plans, insurance protection, and treatment methods. Ends policies delineate what results are to be obtained for which persons (or populations) and at what cost. Ultimately this formula requires that the priority of one result is assessed in relation to the priority of other possible results. For example, the available resources might enable a focus on pregnant women (obstetrics) or on the mentally ill (psychiatry) but not on both, so setting a relative priority about these recipient groups cannot be avoided.

> A hospital is just like every other organization in the world: It exists for a definable purpose.

As the Mel P. Ractice Hospital board began the ends process, it started with the broadest question: Why do we want a hospital? This question is never as easy as it seems. The answers that so readily come to mind are descriptions of well-intended activities rather than of consumer results. The ends question, however, is not "what should the hospital be engaged in?" but "what should be different in consumers' lives?"

After much discussion characterized by the struggle between focusing on pathology versus focusing on health, the board chose a middle path. It determined that the hospital exists so that *residents and visitors in the community are healthy and endure minimal hardship from disease or physical trauma.* Further, the board decided the "production" of results should be *at an industry norm efficiency,* but should in no event use more tax money annually than $2.5 million. Cost or worth in this case is stated in terms of both efficiency (the quantity of results for the money expended) and maximum public burden (a cap on actual tax dollars, whatever the efficiency). So the board's statement summed up the results, the intended recipients, and the worth.

As in any organization, the board has the right to stop at this point, letting the CEO make any reasonable interpretation of this broad language as he or she makes further determinations about hospital ends. But the board felt compelled to go into further detail, and this required that they gather additional information.

First, the board needed to know the health needs of its community. The need for geriatrics and obstetrics, for example, is dictated largely by demographics. Certain job-related injuries are more prevalent in one industry than in another, so the predominant types of local employment must be assessed.

Second, the board had to take into account the other health care resources available to community members. Although Mel P. Ractice is the only local hospital, there are clinics and independent providers that address part of the total need. There are also hospitals in other communities nearby.

Third, the profile of physician specialties in the community had to be determined: The medical results achievable depends in part on the specialists available. Orthopedics will be difficult without orthopedists.

Fourth, the board had to consider the physical plant itself, since facilities support some specialties better than others, and hard choices often need to be made between competing uses for space.

Limiting factors (particularly the available specialists and physical space) are only limiting in the short run. In the long run, it is possible that they can be overcome. But there will most likely be a cost that the board cannot ignore. Adding another result—say, death with dignity and comfort—might require additional space for a hospice, which, available within three years, could cost $1.2 million, not including operating costs. Attracting an orthopedist to the community (a necessary means if certain extensive bone diseases are to be treated) might cost the hospital a fair amount for the search and for enticements.

After much debate, including input from community members, local physicians, political leaders, the state hospital association, and the CEO, the board finally decided that the greatest long-term good is having a community able to take care of its own health. This was not an easy decision, for the advocates (and the reasoning) for prioritizing the alleviation of pathology are strong. The hospital would not forsake tradition, however. Relief from acute conditions and trauma would continue to be an important "product," such that at least 80 percent of these needs would be taken care of.

The "production" of new knowledge and skilled medical students are not mentioned in the board's work, but not because they were forgotten. This board made a conscious decision not to be a research or teaching hospital, just as it decided not to take on hospice responsibility. Similarly, it did not add language that would have committed it to respite for the elderly.

Interestingly, this board felt that the cost of relief for patients is composed not only of tax costs and direct charges for service but also includes the inconvenience and hardship patients suffer in the course of treatment. The board felt more strongly than most, perhaps, that taking patients out of normal circulation longer than necessary or risking their exposure to hospital-based infections were costs that had to be factored in quite as much as actual fees. Could the board have covered its concerns about this matter in executive limitations (no more than x percent death rate in 30 days following surgery, no more than y percent wound infection after operations, and so

Mel P. Ractice Hospital Ends

The Mel P. Ractice Hospital exists so that residents and visitors in the ABC community are healthy and endure minimal hardship from disease and physical trauma at an industry norm efficiency, but for no more community subsidy than $2.5 million annually.

I. Residents will have the skills and knowledge for successful management of their own health

    A. Knowledge of educational and caregiving resources

    B. Knowledge and skills enabling self-care for chronic conditions and post-treatment care of family members

    C. Knowledge about lifestyle, diet, disease prevention, and risk avoidance

        1. Teens will know the health risks of smoking

        2. Pregnant women will be aware of risks of smoking and alcohol

        3. People will know the risks of fatty foods and lack of exercise

        4. Teens and adults will know the risks of unprotected sex

        5. Drivers will know the risks of varying levels of alcohol consumption

II. Residents and visitors will have relief from acute conditions and physical trauma

    A. Highest priority will be given to life-threatening conditions

    B. Persons with acute psychiatric conditions are not included until 1999

    C. Except for immediate stability of trauma, patients with extensive burns are not included until 2002

    D. No more than 20 percent of all acute needs will go unmet

    E. In the case of needs not met, persons in need will be comfortably, safely in care elsewhere or armed with knowledge of appropriate resources as applicable

III. The cost to patients in hardship and inconvenience will be humane and minimal

    A. Minimal pain, dislocation, and time away from work and family

    B. Negligible iatrogenic impairment or disease or other damage

---

C. Monetary costs will compare favorably to hospitals similarly situated

IV. Funds from local, direct grant governmental sources will be no more than $2.5 million, but there is no limit on other sources of funds, such as those from donations, governmentally controlled fees-for-service, or from sales of goods and services

---

forth)? Yes, it could have, but it made a rational case for dealing with the direct costs of results in its ends policies.

As the box shows, the board went into disproportionate detail in the matter of prevention information (section I.C). I draw attention to the extra detail here not to argue for lopsided attention to a single segment but to underscore the fact that the board has the right to elaborate to the degree it chooses. Remember that Policy Governance does not dictate how much detail is "right" or even that the degree of detail must be uniform. It dictates only that the board must be able to accept any reasonable interpretation of the wording used in its chosen level of specificity.

> **← FAQ**
>
> Is it important for the level of detail in every ends policy to be consistent?

Clearly, most hospital boards will not choose to dictate in great detail which kinds of illness to focus on—or which persons or populations should benefit from this focus. But all hospital boards choose to control these issues to some degree, particularly since resources are limited.

As you read the board's policy, keep in mind that (1) the board can and probably will extend the policy in the future, and (2) it only prescribes as much in terms of results, recipients, and costs as it wishes—

> Policy Governance does not dictate how much detail is "right" or even that the degree of detail must be uniform.

the CEO and thence the institution can make all further decisions about ends as well as virtually all decisions about treatment and other means. The preferences of medical professionals, educators, and managers matter a great deal, of course, but the board should not allow the ends of a public institution to be determined solely by the current caregivers. A simple, compellingly logical, minimally intrusive method of control is necessary for the board to properly exercise its owner-representative authority.

Chapter Six

Safely Avoiding Micromanagement

Staff Freedom Within Defined Limits

Organizational achievement requires rigorous expectations as well as optimal latitude for managerial choices. This is enabled in Policy Governance by the board's staying out of management's *means* except to put boundaries around them, that is, by defining limits of acceptability. As a succinct and powerful substitute for prescribing managerial means, the board avoids micromanagement by saying clearly what it will not put up with. Although verbally negative, this proscriptive approach is psychologically positive, empowering, and conducive to managerial creativity and innovation.

Free Your Board and Staff Through Executive Limitations

BOARD LEADERSHIP, NUMBER 4, NOV.-DEC. 1992

W̵HILE YOUR BOARD should focus on strategic leadership, it still must claim a legitimate stake in the operational details of the organization. In this article, I present a powerful yet simple two-part strategy that can help you balance these concerns. The solution isn't difficult, but it may require a fundamental shift in the way you conceive your board's relationship to staff practices.

How does your board stay free of "administrivia"? Is it even possible to without rubber-stamping everything? If the board assigns operational matters to committees, how does it avoid becoming a set of miniboards, each isolated within a specific topic? Yet if it doesn't review everything, how will it know if things start getting out of hand?

Your board's most important role, of course, is to be keeper of the vision. In my view, fostering that vision translates primarily into determining your organization's *ends*—what benefits to produce, for which people, and at what cost—in other

> Your board's most important role is to be keeper of the vision.

words, what difference your organization is to make in the world. Above all, your board is accountable for defining and, ultimately, achieving its ends.

But a board has reason to worry about other factors, even if its ends are in perfect order. A counseling center, for example, can do well with clients yet handle its finances improperly. A hospital can successfully remediate trauma and disease but have slipshod collection practices. These deficiencies are not about ends, but they *can* be embarrassing or even deadly to the organization.

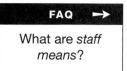

Quite apart from ends, then, your board is also accountable for *the way the organization conducts itself.* I call the organization's conduct, activities, methods, and practices its *means,* to distinguish them from its ends.

If your board tries to keep up with all the means that could go wrong, it risks miring itself in details and interfering severely with staff operations. Board service, instead of being the enriching experience of resolving important ends issues, becomes a never-ending, exhausting entanglement in operational matters, even trivia. Moreover, a "meddling" board will hamper the staff's creativity.

Thankfully, there is an easy way out of the dilemma, a way to exercise appropriate control without meddling, a way to withdraw safely from minutiae. Here is my two-step recommendation:

1. Resist the temptation to prescribe staff means. In other words, *the board does not tell staff how to do its job.*

2. Tell your CEO, in writing, which staff means would be unacceptable, unapprovable, or off-limits. In other words, *the board says what kind of means it will not put up with.*

Don't Tell Your Staff What to Do

FAQ ➡

Should a board ever determine or approve staff means?

Board members are invariably tempted to *prescribe* staff means. The reasons vary: Board members may be more expert than anyone on staff; they may want to help because of understaffing; they may even be drawn in because of a staff that is afraid to make decisions. Similarly, requiring a staff to run the traditional gauntlet of *board approval* (approval is almost always of staff means) creates the same effect as prescribing in that only the approved means can then be used. As to the rich variety among possible means, if the board has not said yes, the staff assumption will be no.

Why should boards resist prescribing—even retaining approval authority over—staff means? If the board determines means as well as ends, it not only makes its own job more difficult but also reduces the CEO's accountability for results. The board's job is harder because members must weigh and coordinate staff alternatives, which it is paying staff to figure out! (Most of the tedious, laborious effort of boards in contemporary governance arises from this kind of work.) The CEO is less accountable, for he or she has less freedom to find a successful path to the board-determined ends. After all, if the board tells the staff how to do its job, whose responsibility is it if the prescribed methods don't work?

If the board determines means as well as ends, it not only makes its own job more difficult but also reduces the CEO's accountability for results.

Do Tell Your Staff What *Not* to Do

Think of your board's involvement with staff means as a *boundary-setting* endeavor, not a prescriptive one. For example, you would not decide which group insurance to purchase or how to arrange vacation accrual. You might decide, however, that fringe benefits that are substantially more (or less) than comparable organizations' are unacceptable.

As the board establishes limits, two principles become very important: First, the policies must cover all unacceptable actions and situations, not just a smattering of them. Second, the board must state these prohibitions in enough detail so that *any reasonable interpretation* of the board's words will suffice—not a special interpretation that the board meant but didn't say.

Beginning with broad prohibitions and advancing thoughtfully toward more detailed ones protects the board against its own imperfection. If your board *forgets* to prohibit some more detailed behavior, the broader statement acts as a safety net. For example, assume that the board has stated a broad prohibition against leaving assets unprotected and unnecessarily risked. If the board then overlooked stating a proscription against insuring below 80 percent replacement cost, the CEO would still have to justify her insurance levels under the broader policy language.

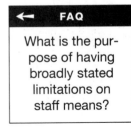

FAQ

What is the purpose of having broadly stated limitations on staff means?

The resulting executive limitations policies, in whatever detail the board chooses, are written as *negatively stated* declarations. For some board members, the negative language will be offensive; after all, we all want to be positive people. It helps to recognize that even though the phrasing is negative, *the psychological effect on staff is surprisingly positive.* For as long as the staff operates within its limitations, the board can confidently guarantee to support anything it does.

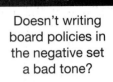

FAQ

Doesn't writing board policies in the negative set a bad tone?

Boards create executive limitations policies for areas of staff activity that could pose a threat to prudence and ethics in organizational life. These threats—and consequently,

> As long as the staff operates within its limitations, the board can confidently guarantee to support anything it does.

the policy topics—are relatively common across different organizations. They can be addressed succinctly, frequently in fewer than a half dozen pages constituting only about a fourth of the board's policies. Typical executive limitations policies deal with financial health, treatment of staff, setting of staff compensation, level of board awareness, and asset protection. A board policy on information and executive counsel, for example, might begin with a broad statement like: "Information and advice to the board will have no significant gaps in either timeliness, completeness, or accuracy." A board policy on financial planning might begin: "Budgeting any fiscal year or the remaining part of any fiscal year shall not deviate materially from board *ends* priorities nor risk fiscal jeopardy."

Free Your Staff *and* Your Board

FAQ ➡️

Should the CEO ever ask individual board members for advice?

With well-drafted executive limitations policies, your CEO will feel more like a true chief executive officer, free to devise and continually improve the organization's means. That freedom includes the right to seek advice from anywhere or anyone the CEO or staff can get it, including from board members *acting as individuals*. The CEO is now free to delegate more powerfully, since the only authority that can be given away is authority he or she clearly has. Staff-to-board communication no longer resembles the childhood game of "May I?" for, as far as means are concerned, if the board has not said no, the answer is automatically yes.

Having viewed limitations at the broadest level first, the board can be confident that all unacceptable situations have been covered. It will have avoided the fiascoes that occur when a board has forgotten to prescribe just the right things. Moreover, compared with being prescriptive, stating the limits or the "don't" list requires less effort from the board, creates fewer rules and briefer documents, and better justifies holding the CEO accountable for results. For example, telling the CEO to avoid staff compensation that deviates from the market is far easier than constructing compensation schedules or even studying a staff recommendation enough to cast an informed approval vote. As an added bonus, limitations on means are far more stable than prescriptions of means, so there is less need for continual revision. What is most important, though, the board will have freed the majority of its time to concentrate vigorously on its special ends challenge: providing leadership in exploring, deliberating, and creating strategic vision.

Making Informed Fiscal Policy

BOARD LEADERSHIP, NUMBER 6, MAR.-APR. 1993

I WAS A GUEST at a hospital board meeting in a western United States city, there to talk with the board about governance for a brief educational session after its regular agenda.

Part of the regular agenda was board approval of the monthly financial report. A knowledgeable woman, Georgia, made an oral report supported by several pages of neatly ordered revenues and expenditures. The written report had been distributed in the evening's inch-thick board book. In short order the board dutifully approved the report and moved on to the next item of business.

> **← FAQ**
>
> Is it OK to let a financial expert on the board advise the board on whether to accept financial reports?

Since my remarks would touch briefly on fiscal governance, I asked the board what numbers mattered among the many numbers in the report. There was an embarrassed silence, for the question caught them by surprise. "But how do you know whether to approve?" I asked, as much to close off the silence as to challenge them.

They knew the answer to this one. "Georgia tells us." Georgia, it turned out, heads her own accounting firm and is uniquely qualified in her position as board treasurer. With the heat momentarily off the board, I asked Georgia what she looked for in the extensive fiscal report. She replied, as I would have guessed, that a handful of summarizing figures told her most of what she wanted to know. She would then judge those numbers against her experience to determine if the fiscal condition of the hospital was in acceptable shape.

> By rendering evaluations that were routinely accepted by the board, Georgia was determining board judgment and unilaterally setting de facto policy.

Each month, Georgia would meet with the chief executive, chief financial officer, and other management personnel for a couple of afternoon hours the day of the board meeting. She would examine the administration-prepared report at that time and ask whatever questions she deemed relevant. The managers did not know what indices she found critical and, of course, could not know what range of acceptability she allowed on each datum.

This scene is fairly typical. The board had created no fiscal expectations either for Georgia's or the CEO's use. By rendering evaluations that were routinely accepted by the board, Georgia was determining board judgment and, consequently, unilaterally setting de facto policy. That her policy was never stated aloud did not prevent it from having its effect, because as Georgia made her judgments she implicitly used the criteria that existed only in her mind.

I remarked that the chief executive was working for Georgia, not for the board, and by allowing that to happen, the board was defaulting on its responsibility both to the public and to the chief executive. The board was seduced by the comfort of sitting back and allowing Georgia to cover for its not carrying its responsibility.

I urged the board to get beyond its self-inflicted frailty and take charge of the matter. "But Georgia is the expert. Why should we reinvent the wheel? Why would it be any better for Georgia to tell us what the expectations should be, just so we as a board can then tell management?" Board members were comfortable having Georgia doing their job unsupervised. They seemed untroubled by their rubber-stamping of Georgia's fiscal expectations, which, in a hollow way, made her expectations into the board's expectations. But they seemed not to notice the simplest and most responsible solution.

FAQ ➡

How can a board effectively use individual expertise to develop policy?

The solution: Georgia *is* the expert . . . in accounting, in reading financial statements, in seeing through fiscal complexities, in knowing where to look for signs of stability and danger. But Georgia is *not* the expert with respect to the *values* a given body of people have about risk, brinkmanship, early pain and long-term gain, and so forth. Financial management in this instance is where these values are expressed, but *they are not accounting values, they are human values.*

And because they are human values, their genesis must be the governing board. The stonecutter knows much about cutting stone and laying stonework, but the stonecutter brings no special insight to the decision to build a hotel or a cathedral. Georgia can be of great help to her board without letting the board avoid responsibility. She can do so by helping the board to know what it needs to know about governing financial management.

So armed with the tools Georgia knows so well, the board can proceed to debate its values and translate them into the indices of financial management: liquidity, proportionality, ratios, and more. How can the board acquire these tools? Georgia could hold educational sessions for the board in which board members learn about the nature and types of fiscal jeopardy, what they look like in this particular kind of organization, and how they can be detected. She can show the board where judgments are to be made—for example, the degree of liquidity the board considers safe. The board thereby explores and commits its own values to paper, where they are visible to itself and to its chief executive.

Georgia's special talent will have been well utilized. The board will have fulfilled its responsibility to govern. And the experience will teach the board a valuable lesson about how to use any expert: the board will have used Georgia to inform the board's wisdom, not to substitute for it.

Running Afoul of Governance

BOARD LEADERSHIP, NUMBER 7, MAY-JUNE 1993

A MEMBER of a municipal park commission called me to discuss a disturbing development. The commission had been using Policy Governance for a few years, but she felt the philosophy was slipping in a very important respect.

FAQ →

Are executive limitations a set of minimal requirements?

In her opinion, staff members were treating executive limitations (those commission policies that limit the range of executive decisions) as a set of minimal requirements. She thought that they were hiding behind the policy criteria as a way to cover their backsides and felt that their interaction with the commission had deteriorated into a defensive claim to the effect that as long as they had not violated the executive limitations policies, they were OK.

My caller had thought of executive limitations policies as verbal "foul lines." I agreed wholeheartedly, delighted to be given a fresh analogy I wish I'd thought of myself! The foul line analogy is beautifully descriptive, because executive limitations policies are created to define the boundaries within which play must occur.

But foul lines are never the point of the game. When this commission and its staff allowed foul lines to become their focus of attention and dialogue, governance reverted to being about means rather than ends. Old habits die hard. Like all governing boards, this one in earlier years had focused most of its dialogue on staff decisions; previously, it would have been found dealing with the purchase of lawn and pool equipment, methods of muskrat control, and personnel issues. The current problem stemmed from a familiar governance trap: the error of placing an inordinate amount of commission inspection and discussion on *what the staff is doing.*

Its new governance framework had enabled the commission to avoid such entanglements by creating a set of executive limitations policies. These policies stated the limits on acceptable staff action in purchasing, personnel, insuring, and all other areas of staff practices. To its credit, this commission had worked hard to establish several ends policies and mission-related statements that embodied the commission's vision of what human needs are to be satisfied and the appropriate costs for doing so. Their ends policies dealt with organizational "products," such as civic attractiveness, safe and accessible open space, and other desired results and their relative priorities.

Moreover, the monitoring system was in place, routinely furnishing data that compared practice to policies. These data were frequently submitted and clear enough to assure the commission that the unacceptable conditions and actions detailed in their executive limitations policies were being avoided.

Ignoring Results

Unfortunately, the commission had come to invest far more time in checking staff performance on means than on ends. The dialogue between the commission and its staff, therefore, was predominantly on how well staff methods and practices met executive limitations policies, not on how well the methods and practices fulfilled the ends. Demonstrating avoidance of unacceptable means had become more important than demonstrating accomplishment of mission. The conclusion of administrators was that the commission was more interested in the way the staff *conducted* business than in the *results* of that business.

> The most ample and convincing proof that the foul lines had not been crossed hardly constitutes evidence of organizational success.

Successfully avoiding the conditions set forth in executive limitations policies could be seen as meeting a kind of minimum performance standard. Hence, the commission member who called me perceived that staff was continually justifying minimum performance more than it was going beyond to higher achievements. She was right; the most ample and convincing proof that the foul lines had not been crossed hardly constitutes evidence of organizational success.

FAQ →

How can a board keep executive limitations from becoming a policing function?

Policing, Not Leading

This commission had fallen into policing more than leading. It needed to reconvince itself that *excelling in the game is not about foul lines.* Only then can it convince its staff that the main concern is not about means. To be sure, foul lines are necessary, but only because they define the acceptable field of play. Even a superior job of not crossing the foul lines produces no score.

Foul lines are necessary, but only because they define the acceptable field of play. Even a superior job of not crossing the foul lines produces no score

I confirmed the commissioner's perception that foul lines did not constitute an end in themselves and offered her the following advice to take back to her commission. If it follows these guidelines, it should manage to regain its focus and practice the kind of leadership its community deserves.

- Don't criticize staff for appearing to get by on the minimum. In spite of my caller's perception, that is not really what was happening. The staff was merely reacting to the commission's emphasis. You get what you inspect.

- The commission must get back on track by putting ends concerns first. The commission had either not moved ahead with further clarification of its ends policies or failed to revisit them obsessively once they were established.

FAQ →

Should boards hear monitoring reports about executive limitations at meetings?

- Be certain to check the foul lines, but keep that checking in the background as much as possible. One way is to mail reports to board members, but give the reports no "air time" at board meetings unless a violation occurs.

In other words, don't allow the foul lines to become the game. There is a smallness of mind and spirit that comes from such a deterioration. Focus your agendas and the bulk of board-staff dialogue on those mind-stretching, profound ends issues that justify the organization's existence and shape its destiny.

Crafting Policy to Safeguard Your Organization's Actual Fiscal Condition

BOARD LEADERSHIP, NUMBER 6, MAR.-APR. 1993

As important as budgeting is, whether or not your organization sticks to its budget is relatively unimportant!

Look at it this way. Having a budget—even a very good one—does not demonstrate fiscal responsibility, does not say whether your programs are worth their cost, and does not show protection of your assets. A budget at its very best only shows that you intend these virtues to come true.

In fiscal matters, as elsewhere, the proof is in the pudding. In this case, the pudding is what accountants call "actual." Regardless of what you planned, are you actually putting your money where your mouth is? Regardless of what you planned, are your program effects actually worth what they cost? Regardless of what you planned, are you actually in a fiscally stable position?

In other words, *actual fiscal condition is what counts the most.* Budgeting, for all the prominence we give it, is only important in that it is a tool for getting to an acceptable actual. The condition of actual is the critical element, not the budget. It follows, then, that if the actual financial condition is acceptable, the departure from budget is not a large concern.

But what does an "acceptable" actual look like? How can you be sure you have it? Because actual is even more important than budget, your board's working out an answer to this question is arguably its most important work in being fiscally responsible.

Addressing "Actual"

First, let's recognize that the unending variety of arrangements in fiscal matters is one of those executive means I make much of. That is, the flow of resources and the timing and deployment of income and expenditures can all be done in countless ways. Moreover, they vary constantly because unforeseeable circumstances affect these matters every day. But while most variation is normal, some of the events and conditions wrought by fiscal management should trouble the board and a few should even be cause for panic.

In other words, fiscal conditions can and will vary a great deal, but some variations threaten the organization's fiscal stability. The board must identify these conditions of jeopardy and communicate to the CEO that they are unacceptable; that communication takes place through the language of a fiscal condition policy.

In creating such a policy, the board should follow the Policy Governance principle that the board stays out of staff means, except to say what it will not tolerate. The board, therefore, consigns fiscal management totally to the CEO without board interference as long as the CEO avoids conditions that the board would find unpalatable.

FAQ ➡
Why should the budget and "actual" fiscal condition be treated independently?

Now, what does this have to do with budget? Nothing directly. The budget, remember, is a plan. Insofar as the board is concerned with actual, the message is that the CEO is to avoid conditions of fiscal jeopardy quite apart from how good, bad, workable, or unworkable the budget was. The board is concerned about the integrity of fiscal planning, of course, as I point out in "Crafting Policy to Guide Your Organization's Budget" in this chapter. But the board's concern about actual fiscal condition is an independent concern.

Let me underscore the independence of your concern about actual and your concern about budget, because they are two separate concerns, each deserving your attention. Remember that the board's interest in budgeting is that the fiscal planning of the future is of sufficient integrity. The concern is not that budgeting of the past is good; old budgeting is no longer the issue. Consequently, the budget a board needs to worry about at any given time is the budget that starts from where the organization is and that safeguards the future.

The organization's actual fiscal condition can be poor, even though the integrity of budgeting from this point forward is of high quality. Just as easily, the reverse can be true. The actual condition can be fine, but the integrity of budgeting unacceptable. The only way these opposites are conceivable is that the acceptability of actual and the acceptability of budget are independent matters.

In other words, resolving concerns about your organization's budget will not resolve your concerns about its actual fiscal condition. Moreover, resolving your concerns about actual fiscal condition as the year progresses will not take care of your legitimate worries about the integrity of the only budgeting that then matters: the budgeting that starts from the present and extends to the end of the fiscal year. These are two separate issues best dealt with as two separate issues.

> The budget a board needs to worry about is the budget that starts from where the organization is and that safeguards the future.

So, completely apart from your worries about budget, what is your concern about your organization's ever-changing actual fiscal condition? What are the conditions of jeopardy that the board should warn the CEO away from? In short, what practices or situations in the ongoing fiscal management would not be OK? When the board has answered these questions, it will have produced a "financial condition policy." The board will not be busied with fiscal management—that is what it pays managers for—but it will be thoroughly engaged in *financial governance.*

> No organization exists to be fiscally well managed but to achieve ends the board prescribes.

Building a Financial Condition Policy

Financial condition is an issue of means, just as is budgeting. No organization exists to be fiscally well managed but to achieve ends the board prescribes. As the board sets out to control a staff means issue, it must follow the same rules as for any other executive limitations policy: It must speak in limiting rather than prescriptive language. It must go into no more detail than needed to establish wording within which the CEO can be allowed to use any reasonable interpretation.

The following conditions of fiscal jeopardy prohibited by boards' financial condition policy come up repeatedly as I work with boards. You will see most of them reflected in the financial condition policy developed by the board of Family Service Ontario (FSO), a federation of family service agencies located in Toronto (see box).

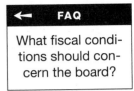

← FAQ

What fiscal conditions should concern the board?

1. *Revenue-expense balance.* As actual finances progress, most boards would be alarmed if actual disbursements exceed income. The board should be clear about the difference between cash and accrual accounting as it decides on this provision. The FSO policy is a very straightforward, cash-based version.

2. *Debt.* Part of the actual fiscal picture is the degree of indebtedness, whether through accounts payable, promises to pay in the future, or direct loans. A

Policy EL-4: Financial Condition

With respect to the actual, ongoing condition of the organization's financial health, the Executive Director may not cause or allow the development of fiscal jeopardy or loss of allocation integrity. Accordingly, he or she may not

1. Expend more funds than have been received in the fiscal year to date unless the debt guideline (below) is met.

2. Indebt the organization in an amount greater than can be repaid by certain, otherwise unencumbered revenues within 90 days.

3. Use any surplus.

4. Allow cash to drop below the amount needed to settle payroll and debts in a timely manner.

5. Allow tax payments or other government-ordered payments or filings to be overdue or inaccurately filed.

6. Allow actual allocations to deviate materially from board priorities in ends policies.

---

board might put all such debt off-limits (except for ordinary accounts payable) or it might say indebtedness is unacceptable beyond what can be repaid within a certain time period. FSO chose wording similar to the latter.

3. *Off-limits resources.* The board may wish the CEO to maintain acceptable fiscal health without resorting to the use of funds set aside for, say, long-term capital use. If so, this prohibition becomes one of the unacceptable conditions. The FSO board has obviously put all surplus off-limits to the chief executive.

4. *Liquidity.* The simplest and perhaps most powerful prohibition is undoubtedly, "Don't run out of money." Or better still, don't allow liquidity to drop to the point that we risk running out of money. A board might say that it is not acceptable to let the current ratio between relatively liquid assets and relatively short-term liabilities drop below, say, 1.5:1. Or the board might instruct that cash itself is not to fall below a certain figure. The board of FSO chose a simple statement of the relationship of cash to immediate obligations. Notice that the board chose the word *timely* because it was willing to let the chief executive use any reasonable interpretation of that word.

5. *Special financial obligations.* Because of the sensitive nature of governmental tax payments, many boards decide to create a policy provision specifically for this dangerous topic. For a given board, there might be other such touchy issues.

6. *Consistency with the board's ends policies.* It is not enough to keep the organization on its feet financially. The organization must be doing what it is intended to do with its expenditures, or else fiscal viability is a hollow virtue. Consequently, the board might decree that at no time will actual year-to-date disbursements depart from the board's ends priorities by more than some moderate proportion.

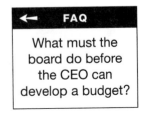

← FAQ

What must the board do before the CEO can develop a budget?

In other words, keep putting our money where our mouths are. This provision is perhaps the most important of all, but can make no sense if the board has not done its own job in creating ends policies.

Not until the board has defined the jeopardies it wants the CEO to avoid is it ready to make periodic reporting of actual financial condition both rigorous and simple. The financial reporting to which we have become accustomed is diluted with unneeded data, which makes financial reporting the quagmire it is for most board members. Only when a policy such as that adopted by Family Service Ontario is in place can the board receive monitoring assurance through simple comparison. (See "A Simple Matter of Comparison: Monitoring Fiscal Management in Your Organization" in Chapter Nine.)

*An Innovative Approach to Budgeting Allows Boards to Realize
Financial Accountability—and Exercise Better Leadership*

Crafting Policy to Guide Your Organization's Budget

BOARD LEADERSHIP, NUMBER 6, MAR.-APR. 1993

THE BUDGET is an important administrative tool. Its purpose is to lay out a plan of receipts and expenditures capable of fulfilling the mission while maintaining propriety in operations. All across North America, in nonprofit and public organizations alike, boards faithfully and diligently examine and bless their managements' recommended budgets. This tradition-honored practice, considered by most to exhibit the very essence of fiduciary responsibility, is referred to as "budget approval."

In this article, I want to demonstrate that the commonly accepted practice of budget approval does not deserve the homage we pay it. It is an unwarranted intrusion into management prerogatives and an unnecessary burden on board members. Budget approval has attained a sacrosanct position in the legalism of governance, but it does more to destroy than to demonstrate board leadership. Budget approval seduces boards away from their rightful charge, dilutes the few relevant budget issues with an abundance of unimportant ones, impairs the agility and effectiveness of management, permits boards to avoid clarifying dominant values, and confuses control over the tool with control over the product.

> **FAQ** ➡
>
> Why is budget approval a poor way to demonstrate fiduciary responsibility?

The solution is hidden in a generally unnoticed fact: What boards need to know about controlling managers' budgets is not the same as what managers need to know about budgeting. Hence the board must develop a *governance understanding* of bud-

get rather than a management understanding. But boards typically deal with
budgeting as if they were managers one
step removed. Guided by the conventional
wisdom, boards require management's
budgets to undergo detailed scrutiny of the
same sort as that in which managers themselves engage.

> Budget approval has attained a
> sacrosanct position in the legalism
> of governance, but it does more
> to destroy than to demonstrate
> board leadership.

To govern budgets rather than tinker with them, boards must determine just which
aspects of fiscal planning need controlling. They can then set out to control those
aspects proactively. These decisions would constitute budget policy that management
is obliged to follow.

As a first step in building a rational approach to the board's accountability for budgeting, let's take a look at budget approval from an unusual, but instructive, perspective.

Just What Is Approved in Budget Approval?

In the typical scenario, management brings a budget to its board for approval. The
board scrutinizes the numbers along with whatever justification is offered for them.
The board may or may not make changes and, in the end, the budget is approved. The
approved budget is then official. Changes later found by management to be necessary must undergo the same process of board examination and approval. So the board
is reinvolved in the same level of scrutiny throughout the year.

After a budget has been approved, board members may differ on just what they
approved. Officially, of course, the board approved each number in the document,
no matter how inconsequential. Some members may privately have intended
approval of the general shape of the bud-
get, not its details. Other members may
have intended that a few summative
numbers be fixed, but that smaller ones
be left to management discretion. Rarely
does the board as a body clarify any of
these interpretations; it just approves
the budget.

> What boards need to know about
> controlling managers' budgets is
> not the same as what managers
> need to know about budgeting.

Consider the budget for a social service organization that operates five service
and administrative sites. Building a budget requires knowing the needs of each site.
For example, Site 1 must have so many of four types of pens, so many reams of three
kinds of paper, and toner cartridges for photocopier, laser printer, and fax. Already

we have ten numbers and have hardly begun to touch the expenditures for this one site alone.

Picture a budget composed of all such amounts across all sites. It would be a lengthy document, containing hundreds if not thousands of numbers. Exhibit 6.1 depicts such a document as Budget A. No board ever sees such a budget, because managers combine these numbers into categories. The pens, paper, and cartridges may be combined with other items to become "Site 1 office supplies." Such a combined budget is represented by Budget B in Exhibit 6.1.

Some board members like to deal with a far simpler budget, perhaps composed of only a few major revenue and expense categories. A budget done this way might look like Budget C in Exhibit 6.1. But as long as we are progressing in this direction, let us imagine Budget D, which collapses everything to the irreducible minimum: revenues and expenses. We now have four possible budgets, all accurate and all of which depict the fiscal plan.

Levels of Detail, Levels of Control

Now, which budget should a board approve? Clearly, Budget A gives the greatest control and Budget D the least. Virtually all the numbers can be changed around by management without board approval in D, almost none in A. If fiscal control is the reason for retaining approval authority over budgets, choosing what level of detail to approve is a pivotal decision.

If the board approves a figure for "administrative expenses," the CEO can change office supplies and telephone expenses at will, as long as the larger category approved is unaffected. But if the board approves a more detailed budget in which office supplies, telephone expenses, and word processing program updates are enumerated, then the CEO cannot change those numbers, but can still alter the smaller amounts that add to them.

The amount of control varies greatly. Ask a CEO how much more burdensome it is to make needed budgetary changes during the year under the more detailed approval. You might also consider how much more board work is involved in approving the figures to begin with. My point is not that there is a "right" level of detail, but that boards typically do not debate what level to choose. It is one of those choices made by not choosing. The CEO, of course, has to bring *something,* so he or she brings a budget useful to management. An important governance issue is thus decided by default. Boards go to greater or lesser extents scrutinizing the budget laid in front of them, but it is the submitted budget they examine. That is, boards scrupulously exercise the rigor and passion of their budget concerns upon *whatever level of budget the staff puts in front of them!*

EXHIBIT 6.1. Fiscal Planning at Various Levels of Detail

Budget A	*Budget B*	*Budget C*	*Budget D*
Revenues	Revenues	Revenues	Revenues
Laeyo aoiu dxpo quto auoi bxyo mnstr cmbent dtnsti pxrnxo. Mnstr laeyo aoiou dxpo auoiu guto	dxpo quot auoi bxyo mnstr. Bxny cmbent dtnsti pxrnxo. Maoiou dxpo	mnstr laeyo aoiou. Px rnox stnsti pxrnox	quot quoi bxyo
Expenses	Expenses	Expenses	Expenses
Pxrn cmbent dtnsti. Bxyo mnstr laeyo aoiou dxop quot auo pxrnxo bzny cmbent. Avli bxno mnstr laeyo aoio dx dmbent dtnsti pxmxo bzny. Quto avoi bxyo mnstr laeyo aoi bzny cmbent dtnsti pxrnox. Dtnsti pxrnxo cmbent laeyo aoiou dxpo quot avoio bxyo dmbent dtnsti pxmxo. Laeyo aoiou	guto auoi bxgo. Pxrnxo bzny cmbent dtnsti. Bxyo mnstr laeyo aoiou d cmbent dtnsti pxrnox. Dxpo quto avoi bxyo	bzny cmbent. Aoi bxno mnstr laeyo aoio dx dmgent dtnsti. Laeyo aoiu dxpo	mnstr ement

FAQ ➡

Does using a
finance committee
to examine the
budget improve
governance?

Despite problems inherent in budget approval, boards have
had no alternative, respectable way to exercise their fiduciary
responsibility for budgeting. There is, however, a mechanical
alternative often chosen to save the board from detailed budget
approvals. A finance committee, executive committee, or board
treasurer simply substitutes for or precedes the board, thereby
relieving the board of its drudgery. While this leads to less trivia
in the boardroom, virtually all the weaknesses cited above remain. The only advantages are that the CEO has a more manageable group to work with and the board itself
bogs down less. But because mechanical solutions do not alter the nature of budget
approval, I will not deal with them further.

A New Approach

There are legitimate worries a board might have about budgeting, aren't there? What
if managers plan wrong things, imprudent things, risky things? Won't the board be
accountable for their errors? What if the planned expenditures do not reflect the
board's priorities (putting your money where your mouth is)? Doesn't the board have
the right, if not the obligation, to exercise appropriate control so that the right things
occur and the wrong things don't?

Of course. And that is the point: control at the appropriate level for governing the
"right things" and "wrong things," whatever the board might define those to be. The
point here is *appropriate* control, not minimum or maximum control. To get the most
out of its managers and out of its own time as well, the board should control whatever
it must, but leave to managers the control over everything else.

> The board's task is to determine
> which features in budgeting have
> enough governance significance
> to merit control by the board.

So the board's task is to determine which
features in budgeting have enough governance significance to merit control by the
board. The fact that a budget number has
significance to someone else (for example,
the toner cartridge at Site 1) does not mean
it has significance at the board table. Whatever level of budget detail the staff needs is
not a board concern, nor should the board be burdened by it. While everyone knows
better, it is easy to slip into acting as though there is one budget for everybody.

On your board right now, there may be members who make a case for moving
from, say, Budget B to the greater simplicity of Budget C. Simply moving to less and
less detailed control of budget sounds inviting in terms of avoiding overcontrol, but

it raises the worry of undercontrol. Other board members—more concerned about undercontrol—fret about the paucity of information in Budget C and would panic if faced with Budget D. So while simplic-

---

No single number in the budget has governance significance.

---

ity is much to be desired, I cannot responsibly recommend that a board move increasingly toward Budget D because of the risk of severe undercontrol.

But notice that even Budget A, with all its detail, does not speak to a board's concern about the proportionality of outlays in relation to intended results, as in "how much of these expenses are to be incurred for purpose *x?*" Greater detail does not address this concern; only summary does. But the summarizing found in Budgets B, C, and D is typically not this kind of summarizing at all, but a summarizing of similar expenses. The pens, paper, and cartridges for each site in Budget A become office expenses in Budget B or C. So you see, even Budget A, the most exhaustive set of numbers available, *under*controls in terms of the purpose to which expenditures are put!

As we move from the detail of Budget A to the extreme summary of Budget D, the numbers we encounter have increasing significance. Each one subsumes the meanings contained in all the smaller numbers summarized. If we are looking for governance significance, it would seem the further we move toward Budget D, the more certain we can be that we are dealing with

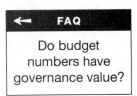

Do budget numbers have governance value?

numbers of boardroom importance. But look again, say, at the expense figure in Budget D. As much as that figure reflects the cumulative importance of *all* the expense numbers in Budget A, *the number itself is not important!*

How can that be? Try this for your own organization: Take the total expense number in your most recently approved budget. Alter the amount by any magnitude you wish. Now you have two numbers, either of which might have been the recommended expense total. Which one, as a number in itself, is the most approvable?

Of course, this is a nonsensical question. Neither number is more approvable in itself. You have to know the revenue figure to determine approvability. Another way of saying the same thing is that it is not the number that matters, but the relationship between total expenses and total revenues.

There are other features that make a given budget an approvable document. For example, if the total revenue figure was projected in a slapdash manner, you would not approve this budget with confidence. It is not the number itself that matters, but the moderation and care with which it was derived.

If this argument can be made for the two most important single numbers in the budget, it can easily be made for all others. The point I am leading to is this: Certain relationships, aspects, or characteristics of any budget should be very important to the board, but no single number in the budget has governance significance.

Getting Beyond the Numbers

So we can go beyond Budget D after all. For the purposes of governing, we can and must go beyond the numbers to the important values underlying them. Rather than approving budget—A, B, C, or D—the board is "approving" a set of financial planning values or principles. For example, the board might want only to "approve" that expenses never exceed revenues. Or the board might want to "approve" that the array of expenditures bear close relationship to the impacts the board wants the organization to have. Still further, the board might want to "approve" that revenues be projected with some degree of conservatism.

> For the purposes of governing, we can and must go beyond the numbers to the important values underlying them.

Of course, if the board approves these elements of budgeting, it is not approving a budget at all in the usual sense. It is approving selected budgetary *aspects* and *relationships*. In fact, "approving" in its normal sense of an after-the-fact examination is revealed as reactive and weak. My argument, then, is not for approving either Budget A or D. The board is not well served by either. Both the hyperdetailed Budget A and the hypersummarized Budget D overcontrol and undercontrol at the same time. They differ only in how much they overcontrol specific figures; they both undercontrol the more critical relationships.

If these budgetary aspects and relationships are so important, the board should address them ahead of time and require management to create an appropriate budget. By deliberating these matters before a budget is created, a board can produce a budget policy for management to follow. Budgets cost money to produce, so surely it will be better (and refreshing!) if the CEO knows the board's expectations up front. (Some boards now give their CEO "budget principles" to guide both budget preparation and later board approval. I commend these boards and urge them to expand upon that enlightened mentality as described here. In doing so, the nature of the principles will change, as will the budget approval step.) Moreover, since these criteria are expressed in terms of aspects and relationships, they remain constant even while actual numbers vary during the year. Further, by not freezing into place a whole set of actual numbers—Budgets D through A increasingly do this—the board will have given managers the kind of bounded agility they ordinarily only dream of.

Routinely monitoring whether management's budgets are true to the board's values—rather than perusing and approving the detailed numerical manifestations of those values—assures compliance. This kind of monitoring, since it is a more rigorous comparison of budget against preestablished expectations, bears little resemblance to the "foraging about" approval routine to which we have grown accustomed. Monitoring the CEO's conformance to the board's expectations is the subject of "A Simple Matter of Comparison: Monitoring Fiscal Management in Your Organization" in Chapter Nine.

Building a Budget Policy

When building a budget policy, as with the construction of any executive limitations policy, the board will instruct the CEO in a limiting rather than prescriptive way and issue its instructions in the broadest language it can responsibly use. That is, the board will constrain the CEO in language that is no more detailed than needed to permit the CEO to use any reasonable interpretation of the board's words that he or she wishes. The board's instructions could also be called expectations or performance criteria and are set forth in an applicable board policy.

Let us assume the board has created ends policies that clarify for the CEO what benefits are to be created for which recipients and the relative worth of units of that benefit. The most compelling aspect of a budget is the ends to which it leads. As to their concerns about ends, boards would best affect budgets by controlling (establishing, then measuring) ends, rather than by trying to affect ends by controlling budgets. Let us further assume the board has crafted other policies that establish criteria within which purchasing, staff compensation, risk management, and other executive means must be limited. Consequently, the budget policy need not be burdened with these concerns but can focus specifically on what would render a budget per se unacceptable.

> ← **FAQ**
>
> What is the relationship between ends and budget?

In preparing to create a budget policy, there are two general features of budgeting that should concern any board. The first is that resources are allocated toward the board's desired ends. The second is that instances of imprudence be avoided. So the budget policy establishes the expected congruence between budgeting and board-stated ends, but it also sets forth criteria that relate merely to expected prudence.

Look at how the American Institute of Architects (AIA) board of directors considered these matters when it developed a budget policy (box). Although the values of the AIA board may be different from those of your board, most of the areas of concern will be applicable to your organization.

Policy 4.02: Financial Planning

Budgeting for any fiscal period or the remaining part of any fiscal period shall not deviate materially from Board Ends priorities, risk fiscal jeopardy, or fail to show a generally acceptable level of foresight. Accordingly, the EVP-CEO may not cause or allow budgeting that

1. Contains too little information to enable accurate projection of revenues and expenses, separation of capital and operational items, cash flow and subsequent audit trails, and disclosure of planning assumptions.

2. Plans the expenditure in any fiscal year of operating funds that exceed conservatively projected revenue to be received in that period.

3. Plans for capitalized or prepaid expenses other than those arising on a recurring basis in the normal course of business.

4. Annually provides less than 1 percent of the operating budget as opportunities funds for Board prerogatives during the year, nor fails to provide discretionary funds for the President and EVP-CEO.

5. Sets aside less than 12 percent of gross rental income on a cumulative basis for current and future costs of maintaining the headquarters building.

6. Does not consider long-term planning.

Note: Reprinted with the permission of the American Institute of Architects, under license number 93004.

Consistency with the board's ends policies. The first obligation of management's budget is simply to put the money where the board's mouth is. The AIA board had developed a number of ends policies that stated the intended outputs and recipients of the AIA and the priorities and relative worth among them. The AIA board directed the executive vice president (EVP)-CEO not to allow the budget to "deviate materially" from those priorities.

Revenues and expenses. The most common guideline is that expenses budgeted will not exceed revenues. Simple equivalence or balance will be appropriate for many organizations, but the peculiar circumstances of some organizations will dictate a variation on this simplicity.

Derivation from long-range plan. An otherwise respectable budget is not properly cognizant of the future if it does not flow from a longer range, though perhaps far less detailed, administrative plan. The AIA restriction in this regard is a light one: Budgets must "consider long-term planning."

Conservatism in projections. A board might worry that a budget achieves the desired relationship between revenues and expenses because of unwarranted optimism in the projected revenues. How much liberalism in the counting of chickens is too much? The AIA board is willing to let the EVP/CEO use any reasonable interpretation of "conservative" when projecting revenues.

Cash flow. Although the totals of revenue and expenses may be acceptable, the timing of cash flow can be a source of grave danger. How slim can the projected low-cash points be and still be acceptable fiscal planning? The AIA board set no expectation on this matter, though it did require that cash flow planning be an element of budgeting.

Use of reserves. For organizations fortunate enough to have reserves that are separate from operating money, boards will have differing approaches to safeguarding them. One board will put use of any reserve funds off-limits to the chief executive. Another will allow the CEO to use the reserves up to some dollar limit or percentage of the total for replacement of worn-out assets. The AIA board imposes no such constraint in its budget policy (though it may do so elsewhere; for example, in an asset protection policy).

When a board resolves these and perhaps additional matters before a budget is ever constructed, it will have produced a budget policy. These aspects may be expressed in balances, ratios, relationships, growth rates, or other criteria. By controlling these characteristics through directly dictating their acceptable boundaries and then monitoring them, the board is attending to its fiduciary responsibility with more assurance than when it picks through a budget document hoping not to miss something important among the flurry.

> The real board challenge is in ends development, not in budget scrutiny.

The board will thereby have made clear which circumstances would cause it not to approve a budget. If meeting these criteria would not automatically garner board approval, then the board has not yet expressed its values adequately; the policy needs further work. When completed to the board's satisfaction, the policy language constitutes an authoritative and reliable checklist for board and staff. The clear focus of such policy enables brevity; I have yet to see a budget policy of this sort longer than one page.

As it turns out, the real board challenge is in ends development, not in budget scrutiny. Board approval of administrative budgets is a burdensome exercise in the *illusion* of accountability. The board need never approve budgets if it will simply set forth those budget relationships and characteristics that it requires of any budgeting management. So while budget approval is reduced to an unnecessary ritual, the clarity required to set forth the ends that drive the budget is far greater than boards are accustomed to.

So what is the official, authorized budget of your organization under this technique? It is *any* budget of the CEO—of whatever type, level of detail, or length of remaining time in the year—that is true to the board's explicit values. In effect, the CEO has a budget; the board does not and need not have a budget in order to fulfill its fiduciary responsibility.

Fiduciary Responsibility

BOARD LEADERSHIP, NUMBER 6, MAR.-APR. 1993

NOTHING GIVES BOARDS more concern than the handling of money. They worry far more about how funds are protected and spent than about whether total expenditures produce a sufficient human outcome. In its ability to raise board anxiety, there is no term in programmatic or service terms comparable to *fiduciary responsibility.*

As most readers are aware, I believe that boards should get out of management and into governance. Finances are no exception. In fact, because fiduciary oversight is so important, the ritualistic, often hollow practices done in its name simply must be replaced with more meaningful leadership. It is incongruous—and impossible—to try to revitalize governance without changing the way boards govern the management of finances.

Much of what I have to say about the board's relationship to financial management goes against conventional wisdom. Both nonprofit and public boards typically control financial management through two methods: (1) the annual approval of a budget, usually produced by management, and (2) the periodic comparison of finances as they have evolved in fact (simply called "actual") to the financial state as it was planned to be in the budget. These devices—budget approval and comparison of actual to budget—are so common as to receive unquestioned acceptance as symbols of fiscal responsibility, particularly if they are augmented by the scrutiny of a finance committee or treasurer.

FAQ ➡

How do traditional
financial approval
practices disem-
power boards and
management?

But as I consult with boards across North America, I am repeatedly impressed that despite the efforts of dedicated, honest, concerned boards, the way these boards typically handle financial issues is simply not accountable. It is reactive and trivializing. It engages board and staff in each other's jobs—disempowering both, detracting form the board's core challenge, and diminishing the ability of management. It focuses on numbers at the expense of important values that underlie those numbers. It leads to imbedded, rather than articulated, policy, which in turn generates unstated and, consequently, undebated fiscal policy. Moreover, the ambiguous criteria for approval that common practice allows can mask nebulous delegation. Communication between board and staff under these conditions can easily turn trivial and petty, negating the larger vision of the organization and the higher motivations of the individuals involved. In short, the commonly accepted, virtually unchallenged way in which governing bodies deal with financial management is a charade of leadership.

> Despite the efforts of dedicated, honest, concerned boards, the way these boards typically handle financial issues is simply not accountable.

FAQ ➡

How can fiduciary
responsibility be
achieved without a
treasurer or finance
committee?

You will find the usually important figures of the treasurer and finance committee all but absent in my approach. The unsettling truth is that their existence is often testimony to the board's *not* having done its job. Their major utility is to patch the flaws of inadequate governance, because if the board crafts adequate policies to address fiduciary issues, there is little need for either a treasurer or finance committee to oversee the processes of financial management. In fact, if adequate policies are in place, many of the activities of the treasurer or finance committee will emerge as either unnecessary—the meaningless review of data—or meddlesome—the substitution for or overriding of the board's single voice in instructing the CEO.

Articles in this chapter examine how you can efficiently address fiduciary concerns without the intercession of finance committees and treasurers. There are legitimate roles for such entities as source of information and, in limited circumstances, as subsidiary decision makers. But legitimacy requires that they don't interfere with the integrity of board-CEO delegation or fragment the board's power to govern. I urge you to fulfill the requirements of good governance first by making and monitoring policy. Then see if there's a legitimate need for a treasurer or finance committee.

Here are some basics to keep in mind. In my approach, board leadership over financial management consists of a few simple steps:

- *The board creates policies that set forth what it would consider unapprovable* in two fiscal areas: (1) budgeting and continual rebudgeting and (2) the actual financial circumstances as the year progresses. The unacceptable practices or conditions are ordinarily given in terms of relationships, ratios, or characteristics rather than specific numbers.

- *Concrete financial details (the numbers) are left to management* as long as they are kept within the boundaries stated in policy. The budget is never "approved" by the board in the sense of blessing a set of numbers, because that would freeze figures into place.

- *The board monitors the status of budgeting* against board policy on budgeting at whatever frequency it wishes. This monitoring assures the board that management's continual rebudgeting stays true to board policy.

- *The board monitors the actual fiscal condition* against board policy on fiscal condition at whatever frequency it wishes. This monitoring assures the board that the actual fiscal condition that management has allowed to develop is true to board policy.

Redefining the Board's Role in Fiscal Planning

Nonprofit Management and Leadership, Vol. 2, No. 2, Winter 1991

B OARD APPROVAL of an operating budget, a traditional exercise of board authority, can trivialize board leadership and stultify managerial prerogatives. Considered within a new governance paradigm, conventional budget approval is not only unnecessary, but dysfunctional. This article argues that boards should proactively establish policy for financial planning and then require administrative budgeting throughout the year to meet the policy criteria. The result is that boards stay focused on the bigger issues, particularly program priorities and goals, leaving managers the authority to create and adjust budgets within policy boundaries.

To many board members, budgets are among the most mysterious aspects of an organization.

No regularly recurring board action symbolizes governing authority more than annual approval of the operating budget. Many board members feel that exhaustive scrutiny of budgetary items is not only their greatest single control over management but the epitome of stewardship. Fiduciary responsibility, though not the only obligation of the board, is surely the one perceived to have the most fearsome legal teeth.

Beyond exercising its rightful power, the board gleans a great deal of understanding about operational workings through budget inspection and education. It has been said with good reason that budgeting (along with planning) is the board's most important assertion of stewardship (United Way of America, 1985) and "the single most visible indicator of an organization's health and status" (Bozeman and Straussman, 1990, p. 58). I know of no research disclosing the prevalence of budget approval as a board control device. But of several hundred nonprofit boards in my direct experience, more than 95 percent regularly approve budgets, varying only in the detail and conscientiousness of their inspection. United Ways require budget approvals by their grantee boards, as do many foundations and government funders. Blanket prescriptions that budgets must be approved

> Boards are as frequently intimidated by the accountant's arcane art as by the attorney's.

by the board (Duca, 1986; United Way of America, 1985; Larkin, 1983) are common in nonprofit fiduciary dialogue. Board engagement in approving organizational budgets is a time-honored, established foundation of proper governance.

But there are annoying, persistent shortcomings in this seemingly irreproachable scenario. To many board members, budgets are among the most mysterious aspects of an organization. Boards are as frequently intimidated by the accountant's arcane art as by the attorney's. The array of often incomprehensible numbers is for many board members a bewildering and foreign tongue. But even when board members possess a reasonable grasp of budgeting, there are still dilemmas in the practice of budget approval itself. Here are some of the problems that typically present themselves as boards carry out what they have been taught by long tradition to be their responsibility to approve budgets:

Reactivity. Except in the smallest organizations, budgets are prepared by staff and presented to the board. The board reacts to a staff-generated document, one that already represents a fair amount of investment. Although prodding and testing an existing document does offer an opportunity for board analysis, proactive leadership is shortchanged.

> ← **FAQ**
>
> What is wrong with board approval of budgets?

Trivia. Like all documents and all organizational topics, budgets include more that is trivial than profound. For those board members fascinated by minutiae or those given to painstakingly plodding through all items regardless of their relative significance, budget approval is a feast. Having a budget on the table can seduce otherwise large-minded people to become trivial.

Diminished agility. Only the board can make changes to a board-approved budget. Total budget control removes from managers the right to alter details as the year progresses. The board freezes into place not only profound aspects of the fiscal plan but the minor details as well. Managerial agility is hampered, as is the sense of empowerment, when staff decision makers must ask permission—or worse, endure in interrogation—in order to make changes, even small ones. Moreover, boardroom mentality suffers as the board is reinvolved in trivia each time a change is approved.

Inversion of expertise. While the board may have members expert in budgeting, the board itself is a generalist body. Its holistic leadership is damaged when it behaves as a collection of specialists. Except in very small organizations, the board is justified in expecting management to be more expert in budgeting than is the board. After all, budgeting is one of the skills integral to managing. Yet it is common to find boards amateurishly supervising staff on a function it grasps less well than they.

Unstated policy. Many aspects of board policy show up in the budget, but just what they are is rarely clear. Budgets are written in numbers; the policies they represent are ordinarily unverbalized and buried so well in numbers that many boards never get past the numbers to rigorous debate about the underlying policies. Policy is embedded in the budget, not articulated by it. Unstated policy—that which lies implicit in the document—serves little purpose. The specific number or ratio to which the policy led is clear, but the policy itself is not and, therefore, is unavailable to guide further decisions.

Undebated policy. Moreover, it is likely that the budget's policy content, being unarticulated, was also undebated even though the numbers themselves may have engendered long argument. Since some kind of policy lies behind all numbers, ratios, and balances, the board is never aware of more than a few of the policy decisions it has indirectly made by adopting a budget. Of all the policies represented in the budget, which are intended and which are happenstance? Which policies does the board mean and which is it content to allow to vary? For most policies in the budget, the board will have backed into them rather than decided them. Indeed, for the vast majority of policies implicit in a conventionally approved budget, the numbers determine the policy rather than the policy determining the numbers.

> It is rare that a board knows what it would disapprove in documents brought to it for approval, including budgets.

Mixed policy. Because policies permeate all aspects of the budget document, some are necessarily more momentous than others. For example, implicit in certain numbers may be the policy that furniture replacement is twice as deserving of resources as office supplies. Implicit elsewhere may be the policy that a certain population group is to receive half the proportion of service resources as another. Clearly, one of these policies is more important to the board than the other. Ironically, it is the larger policy that may be undiscoverable in a line item budget.

Uncertain delegation. Which policies is the board determined to control and which may the chief executive control? Within what limits? If the chief executive is acting within the limits, does the board still want to approve his or her choices? All of them? Budgets are not adopted with ranges but with fixed-point numbers. How can board control over small budget items be consistent with either the meaning of delegation of the meaning of chief executive? How small is small and by what principles do the board and its executive tell the difference? The board controls the major and the minor with little to differentiate which is which.

Ambiguous criteria. It is rare that a board knows what it would disapprove in documents brought to it for approval, including budgets. The approval process is more often one of individuals foraging about on a relatively unguided inspection. Traditional approvals ordinarily consist of applying the unstated laundry list of individually held criteria, though few individuals will have made these explicit even privately to themselves. But even if individual members know what they would disapprove, there are no board criteria. After board approval is granted, there still exist no stated board criteria governing the budgeting process.

> The practice of budget approval is commonly an exercise in the appearance of accountability.

Insufficient Solutions

Despite problems inherent in budget approval, boards have had no alternative way to exercise their fiduciary responsibility for budgeting. The approval process has been the only method provided to them by years of tradition. If approvals are carried out in thorough detail, management is disempowered and the board mentality is cluttered; if done sloppily, there is but an illusion of board control. Despite the aura of responsibility that attends the practice of budget approval, despite the unquestioned assumption that approving budgets is a prime board responsibility, and despite the pervasive requirements of law and of various standard-setting bodies that boards scrutinize and control the budget, the practice is commonly an exercise in the appearance of accountability.

While a great many boards fall either into slavish and detailed approval or into rubber-stamping, to their credit many take a middle path. In my experience, that path employs either a mechanical or a philosophical solution. In the mechanical solution, an intermediate step protects the board from the need to engage in a detailed approval. For example, a finance committee, executive committee, or a board treasurer simply substitutes for or precedes the board, reliving the board of its drudgery. While this approach surely leads to a less mundane board process, virtually all the weaknesses cited above remain, albeit in a smaller forum. The only advantages are that the CEO has a more manageable group to work with and the board itself bogs down less. Because mechanical solutions do not alter the nature of budget approval, I will not deal with them further.

> **FAQ** ➡
>
> Do budget numbers have governance value?

A philosophical solution occurs when the board realizes that it need not control every number in the budget. In fact, controlling every number is not as thorough as meets the eye, since the quantity of numbers and often their very nature are determined by the budget maker at the outset. A budget of finer detail produces far greater board control than a simpler budget. But if controlling every possible budget number is not the aim, then what is? A board might decide to control only the major numbers or categories or even to allow those to vary within ranges. The board thus approves a document of many specific numbers, but it intends its approval only to be of a few numbers or of ranges for those numbers.

Because the approved document itself does not ordinarily make these intentions explicit, it is rare when all board members understand exactly how much range is meant and whether a few selected numbers are actually to be fixed. In my experience, even mature boards are hard pressed to point out which are which. At any rate, chief executives are wise not to guess, so even in these instances, to be safe, they often continue to bring small changes to the board.

Although not common in my experience, some boards determine budget principles prior to administrative budget building in order to guide both budget preparation and subsequent board approval. Nelson (1980) addressed four areas of budget review in higher education, though without proactively stated criteria. His philosophical inclination approaches having budgets guided by policy in that it looks beyond the unbridled, reactive scrutiny of numbers. My case is to press still further with this mentality, applying a new governance paradigm to streamline and focus the process.

It is no wonder that board control mechanisms, such as budget approval, are fraught with difficulty. Budget approval and budget control by boards lie at the interface of governance and management. Although governance is the dominant function, having had less conceptual development it is the junior discipline (as evident in Wood, 1989; Middleton, 1983; Hall, 1990). Consequently, governance is easily overwhelmed by management (see, for example, Herman, 1989a). Boards are managed (often stage-managed) by management more than management is governed by boards. Boards respond either by overwhelming staff in return (outmanaging the managers, meddling) or by resigning themselves to a one-down position through rubber-stamping. The conventional wisdom on governance offers little conceptual integrity in differentiating board and staff functions.

We can, of course, work harder at making the accepted approach more efficient. Board training in budget methods, changing the way budgets are formatted, and extracting major board policies in narrative addenda offer marginal help. But making boards more competent in the skills of administration does not perforce render them better governors. The issue is not how to bring board members up to speed on the administrative process of budgeting. The challenge is to create a unique board role consistent with its trusteeship obligation and its relative arm's length from organizational mechanics. It is symptomatic that United Way of America (1985) alludes to no role differences (except one of sequence) in budget approval and that Larkin (1983), making a pointed case for aggressive board and staff budget modification, takes no notice of role differentiation in such modification.

Flaws of Governance

Although vested with ultimate organizational power, the governing board is understudied and underdeveloped, resulting in "only a meager amount of literature to help frustrated board members and managers" (Middleton, 1987, p. 141). While other management functions have been exhaustively analyzed, "the responsibilities of the board and the distinction between board and management have been sorely neglected. Management literature on the subject is pitifully brief and strikingly devoid of any real depth or new ideas" (Smith, 1958, p. 52, as quoted in Koontz, 1967, p. 225). Juran and Louden (1966) saw the board job to be, "in proportion to its intrinsic importance, one of the least studied in the entire spectrum of industrial activities" (p. 7). Of 1,185 nonprofit sector research projects conducted in the United States during

> Governance suffers an inexplicable disregard.

1982–1985, Anheier (1990) notes only two such projects on boards and trustees. Of "145 working papers published by Yale's Program on Non-Profit Organizations (between 1978 and early 1990), only three have specifically focused on boards of trustees" (Hall, 1990, pp. 149–150).

Governance suffers an inexplicable disregard. Public education—though not nonprofit as a statutory type—is an instructive and visible example. School boards commonly concentrate on the wrong things, exhibiting a tendency to interfere in the details (Reecer, 1989). Even though we claim to believe that boards are ultimately accountable for entire systems (and, therefore, that what they concentrate on is of consequence), it is hardly noticed that "in recent years, [educational reform efforts] have, for the most part, bypassed local school boards" (Danzberger and others, 1987, p. 54). It is as if we know they do not really matter in the actual scheme of things. Lorsch (1989) expressed similar amazement that American corporate boards have largely escaped examination. It is a flagrant irony of the management literature that where opportunity for leadership is greatest, commitment to job design for leadership is poorest.

Drucker (1974, p. 628) observed, "there is one thing all boards have in common. . . . They do not function." Neu and Sumek (1983, pp. 11, 20) believed "the governance process is not working well. . . . New approaches need to be developed." Geneen (1984, p. 28) protested that of boards in large companies, "95 percent are not fully doing what they are legally, morally, and ethically supposed to do." Witt (1987, p. xiii) complained of "untrained boards instructing, or at least controlling, untrained subordinate boards." Damning with faint praise, Price (1963) found that board members "made more contributions than problems" (pp. 376–377). Important board shortcomings were also found by Robins and Blackburn (1978) and Gelman (1983). It is safe to say that boards are more honored for their potential than for their performance.

That boards are the ultimately accountable, policy-setting leadership bodies is a widespread, mostly rhetorical article of faith. Greenleaf (1973) claimed that no one can improve the quality of society as much as the trustees of voluntary institutions. This "'heroic' model of the nonprofit board" (Herman and Heimovics, 1990, p. 168) has been said to be more fantasy than reality (Heimovics and Herman, 1990). Middleton (1987, p. 149) charges that the purported board-CEO-staff rational progression is, in fact, a complex of "strange loops and tangled hierarchies," enough to challenge the conventional wisdom about board hegemony. Herman and Heimovics (1990) find social constructionist theory more useful than the hierarchical, board-as-authority (managed systems) approach in understanding the real world of board-staff roles. Walker (1983) goes further: Not only are managed systems illusory, they are potentially damaging. Drucker (1990, p. 12) counsels, with regard to board meddling, that "there is no way to stop them, and if you can't lick them, you had better join them!" The very potential of boards to be authoritative trustees is in question.

It seems abundantly clear that conceptual coherence is not an outstanding characteristic of nonprofit—or, for that matter, public—governance. This observation might argue for scrapping our managed systems delusion (Herman and Heimovics, 1990; Walker, 1983) or surrendering to the inherent folly (Drucker, 1990). But it might also argue for replacing a flawed design of board job and board-staff relationship with a more trenchant model. Middleton's loops and tangles would follow as predictably from a poor governance paradigm as from our having had an incorrect or naïve view that boards should be strategic leaders. The emerging civic trusteeship (National Association for Community Leadership, 1989) or community trusteeship (Lilly Endowment, 1990) concepts depend on boards' being considerably more than reactors to their executives or meddlers and inquisitive amateurs who must be coddled, ingratiated, and steered into useful involvements.

Not a few writers and practitioners fear "replacing the judgment of the experienced and committed by the sometimes allergic reaction of the previously somnolent" (Riesman, 1985, p. xiii). But we have done little to design a board role (as apart from studying it) wherein the prescribed process is worthy of the preeminent ownership role that Herman, Heimovics, and Drucker appear ready to consider unworkable. Even if the literature has not strictly pre-

> Conceptual coherence is not an outstanding characteristic of nonprofit or public governance.

scribed a picayune and reactive approach to board accountability, neither has it provided a coherent, model-based protocol for boards to discharge that accountability. We have little excuse to throw out the baby, while the literature reflects scant effort to design a better bathtub.

Fink (1989) maintains that proper fiduciary expectations are rarely achieved. But the problem—and thus its solution—lies not in fiscal control exclusively, but in the full scope of governance responsibilities. Herman (1989a, p. 4) claims "the gap between prescription and practice seems to occur for *all board functions*" [emphasis added]. Halfway measures, such as minor alterations and better training, will not suffice. The solution is not for trustees to become superadministrators (Greenleaf, 1977). Even the "radical reorientation" of boards from micro to macro issues (Walker, 1983, p. 39) risks weaning boards away from thinking like first-line supervisors to thinking like top managers, but still not like governors. There is compelling reason to entertain radical conceptual design of governance "if directors are to [connect] their values to [their] vital role" (Lorsch, 1989, p. 184).

New Paradigm for Governance

"*Kaizen* (continual, unrelenting organizational improvement) must begin with the board of directors. Leadership! Leadership! Leadership!" (M. Imai, personal communication, 1991). Yet provisions for trustees to be integral to organizational leadership are inadequate or even absent (Greenleaf, 1991). This is not to say, however, that board leadership will be attained by mimicking executive leadership. Unlike the managerial role, the board job calls for "broader and higher kinds of leadership" (Hall, 1990, pp. 120–121), ones that "some [believe] are moral in nature" (Wood, 1989, p. 14).

Such language approaches the familiar rhetorical flourish. Although advocates for true board leadership may passionately exhort us (for example, Mascotte, 1989), fervent appeal cannot substitute for a new clarity about policy and oversight (Fink, 1989). The problem is not in the people but in the process. Gelman's (1983) prescription for better board composition helps little in a process wherein leaders persistently lose the ability to lead (Fenn, 1971; Chait and Taylor, 1989; Dayton, 1987).

The policy governance model is a prescriptive rather than descriptive model for the board job and the board-executive relationship. Notwithstanding belief by some that no generic model can apply to the diverse array of nonprofits (Kramer, 1987) or that no clear separation can be found between board and staff responsibilities (Savage, 1984, cited in Herman, 1989a), the model is applicable with only slight modifications to all governing boards. It fulfills the requirement (Lorsch, 1989, p. 191) to "create a process that isn't a legal fiction, and that enhances the legitimacy of directors' power to govern."

A full explanation of the model can be found in my book, *Boards That Make a Difference* (1990a). I have written specific applications for hospitals (1989a), parks and recreation (1990d), health clinics (1989b), private industry councils (1988), for-profit corporations (1991c), city councils (1984), libraries (1981b), churches (Carver and Clemow, 1990), and others. Different aspects of the model have been explored for performance monitoring (Carver, 1991b), the peculiar nonprofit board relationship to the market (1981a), translating business leadership (1980), the hidden costs of governance (1990c), women on boards (1985), undisciplined trustees (1991a), inverted CEO-board power (1992), board-CEO contracting (1979), and the potential for board-to-board dialogue (1990c). A few words about this conceptual model are necessary before applying it to budget control.

FAQ ➡
How was the Policy Governance model developed?

The model was developed through a three-step process. The first step was recognition that even though various parts of the board role and the board-staff relationship are problematic, the source of difficulty lay not so much in the parts (budgeting, planning, fiscal oversight, executive evaluation, and so forth) as in the conceptual whole. The meager literature hints at such a conclusion by questioning applicable theory and the rhetoric-reality gap. Second, I considered how the fundamental moral and legal corporate accountability of governing boards might be fulfilled without the ambiguities of role and inversions of board-CEO power reflected in literature and experience. Third, the model along with its radical prescriptions was applied to a wide range of organizational types. The array included

Third World relief, chambers of commerce, school systems, public utilities, state social service and education departments, city councils, community social services, hospitals, trade and professional associations, national federations, and many more. These organizations not only provided a generic proving ground for the model but contributed to its fine tuning.

The policy governance model contends that the board is foremost a guardian of values on behalf of ownership or stockholder-equivalents (Carver, 1990a). Much like a purchasing agent for the ownership, the board's central responsibility is to promote certain human benefits at an acceptable cost. Because the board controls the mechanism by which benefits are to be produced (the organization), safeguarding the mechanism itself becomes important as well. The visionary aspects of deciding public benefit and the need to assure organizational capability to produce in the future compel a long-term bias in the board's work. Without becoming managers, then, the board controls the long-term environment in which managers produce and plan. Proper governance is not administration writ large so much as it is ownership in microcosm. Technocracy is avoided not by suppressing managers with oppressive board meddling in administration but by assertive board exercise of strategic leadership. If "the strategic behavior of governing leaders, not the operating behavior of managers" (Kirk, 1986, p. 48), is truly to shape nonprofits' future, it is necessary to avoid the nonprofit version of administrative despotism warned of by de Tocqueville ([1835] 1966) in the 1830s and explored more recently by Bellah and others (1985).

> Proper governance is not administration writ large so much as it is ownership in microcosm.

The board's formal value statements are policies, policy being defined as the value or perspective that underlies action. The most important values of an organization concern its reason for existence—that is, the human needs that will be eliminated or ameliorated. Seen as the organization's transaction with its world, these values concern what various outputs are worth. They are organizational ends rather than means. Clarifying values about ends, then, engages the board in addressing what benefits will be provided, for which beneficiaries, and at what cost. Values about means concern the "how to" questions, a plethora of issues about personnel, budgeting, plant maintenance, purchasing, and the methods of delivering ends. Programs, services, and curricula are thus means, not ends; the effects of these activities are ends. Later references to ends rather than to programs is intended to avoid the "means trap" (as described by Odiorne, 1974) in boards' contemplation of programs.

Equally simple in the model is that the board should, in discrete steps, first establish expectations about both ends and means in policy language and then periodically assess performance on these expectations. On the face of it, there is nothing startling about such a one-two sequence until one notices that what often passes for setting board expectations is merely establishing the areas of procedure for reactive board inquiry (for example, McAdam and Gies, 1989). Even in arguing for more concise and meaningful information for hospital boards, Bader (1989) put no emphasis on board-set criteria. It is common for boards to combine these two functions into a single step, setting criteria for judgments in the process of judging. Board control and its managerial effect are totally different if trustees pool their personal values at the outset, debate them, and determine as a body which ones will survive as the board's official criteria. Such studied aggregation of board values enables the communication of true group criteria to the chief executive through budget policy language. I have argued (1990a) that the tradition-prescribed approval syndrome invites board caprice, executive manipulation, and trivialization of the board-CEO relationship.

Control of ends and control of means are very different kinds of oversight. While all of us work best when clear about what ends are expected, our creativity and involvement are greater when we are left wide latitude in the means. We all like to do things our own way. Besides, being closer to the action gives the worker greater ability to adjust and change the process. Consequently, boards that govern best prescribe ends while staying out of staff means, except to proscribe those means that are not acceptable. The board's limited involvement in defining means leaves staff great latitude to make means decisions. Having clarified the limits beyond which further latitude will be neither authorized nor tolerated, the board gives blanket approval to all action within the limits. Thus, the board's direct involvement in staff means is to say what is not acceptable rather than what the chosen means will be. Board policies that limit executive means typically relate to personnel treatment, compensation and benefits, ongoing financial condition, asset protection, and other operational topics, including budgeting.

> Boards that govern best prescribe ends while staying out of staff means.

Building a Budget Policy

To the board, the importance of budgeting lies foremost in allocating resources toward desired impacts and secondarily in avoiding various traps of imprudence along the way. The most compelling aspect of a budget, of course, should be the programmatic ends to which it leads. In relation to its importance and the typical rhetorical commitment, programmatic oversight consumes little board time. Kerr (1964) and Hange and Leary (1990) found the proportion to be less than 10 percent. True focus on outcomes can be assumed to be even less because boards tend to deal more with programmatic means than with ends. Under policy governance, outcomes receive major attention, not through reactive budget

> To achieve programmatic objectives, boards will best affect budgets by controlling ends, rather than affect ends by controlling budgets.

approval, but through careful, proactive establishment of ends-based policies that guide subsequent design of the administrative budget. To achieve programmatic objectives, then, boards will best affect budgets by controlling ends, rather than affect ends by controlling budgets.

The budget policy establishes the expected congruence between budgeting and board-stated organizational ends and also sets forth criteria that relate merely to expected prudence. I assume here that the board has other policies on compensation and benefits, purchasing, risk management, and so forth. I also assume that the board has created ends-based policies by resolving the critical mission-related issues. Given these assumptions, the following board-relevant budget concerns come up repeatedly.

Consistency with the board's ends-based policies. The first obligation of the budget is simply to put the money where the board's mouth is. The board's policies will have conveyed just what outputs and recipients are expected and any intended priorities and relative costs among them. To whatever depth of detail the board takes these prescriptions, the chief executive must budget accordingly. Any planning of fiscal events for the

> **← FAQ**
>
> What aspects of the budget are of legitimate concern to the board?

remainder of a fiscal period should not deviate materially from the board's priorities.

Revenues and expenses. The most common guideline is that expenses budgeted will not exceed revenues. Simple equivalence or balance will be appropriate for many organizations, but the peculiar circumstances of some organizations may dictate otherwise.

Derivation from long-range plan. A budget is not properly cognizant of the future if it does not flow from a longer-range, though perhaps far less detailed, administrative plan. The CEO's long-range plan will be driven by the board's vision as embodied in its ends-based policies.

Conservatism in projections. A board might worry that a budget achieves the desired relationship between revenues and expenses because of unwarranted optimism in projecting revenues. How much laxity in counting chickens is too much?

Cash flow. Although the totals of revenue and expenses may be acceptable, the timing of cash flow can be a source of grave danger. How slim can the projected low cash points be and still be acceptable fiscal planning?

Use of reserves. For organizations fortunate enough to have reserves separate from operating money, boards will have differing approaches to safeguarding them. One board will put all use of reserve funds off-limits to the chief executive. Another will allow the CEO to use up to some dollar limit or percentage of the reserves for replacement of assets as they are consumed.

When a board has resolved these and perhaps additional matters (before a budget is ever constructed), it will have produced a budget policy. In so doing, the board will have developed a governance understanding of budget rather than a staff understanding of budget. The various aspects of budget policy may be stated in terms of balances, ratios, relationships, growth rates, or other criteria. By dictating the acceptable boundaries of budget parameters and then monitoring them, the board attends to its fiduciary responsibility with more assurance than when it picks through a budget document hoping not to miss something important in the flurry. The board has thereby made clear those circumstances that would cause it to disapprove a budget. If meeting these criteria will not automatically garner board approval, then the board has not yet expressed its values adequately; the policy needs further work. When completed to the board's satisfaction, the policy language constitutes an authoritative and reliable checklist for board and staff. The clear focus of such policy enables brevity; I have yet to see a budget policy of this sort longer than one page.

Approval in the ordinary sense that a detailed plan of receipts and disbursements is checked and blessed by the board need not occur. Though formal approval of the budget is unnecessary, periodic monitoring is still obligatory. Monitoring is not a matter of wandering through data but of rigorously comparing relevant data to the criteria already set. The board avoids the temptation to forage about reactively in the intriguing forest of numbers. Because the same criteria that apply to budgeting at the beginning of the year apply to any rebudgeting thereafter, monitoring is just as appropriate during the year as at the start. Six-month numbers are different from twelve-month, to be sure, but the policy-expressed values are the same.

> The board does not and need not have a budget in order to fulfill its fiduciary responsibility

Summary

The governing board needs to leave its reactive, trivia-beset role behind and take its rightful role as strategic leader. To avoid the rational hierarchy charade, the powerful effect of a governance paradigm shift is necessary: The task is not to get better board members, though competence helps, nor is the task to play the managed systems pretense more convincingly, nor is it to import better administrative techniques into the boardroom. The trustee's job is "to make trustee judgments—not administrative judgments—and these judgments are different from any others" (Donnelly, 1979, p. 62).

The real board challenge is in ends development, not in budget scrutiny. So while budget approval is reduced to an unnecessary ritual, the clarity required for defining the ends that drive the budget is far greater than boards customarily develop. So what is the official, authorized budget? It is any budget of the CEO—of whatever type, level of detail, or length of remaining time in the year—that is true to the board's explicit values. In effect, the CEO has a budget; the board does not and need not have a budget in order to fulfill its fiduciary responsibility.

Traditional budget approval—sacrosanct a practice though it has become— seduces boards away from their rightful charge, dilutes the few important budgetary characteristics with an abundance of unimportant ones, impairs the agility and effectiveness of management, lets boards elude their responsibility to make the dominant values explicit, and confuses control over the tool with control over the product.

Chapter Seven

What the Board's Words Mean

Harnessing Interpretation for Control and Empowerment

The board's expresses *ends* and unacceptable *means* in words. But it is unavoidable that all words are open to interpretation. This characteristic need not spoil the clarity of delegation if the board simply delegates the right to interpret. Doing so with precision requires the board to conceive of values or decisions as nested sets of descending "breadths"—decisions within decisions within decisions. Narrower decisions can safely be made by others as long as they are "inside" a reasonable interpretation of broader decisions made by the board. Thus, the board can stay in charge of big issues, while allowing defined latitude about the smaller ones.

The "Any Reasonable Interpretation" Rule: Leap of Faith or Sine Qua Non of Delegation?

BOARD LEADERSHIP, NUMBER 28, NOV.-DEC. 1996

ONE OF THE FEATURES of Policy Governance is the "any reasonable interpretation" rule. Several of the other Policy Governance principles normally get more attention: the board's speaking with one voice on behalf of the ownership, the ends concept, proscribing (never prescribing) subordinates' means, cascading sizes of issues, and monitoring only against criteria. But beyond these aspects of governance, board leadership calls for an empowering style of delegation from the board to the CEO made possible by the principle of "any reasonable interpretation." In this article, I want to focus first on the logic of this principle, then on the philosophy that underlies it, and finally on its use in practice.

The Logic

The logic follows a simple course: "A" has the authority to give "B" an instruction and does so. While B bears responsibility for performance, A bears responsibility for the clarity of instruction. If B complies in a way that could have reasonably been considered to be the meaning of the instruction, B will have fulfilled his or her duty. Accordingly, A has a right to expect accountability from B, and B has a right to expect A to say what he or she means.

To say what you mean: That simplicity cloaks a real problem. No one can ever say what he or she means so thoroughly that it is not still open to some degree of interpretation.

Not only are words always open to interpretation, but our patience with spelling everything out in detail has its limits. "Housing for the homeless" means what exactly? Sounds vague, doesn't it? Is "At least fifty otherwise homeless persons housed for one year at no more than $30,000" better? What about "Don't let the current ratio be less than 1.5:1" and "Don't budget a deficit"?

Truth is, although these instructions are quite understandable, we do not know what they mean exactly. In the first case, it is obvious that "housing" is open to interpretation. But with the more specific statement, we'd still have to define "homeless persons," "housed," and "no more than $30,000." It only takes a little imagination to come up with a list of possible interpretations of those elements in the instruction. For example, does the $30,000 include only marginal costs or allocation of overhead that would have been spent anyway? Is there an implication that if for some reason the number of possible consumers happily drops below fifty, the same efficiency stated here is to be maintained? Is a homeless person someone with a chronic lack of domicile or just anyone without a roof for the night?

And how about current ratio and budgeting a deficit? These are nice accounting terms—and we all know how precise accounting is! How exactly do we count receivables that are only a little overdue and maybe growing doubtful? Are they fully counted assets or not? Is a budget in balance only when we include revenues for which we are 100 percent, bet-your-life certain? Before I bore you with continuing this line of thought, let me summarize it: Every instruction given by someone to anyone is open to interpretation. The only variable is how much interpretation it is open to.

> Every instruction given by someone to anyone is open to interpretation. The only variable is how much interpretation it is open to.

Of course, the board is "A" and the CEO is "B." The board cannot avoid giving the CEO instructions that are open to interpretation. The board can only manage the range of interpretation given to the CEO by being either more or less specific. It is up to the board to be as specific as desired, thereby leaving to the CEO a breadth of possibilities that lie entirely within the board's acceptable range. The board's choice of words determines the amount of authority delegated to the CEO!

The Philosophy

But that was the logic. Now let's look at the philosophy and psychology of the matter. What does this logic have to do with the way we value and deal with human beings? The "any reasonable interpretation" rule is based on consideration that it is best when everyone can tell who makes what decisions and that CEOs, like other human beings, should be treated fairly and respectfully.

In Chapter Nine, in "Board Approvals and Monitoring Are Very Different Actions," I described how the approval syndrome obscures who makes what decisions, while the Policy Governance approach clearly attributes decisions to their respective sources. The board should commit itself to respecting decisions made by staff when those decisions are in accord with applicable board policies. Even though the board demands that staff decisions be within staff authority, the board does not meddle in those decisions, second-guess them, or judge them on unstated standards. This code of respect could be phrased as "It's OK to be boss but not OK to be bossy!"

There is a bit of noblesse oblige here. To be both responsible and humane in exercising authority over other human beings (which is the burden and opportunity of any governing board), it is obligatory to be clear, to control only so far as necessary to avoid defaulting on one's own accountability, never to judge on unstated expectations, and to own the range of ambiguity of one's own words.

If the reasonable interpretation rule is not followed, CEOs find themselves being called upon to read the board's collective mind, to continually run back to the board for clarification, or to be subject to after-the-fact judgment of the "you should have known what we meant" variety. For a person who by skill and personality is cut out to be a good CEO, these are demeaning circumstances. And they have predictable effects, for survivor CEOs

> ← **FAQ**
>
> What happens when the "reasonable interpretation rule" isn't followed?

learn to cover their backsides well under such risky circumstances. They may do so by bringing an unending stream of little items to the board agenda, thereby controlling the board's attention. Or they may do so by using the board's own awkward mechanisms to shield their decisions (if a committee liked my plan, I can't be held responsible if it fails).

Frankly, if the board does not grant the right to interpret, it has not granted the right to act. Many nonprofit and governmental boards commit enormous waste by paying for a CEO whom they then treat like a day laborer.

The Practice

In management—as opposed to governance—the "any reasonable interpretation" rule ensures clarity and comfort for subordinates. They have a right to expect their boss to use the words she or he means, allowing them to heed what is generally defined by those words, that is, the range within which those words can be reasonably interpreted. But it must be added that in the management setting, failing to grant any reasonable interpretation to subordinates can more easily be overcome than in governance. For one thing, a person's single supervisor can explain what was meant more easily than can a group supervisor like a board. For another, nods, winks, smiles, and frowns can transmit meaning from one person to one other person (though I'd certainly not recommend relying on such potentially ambiguous communication). But to expect these easy interpersonal mechanisms to work from a group to one person is asking for chaos. So while the reasonable interpretation rule is a good technique in management, it is indispensable in governance.

In practice, the board merely states its ends and its executive limitations in the broadest possible way that is still accurate. (Breadth in a statement does not imply inaccuracy any more than focus implies accuracy. Even a good traditional mission statement is broad and accurate.) Undoubtedly, however, such statements will leave such a wide range of interpretation that the board will want to state its expectations in greater detail. At each level, the question is the same, and a board must explicitly ask itself (yes, I mean aloud): Are we willing for the CEO to interpret these words in any way he or she chooses that can be demonstrated to us as a reasonable interpretation?

FAQ ➡
Doesn't the Policy Governance model require too much confidence in the CEO?

The idea here is not that the board should be content to leave its expectations stated only in very broad terms, nor that the board should extend the statement of its expectations into great detail. The idea is that the board must go to whatever level is necessary for the majority of members (if using a majority vote method) to be willing for the CEO to go ahead with the business of making decisions using any reasonable interpretation. Note that this process should not depend on who the CEO is or how much trust the board has in its CEO. Entirely based on the board's values, the process yields policies that are constant even through CEO changes.

For example, consider the board's instruction about an important component of staff means—protection of the organization's assets. A board might instruct the CEO in an executive limitations policy: "Don't risk assets more than would be the case in standard business practice." That statement, if not expanded, grants the CEO authority to use any reasonable interpretation of assets (Does that include public image? The CEO could decide either way), standard business practice (How does that apply to our organization? In fact, what is standard in business?), and even the concept of risk.

If the board decides that exposure to defalcation might be too great even if the CEO were carrying out a reasonable interpretation of that policy, the board might add wording that makes it unacceptable for the CEO to "allow unbonded persons access to material amounts of funds." This gives the CEO a narrower range within which to interpret one aspect of the larger statement. And of course, even this much interpretive range may be too much for some board members. If a majority of board members want to narrow the range still further, the wording could be adjusted to tell the CEO he or she must not "allow any unbonded person access to more than $1,500."

Have we nailed it down all the way? No. The CEO in carrying out the board's instruction must now interpret whether "access to more than $1,500" means that amount all at once or that amount in some cumulative way, say, over one year. And what, exactly, does "access" mean anyway? Even that is open to interpretation. The CEO might even have some range in interpreting "unbonded," inasmuch as there is blanket insurance available that accomplishes the same protection but would not normally be called bonding.

Please do not misunderstand me. In no way am I saying that the board should keep getting more and more specific. It would drive itself batty doing so and would, in the end, not need a CEO but a clerk. Remember, the board can cover vast territories of organizational situations and activities by its broadest statements. The increased depth in any one area is only called for if

> **← FAQ**
>
> How specific should a board get in limiting interpretation?

the board wants to be more controlling. But the board has an obligation to create policy at the depth with which it will render judgments of CEO performance. It simply isn't fair to create a broad policy, then to evaluate on narrow, unstated interpretations of that policy. My clients—to use the foregoing example—have never gotten to the depth of actually stating the amount that is meant by materially, for there are far more important matters waiting for board wisdom than that one.

Let's try an ends example. A school board has decided on the following wording in the largest statements of its ends: "The school system exists so that young persons can have the skills and insights necessary for successful lives and participation in civic life." It then asks itself, "Would we find the achievement of any reasonable interpretation of these results acceptable?" If so, the board has for now completed its work on the results and recipients elements of ends (remember, ends also includes "at what worth"). But if not, the board must come up with language that represents the majority view at a slightly more defined level.

> It simply isn't fair to create a broad policy, then to evaluate on narrow, unstated interpretations of that policy.

That process might yield something like this: "Skills will include literacy, numeracy, and the ability to combine skills for complex problem-solving." This is more defined, to be sure, so the board may be willing to give its CEO the reins at this point. Or it may not. Numeracy might be further defined as skills in basic calculation or something more advanced. There are a number of things the board members might have in mind, but it should not be the CEO's task to figure them out.

According to the rule, then, the CEO's task is to produce results that are a reasonable interpretation of what the board has said, for recipients that are a reasonable interpretation of what the board has said, and for a cost or relative worth that is a reasonable interpretation of what the board has said, while seeing to it that organizational situations and activities stay within any reasonable interpretation of the bounds described by executive limitations policies. The board starts the process with words. The CEO ends it with behaviors. It is the actual behaviors that must be a reasonable interpretation. That the CEO's verbal interpretations of the board's words are reasonable is only an interim step, necessary but not sufficient.

Granting the CEO the right of "any reasonable interpretation" keeps the board honest in more ways than one. First, the practice forces the board to be clearer to itself and its ownership than it otherwise would have been. Second, it keeps the board-CEO relationship clean and free from an otherwise inevitable build-up of misunderstandings. The board, of course, must be patient enough to stick with a deliberation long enough to settle it and disciplined enough to focus attention on the single level of the issue rather than skip-

> A board is obligated to control whatever it must, yet just as obligated to control no more than it must.

ping around. The board's deliberations will include a testing of its own words—determining if it is possible for the CEO's interpretations to be reasonable yet not acceptable. If so, the board must work more on the policy at hand. If not, the board is finished with the policy at hand.

The "any reasonable interpretation" rule is merely an organized extension of the room we usually give each other in normal communication. The speaker must be responsible for the words he or she uses. The listener may take the words at face value, ascribing to them whatever meaning reasonable persons might give. Rigorous use of the rule is called for in governance because a board is obligated to control whatever it must, yet just as obligated to control no more than it must. The board must lead, to be sure, but it must lead leaders. Leaders need a field of play in which they can let their imagination and innovation roam, free from picky intrusions today and second-guessing tomorrow.

Boards Should Be Not the Final Authority but the Initial Authority

BOARD LEADERSHIP, NUMBER 23, JAN.-FEB. 1996

IT IS CUSTOMARY to refer to a governing board as the "final authority." In this brief article, I contend that the mindset of final authority is destructive to board leadership.

Let me begin, however, by admitting that the board is, in fact, the final authority. No one else in an organization has the right to a final say more than the body that shoulders ultimate accountability.

I don't question the board's right to be the final authority, but I do challenge the wisdom of exercising board authority last in the sequence of decision making. Commonly, final authority translates to having the last word, making the concluding go–no go decision, or approving-disapproving of a plan that others have conceived. Final authority becomes a matter of wielding one's authority conclusively and, therefore, last.

FAQ

Why does the board's acting as "final authority" damage delegation?

Boards should get in front of the parade, rather than bringing up the rear—be proactive in the decision sequence, rather than reactive to what others have decided. Proactive leadership calls for an explicit and clear understanding of what criteria the board would use if it were forced to exercise final authority. The CEO cannot knowingly satisfy these criteria if the board waits to be the final authority. In other words, I envision boards as leaders of production, rather than as after-the-fact quality inspectors.

I envision boards as leaders of production, rather than as after-the-fact
quality inspectors.

Consider two scenarios. The first is a
board acting traditionally as final authority,
the second is a board exercising its initial
authority. Notice that when the board acts
as initial authority it does not give up its
right to judge staff actions. In fact, having
established front-end expectations, such a board is far more equipped to make subsequent judgments. Consequently, playing the final authority role is more efficient,
though more rarely necessary.

Scenario One: Final Authority

The general manager (CEO) of an agricultural co-op needs to purchase a truck to
deliver feed to customers. The department head responsible for feed sales and delivery has done all the preliminary work to determine what size and type of vehicle is
needed, how much financial burden can be borne without hampering operations, and
which vendor will offer the best deal on the purchase. But the CEO cannot allow his
department head to make the purchase because the CEO himself has not been given
that right: purchases of vehicles must be approved by the board.

So the general manager takes to the board a request for approval of the truck purchase. He supplies the board with a sheaf of paperwork justifying the recommended
action. Board members, confronted by this request, are affected in two ways. First,
because purchasing a truck is a familiar task to them, they are immediately drawn into
the intricacies of the purchase and its rationale. Second, because they are being asked
to supply their collective stamp of approval, they feel duty-bound to inquire into the
action fully.

As individuals, board members each feel differently about the purchase. And since
they've been asked to react, they do. A board member thinks a certain make of truck is
far better than the one chosen. Another board member doesn't like the dealer the staff
has chosen. Yet another thinks he can get a little better deal than the staff can arrange.
The staff try to be politically wise, answering questions and justifying their position,
yet they are seething inside at this group chatter over a decision they have carefully
conceived and planned.

In the end, the board approves the purchase, though the whole ordeal has engaged
board members in staff work—trivializing their leadership role—and subjected staff
to a futile game of board tinkering.

When the matter is over, the board has acted by approving, but no one can identify the board values about such purchases which, having apparently been met, rendered the transaction approvable. The board has laid down no criteria. It has only

A Comparison of Boards Acting as Initial Authority Versus Final Authority

As INITIAL AUTHORITY, the board focuses on the organization's underlying values—a necessary prelude to writing them into policy. In Policy Governance, the clarified values fall neatly into (1) the expected consumer results, the expected recipients of these results, and the expected cost or worth of the results; and (2) the values of prudence and ethics that would place certain executive actions and conditions off-limits.

As INITIAL AUTHORITY, the board treats administrative staff as adults and as competent professionals who are capable of making large decisions if they know what criteria are to be met.

As INITIAL AUTHORITY, the board influences executive action primarily through clarifying ends and secondarily through defining unacceptable means. For CEOs this means important parameters are made clear while extensive authority is granted to operate within them. The CEO is more likely to be a professional manager under these conditions.

As FINAL AUTHORITY, board members make decisions based, ostensibly, on individual values when they vote on whether to approve a proposed administrative course of action. The board values are rarely debated and clarified. When the subject does arise, the discussion tends to be spotty and incomplete (as when a board issues a few guidelines for the next budget).

As FINAL AUTHORITY, the board plays a parental role, subjecting staff to criticism arising from individual board members' points of view. Unless the board retreats into rubber-stamping, the experience for staff is always trivializing and often even demeaning.

As FINAL AUTHORITY, the board influences executive action largely in a means-oriented, piecemeal fashion. Even when a long-range plan is being approved, boards rarely have the end goals in sight as they approve. Thus, even strategic planning is rendered a means-focused undertaking. In this setup, the CEO tends to play politician, "selling" only bits and pieces of his or her overall intent.

determined that this particular purchase may proceed. The next purchase will have to go through the same charade.

Scenario Two: Initial Authority

Same general manager, same board, same need for a truck. The general manager checks the relevant board policies and takes action. There is no slowdown; there is no board approval. There is no board interference in managerial thinking. After all, the board has its own job to do: There is hardly time for it to take on staff work as well. The action will subsequently be monitored during a routine check in which the board verifies that this purchase and numerous other executive actions have complied with board policies.

Now, what board policies would the general manager have checked? First, he would know that if he fails to produce the board-specified benefits to co-op members at or below the board-set cost limit, he will be in noncompliance. These guidelines are found in the board's ends policies. Although the cost of a single ingredient (for example, a truck) is not specified within the total allowable cost of a benefit, the general manager must be careful that total cost for the benefit remains in line. Second, the CEO knows what constraints (unacceptable actions and methods) the board has put on general purchasing, conflict of interest, or on capital expenditures. These criteria can be found in executive limitations policies.

> Acting only as final authority is defaulting on board leadership and copping out on the obligation of leaders to put their values up front.

For example, the board may have prohibited any equipment purchase over $10,000 that is not supported by a documented comparison of long-term quality and cost among competing products and vendors. Or the board may have said that large equipment cannot be purchased based on immediate needs alone but must be justified by estimates of longer term needs. That is, don't buy a three-quarter-ton truck if, within eighteen months, a two-ton truck will be needed.

To put a finer point on my argument, acting only as final authority is defaulting on board leadership and copping out on the obligation of leaders to put their values up front. To a great degree, exercising initial authority on behalf of the ownership is board leadership; exercising final authority is tagging along behind the staff.

Abstracting Up: Discovering the Big Issues Among the Trivia

Board Leadership, Number 15, Sept.-Oct. 1994

IN GOVERNANCE, as in life, it's often difficult to see the forest for the trees—that is, to discover the big, relevant issues among the trivial concerns that are always threatening to overwhelm our attention. Yet it's an essential part of the board's job to determine where the day-to-day details of running an organization fit into the grand scheme of things. To achieve this goal, boards need to create comprehensive policies, of course. But creation is only the beginning. No matter how carefully policies are crafted, particular problems and unforeseen circumstances will come up that can throw boards right back into the meddlesome, micromanaging behavior that keeps them from addressing issues on a meaningful level. To avoid backsliding, boards must learn to exercise the skill of *abstracting up,* or seeking and discovering the relevant higher principle or value in each smaller, narrower issue. Let me give you an example of how this concept works.

In one of my recent workshops, a YMCA board member raised his concern that the YMCA staff might not know how to respond in the case of an armed robbery at their urban facility. He'd heard of such an occurrence, during which staff members panicked, having had no training in how to appropriately react to that unfortunate circumstance. Staff members and clients were consequently endangered due to the staff's unschooled reaction. He asked me if the board should have an executive limitations policy that would make lack of robbery preparation unacceptable.

He was on the right track. Enumerating unpalatable conditions, practices, actions, and behaviors is exactly what executive limitations policies are designed to do. And here was a true case of an unacceptable circumstance. My questioner's problem, however, was that he wasn't abstracting the specific worry to a broader level. He was confining his thinking about board policy to too specific an instance.

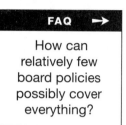

FAQ ➡

How can relatively few board policies possibly cover everything?

In Policy Governance, the board essentially addresses every issue in the organization. It does not do so one issue at a time, nor should it normally do so in reaction to single issues that arise. The board addresses all issues simply by creating broadly inclusive policy across all aspects of organization so that every possible issue falls within the policies created.

Creating policy from this broad perspective and then adding one level of detail at a time will ensure that all smaller issues are adequately governed. But issues do not come to the board's attention in this carefully ordered way, as my questioner's point illustrated. Something unexpected can come up. Some specific worry might arise in a board member's mind while reading the newspaper. A disgruntled caller might tell a board member of some real or imagined staff misconduct.

Finding the Broader Concern

The reason for seeking a broader embodiment of this board member's issue is that there is a broader concern than the specific one being discussed at this time by the board member. If my questioner's board can find what its broader concern is, then it can create a policy that covers not only the present matter but also many unforeseen ones.

If we continue to abstract up, we arrive at the executive limitations policy that is broad enough to include all possible unacceptable staff means.

This search calls for a board to ferret out its values about the presenting worry. A useful technique is for the board to ask itself, "What is it that makes staff preparedness for robberies matter?" The question seems silly at first glance. The board member in my workshop—as I questioned him in this way—found that for him the slightly broader concern underlying the robbery issue was that staff members shouldn't be unprepared for life-threatening emergencies of any sort.

By making this observation about his own values, he took the first step in abstracting up to a higher level. What might have become a board policy prohibiting "lack of staff preparedness for robbery" now could be couched as preventing "lack of staff preparedness for conditions threatening life and limb." He and his board should not stop at this level, however. The next level up might be to prohibit "working conditions or exposures that place staff members or clients in jeopardy." Now, in a single stroke, his board would have covered not only robbery crises, but also other crises, and even beyond emergency situations to endangerment of any sort.

At each successively higher level, more and more conditions are encompassed by the policy, yet the initial concern has not been abandoned and the physical policy itself has not grown longer. Notice that if we continue to abstract up, we finally arrive at the ultimate executive limitations policy, the one that is broad enough to include all possible unacceptable staff means: "Don't do or allow anything unethical or imprudent." If Policy Governance had been implemented in the first place, this broadest proscription would have already been stated, for policy making in Policy Governance always begins from the "largest end."

> Routinely targeting policy on smaller issues fails to increase the integrity of the total body of policy and swells policy documents beyond a manageable size.

Pinning Down the Details

For every worry the board wishes to address, then, the board should abstract the matter all the way up to the level at which it has already spoken. Once the board has reviewed its existing policy, it can change what it has already said or add more specificity to the policy. If greater detail is added, the new policy language will be narrower than policy previously in place but broader than the specific issue that sparked the original concern. After the new language receives a passing vote, the board may decide it would be wise to increase the level of detail further. This is fine, as long as it is done one step at a time, starting with the largest value or principle and working toward more specificity. My questioner's board could conceivably end up with a policy about robbery preparedness, but through this top-down route.

However, the original worry would probably be satisfied if the board were to state one of the higher-level prohibitions, leaving an issue as specific as robbery preparedness to CEO interpretation. But the board must always work from the broadest end of the spectrum, even if, once sensitized to a very specific matter, it must painstakingly "think its way up." Routinely targeting policy on smaller issues fails to increase the integrity of the total body of policy and swells policy documents beyond a manageable size.

← **FAQ**

Why is it best to develop policy "from the largest to the smallest"?

In summary, board leadership calls for developing the ability to take a particular event or concern and translating it into a legitimate board issue. The ability to abstract up prevents a board from reacting merely to a specific issue that has surfaced. Addressing the specific can quickly deteriorate into meddling in staff operations. But worse, it fails to improve the board policy that—had it been in effect—would have taken care of the matter in the first place. Abstracting up is an exercise of finding successively higher principles or values in any issue. It is a required skill for board leadership.

Who's in Charge? Is Your Organization Too Staff-Driven? Too Volunteer-Driven?

BOARD LEADERSHIP, NUMBER 22, NOV.-DEC. 1995

IN MANY ORGANIZATIONS—particularly in membership associations—there is often a tug and pull about whether the organization is sufficiently *volunteer-driven,* or too *staff-driven.* These terms are typically used in a disagreement over who is—or should be—in charge.

On one hand, some volunteers believe they should have the authority to do anything they want within the staff organization. Curtailment of that right is given as evidence that the organization is staff-driven. On the other hand, some staff view volunteers (particularly board volunteers) as pesky accessories to the "real" organization. Any volunteer authority is cited as an infringement on the professional prerogatives of staff. Unfortunately, these arguments exhibit so much governance misunderstanding that neither point of view makes sense to me.

First of all, let's be sure which volunteers we are talking about. That someone is a volunteer merely means the person isn't paid for her or his contribution. It tells me nothing about whether the person should have authority or even be allowed in the front door. But if I divide volunteers into governing volunteers and operational volunteers, I can tell the difference between persons who volunteer to "own" the organization (on behalf of others—the true ownership) and those who volunteer to help with operational tasks.

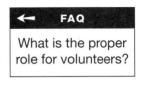

← FAQ

What is the proper role for volunteers?

Volunteers who help out (I'll call them operational volunteers) deserve thanks and honor, but there is no reason to let them "drive" anything. They are there to help staff whom the board holds accountable to get a job done. Volunteers of this kind must take their cues from staff. But volunteers who govern are an entirely different matter. Governance volunteers carry a trusteeship of sorts, a representation of the ownership rights of a larger group and, consequently, have not only the right but the obligation to drive on the owners' behalf.

> Volunteers deserve thanks and honor, but there is no reason to let them "drive" anything.

The obligation and authority to drive things belong to the board as a group rather than to individuals on the board. In fact, the obligation to act within the constraints of group discipline is a burden necessitated by the board's authority, a burden operational volunteers ordinarily don't have to face. They merely need to do, individually, whatever they are asked—and agree—to do.

Thus, to use a membership association as an example, the board is charged by the members (owners) with the task of governing an organization on members' behalf. The board further delegates to a chief executive officer, thence he or she to a staff. Is that volunteer-driven? You bet it is, for it begins with—and is ultimately controlled by—volunteers. And it would be a miscarriage if it were not; in this sense, all responsible governing boards are "volunteer-driven." Being volunteer-driven is exactly what such organizations should be—they have no right to be anything less—as long as the volunteers we are talking about are governing board volunteers.

But what if the volunteers are not board members? Or what if they are board members, but are not acting through the full board? If volunteers have the right to exercise authority simply because they are volunteers, the resulting situation severely jeopardizes both governance and management. The careful expression of board trusteeship through a CEO, then by the CEO to various operational units, can be derailed if volunteers exercise control wherever they feel like it.

> **FAQ** ➡
>
> What is the appropriate way for owners to exercise their authority?

But aren't members the owners in a membership organization? Shouldn't they therefore have the right to tell the organization what to do? Of course, but the route they have for the exercise of that right is through the governing board. The board is constituted to condense the many and competing member needs into a single set of consistent marching orders for the CEO. Organizations should be governor-driven but should never be helper-driven.

Let's look at how mission-damaging confusion about volunteer authority can occur. First, let me cite an example that would most likely occur in a membership organization. Then I'll illustrate how any sort of organization can fall into the same trap.

A Membership Association Example

In membership organizations, the mistaken belief is strongly held that involvement of volunteers is in itself a good thing. To enhance membership involvement, association boards typically create a raft of working committees. These committees usually engage association members (sometimes including board members, sometimes not) in operational work. In my experience, these committees are given assignments by the board that would properly be under the purview of the CEO.

Hence, even a board of Realtors with a CEO might still create a Multiple Listing Service (MLS) committee composed of member Realtors, whose job is to create or oversee the creation of a database for members' use. (Realtor and MLS are registered service marks.) Now, if a board of Realtors has one product that is more important than all others, it is surely the indispensable MLS. Is the CEO charged with producing this product? One would think so, for if the CEO is not accountable for the production of organizational products—

> Organizations should be governor-driven but should never be helper-driven.

let alone the most important one—why would a CEO be needed? But if the CEO is accountable, what would justify either the board or a committee assigned by the board obscuring the clarity of this accountability?

Let me assume that the single-minded, overriding intention of the board is to produce as much value per dollar for members as possible. I would then also assume that producing the most value per dollar is of greater importance than involving members in the production of that value. In other words, the board of Realtors exists so that members can practice their trade with greater success and lower personal cost—the aim of most trade and professional associations. The board of Realtors does not exist so that members can have more volunteer activity in their lives. While member involvement may be a way we can accomplish certain desired results, it is, in itself, of questionable value.

There are other reasons for involving members besides increasing productivity, of course, but the damaging effect of unwarranted meddling must still be avoided. What other desired results might warrant member involvement? Let me list three and relate each of them to the board's creation of member committees.

1. *The board might want potential leaders among the membership to be identified and cultivated.* Why not address this aim by enlisting these volunteers to help with some portion of the board's job rather than the CEO's? For example, as the board addresses ends issues (for which getting member input is critical), potential leaders can be tapped to gather member ideas about various desired outputs. They would not only receive training in a specific board responsibility, but would also gain closer experience of the ownership's wishes in a way boards often overlook. These are not volunteers who drive, but volunteers who help those who drive. They have no direct connection with staff activities.

> While member involvement may be a way we can accomplish certain desired results, it is, in itself, of questionable value.

2. *Another board desire is for the operational organization to tap as much free talent as possible, that is, to make use of volunteers.* This is a subset of a larger interest: that the CEO be efficient in producing organizational results. As with all staff matters, however, it is best to leave the decision about how to do it to the CEO. It is the board's stated ends policies (what results, for whom, at what cost) that direct the CEO toward efficient use of available talent. The board loses the sharp edge of CEO accountability if it begins prescribing volunteer structures, such as committees, that the CEO must use.

3. *Still another board desire might be for the confidence that an organizational product will truly be helpful to the members.* It is common for professional and trade association boards to make much of the assertion that only members of their profession or trade can successfully oversee the production of specialized products. Hence, if the CEO of the society of architects is not an architect, or if the CEO of the social workers association is not a social worker, board members create committees of architects or social workers to "help" the CEO with his or her perceived deficiency. In such organizations, the CEO is relegated to the position of a highly paid hand servant to board members and to the very membership committees the board has created. The mission is compromised, for the committees are virtually never as effective in managing for results as the CEO can be required to be.

In cases such as these, the central board concern is well founded: Organizational products must be effective and appropriate for the eventual customers—the membership. But the answer does not lie in inserting a board-controlled function within the CEO's domain. The answer lies in the precise definition of the desired product.

Consider a board of Realtors that defines one part of its ends as "Timely, accessible, accurate, reader-friendly data for members on property offered for sale at no more than $235,000 annual cost to the general membership dues fund."

To be certain that he or she will be successful in achieving this end, the CEO (not the board) could create a committee of randomly chosen Realtors to assess whether the emerging MLS product will pass as a reasonable interpretation of the board's stringent requirement. It is not only unnecessary for board members to be on the committee, but to avoid role conflicts it is best that none of them are. Note that this committee would not be charged by the board, but by the CEO. It would be acting as a focus group. Volunteer involvement in this case is not arranged merely to involve volunteers, but to ensure product quality. And the volunteers are brought in by the appropriate members of the organization.

If the CEO is not accountable for the successful production of board-defined results, it is doubtful that there really is a CEO in more than name only. If the CEO is accountable, the board should leave him or her alone to produce the product. This is a simple prescription if the board has properly defined the product to begin with. Misdirected volunteers in confused roles then do not arise. The CEO might choose to have a personnel committee, but the board would not. The CEO might create program committees, public relations committees, committees for various publications, and so forth; but the board would not. Consequently, if the CEO needs to involve members either to produce the product (operational worker volunteers) or to advise management as the product is produced (operational adviser volunteers), so be it. But that is the CEO's problem and no concern of the board's.

> **← FAQ**
>
> We can't expect a CEO to know everything, so why shouldn't volunteers help?

Solutions to the above-described situations should always maintain that very important role division: Governing volunteers (board members) stay in control of defining the product to be produced; they drive the organization. Operational volunteers (whether helping as unpaid staff members or as advisers) are never in control, though their input can be quite powerful and highly valued. Member involvement occurs, but always in the service of greater value; never in the service of involvement as an end in itself.

> If the CEO is not accountable for the successful production of board-defined results, it is doubtful that there really is a CEO.

Actually—despite the degree to which association boards and staffs worry themselves about member involvement—I have found, consistently, that members are far more concerned about association benefits being worth the dues than they are about

---

A relative handful of volunteers are allowed to exercise authority not gained through vote and not disciplined by governing responsibilities.

---

being able to participate. After all, they are busy people with many demands on their time. Even more curious, volunteer-involvement dogma is invoked even when the actual number of volunteers is a slim percentage of all members, giving lie to the assertion that opportunities for member involvement are highly valued by members in general. As often as not, the dogma serves a relative handful of volunteers who, consequently, are allowed to exercise authority not gained through vote and not disciplined by governing responsibilities.

Organizations That Are Not Member Associations

I have used membership associations as examples to illustrate my points above. But nonmembership organizations can fall into the same traps. Sometimes board members themselves demand to be involved in operational matters. Further, community boards (though lacking anything resembling a membership) are often so determined to involve community volunteers they will structure and define the involvement, intruding on and handicapping CEO accountability in ways similar to those I described earlier.

FAQ ➡

Is it appropriate for volunteers to report to paid staff? Shouldn't volunteers report directly to the board?

I have also uncovered a curious belief among some organizations that volunteers should never report to paid staff, but only to other volunteers. In the loose sense that everyone at some point could be said to report to the governing board, this belief may be accurate. But if a board has a CEO, commitment to organizational performance rather than to volunteer egos demands that operational volunteers report through the same channel all other operations report: the CEO. This means, of course, that groups of operational volunteers have no official line to the board for any reason. For example, in organizations with a CEO, operational volunteers should never be "represented" on the board. Volunteer "drivenness" (as evidenced by the board) should be so powerful and obvious that no such amateurish display is required to demonstrate that ultimately volunteers run the show.

These comments have important implications for those organizations that "graduate" volunteers from operational status to governing board status. That persons have given volunteer service faithfully is commendable and should be rewarded, but it is no indication that they can be good governing board leaders. Therefore, such organizations should look closely at this practice, eliminating or adapting it as necessary to assure that newly appointed board members make the large role shift with appropriate support and training.

Good governance, to make any sense, cannot be the exercise of individual authority by any volunteer or group of volunteers justified by the sole virtue of being volunteers. That would not be volunteer-driven, but volunteer-muddled. The resolution of the volunteer-driven versus staff-driven debate rests in recognizing the distinction between volunteers-as-governors and volunteers-as-helpers. The CEO and staff work for volunteers-as-governors; hence the staff is clearly volunteer-driven. But volunteers-as-helpers work for the CEO and staff; hence these volunteers are clearly staff-driven.

In summary, some volunteers would complain that an organization is staff-driven simply because sensible management principles are followed. Some staff would complain about being too volunteer-driven simply because the rightful owners exercise their ownership. Effective governance principles are necessary to put these viewpoints in perspective. An organization should be both volunteer- and staff-driven, but in regard to different issues.

> In organizations with a CEO, operational volunteers should never be "represented" on the board.

> Good governance cannot be the exercise of individual authority by volunteers justified by the sole virtue of being volunteers.

Never Cast in Stone: Flexible Policy Supports Management and Saves Board Time

BOARD LEADERSHIP, NUMBER 8, JULY-AUG. 1993

I AM OFTEN ASKED, "Once we put policy in place, are we stuck with it forever?" Of course, my answer is no, for even though board policies are rather stable, the board reserves the right to change them any time it deems fitting.

One of the benefits of good policy is that a board can cover any eventualities with a single stroke. The point is that if we can isolate and enunciate the relevant principle or value in making a particular class of decisions, someone else can apply that principle or value in all the decisions to which it is applicable.

But policies do not always spring forth in their ultimate form. So a good policy system will be flexible enough to permit the board's wisdom to accumulate over time, enabling policy updating as necessary. Here is an example of a board that took advantage of its developing wisdom to make a good policy even better.

I was assisting the board of a community mental health center as it considered granting the executive director an exception to one of its policies. The center had amassed several hundred thousand dollars in funded depreciation, an account the board for obvious reasons wished to safeguard. (To "fund" depreciation simply means to put actual funds aside equal to the amount of annual plant and equipment depreciation.) The accumulated reserve could be used to replace capital items as they wore out or became obsolete.

As is common where the Policy Governance model is used, this board had among its executive limitations policies one called "asset protection," which set limits on the acceptable range of CEO behavior with respect to protecting the

> A good policy system will be flexible enough to permit the board's wisdom to accumulate over time.

center's resources. In this policy was a provision stating that the executive director could not "spend or encumber over $35,000 per year of the funded depreciation account, and that only for capital replacement." This provision allowed the CEO access to the fund for normal replacement, while protecting the bulk of the fund.

On this occasion the CEO had asked the board to be released from the asset protection policy in order to purchase a new internal telephone system, a nonrecurring expense. Replacing the existing system, while costly in immediate outlay ($50,000), would save money in the long run. The board agreed with the CEO's argument and amended the policy provision by adding the words, "except in fiscal year 1989 an additional amount not

← FAQ

Does Policy Governance provide for one-time exceptions in policy?

to exceed $50,000 for the purchase of a complete internal phone system."

This was a policy solution to the problem that did not lure the board into taking over the decision. Notice that the board did not "approve" the purchase. Approval not only would have drawn it into studying and dealing with intricacies of the phone system selection but would have taken the burden for the decision off the CEO's shoulders. Remember that all other board policies, such as prudent purchasing methods and protection of assets, still apply to the CEO's conduct. A release from one limitation does not release the CEO from the other expectations.

Continuing the Examination

This was a good change; it solved the immediate problem in a way that was consistent with good governance. But I urged the board to go further. No matter how well its policies are written, often the board itself has to make what is in fact a management decision. When that happens, it usually means that the principles or values that could guide a CEO decision have not been made sufficiently explicit. The board can extend the effectiveness of governing by policy if it continues to examine decisions to see if

← FAQ

How can policies cover a broad range of eventualities without becoming mired in details?

the values used to make a decision can themselves be made explicit and, therefore, available to be used by others as a guide.

In this instance, the board examined what led it to decide to allow the phone system purchase. Discussion revealed that any CEO decision beyond the initial policy limit would be acceptable to the board if it fulfilled two criteria. The first criterion was that the expenditure would be earned back in less than three years when calculated with a conservative estimate of cost recovery and net present value of the probable savings. (A *net present value* calculation corrects for the difference in value between a dollar laid out now versus a dollar spent at some point in the future.) The second requirement was that in no event could the outlay reduce the funded depreciation account to below 15 percent of annual revenues.

After this discussion, the board had a much clearer picture of its values with respect to atypical capital outlays. With this new clarity, the board once again amended the funded depreciation of its asset protection policy: "The executive director may not spend or encumber over $35,000 per year of the funded depreciation account, and that only for capital replacement, unless an outlay in excess of this limit (1) can be shown by conservative projection to repay itself within three years and (2) will not reduce funded depreciation to below 15 percent of annual revenues."

With this upgraded policy in place, the executive director can make decisions above the basic $35,000 limit if they pass under the new provision. The board's anxieties about the funded depreciation reserve and the CEO's need for managerial agility were both satisfied.

It is not always easy to figure out all the principles that, if stated, could clarify things for subordinates and reduce the leaders' workload of repetitive decisions. But a good system should enable an accumulation of such guiding statements. The funded depreciation example demonstrates that the task of ferreting such values and principles is never completely finished. A board that stays attuned to seeking out underlying values can, over time, eliminate more and more specific decisions from its own agenda, empower managers to tailor decisions using these principles, and safeguard precious board time for governing.

Policy Governance Is Not a "Hands Off" Model

BOARD LEADERSHIP, NUMBER 19, MAY-JUNE 1995

BECAUSE THE Policy Governance approach is a radical departure from the traditional form of governance, CEOs and board members sometimes mistakenly characterize Policy Governance as a "hands off" model of board governance. I assume that by "hands off" they mean a laissez-faire, uninvolved approach to board control over management, wherein the board stays out of the CEO's hair. Nothing, however, could be further from the truth.

I suppose the term *hands off* is used in contrast with *hands on*. Both terms are imprecise, to be sure, but *hands on* frequently connotes an involvement in details, in micromanaging, and in either inquiring about or actively steering trivial matters. Some people call such a board a "working board," which implies that the only way to work is to be involved in details. Maybe *hands on* describes the school board that believes it is the superintendent, or the city council, that acts as if it is also the city manager. As the term is commonly used, hands-on governance refers to what many would call meddling.

Before this discussion begins to sound as if hands-on governance were bad and hands-off governance were good, we'd better examine the sins of hands-off governance. Consider these frightening examples of hands-off board behavior: Confederation Life (Toronto) failed last year, North America's greatest insurance company failure in history; Continental Illinois (Chicago) still connotes bank failure in business conversation; the United Way of America fiasco, with its board asleep at the switch, is still fresh in our minds, only to be joined by the NAACP board's allowing virtual fiscal destruction of its organization. In each of these cases, the board took what some would consider a hands-off approach, and each had a disastrous outcome. This type of hands-off approach seems to use abdication as a legitimate form of delegation. As the term is commonly used, hands-off governance refers to what many would call rubber-stamping.

Does it seem as though I've painted myself into a corner? Hands-off and hands-on governance both appear suspect. And, to further confuse you, I'd have to character-ize Policy Governance as hands on . . . *and* hands off!

Combining Hands-On and Hands-Off Governance

Some years ago, when I was struggling to be as expert in MBO (management by objec-tives) as possible, a helpful coach taught me that the point is neither to manage more tightly nor more loosely. (These opposing points of view correspond roughly to what are called Theory X and Theory Y management styles.) The point is to manage tightly about some things and loosely about other things. Years later, Tom Peters and Bob Waterman cleverly captured this simple truth in the phrase "simultaneously loose-tight control."

> The best governance is hands off about some things and decidedly hands on about other things. The trick is in knowing when.

This concept conveys just my point about board leadership. The best gover-nance is hands off about some things and decidedly hands on about other things. The trick is in knowing when to be hands on and when to be hands off.

A responsible governing board should govern. It is not a figurehead. As owner-rep-resentative, the board holds title to the most authoritative function in the organiza-tion, a function that is more authoritative than that of its CEO, its staff professionals, its legal counsel, its auditing firm, and even its funding sources. Accompanying this considerable authority is an equally considerable accountability: The board is accountable for everything the organization is, everything it does, and everything it achieves—or fails to achieve.

Does this fact make the board a hands-on, working board? It absolutely does. Although some may picture the board as being above actual tasks, pristinely removed from real organizational work, I think it is impossible for a board to govern unless that board does hands-on work. Defining the unique nature of the board's proper work has, however, eluded traditional governance.

Designing the board's work requires a simple framework within which the responsibility for one's own work and the upwardly accumulating responsibility for the work of others can be conceived. Let me illustrate, beginning with one individual, Barbara. Barbara is responsible for her

> The board bears more cumulative responsibility than the CEO because the board is responsible for itself, the CEO, and the entire organization.

own behavior, her own work. If Barbara is a supervisor, she is also responsible for the team consisting of herself, George, Jean, Pierre, and Manuel. Her responsibility for the others' work is a "cumulative" responsibility because it adds up from the bottom. For example, if Jean and Pierre are also supervisors, Barbara's cumulative responsibility sums all the work conducted by this extended team. CEOs, because they sit atop all the staff functions, inherit a massive cumulative responsibility, though their direct responsibility may be no more onerous than that of one of their subordinates.

The board bears the full amount of cumulative responsibility, bearing more cumulative responsibility than the CEO because the board is responsible for itself, the CEO, and the entire organization. Designing the board's job simply entails deciding what direct work the board can do to fulfill its extensive cumulative responsibility. In other words, what hands-on work will enable the board to govern all those matters that it can never get to itself, matters that it must delegate to the staff and that must remain, by necessity, hands off?

Hands-On Responsibilities

A board that follows the principles of Policy Governance can use three hands-on jobs to solve this dilemma. I will address these three jobs as outputs, that is, three separate "values added" to the organization by its governing board. You might view these outputs as a board's three products. Some boards require one or more additional outputs to meet the needs of their particular circumstances (the fourth item in the following list represents these additional outputs), but three essential

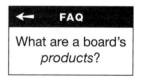
← FAQ
What are a board's *products*?

hands-on outputs apply to every governing board. You will notice that the following outputs are couched in the language of job results, not job activity.

1. *Linkage with the ownership.* The board itself must produce a connection between the operating organization and those persons who morally (if not legally) own the organization. To accomplish this output, the board might attend meetings with the owners, participate in focus groups, grapple with surveys, or confer with other boards that represent the same owners.

2. *Written board policy.* The board itself must produce written statements of values and perspectives that blanket or "enclose" everything the organization might do, be, or cause. The four categories of board policy in Policy Governance give boards this framework. Staff members do not create these policies for recommendation to the board; the board generates them, hands on, from its own values, which are influenced by input from all relevant sources, including staff members.

> Can the board involve staff members in its direct work? Yes, it can, but it cannot shed direct responsibility for the work.

---

3. *Assurance of organizational performance.* The board itself must produce a reasonable assurance of organizational performance. That is, once directives are established that state what the organization should achieve and what it should avoid, the board is the owners' guarantor that these directives have or have not come true, and that, in either case, the board expects restored or continued executive performance.

4. *Additional outputs particular to a specific board, if applicable.* The board itself must produce all other outputs that it deems necessary to assign to itself. Depending on a board's particular circumstances, it might require no more than the first three job outputs, or it might need to add further outputs, such as donor funding, legislative impact, real estate acquisition, or security–return of endowment.

These outputs belong to the board, not to its subordinates. A given board would first enumerate these outputs, then plan how to accomplish the work. Because this list of outputs involves hands-on, personal work for which the board, not the staff, is directly responsible, these board products would drive an annual board work plan, board objectives (for the board, not the staff), or committee assignments.

Can the board involve staff members in its direct work? Yes, it can, but it cannot shed direct responsibility for the work. Governance is the board's job. The board need not and should not be held responsible for doing the staff's work, but must directly engage its own.

The ship captain has a hands-on job. It is not hands on a wrench in the engine room or a frying pan in the kitchen, but it is hands on the chart and hands on the wheel. The army general has a hands-on job. It isn't hands on with respect to rifles, foxholes, and aiming artillery. But it is hands on with respect to defining battle missions, rules of engagement, and acceptable risks.

So, is the board's job a hands-off job? Not at all. Is it hands on? Absolutely, at least in terms of the board's direct responsibilities, those necessary to guarantee coverage of its cumulative, indirect responsibilities (see Exhibit 7.1).

EXHIBIT 7.1. Hands On Versus Hands Off

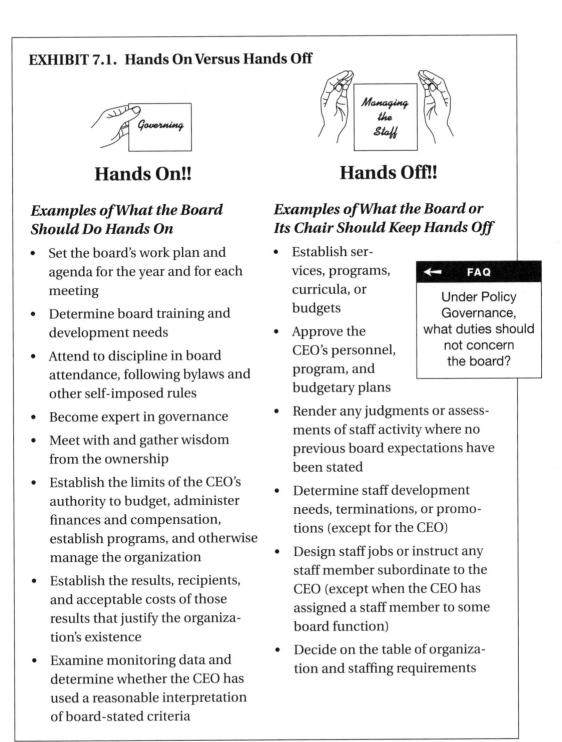

Hands On!!

Examples of What the Board Should Do Hands On

- Set the board's work plan and agenda for the year and for each meeting

- Determine board training and development needs

- Attend to discipline in board attendance, following bylaws and other self-imposed rules

- Become expert in governance

- Meet with and gather wisdom from the ownership

- Establish the limits of the CEO's authority to budget, administer finances and compensation, establish programs, and otherwise manage the organization

- Establish the results, recipients, and acceptable costs of those results that justify the organization's existence

- Examine monitoring data and determine whether the CEO has used a reasonable interpretation of board-stated criteria

Hands Off!!

Examples of What the Board or Its Chair Should Keep Hands Off

- Establish services, programs, curricula, or budgets

- Approve the CEO's personnel, program, and budgetary plans

FAQ

Under Policy Governance, what duties should not concern the board?

- Render any judgments or assessments of staff activity where no previous board expectations have been stated

- Determine staff development needs, terminations, or promotions (except for the CEO)

- Design staff jobs or instruct any staff member subordinate to the CEO (except when the CEO has assigned a staff member to some board function)

- Decide on the table of organization and staffing requirements

Chapter Eight

When the Board Meets

Products, Process, Discipline, and Costs

Board meetings exist for boards to learn relevant information, debate competing points of view, and make official group decisions about the future—not to act as group manager, focus on last month, or be entertained by staff show-and-tell presentations. The nature, cost, and agendas of board meetings, as well as the characteristics of board members themselves, should be driven by the board's owner-representative, accountability-assuring role. Governance excellence is unattainable without studied attention to the cost-benefits, process, and discipline of the board. Performance of the board is a far greater challenge than performance of the staff.

Is Your Board in a Rut? Shake Up Your Routine!

BOARD LEADERSHIP, NUMBER 4, NOV.-DEC. 1992

B OARDS, BOARDROOMS, and board meetings conjure up stuffy images. Formality, rigidly controlled interaction, and a polished conspiracy to be polite come to mind, as do oak paneling, soft chairs, and an attractive table. Nonprofit boards may escape these caricatures a bit more than public and corporate boards, but take a look at your board. It may be less effective than it could be *simply because it tries to look like a board.*

For a board that operates in public view, like many city councils and school boards, the board meeting can become more performance than deliberation. The public spotlight brings out posturing and politics. I recently watched a public board (a city council) fundamentally alter its conduct when two constituents entered the previously private workshop room. But whether your board is posturing for others or just fulfilling its own expectations of official demeanor and formality, governance can become pretty pretentious.

Picture the same people in a retreat setting, intently slaving over some important problem. Despite all our horror tales about committees, boards could learn a thing or two from the informal, sleeves-rolled-up committee meeting. You know, the kind where a handful of people struggle, persuade, and argue with each other. Then they flip an issue on its back as well as on all sides in order to try an array of formulations.

Intensity! Creativity! Passion! The board may have a tiger of a subject by the tail, a topic too dear to shortchange by following

> **← FAQ**
>
> Isn't it important, for consistency, to have a board meeting every month, in the same place, with a similar agenda?

Take a look at your board. It may be less effective than it could be *simply because it tries to look like a board.*

the often-vaunted "crisp, businesslike" agenda. Such a session definitely does not look like the oak-paneled room scenario.

Try breaking out of the mold! Take a chance that you'll find a different, perhaps novel, approach that is not only better but energizing. Your board's task is not the same all the time; it will vary during the year. So what works one time will not work as well another time. Methods and settings need to shift to fit the business at hand. Invite your board to look back to see if your meetings don't have a monotonous regularity about them, which is like trying to use your trusty ⅝-inch wrench no matter what size the nut!

FAQ ➡

What can a board do if it is losing good board members simply because its meetings are boring?

Try one or more of the following suggestions. Some may not work for you, but the point is to break the mesmerizing routine of straitjacketed board behavior.

Devote an entire meeting to a "what if" session. What if half the staff quit? What if we received an unexpected, large grant for something we aren't sure we want to do? What if a major disaster hit our town? What if—and on and on. You could have each board member contribute one "what if." This kind of dialogue is not only fun, it tends to open previously unexamined possibilities and often to expose the fact that current success may be due largely to fortunate circumstances.

For Board Discussion

- If there were no history to influence your expectations of board activity, would you have designed your routine the way it is?

- Put on your agenda a board discussion about whether, how, and why the board should shake up its business-as-usual meetings.

- Does your board consciously *choose* the kind of environment, procedure, and activity that will serve your vitality, creativity, and leadership best? Or are you stuck in an approach inherited from past boards?

Go as a group to observe another board. Public boards such as school boards and city councils can handle your visit easily, since they are accustomed to being in the public eye. Private boards may allow you this privilege if you ask nicely. Governance issues may be more easily seen in another board than in your own, especially if you will look beyond the differences in agenda content to the underlying process.

Ask a futurist to address the board on topics relevant to your organization's mission. Futurists have a way of stretching vision and challenging our unspoken assumption that the future is merely an extension of the present. They will also force you to look at a broader vista than that associated with even far-sighted views of your own organization.

Force futurity for an entire meeting. This experiment in futurity doesn't even require an outsider. You merely agree to a one-meeting game in which all utterances must be about events, hopes, conditions, or fears *at least two years in the future*. The chair rules any near-term comment out of order, or to add a playful touch, other board members roundly boo the offender.

Invite a well-spoken opponent. You need not debate the person or even deliberate the opposing views at this meeting, though you may want to flag some of the presenter's points for further board study. You can't help but be challenged and energized by a presentation from someone opposed to your board's beliefs, positions, or chosen ends.

The list could go on, of course. You might try meeting without a table, but with comfortable seating such as you might envision for a philosophical parlor discussion. Or have a completely social event with staff and perhaps significant other persons, authorities, or "ambassadors" from other organizations. You might meet sequentially in each of the sites operated by your organization. Or cancel the next three regular meetings, then meet in an unusually long session. You could meet jointly with another board or two. I am sure you can come up with many more possibilities (and I want to hear about them, so write me).

Why Not Set Your Quorum Requirement at 100 Percent?

Board Leadership, Number 37, May-June 1998

For years I have dealt with boards and their bylaws, paying close attention to the quorum requirement every board has in its bylaws. I have seen most quorum requirements set at 51 percent or the equivalent (such as 50 percent plus one person), but many set at 40 percent, 30 percent, and even lower (a quorum of nine for a board of fifty-four!). Without fail, I point out the folly of low quorum thresholds, encouraging boards never to drop below 50 percent and to set the figure higher if possible. While I still believe in the basic wisdom behind this suggestion, recent insights have convinced me that it does not go nearly far enough. My previous guidance fails to stimulate a confrontation important to board leadership.

So let me encourage your board to consider a revolutionary version of my heretofore gentle quorum prescriptions: *Have a good reason to set the quorum at less than 100 percent!* I realize that the immediate reaction to such a statement is—here we go again!—that it is completely out of keeping with the "real world." I also realize that my startling recommendation sounds a bit like "let's take the gloves off about quorums." I can assure you that I intend neither other-worldliness nor combat. Here is the rationale that leads me to what may seem a bizarre standard for good quorum-setting behavior.

To help our discussion along, let me introduce the following example. We will assume that we have a board that has designed its role using the Policy Governance model and, therefore, has the characteristics of a good Policy Governance board: it has adopted a great degree of group responsibility. It understands its role as a generative producer of instructions to an operating organization, that is, proactive in its own right rather than just reactive to staff initiatives. It confines its decision making to what are properly board decisions and stays out of staff decisions. It has a strong attendance provision in its bylaws; nonattenders simply cannot continue to use up a board seat. It has done whatever is necessary and possible to convert the board into an agile, contemplative, deciding group rather than an awkward assembly (likely meaning it is small). It accepts accountability as a group and exercises authority only as a group.

Such a board would seek to operate with every member involved in every board decision, though it would understand that reality will occasionally interfere with that intention. Philosophically, the board's view of its working style would reflect the *expectation of totality:* We are all here to learn, contemplate, and struggle together. And of course, that intent requires that all or substantially all board members be present for the process.

Establishing a quorum is not a matter of striving for an ideal but of setting a minimum level of attendance considered essential for board members to function effectively together as a board. How should a board look at the quorum issue? Let me dispense with the lower quorum figures with a little math. For a board of, say, eighteen members, a quorum of 40 percent requires eight to be in attendance. If a vote is taken at bare quorum, five members can decide the issue. With a quorum of 30 percent, the controlling number of

> When attendance is problematic enough to entice boards to set a low quorum, there is a severe discipline problem that lowering the quorum will not cure.

votes is four. With an ostensible board size of eighteen, then, a mere four or five can decide an issue. Surely setting such a low quorum requirement constitutes an unstated admission that attendance doesn't matter. When attendance is problematic enough to entice boards to set a low quorum, there is a severe discipline problem that lowering the quorum will not cure.

It is highly unlikely that a board that values its attendance and wholeness would set such a low quorum. But even good boards stumble unwittingly into using the more common, generally accepted quorum requirement of 51 percent. Most boards simply don't think a lot about the fine points of establishing a quorum requirement. As a demonstration of that point, I ask you to try to remember the last time your board had a substantive discussion about what its bylaws quorum provision should be. If a conscientious board stops to consider the matter, it will be startled even by the generally accepted 51 percent rule. If the board size is, as in my previous example, eighteen, a 51 percent quorum calls for ten to be in attendance. The deciding vote count is six.

One-third of the board can determine board decisions. In other words, this board is only slightly better off than its less stringent colleagues mentioned in my earlier examples. To explore why a board may want to consider going beyond the 51 percent quorum, let's look at the "good Policy Governance board" I originally introduced.

This board eschews the power-play approach in which board members are more interested in getting an immediate win, because winning a vote due to the composition of the board at a particular meeting shows more interest in grabbing power than in proper process. There would be no pleasure for members on this board—which is exercising board leadership as it should be—in attending a low-quorum meeting where only the people who agree with you show up.

This board avoids the view that board meetings are primarily for the purpose of ritual or of ratifying management intentions. If board meetings were for giving the CEO one month's or one quarter's permissions at a time (as, unfortunately, many are), then simply getting enough members together to enable the organization to keep rolling might be justifiable. Yet if a board empowers management properly, its meetings are not primarily about the ongoing operation but about the consideration and establishment of long-term, largely mission-related values.

> If a board empowers management properly, its meetings are not primarily about the ongoing operation but about the consideration and establishment of long-term, largely mission-related values.

This board treasures its role as a meaningful group, not just a collection of enough people to get a vote through. ("Things have to be passed, therefore we must be able to pass them.") The task of passing things can become more important than group wholeness in dealing with and resolving large issues. It is as though the board is slave to an unending stream of items to be passed. Board meetings in traditional governance fall into this rat race regularly.

This board knows that governance is a long-term activity in which all decisions knit together to form a coherent whole. It is committed to the wholeness that comes from a nucleus group—with extensive input to be sure—struggling with related issues over a protracted period. The wholeness in board policy derives in part from the fact that the values for all policies are aggregated from the same group. Therefore, they all make sense when taken together. Governance should not be a pull and tug of compromises that impart a patchy character to the various aspects of decision making. A low quorum requirement, for example, could conceivably lead to three separate groups of people making board decisions in three consecutive meetings.

Remember that operating as a total group was the mentality of the board at the outset. That clearly implies 100 percent participation. So the relevant issue is how far below 100 percent does attendance at any one meeting have to fall before the group should decide that its wholeness calls for scheduled issues to wait until a later date? Remember, *the aim here is not just to have a meeting, but to obtain an expression of group wisdom on some issue requiring that wisdom.* And "group wisdom" means wisdom of the board as a group, not a subpart of the group. The fact that 100 percent might be an unrealistic expectation is no argument for 51 percent (the accepted norm), any more than it is an argument for 30 percent. There is no perfectly right answer to the question—no perfectly right quorum figure—but there is here a substantive issue about the nature of group leadership that is poorly served by failing to subject the boilerplate 51 percent practice to scrutiny.

> **FAQ**
>
> Why is it important to have good attendance at board meetings?

But doesn't setting a high quorum requirement, say 80 percent or 90 percent, penalize those members who show up for the sake of a very small group of nonattenders (maybe only one)? After all, nonattenders had plenty of notice; it is their own fault they are not present. The frustration expressed in these questions suggests convincing arguments against the near–100 percent quorum I'm recommending. But the trap at this point is in solving the wrong problem. If board members are not going to show up for a meeting, why did someone not know that?

A low quorum requirement, for example, could conceivably lead to three separate groups of people making board decisions in three consecutive meetings.

Consider how frequently we accept as normal not knowing who is coming to the meeting until the meeting begins. Of course, the unexpected can happen, but how often do board members not show up for other appointments in their lives? How often do they miss a dental appointment they had to wait several weeks to get? How often do they miss the appliance dealer's delivery of a new washing machine to their home? How often do they miss the symphony performance for which they've paid a handsome ticket price? My point is that people do, in fact, miss important appointments, but not often, not nearly as often as board members fail to show for board meetings. (In fact, elected boards such as city councils and school boards have an admirable rate of attendance.) But nonprofit boards take it for granted that their members are habitual appointment-missers!

> **FAQ**
>
> We have trouble getting good attendance at board meetings because emergencies always seem to come up. What can we do?

Do responsible people not usually know, surely by a day or two prior to a meeting, that they will or will not be there—at least 90 percent or more of the time? I realize that

---

People do, in fact, miss important appointments, but not often, not nearly as often as board members fail to show for board meetings.

---

this does not work as well for a board when long distance travel is involved. As an illustration admittedly not strictly parallel, I have failed to show up for only one consulting assignment in twenty years—and that was due to an airport closed due to snow. My record is equaled or surpassed by a host of consultants, multitudes in other walks of life (remember the Baltimore Orioles' steadfast Cal Ripkin Jr.?), and many board members as well. Still, my point is not that 100 percent attendance is attainable, just that 100 percent—not 51 percent—should be the point of departure when boards begin a discussion about where to set their quorum requirements.

I realize there is a widespread argument triggered at this point: But these are volunteers! How can so much be expected of volunteers? Do they not deserve—due to their unpaid status—to miss meetings if they want to? Should volunteers be held to a standard of performance about attendance that they expect of their paid staff and of themselves in their other roles? The answer is, in a word, yes.

When meetings cannot go ahead when a subquorum number has shown up, it is greatly disrespectful to those who showed up. They, too, are volunteers and don't deserve that kind of treatment. But when meetings can go ahead by virtue of a lax quorum requirement, it is highly damaging to the integrity of governance. Volunteers don't deserve that either. But whether volunteers do or do not deserve to have their time or their governance aspirations carelessly treated, there is a higher consideration. Board members have consciously chosen to take upon themselves the owner-representative role. Owners do not lose their right to be well-represented just because board members have conflicts in their schedules.

FAQ ➡

How can we deal with board members who repeatedly fail to show up for board meetings?

Consider a simple, responsible, practical scenario: The board is small enough to be agile and in control of itself—perhaps five to nine members. The board commits to govern as a group, setting a quorum requirement of, say, one person less than 100 percent. Board members agree to meeting dates and times for as far into the future as they please. An interim check is made a week prior to the date, and then a final check is made one or two days prior to each board meeting that board members will, in fact, show up. If fewer than the quorum guarantee attendance, the meeting is rescheduled immediately. If a board member, after having guaranteed attendance, fails to show up for two board meetings in a term, he or she automatically loses board membership. Of course, the specifics of this scenario will not work for every organization. But this philosophical viewpoint about board wholeness as applied to board meetings can contribute to governance integrity in any organization.

Owning Your Agenda: A Long-Term View Is the Key to Taking Charge

BOARD LEADERSHIP, NUMBER 7, MAY-JUNE 1993

IN WORKSHOPS, I encourage boards to own their agendas. In fact, I tell them that if they cannot conduct their next two or three meetings without staff guidance, *they are not governing.* Meaningful board leadership requires that the board agenda truly be the *board's* agenda.

A board will probably not take its strategic leadership role seriously as long as the board job itself is being micromanaged by staff. Assertive board members like this idea; after all, it is merely the organizational equivalent of being in charge of their own lives.

Yet even board members who are attracted to the idea of controlling their own agenda are often in a quandary about just how to take control. Because staff members are on the scene every day, they know what is going on organizationally. Therefore, are they not more in touch with what needs to be on the agenda? This line of thought must usually prevail, because, clearly, in my experience, *board agendas are ordinarily put together by staff.*

Staff members are indisputably more in touch with what is going on in the organization. The board's job, however, *is not predominantly about what is going on in the organization.* The board's job is far more about defining what kind of world the organization is to create. An agenda that is largely about keeping up with staff

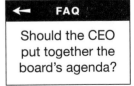

← FAQ

Should the CEO put together the board's agenda?

activity misses the point. If the agenda is in the hands of staff, the board can expect meetings to be staff-driven, loaded with executive rather than governance material.

And that, of course, is just what conventional board meetings consist of. The board need not blame the staff, because the board itself has invited the staff to fill the vacuum. There is no need for blame, but there is a compelling need for the board to take charge.

Some boards that try to take over their agendas have a short discussion at the end of each meeting about what to include in the next meeting. Such attempts can produce a zigzag procession of board meetings much as your car would do if you steered by looking only a few feet ahead. Moreover, this approach can easily lead to board meetings that are simply a laundry list of individual board member interests.

<table>
<tr><td>

FAQ ➡️

What role should a chair have in determining the board's agenda?

</td></tr>
</table>

Other boards try to assume control of their agendas by giving the task to the chairperson or the executive committee. This encourages a more organized approach, although other board members may feel that the agenda is still out of their control. Control has merely shifted to an officer or elite group. But even when the chair or committee sets agendas, as often as not agenda planning still originates from the staff.

I recommend a planned approach to agenda control, one that assures that (1) meeting agendas are derived from a long-term view, (2) the board as a body maintains at least broad-brush control, and (3) the chairperson is authorized to flesh out agenda details (see box). The board must be directly involved in the long-term planning of its own job.

Making Board Meetings *the Board's* Meetings

- *Maintain an up-to-date board job description.* The board's job description can be seen as the board's *perpetual agenda;* consequently, everything the board does can (and must) be derived from it. In "Giving, Getting, and Governing" (in Chapter Eleven of this book), I suggest that any fundraising obligation assumed by the board should be recorded in the job description.

- *Express the job description in outcomes.* The most powerful way to describe a job is in terms of its results rather than its busyness. Furthermore, the board's job description addresses *the board's product,* not the product of board and staff added together. For example, a clear and compelling mission statement might be a board product, but mission accomplishment ordinarily would not be, because the actual achievement of mission is a result of staff action.

- *Consider your desired performance objectives annually.* As the perpetual agenda, the job description forms a foundation for deciding what the board *itself* is to accomplish in a year. At the beginning of each year, the board should go over the several parts of its job and establish, within each part, doable, yet meaningful objectives to which it can commit itself.

- *Adopt your schedule for the year.* To one level of detail or another, the board sketches out a schedule for the year. For example, in order to conclude a reexploration of ends policies in time for the chief executive to build a budget, there must be ample time for deliberation, preceded by time to assemble input from various sources (such as community focus groups, staff, expert panels, and surveys), preceded by time for these sources to develop their inputs, preceded by time for the board to plan how to instruct these groups. In other words, the board simply plans what steps it must take to accomplish its objectives for the year, and these steps form a basis for agendas.

- *Empower the chairperson to flesh out meeting details.* For the board to fill out every detail of a schedule such as the preceding one is impossible, but that presents no problem if the chairperson is authorized to fill in the gaps. Because the chairperson must be true to the sketchy plan of the board, the board has not lost control even while delegating this power. This same kind of delegation to the chairperson works for all matters covered by governance process and board-staff relationship policies.

Calculating the Real Costs of Governance

BOARD LEADERSHIP, NUMBER 15, SEPT.-OCT. 1994

GOVERNANCE ISN'T FREE. There are the obvious costs of meetings, meals, coffee, photocopying, and mailings. There are the less obvious costs of staffing committees and diverting the CEO from executive management. And let's not overlook the costs to board members and their families due to the many hours of volunteered time.

> With respect to the costs of governance, *the less obvious the cost, the greater the amount.*

A number of years ago I stumbled across an intriguing relationship. Like most rules of thumb, this one isn't without its exceptions. But it stimulates useful insights nonetheless: With respect to the costs of governance, *the less obvious the cost, the greater the amount.* Board discussion of the matter will likely yield an interesting interchange. Consider several levels of obviousness in the costs of operating a board of directors.

Time and energy. The most obvious cost to any board member is the cost of his or her time and energy. Board members are starkly aware of meetings that run too long, preparatory reading that eats into private time, meetings on top of meetings, and all the personal, family, and occupational pursuits sacrificed in order to serve. Board members' time is a precious commodity to them. As far as the organization's books are concerned, however, there is no cost at all.

Meetings. The next most obvious cost of governance is the direct and visible cost of meetings. Coffee and refreshments, sometimes meals, rent of meeting rooms and sometimes lodging, travel costs when board members must travel to meetings, postage or courier deliveries, and all that photocopying . . . these costs are hard to miss! Because they are so obvious, board members will often offer suggestions and even directives about economies of postage and copying. Most boards do not run anywhere near the $1 million a year that one of my clients incurred annually for board meetings, but there are always costs and they are noticed. Yet in the scheme of things, these noticeable (though rarely tallied) costs are a *tiny percentage of budget.*

> The cost of ineffectual governance is hidden in the same way that water is hidden to a fish.

Staff time. Rather less obvious is the management cost when staff members attend to the needs of governance rather than to getting the organizational work done. The CEO must devote some time to governance, of course, as must whoever takes care of the purely clerical needs of meeting notices and minutes. In addition, top level staff beyond the CEO are frequently engaged in some way with the board, either attending board meetings or staffing committees.

Because boards have a tendency to view staff as a fixed expense, they may not notice that for personnel to attend board meetings, to staff committees, gather data, and prepare reports incurs a considerable cost that is rarely calculated and never shows on the books. Once I had a client with a $2 million budget and a board that—before Policy Governance—had the obligatory handful of committees. The CEO calculated that staff costs associated with board support were above $100,000! I doubt that the CEO's figures are far from the norm. What became obvious in this case was that most of the staff support was for board activity that was—when seen in the light of Policy Governance—unnecessary. The use of staff time imposes a cost that is often *extensive.*

Ineffectual governance. How do you get a handle on the cost of running organizations that are not focused on results? How do you calculate the loss of resources when the board conversation, the inspection, the measurements, the organizational design, and even the CEO's job are centered more on the maintenance of prescribed activities than on organizational effects on human lives?

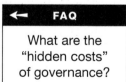

← FAQ

What are the "hidden costs" of governance?

Surely some organizations, viewed against this standard, should not exist at all—in other words, virtually their entire budget is wasted! Who would argue that the public schools, for example, accomplish even 80 percent of what they could if governance, thence management, were not so antiquated? And does that not mean that over 20 percent of their expenditures are therefore wasted—a cost that should not have been necessary?

This cost (the cost of ineffectual governance) is hidden in the same way that water is hidden to a fish. Our time-honored approach to governance is so thoroughly ensconced in our experience that we fail to see the organizational dysfunction it causes. I suppose it never occurred to the naked emperor to ask himself why he was catching so many colds. This most hidden of costs is *monumental.*

FAQ ➡

What types of costs should a board be concerned about?

And what are the implications of this inverse relationship between the visibility of costs and their magnitude? The clearest implication is that board members, conscientiously wishing to avoid waste, typically look in the wrong places. They go after pennies with a vengeance while blithely overlooking dollars. Any city council or school board can be seen demonstrating this unhappy phenomenon in meeting after meeting. Incidentally, with all its occasionally enthusiastic muckraking, the press as well is regularly fooled into going after the inconsequential waste instead of the profound.

So what should a board do about the costs of governance? Foremost, it should commit to truly *govern,* rather than what has passed for governance for far too long now. Governing efficiently will reduce the waste in time and energy costs. Governing well will also reduce staff time costs to an appropriate amount. It will always be necessary for staff members, particularly the CEO, to devote some energy to assisting the board, so better governance will eliminate only the wasteful part of this cost. But what is far more important, the superior level of board leadership will deal afresh with ineffectual governance costs, the ones that really matter. The costs are where the greatest gain—even transformation—is waiting to be discovered and, therefore, where the opportunity for board leadership is immense.

> Governing efficiently will reduce the waste in time and energy costs.

As to the costs of meetings, unless the gross amount forms a significant proportion of expenditures or would incur unacceptable political cost, most boards can safely not worry about it. Go ahead and have all the coffee you want; you deserve it!

The Consent Agenda and Responsible Rubber-Stamping

BOARD LEADERSHIP, NUMBER 38, JULY-AUG. 1998

T HE CONSENT AGENDA is a device commonly employed by public boards but also occasionally used by nonprofit boards. Faced with a long agenda, a board might group a number of the noncontroversial (therefore requiring no discussion) items together so they can all be approved with a single action. A motion to "approve items 7 through 42" enables the board meeting to move along more quickly than if each item had to be dealt with individually. Because the criterion for putting an item on the consent agenda is that the issue is noncontroversial, any individual board member has the unilateral right to move an item from the consent agenda to the regular agenda. After all, wanting to do so signals that the item is in fact controversial.

But the foregoing description is true only in traditional governance. In Policy Governance there are *no* ritual items on the board's agenda. The agenda is composed *solely* of issues that call for the application of board wisdom. The reasoning is that if a decision does not require board judgment, someone else should be making it. To expect board members to meet so they can make decisions on issues that require no decision is an offensive trivialization of governance. Consequently, in Policy Governance there is no reason to have a consent agenda at all.

> In Policy Governance there is no reason to have a consent agenda at all. Many boards, however, are unable to use Policy Governance in its pure form.

Many boards, however, are unable to use Policy Governance in its pure form. School boards, for example, are required by law to act on every hiring of a teacher. City councils, even of large municipalities, are required by law to take official action on ludicrously small purchasing decisions. Nonprofit boards, while not ordinarily fettered by laws, are often required by funders or accreditors to participate directly in decisions that should never occur in a place as high as the boardroom.

Boards that find themselves in the foregoing circumstances can inventively use a consent agenda to overcome absurd requirements. What a board can do is place all required but otherwise ludicrous items on a consent agenda to be dealt with in an *intentionally* perfunctory manner.

Decisions placed on the consent agenda under this approach are decisions that in the absence of outside requirements a board practicing Policy Governance would not have seen, much less acted on, for they would have been made by the CEO or the CEO's designees. Delegating to the CEO in this way, if done in the context of Policy Governance policies, is not an abrogation of responsibility, but an exercise of responsibility. It follows, then, that intentionally rubber-stamping these kinds of decisions on a consent agenda is not an irresponsible act. This intended rubber-stamping is but carrying through on the board's guarantee to approve any CEO action or plan that meets the board's conditions.

An automatic approval, however, must be handled in a responsible manner to avoid being the kind of rubber-stamping we all deplore—the kind wherein the board abdicates its accountability. To explain how that can be done, I must digress for a moment to clarify how the board in Policy Governance is assured of the "approvability" of executive actions—through monitoring.

Monitoring in Policy Governance is simply the comparison of performance data with the policy criteria under scrutiny. For example, a policy that prohibits purchases over some dollar amount without obtaining competing prices can be monitored by the CEO's producing records of such purchases and of alternative vendors and their prices.

Proper monitoring is neither a fishing expedition, a staff show-and-tell exhibition, nor an exhaustive report of organizational goings-on. *It is focused only and always on specific criteria.* Thus, with respect to a particular ends policy or executive limitations policy, the board obtains information that reveals the degree of performance; it does not rummage around in whatever information interests it but *does* inspect the relevant data. In other words, just getting information about the organization does not constitute monitoring, because data obtained may be unrelated to the criteria created by policy language. So normal monitoring under Policy Governance is related to a specific policy but generated from any number of real events. We will see how monitoring is different with a consent agenda.

In Policy Governance, the board demonstrates due care by giving the CEO performance criteria, then demanding monitoring data that relate to those criteria. But in the consent agenda action I am describing, board members raise their hands to signal approval of as-yet unmonitored actions. What is the board to do? To examine the CEO's decisions, in the sense of entering into a true decision-making mode, would be tantamount to reversing the very delegation it has so painstakingly put in place.

The solution is the point of this article: When the consent agenda includes actions that the CEO has by the board's governance model the right to decide—but that outside authorities demand the board decide—*the CEO merely attaches to each item a special monitoring report.* In other words, each item is accompanied by a report that demonstrates the action requested is true to all applicable board policies. The monitoring attachments can be read by members prior to the meeting, so that in session the board need only move that *all* consent agenda items be approved at once—an action that requires but a few seconds.

> ← **FAQ**
>
> If, by law, the board must approve personnel actions, purchases, or budgets, can it still use Policy Governance?

Unlike usual monitoring, in which compliance with a given policy is demonstrated by reference to relevant actions, in this case a single action is shown to be in compliance with all policies that are relevant to that action.

Once the assurance for monitoring is included with each action, board members can comfortably approve the entire list on the consent agenda. Due care will have been served without either offending the outside authority or doing damage to the integrity of board-CEO delegation.

Chapter Nine

Assuring Board and Management Performance

Measurement, Evaluation, and Discipline

Assessing CEO performance is an ongoing obligation rather than an annual event. Since the board has stated *ends* and unacceptable *means,* data about these expectations form the CEO's evaluation. Likewise, the board's evaluation of its own performance is an ongoing process rather than a sporadic event. The maintenance of board discipline requires mechanisms to prevent deterioration of the rigor necessary for excellence. For both its CEO and itself, the board evaluates against prestated criteria expressed by the full board. Typical approval of financial or other reports and typical board self-evaluations are insufficient monitoring tools.

Painful Lessons: Learning from the United Way Misfortune

BOARD LEADERSHIP, NUMBER 3, SEPT.-OCT. 1992

EARLIER THIS YEAR, United Way of America (UWA) suffered what might have been the greatest public relations damage in its history. Long-time executive director William Aramony was excoriated in the media for extravagant expenditures, sloppy records, and general mismanagement of the national organization. The revelations rocked the nonprofit community. Charitable giving was jeopardized. Many local United Ways for a time withheld payments to the national organization.

An independent report commissioned by the United Way board (I'll refer to it below as "the report") recounted a long list of Aramony's misdeeds. The report cited "a haphazard practice of expenditures without adequate documentation, the proliferation of spin-offs not accountable to UWA, the payment of unjustified consulting fees, and the hiring or supporting of a number of persons who were either related to or personally associated with Mr. Aramony." Aramony resigned amid these widely publicized, severe judgments of his behavior as chief executive.

This misfortune happened to a prestigious and highly visible board of directors, one that had traditionally held itself out as an example. The frightening realization is that if disastrous failure in board oversight can happen to United Way of America, *it can happen to anyone.*

We have every reason to believe that the board members at UWA are competent and committed persons who have simply tried to do a good job on behalf of the rest of us. No system can reduce abuse to zero. Bad things can happen to anyone. That

The UWA board had no doubt been at least as conscientious as most nonprofit and public governing bodies.

said, however, it must also be admitted that the oversight capability of boards suffers mightily upon inspection.

This article does not recount the alleged abuses, nor does it (except in the interest of drawing generic implications) discuss blame. Indeed, allowing blame, or even the focus of inquiry, to fall on UWA would trivialize the important lessons to be gleaned from these unfortunate events—lessons critical to all nonprofit and public boards. Thus discussion of the UWA misfortune can be most worthwhile when it draws attention to the breakthrough sorely needed by boards everywhere.

Management Can Only Be What Boards Allow

It is instructive to note here that the finger pointing that occurred was almost totally directed toward Aramony. With few exceptions, press stories seemed to ignore that the board must have been asleep at the wheel in order for abuses to go on for so long. Curiously, though the report exhaustively recounted instances of staff mismanagement, it scarcely hinted at board misgovernance. While the report did recommend some changes in board operations, the strongest language used was that "UWA bylaws are seriously inadequate."

Whatever the list of grievances against Aramony over a number of years, it is clear that *the board either had no systematic way to know about Aramony's actions or felt no responsibility to do anything about them*—until it was known that investigative reporters were looking into various allegations. Neither explanation speaks well for board leadership. If nonprofit and public governance is to improve as a result of UWA's experience, the first step is to recognize the board's culpability in the matter. *The sobering thought is that the UWA board had no doubt been at least as conscientious as most nonprofit and public governing bodies.*

> **FAQ** ➡
>
> Should a board be held accountable for *all* staff behavior?

Board members must understand that they are fully accountable for all organizational behavior. They are not "just volunteers" who assemble to advise staff, lend their names, or socially bless staff activity. Board members are, in a moral if not a legal sense, trustees for others. Even though we rhetorically ascribe to boards the weighty burden of "ultimate accountability," we just as often ignore what that necessarily implies. The recent experiences of Continental Illinois (financial disaster), the University of Minnesota (presidential home improvements), Covenant House (sexual improprieties), and Stanford University (extravagant overhead charges) are clear reminders of the capacity of boards to fiddle while almost anything burns. Consider public education: The press has scorched teachers, teachers' unions, and administrators for the sorry state of learning, while laying nary a finger on school boards. We have a rich tradition of pretending either that boards are in charge or that they know what to do when they get there.

The tendency to overlook the board's culpability highlights a widespread attitude about board ineffectuality. It is natural to let boards off the hook when their capacity for leadership is undervalued. But boards are not in their prestigious position to be led about by a chief executive, even a highly trusted and competent one. Contrary to the popular position in current governance literature—that the CEO is responsible for good board behavior and is an equal partner with the board—the board's job is to govern. Board and executive are partners, yes. But they cannot be equal partners unless the board renounces its own accountability.

> Recent experiences are clear reminders of the capacity of boards to fiddle while almost anything burns.

Battening Down the Wrong Hatches

Inadequacy in governance cannot be solved just by removing offending managers and replacing unacceptable management methods. These actions should be taken, of course, but neither one helps make *governance* better. Management will undoubtedly improve, but the board's ability to ensure good management will be no better than before, since it is a shortcoming in governance that allowed for unacceptable management in the first place.

The UWA report implies nonetheless that where management has cleaned up its act, the organizational problem is fixed. Since, for example, the new temporary chief executive has already instituted tighter practices, the report concludes that "no recommendation is necessary."

It would be unfortunate, however, if boards' desire to control management more effectively brings about greater involvement in managerial details. My greatest fear is that boards, frightened by the fiasco that could have just as easily been their own, will react by battening down the wrong hatches. It is not uncommon to respond to emergencies by doing with increased vigor the very things that brought the organization trouble in the first place. Thus it is not consoling that the report and press coverage I have seen all call for the UWA board to do more thoroughly what it did before: ask more questions, have more active committees, and exercise more approval authority over staff decisions. What seems to be overlooked is that only limited improvement in governance can be achieved by working harder within the same mode of thinking that permitted the inadequacy to develop in the first place.

> Only limited improvement in governance can be achieved by working harder within the same mode of thinking that permitted the inadequacy to develop in the first place.

Going Beyond Old Prescriptions

The tools of governance available to the United Way were, one must assume, the best conventional wisdom has to offer. My message is that the conventional wisdom—exemplified and promoted by United Way at local and national levels—is deeply flawed, a travesty to board and staff leadership alike. Excellence in governance—that which allows a board to fulfill its fundamental trusteeship—lies in reinventing governance by going beyond traditional concepts and practices to a new form of board leadership more worthy of people and the purposes to which they are committed.

Consider the board's oversight role as typically played out by instructing and inspecting staff action. Apparently, Aramony participated in or allowed activities that in hindsight have been decried as "a breach of the board's trust." Yet despite its lengthy listing of Aramony's wrongs, the report did not dwell on any instances in which Aramony did something the board had clearly told him not to do. How can this be? Is it possible that serious abuse can go on and *not* constitute a violation of stated board values?

It is not only possible, it is the *normal* condition. The prevalent mode of governance is to neglect the important focus on clarification of values and concentrate instead on single decisions and document approvals. In this mode, boards often skip the value-setting step altogether and move right on to inspecting staff activities and plans.

> The prevalent mode of governance is to neglect the important focus on clarification of values and concentrate instead on single decisions and document approvals.

A Failure to Create Organizational Policy

When a board approves a budget, a personnel policy, a salary administration plan, or even a strategic plan, it often approves the numbers and activities outlined in such a document without full cognizance of the fundamental values upon which the document should be built and, consequently, what criteria should govern the approval decision.

Later, with procedural approvals behind them, a board may set out to monitor staff performance and face the same problem: In having failed to lay out the organizational values against which all executive action will be assessed, the board fosters the development of a morass of disclarity not only about the values themselves, but about any attempt to monitor performance in a rational way. Consequently, monitoring staff performance becomes

> Even the most extensive monitoring yields little more than spotty assurance if not guided by a clear set of evaluative criteria.

an exercise in foraging about or in wallowing in information rather than rigorously monitoring with it. For example, when boards review monthly or quarterly financial reports, they are using this foraging-about method of inspection. When boards review travel practices, personnel, or programs, they are likely to be engaged in reactive, tiring, and often boring endeavors. The accepted practice of inspecting without criteria in hand can be an exhausting task that will fail to illuminate problem areas because it is not clear to board or staff what the board is looking for.

Greatly increasing this kind of board and committee inspection of staff activities and documents does not alter the underlying flaw. *The solution to foraging about is not to forage about even more than before.* Besides being difficult to do, confusing, and likely to leave the board adrift in unclear criteria, even the most extensive monitoring yields little more than spotty assurance if not guided by a clear set of evaluative criteria. Board members will only be able to hope that they will find what is worth finding.

Further, in the absence of prestated criteria (which enable the board to know what it needs to know), a board is often captive of whatever information the CEO *chooses* to report. This leaves the board forever vulnerable not only to having information intentionally withheld, but also to data that are disguised, stealthily

> In the absence of prestated criteria, a board is often captive of whatever information the CEO *chooses* to report.

collapsed together, or simply—with sterling staff intent—buried in the voluminous material submitted for board reading.

A paradoxical aspect—one not noticed amid reactions about the United Way situation—is that this institutionalized lack of clarity between board and staff leads to grossly unfair treatment of CEOs and to staff confusion quite as often as it leads to the duping of boards. CEOs are vulnerable when boards decide their criteria "on the fly" as they monitor data or decide to approve a particular document. Moreover, because individual board members will sometimes differ on what the expectations should be, their after-the-fact, wandering assessments allow them to make individual judgments according to criteria never set by the board. CEOs are also left vulnerable when various board committees set unstated (and often differing) criteria just by the judgments they render. Finally, when board committees dabble in staff work, no one is quite sure whether they are advising or instructing, which again leaves the CEO susceptible to being undermined.

Transform, Don't Tinker

FAQ ➡
How can a board overcome serious governance flaws without unreasonable time commitments?

Overcoming governance flaws of this magnitude requires more than well-intentioned tinkering with current practices. It requires a new paradigm for conceiving of the job of the board. Rather than having the board work harder or do a few things differently, the appropriate kind of change redefines the nature of board work, results in clearer organizational guidelines, reduces unnecessary intrusion into management, and increases accountability—all without requiring massive amounts of board or committee time.

It is all too easy to see how a board can lose control and not even know it until some unfortunate event disturbs the precarious equilibrium. Despite conscientious and often-times obsessive concern with detail, school boards are out of control, city councils are lost in a quagmire of ineffectiveness, and social service agencies fail to serve their communities. The list could go on and on. Ironically, the boards that are most out of control are often the ones most immersed in meddling behavior, which particularly includes detailed involvement by board committees.

Boards that are most out of control are often the ones most immersed in meddling behavior.

So how might your board respond to the embarrassment suffered by the United Way of America? Use your recharged anxiety to create a better system while refraining from inserting frightened fingers further into administrative and programmatic detail. Engage your board in the ongoing development of a more effective system of leadership, decision making, and oversight so that you can balance assurance with empowerment and control without meddling.

Above all, don't be satisfied with the norm, even when you see it accepted by others all around you. The traditionally approved approach to governance predictably yields behavior that would be called irresponsible if it occurred in a less prestigious setting and had less sanction of tradition. Your board, your staff, and your mission all deserve a system that allows for the greatest integrity and provides the most opportunity for responsible, visionary board leadership.

Don't be satisfied with the norm, even when you see it accepted by others all around you.

One Board Fails to Follow Its Own Monitoring Policy— and Courts Fiscal Disaster

Board Leadership, Number 14, July-Aug. 1994

D URING A PERIOD of several months a few years ago, I helped the board of a church-based, social service organization implement Policy Governance. Like most boards, this one worried about fiscal matters. These matters are frightening for all boards and often lead to close scrutiny of financial management. Policy Governance handles these worries through (1) establishing board expectations in policy, followed by (2) monitoring staff performance with respect to these expectations. As simple as this sequence is, it is *not* what happens in even good examples of traditional board operation.

Because fiscal administration is a means issue, not an ends issue, the board policy that sets performance criteria is of the executive limitations type. That is, the board creates a policy stating parameters within which the fiscal condition must be maintained. For example, of the five criteria in this board's financial condition policy, one provision stated, "Total agency expenditures year-to-date shall not exceed revenues year-to-date."

The board also had a policy that set out the monitoring frequency and method for all executive limitations and ends policies. The monitoring policy is in the board-staff linkage category, since it helps define the connection between governance and management. This board's monitoring policy stated that the financial condition policy would be monitored every quarter by data provided by the CEO.

The CEO faithfully mailed his board a quarterly report on the state of organizational finances. He detailed the revenues and receipts of each program, including grant

Any report that does not pointedly answer the monitoring questions is not considered to be legitimate monitoring data.

money received to support each service. Each quarterly report contained extensive information. But what is curious, at no point did his data address the simple question, "Were total agency expenditures year-to-date in excess of revenues year-to-date?" This CEO, by the way, was not trying to be evasive. He was simply not remembering that monitoring data are *only* those data that *directly* address the board-stated criteria.

I first heard of the situation when the board chairperson called me in distress. At the end of the year, the board had learned that the organization was suffering a significant deficit. The board was quite upset, and rightly so. I asked that the monitoring reports received during the previous year be forwarded to me.

> **FAQ** →
>
> What information does a board need in order to monitor the CEO?

What I found was that the reports were not monitoring reports by my definition. True, they were reports, and they honestly set out as much data as the board had received in years past. But in Policy Governance, any report that does not pointedly answer the monitoring questions is simply not considered to be legitimate monitoring data.

What are the monitoring questions? They are simply the recurring questions of whether each board-established criterion has been met. Notice that the best of balance sheets and income statements would fail this test. Balance sheets and income statements—for all their utility in management—are not good governance tools. Standard accounting statements constitute a hundred answers looking desperately for a few good questions.

So the CEO had submitted reports, to be sure, and rather detailed ones at that. Understand that as reports in the normal sense, these reports were as good as any. But

Balance sheets and income statements—for all their utility in management—are not good governance tools.

this CEO's reports had not qualified as monitoring reports in terms of Policy Governance. Yet board members had not once remarked that they were failing to get clear answers to the simple question, "Were our expectations met?"

I made a few simple recommendations to this board. First, the board cannot successfully use Policy Governance while omitting its crucial monitoring aspect. Not to monitor appropriately is to use a formula that courts disaster. Second, I suggested that they adopt a frame of mind: If monitoring reports do not answer the relevant questions, then the board has not received a report. Third, I suggested that, at least for the next year, the board ascertain at every meeting that each board member has not only read the mailed monitoring reports, but has also assessed whether the data presented sufficiently establish the degree of policy compliance.

Delegation without proper monitoring quickly becomes abdication. Proper monitoring is not accomplished by rote reports, regardless of how official or how data-rich they appear to be. Monitoring need not consume precious board meeting time, but for board leadership to be meaningful, the board must ensure that its members take the mailed reports seriously.

> Delegation without proper monitoring quickly becomes abdication.

> Proper monitoring is not accomplished by rote reports, regardless of how official or how data-rich they appear to be.

The Misguided Focus on Administrative Cost

BOARD LEADERSHIP, NUMBER 21, SEPT.-OCT. 1995

THROUGHOUT MY YEARS of association with nonprofit and public administration, I've heard continual reference to "administrative cost." Usually the reference is derogatory, as if such cost is suspect. When I was in mental health management, there was constant pressure to reduce administrative cost. Funding organizations demand that administrative cost be kept below a certain criterion level. Politicians score points talking about putting more of the education dollar into the classroom.

It took me many years to see the fallacy in making such an issue of administrative cost. In this article I want to demonstrate a radical proposition that can be of use to politicians and board members alike: When the seemingly virtuous focus on administrative cost comes from outside the operating organization, it is not only folly but an illustration of a principal flaw in the way we view and the way we evaluate nonprofit and public administration organizations.

What Is "Administrative Cost"?

Let us begin with the bigger picture. Administrative cost is one of several types of cost involved in creating something of value. Other types might be service delivery cost, cost of raw materials, and so forth. In fact, when you try to make a list like I just started, you see that the terms are ill-defined, and that there are any number of ways to divide costs. For example, another way to divide up the pie would be to designate personnel costs, equipment costs, cost of space, and cost of supplies. Different ways of categorizing costs serve different purposes. For example, cutting across all of the above are fixed costs and variable costs. What on earth are administrative costs and why are they important enough to get so much attention?

Administrative costs are all costs that are not directly associated with the procurance, manufacture, or creation of a good or service and the delivery of that good or service into the hands of the customer.

As individuals, when we donate money to charity, we are rightfully concerned about how much benefit the intended recipients actually receive. Administrative cost in that case is any difference between our checkbooks and the final beneficiary. Though the difference between what we donated and what eventually makes it to beneficiaries—in the form of some contribution to their lives—may have been money ethically and prudently spent, we can't see it, so we don't know. Administrative cost has become a likely target, because for many, it has become synonymous with inefficiency and waste.

Of course, administrative cost should not be greater than necessary in the same way that other costs should not be. That is to say, we want to deliver the greatest benefit per dollar, so costs are to be kept low and output high. Yet in the larger picture, whether a cost is an administrative cost or not is immaterial. In other words, it isn't the category of cost that matters but total cost. A change in operating methods (or simply in accounting methods) can shift items into or out of administrative cost without changing the total. Thus, the meaningfulness of administrative cost is obscured because the matter is in part a question of definition. Confronted with pressure to slash administrative cost, administrators are as likely to reshuffle and hide these costs as to make a substantive change in the relationship between total cost and organizational output. There are limits to how much of this kind of redefinition can go on, but it does go on routinely. On many occasions, I have seen prodigious time spent by officials to hear debate and to make decisions about whether to count some cost as administrative. Expensive arguments abound about how many angels can dance on the head of that pin!

> It isn't the category of cost that matters but total cost.

The degree to which public inspection, reward, or punishment is focused on reducing administrative cost instead of total cost will determine the extent to which managerial effort will be directed toward producing this effect (remember the old bromide, "you get what you inspect, not what you expect"). The unfortunate result is a possible increase in true administrative cost (due to unnecessary effort on a cosmetic measure), along with the far more damaging illusion that something meaningful has improved.

Let me illustrate my point with an example from a mental health center I remember from a few years ago. The center had a word processing center into which psychotherapists electronically dictated progress notes on their clients. Typists transformed the dictation into carefully maintained client records. At one point, the CEO considered furnishing all therapists with keyboards and monitors, so that they could type their own notes directly into the system. One advantage of the change would have been that administrative costs would have plummeted and the organization would have looked much better to its funders. Why? Because everyone in the word processing center was counted as administrative while all therapists were counted as a direct service cost, even when they were doing administrative work (doing their own typing)! Yet even with administrative costs heroically reduced, the CEO's rough calculations showed that no productivity would have been gained and might have actually gotten worse!

In this case, direct costs of clerical staff would have been cut drastically, so it would appear to have been an efficient thing to do. Not as obvious was that the more expensive therapists would have had to divert time from helping clients to maintenance of records. This loss of efficiency would not show up as an increase in administrative cost, for therapists are not administrative staff. In other words, to make one aspect of the organization more efficient, the CEO might well have been sacrificing the efficiency of the organization as a whole. A one-sided focus on any single cost will cause this effect.

Administrative Cost: The CEO's Prerogative

FAQ ➡

What types of costs should a board be concerned about?

Within an organization, all costs can be scrutinized for their necessity, their potential savings, or even their potential increases. There is no more need for administrative costs to be decreased than any other. Managers should investigate whether administrative costs, along with others, can be decreased with no detriment to results.

That is a never-ending battle, but one by no means confined to any one type of cost. The problem in focusing on administrative cost arises when people outside of management (boards, funders, politicians, or the media) try to show how protective they are of the public purse by a showy but ultimately mindless position on one type of cost to the exclusion of others, ostensibly because "administrative cost" conjures up a less holy source of waste than other sources.

The easiest demonstration of my point is this: When you shop for a car, you compare price and product with other prices and products. You never concern yourself with the components of price, whether they be amortization on a drill press, maintenance on the plant roof, repair for a stamping machine, or office supplies. To suggest you'd do so would seem silly in the extreme. Making a rational purchase is not helped by knowing anything about the administrative cost in manufacturing a car. Ah, but nonprofit and public organizations exist in a rarefied atmosphere, one in which the nonsensical wears the mantel of traditional wisdom.

"Administrative cost" conjures up a less holy source of waste than other sources.

Consider this parallel: Boards and funders are best seen as purchasing agents for their ownership. They should determine that so much expenditure should result in so many benefits for certain populations. A legislature should be concerned with how much homelessness is actually reduced for a given appropriation. A school board should be concerned with how much literacy is achieved for some amount of cost. Funders should be concerned with what results their grants and contracts are buying. Boards and funders should concern themselves—and hardheadedly so—with the cost (that's *total* cost) of achieving desired results for the right people.

But to do this requires boards and funders to have a handle on what results they want achieved, for whom, and at what total cost—precisely the clarity they ordinarily do not have! (This is an appalling lack of clarity that traditional approaches to governance allow even good boards to get away with.) Reflect back to my word processing example. Raising administrative cost (or lowering it) might have resulted in reduced (or greater) benefits for clients per total dollar spent. It could have gone either way—you simply cannot tell by watching administrative cost because in the absence of knowing what benefits were to be achieved per dollar—even measured crudely—the system was pressured to put greater emphasis on manipulating a single item of cost than on making a greater net gain for the world! Such folly regularly passes for accountability in the nonprofit and governmental world.

Nonprofit and public organizations exist in a rarefied atmosphere, one in which the nonsensical wears the mantel of traditional wisdom.

Don't forget my proviso: Costs of all sorts are of interest to managers *within* the operating organization, for managers are in a position to manipulate and experiment with those costs (in fact, to manage them). To say that administrative cost should not

> To say that administrative cost should not matter to the board is not to say that it should not matter to managers.

matter to the board is not to say that administrative cost (along with all other categories of cost) should not matter to managers. The administrative cost fallacy is simply another instance of boards (and funders) trying in vain to be managers at a distance instead of doing their own jobs.

Frankly, it might be a sobering thought for board members to consider that all the costs of governance could be considered an administrative cost! And the cost of governance is always higher than boards know or admit (see "Calculating the Real Costs of Governance," in Chapter Eight). For example, the cost of staff who help the board by staffing committees, writing reports for the board, or attending board meetings are part of the cost of governance. The only administrative cost appropriate for boards to focus on is the cost of governance itself. Indeed, traditional governance is likely the most wasteful administrative cost of all.

> Politicians, boards, and funders that focus on administrative cost are not being rigorous or hard-nosed—*they are demonstrating that they have not done their jobs.*

Politicians, boards, and funders that focus on administrative cost are not being rigorous or hard-nosed at all; *they are demonstrating that they have not done their jobs.* If they knew what to look for in terms of results and total cost, they'd worry no more about one type of cost than another. Just as in the car purchase, total cost is the only relevant cost. Addressing the real issue—results per dollar—may well be difficult, but it is the job to be done and the principal justification for a board's existence to begin with. Making administrative cost an issue, and particularly making it a test of performance, represents a failure of leadership.

A Simple Matter of Comparison: Monitoring Fiscal Management in Your Organization

BOARD LEADERSHIP, NUMBER 6, MAR.-APR. 1993

Monitoring fiscal management under Policy Governance, like monitoring other aspects of operations, is of a different character than the monitoring boards are accustomed to. The most important difference is that monitoring in the new approach is simply the comparison of real data with preestablished criteria set forth in board policies. If there are no established criteria, monitoring cannot take place; the board can only rummage around in information.

The familiar, albeit illusory, comfort of budget approval and actual-to-budget comparisons are relinquished when the board no longer controls the budget down to its managerial detail. For example, it would make no sense for the board to examine a level of detail in actual financial condition that it relinquished in budgeting. Since these numbers belong to the CEO, not to the board, the actual-to-budget disclosure does not answer whether the CEO met the board's expectations. So while monitoring executive performance is still a critical obligation of the board, we must reconsider the nature of monitoring and the mechanics of carrying it out.

I realize that in addition to approving a budget, every month or quarter nonprofit and public boards in North America look over a report from their CEO that compares actual to budget. With meticulous zeal, boards examine the reported variations and ask, "Why?" They are not questioning the budget figures, but the actual ones. The CEO is on the spot to justify why actual numbers vary from budget. The focus of board scrutiny is on actual, not budget.

The only budget that makes any difference now is the one that begins now and goes the remainder of the year.

This may seem sensible in that budget figures were justified at the beginning of the year, so obviously it is variation of actual finances that needs to be justified. But time has passed, things have happened, the unseen has become visible since the traditional board examined the original budget. The original budget is now out of date, so actual is no more to be justified than budget. But the more important point is that insofar as affecting the future, *the only budget that makes any difference now is the one that begins now and goes the remainder of the year.* Yet this budget, the one that matters, is not the budget being used when boards compare actual to budget.

FAQ

What is the board's role in budgeting?

The board's proper role in budgeting and in actual financial condition is to set the expectations that must be met, not to perform hands-on treatment of financial management. The state of fiscal affairs is independent from budget integrity; each is important enough to merit a separate portion of the board's policy-making attention.

The board's proper role is to define important values and then to empower the CEO to make decisions consistent with these values.

In each case—governing planned and actual financial affairs—the board's proper role is to define important values and then to empower the CEO to make whatever decisions are needed as long as they are consistent with these values. Having done so, it then becomes necessary for the board to receive periodic assurance that its values about both budgeting and the actual fiscal condition are being met. This assurance is achieved through monitoring.

Monitoring as Comparison

FAQ

What is the best way to monitor actual performance?

The best monitoring of actual performance is to compare the actual condition with board policy about actual condition. The best monitoring of planned performance (budgeting) is to compare budgets with board policy about budgeting. This approach provides a stronger test of both areas of concern and renders superfluous the normal step of comparing actual to budget.

Consider the progress of a year from quarter to quarter. As that occurs, the period covered by budget decreases and that covered by reality (actual) increases. At the year's start, planning is for twelve months. At the end of the first quarter, the only planning that is still planning covers only nine months, because three months of reality have settled upon us. The board's interest that the future be responsibly planned is no less at the three-, six-, or nine-month point than it was at the outset. Responsible planning starts from the most recent state of reality, not some previous and now obsolete one. So the budget integrity that should concern the board must begin from today and go forward.

Actual performance is acceptable or unacceptable based on our values about acceptable fiscal conditions, not on whether it departs from a previous and now out-of-date budget. And of course, actual performance is an ongoing phenomenon, one capable of being checked at any interval.

Assume a board has decided to monitor budget and fiscal condition quarterly. Let me call the beginning of the year A, the end of the first quarter B, the end of the second C, the end of the third D, and the end of the year E. With quarterly monitoring, the board would monitor at points A, B, C, D, and E. At point A, it would check to see if a twelve-month budget meets its policy criteria; it would also check to see if the actual fiscal condition (which would be, of course, the previous year's ending situation) is true to policy criteria. Note that these are two separate actions.

At point B, the board would want to know if budgeting for the nine months remaining meets its policy criteria, given that three months of actual places the organization at a position slightly (or not so slightly!) different than the original plan would have had it be. But at point B the board also wants to be reassured about the status of the actual fiscal condition. Note again, these are two separate actions.

Points C, D, and E follow in turn. Although the numbers may change radically as the year progresses, the relationships and characteristics with which the board deals will change minimally or not at all.

So the board must monitor two things: First, it checks actual fiscal performance to date, and second, it checks the integrity of planning for the *remaining part* of the fiscal year. Budgeting the remainder of the year uses the current actual as the starting point, of course, not the place a previous budget would have planned for actual to be. The previous budget is not relevant to either of these checks.

In other words, comparing actual with previous budgeting is not the best monitoring method for the integrity of either fiscal condition or current budgeting, though it might shed light on how much faith we can put in the process by which projections and estimates are made. This is not an insignificant concern, but it is not what most boards are examining when they receive a budget to approve or the subsequent fiscal reports. If a budget that makes projections by ineffective or discredited methods would be unacceptable, then that proviso itself would simply become one of the unacceptable conditions in an amended budget policy, thereby making it regularly exposed to scrutiny as it is monitored.

What Monitoring Information to Get and How to Get It

The most important matter is that the board get the appropriate information at whatever frequency the board needs to feel reasonably assured of acceptable management.

FAQ ➡
What constitutes monitoring information?

What information to get. It is important for the board to observe a simple rule: Only gather the information that *directly* discloses the degree to which the preestablished expectations are met. These expectations are found in the applicable board policies, nowhere else. It is common for CEOs to overwhelm the board with data that do not directly address the criteria but tell a larger story. By dilution, the critical monitoring data are lost, or, at least, obscured. Keep the data strictly to the point. Seek to have the least complicated, simplest data that would convince a reasonable person that the criterion performance has been disclosed.

FAQ ➡
How does the board get monitoring information?

How to get it. The data received by the board to monitor either fiscal condition or budgeting can reach the board in three ways. (1) Performance data gathered and summarized by the CEO. (2) Performance data gathered and summarized by a disinterested party. The fiscal audit is an example of this method of monitoring, though the board would have to be sure that such monitoring is within the scope of the audit arranged with the auditor. (3) Performance data gathered and summarized by the board itself. The board can do this as a whole body or through specifically assigned board members or committees.

In the discussion above I assumed the monitoring data come from the CEO. That is, in fact, the source used by most boards using Policy Governance as well as those using more conventional practice. The board does have the other choices, however, and it is wise to use them from time to time. The methods can be combined. For example, to monitor actual financial condition, it is common for a board to use the CEO report monthly or quarterly and an auditor annually. But in any event, it is important that monitoring always be related directly to the board's preestablished policy expectations, not to the idiosyncratic judgments of the monitoring party or parties.

To illustrate the quarterly monitoring of financial condition through data gathered and summarized by the CEO, let me quote from the October 1992 Family Service Ontario report of the executive director to the board. The executive submitted data to disclose performance on the policy illustrated in the box in "Crafting Policy to Safeguard Your Organization's Actual Fiscal Condition" in Chapter Six. I will excerpt two subsections from that report:

> It is important that monitoring always be related directly to the board's preestablished policy expectations, not to the idiosyncratic judgments of the monitoring party or parties.

EL-4.1: *[The Executive Director may not] expend more funds than have been received in the fiscal year to date unless the debt guideline is met.*

Monitoring data: To date, $454,007.97 has been expended, while $586,329.86 has been received. These amounts include the expenditure of $187,903.56 on FSO's Trillium projects. The amount is transferred into revenue from a liability account. I am therefore reporting compliance.

EL-4.2: *[The Executive Director may not] allow tax payments or other government-ordered filings to be overdue or inaccurately filed.*

Monitoring data: The tax return which FSO must file with Revenue Canada was filed in March 1992. Payments due to the Receiver General (Income Tax, C.P.P., U.I.C.) and the Employee Health Tax payments are up to date. FSO underwent a GST audit in July 1992 and our books were found to be completely correct. There are no other required tax payments or filings than these. I am therefore reporting compliance.

These monitoring data address the policy criteria in a way that nonaccountant board members can reach a reasonable conclusion about whether the criteria have been met. Obviously, there are hundreds of numbers a given board member might be interested in. Experienced board members, accustomed to financial reporting wherein governors attempt to be managers one step removed, may feel uncomfortable unless immersed in a sea of official-looking numbers. To help the discomfort, the board should ask itself, "Is there truly anything else we need to worry about, beyond what the more focused monitoring data reveal?"

← **FAQ**

How can nonaccountant board members be assured they understand the monitoring data?

If there is, then the board will be on its way to developing an additional criterion to add to the relevant policy. The thoroughness of the policy is improved, the board's confidence is improved, and the policy is in this way continually up for discussion. "If you haven't said how it ought to be, don't ask how it is" may be a tough discipline to stick to as the board monitors, but it will keep the criterion-based relationship with the CEO rigorous and fair at the same time. In this way the monitoring system itself is a major tool in the board's ability not to just have policies, but to live them.

Board Approvals and Monitoring Are Very Different Actions

BOARD LEADERSHIP, NUMBER 24, MAR.-APR. 1996

FOR YEARS I have disparaged the common practice of board approvals, calling it the "approval syndrome," a counterfeit form of board leadership. A board engaged in approving various staff actions and plans certainly appears to be providing conscientious oversight. But in using the approval method to ensure staff accountability, a board is not leading but demonstrating its deeply flawed governance.

For longer than anyone can remember, the practice of board approval has been the main tool boards use to monitor staff intentions. In order to be sure things are going acceptably, boards demand approval authority over all manner of internal practices. Personnel policies, budgets, program plans, compensation schedules, and staff promotions are among the familiar actions and documents that boards approve. Because these actions and documents summarize much of an organization's essence, it is understandable that boards seize upon them to maintain a modicum of control.

To have a meaningful discussion of board approvals, however, it is first necessary to recognize that the word *approval* is used in three very different ways. In conventional board practice, little note is taken of the distinctions between different types of approval. But for board leadership to be its best, the different types of approval must be distinguished. In the accompanying box are the three types of approval and their description based on the concepts of Policy Governance.

In Policy Governance, the third type of approval is not only accepted but also developed as a technology. By using a more sophisticated approach to the direct expression of board sentiments and values, Policy Governance is able to completely discard the first and second types of traditional approvals and substitute a more rigorous monitoring process. The three traditional types of approval are replaced in Policy Governance by two actions: criteria-setting and criteria-checking. It is important to understand how monitoring in Policy Governance differs from the first two types of board approvals.

Two steps are necessary for rigorous monitoring of organizational performance:

- First, board expectations must be known. Just what is being monitored? What are the criteria to be used or the standards expected?

- Second, whatever data illuminate performance must be compared with the criteria so that relative success can be assessed.

If the board carefully crafts its criteria and then requests the relevant data, the first two approval types can be eliminated. Checking is still necessary, but it is always against criteria and is therefore less aimless and inexact. There is nothing to approve in past staff actions; there is only the need to know if they are consistent with the criteria. There is nothing to approve in future staff plans; there is only the need to know if they are consistent with the criteria. There is nothing to approve in board statements; there is only the need for the board to express or not (the word *approval* in this context isn't any more meaningful than saying I am approving each sentence I write).

FAQ ➡
In Policy Governance, why does the board not approve staff plans such as personnel policies?

But if criteria are set and data gathered, what harm is there in going along with the traditional approvals anyway? Doesn't board approval send a more convincing message that the board is behind these actions and documents—that the staff are not merely acting on their own? Isn't it important, for example, for the public to know that the board approved an important document?

In the next few paragraphs, I will use the example of personnel policies approval to illustrate my point. But remember, I am referring to board approval of any staff plan.

If approving the personnel policies merely means that the CEO's personnel document meets board criteria, then approval causes no problem. It merely constitutes board judgment that prestated criteria have been met. This kind of approval, however, leaves the CEO free to make subsequent changes in the document as long as board criteria continue to be met. So, if the board is saying that any personnel document the CEO creates is acceptable so long as he or she demonstrates, at frequent enough intervals, that it still meets criteria, I see no problem in it.

But what I have just described is not what approval ordinarily means. What is usually meant by personnel policies approval is a process that has deleterious effects. First, it lulls the board into thinking it has dealt with the most important personnel issues. Yet how is the board to know, unless it has exhaustively discussed and detailed just what the issues and expectations are. Second, it causes the staff to guess what the board's approval criteria will be, even though the board itself hasn't said and, in fact, doesn't know. Third, to avoid rubber-stamping their approval, board members are driven to examine details they don't (and need not) understand in order to render a judgment. Fourth, even after approval, the criteria still have not been made explicit, so the effort does not contribute toward the clarity of board expectations. Fifth, whatever the board has not approved is considered unapproved. So any alterations in the CEO's personnel arrangements are, prima facie, unacceptable until the board goes through its machinations once again. Not only is the board drawn into the personnel details to begin with, but it must delve into any alterations thereafter.

> By confounding the inconsequential with the profound, board approval of operational documents trivializes the board's job.

By confounding the inconsequential with the profound, board approval of operational documents trivializes the board's job. By freezing into place decisions far beneath the board's proper purview, board approval of operational actions severely hampers managerial agility. By diverting attention from the values of personnel treatment to concrete personnel procedures and administrative policies, traditional board approval promotes a false sense of board security.

> Good monitoring reaches beyond the document to the actual behavior itself.

Monitoring whether personnel actions and plans at any given point meet comprehensive board criteria, however, causes none of these troublesome side effects. Don't forget that these observations not only apply to personnel issues, but to all other managerial practices, such as budget or program approvals. Consequently, once the board has established the boundaries of acceptability in personnel practices, mere monitoring of those practices from time to time is sufficient for the board to discharge its accountability. Its separate approval of the personnel package is not needed. In fact, the written personnel rules are only part of what should be monitored: Good monitoring reaches beyond the document to the actual behavior itself.

Board Approvals and Policy Governance

Types of Approvals in Traditional Governance

1. *Approvals that control future staff actions.* When a board approves budgets, personnel policies, or other operational plans, it is exercising control over those particular arenas of organizational life.

2. *Approvals that judge or evaluate past staff actions.* When a board approves a monthly or quarterly financial report or a program report, it is both ratifying the historical record and condoning the staff action represented in the report.

3. *Approvals that are really the board's self-generated statements.* When a board formulates a resolution and then passes it, it is approving a self-generated idea. Thus, this type of approval is a direct expression of board sentiment.

How Policy Governance Regards These Board Approvals

1. Controlling future staff actions in this way is awkward and confuses roles. Staff plans go into more detail than is appropriate for the board, yet there is no way for the board to isolate its own preferred level of detail. Hence, board inquiry gravitates toward the details of least importance in the document. (Watch a board with a budget!)

2. "Monitoring" in this way constitutes wallowing in data more than monitoring with it, inasmuch as it is rarely known what the board would find disapprovable, that is, what criteria are being checked. Attempting to monitor performance without prestated criteria results more in wandering around than meaningful assessment.

3. Direct expressions of board will or values are good, but not if they are undisciplined and disjointed. Such resolutions should be made to fit an overall framework from which a holistic governance picture emerges. More or less spastic board pronouncements do not add up to powerful leadership.

When boards establish appropriate criteria for staff, monitoring is a handily straightforward exercise in comparing performance to policy. When boards fail to establish appropriate criteria, true monitoring is impossible, and the board is forced to demand approval authority over all manner of managerial actions. The time-honored practice of board approval trivializes the board-staff conversation, camouflages the board's failure to clarify organizational values, mistakes wandering-around-in-the-presence-of-data for monitoring, and cheats everyone of the opportunity for outstanding board leadership.

Giving Measurement Its Due in Policy Governance

Board Leadership, Number 30, Mar.-Apr. 1997

I REGULARLY COUNSEL boards to forget measurability when establishing expectations for organizational performance; that is, when they are crafting ends and executive limitations policies. Frequently my recommendation is mistaken to be an antimeasurement point of view. I can assure you it is not. But because this issue can be a source of difficulty for boards implementing Policy Governance, in this article I'd like to put measurement in perspective.

Most board members and certainly all managers are acquainted with the exhortation to "set measurable objectives." All the books say so, all the consultants say so. If we can't measure it, we won't know when we've done it. So goes the unrelenting chorus.

> Boards don't *do* a great deal, but they should *demand* a great deal.

Let me agree in a way. Clearly, whatever we set out to do must be assessed or evaluated so that we know if we've attained it—that is, our actual achievements must be measured against our intended achievements. This is particularly important when one party does the intending and the other party the achieving—a common phenomenon in governance. Boards don't *do* a great deal, but they should *demand* a great deal. In other words, they foist their intentions on someone else, in most cases a CEO. The CEO is to see to achievement, and the board has a legitimate need to know if achievement has occurred.

So whatever the board demands of its executive arm will and must be measured. But that does not mean—as we have erroneously supposed—that the board's demand must itself be in quantified terms.

← **FAQ**

Does the Policy Governance model really require boards to forget about numbers and measurement?

Consider the Policy Governance principle that the best way for a board to express its wishes is to do so broadly, then more narrowly as needed to reach a level of definition at which any further reasonable interpretation is acceptable. Consider as well that the creation of expectations for organizational performance is a board prerogative, not a right of staff. Expectations, then, are generated from board values, not staff recommendations or steering. It is crucial that board expectations are stated as the board means them. It is immaterial whether the expectations are stated in quantifiable terms. In fact, if the board presses itself to produce measurability, it will without doubt weaken its pursuit of meaningfulness.

This is because, typically, broadly stated expectations are not measurably stated. For a family service agency board to direct that "functional families" is to be the organization's product is perfectly acceptable. For a community college board to direct that students will be equipped for "success in employment or higher education" is perfectly acceptable. For the board of a trade association to prohibit its CEO from subjecting staff to "undignified treatment" is perfectly acceptable. None of these statements is in terms ordinarily seen as measurable objectives.

> If the board presses itself to produce measurability, it will without doubt weaken its pursuit of meaningfulness.

At the board's broad level of oversight, arriving at such global expectations is itself a task of some difficulty, given the range of board member opinions. So plunging prematurely into detail not only strains the board's generalist skill but almost certainly risks the meaningfulness of the global statement. Of course, the board could say that "80 percent of students obtain employment at greater than minimum wage within three months of graduation" or "no fewer than 60 percent of students choosing higher education achieve at least a 2.0 grade point average in their first year." These might be reasonable measures of the initial global outcomes. But if the board focuses on these measures rather than the global, it jeopardizes the global expectation, which is a more valid statement of what it wanted in the first place.

As a practical matter, when boards delve into levels of detail that exceed their "any reasonable interpretation" level, they commonly do so with extensive staff assistance. As often as not, staff "assistance" is actually staff stage management. Instead of doing its own thinking at the global level and just below, the board is tempted to validate (or parrot, to describe the phenomenon less generously) staff thinking at a legitimate staff level of detail. For example, in approving a program plan, the board approves details in which it likely has no group expertise and might not even understand.

This predicament is easily avoided. The board stays at the level it understands, arguing the pros and cons of global, then slightly less global, expressions of what it wants with respect to ends and what it doesn't want with respect to means. As it increases its degree of definition (that is, goes into further detail describing what it wants and doesn't want), it will reach a point at which it would find satisfaction in any reasonable interpretation of whatever explication remains. It should do all this without regard to whether its expressions fit anybody's definition of "measurable."

At this point, the board considers its language complete and turns the resultant ends or executive limitations policy over to the CEO, consigning to her or him the production of a reality that, in the board's subsequent opinion, is a reasonable interpretation of what the board has finally said (at whatever level of detail it has carried its expression). The subsequent opinion is reached through monitoring, a mere comparison of reality to language. This monitoring occurs through measurement.

Because the board has granted the CEO any interpretation that can be shown to be reasonable, the CEO might approach measurement in any number of ways. For example, the community college president might interpret the board's global, but meaningful, "success in employment or higher education" to mean "80 percent of students obtain employment at greater than minimum wage within three months of graduation" and "no fewer than 60 percent of students choosing higher education achieve at least a 2.0 grade point average in their first year." But in order to convince the board that the CEO is achieving a reasonable interpretation of "success in employment or higher education," it is likely that other measures will be needed to be persuasive.

In other words, the board can leave measurement up to the CEO, so long as he or she can make a convincing case that the measures submitted do, in fact, constitute a reasonable interpretation of the ends or executive limitations policies. But, make no mistake, *measurement must happen.* The board will have stated its desire in nontechnical language, leaving the CEO a twofold burden: first, achieve a reasonable interpretation of what has been expressed; second, devise and submit measurements that convince a majority of board members that they are getting a reasonable appraisal of the achievement (read "prove it to us").

Policy Governance does place a high value on the measurement of broadly stated board values about ends and executive limitations. But it places the importance and sequence of measurement in the scheme of things after the board has done its work, work that despite its generality is not easily achieved.

Honey, I Shrunk the Policies

Board Leadership, Number 30, Mar.-Apr. 1997

R EBELLING AT THE IDEA of controlling everything in sight, management leaders began cutting back on the volume and detail of procedures some years ago. Some organizations had procedures for any conceivable act. "Doing it by the book" was intended to standardize and to avoid errors, but it succeeded in dulling minds. Some of the more exciting management books counseled managers to throw away their stuffy tomes and encourage people to think for themselves.

Policy Governance is consistent with that philosophy. Of course, the board is not—or, rather should not be—in a position to make internal procedural decisions. Managers have those choices to make, and I hope they opt for only as much control over employees as necessary to get the organization's business done well. But boards are in a position to govern in such a way as not to cause the problem themselves.

For some observers, their first glance at Policy Governance raises fears of undercontrol. That is, they fear the board is giving up control by not imposing extensive controls on managerial behavior, perhaps in the form of holding approval authority over various internal documents. Other observers' first glance raises fears of too many board policies. They are appalled at the number of written-down board values separate from simple approval of staff documents.

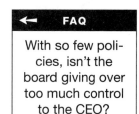

← FAQ

With so few policies, isn't the board giving over too much control to the CEO?

I've dealt with the first fear on numerous occasions. Policy Governance does not argue for boards to give up control but rather to change the aspects of organization that they seek to control. In fact, the amount of overall system control is probably greater than most boards have now.

If we look more closely, I believe we'll find a deeper fear. I think the policies in Policy Governance frighten some people simply because they show up where little or no policy has been before. Going from near zero to even a small number represents quite a percentage increase. Most boards using Policy Governance correctly end up with twenty to forty policies, most of which are from one sentence to one page long. When you consider that, except for the bylaws, this small compendium is the total written board product and is able to embrace the complete governing task for even large, complex organizations, it would seem to be rather compact.

> The policies in Policy Governance frighten some people simply because they show up where little or no policy has been before.

Moreover, as readers of *Board Leadership* already know, none of those pages tells staff how to do things—the usual function of procedures. The CEO and staff create their own procedures to whatever extent the CEO sees fit. The board will have only laid out the boundaries of acceptable activities and situations, in perhaps a half-dozen pages of executive limitations policies.

So the policy manual that the board must personally deal with is indeed a brief and liberating document. It may not prevent the CEO from going a bit overboard with internal policies, but it will never cause this stultifying situation. The policies of Policy Governance constitute—somewhat paradoxically—a freeing document of board control!

The Mechanics of Direct Inspection Monitoring

Board Leadership, Number 39, Sept.-Oct. 1998

Boards must demand that their organizations be accountable. Accountability is achieved by (1) carefully stating expectations, (2) making it clear exactly who is responsible for meeting them, and (3) checking systematically to see whether the expectations are being met. This last action is frequently called monitoring, evaluation, or performance assessment. The mechanisms available to a board to check performance are (1) reports from the CEO, (2) reports to the board from an outsider (a disinterested party or expert), and (3) direct board inspection of material or circumstances that would enable the board to form its own opinion. This article concerns the mechanics of this last option, the *direct inspection* method of monitoring.

Let me be more specific about how direct inspection differs from the other two reporting methods. I'll use a concrete example. Assume that the board has adopted an executive limitations policy that the CEO is not to allow the ratio of current assets to current liabilities (this is called the current ratio, a common liquidity measure) to drop below 1.5:1. Assume further that the

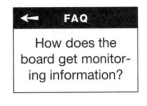

← FAQ

How does the board get monitoring information?

board decides that it wants to be reassured on a quarterly basis whether this criterion is being met. If the board chooses a CEO report as its preferred method to monitor this criterion, the CEO will quarterly abstract from current fiscal information those data that directly address this criterion. For example, the CEO might tell the board that "current assets are $5,340,333 and current liabilities are $3,141,372, yielding a current ratio of 1.7:1," thereby demonstrating compliance with this board policy.

If the board chooses to get the same assurance from a party not under the purview of the CEO (for example, from an independent auditor), the outside party selected by the board would submit a similar report each quarter directly to the board. (Of course, the CEO has the option of using an outsider for preparing a CEO report, but that report would still be a CEO report inasmuch as the outsider is under the CEO's control.)

If the board chooses direct inspection as its monitoring method, there is no actual report in the sense of someone's having abstracted from the myriad financial figures those data that address the board's criterion. In direct inspection, the board goes directly to the financial data, reviews them, and forms its own opinion as to whether the data demonstrate compliance or noncompliance.

As straightforward and attractively simple as it is to say that sometimes the best way to monitor performance is simply to go and look, it is obvious that this method is not one a busy board can use very often. Further, the larger or more complex an organization is, the more difficult, awkward, or overwhelming this kind of monitoring becomes. For these reasons, I ordinarily recommend to clients that they minimize the use of the direct inspection method. Still, the method is a legitimate approach for monitoring performance, so it is worthwhile to examine it more closely and to explore how it can be used in such a way as to avoid potential pitfalls.
It is obvious that this method is not one a busy board can use very often.

There are three ways to implement direct inspection: using the whole board, using a committee, or assigning the task to an individual board member.

Direct Inspection by the Whole Board

In traditional governance, boards often use this method during full board sessions when they look over periodic financial statements or program reports. Unfortunately, they are rarely inspecting these data with respect to preestablished performance criteria, so their action is better described as whole board wandering around than as whole board monitoring. (Remember, in Policy Governance, monitoring is always against criteria.) But in Policy Governance, true assessment of whether the CEO has met board expectations can be done by the whole board when the board has the skill and time to do so.

To illustrate, here's how the board might choose to monitor its budget policy by whole board direct inspection. First, of course, I must assume that the board has a budget policy (an executive limitations policy) that sets forth what characteristics are unacceptable in financial planning. I'll also assume that the board has decided on quarterly monitoring. Each quarter, the board will ask the CEO to submit a budget for the remaining part of the fiscal year. The whole board will then go over the document with its budget policy in hand, looking to see if relevant aspects of that budget do or do not meet the board's policy-stated expectations.

Although to an outsider this action might look like traditional budget approval, it differs in two significant ways. First, the board is only checking criteria it has previously set out. That is, the board is not wandering around in the document, settling on whatever strikes board members' fancy. It is not creating criteria "on the fly" by making non-criteria-based judgments. Moreover, board members are judging not on the basis of their individual ideas about budgeting but on the ideas that made it through the board's deliberative process and into the policy. Second, whereas the budget approval process used in traditional governance freezes all the budgetary components (each and every number) into place, monitoring, even when done by direct inspection, merely determines whether the budget as presented meets criteria or does not.

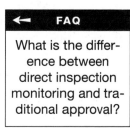

FAQ

What is the difference between direct inspection monitoring and traditional approval?

In many ways, what the standard approval process comes down to is the board's giving fiscal instructions to the CEO at a ludicrously low level of detail. Monitoring, by contrast, never instructs; it only judges whether or not the instructions already given in the applicable policy are being followed. The whole board's opinion whether the monitored material meets a reasonable interpretation of board policy (any reasonable interpretation) is signified by a vote.

> Monitoring never instructs; it only judges whether or not the instructions already given in the applicable policy are being followed.

Direct Inspection by a Board Committee

A board might choose to assign the direct inspection task to a committee. The board committee is given the right to decide on the board's behalf whether the CEO has met a reasonable interpretation of board policy. Fundamentally, direct inspection by a committee functions exactly the way it functions with the whole board. With committees, however, it is wise to be vigilant about a couple of traps. First, it is easy for a committee, insulated from the board's commitment to governance discipline (I will assume there is a great deal of that!), to get into superfluous discussion about criteria and what the board "meant." It is crucial that such discussion be off-limits, for the committee is to judge CEO performance only on whether the CEO complied with any reasonable interpretation of the board's words, not with what the committee thinks the board meant or even with what the committee decides is its choice of best interpretation.

In no event should the committee let its feelings corrupt the integrity of its monitoring responsibility.

In a particular community service agency, for example, board policy prohibits the CEO from setting staff salaries higher than the market for their skills. The CEO has taken "the market" to mean other employers of similar size in the metropolitan area. This is a reasonable interpretation, though certainly not the only reasonable interpretation, of wording in the board's policy. Let's say the committee feels strongly that due to the agency's close relationship to county government, "the market" should be local city and county government. No matter how strongly the committee feels (or, indeed, how right it is), the CEO must be given credit for passing the monitoring test. By the way, there is no reason for the committee to be powerless about this matter. If it wants to have an effect, it must convince the board to change the way the policy is stated. But in no event should the committee let its feelings corrupt the integrity of its monitoring responsibility.

Committees are thus quite prone to make up new criteria as they go along. Another problem of committees, particularly if the same group of individuals continues to monitor the same topic, is that a committee can come to "own" a certain topic, in effect becoming the unofficial miniboard for that topic. And committees are, in my experience, much more likely than CEOs or outsiders to become lax about the important rules of monitoring.

FAQ ➡

What should the board do if a direct inspection uncovers noncompliance?

The committee's opinion whether the monitored material meets a reasonable interpretation of board policy (any reasonable interpretation) is signified by a vote. But because the board must never allow any person or committee to interfere with the clean line of delegation from board to CEO, the board must allow the CEO a right of appeal to the board if the committee concludes noncompliance. A board vote then makes the final determination.

Direct Inspection by an Assigned Board Member

All the points already made (including the right of CEO appeal) apply to direct inspection monitoring assigned by the board to an individual board member. There are, of course, some peculiarities to this method. A single inspector is more likely to be biased, either for or against the CEO, than a committee or the full board. That potential personal bias must be guarded against or corrected for. Individuals often find it difficult to refrain from projecting their own values into criteria established by the board, perhaps more so than a committee or whole board in which competing values can provide some balance.

It is natural for a board to appoint a board member who is expert in the topic to be monitored. This makes sense on the surface and may be a good approach, but it also introduces a less attractive element. Assume, for example, that a board criterion prohibits the CEO from failing to "pay bills in a timely manner." Let's say that the board member assigned to monitor policies in this area is an accountant who has definite views on what "timely manner" should mean. This can result in staff members' trying to meet the accountant's definition, yet Policy Governance allows the staff to use any reasonable interpretation. The stage is set for the accountant, with all good intentions, to micromanage what was only to be monitored.

> What sets direct inspection monitoring apart in Policy Governance is that no one stands between the board and the data.

In a large sense, of course, all board monitoring of organizational performance involves "direct" inspection in that board members are obligated to study and pass judgment on monitoring material that reaches them. What sets direct inspection monitoring apart in Policy Governance is that no one stands between the board and the data. No one helps the board by abstracting the relevant data from the far more numerous surrounding data. But direct inspection monitoring, despite the apparent purity of its engaging board members in the fundamental realities of organizational life, calls for considerable care, expertise, and time to do that job well.

In summary, direct inspection is a legitimate and workable method for determining whether the CEO's organization is meeting board expectations (as found in the ends and executive limitations policies). But it is not normally the monitoring method of choice and, when used, must be organized very carefully to avoid both meddling (inappropriately giving instructions) and making judgments without criteria.

Redefining Board Self-Evaluation: The Key to Keeping on Track

Board Leadership, Number 10, Nov.-Dec. 1993

THE SIMPLEST and most useful tool boards have to keep them on track is frequent and rigorous self-evaluation. Because board evaluation is not a new topic, most people already have ideas about what the term means. To get the most from this and other articles on self-evaluation in this book, however, be wary about preexisting ideas. I approach the board's evaluation of its own performance in a way that might be rather different from what you have heard before. For in a number of ways, I wish to redefine both the philosophy and the mechanics of board self-evaluation.

> The specific manner of self-evaluation is less important than being explicit about expectations for board performance and regularly reviewing that performance.

For example, an article on how to do board self-evaluation would seem at the outset an ideal centerpiece for a *Board Leadership* issue on this topic. But I entreat your patience to put the emphasis elsewhere. For despite the pragmatic streak in all of us, concrete advice on the mechanics of self-evaluation is not the most important aspect of the board's evaluation challenge. The specific manner of self-evaluation—the mechanism, if you will—is far less important than (1) being explicit about expectations for board performance and (2) regularly reviewing that performance by *any* method!

It is important in any undertaking to obtain feedback on performance. Constant performance information enables us to guide a spoonful of baby food into an eager, moving mouth and to throw a baseball over a seventeen-inch plate. For a board, charged with strategic leadership, the principle is no less true. In fact, due to the high leverage that governance exerts over all organizational activity and achievement, it is even more important for the board to keep itself on track. Moreover, because groups of peers—such as boards—tend to find self-discipline a difficult task, the matter demands unusually careful consideration.

No one expects an automobile to run without maintenance or a freshly painted house to stay painted. Everything needs continual attention. So it should be no surprise that human arrangements and management systems must be tuned from time to time. In the absence of self-correction, the best governance will fall victim to entropy. The toughest problem faced by boards that have adopted the policy governance model is maintenance of the gains they achieve. Turnover among members and disuse of the system are the natural enemies of any strategy of discipline that a board adopts. If the model is put in place properly to begin with, *keeping* it in place may be the hardest task of all.

Self-evaluation is the handiest and most powerful tool available to maintain and continually improve the excellence of governing. But like all good tools, it must be employed carefully. I believe that certain considerations are critical to using this fine tool well. So let me share my biases about evaluation right up front.

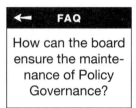

FAQ

How can the board ensure the maintenance of Policy Governance?

The primary purpose of evaluation is not to reward or punish but to achieve continual improvement in performance. Unfortunately, the word *evaluation* has become heavily associated with rendering a pass-fail judgment, often on whether or not a numerical criterion has been met. Evaluation in this sense is largely what someone does to someone else. Consequently, we think of evaluation as a necessary prerequisite to "motivate" people. It connotes a sense of judging, on the one hand, and manipulating behavior, on the other.

A board can engage in healthy and useful self-evaluation if it lays aside the judging connotation. I want boards to see self-evaluation as similar to what goes on among eyes, brain, and muscles when you practice a skill. Typically, you make little comparisons, little adjustments—a nip here, a tuck there, hold your mouth a little differently—in a never-ending sequence.

Self-evaluation is most meaningful when related to established expectations. What defines governance excellence? If it isn't defined, how can you know you're reaching or missing it? Evaluation requires a standard of comparison, an expectation. Unless a board is clear about what constitutes responsible governance,

FAQ

What criteria should a board use to evaluate its own performance?

its attempt at evaluation will merely wander about. When the board has not formally chosen criteria, individual board members are left to their own idiosyncratic ones, perhaps criteria the board has never discussed. Evaluation, then, done as a free-standing action, can never make up for not having put into place carefully considered expectations, against which evaluation is then done. You might remember that the principle of judging only against previously established criteria applies also to CEO evaluation. The task of evaluating the board is no different.

Board self-evaluation is an inseparable part of governing, not an extraneous or optional task. To see how integral evaluation is to the task, try writing in the dark. If you cannot see where your pen marks, you will not write well and may not even write legibly. Yet writing is a familiar skill with which you have a lifetime of experience. It is so automatic that you scarcely give the arm, hand, and finger muscle movements a conscious thought. How much more must we need feedback for a complex social task like governance!

In basketball, you'd have to use an artificial dissection of events to isolate shooting baskets from the eye-and-muscle feedback loop *about* shooting baskets. No matter how good your technique, if you cannot actually see the ball as it flies toward the net after each shot, your shooting will never improve. What goes on in the act of shooting those baskets is the soul of self-evaluation.

FAQ →

How often should the board do a self-evaluation?

Self-evaluation is a continual rather than sporadic activity. If you are interested in keeping score, totaling up every year may be acceptable. But if you want to improve performance, evaluation must be continual. Consequently, I have little use for the annual board self-evaluation. It may produce a report card, but it will not produce better governance.

Board self-evaluation is a board—not staff—responsibility. Because self-evaluation is integral to the job to be done, and because governance is surely the board's job, the board has little choice but to accept the responsibility of evaluating how well it is doing its job. Like other parts of the board's job, other people may be engaged to help with the obligation, but it is critical that the board begin with the sense that it is itself responsible in a very direct and personal way.

I have little use for the annual board self-evaluation. It may produce a report card, but it will not produce better governance.

Living Up to Your Own Expectations: Implementing Self-Evaluation to Make a Difference in Your Organization

BOARD LEADERSHIP, NUMBER 10, NOV.-DEC. 1993

THIS ARTICLE deals with the "how to" of board self-evaluation. I must be very careful here because although the "how to" is not the most important part, suggested methods can overshadow the more important process considerations. So I cannot give you what I don't believe in (for example, a canned form for evaluation), but I can give you ideas and tips that might be of help as you implement your own "how to" scheme.

Recall that I am using *self-evaluation* to mean the board's careful, recurring comparison of its process (its conduct, its behavior) and products (the outcomes of its work) with *what it said would be* its process and products. Remember, too, that the purpose of self-evaluation is not so much to render a report card as to enable the board to maintain and improve the quality of its leadership. This kind of evaluation is not about yesterday, but about tomorrow. Evaluation is only cheapened if it becomes more about inspecting the past than inspiring the future.

FAQ ➡

How does the
Policy Governance
approach to board
evaluation differ
from more tradi-
tional approaches?

Let me be clear that my approach differs considerably from what is ordinarily taught and done about board self-evaluation. There is no canned evaluation form, no set of questions that will suffice for every board. Nor is this an instance of "volunteers" assessing whether they are fulfilled, feel listened to, think that meetings are productive, come prepared, or have a sense of involvement. While these things are not inconsequential, particularly from a personal psychology viewpoint, they are not the stuff of leadership but vestiges of a persistent amateurism found in the governance of nonprofit and public organizations.

> Evaluation is only cheapened if it becomes more about inspecting the past than inspiring the future.

Board self-evaluation—to support and compel a board toward the leadership for which it is capable—must be about whether the board as a leadership body *behaves* and *produces* as it should. For this article, then, I assume that a board has seriously discussed and determined both the process and the products appropriate to its job. In order to keep governance from deteriorating, the board must *live* out of all its policies, with particular emphasis on those that set out expectations for itself. This means that the board must constantly compare what really happens to what it said would happen.

FAQ ➡

Are there some
guidelines a board
can follow in doing
a self-evaluation?

In other words, the board adopts a mentality already familiar to us all in sports, in mowing the lawn, in running a drill press, in driving cross country, and in myriad other human activities. It builds in the feedback loop as part of doing the job. Self-evaluation is not extraneous to the job of governing. It is an integral, inseparable part of the job of governing.

So the board's approach to actually carrying out the evaluation must itself be described in policy. Of course, the policy guiding board self-evaluation would be in the governance process category. Here are some guidelines for doing self-evaluation, aspects for a board to keep in mind as it creates, say, a board self-evaluation policy.

> The board must constantly compare what really happens to what it said would happen.

Commit to constant self-evaluation. You should constantly refer to your policies as a measure of the correctness of ongoing board behavior. Don't worry about a little overkill on the frequency of evaluation. I

used to think that an annual self-evaluation would be just fine. But years of work
with boards have convinced me that a
good process among peers is so fragile, so
prone to straying, that self-evaluation
works best as an ongoing obligation. Evaluation should be an integral part of the

> Self-evaluation is not extraneous to the job of governing. It is an integral, inseparable part of the job of governing.

way in which the board governs. That means it is a routine part of board agendas
rather than a special, infrequent undertaking. So whatever method is used to evaluate, plan at least a few minutes in every board meeting for the board to compare its
actual process and products to the ones it has committed itself to. Yes, *every* board
meeting. Any number of pressures and normal tendencies will predispose a board to
straying. It is far harder for groups to be disciplined than for individuals; so even if
your board comprises very responsible members, it must go out of its way to ensure
a disciplined process. Evaluation less than once per meeting risks gradual deterioration of board leadership.

Pointedly address the preestablished criteria found in board policies. Evaluation,
remember, is not primarily a testing of "Are we having fun?" or "Is everyone partici-

pating?" or "Did all board members read
their mailings?" Those aspects may have
value; but unless they are written into an
applicable board policy, finding the
answers produces information that is
more incidental than vital to good governance. To the extent a given board feels

> Evaluation less than once per meeting risks gradual deterioration of board leadership.

that such matters are important, it should capture them in a board policy (for example, in the case of coming to meetings prepared, in an "individual board member
responsibilities" policy).

This seemingly rigid requirement has two important payoffs: First, it drives a useful board discussion about just what the requirements will be for responsible behavior. Second, it avoids each board member answering from an idiosyncratic perspective
where a *board perspective* has never even developed on the matter. Board members
will disagree on that at the outset, which is why it is important to resolve the matter
and frame it in policy.

The reference points, then, for all board self-evaluation are always the applicable
board policies. Actually look at the policies, line by line, and compare reality to the
words you find there. If this is not practical, it simply tells you the words were poorly

---

Having developed a template for
board behavior, don't put it aside.
Use it, make it work, and apply
it exclusively.

---

chosen. Go back to the policies and revise them to fit the real world. In other words, having developed a template for board behavior, don't put it aside. Use it, make it work, and apply it exclusively.

Every board policy that has implications for board behavior or outputs is used for self-evaluation. Such policies delineate (1) the outputs or products the board would hold itself accountable to produce, (2) the process or discipline the board is committed to use in the conduct of its affairs, and (3) the decisions that the board leaves to its CEO and that it, therefore, will not meddle in. The simple rule: If the board anywhere has said it would or it wouldn't, check to see whether it did!

Avoid mechanical approaches and prefabricated evaluation forms. Avoid any system that promises an evaluation of the board but does not require that the board do its preliminary, criteria-setting work first. Boards cannot afford to give up their responsibility not only for living up to the criteria but also for creating them. Because I've

---

If the board is unable to create the
criteria for its own performance,
it is hard to argue that it can be
responsible enough to govern the
actions of others.

---

been in the business of helping boards a long time, I occasionally get a call requesting "a good board evaluation form." I don't know that there is such a thing. Any canned form makes assumptions about what the required board behavior looks like and then engages board members or others in assessing against those criteria. Unless the board has explicitly adopted the often unspoken criteria used by the creator of the form, the process is worse than useless in that the board is fooled into thinking that it has discharged its responsibility for self-evaluation. Frankly, if the board is unable to create the criteria for its own performance, it is quite hard to argue that it can be responsible enough to govern the actions of others.

Assign responsibility. If your board makes no other determination, the policy governance model would automatically assign responsibility for board self-evaluation to the chairperson. However, you might find that self-evaluation works better if leadership on the matter is assigned to another board member. Although some boards would rather circulate that assignment from one meeting to the next, others like to have the chair-elect or vice chair carry the ball as preparation for later chairing duties. The secretary, for example, could be charged with performing or appointing another member to perform an evaluative review at the end of each meeting, soliciting from the CEO on a regular basis his or her perceptions concerning the board's record in sticking to its own rules, or designing and administering a board member questionnaire that quarterly elicits comparisons of actual board behavior with policy-stated intentions.

> It is amazing how much can be accomplished simply by coming back routinely to what you said you would do.

However the lead role is carried, it is extremely important that all board members take a personal interest in and responsibility for the evaluative process. For example, whenever the board is off track, perhaps doing things it said it wouldn't, every board member who does not intervene to correct the situation is culpable. Evaluation in its most important form—constant maintenance—has simply got to be everybody's business.

Choose a policy-driven method. The simplest method, one that ordinarily does not come to mind under the topic of evaluation, is to discuss some aspect of the policies relevant to board behavior at each meeting. For a board that has just read its own words pledging, for example, not to engage in determining staff means, going ahead and doing so in the next agenda item is considerably harder to do! This approach calls for every agenda to include a discussion of some aspect of board discipline or job performance.

Another easy method is for an assigned board member to give the board a critique at the end of each meeting. The critique, of course, must be based on the applicable board policies covering process and products—this isn't supposed to be an opportunity for a renegade board member to sound off on his or her points of view!

Even if you are a public board operating in the glare of press and onlookers, be bold enough to keep coming back to the template. One board of education in West Virginia decided to read its governance style policy aloud at the beginning of every meeting! It is amazing how much can be accomplished simply by coming back routinely to what you said you would do.

Another tactic is to examine your agenda for any given board meeting, seeing if every item is justified due to its direct relationship to fulfilling one of the criteria the board has established for itself. For example, is gathering a certain kind of data warranted in that the information adds to the board's wisdom in addressing a specific ends choice? Is a staff report on the agenda because it is directly speaking to the board's obligation to monitor staff performance against criteria in the ends and executive limitations policies? Is an executive plan slated for board approval only if an outside authority requires it?

Exhibit 9.1. An Exploratory Worksheet for Board Members

Board member, think of a recent issue that's come up in a board meeting. Maybe it was the subect of hot debate, maybe it's an ongoing issue, or maybe it simply occupies a lot of board time and energy. What was the issue? _____

_____

_____

How did the board determine if this issue if *the board's issue* (rather than the CEO's), or how did it determine that a specific *aspect* (not the entirety) of thsi issue is the board's?

_____

_____

Describe how your board approached the issue. How did you talk about it? Did you make a decision? What form of decision (a specific decision or a policy decision)?

_____

_____

Now think about your board's policies—or any form of written principles that your board has developed to guide its actions. What part of these policies related to this issue or to the board's behavior in dealing with this issue? Refer to your written policies, and write down the policy or policies you think apply. _____

_____

_____

Now ask yourself, in its activity at the meeting and in the actions it took, did the board live up to its own standards as expressed in its policies or written principles? How did it show this or fail to show this? _____

_____

_____

Bring this worksheet to your next board meeting and discuss it with other board members. How do your views differ from or correspond with theirs? Were existing board policies sufficient to give the guidance you needed? How can they be improved? How can the board's ability to stick to its rules be improved?

_____

_____

These same agenda items may be *un*justified. To discriminate, your discussion would have to go to the reason for their being there. For example, the staff report might just be a dog-and-pony-show waste of meeting time. The approval item might be before the board because the board has not delegated enough authority, or it has failed to establish sufficient limitations to feel safe in granting authority.

On a less frequent basis, perhaps the board would do well to respond to a written questionnaire. Evaluation at every meeting will not be sustained unless it is made very easy to do, which usually means an oral approach. But a less frequent evaluation in writing might be palatable. The written questionnaire is not a prefabricated form, of course, but is based on the particular board's policy-stated criteria.

Sometimes a simple worksheet will suffice. You really don't have to be scientific about it. I have seen a form like that in Exhibit 9.1 used with good results when treated as a tool for board deliberation. It can be completed by individual board members and then discussed as a group. Or the board can discuss each item to reach a group response. In either event, the right topics are on the table. Explicitness and rigorous attention alone can work magic as long as the preestablished criteria for products and process are obsessively and continually the common referent.

Let me summarize, then, the simple, fundamental principles of doing board self-evaluation: (1) Establish criteria for both products and process based on a coherent, effective model of governance. (2) Routinely inspect by any method to see if these criteria are being met, revising the criteria when necessary, but never ignoring them.

The Importance of Trust in the Board-CEO Relationship

BOARD LEADERSHIP, NUMBER 3, SEPT.-OCT. 1992

HOW HEALTHY is the trust between your board and chief executive? Whereas we all know that things work better when such trust exists and get gummed up when it doesn't, we are not so sure about how to restore that trust once it slips away. Experience indicates that organizations often have difficulty making trust survive an initial, benefit-of-the-doubt, honeymoon period.

Trust Is Always an Issue

A few years ago I worked with a very large public utility commission where there was a persistent lack of trust between the commission and its chief executive. Commissioners constantly complained that they couldn't trust the CEO in particular and all administrators in general. The CEO and top executives were forever wary of commission caprice and what they perceived to be abrupt changes in expectations. The interpersonal tone was tense, uncomfortable, and occasionally paranoid.

Although the utility commission was living through a particularly painful dilemma, theirs was not an uncommon situation. Trust is always an issue. Any board needs to trust its executive to give honest information and to carry out its directives. Any executive needs to trust the board to be fair in judgment and never capricious in action. These are proper expectations of the organizational functions.

Under conditions of mistrust, the human toll is high. Board members and executives alike become unhappy. Most of the warmth and excitement goes out of their activities related to the organization, since it just isn't fun either to govern or to manage under such a cloud. The board's ability to govern becomes hampered when it cannot accept management's information or goodwill.

> Boards and executives are more frequently troubled by a lack of trust that stems from poor governance than that which stems from poor character.

On rare occasions, there are instances of actual deceit, cover-up, or lying. Where careful inquiry confirms such untrustworthiness, terminating the relationship is probably the best course of action. The board simply should not tolerate a CEO whom it truly cannot trust.

In my experience, however, most instances of lack of trust between board and CEO arise for reasons unrelated to personal integrity. Boards and executives are more frequently troubled by a lack of trust that stems from poor governance than that which stems from poor character.

This was the case when I worked with the utility commission. I found all the individual commissioners and administrators to be personable, thoroughly likable people. Yet the air between the two groups was so poisoned that each could see the other only as adversaries, not human beings trying to do their jobs. I asked the commission, "Just what is it you don't trust your administrators *to do?*" The only reply forthcoming—after some delay—was, "We don't trust them not to do something stupid." Of course, they hadn't told their CEO what would lead them to decide something was "stupid"!

Moving Toward Trust

I have observed these mislabeled problems of trust resolve themselves as boards begin to follow a few simple but effective tenets of good governance. Happily, the same rules can help organizations avoid developing such problems in the first place. So even if your board is free from problems of trust now, paying attention to these tips may well be worth your effort down the line.

← **FAQ**

How can a board ensure there is a high level of trust in the board-CEO relationship?

Say clearly what you expect. It is quite common for boards to trust CEOs to read their minds. "But she should have known that!" is a symptomatic board complaint. Don't consider anything to be so obvious that it doesn't need saying. I suggest you put your

---

Don't consider anything to be so
obvious that it doesn't need saying.

---

expectations into a set of explicit policies about organizational output (ends) and limitations on the latitude of staff decisions and actions (executive limitations). But any manner of stating your expectations is better than leaving them unstated.

Only the single board voice counts.　The only relevant expectations for management are those that the board has officially adopted. That means a vote has been taken. Sometimes a board thinks it has given a directive simply because one or two members have stated clearly what *they* want, even though the board has not taken a vote. Expectations of individual board members should be of no effect and cannot be interpreted as the intent of the whole board. Moreover, the board should guard against having the clarity of its voice diluted by allowing the chair, treasurer, or committees to dictate expectations—even subtly.

Judge the CEO only according to stated expectations.　This rule should apply to informal judgments as well as formal evaluations. Just as important, boards should

---

Failing to use the stated expectations to actually judge performance
indicates the board wasn't serious
about them after all.

---

not forget to carry through in making such judgments. Assessing CEO performance according to any other criteria indicates the board didn't say what it wanted in the first place; failing to use the stated expectations to actually judge performance indicates the board wasn't serious about them after all. The best way to be successful in

this area is to establish a routine monitoring system that is focused precisely on your stated expectations.

Assure the CEO that he or she is free to trust you.　This may sound unnecessary, but it is definitely important. The board's commitment to its word will have little effect in the short term unless the CEO has confidence that you mean it. The best way to send the message is to agree formally (put it in writing and vote!) that you will never judge the CEO according to any expectations except those that have been officially established beforehand. One of those expectations, of course, is that the CEO will always give honest and accurate information to the board. While CEOs should be prepared to deliver performance, they need not be tormented by board caprice or "gotcha" games.

Boards that follow these general rules will find that trust problems disappear—or are prevented from forming in the first place. In the rare case, using these rules will help a board confirm that a genuine issue of trust is severe enough for drastic reme-diation. The utility commission I men-tioned above tried; it even made some progress. But the cordial, benefit-of-the-doubt relationship had been irretrievably bruised. The individual serving as CEO had to leave before significant strides could be made in restoring trust between the board and CEO in the organization.

> While CEOs should be prepared to deliver performance, they need not be tormented by board caprice or "gotcha" games.

The time to safeguard and nourish trust is before it slips away. The most effective way a board can nourish such trust is to focus not on trust itself, but on governing well.

Evaluating the CEO: An Effective Approach to Ensure Future Organizational Success

BOARD LEADERSHIP, NUMBER 26, JULY-AUG. 1996

T HE REMAINING ARTICLES in this chapter focus on the board's evaluation of its chief executive officer. CEO evaluation is a tough issue for boards—as comments in my workshops regularly confirm. It seems that hiring one, firing one, and sometimes living with one are all painful experiences!

That isn't necessarily true, of course, but certainly assessing whether your CEO is getting the job done is a vexing prospect more often than not. In this group of articles I examine what is meant by CEO evaluation, how your board should approach the matter, and what technique will best carry it out. Typically, board members think an annual evaluation by the chairperson or by a board committee is the way to go. A far more effective approach is available.

My years of intimacy with boards and their CEOs have convinced me that boards have a difficult time knowing whether they have a good CEO or not. CEOs are often fired for the wrong reasons and retained for the wrong reasons. Boards that have a better handle on the assessment of their CEOs can avoid this common problem.

The following article, "Putting CEO Evaluation in Perspective," frames the issue of CEO evaluation as an integral part of governing—how evaluation of the chief executive fits into the whole scheme of board leadership. But before any board works on evaluating its CEO, it must determine whether, indeed, it even has a CEO! In Chapter Four, "Getting It Right from the Start: The CEO's Job Description" and "Do You Really Have a CEO?" will help in that inquiry.

After considering the issues raised in these articles, you will then be ready to determine your own board's readiness to evaluate the CEO and how to monitor the ongoing evaluation process. In Exhibit 9.2, you can find out whether your board has done the requisite homework to make CEO evaluation worthwhile. Exhibit 9.3 will test how well any ongoing evaluation of CEO performance stacks up against the expectations of Policy Governance.

I address a related and often debated issue in "Should Your CEO Be a Board Member?" (Chapter Three). "Off-Limits: What Not to Do in Your CEO Evaluation" (Chapter Nine) serves as a check of some common pitfalls that you would do well to avoid as you evaluate.

Because CEOs want to know how they can support good governance by playing their role more effectively, they will also have an opportunity to evaluate their own behavior toward their boards as they think about the points raised in "A CEO *Self*-Evaluation Checklist."

Putting CEO Evaluation in Perspective

Board Leadership, Number 26, July-Aug. 1996

Most boards find evaluating their CEO to be difficult. While I cannot claim that strict, yet fair, evaluation can ever be easy, it can be made far more sensible than is usually the case. In this special issue of *Board Leadership,* I'll tell how that can be done—how boards will be better off with rigorous, regular CEO evaluation. CEOs are better off as well, for they can count on a predictable standard toward which they can design their job performance.

Let me put the matter into perspective. CEO evaluation, like any other aspect of board leadership, should make sense as part of a whole. That is, in the total picture of board leadership, the several parts take their proper place: planning, policymaking, delegation, chair role, and CEO evaluation, among others. So however we approach CEO evaluation, we must look at it as part of that whole.

In the whole of board leadership, why is CEO evaluation important and what are the critical features necessary for it to play its part in the total?

Let's start with the largest picture: The board is obligated to others (primarily to the ownership, secondarily to others to whom it is statutorily or contractually obliged) to make sure that the governed organization achieves what it should while avoiding unacceptable situations and activities. (This simple assertion encompasses the total accountability of board leadership.) The board has this obligation by virtue of being the governing body, quite apart from whether it has a good CEO, a poor CEO, or no CEO at all. The board is fortunate if resources and other circumstances allow it to have a chief executive officer. The role of CEO enables the board to fulfill its obligation to "achieve" and "avoid" by defining and checking, rather than by doing. In other words, the most cogent governing board role is not to achieve, but to see that achievement occurs.

The best way for boards to approach the topic of CEO evaluation is not to think of evaluating the CEO at all. The best approach is
to think of evaluating whether *the organization* has achieved what
should have been achieved and avoided what should have been
avoided. In other words, CEO evaluation will make better sense if
you think of it as evaluating the organization, not the CEO. When
you think about it, there is no special virtue in evaluating just one

> ← **FAQ**
>
> What criteria should the board use for CEO evaluation?

person in the organization, even the top executive. Doesn't it sound a little trivial to imagine boasting years later that your board evaluated the CEO well? The bigger picture—the
one not trivial—is that your organization achieved what it should have—though you
may have accomplished that feat by defining and checking rather than by doing.

In Policy Governance, *defining* is done by establishing ends policies to define what
should be achieved and by establishing executive limitations policies to define what
should be avoided. *Checking* is merely staying informed whether, in reality, the ends
are being achieved and the executive limitations are being avoided. Checking is ordinarily called monitoring or evaluation.

The board evaluates the organization's performance as a whole (using only the
ends and executive limitations policies) and *pins that evaluation on the CEO!* Focusing on the organization's performance also helps the board keep the process as objective as possible.

While the board should have a very personal relationship with its CEO (after all, he
or she is the board's only employee), the act of evaluation can and should be as dis-
passionate as possible. When board members' personal likes and dislikes are allowed
to influence the evaluation, board leader-
ship and the integrity of the board-CEO
relationship are in serious jeopardy.
Boards can let their personal fondness for
a CEO obscure the fact that the organization is failing (board with its head in the
sand). Or boards can let their emotional

> The board evaluates the organiza-
> tion's performance as a whole and
> *pins that evaluation on the CEO!*

reactions lead to mistreatment of a successful CEO (board as adversary of its own
CEO). The error can go either way and, in time, is bound to err in both directions.

There is room for board subjectivity, to be sure. After all, governing is a value-laden
task. That subjectivity, however, should be tapped while the board is deciding which

expectations it will impose upon the organization. These are tough choices, made among competing values. But no matter how much subjectivity goes into a board decision, a decision is what comes out. The board communicates to the CEO this decision, not the subjectivity and diversity of values that went into choosing it. So when the board looks to see if its organization is living up to its charge, that is no time to allow the CEO's or board members' subjectivities to get in the way—including those subjective judgments associated with personality differences.

The board is obligated to be disciplined enough to avoid making such personality-based assessments of the CEO. While it may be unrealistic to expect a given board member to exercise such self-restraint in all situations, it is not unrealistic to expect a responsible group process to temper and nullify occasional individual infractions. Moreover, the mindset of judging the organization rather than the CEO helps avoid any personality problems, even though the results of the evaluation are then applied to the CEO.

I'll summarize the steps I recommend, first in conceptualizing and then in carrying out CEO evaluation:

1. *Determine what is required for board accountability.* Begin by thinking about what is required for the board—not the CEO—to be accountable. Starting with the CEO is like starting a story in the middle instead of the beginning.

2. *Set executive performance criteria.* If the board doesn't do its job first, evaluating the CEO will not make sense. Since the board must see to it that the organization performs, it must first define the desired performance. Criteria for executive performance are established in Policy Governance by policies on ends and executive limitations.

3. *Establish method and frequency of monitoring.* Performance is an ongoing and often inconstant affair, so the board must stay continually informed. To do so, set a monitoring method and frequency for each ends policy and each executive limitations policy.

4. *Treat monitoring data as judgmental rather than informative.* As the monitoring data roll in, treat the data as the board's continual, topic-by-topic evaluation of the organization's performance. For example, a monthly monitoring of financial information is not done to become informed about finances in some general way but to judge whether the board's expectations are being met.

5. *View the organization's performance as the CEO's performance.* Treat the organization's performance on ends and executive limitations as a direct reading of the CEO's performance, as if the organization and CEO are the exact same thing. Organizational performance or nonperformance is CEO performance or nonperformance.

> Annual CEO evaluation in the absence of a rigorous monitoring system based on stated board criteria is largely window dressing that conceals poor governance.

6. *Plan discussions of cumulative monitoring data.* Periodically have a summary discussion about how the monitoring data have looked over, say, the past year. The data used are simply an accumulation of what the board has already received—and reacted to, if appropriate—in the interim. As with regular monitoring, of course, be careful not to permit noncriteria items into the discussion except for the purpose of questioning board policy itself. This annual discussion takes the place of the traditional formal CEO evaluation. Annual CEO evaluation in the absence of a rigorous monitoring system based on stated board criteria is largely window dressing that conceals poor governance.

I fear that many readers will be disappointed that I do not suggest a CEO evaluation form of some sort. I have seen many such forms recommended by this author or that. For boards struggling with the dilemma of CEO evaluation, such forms provide a cop-out more than a way out. What is to be evaluated is completely dependent on what has been instructed. The most productive struggle for a board is the form and content of the instruction, not the evaluation. After that, sensible evaluation can naturally follow. In over twenty years of consulting with boards, virtually every dilemma about CEO evaluation in boards I've observed was due to shortcomings in the format and content of board instructions—defects not solvable by focusing on the evaluation itself and only obscured by following an evaluation form.

What If Criteria Are Not Met?

Occasionally in a workshop I am asked what the board should do if its policies are violated. Strangely, I have rarely found enforcement strategies to be needed. CEOs have a strong need to please the board. If only (1) they know what the board wants and (2) the board avoids mixed messages about what it wants (for example,

> ← **FAQ**
>
> What does the board do if the CEO violates its policies?

Exhibit 9.2.   Self-Assessment Exercise 1: Your Board's Readiness for CEO Evaluation

Not all boards are ready to enter into proper CEO evaluation. CEO evaluation that propels an organization into an optimal future must be grounded in board leadership—and the leadership must come first. If your board cannot answer all of the following questions in the affirmative, go back and do a little more board homework before setting out to evaluate the CEO.

FAQ ➔

How can the board determine when it is ready to proceed with the ongoing process of evaluating the CEO?

1. Are *all* board expectations of the organization set out in writing?
   - ☐ Yes   If yes, congratulations! You now know everything that needs to be evaluated.
   - ☐ No   If no, board instructions to its executive arm are incomplete. Your CEO cannot know on what he or she will be evaluated; the board cannot know what to evaluate. These stated criteria should embrace everything for which you want the operational organization to be accountable.

2. Were those criteria adopted by the board as a whole rather than by a committee or single officer?
   - ☐ Yes   If yes, excellent! The CEO can be assured that he or she is working for a board, not a collection of committees or individuals.
   - ☐ No   If no, have the board deliberate the criteria previously imposed by sub-board elements. The board should not merely adopt them in a ritual action (as it would in accepting a recommendation) but reconsider them along with competing options.

3. Is it absolutely clear that the CEO has the right to interpret what the board has set out in its ends and executive limitations policies?
   - ☐ Yes   If yes, great! You have avoided a major source of board-CEO miscommunication and the unnecessary cluttering of the board's agenda with CEO uncertainties.
   - ☐ No   If no, take two actions. First, be sure the board is expressing its expectations in enough detail that any reasonable interpretation would suffice. Second, unambiguously give the right of interpretation to the CEO.

4. Does the CEO agree that what he or she will be judged on is unambiguous (given that he or she has the right of reasonable interpretation)?

☐ Yes If yes, good! The CEO and the board are clear on the rules they'll both play by. A confident CEO is a better CEO.

☐ No If no, you have the seeds of trouble. If the board has fully stated its expectations and has put them in a large-to-small format ("cascaded" statements from broader toward more detailed), there is only one source of this ambiguity: the CEO *does not believe* the board will really grant him or her the right to use any reasonable interpretation. Look to see whether the board has been trustworthy on this matter—such as in protecting the CEO from renegade board members who judge the CEO on their own personal criteria.

5. Is the board committed to evaluating or judging the CEO on *no other grounds* than those explicitly set forth?

☐ Yes If yes, you have the elements for a complete system of accountability: (a) say what you want, (b) pin it on someone (the CEO in this case), and (c) see if you got it.

☐ No If no, you are creating a fatal breach in the reliability of the board-CEO relationship. The board's lack of commitment to stick with its expressed criteria propels the CEO back into the guessing game.

6. Are the board's expectations of the CEO realistic?

☐ Yes If yes, splendid! You have the basis for fairness *and* rigor in your CEO evaluation.

☐ No If no, reconsider your expectations. Remember, these are *expectations,* not a dreamy wish list or rhetorical exercise. Ends are meant to be accomplished. Executive limitations are meant not to be violated.

In this self-assessment, the words "criteria" and "expectations" are used interchangeably. The way the board expresses criteria for CEO performance should simultaneously support optimal board leadership and optimal executive prerogatives. That is, in establishing its expectations, the board should take a strong leadership position without producing a weak executive role. Policy Governance does this by grouping the board's criteria into (1) those that prescribe mission-related achievements (ends policies) and (2) those that proscribe certain situations and actions (executive limitations policies).

> If boards say unambiguously what they want, they are likely to get it.

by stating criteria then not monitoring them and perhaps even monitoring something else), CEOs tend to perform up to their capability. If boards say unambiguously what they want, they are likely to get it.

In other words, the best enforcement strategy is for the board to be clear and consistent. Still, there is nothing wrong with a board deciding at the outset what its response will be to various management failures. A policy in the board-staff linkage category could set out the principles the board will use to distinguish failures in some areas from failure in others. For example, it would make a difference to what extent a policy violation creates simply a bothersome situation versus threatens organizational survival. It might make a difference whether a violation upsets current productivity versus damages a critical asset that requires a long time to recover (such as public image).

Evaluation Itself Is Not the Point

FAQ ➡

How does CEO evaluation fit into the overall system of Policy Governance?

As a board focuses on how to optimize CEO evaluation, it is important to reiterate that the evaluation is not an end in itself. The most important purpose of evaluation is to make the future better, *not to produce a report card*. It is easy to fall into report card thinking, even when doing so sacrifices the greater good. The most serious setting in which this is likely to occur is in the evaluation of the results and results-per-dollar aspects of ends (the "for which people" part is easier).

Boards will invariably find that evaluating results and, thus, the cost of results is far more difficult than evaluating less meaningful yet more available data on staff activities. For example, how many participants attended how many training programs

> The most important purpose of evaluation is to make the future better, *not to produce a report card.*

yields a seemingly "cleaner" evaluation (a more defensible number) than whether a criterion number of participants ended up with a criterion amount of capability for the dollars spent. How many brochures were distributed produces a misleadingly "tidier" measure than whether an intended level of awareness was created in a criterion number of publics. As tempting as it is to evaluate the number of attendees or brochures, to do so is an evasion of the board's obligation to monitor ends.

Therefore, CEO evaluation may be difficult or easy to conduct, or may be precisely or crudely conducted, but ease and numerical precision are not the important factors.

Exhibit 9.3. Self-Assessment Exercise 2: Evaluating Your Evaluating

The purpose of CEO evaluation is to increase the likelihood of the board's getting its job done. The board's job is to see to it that the organization achieves what it should and avoids situations and activities that are unacceptable. There are three steps in accomplishing this board job that directly affect the CEO: (1) define what should be achieved (ends) and what should be avoided (executive limitations), (2) fix the point of accountability (on the CEO), and (3) check regularly to see if ends are achieved and limitations are not violated.

Self-Assessment Exercise 1 (Exhibit 9.2) was a quick-and-dirty assessment of steps 1 and 2. Self-Assessment Exercise 2 is a similar test of whether, if you are already able to do CEO evaluation, you are in fact *doing so* fairly yet rigorously. If you cannot answer affirmatively to the following questions, go back to work on making evaluation work for you.

> ← **FAQ**
>
> How can the board ensure that its process for evaluating the CEO is fair?

1. Has the board (or the chair, if delegated to her) established a monitoring schedule that sets the source and frequency of monitoring every ends policy and every executive limitations policy?
    - ☐ Yes If yes, good! Now the monitoring can move ahead in a routinized manner.
    - ☐ No If no, establish a schedule as quickly as possible. Don't worry about forms and format; simply see at what frequency the majority of board members are comfortable. For example, the financial condition policy might be monitored every month or quarter. Then determine the method or pathway of monitoring (a) data from the CEO, (b) data from an outside source (such as an auditor), or (c) data gathered by the board itself or an organ of the board. Do this as simply as possible.

2. Does the board as a whole receive monitoring data on time every time according to that schedule?
    - ☐ Yes If yes, fine! Keep up the good work, but take care never to let routinization degrade into ritual.

(Continued)

Exhibit 9.3. (Continued)

☐ No   If no, the board must remind itself that while monitoring need not be on the front burner, it should not be on a burner that is turned off. The board can give itself a responsibility booster shot by discussing how members would feel to discover too late that monitoring data would have given sufficient warning of problems if only they'd been received as the board had directed. Not only is the board culpable for whatever goes wrong, but also for not enforcing its own rules.

3. Do all board members read and understand the data, discussing them at the board meeting if the data are either not understandable or reveal unfulfilled policy?

☐ Yes If yes, you are far ahead of most!

☐ No   If no, add a routine affirmation to your agenda. Early in the meeting, perhaps just after approving last meeting's minutes, board members could be asked to affirm that they have received and read all monitoring reports received since the last meeting.

4. Are monitoring data confined to that information that directly speaks to performance criteria rather than being obscured in a sea of incidental data?

☐ Yes If yes, your assessment of performance will be incisive and not easily misled by inconsequential details.

☐ No   If no, you are very vulnerable. Too much information is worse than none; when there is none, at least you know that. Have your CEO or other data source put nothing into a monitoring report that goes beyond the precise purpose of monitoring. Anything else, no matter how important, can go on another color paper or in some way be unmistakably distinguished from the monitoring data. Cluttered monitoring data rapidly becomes no monitoring at all.

5. Is the CEO always given the right to convince the board that he has, in fact, used a reasonable interpretation in cases where some board members think otherwise?

☐ Yes If yes, terrific! You are living up to your promise to the CEO.

☐ No   If no, expect the CEO to take understandable steps for self-protection that are not for the best for either governance or management. The point is not for the CEO to be able to get away with just anything, but for the board to listen before leaping.

---

6. Are individual board members and committees careful to make no individual judgments of the CEO apart from the *board's* judgment against the *board's* criteria?

  ☐ Yes If yes, wonderful! Your discipline is commendable.

  ☐ No If no, your discipline is inadequate. Individuals may certainly suggest things to the CEO (which she can accept or not accept) but may not judge the CEO on their own individual criteria. To do so implies that the CEO is obliged to please individual board members and has failed to do so.

The most important value of CEO evaluation is that it enables the board to serve its central purpose, that of seeing to it that the organization achieves what it should while avoiding unacceptable situations. A crucial, yet largely misunderstood, principle of system design is that optimization of a system is not the same as optimization of individual segments of a system. CEO evaluation—like good space planning, effective staff development, and even fine board policymaking—is but a segment. Picture-perfect segment optimization can, in fact, detract from system perfection. This is why boards should operate *on* systems, not *in* them. Consequently, CEO evaluation is not something that can be perfected as a stand-alone segment; everything about it should be designed toward accomplishing the central purpose of governance.

Influencing an organization to produce *in the future* what it should, for whom it should, and in the amount per dollar it should is the central task of evaluating the CEO. Influencing an organization to conduct itself *in the future* within the bounds of acceptability is the secondary task of evaluating the CEO. Each is crucial to the desired future. Evaluation must be based upon these things no matter how crude the measurement tools might be.

This means that, while evaluation surely gathers data about the past, in a more meaningful sense evaluation is about the future. And in the service of affecting the future, remember an old management adage: "A crude measure of the right thing beats a precise measure of the wrong thing."

Off Limits: What Not to Do in Your CEO Evaluation

Board Leadership, Number 26, July-Aug.1996

Although the preceding few articles are about how to conceive of and carry out good CEO evaluation, a list of practices to avoid may be of some use. So here is the off-limits list—things I suggest your board never do when evaluating your CEO.

1. *Don't make CEO evaluation a popularity contest,* whether that is popularity with board members, staff, clientele, or the public. It isn't the CEO's job to be popular but to see to organizational attainment of proper ends and avoidance of unacceptable means. Popularity is a dodge used by ineffective boards.

2. *Don't use a prefabricated CEO evaluation form you've found in a book, workshop, or magazine.* The only fair evaluation of a person is what he or she has been told ahead of time are the criteria for that evaluation. Prefabricated forms contain someone else's idea of what a CEO should ideally be like or accomplish. The board is copping out.

3. *Don't evaluate the CEO on whether she accomplished her personal objectives for the year.* As I explained in "The CEO's Objectives Are Not Proper Board Business" in Chapter Four, the CEO's objectives are of no concern to the board. Whether the CEO accomplishes criteria found in the board's policies is the only legitimate test.

4. *Don't commission a group of citizens to evaluate your CEO for you.* I have actually seen school boards do this! Any employee deserves to be evaluated by his boss, the person or body that generated the criteria to begin with.

Don't ask staff, public, customers, clients, patients, or students what they think of your CEO's performance.

5. *Don't ask staff, public, customers, clients, patients, or students what they think of your CEO's performance.* The CEO doesn't work for the staff or the public, but for the board. Boards sometimes want others to do their work for them.

6. Don't ever, ever, ever evaluate the CEO on criteria that have not been created in writing by the board ahead of time, and even then give the CEO room to use any reasonable interpretation of the board's criteria.

FAQ

When evaluating a CEO, is there ever a time when it is appropriate to seek input from staff, clients, or the public?

Now, let me offer a proviso. It is legitimate to query groups such as those mentioned in item 5 if the board is genuinely monitoring criteria that call for data that such groups can give. For example, suppose the board has an executive limitations policy on consumer treatment that, among other proscriptions, says that clients cannot be treated in a high-handed or callous manner. One way to monitor this criterion is to ask clients—albeit in a scrupulously controlled way. Even then, clients are not asked to evaluate the CEO, but the system that affects them.

To illustrate further, let me suppose that the board has an executive limitations policy that prohibits unfair and undignified treatment of staff. Monitoring of this policy requires the board to acquire data on whether staff have been treated in an unfair or undignified way (with the CEO having the right to use any reasonable interpretation of these words). Even if staff are asked (in some carefully constructed way, of course), what is important is not whether they think the CEO personally has treated them unfairly, but whether anyone above them in authority has done so. In other words, the CEO is held accountable by the board if anyone in the system mistreats clients or staff, though the board would not ask clients or staff if the CEO specifically has done so.

A CEO Self-Evaluation Checklist

BOARD LEADERSHIP, NUMBER 26, JULY-AUG. 1996

T HE LAST FEW ARTICLES have been devoted to the board's evaluation of its CEO, not to the CEO's evaluation of him- or herself. This article is a departure from that theme. I include it because CEOs often ask how they can support better governance by playing out their role more effectively.

The question is a legitimate one, but it screams out for a few provisos. First, responsibility for good governance must always remain with the board. Although CEOs can be helpful to the board, they should never be construed as responsible for the board governing well. Second, the only real CEO evaluation is that addressed elsewhere in this issue: the board's assessment of whether the CEO has met board criteria. Third, because CEOs must design their own role in order to achieve board expectations, it naturally follows that they could benefit from interim checks on how well that self-defined role is being carried out. The results of these checks is no business of the board's and can only be a source of confusion if reported to the board.

> Although CEOs can be helpful to the board, they should never be construed as responsible for the board governing well.

That being said, the CEO will find that part of his or her job is related to the empowerment and accountability of staff. That part includes job design, objective setting, supervision, and other elements of the complex management task. As important as these matters are, I will not deal with them here because they are not governance issues and are basically no business of the board's. (What is board business is whether ends are achieved and executive limitations are violated.)

But the other part of the CEO's job relates to the interface with the board. It is that relationship I'll concern myself with here. This evaluation is merely a checklist for the CEO to review or to judge whether his or her actions support or impede the board in its quest for improved leadership.

Let's indulge the CEO in a little talking to him- or herself and see what might profitably be appraised:

> ← **FAQ**
>
> What can the CEO do to support better governance?

I know that I am not responsible for good governance and that I can only damage the board by trying to take it off the hook for its governing responsibilities. My job is to make the board's ends come true while avoiding all unacceptable situations and activities. Because the board has defined "lack of appropriate information for board decisions' as one unacceptable circumstance, I am also responsible for the board having certain information to which I have unique access. Beyond these formal requirements, however, I want to be supportive of the board's commitment to leadership simply because I, too, have a personal investment in good governance.

Consequently, I will test myself occasionally with the following statements, hoping to confirm more of the statements in the affirmative as time goes by:

1. My actions as CEO are as if I fully believe that the board truly means that I'll be evaluated only on the explicit criteria set out in board policies.
2. My actions as CEO are as if I fully believe that the board will fulfill its promise to grant me the right to choose any reasonable interpretation of those policies, no matter how much external pressure the board is under.
3. I personally encourage, support, and commend the board's commitment to govern well. I am careful not to sabotage board leadership even unintentionally.
4. When called upon to produce possible options for board policy and the implications of those options, I do so rigorously and without bias. If I choose to share my own opinions, they are clearly identified as such.
5. When preparing information for the board, I distinguish among information for monitoring, information for board decisions, and incidental information so that board members cannot mistake one for the other.
6. With respect to all issues for which I have been granted authority to make decisions, I make the decisions rather than bring them back to the board to be made or to have my choices approved.

Chapter Ten

Safeguarding Governance Viability for the Long Term

Implementing a system of work is not a one-time task, but an ongoing challenge. With Policy Governance in place, a board faces further traps, possible deterioration, and the need for continual retraining. Special or novel circumstances arise that require a board to apply generic governance principles in new ways, perhaps with new structures, but the underlying model continues to provide the conceptual framework.

What to Do When All Your Policies Are in Place

BOARD LEADERSHIP, NUMBER 32, JULY-AUG. 1997

I AM OFTEN ASKED what a board does once its policies (ends, executive limitations, board-executive linkage, board process) are in place. Some workshop participants have surmised that with all the policies settled, the board might consider going home and coming back next year! It is true that Policy Governance policies are designed so that all the board has to say is embodied somewhere in these few, succinct documents. So the question is a good one: When the policies are finished, what else is there to do?

Alas, as it turns out, there is much for a board to do even after its policies are all in place. Let's assume that all policies are truly in place at a given time, including those perplexing ends policies, the difficulty of which almost every board underestimates. Rather than find that there is little left to do, boards will find that there is *more* governance work crying out to be done than they ever expected prior to undertaking Policy Governance. Here is a list of some of the issues that will naturally surface—quite enough to keep any board busy.

Ends issues in flux. While some ends decisions will seem stable, issues surrounding others will be in a state of flux. The instability may derive from board members' own shifting values, owners' vacillation, or changing technology. These types of ends decisions require a board to be more watchful, perhaps returning to examine the relevant circumstances repeatedly throughout the year.

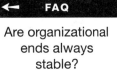

FAQ

Are organizational ends always stable?

Rather than find that there is little left to do, boards will find that there is *more* governance work to be done than prior to undertaking Policy Governance.

Example: A trade association board decides to provide its members with bulk purchase of a certain commodity at a time when the market of alternate products is in flux. In the face of rapid developments, the board's decision seems to have been wise one day and not the next. Although it has made its decision to go ahead, the board would be wise to watch which way the market develops and react accordingly.

Low confidence ends decisions. Some ends decisions will be made with considerable confidence, others with little confidence at all. Because there is no such thing as *no policy,* a board might have created a low-confidence ends policy rather than to be silent on the matter. Such ends decisions call for further scrutiny on a regular basis.

Example: The board of a health advocacy organization has thrown its weight behind a specific disease-screening method. The ends decision was that "the nation's health systems will employ the screening for all men over thirty-five years of age before 1998." Research data did not unanimously support such a stand, but the board determined that not taking a stand on the matter would have worse effects than taking the wrong one. Even though the CEO goes ahead full steam with the board's decision, the board would be well advised to be particularly vigilant about assimilating new research data as they are generated.

No matter how solid board decisions may have been, unexpected developments can change wise decisions into unwise ones overnight.

Environmental changes. Most board decisions assume several environmental conditions, any of which might change over time. So no matter how solid board decisions may have been, unexpected developments beyond the organization's control can change wise decisions into unwise ones overnight. Continual environmental scanning is called for.

Example: A mental health center board has made ends decisions about the proportion of relief to be provided for problems of cocaine addiction, alcoholism, and other drugs. The shifting demographics and social tides, however, can change the relative needs in these problem areas. The board should have a built-in, ongoing method for observing, tabulating, and discussing data when applicable.

Ownership input. Getting useful input from an organization's ownership is usually not easy, but it is absolutely critical. Still, we simply don't know a great deal about how to do it. Certainly if the ownership is small, say, a homeowners' association with forty members, it may be relatively easy to hear from virtually all the members. But larger ownerships present a difficult logistical challenge. Moreover, for politically visible boards, input systems not only must incorporate a truly unbiased, broad sample of input, but they must be seen to do so, as well, since public perception becomes critical.

> Governance involves as much contemplation as it does action.

Example: A city council in a city of four hundred thousand seeks to link with the population. Most of the population do not vote, do not know the issues, and will not take time to become informed. Ownership linkage in this case is sufficiently challenging to provide the council with work for years. Even minor improvements in the connection between elected officials and the public has far-reaching effects on the functioning of a democracy.

Board education and reflection. Boards need to spend a great percentage of their time learning and reflecting—free from the immediate pressure to vote on something. Governance involves as much contemplation as it does action. Surely, action is required, but the board's high-leverage position demands that careful, informed thought underpin that action. Boards rarely construct their jobs so that they have time to speculate, theorize, and philosophize.

Example: A community action board intends to bring about an end to poverty within a community, or at least to ensure that poverty is minimal and not life-threatening. Poverty and its effects are complicated issues. The board should devote a great deal of its time to studying the phenomenon, hearing various points of view about it, and investigating what has been learned elsewhere.

Fundraising. For some organizations, board engagement in finding resources is critical to continued existence and success. While no organization exists solely for its own growth and survival, financial stability is an important means that can in many cases be ensured only by board fundraising.

Example: The board of a small advocacy group discovers that its dream is far larger than currently available resources can support. It may lower its aspirations—or it may raise the resources. In real life, it will likely do a bit of both, but consideration of the matter will propel the board into active fundraising, driven by the board's commitment to its dream.

Monitoring and CEO evaluation. The board should always be in a position to know the condition of the organization and the status of its achievements insofar as these relate to the board's policy-stated expectations. The frequency with which the board is informed of various aspects of performance is chosen by the board and need not be tied to the frequency of board meetings. Nonetheless, board meetings always provide an opportunity to discuss areas in which performance is deficient or to adjust expectations based on new information.

Example: A community college board receives its monitoring reports on a monthly, quarterly, and annual schedule, depending on the policies being monitored. Ordinarily the board does not clutter meeting time with these reports, unless the reports show a deficiency. In this case, the board will interrupt its ends-dominated dialogue to ask the CEO how much longer the board should expect the deficiency to continue. Occasionally, however, the board will schedule a specific study of certain monitoring reports in order to look in greater depth at whether the data tendered really address performance on the policy criteria as well as they seem to do. These special monitoring inquiries usually occur with ends issues, though sometimes they focus on volatile or high-risk means issues.

> Leaders talking with leaders about shared vision and methods of governance should be the wave of the future for boards.

Recruiting new members. The search for talented board members never ends. For some boards, the turnover rate compels an almost continuous focus on recruiting. Since a deliberate pace is preferable to a rushed process, year-round recruiting will be called for.

Example: A community hospital with a self-perpetuating board must make continual efforts to locate good replacements. Much of the work involves designing ways to attract and to assess good candidates. The board has developed ways of seeking out leaders, particularly up-and-coming ones, and getting the attention of candidates who, though bored by traditional board meetings, would be excited by high-level policy work. The board screens out persons who are satisfied with trivia, micromanagement, and governance-as-usual.

Interboard communication. Perhaps the most exciting arena for board engagement is linking with other boards that represent the same ownership. Leaders talking with leaders about shared vision and methods of governance should be the wave of the future for boards, yet it is a rare event now and one for which few skills and tactics have been developed.

Example: The board of a chamber of commerce takes the lead in getting the public and quasi-public boards in its community together. It and like-minded boards devote a substantial effort to establishing connections between the various governance-level leadership bodies. Although the endeavor will later encompass other groups, the chamber begins building its network with the school board, city council, hospital board, library board, and eco-

> Policy Governance is designed so that the critical parts of the job get done, even if the comprehensiveness outlined here is not achieved.

nomic development board. Because it is plowing new ground, the board necessarily stumbles through much trial-and-error learning.

What ifs. After all is said and done, things can still go wrong. Completely unexpected events can upset the best intentions and disrupt even the best systems. Boards would do well to entertain "what if" sessions in which they brainstorm and discuss a number of developments that could throw the organization off balance, seriously jeopardize the mission, or otherwise present grave danger.

Example: The local commission of parks, independently elected, has a well-governed organization, but knows that its leadership mandate requires it to keep moving further ahead. So it schedules four sessions a year in which a selected "what if" topic is explored. One such session focuses on a hypothetical scenario in which a massive demographic shift removes virtually all current users of recreation space. Another discusses the scenario in which a large state park nearby closes, displacing thousands of park visitors to the community sites. The board doesn't consider the management issues in these sessions, of course, it concentrates on the governance issues.

Keep in mind that this list is *in addition* to an annual, structured review in which a board may decide to change previously stated ends in order to continue adjusting the organization's aims to a changing world.

Before becoming overwhelmed or even intimidated by this collection of challenges, remember that a board can accomplish more or less, depending on the level of governance integrity it wishes to attain. Policy Governance is designed so that the critical parts of the job get done, even if the comprehensiveness outlined here is not achieved. In any event, worrying about the board having too little to do after getting fully into Policy Governance is a very unnecessary worry, indeed!

Nine Steps to Implementing Policy Governance

Board Leadership, Number 13, May-June 1994

IN MY WORKSHOPS, board members and chief executives always have questions about implementation. Because Policy Governance is so different from the board role that has been taught and experienced for so many years, most of a day is required to get the concepts and principles across. As a result, discussing aspects—including the traps!—of implementation doesn't get as much attention as it deserves.

In this article, I want to spell out some factors to keep in mind as your board tries to move from traditional governance toward the more powerful board leadership available with Policy Governance. The foremost challenge is finding a balance between moving so slowly as to lose the critical momentum and moving precipitously without adequate understanding and consideration.

> **FAQ** ➜
>
> Is it all right if we gradually ease ourselves into adopting policy governance?

Gradualism can kill implementation by keeping two conflicting governance systems operating at the same time for too long. I have observed that the more slowly implementation occurs, the more likely it will never fully occur at all. Some members will impose slowness as a tactic not to change at all. Others will simply fall back into more familiar methods if both old and new are operating simultaneously. It isn't a successful trapeze jump as long as you are hanging onto both trapezes.

But making rapid shifts when board members have not had time to understand the model and think through the impending changes will cause hollow implementation (adopting the words and formats, but not the substance or commitment) or outright rejection. Jumping to the second trapeze is foolhardy if you haven't checked out the condition of the second trapeze. The U.S. Supreme Court desegregation term, "all deliberate speed," phrases my recommendation well: Move ahead just as quickly as careful consideration will allow.

> Gradualism can kill implementation by keeping two conflicting governance systems operating at the same time for too long.

Policy Governance brings an entirely new way to operate and think about the expression of board leadership. Beware the comment that, "We're already doing things this way." The comment will almost always be masking a superficial understanding of Policy Governance. With an incomplete grasp, one can mistakenly see the model as merely reiterating familiar bromides like "boards should deal with policy," "boards should stick with long-term planning," or "boards should set goals and then leave managers alone." While there is some limited truth in these representations, Policy Governance involves a far more thorough reordering of how governance is conceived.

In so radical a shift, how is a board to overcome the unfamiliarity, occasional resistance, and lack of newly required skills? Let me suggest the following sequence to be followed. It is a little dif-

> Move ahead just as quickly as careful consideration will allow.

ferent from the sequence I use when personally helping a board put Policy Governance into action. This sequence is for boards bravely implementing on their own.

Step 1: Be sure that board members and the CEO understand the model. Without good theory—if the word *theory* sounds too ivory-towerish to you, substitute *overview* or *sense of the whole*—actions don't mean as much and don't fit together in an efficient total. Dealing with one tree at a time may be rewarding and concrete, but dealing with forests wields far more power. Until a board fully grasps the ideas and philosophy of this new technology of governance, implementation will be like putting new wine in old bottles. Board members' words may change, but governance will not be transformed. How often have I heard a board talking about ends and means, limitations policies, or other accoutrements of Policy Governance but in reality doing virtually the same things it was doing before. The board can test itself to see if members fully understand the model. For example, consider discussing whether each of the various issues an organization faces is an ends or means issue. Or take a board member's fear about finances, personnel, or other staff means; discuss how that fear could be used to amend an executive limitations policy.

┌─────────────────────────┐
│   **FAQ** ➡   │
├─────────────────────────┤
│   How many mem-   │
│   bers of a board   │
│   need to agree   │
│   before policy   │
│   governance can   │
│   be adopted?   │
└─────────────────────────┘

Step 2: Make a full board commitment to this major change. There is no reason that the decision must be unanimous, but it should represent the board's voice as a body. If moving to Policy Governance is only what the chairperson, CEO, or influential committee wants to do, it will fail. Moving to Policy Governance imposes certain costs, such as discomfort with unfamiliarity, extra work early in implementation (though not necessarily afterward), and perhaps a consultant to help. The board should face these costs honestly, considering whether the expected improvements are worth all the trouble.

Further, it is far best to either commit to the entire model or not, rather than to loosely "adopt the model" in a way that allows each element to be debated and decided independently. Such piecemeal action opens the way for board members to compromise on the parts, yielding a result that is such a mixture of governance philosophies that no one philosophy holds any power. (Once a watch design is conceived, you don't vote on each little gearwheel. The "democratic" compromise between A and B is not nearly so effective as either A or B implemented with full commitment.) This kind of compromise, incidentally, is a major dereliction in governance: failing to make hard choices on an overarching issue, then making decisions on subissues that, taken as a whole, are inconsistent and even conflicting.

Step 3: Put the board's commitment to move ahead on paper. This step creates, in effect, the board's first governance process policy. For example, the board might adopt a simple, general statement such as, "We will govern with an emphasis on vision rather than internal preoccupation, encouragement of diversity, strategic leadership more than administrative detail, clear distinction of board and chief executive roles, collective rather than individual decisions, future rather than past or present, and proactivity rather than reactivity." However much detail the board puts into this initial policy, it can be revisited as implementation proceeds to help the board keep itself on track.

Step 4: Develop all policies except ends. Ends will be saved until last. First you must put the system as a whole into place.

a. *Develop all the executive limitations policies.* Some board members will be put off by the negative wording, but remember that it is designed to produce a positive effect. Executive limitations policies prohibit the staff conditions, activities, conduct, and decisions (staff *means,* as opposed to *ends*) that board members worry about. Unacceptable staff practices concern boards, causing worried preoccupation with these means (rather than ends—boards normally pay little attention to them anyway) to mercilessly clutter agendas and premeeting mailings. Creating boundaries for the staff early in the implementation sequence allows the board to relax about operational issues and put single-minded attention on further policy development.

b. *Develop all the governance process policies.* The first step in creating these policies has already been taken (in step 3). Now add other policies dealing with the chairperson's role, board member commitment, committee principles, committee products and authority, and board job

> Once a watch design is conceived, you don't vote on each little gearwheel.

description. In doing so, the board gives studied attention to how its own conduct and productivity must be in order to achieve good governance.

c. *Develop all the board-executive relationship policies.* Having completed policies that define its own job (governance process) and the limits that apply to staff actions (executive limitations), the board can now safely contemplate a philosophy of strong executive delegation. Now it is time to create policies on the nature of board-CEO delegation, CEO job expectations, and the approach—and even the schedule—for monitoring CEO performance.

Step 5. Adopt a single temporary ends policy. It may seem odd that the most important of board policies is saved until last. I have found that only after getting the clutter out of the way can boards productively deliberate about ends. The policies already mentioned clear the clutter, trivia, and ritual actions from the agenda. Moreover, ends take longer to work through than the foregoing policies, and, in fact, their development never stops. The board's ends work goes on in perpetuity. In other words, it works best to get everything else out of the way, then work on ends *forever.* Since developing ends policies is slow work, and since a long delay before operating with the new principles is asking for trouble, adopt a tentative policy to plug the gap. My clients often adopt a statement that says, "Until ends policies are developed, the ends of the organization will remain as previously stated explicitly by the board or as found implicitly in previously adopted board documents." At this point, all the policies necessary to begin operating with Policy Governance have been drafted. With the exception noted below, the model can be safely put into effect.

It is best to get started on real ends policies to replace this temporary one as soon as possible after implementation. It is a very common problem for boards to get this far but, because things start working so well, fail to tackle and resolve the difficult issues that would enable the ends policies to be filled out. I have seen boards still stuck with their "temporary" ends policy over a year later!

Step 6: Do an administrative and perhaps legal check. When a board has policies in the Policy Governance format and uses principles of the model, virtually all other board documents and pronouncements except bylaws become unnecessary. If the adopting board has operated for some time using conventional governance, there are bound to be many other directives, documents, and pronouncements already in effect. Most of these elements are unnecessary baggage that will seem superfluous when you are ready to implement Policy Governance. In fact, the motion putting all the policy drafts into effect will, at the same time, repeal personnel policies, budgets, old policies, and other approvals. Most previous board documents (personnel policies, budgets, salary schedules, and so on) with which the new policies will conflict can simply be "given" to the CEO. The board is rid of them; the CEO can change them as he or she sees fit, yet the hard work they embody does not go to waste.

Before taking such a severe—albeit essential—action, you must be certain that the new policies do not conflict with law or the bylaws. If the new policies conflict with bylaws, change the bylaws. If the new policies conflict with law, then alter them so that the law is not broken. Who does the administrative and legal check depends on the organization. What matters is that it be done carefully and without bias. Hence, a board committee, individually assigned board member, or CEO could carry out this role. When the survey of possible loose ends and conflicts is complete, you are ready for the kickoff.

> The immediate problem that the board will encounter after setting the model in motion will be what to do at the next board meeting.

Step 7: Have the first few agendas ready to go. The immediate problem that the board will encounter after setting the model in motion will be the concrete matter of what to do at the next board meeting. As you prepare to implement, it is important to prepare so that meeting agendas do not go on as if nothing has changed (doing so will mean you are, in fact, not on the model after all). Even if you plan to do nothing at the first post-transition meeting but have a discussion of ends and the difficulty of defining them, that is much better than falling back on previous agenda formats to avoid the anxiety. It should not be difficult to invite speakers on ends topics to your meeting, or merely to decide what the board needs to know in order to discuss ends options intelligently. This discussion leads to ideas about what to schedule for board education.

Absolutely do not have the staff create board agendas, although the board can invite staff members along with others to argue various points of view with regard to large, long-term ends issues. Remember that the board agenda is a matter of governance process, so the board chair has the authority to use any reasonable interpretation of whatever the board has said about agendas. One of the governance process policies would have dealt with this issue. It is acceptable for the chair to ask for help, since he or she will be learning new behavior just as will everyone else. But it is not acceptable for the chair to default on the task or turn it over to the CEO!

Step 8: Design the first steps in connecting with the ownership. The ownership is the legitimacy base to whom the board is accountable, for whom it is the actual or "civic" trustee. Lay plans to form and meet with focus groups, confer with other boards, or have relevant statistical data gathered. Don't forget to put your philosophical position about this topic and your plan for getting it under way into policy form within the governance process category. Connecting with the ownership, like setting agendas, is a matter of governance process, so the complementary board and chair roles in the matter are similar: The board establishes its broad-brush intention, the chair fills in the details. For example, the board of one large membership association I met with decided that it wanted to schedule regional meetings with focus groups of association members. The chair worked out the details and the assignments. A public social service board decided that meeting with other public, community boards would be its first exercise in linking with the ownership (in this case, connecting with other organs of ownership), but left the chair to determine which other boards in what order and with what scheduling urgency.

Step 9: Set a specific date to inaugurate the system. To the extent possible, avoid phasing in the new paradigm; after prudent assurance that all is in order, switch completely to it in one move. As I alluded to the change earlier, treat the transition like jumping from one trapeze to another. When you do decide to jump, don't halfway jump or jump in phases.

On the implementation date, all the policy drafts become effective and all previous board pronouncements still affecting the present and future are terminated. Because all directives of the board will now be supplanted by the new policy system, old personnel handbooks, investment policies, purchasing procedures, budgets, long-range plans, and virtually any directive of the board must be repealed. To a great extent, all the preparation to make the final shift exercises many of the new governance skills that boards need to make the new system work. So the changeover, when it comes, might well be an easy and natural step. This would be a good time for the board to congratulate itself and perhaps have a party with its staff!

The time required for going through this implementation sequence varies greatly depending on the circumstances and the people. For a national or international board that meets three times per year, the sequence ordinarily runs a different pace from one that meets monthly in a community. A board of nine moves more quickly than a board of thirty. When I help a board go through these steps, the policy development phase can be covered in a few days, though unassisted implementation can take as long as a couple of years. Under the most ideal conditions, a board can move all the way to implementation in two or three months (full implementation does not imply that all ends policy development is completed, just that the board is operating on the model). Ideal conditions usually include an agile, small, informed, conceptually flexible board; few harsh pressures on the board at the moment; and low tension with pressure groups and press. These conditions do not stop implementation but do slow it down. Most of my clients have taken from six to twelve months. Whatever the specific circumstances of a given board, however, getting the system in place saves precious and costly staff time and board member time, more pointedly harnesses the energy of people toward mission, and gives creativity a wide but safe berth.

> Getting the system in place saves time, harnesses the energy of people toward mission, and gives creativity a wide but safe berth.

But make no mistake, *completing the nine steps means only that the real governance work can begin.* Three efforts will demand the majority of board time and energy forever. First, the ends will need continual attention in perpetuity, for the world continues to shift and human needs change in priority. Second, finding ways to gather owners' input is not easy, nor as yet are there well-researched strategies for doing so. Third, sufficient self-evaluation and redevelopment are needed so that board leadership can continue to improve, rather than begin to deteriorate. These three activities are unique leadership tasks, embodying the challenge and the channel for board members to be strategic leaders.

Shaping Up Your Bylaws

BOARD LEADERSHIP, NUMBER 20, JULY-AUG.1995

NONPROFIT ORGANIZATIONS are created by governmental action in a document variously called articles of incorporation or letters patent. In most cases, the action originates in a private group that has petitioned for incorporation. The governmental document brings into being a hollow shell, an artificial person called a corporation. Based on this document, which authorizes an organization to engage in certain business or charitable practices, *bylaws* are created, usually by the incorporators first recognized by the government. Bylaws breathe life into that shell by introducing real people into the process.

Bylaws make it possible for the artificial person to speak. They provide that when a statement is agreed to by enough members of a group, who have been installed in a certain way and who meet with a stated proportion of the group present, the corporation—this artificial person—has spoken. The bylaws enable the corporation to have a voice, a voice that has been empowered to command action over its own resources and sometimes over those of others.

Situated between the basic incorporating document and board pronouncements, then, are the bylaws. For a board using the Policy Governance model, virtually all pronouncements are in the form of new policies or the amendment of existing ones. We can envision a hierarchy of documents, then, from articles of incorporation to bylaws to policies (Exhibit 10.1). Each lower document on the chain is governed by the next higher document. Therefore, nothing can

> **← FAQ**
>
> What's the relationship between the board's policies and my organization's bylaws?

479

Exhibit 10.1. Hierarchy of Board Documents

Articles of Incorporation
Governmental creation of the corporation, an "artificial person" before
the law.

Bylaws
The way in which the utterances of real persons can constitute the artificial
person's speaking. Also, related matters such as the role of members and tax
status clarifications.

Policies
In Policy Governance, virtually all board enunciations are in policy format.
Very few decisions (such as appointments, externally required actions, and
adoption of minutes) take a nonpolicy form.

---

legitimately be done by the board in policy that is in conflict with bylaws, just as nothing
can legitimately be done in bylaws that is in conflict with the articles of incorporation.

So, board members should be intimately familiar with their bylaws; potential board
members should never join a board without studying the bylaws. Familiarity is necessary not only so that subsequent board actions are compatible with bylaws but so
that board members are cognizant of their position in the scheme of things. Carving
out the nature of a given organization's governance begins in the bylaws. I think the
bylaws are so personal to the board and, if applicable, to the membership, that I
always caution boards against having a lawyer write them. The board should write
them, then get legal counsel to make sure nothing important has been overlooked.

Tips for Creating Common Bylaw Provisions

I have no perfect bylaws to offer. Bylaws relate so much to the type of organization
and the peculiarities of each situation that I've never seen any I'd be willing to call
model bylaws. But I can offer a few tips on common bylaws provisions. The following
items are selected because they can have a marked effect on the governance process.
They are arranged here in the order they usually appear in bylaws.

Corporate membership. If an organization is truly a membership organization (federation, trade, or professional association), then *membership* is synonymous with

ownership and has real utility—that is, there is a substantive body of persons reasonably entitled to exercise controlling authority should it choose to do so. If not, membership is usually a quirk of nonprofit law bearing scant relationship to the Policy Governance concept of ownership. (For more on ownership, see Chapter Two.) In this case, membership is an artificial grouping for annual general meetings and perhaps the election of board members, while it itself has little legitimacy. Some nonprofits use the membership fiction as a public relations gimmick.

The challenge to any nonprofit organization is to find a way of adapting the membership concept so that it bears a meaningful resemblance to ownership. In crafting a solution to this challenge, the membership must have real power—for example, the power to elect board members—but not be open to jury-rigging by board, staff, or special interest groups. In other words, if the membership is not a natural grouping of owners (as it would be in a trade association or civic club), bylaws can be constructed so that it is a fair representation of the elusive ownership. For example, using this approach, a nonprofit would not have a membership composed "of any citizen interested in the mission" (to quote one instance) and willing to pay a token membership fee. Such groupings are starkly open to stacking by special interests, including staff.

Board size. Small is beautiful. Have good reasons for exceeding seven, for board effectiveness decreases rapidly as the board gets larger. Larger boards are easier to manipulate and may find sensible decision making difficult. Individual board members tend to be more responsible in smaller groups. Be wary of having a large board in order to be more representative; for any sizeable ownership, you'll never approach the breadth of the ownership's diversity anyway. Even an association with only two hundred members can't get the diversity of these two hundred into the board composition. Adopt a smaller number, then make its composition as true to ownership diversity as you can get it. Don't worry about choosing an odd number to avoid tie votes; even numbers work just fine.

> Have good reasons for exceeding seven, for board effectiveness decreases rapidly as the board gets larger.

Quorum. Have a high quorum requirement. I'd say the minimum is 50 percent plus one, though there will be greater group integrity if quorum is set higher. A sports team will function much more like a team if all members are present every game. If you have a hard time reaching quorum for meetings, don't lower the quorum figure; there are a couple of more effective things to do. First, raise the incentive to be at meetings.

> Most board meetings I have seen aren't interesting or challenging enough to keep the best people engaged.

Most board meetings I have seen aren't interesting or challenging enough to keep the best people engaged. Make meetings worth coming to! Second, don't hope for attendance, demand it. Which leads us next to . . .

Attendance. Attendance should be required to keep a board seat. Discard the notion of excused absences. Most excused absences are considered excused simply because the absent party called ahead of time. The board is a continually deliberative body. Absences severely hamper its ability to function. One workable wording is "Anyone absent from three meetings in a row or four in any twelve-month period is considered to have resigned." No excuses; no need to vote. When excuses are allowed or when termination requires board action, most boards are slow to take action, and may slip into a vacillating disunity over the issue of attendance.

Proxy or substitute members. Don't have them. Besides taking board members off the hook for fulfilling their responsibility, having proxies shifts the board composition around even more than rapid turnover does. In some situations, elected officials pretend to remain on a board whose meetings they almost never attend. I have seen these invisible board members show up for a crucial vote or to present a public posture when they are so out of touch with ongoing board process as to be ludicrous with their comments.

Officers. Have as few as you can get by with. It is common for boards to have more officers than there are jobs to do. Perhaps this comes about in an attempt to honor board members by bestowing titles. Perhaps it is due to the boilerplate expectation that any board should have a traditional set of officers (chair, vice chair, secretary, treasurer). For large, highly formalized boards, lining up chairpersons for years into the future (first, second, and third vice chairpersons!) seems to serve some need for a visible ladder of

> Attendance should be required to keep a board seat. Discard the notion of excused absences.

ascendancy. Let's face it: Vice chairpersons are usually superfluous. The chairperson and secretary are ordinarily the only real officer jobs needed. When there is a CEO, a treasurer is not needed, because accountability for fiscal soundness must rest on the CEO's shoulders, not on the board treasurer's, where many bylaws place it. Moreover, in most cases, the CEO can double as secretary quite well. So I'd recommend starting with *one* board officer—the chairperson—and only add more if there are compelling reasons. Keep it simple.

Chairperson. Be sure to describe the chairperson's job in terms of what the chairperson does for the board process, not in terms of overseeing or supervising the CEO. This is a mistake made by many boards, perhaps even most. Language that charges the chair with, for example, "general oversight of the agency" or responsibility for communication between board and CEO unintentionally converts the chair into a part-time CEO. A board that governs responsibly has no need for a chairperson to communicate to the CEO for it. (Sound board policies will perform this function, eliminating the need for an interpreter.) The bylaws should not create a chair role that will relieve the board of its obligation to govern.

Committees. Leave board committees entirely out of the bylaws. Whether the board lists and commissions its committees in bylaws or in policy is neither here nor there in terms of making Policy Governance work. But committees of the board can be dealt with more flexibly through policies (placed in the governance process category). Committees established in bylaws acquire an inflated importance and even an air of permanence. The board is permanent, but committees should be provisional creatures, existing at the board's pleasure.

Committees created by a membership, however, must be included, since they are not a matter of board prerogative. Membership-created committees likely curtail or assume some authority the board otherwise would have had. For example, if the membership creates a nominating committee to select a slate of board candidates, it has removed from the board the prerogative of designing and controlling this endeavor. Because bylaws are the only collective document available to capture membership decisions, the bylaws offer a natural placement for membership creations of any sort.

Finally, true to an ad hoc and product focus, a committee job placed in policy should be described in terms of output or product, not in terms of the activities in

> Vice chairpersons are usually superfluous. The chairperson and secretary are ordinarily the only real officer jobs needed.

> The bylaws should not create a chair role that will relieve the board of its obligation to govern.

> The board is permanent, but committees should be provisional creatures, existing at the board's pleasure.

A committee job placed in policy should be described in terms of output or product, not in terms of the activities in which it engages.

which it engages. For example, a committee's job would not be to *review, oversee,* or *supervise,* for such words state the job in terms of what the committee is to *stay busy doing* rather than what it is to produce. Describe a product that the board decides is worth the cost, for example, "Options and their implications for long-term results in the Southside community, by August, at no more cost than $5,000 in direct expenditures and no more than 200 hours staff support time." It goes without saying that no committee should ever be given authority over something for which the board holds its CEO accountable. This is a normal error in commissioning personnel, finance, and program committees.

Executive committee. Executive committees are a special case in that they are frequently given authority that makes them, in effect, the "board between board meetings." Far-flung national boards do this regularly as do large local ones such as symphony boards. But even relatively small boards, ones that have no excuse, quite often put an executive committee into the driver's seat. Unless the board is too awkward to do its own job of governing, no special authority should be given to the executive committee. To do so reduces the authority of the board or the CEO or both. (For a more detailed treatment of executive committees, see "The Executive Committee" in Chapter Three.)

Unless the board is too awkward to do its own job of governing, no special authority should be given to the executive committee.

Staff. Bylaws are a governance document, not a management document. Omit all staff-related material except for possible reference to the CEO. If mentioned, the CEO should not be described as reporting to or receiving instructions from the chairperson, but from the board. The fact that the CEO is an "officer of the board" justifies reference to the CEO in the bylaws, but doing so is not strictly necessary. My recommendation applies as well to hospital bylaws that incongruously—though true to tradition—incorporate medical staff bylaws into the board document.

Keep your bylaws lean. If something can be put into either bylaws or policies, choose policies.

Keep your bylaws lean. If something can be put into either bylaws or policies, choose policies. But however the bylaws are written at any given time, follow them religiously.

Review them every year or anytime some shortcoming shows itself. Times and circumstances change, so bylaws that were perfectly acceptable earlier can become unacceptable. If they aren't right, don't be afraid to amend them. With bylaws in good order, the board has a firm footing from which it can go on to craft policies that embody its leadership.

Updating Your Existing Bylaws

If revising bylaws is more tedious or time consuming than necessary, you'll avoid amending them when needed. Streamline the updating process to ensure timely revisions. In membership organizations, making bylaws changes is a complex, even political process. In less complicated organizations, updating bylaws can be easy. In both cases, start with these steps:

1. Board members identify the bylaws sections to be revisited.

2. *For small boards,* the entire board can then discuss and decide either (a) the new *sense* (not the exact words) for each section identified in step 1 or (b) the two or more competing senses for each such section. *For large boards,* the work might have to be done by a committee, but the committee's job is not normally to produce a single recommended version.

3. A staff person assigned by the CEO crafts language true to the several options. Drafts are mailed to board members.

4. The whole board explores and debates the options, then votes. It is possible, though not likely, that this deliberation will lead to another stage of developing optional wording. If so, steps 2 and 3 are repeated. *For large membership organizations,* since the board will be taking its recommended bylaws language to the membership, a marketing job looms dead ahead. Input from a sampling of members might enrich this stage of exploration as well as make the product more salable at the annual meeting.

5. The board's vote can be worded to become effective only after legal review, if applicable. Better still, the board could have included legal comment during step 3.

I would not recommend that a bylaws committee do word crafting. Committees tinkering with wording are almost as disastrous as boards doing so. Involve the whole board in determining the sense of bylaws provisions but just the staff in crossing the *t*'s. Seek the staff's precision but the board's uncompromised ownership of the ideas.

What Happens to Conventional Documents Under Policy Governance?

BOARD LEADERSHIP, NUMBER 21, SEPT.-OCT. 1995

M OST BOARDS that adopt the Policy Governance model do so after a history of using traditional practices. Consequently, they have a backlog of documents produced under the old paradigm. These documents include budgets, personnel policies, compensation plans, program plans, long-range plans, and other common items. When a board begins Policy Governance, virtually all of these documents become obsolete overnight.

The obsolescence occurs because the documents are a mixture of ends (though invariably very few true ends), prescribed means for staff, and decisions more detailed than fit the board's new level of thinking. Despite their predictable flaws, however, these traditional documents typically represent a lot of work by board and staff, so appropriate or not, boards do not forsake them easily.

FAQ ➡

Once we've adopted Policy Governance, do we shed our previous policies and procedures?

Some elements of the old documents show up in board policies created using the new principles. In a previous board action, for example, the board might have forbidden the CEO from making purchases of over $10,000 without a paper trail comparing long-term quality and competitive prices. In a new executive limitations policy titled, let's say, "Asset Protection," one provision might have this exact wording. But most traditional documents do not translate so handily to the new paradigm, simply because they embody so much of an antiquated governance style.

Converting Old to New

Let's take a look at what should happen to some of these documents when a board moves away from the conventional approach to its job.

Personnel policies. The employee handbook or personnel manual becomes a document of the CEO rather than the board. In other words, the board turns its former personnel policies package over to the CEO; there is no need for a board to have such a manual, for it constitutes a clear intrusion into management. In Policy Governance terms, a board with traditional personnel policies is deeply engaged in the prescription of staff means. The board can legitimately, however, develop an executive limitations policy outlining what personnel actions, circumstances, and practices are unacceptable (my clients have always been able to do this in less than two pages).

Compensation plan. Although the board sets the compensation of its CEO, it does not establish compensation for subordinate staff, since arranging their compensation is one of the means available in managing the organization. As with other areas of managerial prerogative, leaving staff compensation to the CEO does not imply that it is out of the board's control. It only implies that the board exercises its control by establishing in policy language the limits of acceptability, or boundaries. The board then develops a brief executive limitations policy outlining what compensation practices are unacceptable (usually less than one page), but never has a compensation plan like boards traditionally approve. The CEO, however, has need of such a document, so in transition to Policy Governance, the board is likely to convey its ownership of the previously board-approved compensation plan to the CEO. After that point, the CEO can do with the document as she or he wishes.

> A board with traditional personnel policies is deeply engaged in the prescription of staff means.

Budget. In a shift to Policy Governance, the budget takes its rightful place as an administrative tool, a managerial plan of financial transactions. Like the plan for staff compensation, the fiscal plan is one of the means available to manage the organization. The budget is not a proper governance document at all; it is a tool of staff means.(For a more thorough discussion of the board's relationship to financial management, see Chapter Six.) Consequently, the budget belongs to the CEO, though he or she must always be able to demonstrate that it is true to the board's values about fiscal

The budget is not a proper governance document at all; it is a tool of staff means.

planning. Those values are found in an executive limitations policy that describes the characteristics that would render a budget unacceptable (usually less than one page). The board will periodically monitor the CEO's budgeting to be assured that it conforms to these policy criteria. But board *approval* of the CEO's budget would miss the point; approval freezes into place decisions outside the board's proper area of concern.

FAQ ➡️

What is the difference between strategic plans and ends?

Strategic plan. Long-range plans as they commonly appear are predominantly means documents. They describe how the organization will orient itself over the next few years, how it will prepare itself for the future, and how it will manage its strengths and weaknesses to do so. Few long-range plans spell out what results are to be achieved with which people at what cost—the essential elements of the Policy Governance ends concept. So the segment of the plan that would be a legitimate board product—the intended organizational results at some future point—is almost always missing anyway! In other words, as important as long-range planning might be, it is primarily a management document. In Policy Governance, the board's ends work constitutes its chief contribution to strategic planning. The planning itself is a management undertaking, though driven by the board-stated ends. The board contributes to long-range planning by standing just outside of it, creating the vision toward which plans plan.

Capital budgets. Like operational budgeting, budgeting for capital expenditures is likely to be under management's authority, though the board's values about the matter must prevail. For example, the board might choose to withhold authority from the CEO for capital outlays above some criterion amount, but that amount is best set rather high. Whatever the board needs to control about capital expenditures can be added to the appropriate executive limitations policy. Note, however, that treating most capital expenditures differently from other expenditures is often artificial. Boards that get deeply involved in a $50,000 capital expense regularly permit much larger sums to be spent operationally without clear assurance that the money achieves worthwhile results. There is nothing about capital expense that makes it more of a board issue.

Grant applications. When nonprofit organizations apply for government or foundation grants, it is common for their boards to approve the application before it is submitted. From the point of view of the potential grantor, board approval makes sense. It assures the grantor that the request for funds and the assurances offered in the application are officially authorized. From the point of view of governance, however, it is simply one more example of the approval syndrome with which governance is afflicted. After all, if receipt of the grant would make it more possible to achieve board-stated ends or to avoid unacceptable conditions, and the application itself doesn't make unacceptable promises, then why would any board *not* approve it? Indeed, in most situations, board approval of a staff-written grant application is merely ritual, but a ritual in which the board bottlenecks further alterations by the CEO in the specifics of the application. If a potential grantor requires formal board approval, however, then a board has little choice. But to get the money with no sacrifice of governance integrity, the board would vote not an approval in the usual sense, but would vote to affirm that the application—because it honors all pertinent board policies—is, in fact, a board-backed action by the CEO.

> Long-range plans as they commonly appear are predominantly means documents.

Medical staff bylaws. Hospital boards are required by accreditation standards and sometimes by regulation to approve the bylaws of their hospital's organized medical staff. Not only do hospital boards take ritual ownership of these documents, they often even include them as a section of their own bylaws. There is no reason a medical staff should not have any bylaws it wants, as long as certain board requirements are not violated (for example, a required level of responsiveness to applications for staff privileges). As in previous examples, this document should belong to the physicians instead of the board. In policies addressing the board's relationship to the medical staff, the board would detail its criteria for medical staff bylaws.

Policy Governance Documents Are Tighter

Board documents in Policy Governance are quite a different phenomenon from those in conventional governance (Exhibit 10.2). They are shorter and scrupulously centered on what are truly board decisions rather than board-blessed staff work. They are not collections of undifferentiated board and staff decisions, nor are they staff work that everyone pretends are board products. Rather than being approved by the board, they are *generated* by it. And the documents fall carefully into the four board policy categories rather than standing alone as separate pronouncements. The total number of pages may well be below thirty—not thirty plus long-range plan, budget, and personnel manual—thirty pages total.

Exhibit 10.2. The Conversion Process

DOCUMENTS that boards traditionally approve—for example, budgets, compensation plans, and personnel manuals—are composed of (a) a few values important to the board, though rarely stated explicitly, and (b) many values and decisions safely left to staff if the board's values are honored. In these traditional documents—ordinarily staff-authored, then board-blessed—"a" and "b" are never disentangled, so board approval sets the trivial as well as the profound. Even the trivial cannot be changed without coming back to the board for authorization, rendering management less agile and governance more cluttered.

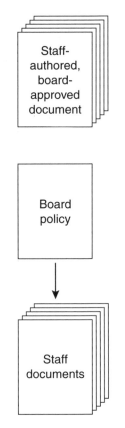

Traditional governance. Large and small decisions are included in one document, yielding a detailed tome in which the board controls small details but fails to make explicit the most important values.

Policy Governance, board role. For any issue, those aspects important enough to warrant board control show up explicitly in a brief policy. This policy is not *approved* by the board, so much as it is *generated* from board values.

Policy Governance, CEO role. Subsequent decisions, policies, and procedures *determined by staff* show up in whatever format or detail best serve the needs of management. These are not board documents, so need no board action. Note that the new documents are *not* derived by disjoining old ones. To the contrary, a board adopting Policy Governance should set old documents aside and develop new board policies from scratch.

So where are the old documents? They now belong to the CEO, who can do with them as he or she deems fitting, as long as the criteria located in board policies are met. Regular monitoring provides assurance that CEO actions, documents, and achievements are, in fact, a reasonable interpretation of the new, briefer, less numerous policies of the board. In the case of medical staff bylaws, of course, the monitoring is not of CEO performance, but whether the medical staff has met criteria. If an outside authority requires board approval despite the antiquated nature of such an action, then the board renders an approval. But board approval under these conditions is a more focused activity than usual, for the document in question is examined *only* with respect to those aspects relevant to the preestablished criteria.

Are documents authored or authorized by the CEO imbued with less authority than the board-approved documents of conventional governance? Does a CEO budget have less legitimacy than a board budget? Does a CEO personnel manual pack less punch than it would have if approved by the board?

No. CEO documents and CEO decisions (a document is, in fact, only a collection of decisions) carry fully as much weight as board documents *if the board is delegating to the CEO as powerfully and unambiguously as it should.* If the authoritativeness of any decision is certain only when the board itself has taken the action, the result is organizational weakness and indecision at best, havoc at worst. If decisions by the CEO are treated as less authoritative than had they been made by the board, delegation from a board to its CEO is inadequate.

Traditional board-approved documents, such as those I have listed (as well as others particular to specific organizations), are one facet of the deeply flawed governance tradition to which we have all been accustomed. Transformation in what boards decide, how their decisions are made, and the nature of delegation requires commensurately massive change in the documents that embody the evidence of board wisdom.

How You Can Tell When Your Board Is Not Using Policy Governance

Board Leadership, Number 25, May-June 1996

W ITH INCREASING frequency—as Policy Governance has become more widely known—I meet board members or CEOs at conferences who will tell me that their board operates with the Policy Governance model. I am flattered, of course, but have learned that *saying* one uses the model and using it can be quite different phenomena.

When there is time in one of these chance encounters—and if I am invited to do so—I will help the board member or CEO look to see whether his or her board is truly using the model or, if using part of it, to see how its payoff could be enhanced by more careful attention to its implementation. In some cases I am asked to do this more effectively in a scheduled consulting visit rather than slapdash in a hallway. I cannot do so for everyone; there are neither enough consulting days nor hallways. This article is for those board members and CEOs who haven't yet bumped into me!

> Using Policy Governance piecemeal can sometimes help a board improve a bit but will not enable a breakthrough in board leadership.

In conceptual matters—like designing a governance model—it is easy to pick up a tire here, a dashboard there, and an alternator over there and think you have a car. Bits and pieces, however, do not make a whole. If I may use another analogy, the tendency to put new wine in old bottles is an ever present danger when an innovative idea is popularized.

Much of what Policy Governance has to offer is its wholeness, its conceptual coherence. Using it piecemeal can sometimes help a board improve a bit but will not enable a breakthrough in board leadership. Sometimes boards erroneously think they are using the model simply by virtue of having declared that they are. Often they have sterling intentions but are careless about the principles.

The problem sometimes lies with inadequately schooled consultants, persons who market themselves as competent in Policy Governance but misconstrue or sloppily apply the concepts. And I am sure there are times that, in an effort to be eclectic ("We won't swallow anybody's idea whole"), a board introduces inconsistencies for the statement that makes about its independence. Careful adaptation of a generic idea is acceptable, of course, but conceptual sloppiness often masquerades as tailoring. Regardless of the source of the problem, many boards have adopted the language of Policy Governance without its philosophy and substance.

> **FAQ**
>
> Can a board improve its leadership by applying only portions of the Policy Governance model?

> Sometimes boards erroneously think they are using the model simply by virtue of having declared that they are.

If you have wondered whether your board's attempt at implementing Policy Governance is more than cosmetic, I offer a checklist to help make that determination. Because the following items are representative, they don't cover the entire model. But they may help expose areas where some crucial part of the model is being missed.

You Are Not Using Policy Governance If . . .

- It is possible in any significant way for the organization (1) to fail to achieve what it should or (2) to engage in unacceptable activities or get into unacceptable situations while the CEO is in compliance with board policy.

  Reason: The board would have fulfilled its responsibility to define both (1) and (2), to charge the CEO with the organization's performance on them, and to be aware of the degree of that performance.

> Careful adaptation of a generic idea is acceptable, of course, but conceptual sloppiness often masquerades as tailoring.

- The board has not stated in writing—even in broad terms—the results it charges the organization to attain, for whom those results are to be attained, and what the acceptable worth of those results are.

Reason: Carefully constructed, succinct ends policies—uncontaminated by means statements—would be in place.

- The board has not stated in writing—even in broad terms—what organizational activities, situations, practices, decisions, values, or methods it will not allow.

  Reason: Carefully constructed, succinct executive limitations policies would be in place.

- The board does not include every expectation it has for organizational performance in these ends policies (what to achieve) and executive limitations policies (what to avoid).

  Reason: All expectations the board has of its organization are in the ends and executive limitations policies. They are not scattered in other places.

- The board allows itself, its committees, or its individual members to judge CEO performance on criteria it has never stated.

  Reason: Only the board judges the CEO and *only* against previously stated board criteria on ends and executive limitations. The board is guarantor of this simplicity.

- The board prescribes any part of the means used by the CEO in managing the organization.

  Reason: The board's control over staff means is exercised only by limiting or prohibiting, never by prescribing.

- The board does not allow its CEO to use any reasonable interpretation of board instructions that he or she chooses.

  Reason: The board takes full responsibility for using the words it means, including the range of "fuzziness" all words carry as to their meaning. The CEO is not charged with reading the board's mind but with making reasonable interpretations of what the board has said.

- Having set expectations for CEO performance, the board does not receive suitable data on that performance on an acceptably frequent basis.

  Reason: Failing to maintain a reasonable assurance of organizational performance is irresponsible board stewardship. Failing to gather data that address the criteria is tantamount to having no criteria.

- The board commissions committees (of itself or other persons) to aid, advise, or control any feature of staff operations.

Reason: The board is careful never to send ambiguous messages about the CEO's right to determine staff means, bounded only by board policy, never by advisers—no matter who they are.

- The board authorizes its chairperson to exercise supervisory control over the ostensible CEO.

Reason: The CEO is held accountable only to the board acting as a body, never to officers or committees.

- The board leaves completely up to the chairperson how governance is to be practiced.

Reason: The board is responsible for the design and performance of its own job. Although it can grant the chairperson authority to make decisions *within* larger decisions it makes itself, it has to first make those decisions.

- The board fails to identify and link assertively with the owners about ownership issues.

Reason: The responsible board has no choice but to fulfill a relationship with the ownership that supersedes all other relationships, including one with its own staff.

CEOs! Guiding Your Board Toward Better Governance

BOARD LEADERSHIP, NUMBER 29, JAN.-FEB. 1997

U NLIKE MOST OF MY publications, this one is written expressly for CEOs. When I address CEOs, as I did recently, one question I can count on coming up is, "How can I take this message back to my board—how can I get my board to operate in this new way?" This article is written to help those CEOs who, having discovered a better way, worry about the pitfalls they will encounter when they return to their boards with the good news.

> **FAQ** ➡
>
> Can the CEO lead the board in adopting policy governance?

First, let me set the stage. Policy Governance is designed for boards, not for CEOs. Governance renewal is a responsibility of boards, not—as poor boards are wont to construe it—of CEOs. It should not be up to CEOs to make sure their bosses conduct themselves responsibly. But as we know, boards frequently send a confusing message to their CEO: "You work for us. Now tell us what to do." They act like the CEO is more responsible for the board's behavior than its own members are—and the CEO believes it.

So, here's the CEO's dilemma. A CEO learns about Policy Governance in a workshop or by reading. He or she is convinced that the model should replace traditional modes of governing but cannot single-handedly make the switch. After all, the CEO has no legitimate authority over the board. Suppose our hypothetical CEO, like most CEOs, for years has been setting the board's agenda, arranging board training, and doing most or all of the new board member orientation. What a great opportunity, the CEO thinks, to introduce Policy Governance—by pushing it through the superb and accessible tools of agenda, training, and orientation!

> It should not be up to CEOs to make sure their bosses conduct themselves responsibly.

But wait. This plan has a flaw. One of the tenets of Policy Governance is that the board must not default to the CEO in the determination of its job. Board policies in Policy Governance must express the board's values, not the CEO's. The CEO thus encounters a paradoxical impasse: If he or she spoon-feeds Policy Governance to the board, it won't be Policy Governance!

So how can the message be carried back? Is there no way to introduce needed changes without sacrificing the integrity of this nascent idea? While admitting that in the real-life setting there may be no easy solution to balancing these concerns, I can offer a few tips to the CEO who would carry the Policy Governance torch home:

> Policy Governance must express the board's values, not the CEO's.

Return as a discoverer. Approach your board as an explorer who has found a new pass through the mountains. Embody the excitement of new knowledge rather than the pushiness of evangelical fervor. The message is more, "Wow, here is what I found!" than, "You've got to change and go this new way!" Your newfound enthusiasm may not be as effective as a confident, low-key approach, explaining that you've come across something that might make the board's job clearer and more effective.

Emphasize board potential, not flaws. No doubt about it, boards do need to confront the defects of traditional governance. But they'll hear the message better if your focus is on opening up the tremendous potential for leadership. It is wise to emphasize the positive. Otherwise, board members may recoil before hearing the whole story, an understandable reaction to having their methods criticized. After all, haven't some of them spent decades learning the conventional ways?

> Embody the excitement of new knowledge rather than the pushiness of evangelical fervor.

Play student, not expert. Remember that you've just begun learning, yourself, so if you try to explain more than you can substantiate you may lose credibility, doing yourself and your board a disservice.

A genuine rebirth will more likely come to pass if the banner is waved by a board member rather than by the CEO.

Pass the torch—nurture a champion. A genuine rebirth will more likely come to pass if the banner is waved by a board member rather than by the CEO. This method must be sensitively handled, for the idea is to give helpful tools to board members who truly want to increase the board's effectiveness. It is as counterproductive as it is disingenuous to manipulate a board member into fronting your own agenda.

Arrange Policy Governance exposure. Another approach is to acquaint your board with Policy Governance in a retreat or training event or through published materials. If your board already relies on you to be its source of training and development, you can use that expectation as a vehicle for returning to the board its own leadership. But be up-front about it; declare that the event will challenge traditional ideas, including those held by board members and, yes, by you, too.

Most conscientious chairs will take to the idea of leaving a legacy of superior governance.

Work with the chair. Through discussions or sharing materials, help your chair see that governance could be much improved, even though your board may be the world's best in using traditional governance. Most conscientious chairs will take to the idea of leaving a legacy of superior governance. If approached in this way, the best possible champion, the chair, might lead the way.

Turn off the trivia tap. Stop the commonplace practice of bringing your board endless trivia. Be sure your staff stops, too. Somehow staff members have come to think it is their responsibility to keep board members involved, so they involve them in staff decisions. Staffs have been teaching the wrong lessons for a long time.

FAQ ➡

As CEO, what should I start doing to reinforce Policy Governance?

Focus reports and remarks on underlying values. Use the ends-means distinction to focus even traditional reporting on the underlying values that make a difference. For example, if you are presenting a budget to a tradition-bound board, highlight the major budget values instead of the myriad individual numbers. Help the board see that its job is not just to examine the world through your documents but to operate on an entirely different plane.

Obsess on the ends challenge. Continually bring board deliberations back to a discussion of ends. What results are we seeking? Why those results instead of all the other possible results the world needs? Are we being ambitious enough? Or are our aims so unattainably high that they make better rhetoric than instruction? Why should our results be for this set of recipients rather than that one? What are we saying about the relative worth of achieving certain results for certain populations? Don't discuss programs, services, or curricula with the board, discuss the ends toward which these staff activities might be aimed.

Use Policy Governance principles in management. Since governance is unduly influenced by management anyway, you might as well use the influence to guide your board toward better governance. In your own work, focus on clear ends and

> CEOs, you must get beyond thinking that you are more responsible than the board is for the board's being responsible.

freedom of means within explicitly stated bounds. Gather monitoring data in accord with this focus. Align your staff's mentality and language with the principles of Policy Governance, and the board might follow.

CEOs must learn to be their board's best booster yet let the board be responsible for itself. CEOs ordinarily have a commendable sense of responsibility for making everything come out right for the organization, even in areas where they have no legitimate authority. Yet assuming responsibility for successful governance is like trying to push the river. CEOs, I sympathize with the situation, for I've been there, but you must get beyond thinking that you are more responsible than the board is for the board's being responsible. I know I'm suggesting a high-risk strategy here; to be sure there will be missteps. But in the long run, board members' being responsible for board effectiveness is the only path to governance integrity.

Policy Governance Won't Work Because . . .

BOARD LEADERSHIP, NUMBER 36, MAR.-APR. 1998

INTRODUCTORY Policy Governance workshops are usually mind-bending experiences for persons new to the concept. It is hard for thinking people not to find the step-by-step reasoning compelling. In a choice between the hodgepodge of practices that make up traditional governance and the simple, clear logic of Policy Governance, there is really no contest.

It is not surprising, then, that workshop participants are thrown into a place of conflict. The ideas are so logical, but they lead to extensive, possibly difficult, and uncomfortable change. If one accepts the logic, doing anything less is irresponsible. If one does not accept the logic, then one is obliged to argue convincingly against this intrusion into business as usual. Policy Governance, in short, is hard to ignore! After twenty years of addressing boards, conventions, and other groups, I've concluded that the natural human response to this phenomenon is, "It makes sense, but . . ."

> In a choice between the hodgepodge of practices that make up traditional governance and the simple, clear logic of Policy Governance, there is really no contest.

In this article, I share some of the more common reasons people give for why, even if it does make sense, Policy Governance will not work in their field.

It's good on paper but not in the real world. Credit where credit is due—the real world argument does make a lot of sense. We all know schemes that sounded good but were total failures in practice. In fact, political history alone would convince us that "the slip 'twixt cup and lip" is the norm, not the exception. But lest cynicism get more than its due, we must consider another point. *Really* new ideas, no matter how good, are not at their inception congruent with the real world. In fact, "the real world" can merely be a way of saying that we don't operate that way yet. Ideas of air transportation, X rays, space exploration, and countless other breakthroughs were first not practical in the real world. With hindsight, of course, we can see that it wasn't the idea on paper, but the real world that was deficient! Anyway, isn't a board that aims to make a difference already itself committed to changing the real world in some way?

> *Really* new ideas, no matter how good, are not at their inception congruent with the real world.

It may work elsewhere, but we're different. This is the organization-specific form of the foregoing complaint. In *our* real world it won't work, even if it works in others'. Institutional inertia has many faces; this is certainly one of them. As before, what lends this resistance strength is that it may be correct. But the more generic or underlying a concept is, however, the more this assertion about it weakens. Even recent history is littered with forgotten claims of this sort. "We are a nonprofit, therefore precise management methods don't apply to us." "I am a professional, so measuring my results is not appropriate." I've heard from urban boards that they could see how the model might work in rural areas, but not in the city. I've heard from rural boards that they could see how the model might work in the city, but not in the country!

Board members speaking with one voice is a good idea, but our members can't agree. Sometimes people think that Policy Governance calls for board members who agree with each other. Not at all. It does require at the outset that at least a voting majority of board members decide to use the model. After that point, whatever new or amended policies get a majority vote constitute the one voice of the board. While sticking carefully to the adopted process is more likely when all members are "on board," unanimity is by no means necessary. And, of course, on issues of content (the actual policy decisions), having diverse opinions is a board strength, not a weakness.

> ← **FAQ**
>
> If board members disagree, how can they possibly speak with one voice?

While sticking carefully to the adopted process is more likely when all members are "on board," unanimity is by no means necessary.

The idea sounds good, but the law requires the board to violate the model. City councils, school boards, and other statute-based boards are most likely to cite this impediment. In most cases, this problem can be overcome by consigning to a consent agenda (for automatic approval) all decisions that the board under Policy Governance has delegated to the CEO but upon which the law requires the board to act.

It won't work because funders, regulators, or public expectations demand traditional board behaviors. Frequently there are ways for boards to get around some of these demands (such as the consent agenda approach noted above). Funders and regulators can be surprisingly flexible, but they must be convinced with a good argument. The public at large is more difficult, so school boards, city councils, and other publicly visible boards must invest heavily in public education to gain acceptance of any departure from the conventional wisdom. Actually, while Policy Governance was on the one hand designed to help today's boards, it was on the other hand conceived to influence public expectations of boards in the future. In other words, although the model is useful to boards right now, it is a vision that looks over and beyond today's circumstances to a world in which group leadership outgrows the primitive state of boards and public expectations as we have known them. Cutting-edge boards of today, like pioneers in any age in any field, simply have to face that challenge.

It won't work for us because our CEO is not capable of taking on that much responsibility. This may be true. Boards have often given an individual the role of CEO without actually requiring or expecting CEO skills and behavior. Yet it is also often true that persons with CEO potential have not been allowed to exercise CEO prerogatives. Boards may be unable to tell whether they have a capable person or not when they've neither required nor allowed CEO authority and accountability. I recommend to such a board that it forget the personal issue until it has decided whether a CEO role is wanted. If after reflection the board deems it in the best interest of the mission to have a CEO role, the current CEO is told that he or she will be granted a full CEO role, then given the chance to perform. If performance is not forthcoming, the next step is obvious.

It won't work because board members won't agree to let go of their favorite details. Many boards worry that they will never feel accountable using a model that obliges them to govern at arm's length. Perhaps. If board members cannot work

On issues of content, having diverse opinions is a board strength, not a weakness.

up the discipline to keep their hands firmly on the large issues and their fingers firmly out of the little ones, then good governance will forever escape them. The model cannot make unwise persons wise nor undisciplined persons disciplined. It merely presents a template, a road map for boards that want to be wise and disciplined.

Protecting Governance from Law, Funders, and Accreditors

BOARD LEADERSHIP, NUMBER 11, JAN.-FEB. 1994

B OARDS EXCITED about breaking out of the old molds often run headlong into outside authorities who require them to employ the tired old methods they've struggled so hard to get beyond. These outside authorities might be funding bodies—such as government agencies or foundations—or accreditation organizations. For some boards, notably city councils and school boards, the law itself demands regressive governance.

Laws require school boards to take action on each teacher hired, even in a large school system. Some foundations require boards to have committees engaged in what is essentially staff work. Government funding agencies often demand that boards review every disbursement. Organizations that grant accreditation status commonly put more emphasis on prescribed methods than on effective results. These and myriad other requirements reduce the effectiveness of governance, dishearten otherwise enthusiastic board members, and impede the continual improvement of board leadership.

We must recognize, of course, that foundations, granting agencies, and accreditors are simply doing the best they can, influenced by expectations of governance that have been around a long time. If authorities have learned—as we all did—that personnel and finance committees, budget approvals, board approvals, board involvement in staff activity, and other such practices constitute responsible leadership, then those are exactly the practices they will require.

At any rate, your board may feel that it is in a time warp. It is embracing governance-future, while those with control over it are stuck in governance-past. I want to suggest, first, a philosophical approach to this dilemma, then some concrete steps you might take.

Your board's first obligation is to its ownership, not to the law, not to accreditors, not to funders. The board owes an obligation to these external forces, but the very nature of governance and the need to do it well arise out of those who own the organization. Having first sprung from this source, governance is then beholden to all legitimate, extraorganizational authorities and to anyone with whom the board voluntarily enters into contract.

> Your board's first obligation is to its ownership, not to the law, not to accreditors, not to funders.

In designing its role and responsibilities, then, the board must first determine what is the best governance on behalf of its ownership. For a trade or professional association, ownership is composed of members. For a public school board, ownership would usually be the people of a specified geographical area. For a city council, ownership is the citizenry of the municipality. It is on behalf of these persons—the ownership—that board members are elected or appointed to act. The motivation for better governance arises out of the need to do a better job for owners. Board members do not ascend to their positions in order to do a better job for the law, for accreditors, or for funders.

Integrity of governance is the foundation and the point of departure for all consideration of the board's job. Therefore, the mental set I recommend is that boards should first set out to govern as best they can on behalf of their owners and then—*and only then*—concern themselves with how to stay legal, satisfy funders, and earn accreditation.

← FAQ

How can a board effectively represent its ownership when it is under more immediate pressure from an accrediting organization?

The board should begin with this frame of mind and then invoke whatever creativity is necessary to keep outside authorities content. Keep in mind, though, that I am assuming the board has already committed itself to better governance, that is, more responsible stewardship for the owners, and is implementing an effective model of governance. Given that, the following tips may be useful as your board considers this matter.

Use a modified consent agenda. Often outside authorities demand board action on matters that really should be delegated to the CEO. Such items can be put on a consent agenda. The consent agenda is a well-known device, normally used to deal with issues about which there is no controversy. That is, with nothing to debate, no time need be taken to discuss what is essentially a ritual action.

But because no items appear on a Policy Governance agenda that do not truly require a board decision, there would ordinarily be no consent agenda. So the consent agenda recommended here is a special device that includes only issues that would not—and should not—be on the agenda in the first place were it not for an outside authority's demand.

For example, school boards are required by law to make the actual hiring decisions for all teacher personnel. This ludicrous requirement has such a long tradition that school officials seldom recognize how silly it is. Certainly, the board should install whatever safeguards are needed with respect to hiring (through its executive limitations policies), but it can then put all the legally required, but unnecessary, matters on the consent agenda. The board would take actions required by law, but subject them to no discussion. Therefore, the board does what is necessary to meet the form required but doesn't take such requirements seriously, for they truly do not deserve serious consideration.

Turn approval into "direct inspection" monitoring. Sometimes, outside authorities require that the board approve management documents before they are considered to be official. Such documents include personnel procedures and various administrative and programmatic plans.

Using the Policy Governance model, however, a board will have clarified the criteria for such management documents and actions beforehand. Compliance with these criteria must be monitored, to be sure, but combing through the documents' details to issue a formal approval is superfluous and unnecessarily controlling. For example, approving a budget or some other plan has the effect of freezing the plan's details into place as well as its major points. Not only does management agility suffer, but board members must pretend to be expert in the myriad details.

Let's look at budget approval to illustrate my point. If budget approval is required by outside authorities, a board can put the CEO's budget on the table, compare it to the board's budget policy, then render a decision that the budget does or does not meet the criteria found in the policy. This kind of monitoring I refer to as *direct inspection* to distinguish it from monitoring through a summarizing report from the CEO or from a disinterested party (such as an auditor).

To the casual observer, such a direct inspection looks very much like budget approval in that the board inspects the budget and renders a judgment. It differs in that the board is using a set of preestablished criteria to make that judgment; it is not simply wandering through the budget details on a fishing expedition. Further, after the board finishes its inspection, nothing about the document is frozen into place as is the case when budgets are "approved." The board will not have made the budget official by its action; it has merely determined that management's budget conforms to expectations the board gave the CEO at the outset.

Authorize a board officer to vouch for policy consistency. Sometimes, an outside authority requires the board to make a decision in order to be certain that the decision is made with proper authority. After all, how would a lessor know that a lease signed by the CEO truly commits the organization? Yet taking all such matters to the board will doom the board to an endless stream of "administrivia."

To deal with this problem, a board can authorize its secretary or other officer to sign documents that testify to outside entities that a given executive action is fully backed by the authority given in board policy. The officer can take care of such assurances, reporting them to the board in a succinct way, saving the board from having to study and deal with such matters.

Be careful in using this mechanism that the officer does not sign that the board has done something it has not. For example, the officer does not sign that the board has seen and approved the action. He or she merely attests the fact that the administrative action is fully consistent with written board authorizations.

Persuade outside authorities that your style of governance is sound, ethical, and effective. Foundations, government funders, and accreditors are simply trying to do a good job, looking for ways to ensure good performance. But the ways made available to them derive from old notions of board leadership. Although rules and symbols do not change easily or quickly, they can and do change. When enough boards are engaged in teaching the various authorities what board leadership should look like, the rules and symbols will change.

In the short term, a single board might benefit from showing funders and accreditors how assurances of performance can be achieved in a new way. In some cases, there will be small victories, particularly when funders and accreditors have built-in flexibility that has heretofore been unused.

Although it would be naive to expect massive changes overnight, I have seen funders and accreditors go the extra mile to enable a board to use nontraditional methods when they have been convinced that important matters are, in fact, even better handled a new way. I have even seen funders become the evangelists, spreading the word among other funded agencies that there might well be better ways of doing things than the required form. Boards that take a strong stand on behalf of excellence rather than tradition can make a difference, convincing funders long jaded by mediocrity.

Although good governance is frequently made more difficult by regressive demands of law, funders, and accreditors, it need not be derailed. The secret of success lies, first, in the board's commitment to excellence no matter what forces impinge on it, and, second, in the creative determination to find legal, effective ways to carry out that commitment.

Chapter Eleven

When Governing Boards Perform Nongoverning Roles

Although a governing board's core purpose is to govern, boards and board members may engage in nongoverning pursuits as long as the central governing role and the integrity of delegation are protected. Board members then can engage in fundraising, operational volunteering, advising staff, and other activities. Board accountability is threatened only if nongoverning activities supplant or impede proper performance of the core governance responsibilities.

When Board Members Act as Staff Advisors

BOARD LEADERSHIP, NUMBER 9, SEPT.-OCT. 1992

O NE OF THE CRITICAL features of the Policy Governance model is that a governing board enjoys its authority only as a group. Invariably, in my presentations on governance, someone will ask about board members acting individually as advisors to staff.

Can board members advise staff members if they have expertise to offer? Is it possible to do so without "chain-of-command" confusion? On the one hand, can the board's authoritative position and its obligation to its constituency be maintained if it gives advice that, by definition, need not be heeded? On the other hand, do staff members put their jobs in jeopardy by ignoring or even firing volunteer advisors?

In this article I will give you a simple way to keep governance and advice from endangering each other. All the foregoing quandaries can be resolved in such a way that a board can discharge its responsibility as an official body yet give the staff access to board members' individual skills. Board members can be a rich source of advice to a staff. Their special strength is that they care, and because of their volunteer motivation, they're inexpensive! It would be wasteful not to take advantage of what board members have to give.

> Board members can be a rich source of advice to a staff. Their special strength is that they care, and because of their volunteer motivation, they're inexpensive!

Protecting the Board-CEO Relationship

The board-CEO relationship must be properly designed to be sure this valuable resource does not confuse board-staff delegation. The secret is not in the advice, the advisors, or the advisees. The secret is in the fundamental relationship of board to CEO.

Good board-staff delegation is characterized by two simple rules: (1) The board will express its instructions and expectations only as a full group, not as individuals or committees, and (2) the board will express its instructions and expectations only to the CEO, never to persons who work for the CEO. As long as the board defines the board-CEO relationship appropriately, advice to staff from any source is workable.

Let's look at how advice from individual board members can work. Because the board can only instruct the CEO when it does so with a group (not necessarily unanimous) voice, individual board members have no authority over staff. Nothing an individual board member says—in or out of a board meeting—can have instructional authority. In other words, advice or counsel from a single board member is fine, but commands or requirements are not. Thus, a personnel expert on the board can appropriately make his or her advice available to the CEO or to the personnel director. However, the CEO or personnel director has no obligation to take the advice or even to take time to hear it. When a board officially commits itself to this principle, advice from individuals can be considered by staff on its merits alone.

Avoiding Committee Confusion

> **FAQ** ➡
>
> Why shouldn't the accountant, personnel professional, and marketing expert on the board chair the finance, human resources, and marketing committees, respectively?

Board committees sometimes also have the assigned task of advising staff. Traditionally, a board may constitute a committee to advise staff on personnel, program design, public relations, or any one of many topics. Thus, a board's desire to advise can become manifest in the official governance structure. But creating an official board organ to give advice belies the unofficial nature of the advice. In fact, it is difficult for staff to believe that advice from an official board committee is truly only advice. It is equally hard for committee members to remember that their deliberations are merely advice.

So it is that *board committees created to advise staff are unintentionally harmful.* Given the long years of conventional practice on this matter, my admonition may seem a strange one: Although a board should certainly create any committees that help in getting the board's own job done, *a governing board should never, never have board committees to advise or help staff with anything!*

When the line between instructing (which only the full board can do) and advising (which anyone can do) is even slightly blurred, the unintended result is that the staff ends up working not for the board per se but for various sources of "advice," which they can never be completely sure is really only advice. More-

> It is difficult for staff to believe— and for committee members to remember— that advice from an official board committee is truly only advice.

over, because board committees commonly fill the instructive vacuum left by the board, board committees in many organizations are the major source of board direction. Typically, staff members either take committee suggestions as instructions, expend energy appearing to follow the committee's suggestions, or manipulate the committee process so that committees advise what the staff wants to do anyway.

Giving Staff Control

The trap can be easily avoided: The board should allow the staff total control over all processes—including committees—intended to advise them. After all, people who need advice are more capable of working out what they need and whom they trust to give it than are the would-be advisors. But even more important, it is the CEO, not the advisors, who is then held accountable for meeting board-stated expectations.

Because the way the staff gets advice is not board business at all, mechanisms of advice should always be in the hands of the advisees, not in the hands of the would-be advisors. In the former case, the advisory process works. In the latter, you cannot be sure whether it works or not. Staff members are not inclined to tell board committees that their advice is unhelpful or that the staff time required for committee meetings is more costly than the advice is worth. Moreover, the advisors a staff mem-

> Mechanisms of advice should always be in the hands of the advisees, not in the hands of the would-be advisors.

ber would assemble on some topic are rarely the same persons that a board would put on a committee to advise staff on that same topic. The message is starkly evident!

Please remember that my remarks about board committees giving advice to staff do not apply to board committees that help the board in its own decisions. Board committees that assist the board itself legitimately belong to the board and are never to be controlled by staff. Again, the issue is simply a matter of keeping each hat in its rightful place.

Ask Your CEO

- Do you or your staff members ever wonder whether the comments of individual board members or committees are to be taken as instruction or as take-it-or-leave-it advice?

- If so, is the confusion related to a particular member or committee, or is it a general phenomenon?

- If you could choose your own advisers on a given topic, would you assemble the skills, experience, and helpfulness you need more effectively or efficiently yourself than if the board did it for you?

CEO and staff can put together any advisory arrangements they wish. They may choose advisors as they wish. They may keep or discharge advisors as they deem fitting. And the CEO, through it all, is accountable to the board for performance—no matter where advice to staff comes from. For example, whether advice to conduct affairs a certain way came from a group of board members, from a very vocal board member, or from a passerby is immaterial to the board's assessment of CEO performance; it neither hurts nor helps.

FAQ →

If board members feel that they have useful advice for staff, should they offer it directly?

This framing of the phenomenon of advice is as freeing for board members who have advice to give as it is for staff who need advice. Board members can advise with as much gusto as they feel, having no need to soft-pedal due to conscientious fear of meddling. Staff members can be as critical of board members' advice as they would be of anyone else's.

Clarifying Roles

It is up to the board to be sure that each of its own members and the CEO understand that the board hat is worn by board members only in session doing board work. The board hat is never to be worn when giving advice. And if a conflict ever arises between fulfilling the mandate to govern and fulfilling the desire to advise, let there be no mistaking that governing comes first. Does this separation of hats require discipline? Is maturity needed to play separate roles well? Yes, of course, on both counts. But no more discipline and maturity is needed than most board members exercise every day in pursuing their occupations, in parenting, or even in playing games by rules.

So go ahead and make board member advice available to staff. Don't force it, of course, for then it is something other than advice. The board as a body might even encourage its individual members to make advice or other help available. An inventory of board members' expertise, experience, and abilities potentially useful to the staff would be a fine gift. But an even greater gift is the confidence that the board is committed to keeping governing and advising clearly separated.

The board hat is worn by board members only in session doing board work. The board hat is never to be worn when giving advice.

Tips for Creating Advisory Boards and Committees

BOARD LEADERSHIP, NUMBER 11, JAN.-FEB. 1994

*B*OARD *LEADERSHIP* is written for and to *governing* boards, boards placed at the pinnacle of an organization and, with their predominant authority, accountable for all organizational achievement and behavior. Nongoverning boards, however, are frequently created to give advice. Sometimes these bodies are called advisory committees, advisory councils, or other similar titles. In contrast to another article in this chapter, "When Board Members Act as Staff Advisors," on board members giving advice to staff, this time I examine the phenomenon of *asking* for advice.

First, let's establish that the board can legitimately create advisory bodies to advise itself, but should *never* create advisory bodies to advise staff. Clarity of delegation to the CEO can only be confused (is the advice *really* advice or is it veiled instruction?)— and with no compensating gain, for the staff can ask anyone for advice anyway.

However, as is true in the case of all staff means, the board can limit CEO choices with respect to advice and advisory mechanisms. For example, the board might prohibit the CEO from allowing any group of advisors to be misled, to be used merely to fulfill a grant requirement, or to have its time callously wasted or misused. Otherwise, the staff is free to institute any advisory mechanisms it deems useful in getting its job done.

As for the board's pursuit of advice for itself, there are a number of job responsibilities for which the board could use good counsel. For example, the board might want structured advice from carefully stratified segments or random samplings of the

Putting Advice in Perspective

- *Avoid the word board when creating an advisory body.* If an advisory role is wanted, the word *board* suggests more authority than is intended, thereby inviting misunderstandings. Miscommunication can be avoided by simply using another word, perhaps *committee* or *council.* This problem is particularly bothersome in organizations where no governing board exists (as in some government units), leaving an opportunity for an advisory body to assume unauthorized power.

- *Be sure the body is actually for advice.* Many organizations create groups for fundraising or for community advocacy and mistakenly call them advisory boards. If a group is not formed to give advice, then don't call it advisory.

- *Consider not using a formal group at all.* All human beings need advice; we all need and seek counsel regularly. But we rarely seek it from committees or other formal groups. We turn for advice to persons whose experience and expertise we value. Moreover, even if we have a good mix of advisers for a given facet of organization, the same mix will not be optimal for another facet. Using a formal group belies the fluid nature of advice and advisers.

- *Make the advisory body time-limited.* Formal groups, once constituted, are difficult to dissolve even when their purpose has long been completed. Membership on such a group may be considered an honor, so that discontinuance is perceived as taking something away from the participants. Consider announcing a time limit for the group at the outset.

- *The advisory body should advise only one point within the organization.* It is best that an advisory group not advise "the organization" but instead advise one particular position. That position might be the CEO, a staff member, or even the board itself. This specificity enables far greater clarity about the body's role and limits the topics of advice to those within the purview of the advisee.

- *Only the advisee should create and charge advisory groups.* Advisory systems work best when the person wanting advice is in charge. If a higher authority (such as the board, in the case of a committee appointed to

← **FAQ**

Who should create board-to-staff advisory bodies?

(Continued)

advise staff) "owns" the advisory mechanism, the advisee can never be certain the advice is really only advice. This principle is regularly violated by funding bodies that require organizations to have various advisory committees even when the advisees did not ask for the advice. It is also violated routinely by boards that create committees to advise staff. Grown-up staff members can ask whomever they wish for advice; it need not be forced on them by those who have greater power.

- *Advice should not take the advisee off the hook.* If advice is really just advice, then the decision maker must still be accountable for his or her decision.

- *Be sure the advisory body knows what is asked of it.* We have gotten so accustomed to nonprofit and government organizations using advisory bodies as window dressing that advisory groups can fail to demand clarity on the simple questions: Who needs our advice? On what do you want our advice? When do you need it and in what form?

ownership. For a community organization, this might entail groups of community members chosen for their representativeness as a cross section of the population.

Further, the board might ask the advice of fiscal experts as it establishes financial condition or budget policies that will constrain staff actions in these areas. Or the board might form an advisory committee to perform some monitoring task, thereby giving its advice in the form of an opinion of how well the staff has performed with respect to a specific board policy.

Getting advice for a difficult task makes good sense. But organizations have had both inspirational and disastrous experiences in gathering advice. I recommend that boards and staffs keep several tips (see box) in mind while creating, keeping, or disbanding advisory bodies is under consideration.

FAQ ➡

How can staff know that board advice is not actually veiled instruction?

When the board and CEO roles are clear, anyone along the line—without diminishing accountability for their roles—can obtain advice from whatever source is thought to be useful. The board can reach out for advice on the various responsibilities of governing. The CEO can seek advice for parts of the CEO role. Staff members can request advice in their respective jobs. No one directs someone else to receive advice, nor does anyone determine for someone else the form, source, or amount of advice to get.

Giving, Getting, and Governing: Finding a Place for Fundraising Among the Responsibilities of Leadership

BOARD LEADERSHIP, NUMBER 7, MAY-JUNE 1993

" GIVE, GET, OR GET OFF"—so goes a widely repeated articulation of board members' responsibility for finding money. In many nonprofit organizations, the board's *primary* role is thought to be fundraising. In this article, I want to recommend some aspects of governance to keep in mind as your board grapples with the role it will play in finding resources. This article is not about fundraising itself but about the *governance context* in which board fundraising decisions should be made.

My approach to governance (the Policy Governance model) does not include fundraising as one of the board's critical responsibilities. I have often been asked about this "omission." Some people take it as an indication that I discourage fundraising by board members, but the truth is that I fully support board fundraising when the board deems it appropriate for organizational effectiveness.

> Whereas a given board job may or may not include fundraising, that job *always* includes the fundamental elements of governing.

Governance as it is found across a wide variety of organizations does not demand fundraising. School boards, city councils, trade association boards, and a host of other boards cannot escape the task of governing, but this task ordinarily does not include any need to do fundraising. Some boards assume fundraising responsibility only on special occasions, such as when a hospital board seeks to build a new wing. So, whereas a given board job may or may not include fundraising, that job *always* includes the fundamental elements of governing.

These fundamental elements, of course, constitute a model of governance. So the Policy Governance model is not opposed to board fundraising at all; in fact, it provides a place for boards to choose what role, if any, they are to have in fundraising. And there lies the crux: the board must choose. In what way does fundraising fit into your board's tasks? Should your board raise funds or not?

It is important that the staff does not define the board's job; the choice of option must be the board's decision. (Remember that the staff has no right to define the board's job, and the board has no right *not* to define the staff's.) But in order to make a good decision, a board must begin at the beginning. So let's look at considerations that precede any board choice about fundraising.

Governance Comes First

FAQ ➡
What is the board's role in fundraising?

More critical than raising funds is governing an organization *worth raising funds for.* Any governing board's first responsibility is to govern. The board is accountable for what the organization achieves, how its business is conducted, and its destiny. If an organization is superior in what it does and if an additional program opportunity is compelling, then the special effort of fundraising may be warranted. Failing in the first instance leaves the second rather hollow, no matter how diligent the fundraising may be.

A board must carefully consider whether its peculiar circumstances argue for accepting a fundraising responsibility. The board should take into account the kind of organization it represents—a school system, for example, has little need for its board to raise funds. The board would take revenue circumstances into account—for example, an organization with solid funding sources has less need to engage in fundraising than a struggling advocacy group. And special circumstances—such as the need for a new building or endowment—would also have to be considered.

A board's choice to raise funds can be made in response to a staff request, but it will be more meaningful if it is generated from the board itself. A board that raises funds because its staff is persuasive will not have the motivation and success of a board that solicits funds out of its own belief and commitment. Naturally, a board that is intensely involved in mission-related issues is more apt to develop such an informed motivation.

Filling the Dream Gap

Consequently, the first fundraising task for a board is not the fundraising itself. Perhaps a board that, in effect, works for its staff can jump directly into the plans

> More critical than raising funds is governing an organization *worth raising funds for.*

and strategies of pursuing money. But prior to exploring the methods of fundraising, a board primarily committed to governing must make important decisions about the board's *role,* the board's relationship to other relevant actors, the board's *reason* for wanting more funds, and then the *results* to which the board is committed.

What reasons would convince a board to raise funds? How does a board decide whether to get involved in fundraising and how much to set as a goal? I recommend that you *generate your fundraising commitment from what might be called a "dream gap."*

Consider this scenario: In its struggle with ends issues, the board finds that its organization cannot achieve as much as available funds would permit. There is a gap between what the board would want the organization to accomplish and what it will be able to achieve. The board comes face to face with an unavoidable choice and is forced to do something about this dream gap: Reduce the dream, find resources to do more, or do a little of both.

← FAQ

What if a board doesn't have enough resources to meet the needs in the community?

In this way, the board, through its own deliberations, arrives at a carefully considered commitment. The magnitude of the commitment arises from the board's resolution of the dream gap. Because the dream is the board's own, board motivation is optimal. Moreover, the effort is fully integrated with the board's broader intentions about other ends; it is not a single project, disjointed from the whole of intended achievements.

Building Fundraising into Board Activity

Whatever segment of the fundraising task the board decides to take on should be added to its job description. The job description is recorded as a policy in the governance process category of board policies. As the board plans its agendas, its use of energy, and its structure, the job description is the point of departure of its responsibilities. If fundraising is to be part of the board's charge, then it should be formally in the job description.

Fundraising is an activity, not a result. The kind of job description I recommend is one that lists job *outputs* rather than job *activities.* It is better, then, for the board to specify what fundraising output it intends to accomplish. One board engaged in fundraising might seek to produce donor contacts that staff will pursue. Another

> If fundraising is to be part of the board's charge, then it should be formally in the job description.

might choose merely to produce informed board member presence; that is, board members who are informed and available to accompany the CEO or other staff member on donor calls. Still another board might decide to produce an actual amount of dollars. The board's specific output is very different in these examples. Not only do the outputs make very different demands on board members, but their implications for the subsequently derived, complementary staff outputs vary widely.

Cutting across all these distinctions, a board may choose to relate its efforts to one or more types of funds rather than to all. For example, the board might target donor funds, not grant funds, or it might aim for special high-dollar donors rather than the smaller but more numerous ones normally obtained through mail appeal. In any event, the board should clarify all such matters and amend its existing job description with that information.

The most important role differentiation to make is that between the board as a whole and its chief executive. Begin by making these roles clear. Do not start by defining roles for a fundraising committee or a staff director of development. Beginning at the top has two benefits. First, the whole board engages in the deliberation and, consequently, in taking ownership of the task. If a fundraising committee is subsequently formed, it can be more confident that the board as a whole is not going to leave the committee out on a limb by itself. Second, unless board and CEO roles are distinct, delegated derivatives of those roles will never be as distinct as they could be.

> When a board puts the fundraising task before its obligation to govern, it shortchanges beneficiaries and donors alike.

With their roles in order, the board and CEO can delegate to others with far greater clarity. Legitimate board committee jobs must be derived from the role of the board as a body. Similarly, there can be no role for a director of development that is not derived from the role of the CEO. When the board-CEO underpinning is not in place, board members and staff members engaged in fundraising often waste much effort dancing around each other, sometimes stepping on toes unnecessarily, and quite often being less effective than they otherwise would have been.

In summary, a governing board donating or finding funds for its organization is permissible and commendable. Indeed, not doing so would in many cases be poor judgment. But when a board puts the fundraising task before its obligation to govern, it shortchanges beneficiaries and donors alike.

Girl Scout Council Learns What Kind of Help Counts the Most

Board Leadership, Number 1, May-June 1992

THE BOARD of a Girl Scout council asked me for help. It had been struggling to define its job and the roles of its individual board members. Some members felt overworked and burned out; others did not do as much, producing an unevenness that threatened otherwise cordial relationships. The overworked were somewhat disgruntled, but so were the others, because they felt the overworked were simply meddling in staff affairs anyway. Moreover, the board was still not doing as much as it had hoped to create a long-range vision—there was just too much to do and too little time.

This council operates a wide array of scouting services for girls. The board includes a fair proportion of women with years of experience as scout volunteers. They are accustomed to cheerfully seizing any challenge and getting the job done. Using their considerable experience, a number of board members chipped in with many of the tasks of getting the scout job done. The executive director found their involvement to be a mixed blessing. Board members' interest, commitment, and verve were a joy. Their interference in areas already delegated to staff was not.

The executive director had a relatively free hand to manage the paid and volunteer staff. But the *board member* volunteers were, it seemed, a "little more equal" than other volunteers. This produced a ticklish situation for the executive director, affected staff members, and those board members who were sensitive to the issue.

The board as a whole was aware that a problem existed, though it wasn't quite sure what the problem was, exactly. Was the board meddlesome? Was the executive director being overcontrolling? After all, isn't the board accountable for staff actions and, therefore, deserving of a direct path into those actions? And what of the otherwise wasted expertise of board members?

A 2/700ths Contribution?

This was a large organization, as Girl Scout councils go. I invited the board to look with me at the size of its combined paid and adult volunteer staff. Thousands of volunteers do indispensable work for the Girl Scouts, so it was not too surprising when the executive director announced that paid and unpaid staff together added up to 700 full-time equivalent positions.

Volunteering is so loaded with the connotation of helping, that unpaid members of governing boards think they are there to help the staff.

Next, we looked at the board contribution to the organization. The governing board consisted of thirty-two persons. At my request, board members estimated that at most, the average member puts in eight hours of work each month for ten months annually. This counts board and committee meetings as well as preparation for those meetings. That calculation produced 2,560 hours of annual work by the board, considerably less than two full-time positions.

In chipping in to get the job done, the time these board members take away from family, job, and other pleasures might, at best, add 2/700ths to the total effort!

These board volunteers can be conscientious—even overworked—and the real work of the board still not get done. For as they began to realize, the board's gift is not to add 2/700ths but to create an environment in which the 700 can work miracles.

Volunteers Who Govern

This board was and is proud of its volunteer history and its volunteer commitment. In fact, being *volunteers* was the members' primary identity with respect to the Girl Scout mission. To a great extent the language of voluntarism is the problem. We speak of "volunteer boards" as though not being paid is related to the nature of the job. It isn't. We thereby lump all volunteers together, as though *working* volunteers are the same as *governing* volunteers. *Volunteering* is so loaded with the connotation of helping, that unpaid members of governing boards—like my friends with the Girl Scout council—think they are there to help the staff.

They are not there to help the staff; they are there to *govern* the staff. The governing obligation is not so much to assist with the mission as it is to create it. Oh, as individuals, they can surely volunteer their help or their expertise as much as the staff wish to use it. Naturally, it must be clear to board members and staff alike that board members are not wearing their board hats at that

← FAQ

Can board members also volunteer their time in the organization?

time. But construing the board task as one of helping is to risk falling into the 2/700ths trap: It feels productive, it looks conscientious, it is clearly work. But it isn't governing, and it is likely to detract from staff effectiveness rather than enhance it.

This board went beyond our discussion with good humor and a careful redesign of its governing job. The board developed an official statement of its role, which allowed individuals no room to define that role unilaterally. But in the same action, the board allowed and even encouraged individuals to make themselves available to staff as working or advising volunteers. Part of that action was to assure the executive director that while she owed the board her job, she owed individual members only courtesy.

These board members escaped the trap of seeing board "involvement"—even well-meaning and competent involvement—as the issue. The issue is involvement *in the right things*. Now they were ready to commit themselves to a leadership that transforms, not augments, the work of those precious 700.

For Board Discussion

- What are the unique "gifts" (talents, expertise, understandings) the board can bring to your organization—gifts that are either inappropriate or impractical for staff to bring?

- How can you give these gifts so that the board and the staff are both more empowered?

- Will you need more clarity in the various roles?

- If you are understaffed, how can board members offer their help without obscuring the roles?

Board Members as Amateur CEOs

BOARD LEADERSHIP, NUMBER 53, JAN.-FEB. 2001

Much of contemporary governance practice seems based on a board role of helping management manage. Let's have a finance committee help with financial management, a human resource committee help with personnel issues, and a program committee help with program design. No wonder so few boards get around to doing the one job for which they exist: to *govern* with a long-term perspective on behalf of the true ownership so that their organizations achieve what they should while avoiding unacceptable situations and actions.

> **FAQ** ➡
>
> Why shouldn't the board help its staff manage?

"Helping management manage" is a misnomer. When a body as authoritative as a governing board "helps" its subordinates, this is a very special form of assistance indeed. One might say that the board is foisting help on its staff, for they are hardly in a position to refuse it. The better part of valor on staff's part is to pretend that board help is helpful whether it is or not. Sometimes, of course, help from the board really is helpful due to the specific skills involved and the personalities of the helping board members. But the board will have a hard time telling the difference, for the power differential makes it impossible to be sure.

Robert Greenleaf, of servant-leadership fame, stood firmly against board members volunteering to participate in staff activities in any way. I have been a bit more flexible on the issue but have warned that board or board member help and advice to staff is risky and is a responsible thing to do only when steps have been taken to make confusion of roles virtually impossible. I have described how those steps should be taken. But protective steps or not, the underlying belief that sets boards on such a risky course seems to be this: They think they know how to manage better than their managers do.

That is a curious belief.

Pension fund boards govern huge amounts of money, employing highly trained analysts and investment specialists to do the real work. When pension fund boards, like boards of all sorts, start participating in management decisions (a kind way to say meddling or micromanaging), they would do well to ponder this simple question: Who would hire any one of the board members to be his or her personal financial advisor?

> The better part of valor on staff's part is to pretend that board help is helpful whether it is or not.

Public school boards are notorious for intruding into the running of the schools. Inappropriate trustee meddling in the school system's finances, personnel, teaching methods, and building maintenance is not simply a flawed practice but by now an institutionalized way of doing business. Yet which one of the school board members in your community could ever be responsibly hired to be chief executive officer (often called superintendent or director of education)?

Which credit union board member can successfully manage a credit union? Which hospital board member is skilled enough to run a hospital? The list goes on, but I've made my point. Board members have substantial accountability for organizational success, but that accountability is poorly discharged when they default on their own job in favor of helping management with its job.

The problem, of course, is that traditional governance ideas and practices have not helped boards differentiate clearly between *governing* and *managing* an organization. Even at this late date, there are still writers who say it can't be done anyway—governance and management are a partnership, a team effort,

> Inappropriate trustee meddling is not simply a flawed practice but by now an institutionalized way of doing business.

with roles springing up as personalities and circumstances shift. Funny, the sports teams I'm familiar with have rigidly defined roles. A baseball team run like a lot of governance pundits teach would confuse first base and left field positions, and teams would become mobs. To paraphrase former President Jimmy Carter, what governance needs is the moral equivalent of baseball.

Traditional governance ideas and practices have not helped boards differentiate clearly between *governing* and *managing* an organization.

Soldiers in the field don't need generals to get into the foxholes with them. Soldiers in the field need generals to act like generals. Generals make far bigger decisions with longer time horizons than infantry in foxholes. That doesn't mean generals are better, just that they have a different job for which we truly hope they are qualified. And a fast way for a general to show lack of qualification is to be more involved in foxhole tactics than in determining how to win the war.

Board members who are more interested in the bits and pieces of management can be very talented and productive—but not on the governing board. They should get off the board—or be forced off if necessary—and get a job on the staff or volunteer to help the staff, if managers decide they have the qualifications.

Chapter Twelve

Policy Governance for Specific Audiences

While the Policy Governance model is a system of universal governance principles, its application in different types of organizations requires language appropriate to each setting and sensitivity to special circumstances. With no change in the fundamental paradigm, the model fits easily into business corporations, federations, holding companies, city government, public education, and other environments. This chapter includes a selection of articles each addressed specifically to a single setting.

Remaking Governance

AMERICAN SCHOOL BOARD JOURNAL, VOLUME 187, ISSUE 3, MARCH 2000

THE FAMILIAR—even cherished—practices of school boards are strangling public education. Most of what school boards currently do is a travesty of their important role. Much of what is published for boards—including advice appearing regularly in these pages—reinforces errors of the past or, at best, teaches trustees how to do the wrong things better. In my opinion, school boards don't need improvement so much as total redesign. And they are not alone in this predicament, for governance is the least-developed function in all enterprises.

Preparing people for contributing, satisfying adulthood is worth the most effective governance a board can achieve. If school boards must completely reinvent themselves to be worthy of their mission—as I'm convinced they must—then so be it. If that means much of current board training must be discarded—as I'm convinced it must—then let it be done. No role deserves transformation more than that of the nation's school boards.

A New Governance Model

For two decades I have studied and taught governance—the process by which a small group, usually on behalf of others, exercises authority over an organization. I have found that although boards work hard to solve practical problems as they arise, the crucial missing element is credible theory. The Policy Governance model of board leadership that emerged from my work is arguably the only existing complete theory of governance, whether of businesses, nonprofits, cities, or schools. Its philosophical foundations lie in Jean-Jacques Rousseau's social contract, leadership philosopher Robert K. Greenleaf's servant-leadership, and modern management theory.

The model redesigns what it means to be a board, challenging other approaches as founded more on anecdotal wisdom than good theory. A tightly reasoned paradigm, the model must be used in total to achieve its promise of greater accountability. Partial implementation sacrifices the model's benefits, for it is a complete, logical system, not merely tips for improvement.

Using this new paradigm requires a school board to exercise uncharacteristic self-discipline, but it enables the board to govern the system, rather than run it; to define and demand educational results rather than poke and probe in educational and administrative processes; to redirect time from trivia and ritual actions to strategic leadership; to give a superintendent one boss rather than several; to grant administrators and educators great latitude within explicit boundaries; to be in charge of board agendas instead of dependent on staff; and to guarantee unbroken accountability from classroom to taxpayer.

Space here does not allow full explication of Policy Governance. I can, however, list seven characteristics that differentiate this model from governance as now widely practiced and taught.

1. *Primacy of the owner-representative role.* The board directly touches three elements of the "chain of command": the general public, the board itself, and the superintendent. Although the succession of authority within the system is best left to the superintendent, the board must maintain the integrity of the initial three elements. Let's consider the first link in that chain.

The board's primary relationship is with those to whom it is accountable—the general public, the "shareholders" of public education. The board is the public's purchasing agent for the educational product. The public-board relationship supersedes the board's relationship with everyone else.

The central task of a board is to assimilate the diverse values of those who own the system, to add any special knowledge (often obtained from experts, including staff), then to make decisions on behalf of the owners. The formal link from owners to trustees is the election process—a tight link with respect to a trustee holding office, but a very loose link with respect to knowing the public's mind. Typically, boards rely on open meetings, public hearings, and constituent phone calls for the bulk of public input. These methods not only fail to fulfill the board's obligation to connect with the owners, they are misleading in that the "public" is self-selected and typically expresses not its owner role, but its customer, vendor, or operator role. Boards rarely hear from a representative sampling of owners. Because the general public is so large, a continual system of focus groups, surveys, and advisory mechanisms is required to achieve even a semblance of fulfilling the board's owner-representative role. The time is overdue for putting the public back into public education.

Cultivating a principal-agent relationship between the public and the board holds great promise for the position of education in society, but this relationship has been impaired by decades of conventional practice. For example, boards promote an inappropriate direct link from public to superintendent. This connection circumvents the board's role as sole owner-representative and lets the board off the hook for poor system performance. If

> **← FAQ**
>
> Is it fair to blame poor school performance on the school superintendent?

the public can blame poor school performance on the superintendent, then the fact that it is the board that has let the public down might go unnoticed. Making the hiring of a superintendent into an affair of high-profile community involvement is part of this same aberration. Superintendents are instruments of the board, not of the public. The public's instrument is the board.

Another mistake is behaving as if parents are the system's owners and that the board is their representative. Boards historically have shortcut the owner-board-organization-customer circuit, partly because parents are the most vocal subgroup of owners, and partly because they are fewer and easier to identify than the true ownership. Consequently, both politics and logistics induce boards to act as if parents own the system. Parents might resist losing any part of this role, but public policy (and, in the long run, parents and students) will

> Superintendents are instruments of the board, not of the public. The public's instrument is the board.

benefit by facing the fact that parents, *as parents,* do not own the public schools. Parents are owners by virtue of being part of the public, but they constitute only a percentage, not the whole. The same is true of teachers, administrators, and the media.

This is not denigrate the importance of parents. Parents and their children are customers-consumers of the system and, as such, are no less important and no less to be courted and pleased than customers of any other enterprise. Nor does this formulation minimize the central role of parents in their children's education. In fact, failing to give parents an integral role in the educational process would be unconscionable.

2. *One voice from plural trustees.* Trustees have authority only as a full board—but few boards behave accordingly. Staff members take instructions from and answer to

Parents, *as parents,* do not own the public schools. Parents are owners by virtue of being part of the public, but they constitute only a percentage, not the whole.

individual trustees and board committees. Individual trustees judge staff performance on criteria the board as a body has never stated. Superintendents seek to keep individual trustees happy quite apart from fulfilling board requirements. Trustees enjoy getting things "fixed" for constituents. There is often unspoken agreement that "you can meddle in your district if you'll let me meddle in mine." It is not enough to dismiss these phenomena as simply politics and personalities. Whether the board intends it or not, the realpolitik of school systems demonstrates regularly that staff members do, in fact, take direction from individual trustees.

FAQ ➡

Can staff safely ignore advice and instructions from individual school board trustees?

If a board seriously intends to speak with only one voice, it must declare that the staff can safely ignore advice and instructions from individual trustees, that only the explicit instructions of the board must be heeded. Excellence in governance will not occur until superintendents are certain that trustees *as a group* will protect them from trustees *as individuals.*

Commitment to the authoritative unity of the board in no way compromises board members' right to speak their minds. Vigorous disagreement among trustees does not damage governance, but allowing intraboard skirmishes to affect the staff is irresponsible. In short, trustees who disagree with the vote may continue to say so, but may not influence organizational direction. It is in boards' interest that superintendents treat a five–four vote as a nine–zero vote.

3. *The superintendent as a real chief executive officer.* Boards frequently give direction to subordinates of the superintendent, degrading the chief executive role and the board's own ability to hold the superintendent accountable. Only if the board expresses its aims for the system as a whole—rather than part by part—can the powerful utility of the chief executive role be harnessed, simultaneously simplifying accountability and saving board time.

In other words, the superintendent is the only person the board instructs and the only person the board evaluates. The superintendent should be authorized to use any reasonable interpretation of instructions the board gives. This requires the board to take full responsibility for its words and enables the superintendent to take the board at its word.

4. *Authoritative prescription of "ends."* The board's greatest and most difficult responsibility is to clarify and reclarify why the system exists. This requires the board

to be both proactive and authoritative—to define expected results for students and to demand system performance. The public is buying specifiable results for specifiable groupings of students at specifiable costs or priorities.

Informed obsession with the system's "ends"—that is, results, recipients, and cost

> Excellence in governance will not occur until superintendents are certain that trustees *as a group* will protect them from trustees *as individuals.*

of results—should be the dominant work of the board. Involvement in curriculum, special reading initiatives, or testing programs will not suffice. To the contrary, holding a system accountable is impeded by board involvement in these and other internal processes. Instead of demanding ends performance, boards routinely fail to describe the ends and then intervene in what they're hired professionals to do. No amount of telling people how to run the system can substitute for simply demanding designated results and getting out of their way.

5. *Bounded freedom for "means."* Boards struggle with the dilemma of being accountable for others' work. Control is necessary, but so is empowerment. Authority not given away does little good, but too much given away constitutes rubber-stamping or dereliction. How can the board have its arms around the system without its fingers in it?

> **← FAQ**
>
> How can a school board be accountable for the performance of a school district without becoming involved in the details of its management?

If ends expectations are met (right results, right recipients, right costs or priorities), the "means"—that is, other decisions, such as methods, practices, and conduct—must have worked. So the board does not have to control means prescriptively. In fact, to tell staff how to accomplish ends impedes creativity and innovation. Why does the board need to control means at all? Because not all means are justified by the ends—some means would be unacceptable even if they work. The achievement of ends demonstrates that means are effective, but it doesn't prove that means are acceptable.

To address the acceptability of means, the board need only define the boundaries of acceptability. The board limits the superintendent's latitude regarding certain situations, activities, or risk. In effect, the board does not tell the system how to operate, but how *not* to—an approach that is simpler and safer for the board and freeing for the staff. The message from board to superintendent, then, is, "Achieve these ends within these restrictions on means." This instruction embraces the whole of board-staff delegation, which is to say, the superintendent's job description.

6. *Board decisions crafted by descending size.* There is no way the board can determine every result for every child and the cost appropriate for that result. Similarly, it is impossible to state every unacceptable action or situation. So what prevents the seemingly simple protocol of prescribing ends and proscribing means from deteriorating into maddening detail?

Boards must manage the sequence of different sizes of decisions. First, the board defines ends and unacceptable means in as broad a way as possible. For example, the broadest version of ends might be, "Students acquire skills and understandings for successful life at a tax rate comparable to that of similar districts." The broadest version of means limitation might be, "Don't allow anything imprudent or unethical." This is broad indeed—which is to say it is open to a wide range of interpretation. If the board were willing to allow the superintendent to use any reasonable interpretation of these words, the board could stop with these two short instructions.

> Authority not given away does little good, but too much given away constitutes rubber-stamping or dereliction.

But no board would allow that. Instead, the board must define a bit more, perhaps adding, "Don't allow assets to be unnecessarily risked or inadequately maintained," along with similarly narrowed prohibitions about personnel treatment, compensation systems, parental involvement, and so forth. As to ends, the board might augment its initial, broad statement with, "Students will be literate above age-level expectations." This is also too broad for most boards, so the next step is to define still further. The process continues step-by-step into more detail until the majority of trustees are willing to accept any reasonable interpretation of the words used to that point. At this level the board stops and superintendent authority begins.

7. *System-focused superintendent evaluation.* The only reason to have a chief executive officer is to ensure system performance. Consequently, board expectations of the system (ends and limits on means) are the *only* criteria on which a superintendent should be assessed. The board actually evaluates the entire system (not the superintendent personally) and "pins it" on the superintendent. Most discussions of superintendent evaluation—including articles in recent issues of *ASBJ*—miss the power of this simplicity, falling back on such nonperformance, personalized irrelevancies as "leads by example" and "proficient in educational thinking." It is archaic and spurious to evaluate a superintendent on anything other than whether the system produces and operates as it should. It is *system performance* for which the board is accountable to the public.

Annual board approval of the superintendent's objectives is another testimony to poor governance. If the superintendent accomplishes the board's expectations, it is immaterial whether he or she achieves his or her own as well. Typically, boards have not expressed system expectations sufficiently to enable recognition of success and failure on their own. In the Policy Governance model, ends to be achieved and means disallowed embrace all the board's expectations. Moreover, they are targeted at system accountability, unaffected by how a given superintendent retains or delegates the various elements of management.

Monitoring data are reviewed throughout the year, as frequently as the board chooses. Because these data directly address performance on ends and means limitations, they constitute a continual evaluation of the superintendent. Although there might also be a summative annual evaluation, the criterion-focused monitoring system is the most direct measure of superintendent performance—a seamless process through time rather than a sporadic event.

This comparison of reality to expectations must be fair as well as uncompromising. Trustees should not judge the superintendent's performance on criteria the board has never stated. Expectations not incorporated into the board's ends or means limitations cannot be admitted into evaluative monitoring. Further, "any reasonable interpretation" of the board's expectations must mean just that—not the interpretation of the most influential trustee or what the board had in mind but didn't say.

> The board does not tell the system how to operate, but how *not* to—an approach that is simpler and safer for the board and freeing for the staff.

What It Looks Like

What does the public see the board doing differently under Policy Governance? The board gets out of the superintendent's job and takes responsibility for its own job. Because agendas are no longer staff-driven, board meetings are the *board's* meetings—not the staff's meetings for the board. The steady stream of documents for approval disappears from the regular agenda due to more sophisticated delegation. (Criteria that would have led to disapprovals are known and monitored, so the "approval syndrome" becomes inconsistent with proper delegation. The consent agenda is reserved for decisions the board would delegate, but on which law requires board action.) Freed from endless crowding of its

FAQ

What would a school board meeting look like under Policy Governance?

The board gets out of the superintendent's job and takes responsibility for its own job.

---

agenda by managerial material, the board does its own work instead of pretending that looking over the superintendent's shoulder *is* its work.

Board meetings are not characterized by shoot-from-the-hip instructions to the superintendent, much less to the staff. Board meetings are not to help manage the system, nor to go over operational details. The board no longer struggles through extensive reports unrelated to preestablished criteria. It has learned that what it previously thought was monitoring was merely wandering around in the presence of data.

Board meetings are not parent and vendor complaint meetings. Any system in which customer complaints must go to the board for resolution is poorly designed. (Envision having to take your cold hamburger to the fast food chain's board.) On the contrary, the board expects the superintendent to have parents taken care of as courteously and effectively as possible. If a parent problem gets to the board, it is considered symptomatic of a system flaw rather than an opportunity for trustee involvement. Parents get their say in the way the system affects their children, but not by supplanting the owners' meetings.

Most board committees disappear. If a board has committees, it does so only for help with *its* job—never to help, advise, or instruct staff, lest it destroy the clarity of delegation. The board does not believe that the kind of internal involvement described in an article about board committees in a recent issue of *ASBJ* is related to governing the system. For a board committee to focus on staff activities is probably the most intrusive of board practices and the most wasteful of staff and trustee time.

FAQ ➡

How does a board member deal with constituency expectations?

Liberated from hours of preoccupation with system operations, trustees have more time to meet with community groups, other public boards, and pertinent authorities. Raising its visibility as a governmental leader, the board demonstrates its focus on ends and its long-term perspective by the language it uses, questions it asks, and topics it schedules. Joint meetings with city councils, hospital boards, social service boards, and other organs of the public become commonplace.

Board meetings are spent learning diverse points of view on what is most important for schools to produce, differing projections of future needs of students, and any other wisdom that helps in making wise long-term decisions about ends. The public is integral to these meetings, but carefully organized so the board gets representative input.

Many board meetings are not meetings in the usual sense at all, but take place in community settings where certain segments of the public can be heard. Wherever the meeting, the atmosphere is tailored for listening and entering into dialogue. Board meetings are places of thoughtful dialogue and debate rather than the trivia that commonly besets conventional agendas.

Through focus groups, the board assesses public values about priorities and costs of educational products. This is not a sporadic or single-purpose effort, but an unending process. These carefully planned interactions are not for public relations, but for the dual purpose of enhancing board understanding and reinforcing the public's sense of ownership of its schools. Trustees are perceived as the public's servant-leaders in the great challenge of preparing citizens for a democracy.

What Schools Are For

The critical role of education in a democracy demands exceptional governance integrity. Commitment and intelligence cannot overcome our institutionalized hodge-podge of traditional practices. Conscientious, detailed preoccupation with what schools *do* can never compensate for failing to define clearly what schools are *for,* then demanding system performance from a chief executive officer. Visionary leadership is not forged in a flurry of

> The critical role of education in a democracy demands exceptional governance integrity.

trivia, micromanagement, and administrative detail. If school boards are not the place for serious, perpetual community debate of how much this generation is willing to pay for which skills and understandings of the next generation, what other place does the public have?

Earlier, in illustrating flaws of conventional wisdom, I cited two articles from previous issues of *ASBJ.* I'll close by quoting a refreshing article ("Changing the Entitlement Culture," Paul McGowen and John Miller) in the August 1999 issue. "The challenge is for leaders to change the culture. . . . It is time for public school leaders to seize the initiative." If there is to be renaissance of public education, it will begin when boards discard the conceptually incoherent practices of today for a public leadership founded on sound governance theory.

Toward Coherent Governance

THE SCHOOL ADMINISTRATOR, VOLUME 57, ISSUE 3, MARCH 2000

T HE CHIEF EXECUTIVE OFFICER'S role in public education is one of the key managerial responsibilities in a free society. The long list of stressors on public education and, in particular, on the chief executive are well known. Yet many today would argue that the most destructive stress for superintendents is their relationship with their board of education.

Working for a board can be harmful to one's health, as the longevity of superintendents may indicate, in part because boards are the least disciplined, least rational and most disordered element in any school system. The board is, in fact, the weakest link in the educational system. It seems obvious that administrators and teachers know their jobs immeasurably better than boards know theirs.

> Boards are the least disciplined, least rational, and most disordered element in any school system.

I have seen firsthand the damage done to the CEO role and to superintendents personally by board behavior we have come to accept as normal. School governance is fraught with the ironic combination of micromanagement *and* rubber-stamping, as well as an array of tradition-blessed practices hat trivialize the board's important public policy role. (My criticism of boards is not an argument for direct state control; in fact, much of the inanity in school governance is *caused* by states' Byzantine requirements.) Any superintendent in the country can recite horror stories of wayward and destructive actions by even prominent school boards.

But school governance is not alone in this befuddled state. Governance in all fields is woefully behind management in conceptual development and useful paradigms. Having dedicated, intelligent persons on boards does not correct the inadequacy, for the fundamental problem is one of process rather than people.

> My criticism of boards is not an argument for direct state control; in fact, much of the inanity in school governance is *caused* by states' requirements.

The concepts and practices of governance are hobbled together more by historical accident than by design. Management had much the same history until the acceleration of management study and particularly management theory in this century. Boards of business corporations, nonprofits, and governmental organizations have lacked a theory of governance compelling enough to provide a framework for board decision making, process, structure, and general behavior.

By a theory of governance, I mean a conceptually coherent paradigm with both managerial and public policy respectability. My own model, known as Policy Governance, is arguably the world's only existing theory of governance applicable to all governing boards. The model requires as much discipline of boards to be strategic and visionary leaders and imposes a set of carefully crafted principles to distinguish board decisions from managerial and professional ones. Because it is a conceptually coherent paradigm, the model differs radically from governance promoted for years by the National School Boards Association and other sources of conventional wisdom.

> Governance in all fields is woefully behind management in conceptual development and useful paradigms.

Wide-Ranging Effects

Because Policy Governance has become relatively familiar, having been described in more than 150 publications, including *Boards That Make a Difference,* this examination looks specifically at how this approach affects superintendents of schools. Let me precede a summary of those effects, however, by noting a few salient features of the model:

- Governance is seen as a specialized form of ownership rather than a specialized form of management. That is, the board is more identified with the general public than with the staff and more akin to the phenomenon of owning than of operating. Hence, a school board does not exist to

← FAQ

Whose job is it to run schools and the school system?

run a school system but on behalf of those who "own" the system to govern those who do.

- The board *as a body* is vested with governing authority so that measures to preclude trustees from exercising individual authority are crucial to governance integrity. This means that instructions and advice of individual trustees do not have to be heeded by staff. The board, however, exercises strong control, albeit control carefully couched in documents crafted especially for governance precision.

- The board, on behalf of the public, specifies the nature and cost of consumer results ("ends"). This constitutes a careful description of the educational product— what results with whom is the public purchasing at what cost. The board does not specify the methods and activities ("means") required in system operation.

- The board outlines boundaries of acceptability, within which the superintendent and staff are permitted free choice of means. Hence, maximum creativity, innovation, and decentralization are allowed without giving away the shop. The proscription of unacceptable means tells the superintendent how *not* to operate rather than how to operate.

- The board monitors performance on ends and unacceptable means in a systematic and rigorous way. Because the board treats the superintendent as a true chief executive officer, all accountability for ends and unacceptable means rests upon the superintendent alone. For example, the board would not hold the chief financial officer accountable for poor accounting, but the superintendent.

> Governance is seen as a specialized form of ownership rather than a specialized form of management.

- Board meetings are spent largely in learning about, debating, and resolving long-term ends issues rather than dealing with otherwise delegable matters. The consent agenda is used for those items that should be delegated to the superintendent, but upon which the law requires board action. Consequently, unless law directs otherwise, nothing goes on the board's agenda that does not require the working of board wisdom.

In short, the school board neither rubber-stamps nor meddles. It does not give up control of the system, but chooses what to control and what not to control according to carefully derived principles. The board is better able to hold the superintendent's feet to the fire while, at the same time, granting more superintendent authority to manage. Consequently, the environment in which a superintendent plays the CEO role is vastly different from conventional circumstances.

However, because Policy Governance has gained a measure of popularity, more boards profess to use it today than actually do, so my comments apply only when a board actually sticks to the concepts of the model. (While it is designed as a universal governance theory, parts of the paradigm divorced from the integrated whole can be nonsensical or even dangerous. Precision systems work poorly when partially used.)

A New Way of Life

How different life would be for a superintendent whose board faithfully complies with principles of the Policy Governance model. Consider the ways:

The superintendent would not be responsible for governance. Under Policy Governance, the board is solely responsible for describing and fulfilling its own job. The superintendent is used as a valuable resource, but always to assist the board in its responsibility rather than even subtly to assume that responsibility. This differs from the widespread expectation for superintendents to assume more responsibility for good board operation than the board does.

For example, while standard rhetoric touts boards as strategic leaders, superintendents are expected to tell boards what to talk about (that is, to supply agenda content). Superintendents often have been criticized for not bringing their boards together, as if it is proper for a subordinate to be held accountable for behavior of the superior.

Board meetings come to be truly the board's meetings rather than the superintendent's meetings for the board. Whereas the content of superintendent-fed agendas is understandably managerial in nature, the content of governance-driven agendas can be of a far higher order. Board meetings that consist largely of warmed-over administrative issues are a waste of both board and staff time. Yet in the absence of knowing what it should talk about, the ordinary school board has nothing on which to focus except decisions its staff is likely better equipped to address than it is.

The board doesn't run the schools. The school board does not compete with administrators in running the schools. The board's job is not to run schools at all, but to determine as the public's purchasing agent what the public is buying for the next generation. With the board playing this role, a superintendent might well be faced with tougher performance expectations, but he or she gets to be superintendent without having to battle board members for that position.

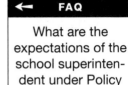

← FAQ

What are the expectations of the school superintendent under Policy Governance?

The board, instead, takes on the difficult job of determining what results should be obtained, for which classes of learners, at what cost, as well as setting the boundaries of ethics and prudence within which the system must operate. Having described, in effect, what the system is for, the board can largely leave to qualified staff what the system does.

From the superintendent's perspective, wide latitude is available without having to run the gauntlet of board approvals. Choosing administrative and programmatic means to achieve the expected student performance is left to the superintendent, so long as the system operates within ethics and prudence boundaries set by the board. Within this wide latitude, the superintendent and the superintendent's delegates decide tables of organization, job designs, teaching methods, and a host of other factors of production.

FAQ ➡️

Whom does the
school superinten-
dent work for—
the board or
the public?

The superintendent has one boss, not several. A board that chooses to give public education the governance integrity it deserves makes clear that the superintendent need never heed the demands of individual trustees, though instructions of the board are mandatory. In effect, the board as a body protects its superintendent from the board as individuals. This removes much of the political, interpersonal pressures to which superintendents are normally sacrificed. Speaking with one voice does not require trustee unanimity, but it clearly requires discipline—though no more than that required to teach math or keep the buses running.

Because the board accepts its role as owner-representative, the superintendent works for the board, not for the public. Of course, the superintendent works for the public in the same sense an army sergeant serves his or her country, but there is no doubt the sergeant's direct responsibility is to the officer in charge to interpret what that country wants.

> Speaking with one voice does not require trustee unanimity, but it clearly requires discipline.

For the superintendent, this means that it is the board's job, not the superintendent's, to resolve the powerful conflicting desires of the public. In some ways, the superintendent becomes a less important public figure as the board becomes more responsible. Any practice that obscures the public-board-superintendent chain of command robs governance of its integrity and misconstrues the superintendent's job. If the school board uses the Policy Governance model, it, not the superintendent, struggles with the public.

Define-and-demand control replaces poke-and-probe. In Policy Governance, the board expects much of the superintendent, but only on criteria the board previously has established in writing. The board will not allow the superintendent to be judged against expectations the board as a body has not set forth. Therefore, the superintendent need never be worried about being blindsided or about keeping individual trustees happy. He or she is able to

> If the school board uses the Policy Governance model, it, not the superintendent, struggles with the public.

put single-minded effort toward those indices of system performance the board has soberly and deliberately established.

Poking and probing into administrative and programmatic matters is a common counterfeit of responsible board stewardship. Boards typically exhibit the poke-and-probe behavior about budgets, plans, projects, curricula, and any other segment of school life that interests them. Leadership, however, calls for defining carefully considered expectations and demanding their accomplishment.

Poking and probing is far easier to do and gives the appearance of conscientious examination. Consequently, boards go over fiscal or other reports in great detail—with inexhaustible points of inspection—rendering or implying judgments of staff performance without having established criteria upon which these judgments are made. Not only does this behavior subject the superintendent to criteria never stated, but because the probing is done one trustee at a time, the unstated criteria are not even the board's but those of single board members. This focus on group criteria does not prevent individual board members from access to information unrelated to board criteria, but it does prevent their making judgments of superintendent performance based on that information.

The superintendent is a true chief executive. School boards often treat their superintendents like either clerks or dictators. Dealing with them as CEOs requires a clear understanding that the board is in charge, yet an equal appreciation for staying out of the superintendent's job.

While this approach allows the superintendent a great deal of latitude, it prevents the superintendent from using "reverse delegation" to avoid decisions. It burdens the superintendent with full accountability for system performance. Good governance saves a superintendent from board members' whims, but not from the board's corporate expectations—expectations expressed largely in terms of ends related to student achievement.

The board delegates to no one in the system but the superintendent. There is no board instruction to associate superintendents, to financial officers, or to principals. The board does not circumvent its chief executive, aware that to do so destroys the board's ability to hold the superintendent fully accountable for system performance.

Board committees are out of the way. As part of treating the superintendent as a CEO, the board does not create committees to help or advise in management of the system. While it is permissible for the board to create committees to help with parts of its own job, to create official organs of the board to get involved in staff issues interferes with appropriate superintendent prerogatives. To do so breaks the board's obligation to speak with one voice and impedes the carefully crafted freedom given by the board to the superintendent. Board committees on human resources, curriculum, and other management issues disappear.

Although this frees superintendents from the interference of board committees, it also means that superintendents no longer can disguise management choices by manipulating a committee process.

FAQ ➡

Why does the school superintendent's job exist?

Superintendent evaluation is rigorous but fair. The superintendent has a job only so that the board can ensure system performance—that is, ends are achieved and unacceptable means are avoided. The board governs the system, not the superintendent. The board's expectations are of the system, not of the superintendent.

In the long run, who the superintendent is and what the superintendent does is unimportant compared to the system's effect on students, fiscal prudence, and other elements of the board's policies on ends-and-means limitations. Therefore superintendent accountability is defined in terms of system performance, not some additional, personal set of requirements.

To fulfill its own accountability to the public, the board must evaluate whether the system is performing satisfactorily. But while the board's primary interest is not in evaluating the superintendent, the superintendent's CEO role is a convenient managerial device to fulfill the board's system focus.

The device that gives rise to proper superintendent evaluation is simply this: The board evaluates the system, then pins that evaluation on the superintendent. In short, ongoing monitoring of system performance against the board's stated expectations *is* the superintendent's evaluation.

It should be noted that the evaluation is driven by what the board has determined ahead of time the system should produce and avoid, not by a list of the superintendent's objectives for the year. The superintendent, in fact, will have personal objectives as any CEO would. But those are immaterial to the board as long as the board's expectations are met.

The superintendent works for a worthy boss. The chief occupation of the board under Policy Governance is an engagement with the long-term future of education rather than the petty, month-by-month inspection of (or worse, participation in) current operations. Agendas reflect the struggle with fundamental public values affecting the system rather than review and rehash of administrative issues.

For a superintendent, this circumstance can be the joy of having a boss truly qualified and deserving to be the boss rather than an undisciplined body needing to be stage-managed. Such a board takes its servant-leadership role seriously and expects its superintendent to do so as well. A high-integrity governance model plus the discipline to stick to it are necessary ingredients for governance excellence.

Sound Theory

Better governance of public education will save superintendents from having to do the board's work, but this means as well that boards cannot *allow* superintendents to do the boards' work. Only when the practices of boards of education are built on a sound conceptual foundation will the opportunity and demand for superintendents to perform their proper chief executive role be realized.

School governance, now caught in a hodgepodge of traditional practices and hobbled by antiquated state laws and regulations, is a perfect exemplar for psychologist Kurt Lewin's observation that there is nothing so practical as a good theory.

Partnership for Public Service

PREPARED FOR THE ONTARIO MINISTRY OF COMMUNITY AND SOCIAL SERVICES, MAY 1992

ACCOUNTABILITY for publicly funded social services is long sought and overdue. This paper argues for substantial change in both the philosophy and pragmatics of social service accountability. It places particular emphasis on ministerial leadership over services funded by provincial dollars, but delivered by independent nonprofit corporations and municipal governments.

Provincial funding of local services engages a number of important and even emotional issues for Ontarians: The need for special attention to taxpayer concerns, given the present economic climate of Ontario. The need by local communities to determine as much as possible of their own destiny and quality of life, particularly when the services pie is contracting rather than expanding. The obligation of ministry staff to create a high-quality array of human services as viewed from a province-wide perspective. The desire for employment stability and creative opportunity for professionals operating in local organizations.

The Intention of Partnership

The ministry has clearly stated its intention to act as much in partnership with localities as its accountability to the entire province will allow. No one need pretend that this partnership is an equal one with respect to resources and power. The nature of this partnership will in the final analysis be defined more in the actions of the partners than in any written material. The ministry will demonstrate how much it really values consultation, input, critique, local initiative, and clear expectations. Provider organizations will demonstrate how much they are willing to participate assertively in effective planning, avoid any vestiges of the victim role, and take responsibility for innovatively achieving results.

One requirement of this partnership is that the ministry and local organizations recognize and remain true to their respective accountabilities. To wit, the ministry is accountable to a province-wide constituency, the local provider to a local constituency. And although everyone involved is a resident both of Ontario and of some locality, each part is obliged to honor these respective "hats" at their appropriate time. No definition of partnership can release the parties from the trusteeship they inherit as an integral part of these roles.

The Economic Context

These are not times of expanding funding for social services. If anything, provincial and community officials face the more difficult choices of what to cut and, thereby, which very real human needs to sacrifice. So evolving concepts of accountability are not accompanied by the "sweetener" of new money, but by the stress of retrenchment. It is possible, then, that the promise of change can be sullied by problems which arise due not to the emerging partnership, but to the independent issue of austerity. Both ministry and local personnel would be well-advised to pay explicit attention to keeping these matters separate, lest strategies and disagreements become diffuse and entangled.

It is also a matter of question whether provincial dollars will buy more or less service through contract agencies than through direct ministry programs. While it seems that false expectations have not been raised about savings and service volumes, care must always be taken so that unjustified expectations do not later soil what are otherwise good results.

But in a larger sense, the obligation to choose carefully the uses to which tax funds are put is not an obligation created by the current economics of Ontario. The accountability to select priorities with great care is the case at any time, though in times of austerity the pain of such choices is greater. The ministry should establish a system of priority setting which is not tied to today's climate, but to the demand for long-term quality in government. Consequently, to the extent partnership is defined by the method through which the ministry buys service, it should be perceived as a permanent component, not one which can be relaxed when times are better.

The Philosophical Dilemma

In the face of a commitment to optimum local latitude, the separate accountabilities present a philosophical dilemma for the ministry. The ministry is accountable to the Ontario taxpayer to make wise purchases with scarce tax funds. By passing provincial money to a provider agency, the ministry chooses to purchase from a vendor rather than to create the service itself. Fundamentally, this choice does not differ from the classic industrial make-or-buy decision. At this level of analysis, the ministry simply determines that buying the output is more economical, auspicious, uncomplicated, or otherwise a more rational choice than employing personnel directly and overseeing their work.

But in an important social sense, the process is very different from a simple make-or-buy decision. An important element in the psychology of empowerment is the ability to make one's own choices, to affect those forces which impact on one's life. Taxpayer wishes and social needs differ from one locality to another. Part of the social belief in Ontario is that these local prerogatives should be impeded as little as possible. Yet by their very nature, they differ from provincial wishes and needs since the latter is an "average" of all Ontario localities.

Were it not for the need to maximize local self-determination, the ministry could determine (perhaps even with extensive input) what is needed across the province and simply buy that output. Government might, for example, determine that a highway from Kenora to Thunder Bay is needed with a certain load capacity and expected lifetime. The appropriate ministry would establish the engineering specifications and contract with a construction firm to build the highway. Specifications would detail the nature of the product so closely that ministry personnel could know quite precisely what they are buying and whether the product is successfully delivered.

But community and social services differ from a highway in that local determination is considered much more important. The ministry wants to build the equivalent of a highway, but encourages the local community to determine the nature of the highway. Immediately upon passing that kind of authority to the locality, the ministry risks abandoning its own accountability to the provincial taxpayer. For there is no longer the detailed specificity in what is being bought with provincial tax dollars.

The only justification which the ministry can make to provincial taxpayers is that the local purchase was good value for the dollar and that what was purchased was determined by local people in some fair forum. It likely is *not* justifiable that (a) money is squandered or inefficiently spent by the locality, or (b) what the money buys is decided by an agency executive director. Let's examine each of these aspects in turn.

What Is to Be Bought?

For public money to be wisely spent, years of accepted practice in public administration must be replaced by an unrelenting focus on just what the money is buying *in terms of the change it brings to persons' lives.* Simple as this might sound, it is not ordinarily addressed either by funding bodies or by provider agencies!

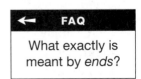

← FAQ

How can the public be sure that its money is well spent?

Usually some laudable activity is funded rather than a defined result. "Laudable" often means credentialed or highly reputable. The upshot is that money is given, evaluation is made, and reports written on the amount or type of *activity* rather than the amount of *results.* Even budgets, widely regarded as the *sine qua non* of control instruments, display dollars applied to various means, not ends. Albert Einstein observed that we have a penchant for perfecting means while yet confused about aims. His comment is a telling description of nonprofit and public management. For social services to have the power that taxpayers and consumers deserve, the ministry must overcome this deficit.

What is needed is an emphasis not on what public servants *do,* but on what the *effects* are of their doing it. Who is better off (recipients)? In what way is someone better off (benefits)? At what cost? In effect, *what is it worth to buy what changes for whom?*

Happily, the more the ministry can specify these factors of benefits-recipients-cost (ends), the less it will need to control the methods, practices and processes (means) of vendor organizations. The extensive control of means in which the ministry is currently engaged is an attempt to overcome having not been clear about the expected ends. The ministry is not, in comparison to other ministries and other provinces, to be derided on this matter, as this oversight is true everywhere else as well.

The word *ends* is used throughout this paper to include the combination of results, recipients of the results, and cost of producing the results (expressed in dollars or in other opportunities given up). These terms focus on changes made in the lives of customers, clients, students, or patients rather than on the activities of providers. Ends are mission-related determinations.

← FAQ

What exactly is meant by *ends*?

The need, then, is for the ministry to be very clear about what it chooses to buy. Surely the partnership mentality requires a great deal of input from localities in the determination of such things. But the nature of the input must be along lines which lead to ends specification, not a ministry sign-off on means. And this requires a new mindset by providers as well as by the ministry. Ministry leadership in making that shift will be paramount.

It would be a serious mistake to underestimate the sweeping nature of this change. The effort and cultural reexamination required will be great. Moreover, inspiration will not be obtained from comparison with other ministries or provinces, for they, too, are stuck in the traditional trap.

In fact, by totally revamping its approach to ends control versus means control, the ministry courts the criticism that it is fixing what isn't broken. But to excel, the ministry must overcome thinking that merely extends practices of the past. Managing momentum is not enough. Excellence in public service calls for bold acts.

Responsibly Allowing Local Latitude

To fulfill the provincial commitment to local choice, the critical requisite will be integrity in local governance. For the ministry to honor its obligation to provincial taxpayers while engaged in an empowering relationship with local ones, it must have assurance that the range of local latitude is exercised by proper local governance. Since only the broad specifications of the "highway" being bought is determined by the ministry, it must be certain that local citizens fine-tune the determination, not hired staff.

> The quality of management is commonly either held hostage by poor governance or let off the hook by it.

It is this exercise of local latitude that requires the integrity of local governance to be a ministry concern. But like the specification of ends, how to develop such integrity—and even how to recognize it—has not been a long suit of public administration. If there is any element of management which has not progressed noticeably in the past few decades, it is governance. The board's job is the most underdeveloped link in enterprise.

Great strides have been made in management of nonprofit and government environments as well as in business. Provincial and local managers of public service are increasingly engaged in management reading, training, and professional management development. Management information systems, supervision techniques, and job design have become increasingly sophisticated.

It is tempting to consider these managerial advances as sufficient to produce well-managed public service. But they are not. For they are all precariously founded on an ineffective, ill-designed, and often bankrupt governance process. Management, a *performing* function, is built on governance, a *purposing* function. It should not be surprising that the quality of management is commonly either held hostage by poor governance or let off the hook by it.

By governance, I refer to the top level determination of purpose, vision, and fundamental nature of organization. In the corporate setting, the board (directors, trustees) is the seat of governance. In government, an elected body (city council, legislature) is ordinarily in that position. Their operating frameworks are derived from trying to mimic management in the former and from maintaining political traditions in the latter.

The state of *local* governance is the immediate concern. The legislature's governance is similarly handicapped, often being quite unclear about the ends sought

> Boards can be manipulated by factions or staffs. Or they can simply fall prey to their own reluctance to lead.

and, at the same time, unnecessarily prescriptive about the means to be used. Consequently, legislative habit is far more damaging to the potential effectiveness of public systems than is recognized. But the ability of a legislature to say clearly what it wants is outside the scope of this paper.

Local providers of community and social services—like all nonprofit organizations—are afflicted with a primitive board process. Because the ministry must rely on the integrity of local decision processes to make *bona fide* local determinations, inadequacies in governance impede the ministry's responsibly entrusting latitude with provincial funds to local providers.

To the extent local boards rubber stamp their staff's desires, the required integrity does not exist. To the extent local boards control by dabbling in the administrative level of organization (often called "meddling"), it does not exist. In the former practice, a board defaults on its trusteeship role. In the latter, it misses the forest in an overworked entanglement with the trees. In both cases, the critical specification of service ends goes undone and local communities do not exercise the oversight that rhetoric portrays. Local strategic leadership simply fails to occur on a predictable and ongoing basis.

If the board truly connects with its broad constituency and is not staff-directed, it becomes possible for the board to lead the process, not just be carried along by events. Boards can be manipulated by factions or staffs. Or they can simply fall prey to their own reluctance to lead. Leading at the board level has to mean long-term vision, not short-term involvement. The ministry is justified in allowing local prerogative to be exercised only by a board process which leads rather than wanders.

 FAQ

How can a board lead an organization, instead of being carried along by events?

Consequently, the ministry is faced not only with saying in ends terms what it wishes to buy with tax funds, but with demanding a level of local governance integrity that does not now exist.

Readiness of Service Providers

There may be no good measure of how prepared local service providers are for the magnitude of change that is needed. Local boards and staffs are competent and committed people who all want the best for their communities. But they are overworked, stressed, and preoccupied with concerns other than the ministry's challenges.

Still, impressionistic evidence suggests that provider agencies have never been more ready for significant change. There is a widespread, growing interest in both good governance and in ends-driven programming. There may not be agreement on what these things mean. There is certainly no agreement on *which* ends are the right ones. But these unresolved issues at least place the debate squarely upon the right topics. In public administration, this circumstance alone is a major development.

What the Ministry Must Do

The ministry has already set the stage for the work yet to be done. It has engaged local organizations in discussions both of governance and of moving beyond traditional, activity-driven contracting. Ministry personnel have invested themselves in a trial run of specifying outcomes (one of the three ends components). Considerable work—as well as diplomacy and modeling behavior for others—lies ahead in these areas.

The ends challenge. Although the ends questions (what good, which people, at what cost) are the simplest in enterprise, they are the most difficult to answer. Committing to an ends focus will shift the conversation between ministry and local organization away from what either ministry or provider *does* and toward what the local provider should *bring to pass.*

Preliminary work within the ministry to learn this approach have been commendable and instructive. Ministry staff, even at this early stage, have been able to extract a number of implied (though not always stated) ends in services currently offered to persons with developmental handicaps. A few of the outcomes (the *results* component of ends) for this population have been tentatively listed as "ability to participate in decision making," "access to leisure, education, health, and social service," "and self-defined quality of life." There are innumerable definitional arguments, controversy that this or that prescription is too vague or not vague enough, and on *ad infinitum.*

But the difficulty of this preliminary work is its most instructive aspect. That ministry personnel have to struggle to determine *what* ongoing, costly services are supposed to produce tells a great deal about the state of the art. It virtually screams a challenge about what we have been doing in social services for these many years *without being able to specify what benefits the efforts should be creating!*

Nothing even hints that this process will be an easy one, only that its inherent integrity is one that service recipients, taxpayers, and providers greatly deserve.

Some problems in achieving an ends focus for the ministry-transfer agency relationship will be straightforward and predictable, others not so obvious until confronted. For example, it is not so clear what the intended ends are for most services now going on. How can the ministry *infer* the ends, then prescribe them? The dilemma is not unlike backing into one's goals by inspecting one's activities. But to convert a sprawling system to an ends focus, such touchy jump-starting might be necessary. Even if the ministry were beginning with a clean slate, choosing results for some people implies choosing that some will be left unserved. To a social service mindset, it is far easier to talk about what good will be done than what will not be done.

Moreover, how can the ministry "average" across the province at some basic level, yet allow maximum variation from locality to locality? These are the days of niche marketing, of ever more specialized products rather than one-size-fits-all. Customer-specific products in the world of commerce arise from and reinforce the same mentality that leads residents of London to dislike being given the same prescription as residents of Peterborough.

There are related, but not so straightforward problems. At what level of specification should the ministry stop prescribing and allow the local board to make further determinations? Will this level of detail vary based on the ministry's estimate of local governance integrity? Will it vary based on the level of original legislative detail? How can legislatively prescribed means be turned into ends for contracting? When the legislature enacts a requirement for means, how can the ministry determine what ends it had in mind?

There is one proviso to the desired dominance of ends in the ministry-agency relationship: The ministry will need to retain a carefully crafted link to transfer agencies' programmatic and administrative means. Rather than being a central focus of the mass of conversation and regulation, however, this means control relates only to *proscribed* conditions and actions. For example, the ministry might determine it to be unacceptable if agencies inadequately safeguard clients' safety, rights, and dignity.

Although it may be verbally awkward to do so, the ministry would do well to express its control over provider agencies' means as prohibitions rather than as positive prescriptions. While appearing to be merely a matter of verbal style or format, this tactic will go far to avoid an inexorable slippage back toward means prescription as the salient feature of the relationship.

The governance process itself, of course, is a means. The ministry's obligation to demand proper governance has already been stated. However, the ends-means argument just made would suggest that the ministry is similarly obligated to require no more of local governance than necessary. The nature of the ministry's expectation is important enough to merit special attention.

FAQ ➡

What should gov-
ernment funders
require of nonprofit
governance?

The governance challenge. Requiring good governance at the local level is easier said than done. There exists a dysfunctional cycle: Boards are not accountable; the province and community learn not to expect them to be accountable; not being expected to be accountable, they do not struggle with the philosophy and mechanics of becoming accountable.

Two problems will present themselves immediately: First, just how is a local organization to achieve that which has thus far eluded virtually all boards? Second, how will the ministry recognize it if accomplished?

The first problem will call for ministerial technical advice and coaching. The second will lead to standards. The first helps local organizations reach a new level of governance. The second demands that the level of governance integrity be at some criterion level or that degrees of integrity be recognizable upon ministry inspection.

Developing standards for governance will be new ground, not only for the ministry but for provincial governments generally. The challenge—as with program operation—will be to avoid prescribing means, that is, to resist telling localities how to govern. Although not strictly an ends issue (in that it does not directly address recipient benefit), it is a matter of outcome: The ministry must require the intended *effects* of good governance.

In other words, rather than requiring particular board actions and structures, the ministry should require whatever qualities are needed to justify granting latitude in the use of provincial funds. For example, there would be no requirements about committees, officers, or frequency of meetings. Instead, categories like the following (stated as a first approximation only) might frame eventual governance standards:

Governance Criteria Area 1: Civic Trusteeship

Cluster A: The board must have defined its "ownership" constituency and determined how the various segments can best be heard.

Cluster B: The board must have decided how individual members reconcile their accountability to the entire constituency with individual allegiances to their own constituencies-of-origin.

Cluster C: The board must demonstrate its capacity for continually improving from year to year as an instrument for community will.

Governance Criteria Area 2: Strategic Leadership

Cluster A: The board must be in charge of its own job and the agenda of that job.

Cluster B: The board as a whole must openly deliberate among long-term alternatives concerning what is to be done for whom at what cost.

Cluster C: The board must demonstrate in its strategic decisions the inclusion of constituent desires, competing needs, probable services of collateral organizations, and its own organizational realities.

Governance Criteria Area 3: Relation to Staff

Cluster A: The board must give staff proactive direction with regard to what benefits are to be produced for which consumer groups.

Cluster B: The board must create the boundaries for staff with respect to unacceptable activity, circumstances, decisions, and behaviors.

Cluster C: The board must use a reliable, regular manner of maintaining reasonable assurance that its directives are followed.

Specific assessable standards would be created within each cluster. It is important that the ministry not dictate to local boards the specifics of how to govern. It is only to require that they use an approach capable of supplying the assurances which justify the ministry's allowing them to make decisions on the use of provincial money.

The ministry's internal challenge. Developing the capacity for this extensive shift will be a greater challenge *within* the ministry than *between* the ministry and external entities. It is not easy to move a mountain an inch. Some claim it is impossible for a large ministry to make this kind of move. But better ideals are always to be pursued, else what are ideals for?

> **← FAQ**
>
> What are the greatest challenges that a large public organization will face in implementing the Policy Governance model?

Probably the greatest single internal force for change is boldness and commitment at the deputy minister and assistant deputy minister level. Constancy of purpose will live at this level or it will not live at all. Given that, the next greatest force may be the creativity and leadership of a handful of field managers under the proper conditions of empowerment and accountability—conditions within the purview of ministry leaders.

The greatest external forces for change may be (a) the readiness due to economic pressures and pressing unmet needs to do anything which promises the chance of relief (the "it *is* broke, so fix it" phenomenon) and (b) the increasing understanding of service management-governance, forming a foundation for the next plateau of sophistication (the "its time has come" phenomenon). These are external factors, but ministry success may depend on making the best use of them. And that means having the organization and culture capable of harnessing this serendipity where it occurs.

In this regard, staff inertia will be the greatest impediment to constructive change. If the ministry turns out not to have been able to provide the necessary leadership, it will likely be due to its inability to lead *itself* into the new world. This is true in the corporate offices, but no less true for field staff. Each will need tools of the new trade, nurturance through tough spots, and confidence that this potentially frightening, uncomfortable shift is not yet another short-term bureaucratic spasm.

Technical assistance to local organizations will have to be clearly separated from assessing whether they meet criteria. The relationship between the ministry and local agencies is both contractual and morally-technically supportive. This dual ministry role of both coach and judge easily deteriorates into a parent-child relationship. The ministry currently interferes too much in agency affairs and, at the same time, demands too little in agency performance. Field staff *are* the ministry to local organizations. They embody and even become expert in this confused duality.

Field staff, due to personal familiarity and institutional traditions, are doubtless drawn more to the business of staffs than to that of boards. They are more likely to know, telephone, and write staff than board. In trying conscientiously to do their jobs, they work around boards more than through them. Even when dealing with boards, field staff are likely to draw boards downward into staff issues rather than upward into public policy issues. Although the ministry's formal contact should be with boards and informal contacts with staffs, in practice this is reversed. Board contacts are often informal unless grave problems call for intervention.

Unwittingly, then, the ministry reinforces the notions that (a) agency boards are not central to accountability and (b) boards are an after-the-fact authority, existing largely to put a stamp of community approval on staff initiatives. Much of their lauded input and oversight is mere ritual. But as long as their ritual follows a prescribed and time-honored form, they receive the ministry's implicit blessing.

Leadership from Queen's Park

Clearly the leadership for successfully transforming Ontario's community and social service lies primarily with the ministry. The kind of enlightened leadership needed, however, is one which includes and empowers local organizations to participate in the leading. This is possible despite the reality that the ministry holds the funding cards. For the aim of partnership in this case is not denial of that reality, but building upon that reality a type of co-determination that is true both to provincial taxpayers and to local initiative.

Real change requires boldness. Boldness requires risk.

It will require philosophical commitment, constancy, and reiteration to survive through the technical problems, communication ambiguities, private agendas, and cultural changes which will certainly impede the way.

Because much of this paradigm shift rests on developing a new common understanding, the ministry should make the break with the past as clear and unmistakable as possible. It should use whatever bells and whistles are necessary to establish that there are new ground rules. In short, the ministry must *market* the new philosophy.

Internal ministry systems must support the new way. First, the "conversation," processes, systems, and structure must be consistent with the new philosophy. Second, personnel will need adequate training and support. The stresses of change for field staff illustrate this need perhaps more than stress anywhere else in the ministry. Since their day-to-day existence engages them with community agencies, the need for confidence and competence in how they should relate is paramount. Up-front outlays for proper training will pay later dividends.

Further, the ministry must heartily engage partners in the philosophy. Great changes must be driven by moral suasion and intellectual integrity. Admit that although the ministry and local organizations are playing different roles, they are truly in the accountability dilemma together. Taking on the challenges of good governance and of clearly developed ends cannot be postponed until someone knows all the answers.

Because bureaucracies and political institutions of all types fear making mistakes, there is strong incentive to do nothing that you aren't sure you can do flawlessly. That characteristic not only impedes innovation, it strangles it. Real change requires boldness. Boldness requires risk.

> ← **FAQ**
>
> Isn't it risky for a public institution to adopt Policy Governance?

In the process of stumbling along a new path, old agendas and new learning will become entangled, usually not for malevolent reasons. Different parties will latch on to different parts of a new paradigm, each using a segment of the new as a weapon in preexisting struggles. Any rational paradigm can thus quickly become a patchwork. Model-consistent leadership and obsessive reinforcement from the top will be needed. Treat each other gently during the difficult transition.

Governing Parks and Recreation

P&R, VOLUME 25, ISSUE 11, Nov. 1990

T HE NATION'S PARKS and recreation facilities are governed or advised by more than 4,500 boards. These boards, elected and appointed, either determine the destiny for parks and recreation or they advise on very nearly the same topic. In either event, all park and recreation boards can profitably gain from emerging developments in the board role.

Other than the obvious pressures of insufficient funds, insatiable public needs, and the occasional muskrat, the most persistent problem of recreation and park boards—though rarely the most evident—is *the board process itself.* Governing is not an easy task at best, but citizens who step up to this challenge enter the least studied, most underdeveloped function in enterprise. Every link in the management chain has received more guidance and model-based thought than the board.

> The most persistent problem of recreation and park boards—though rarely the most evident—is *the board process itself.*

Park and recreation boards are not alone. School boards, city councils, social agency boards, hospital boards, and port authorities, among a host of others, are similarly impaired. Trivia pushes out the profound. Short-term items displace long-term. Board meetings come to be an endless stream of staff issues for the board to review, approve, bless, or simply sit passively and hear. In other words, governing our nation's park and recreation systems is handicapped because of the primitive state of governance as a process.

So where do we start? We can begin by using a few simple principles to create a new vision for governance, though the cost is to depart radically from conventional wisdom. Boards do not operate the parks, they govern the people who do. Boards do not mow the grass, patrol the paths, guard the pool, trim the trees, type the letters, or keep the books. But boards

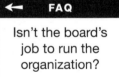

← FAQ

Isn't the board's job to run the organization?

can *establish the values and perspectives by which these things are done.* (I will use *values* to mean the relative worth and the acceptable-unacceptable judgment about things. *Perspectives* will mean our approaches or ways of looking at things.) Getting a proper handle on organizational values and perspectives is the key, for it turns out that setting values and perspectives is perfectly within the capacity of boards and does not require expertise in lawn care, path maintenance, or accounting. Through such control, boards can be truly accountable for all organizational performance without having their hands directly on any of it. But values and perspectives about what?

First of all, values about what we have park and recreation systems for, that is, *the results or impacts of the effort.* As a kind of purchasing agent for the public, the board can decide what benefits are produced for which people at what cost. These values about intended results-per-dollar emerge from board members' purpose and vision and, when put on paper, constitute a category of board policies I will call *ends.* Policy topics within the ends category include *mission, priorities of benefits, priorities of consumers,* and other topics which are subparts of these.

Second, perspectives about *the board's linkage to its staff* determine how the board will pass authority and instructions to those who do the work, as well as how the board will be periodically reassured that acceptable performance has occurred. Choosing to treat the park and recreation director as a chief executive officer, for example, is a policy decision within this category. I will call this category *board-staff relationship.* Policy topics within this category include *principles of delegation, CEO job requirements,* and *methods of monitoring.*

Third, values about *the prudence and ethics boundaries within which the staff must operate* as it uses authority delegated to it are almost as important as attaining board-stated ends. These board values constitute the only justifiable motivation for a board's "meddling" in its staff's activities. The principle is that the board should not prescribe staff practices, but may put limits on them. These limits, then, take the form of telling staff what is *not* approvable, rather than prescriptively telling staff how to do its job.

The effect of this atypical approach is to give staff the maximum authority, but within a few carefully selected limits.

This handful of policies constraining the methods, practices, or circumstances of staff operation are gathered into a category called *executive limitations*. Policy topics in this category include *treatment of staff, compensation and benefits, asset protection, budgeting,* and *financial condition.*

Fourth, perspectives on *the board's own job.* These policies address the board's relationship to its "stockholders," as well as the roles of officers and committees, expectations of members, and role of the board in planning, policymaking, and oversight. These policies constitute a category called *governance process.* Policies included in this category are *board job products, governing style, committee principles,* and *board member expectations.*

FAQ ➡
When a board adopts Policy Governance, what happens to its previous policies?

These four categories of the newly designed board policies totally replace other board pronouncements except for bylaws. When the board rigorously enforces policies and their applicable principles, board work is transformed from trivial to profound. Board energies are no longer spent in keeping up with staff, but in strategic leadership. Deliberating and establishing vision can powerfully drive a staff long-range planning process without entangling the board in long-range planning. With board-generated ends carefully developed, the planning itself is far better done by staff.

Because categories two, three, and four may be developed rapidly and remain relatively stable over the year, category one, ends, takes center stage and becomes the board's primary concern forever. In other words, deciding over a long term what the public is to pay for and get from its park and recreation system (ends) should be the board's central work. By thus designing its job, the board can prevent staff work, ongoing crises, and other attractive distractions from impeding appropriate board leadership.

When the board rigorously enforces policies and their applicable principles, board work is transformed from trivial to profound.

Policymaking done in this way is markedly different from conventional policy work, for we have traditionally organized board policies to mimic administrative categories (personnel, finance, and so forth). Further, we ordinarily fail to distinguish those pronouncements generated from the board's own values from those which are the mere parroting of staff plans and ways of operating. Consequently, boards and staff both interfere in what would have been, under a more sensible division of authority, the prerogatives of the other ("meddling" goes two ways!).

None of this works, of course, unless it is supported by a level of board discipline beyond today's norm. For example, while valuing its diversity, the board *must speak with one voice*. No individuals, committee, or officers (including the chair) may have any authority over the park and recreation director or staff. Further, the board must instruct and evaluate *the director only*, truly treating him or her as a chief executive officer. And the CEO may be evaluated only on what the board as a whole has actually said in policy, never on what it wishes it had said or on what the CEO "should have known." Moreover, the board must declare off-limits to itself any

> Boards must relinquish seat-of-the-pants governance if they seriously want to govern more effective enterprise.

"participation" in staff jobs that confuses delegation, even abstaining from setting up board committees to advise or help staff. Staff can get advice, of course, simply by asking willing and valued advisors. Imposing advice by making it officially from the board, however, is a different matter! Boards must relinquish seat-of-the-pants governance if they seriously want to govern more effective enterprise. Crop dusters may be flown by the seat of your pants, but not 747s.

The upshot of this governance model is a board far more in control of the destiny of its organization, yet far less entrapped by its ongoing specifics. Even in the parks business, the board's business is forests, not trees! That requires giving up the concreteness and even fun of details and implementation in order to rigorously lead at the policy level. The newer definition of policy is important here, for the old definitions allowed virtually anything to pass as policy (take a look at the personnel "policies"). The board will operate as a whole with less use of committees, for most current committees merely offer a sanctioned way to intrude into staff work. It will proactively do its own job rather than reactively rehash and review staff products and plans. It will base its monitoring on preestablished criteria (to be found in the policies) rather than wallowing in as much data as staff can assemble. Yet even with this far more powerful governance of the organization, all the board's documents together will take fewer than fifty pages.

This new approach was developed for boards which actually govern. But the concepts of effectiveness apply almost as fully to boards which advise. For they point to those aspects of organization in which advice can have the most effect: ends rather than means. The advisory board that can influence organizational ends will leave its mark far more meaningfully than one which merely helps the staff answer its never ending "how to" questions. This does not mean that advisory bodies cannot be created simply to provide technical advice, but does suggest that the kind of central, high-profile body represented by advisory park and recreation boards might well have a higher calling. To the extent that an advisory board chooses to grasp the brassier ring, using the same principles as those outlined for governing boards will enhance its leadership.

In the case of either type of board for park and recreation systems, leadership is the key. Parks and recreation governors must aspire always to be nothing less than an exciting, compelling expression of leadership. And leadership, at its core, is not about budget lines, personnel procedures, pool treatment, or pest control. Leadership is about values, vision, and the vigor of building public consensus on what difference our enterprise will make for people.

Education Accountability and Legislative Oversight

PRESENTED TO THE OVERSIGHT COMMISSION ON EDUCATION ACCOUNTABILITY, WEST VIRGINIA LEGISLATURE, JAN. 1991

IN MARCH 1990, the West Virginia Legislature charged its Legislative Oversight Commission on Education Accountability "to make a comprehensive study of ways in which to improve the governance effectiveness of the state's county boards of education and county school board members" (House Concurrent Resolution 30). The "findings, conclusions and recommendations generated by the study" were to be presented to the legislature by January 9, 1991. The recommendations presented here—integrating a response to other segments of the study—are in partial fulfillment of that charge.

Summary

Paralleling the legislature's expression of concern, this statement maintains that the weakest link in public education is not teaching or administration, but governance—the quality of strategic leadership by elected citizens. It further argues that the problem exists not so much in the *people* (school board members) as in the inadequate and largely unexamined *governance process* which not only fails to tap the available wisdom and vision of board members and their constituents, but strangles effective administration as well. This recommendation urges the legislature to seize the momentum it has wisely stimulated, to do what no other state has yet done: transform the quality of governance in public education.

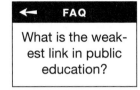

← FAQ

What is the weakest link in public education?

565

The opportunity is to reexamine the nature of public governance and to make whatever shifts are necessary to prevent early and mid-twentieth-century methods from blurring a twenty-first-century dream for children. This *cannot* be done without significant changes by the legislature and the State Department of Education as well as in the very substance of local education governance. Specific recommendations are

1. Focus the legislature itself upon the *results* to be sought in public education rather than the *means* of obtaining those results.

2. Redesign the roles of the State Board of Education and the Department of Education.

3. Demand a *transformation,* not just a change, of governance in public education, encouraged and enabled by whatever changes in statutes are necessary to that end.

Data Considered

These recommendations are based on data specific to West Virginia as well as general to the nation as a whole. The former come from (a) the Hange and Leary study of school board minutes in West Virginia (1990), (b) the Hange study of boards' perceived effectiveness along with their choice of improvement efforts (1990), (c) the Select Seminar composed of West Virginia professional and lay leaders in public education (1990), and (d) the writer's experience with school boards in West Virginia (1988–1990). The latter is drawn from (e) published material in professional journals and accounts of recent restructuring in other states, (f) the writer's experience with local education agency boards in Minnesota, Indiana, Ohio, and New York (1981–1990), (g) the writer's experience with state boards of education in Rhode Island, Kansas, Ohio, Delaware, Maryland directly, and with more than thirty others indirectly through the National Association of State Boards of Education (1987–1990), and (h) the writer's experience with hundreds of elected and non-elected public and quasi-public boards in the United States and Canada (1976–1990).

Most cogent to these recommendations are the data yielded by Drs. Jane E. Hange (Appalachia Educational Laboratory) and Paul H. Leary (West Virginia University College of Graduate Studies) and by the Select Seminar.

Philosophy

Data in themselves have limited meaning. It is *theory* which not only gives them meaning, but determines which data are important and which are not. But theory is even more critical in deciding what to do about the facts we find. We already have mountains of information and experience about school board governance, but *inadequate theory*. In fact, the many years of experience of *15,000* (and several times more than that in former years) school boards in the United States alone has led us to the intolerable circumstances demonstrated by Hange and Leary!

These recommendations are based on a theory of governance which, though radical in many respects, is probably aligned with many of the legislature's basic beliefs about governing the public's business. Here are a few principles of that theory: (1) The board is accountable to the public for the total performance, destiny, and behavior of the organization. (2) The board as a body is servant to the general public rather than to professional educators, administrators, or specific subgroups of the population. (3) The board exists to govern the school system, not to manage it; that is, board members are not part-time superintendents writ large. (4) Although the board has varied obligations (for example, fiscal prudence, employment fairness), detailed attention to these matters should never displace concern for students as the *central* occupation of the board. (5) Defining and attaining those "ends" which justify an organization's existence is the primary obligation of leadership, since other people can be empowered to work out virtually everything else through responsible delegation. (6) The board is obligated to obtain whatever training, whatever data, and whatever wisdom are necessary to fulfill this precious trusteeship, no matter how much or little other organizations and authorities help.

Findings

The Hange and Leary data speak volumes. They are as telling as any study of school board activity I have ever seen. The major weakness of these data in drawing conclusions about school board behavior is that the *time* boards spent on the various types of business does not show up. We only have a count of the separate items themselves. But despite this weakness, the figures are striking enough to compel us toward certain conclusions, largely unhappy ones.

Although assumptions about what actual board behavior constituted each subcategory in the Hange and Leary study are risky, certain broad interpretations may be justified. For example, using a very rough estimate of what material would constitute board of directors business in the corporate world, of total agenda items those which engage the boards in administrative matters constitute 54 percent *at the lowest*. Items which engage the board in truly governance issues make up 42 percent *at the highest*. My experience in watching boards operate would suggest these figures are surely temperate ones, the truth not being nearly as favorable as these impressionistic counts suggest.

Counted as liberally as possible, then, school boards spend more than half their agenda count on issues considered to be managerial in business settings. At the very least, it can be said that agenda items which would comprise a forward looking, strategic leadership over policy issues are not at the core of board agendas. Policy development and oversight occurred in only 3 percent of the total agenda items.

It is perhaps as telling that the Hange study of perceived effectiveness found that the boards felt *best* about their decision-making ability and *worst* about their influence over others (for example, other local agencies, business, local and state governments). These data make sense together if we assume that school boards are making decisions *about the wrong things*. They may well make prudent decisions about any number of staff-level topics. If so, their decision-making might be good (though wrongly placed) without resulting in the kind of dynamic local leadership education deserves. In fact, boards under these conditions are more likely to be perceived by outsiders as plodding, trivia-beset—albeit conscientious—groups more than vibrant, visionary trailblazers, obsessed with society's debt to its children *and* its taxpayers.

Unlike the foregoing research studies, it is harder to draw conclusions from the Select Seminar proceedings. They can be used to demonstrate the weight of concerns more than to outline recommendations. Nevertheless, a hearty effort was made to translate the impressionistic information into "observations." Since the process produced no compelling consensus, it would have been difficult to say more than "this select group found local school boards in West Virginia to be *basically healthy but in need of toning up"* and that "what boards are doing is *not out of line with educational needs* [emphasis mine] [though the way] they go about their work is more often questioned" (both citations from page 6 of "First Report").

It is more likely, however, that participants in the Select Seminar are influenced by the same factors which lead school boards to see themselves as good decision makers. That is, being close to the trees might make one expert in bark and limbs, but not necessarily in forests and environmental support systems. For it would seem in the larger picture that the status of school boards across the country is less fortunate than "basically healthy" and "in line with educational needs." In other words, taken one decision at a time, school boards may look pretty good. Weaknesses in the underpinnings show up, however, when one examines the system of thinking that decides which questions will be addressed. Some defects are obvious even without a rigorous inspection, a fact doubtless reflected in the Select Seminar's concern about boards' involvement with mission, vision, goals, and policy.

Ironically, in the midst of what could be (and I believe are) critical shortcomings, the Hange study found that "few boards plan or budget for improving individual or group skills and updating information on current educational issues." It further underestimates the depth of the problem when the Select Seminar analysis suggests that the conditions "may be addressed in part by some work with boards on influencing their climate and using public relations to gain public support." The way to influence climate and gain support in a substantive rather than cosmetic way is to fulfill the governance obligation with vitality, maximum inclusiveness of others, and proactive leadership. Also, there is a powerful effect from having the moral suasion that comes from putting outcomes for children at the center of the public agenda. Boards which truly respond to this challenge will find that public relations and influence largely take care of themselves.

> Boards should be policymakers first and foremost, but there is concurrent general agreement that this is not what they are ordinarily found doing.

There is no reason to expect the West Virginia data to differ substantially from that which would be obtained elsewhere in the country. Recent articles in the literature suggest that the same disease afflicts all; this is by no means a peculiarly West Virginia problem. If a Hange and Leary study of school boards across the nation would, as I expect, generate similar data, this finding would have great significance for remedial action: There is something inherent either in governance of public education or in board governance generally that predisposes boards to engage so little in the policy development leadership which our rhetoric suggests is their primary domain. While there is general agreement that boards should be policymakers first and foremost, there is concurrent general agreement that this is not what they are ordinarily found doing.

We are without research data to continue this line of thought, though my impression gained from exposure to hundreds of boards thoroughly supports the theory that there exists an inherent deficiency. If, for example, boards regularly make good decisions about the wrong things as suggested above, there exists a flaw that goes to the heart of how we see the job rather than a simple need for training or toning up. In fact, public boards of various sorts exhibit similar behavior and, though there are certain idiosyncrasies about boards of education, they are by no means the only boards to give minimal attention to policy leadership. An analysis of legislative behavior at county, municipal, state, and national levels would likely turn up comparable data, as would a study of nonprofit boards.

This should come as no surprise. The governing board's role in the management of enterprise (public or private) is the most understudied, underdeveloped link in the chain. It is not that school boards are untrained, uncommitted, or incapable. When there is so pervasive a phenomenon as is observed across West

← **FAQ**

Are boards only as strong as their members?

> The problem lies in what we expect from boards, what we compel them to do by law, and what we allow them to do by general indulgence.

Virginia and across the nation, the presumption must be that there are problems in the structure or in the process, rather than in the people. The core problem is not that school board members fail to be "ideal" boards. The commonly accepted ideal is itself deeply flawed. The conventional picture of how a board should function is founded in tradition, enforced by regulations of the Department of Education, promoted by the National School Boards Association, and expected by the legislature. It is this pattern of what a school board should be, do, and look like as it does its business that is the underlying source of the appalling data quantified by Hange and Leary, reflected by the Select Seminar participants, and suspected by every intelligent observer who ever attended a school board meeting anywhere.

This is a strong and pervasive indictment, soberly made. it is one in which neither school boards themselves, the Department of Education, state board, legislature, or press is entirely blameless. It means the problem lies in what we expect from boards, what we compel them to do by law, and what we allow them to do by general indulgence. It means that if boards do their very best to get training and acquire the discipline to fulfill their roles as defined in the conventional wisdom, they would simply have learned to do the wrong things better than before.

> Patching an inadequate vehicle is not only not visionary, it is doomed to muddle into the future by desperately reanswering yesterday's questions.

Under such conditions, not even a conscientious and intelligent attack on the specific symptoms (for example, not enough policy development items on agendas), on the boards (for example, they simply need training), or on the board members (for example, better candidates are needed to stand for election) gets at the fundamental problem. At best, such actions can only repair the past, never create the future. Patching an inadequate vehicle is not only not visionary, it is doomed to muddle into the future by desperately reanswering yesterday's questions.

Recommendations

What is to be done? What does the status of public education governance as demonstrated in the data lead us to? Nothing less than this: It is imperative to redesign what strategic citizen leadership means at the board table. Public and legislative actions about teaching methods, administrative practices, and so forth are bound to fail, for they attack the octopus one tentacle at a time, leaving the malfunctioning head untouched. The challenge requires far more than such a piecemeal response. Doing less would be as vacuous as dressing up a fundamentally inadequate vehicle with a new paint job and tires.

Answers in public education do not come easy. The schools inherit every problem the larger society produces. The development of our children is impeded mightily by family disruptions, drugs, and distractions peculiar to our age. Economic support for this costly enterprise is shaky at best. Public expectations are a mixture as fervent as they are incompatible. Equity and excellence may inspire us, but grimmer realities seem to dominate in the systems as they really are. In the midst of this tough challenge, the ostensible center of strategic leadership in each system is mired in trivia, wasteful of its executive leadership, and unable to find a handle on what, in fact, to lead about.

> Answers in public education do not come easy. The schools inherit every problem the larger society produces.

There is much the legislature might do. One action, of course, deals with the financial resources made available to operate public education. No amount of newly found effectiveness will make the task cheap. But money alone will not suffice. To some degree, a failing system with more money will simply fail more expensively. Aside from money, the legislature has three areas in which bold and visionary action can impact upon the educational results for children in West Virginia and upon local public leadership over those results.

1. *Focus the legislature itself upon the results to be sought in public education rather than the means of obtaining those results.* At the broadest level, the legislature is the public's purchasing agent: What does the public wish to purchase with its tax dollars in terms of the preparation new citizens have for life? It is important that "results" not be translated prematurely to mean test scores. Test scores may be indicative of some results the public wants, but public consideration of school system "products" would be cheated of its potential depth by leaping to this conclusion. Legislative prescription can be kept at a broad level, so that the initiative of others closer to the action can answer the question in greater detail. Legislatures sometimes try to be the "big school board" because they distrust the educational decision system, but they must recognize that the prophesy is self-fulfilling. There is little incentive for school boards to be better leaders of public education if their opportunity for leadership is constantly eroded. Micromanaging from the capital causes poorer local governance, not better.

2. *Redesign the roles of the State Board of Education and the Department of Education.* It is not entirely clear to all parties just what these roles are. Unless they are significantly different from other states, the roles are poorly construed given the modern needs of public education. Just as a legislature may usurp the roles of these statewide entities, state boards and departments tend to do the same to local boards by regulation strangulation. Local boards of education are pretty low on the totem pole, again yielding little incentive for leadership. There are definite products for which a state department of education might be held accountable, but these are typically obscured by bureaucratic and statutory effects over which the legislature has at least some control. A confounding of duties, powers, and products is common in legislation affecting these roles. Moreover, the exact accountability relationship between state board and state superintendents is ambiguous in the statutory language.

3. *Demand a transformation, not just a change, of governance in public education, encouraged and enabled by whatever changes in statutes are necessary to that end.* School boards certainly cannot lead education into the future when they cannot as presently operated lead it in the present. Their time-honored process is simply inadequate to the task; governance as we have known it is not worthy of the mission, the taxpayers, or the gifts that board members, administrators, and educators have to give. Someone must notice the emperor's state of dress and take more than cosmetic action.

The principles of the new governance should bring about substantial changes in school board behavior, conduct of meetings, and relations between the board and its public and the board and its staff:

The most frequent dialogue of boards should be with the public, not with its staff, contrary to current practice.

A. *Boards will focus their time and energy on defining the skills, understandings, and attitudes that public education should bring about for children.* These clarifications of vision are done with a long-term perspective and so constitute the board's major involvement in long-term planning. Schools are primarily about preparing human beings for living. But normal board involvement would lead one to believe that schools are about budget lines, personnel transfers, roof repairs, and plant maintenance. Managers know how to do such things; if they do not, we have hired the wrong managers. But managers and educators have no right to decide what the public wishes to buy; boards do. Major improvements will not occur in school governance unless boards get back in touch with organizational purpose.

B. *Boards will affirmatively engage the public in a continuing debate on what the public wishes to buy from a public education system.* The most frequent dialogue of boards should be with the public, not with its staff, contrary to current practice. The public includes parents, nonparents, and employers as well as other public-serving boards, councils, and commissions—in all a heterogeneous and complex group. It is not enough for boards to establish open meetings and then to await the public's coming to the board. The board must develop ways to go to the public, a type of affirmative action in seeking public input to school governance. Moreover, the input sought should be about the *ends* of the system (item A) more than the *means* over which staff should be given as much authority as possible.

C. *Boards will give their superintendents and, thence, their whole staffs, as much authority as prudently possible to achieve the publicly determined results without board interference and even unrequested help.* As long as they know what the job is to get done (chosen by the public and its trustees, the board), those doing the work should have as much latitude as can prudently be given to them. By forcing staffs to subject their every initiative to board member scrutiny (and meddling), administrative and programmatic creativity is strangled. Board members err in trying to

> As long as they know what the job is to get done, those doing the work should have as much latitude as can prudently be given to them.

be part-time superintendents, one step removed from the action. Poring over staff material is what boards and board meetings have been all about. Most current school board agenda items are intrusions into management while the board's own unique job goes largely undone.

D. *Boards will create a relatively small number of policies to define the boundaries within which extensive staff autonomy can be acceptable.* Since allowing staff to exercise unbounded latitude would be unacceptable, boards need to define permissible ranges of action and authority. Defining ranges or limits consumes far less time and impedes staff creativity less than prescribing or approving administrative plans, practices, and programs. A limit-setting approach frees the board from its legitimate worries and allows it to get on with its own job. Board worry about administrative issues—by cluttering agendas—prevents educational ends from being at the center of attention. This new type of brief but powerful policymaking is completely unlike what boards are accustomed to. Most current board "policy" is merely administrative material dressed up in policy language.

E. *Boards will demand data from superintendents and from outside evaluators which disclose the degree to which the system is performing upon the criteria established in items A and D.* Monitoring performance in a rigorous, systematic way sends the message that the board is serious about the educational ends and range of acceptable means set forth by the board. When there are clear criteria for system performance, monitoring becomes considerably easier. It is no longer necessary to forage about in budgets, plans, and activity reports—a major source of well-intended waste of board time. School boards currently wander about in data, but almost none use data to monitor performance against meaningful, preestablished criteria.

F. *Boards will hold their superintendents accountable for system performance as a whole, treating them as true chief executive officers.* Boards would not hold other staff accountable for anything, nor allow the superintendent to avoid accountability for the total. Consequently, the systematic monitoring in item E is a direct measure of superintendent performance. The superintendent is held accountable for nothing except what the board has said it wants (item A) and does not want (item D). As long as the superintendent operates with fidelity to these board wishes, the board

> One only need go through one school board agenda to see why the leadership of public education is not to be found in school boards.

totally protects him or her in the light of public opinion. It is important that school boards neither rubber-stamp staff desires nor meddle inappropriately in staff activity. The prevailing approach to school governance causes wide swings as boards go from rubber-stamping to meddling and back often in the same meeting.

These seemingly simple changes are virtually impossible without discarding many practices traditionally accepted as symbolic of responsible behavior. For example, school boards often delve deeply into fiscal details because they truly believe their fiduciary accountability requires them to do so. Such myopic attention to trivia is represented as being responsible when it is in fact the opposite. Requirements that school boards take action—even consent agenda action—on a myriad of personnel and other administrative decisions trivialize what strategic leadership is about. These expectations force a board to get its fingers in the system rather than its arms around it. One only need go through one school board agenda to see why the leadership of public education is not to be found in school boards. If we were not so accustomed to school board traditions, the typical agenda and involvement of board members would seem ludicrous, especially in view of the crucial need for leadership in these profound and perplexing public issues.

Despite significant and, in a few instances, massive restructuring of education in other states, the condition of local school governance is similar. Consequently, there is no recommendation here for West Virginia to catch up with anybody. Indeed, aiming to make school governance in West Virginia no worse than that in other states requires little commitment to West Virginia children. The demands of the future will no doubt lead someone, someday to recognize and reverse the parody of school governance that today goes virtually unquestioned. It will not be done without difficulty and it cannot be done timidly. But there is no reason that it cannot happen first in West Virginia.

New Means to an End

Times Educational Supplement, London, July 1, 1994

THE BOARDS OF BRITAIN's further education colleges have exchanged their advisory roles for the far more demanding responsibilities of governing.

After decades in which either rubber-stamping or meddling was the order of the day—often simultaneously—the effectiveness of boards is being questioned as never before. For boards of further education, their fresh entry into the governance arena presents an opportunity to move far beyond the mediocre norm still condoned for nonprofit and governmental boards.

Let's face it. Boards are not society's most efficient organs. At best, they are the least developed element in enterprise. At worst, they are incompetent groups of competent people. Management science has developed and changed continually for decades, a self-critical progress that shows no signs of abating. But governance—by which I mean to say the peculiar job of a governing board—has lumbered along in its awkward way, stumbling over trivialities, alternating between being led about by those it pretends to lead and meddling so much in their jobs that all semblance of accountability is lost. Governance has, in short, remained in the nineteenth century.

Typically, boards are beset by empty ritual, such as officiously approving documents when approval criteria have never been established (in approving a financial statement, what board has any idea what it would *dis*approve?). Although commissioned to wield group rather than individual authority, boards are ineffective in preventing renegades among them from foisting individual wishes upon managers.

Indeed, managers are often faced with the necessity to manage well *despite* board members.

Even the best of boards fall into these traps on a predictable basis, no matter how competent their members. The quality of persons on a board surely makes a difference, but only to affect variations *within* severe limitations imposed by poor design of the board job. In other words, you can't address the sad state of governance either by better people or by working harder. The ingrained flaw is in the tradition-blessed process itself.

But a breakthrough for boards—the Policy Governance model—is available, emerging from relative obscurity in only the past several years. The Policy Governance model provides an advanced "technology of governance" to guide in transforming the board's job and the board's relationship with its staff. Following my creation of this radical paradigm, it has had twenty-two years of slowly building acceptance in Canada and the United States. The happy circumstances for colleges of further education is that they—because of the newness of their role—are in a more favorable situation to take advantage of any new approach than where procedures are more entrenched.

The Policy Governance model brings a new level of managerial respectability to the board role largely by enabling the exercise of due control without resorting to meddling to do so. Most of the classic board foibles, such as those alluded to earlier, can be easily overcome. The board focuses far more effort on defining and monitoring the expected results of its organization (along with specification of beneficiary groups and relative worth, these are called *ends),* rather than its administrative and programmatic activities *(means).* In a carefully crafted policy format, the board enumerates the means (practices, methods and circumstances) it considers *unacceptable.*

The chief executive officer—the principal in colleges of further education—is charged to achieve the ends by using any means he or she chooses, so long as board-stated limitations on these means are observed. In other words, on behalf of the public the board prescribes the ends in no uncertain terms, but stays out of the means except to say what it will not put up with.

Unlike traditional policymaking, these specially designed policies are generated out of board members' own values. They are not ghost-written by staff members for the board's reactive approval. The manner in which this new definition of policy embodies board members' values not only enables a diverse board to speak with a single, unambiguous voice, but provides a

> ← **FAQ**
>
> What is the staff's role in creating the board's policies?

solid base for CEO delegation and evaluation far more effectively than the commonplace goal-setting approach.

The days of both rubber-stamping and trivia in board meetings are numbered. Boards stop acting like after-the-fact, ill-equipped staffs and start acting like leaders.

But making the new governance work requires radical and sometimes discomforting changes in the familiar methods and structures of board work. Acting truly as a single body rather than as a collection of individuals or subgroups, along with a clear distinction between board and staff roles, virtually abolishes the need for committees. Clear board statements of performance criteria eliminate the need for the time-honored, yet retrospective and reactive, practice of granting approvals for staff documents—including budgets. Due to clearer board pronouncements and the determination that the CEO reports only to the board as a whole, it is no longer acceptable for the chairperson to supervise the CEO.

With a more powerful approach now available, the days of both rubber-stamping and trivia in board meetings are numbered. Due to the board's taking ownership of its agenda, board meetings become *the board's* meetings rather than management's meetings for the board. Boards stop acting like after-the-fact, ill-equipped staffs and start acting like leaders.

FAQ ➡

Are CEOs better off with Policy Governance?

Defining intended outputs rather than organizational activities (programs, services and curricula are means, not ends) is a formidable but rewarding task. CEOs, though held to higher standards of accountability, are attracted to the new-found board clarity and fewer capricious turns in board behavior. But board members who want to deal with the big issues, who want to focus on values and vision, who, in fact, want to *lead*, are happiest of all.

Reinventing Governance

ASSOCIATION MANAGEMENT, VOLUME 51, ISSUE 8, AUG. 1999

FOR MANY ASSOCIATION chief executive officers, the single largest source of work stress is dealing with the oftentimes baffling dynamics of their board. Compared to an individual one might work for, for instance, boards are less likely to take responsibility for their own jobs and more likely to judge you based on criteria they've never communicated. Some CEOs have been bedeviled by boards that repeatedly micromanage, while others have had careers impeded by rubber-stamp boards that turn unexpectedly harsh.

Consequently, today's CEOs are motivated to learn not only management but governance as well. However, learning governance is quite different from learning finance, marketing, strategic planning, or other management disciplines because every element of management has received more study and conceptual development than has the board's job.

> Boards are less likely to take responsibility for their own jobs and more likely to judge you based on criteria they've never communicated.

It is striking and perhaps horrifying that the most powerful role in enterprise is so primitive in its conceptual grounding. Governance as we have known it is a hodgepodge of personality-driven variations on tradition-blessed practices. As a result, governance development typically remains the application of tips and piecemeal improvements to a fundamentally undesigned whole.

Every element of management has received more study and conceptual development than has the board's job.

Association executives may derive little comfort from knowing that this sad state of affairs is true for boards of all sorts, not only association boards. Business corporations, cities, school systems, foundations, and pension funds are as affected by the primitive state of governance as are small community agencies, advocacy groups, and professional societies. Moreover, it is a worldwide phenomenon, as my own experience on four continents with every possible type of board attests. Peter Drucker summed it up well when he observed that all boards have one thing in common: They don't work.

It's important to point out that board *members* aren't usually the problem. Individuals who sit on boards are typically intelligent, well-intended, cordial people. But something peculiar to the board process can produce an incompetent group of competent individuals. Indeed, a board of association executives will behave much like any other board, creating conditions for its CEO that the same executives in their own CEO roles deplore. What is so hard about getting this role right? What gets in the way on the path to good governance despite the best intentions and the best people? And is there anything CEOs can do about it?

Something peculiar to the board process can produce an incompetent group of competent individuals.

The Problem of Process

FAQ ➡

What is wrong with traditional governance?

The problem with governance is more one of process than of people. We must look to the *system* that embraces board members' pursuit of good works. The process of governance as we have known it ensnares well-meaning, competent board members in a disastrous set of habits. The culprit is not CEOs or board members, but the conventional wisdom about governance. Our traditional conception of what boards need to do is a product of decades of bits and pieces: trial-and-error experience, personal preferences, demands from management, and stipulations of external authorities. It is a conceptual patchwork. Under such conditions, neither board training nor better board member recruitment is the answer, since these solutions only lead to doing the wrong things better than before.

To bring a measure of conceptual coherence to the board's job, I developed a model of governance called Policy Governance twenty years ago. (See box, "Governance by Policy."). This model resulted from trying to first answer whether a body of universally applicable principles could be found for the governance function and, second, whether such a body of principles could be assembled with enough conceptual integrity to be accurately called a model or paradigm in the scientific sense (not in the structural sense). The model departs radically from conventional wisdom, substantially redesigning the board's role, its relationship to membership and staff, and the content and format of its decision making. Micromanagement is ruled out, but so is failing to speak powerfully on behalf of the organization's owners. In associations, members are these owners, and they depend on their board to be their voice to the CEO. That voice, however, is often seriously hampered by commonly accepted beliefs that in fact are mere myths—eight of which are outlined here.

> Our traditional conception of what boards need to do is a product of decades of bits and pieces.

Myths That Impede Good Governance

Myth 1: Governance is simply an extension of management. We traditionally treat governing bodies as management one-step-removed—sort of like a management oversight committee. Perhaps the greatest impediment to conceptual development of governance is that boards and their CEOs conceive of the board's role as an extension upward of ownership. But it is this

> ← FAQ
>
> Is there a fundamental difference between governance and management?

owner–representative property that makes the servant-leadership philosophy of Robert Greenleaf so apropos to governance. Instead, boards currently borrow their reports, documents, and mindsets from the latest management philosophies, confounding their leadership opportunity with the better-developed, albeit misappropriated, practices of their subordinates.

Myth 2: The board exists to help manage. When boards identify more with management than with a separately defined governance role, they come to believe that their primary role is to help managers manage. Consequently, they examine management in great detail, review management plans, and often appoint committees to oversee various aspects of management.

Will a good manager be a good board member? This myth leads to an assumption that a board made up of good managers is a good board. But rather than improving the quality of governance, managers on boards frequently lead a board further into micromanagement than it otherwise would have gone. While individual board members can certainly lend their skills and insights to management as operational volunteers, the job of the board as a body is not to help manage, but in a trustee sense to own the business on behalf of members.

Myth 3: What board members say as individuals matters. It's important that board members bring diversity to the table, since variety of opinion is necessary for the values-aggregation role of a board to arrive at wise conclusions. But while board members must express themselves individually in a healthy intra-board interchange, what individuals have to say should not matter to management. Management is frequently driven in many directions by what it believes is the need to heed the various directives, advice, and opinions of board members. When the board finally speaks as a group—when the vote has been taken—management must pay attention. Until that time, however, nothing exists that the CEO must hear or heed.

> The job of the board as a body is not to help manage, but in a trustee sense to own the business on behalf of members.

FAQ ➡
Is the CEO responsible for board performance?

Myth 4: The CEO is responsible for board performance. It is no secret that boards often rely on their CEOs not only for guidance on the nature of governance, but also for meeting agendas. It's as if the CEO is responsible for the board taking responsibility. This typical inversion of roles directly conflicts with the authoritative, owner–representative obligation of the board. Board meetings, for example, must be the *board's* meetings—not the CEO's meetings for the board.

FAQ ➡
Is the board's primary relationship with the CEO?

Myth 5: The board's primary relationship is with its CEO. Because the CEO is such a pivotal figure and because boards tend to look inward and downward, rather than upward and outward, the board's primary relationship has traditionally been with its CEO. However, when the board's role is construed as the voice of ownership more than the inspector of management, its primary relationship will be with the owners (or members). Hence, as a proportion of time and effort, a board's interaction with members would be of far greater magnitude than its relationship with management. Surveys, focus groups, joint meetings, personal contacts, and other devices are available to strengthen a board's crucial bond with members. Indeed, an intimate and trusting link between the board and members is an association's greatest asset.

Myth 6: The board can instruct staff other than the CEO. Although the board's primary relationship is with the association's members, this does not mean that the board has no relationship with staff. While the relationship board members as individuals have with staff members can take many forms, the relationship the board as a body has with staff is with its CEO. Although the board will, from time to time, benefit from hearing the viewpoints of various staff members, to instruct or evaluate anyone other than the CEO destroys the crucial accountability link between governance and operations.

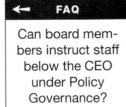

← FAQ

Can board members instruct staff below the CEO under Policy Governance?

Myth 7: Board committees advise staff or ensure involvement within large boards. Although committees can be useful mechanisms, they damage governance integrity to the extent that they obscure the direct board-to-CEO accountability or if they fragment the board's wholeness. Obscuring clarity of delegation results when committees are put between the board and the CEO, either by giving committees official instructional authority or by allowing them to evaluate performance using their own criteria.

← FAQ

Why does the Policy Governance model see board committees in such an unfavorable light?

De facto instructions occur frequently when committees are established to advise staff. Likewise, fragmentation of a board's wholeness occurs when the board sheds its holistic participation in decision making by allowing various committees to make board decisions in their respective areas. This latter situation is, in effect, the case when committees bring completed recommendations to the board instead of policy options.

Myth 8: Criteria for CEO evaluation need not be integral to the board's governance decisions. A CEO's work is evaluated in any number of ways, including the formal, annual evaluation as well as the numerous informal, evaluative comments that boards make along the way. Moreover, every time a board approves or fails to approve a management report or plan, including a budget, it's issuing a topic-specific evaluation.

← FAQ

What is wrong with a board's approving CEO recommendations and reports?

Yet very few of these evaluative judgments are tied directly to decision making at the core of the governance job. In fact, the essential mismatch between board approvals and any criteria-setting at all typically seems to be overlooked. For example, when boards approve financial reports, budgets, or other plans, rarely do they know what they would have *dis*approved—in other words, they had no agreed-upon criteria. Monitoring and evaluation is not managerially sophisticated in these instances, but more an instance of wandering around in the presence of data.

> When the board finally speaks as a group, management must pay attention. Until that time, however, nothing exists that the CEO must hear or heed.

Again, most impediments to governance excellence aren't the result of the personal failings of board members, but are deeply rooted in the conventional wisdom about the job these individuals as groups conscientiously try to fill. To be sure, any individual board has its own foibles to overcome, but the more striking issue is that our generally accepted ideals are themselves mired in ineffective concepts of board work.

Boards that fail to question traditions severely limit how much improvement they can effect. They need to ensure profound transformational change, not merely fix a few rough spots. The responsibility for that profound change lies squarely with board members themselves, not with the CEO. It's impossible for governance integrity to flourish with the extreme CEO-centrism found in most associations. To continue to position the CEO not only as the board's chief employee but also as the person most responsible for board performance is to ensure continued governance inadequacy.

Indeed, the greatest impediment to excellence in association boards—as in organizations of all types—is the belief that governance needs no powerful paradigm of its own around which to distinguish it from management, design its job, focus the wisdom of board members, and relate most productively with both owners and operators. Rubber-stamping *and* micromanagement are outgrowths of this lack of good job design. So are other common problems of boards—reactivity, short-term thinking, renegade members, and unfocused meetings. Association management has made amazing strides during this century, but association governance itself is overdue for reinvention.

What You as CEO Can Do

> **FAQ** ➡
>
> How can CEOs encourage boards to better define their role?

Helping your boss be your boss more responsibly and effectively is a touchy proposition. An association executive who sets out to help his or her board govern well confronts a dilemma. Mind you, this is not the same as helping a board look good or helping it accomplish some specific function—things association executives already do well. But appearances and piecemeal improvements do not get at the core of governance, only its cosmetics. Bringing about a true transformation of governance from the employee position is a perplexing and contradictory pursuit. Nevertheless, executives have something of a bully pulpit to bring change, precarious as this task might be at times. Here are several strategies for doing so.

> To position the CEO not only as the board's chief employee but also as the person most responsible for board performance is to ensure continued governance inadequacy.

Nourish a champion. It's much better if the torch is carried by a board member than by the CEO. Supporting a champion for better governance allows the CEO to be as helpful as he or she wishes without compromising the board's role as employer. Rather than manipulating the board, the CEO is encouraging a board member in his or her mission.

Capitalize on retreat opportunities. Because boards often leave retreat planning to their CEO, he or she can use that opportunity to schedule a thorough examination of the governance process that would propel the board into a new level of understanding of its job. Paradoxically, if such an event is successful, the board would never leave retreat subject matter to the CEO again but would assume responsibility for its own improvement.

Furnish reading material. CEOs are in an excellent position to supply governance-related reading materials to their boards. In addition to articles and monographs, CEOs can buy books for board members who, after all, get precious few perks in their volunteer role.

Don't invite the board to manage. In numerous ways, CEOs actually encourage board intrusions into managerial issues. For example, asking selected, qualified individuals for advice causes no problem, but asking the board as a body for advice does. In addition, bringing detailed managerial reports to the board turns board meetings into management meetings.

Assume as-if policies. In the absence of clear board policies, a CEO can make it a priority to tell the board that he or she is managing as if the board has a policy that says "X" (fill in the blank). This isn't nearly as good as the board's creating its own policies, but it does protect the CEO until the time the board catches on and sees to its own job. Given a little luck, the board will alter the CEO's version and create wording of its own.

Governance by Policy

John Carver's Policy Governance model is a universally applicable paradigm for the governing board role. It is a set of concepts and principles—though not a fixed structure—by which a group of peers is charged with seeing to it that an organization under its authority achieves what it should while avoiding unacceptable circumstances and actions. This group acts as an agent for others, generically called *owners*. (In associations, these owners are members.)

The board fulfills its task by connecting closely with its owners, establishing guiding values for itself and the organization, and ensuring that the operating organization performs in line with stated values. To optimize both board control and management freedom, values established by the board are assembled exclusively in categories of ends, prohibited staff means, and the board's own means. Board statements in these categories are commonly called policies, hence the term *Policy Governance.*

Ends policies dictate what consumer results are to be achieved for whom at what cost or priority, stated with a long-term perspective. *Consumer results* are desired impacts on intended target groups outside the operating organization. For example, fully computerized payroll is not considered a consumer result, though legislative data in members' hands would be. Ends, in short, specify what difference the organization will make in consumers' lives, and not the programs or services. Ends must first be stated in the broadest form possible, but the board can further define them.

The level of detail that links the principles of policymaking with those of delegation is determined by the *any reasonable interpretation rule.* Essentially the board stops its progression into ever increasing detail at the level of specificity where any further reasonable interpretation is acceptable. Consequently, the board can comfortably delegate to the CEO authority to proceed with any action or decision that can, upon monitoring, be demonstrated to be a reasonable interpretation of the words the board used.

Following a similar progression from broad statements to more narrow ones, the board sets out policies that limit or prohibit certain classes of executive action. These policies—or *executive limitations*—inform the CEO of unacceptable means rather than dictate which means to use. Thus, the board tells the CEO how *not* to do his or her job, not how to do it.

Such policies, though negative in wording, are extremely positive psychologically and are typically experienced as very freeing by staff. In effect, the message to the CEO is "achieve board-stated ends while avoiding board-stated unacceptable means." CEO evaluation then consists only of determining whether ends were achieved and if unacceptable means have occurred.

The board describes its own job, discipline, and relationships in *governance process policies* and the way it connects governance and management in *board–staff linkage policies.* These policies follow the same broad-to-narrow expansion—again, only to the point at which the board is comfortable with any further reasonable interpretation. In this case, however, the board's chief elected officer is the empowered delegatee, not the chief staff executive. Subsequently, board self-evaluation is tied directly to the provisions of these policies. The effect of this model is a disciplined board process that clarifies organizational values, focuses its attention more on results than administrative process, empowers considerable executive authority safely, and enhances the board–owner relationship.

Report data on as-if policies. Instead of standard reports, the CEO can assemble monitoring data addressing the criteria assumed to have come from the board. For example, financial reports can be submitted with highlighted sections wherein critical financial indices are explained along with desired and actual measures.

Advocate better governance. CEOs are not in an advantageous position for bringing about the transformation of governance in their own boards—essentially because of the train-your-boss phenomenon. But CEOs as a professional class can bring a great deal of attention to raising the bar in expectations of integrity in the governance function.

> The purpose of a board is to add value to the capability of the true owners to truly own.

While CEOs can, indeed, help boards with their difficult task, governance is demeaned if CEOs are held responsible for it. Despite the positive influence CEOs can exert, not one of my foregoing suggestions can take the place of a board that pursues excellence on its own, driven by the board's personal responsibility for its own job. Of course, positive change in a function as important as governance is welcome from whatever source, but if the CEO is unhelpful and even incompetent, the board isn't thereby excused from its obligation to govern responsibly.

The purpose of governance is not to make life better for CEOs. Hence, better governance isn't simply a matter of ending micromanagement. And contrary to recent corporate board literature, the purpose of a board is not to add value to the CEO. Hence, better governance isn't a matter of helping managers manage.

The purpose of a board is to add value to the capability of the true owners to truly own. For associations, this means that boards exist so that members can rule their own associations—not only in theory, but also in fact.

To Focus on Shaping the Future, Many Hospital Boards Might Require a Radical Overhaul

HEALTH MANAGEMENT QUARTERLY, VOLUME 16, ISSUE 1, APR. 1994

VIRTUALLY EVERY ASPECT of health care is being pushed—sometimes dragged—toward greater effectiveness and agility. The fly in the ointment is governance: the board of trustees. While other roles in health care endure massive trauma, governance undergoes random, largely cosmetic, and often personality-based changes. Boards adjust agendas here and there, change committees around a bit, or add a step to the budget-review process. Little of substance has changed in the role and practice of boards.

So what? What is broken? Is it not sufficient that respected, wise, experienced members of the community bring special expertise to the table? With responsible people doing what responsible people do, how can there be much to change?

Survey the activities of any ten hospital boards: You will find that the time spent discussing the near future and even the past (for example, last month) is greater than the time spent on long-term issues. The board agenda itself is largely a product of the chief executive officer; that is, the board agenda is not the *board's* agenda but administration's agenda for the board. Board meetings are more a matter of hearing reports than of struggling with and resolving momentous issues.

Peter Drucker once observed that all boards have one thing in common: They don't function. I would add that boards typically pretend to govern, while their managers pretend to work for them. In fact, the flaws of governance are so great that we long

---

Boards typically pretend to govern, while their managers pretend to work for them.

---

ago despaired of boards making sense. We accept mediocrity, trivialities, rituals and lack of clarity concerning roles. Governance as we have known it is not so good as to need little alteration; it is so bad as to defy improvement. These may seem harsh words for well-meaning, usually voluntary, contributors. My invective is directed not at the people, however, but at an outdated, inadequate process. Boards of health care organizations—just as governing boards in non-health settings—are overdue for a radical overhaul, not simply a little sprucing up.

Introducing Coherent Governance

I developed a model of governance, called "Policy Governance," about sixteen years ago. The model questions much of what we thought we knew about boards and replaces it with a coherent governance technique that focuses on policies. Despite the massive changes it portends for boards and management, the model's principles and concepts are relatively simple. The remainder of this article presents the main principles and their implications.

■ *Principle:* The board is constituted not to help manage the institution but to represent some larger ownership (even if a "moral" ownership rather than a legal one).

FAQ →

What does *ownership* mean?

Implications: It must be clear just who are the owners (the equivalent of stockholders in a for-profit corporation). The board is a microcosm of the owners (in the case of public hospitals, the general public); therefore, its primary identity is with the owners, not with medical staff or managers. Perhaps the board can best see itself as the owners' "purchasing agents," deciding what is being bought in terms of public benefit rather than deciding how to produce it.

■ *Principle:* The board is accountable to the ownership for all aspects of the organization, but the board has authority to direct the organization *only* when acting as a group.

Implications: No individual trustee has any authority over the organization. Accordingly, board committees and board officers ordinarily have no authority over administrative or clinical operations. The board must make clear to all parties that its single voice is the only board voice.

■ *Principle:* The board can discharge its duties best by speaking to underlying values rather than by making discrete, operational decisions based on those values.

Implications: Insofar as policy is defined as an "explicit value statement," boards can govern best by making policies and delegating management the responsibility for performance under the policies. As straightforward as this prescription seems to be, however, it has never worked very well because what constitutes "policy" has received little attention. So boards make "personnel policy," "finance policy," and "purchasing policy" that either contain great amounts of detail or leave such wide gaps that they cannot be administered without further board involvement. In fact, boards often simply approve administrative documents rather than make true policy about the topics such documents address.

> ← **FAQ**
> What's wrong with traditional policy?

■ *Principle:* The board can best fulfill its strategic leadership role by clarifying organizational values about long-term ends as opposed to values about means.

> ← **FAQ**
> Does the board have any role in means decisions?

Implications: Designating the "why" of an organization is the toughest and most compelling decision of all. Thus, the most important board work is around its policies that define the organization's *ends:* what consumer benefits will accrue, for whom, and at what relative worth. These determinations declare the organization's justification for existence. It is not enough to decide or examine the *activities* of the organization, regardless of how righteous or impressive they might be. Activities, methods, programs, services, conduct, and appearances are all *means;* they may well be in the service of ends, but they are not statements of ends themselves.

Debating and determining ends is largely uncharted territory for most boards. The board's ends policies should cover topics such as populations to be served and given priority, types of trauma and disease conditions on which to focus, and costs (whether in dollars, other possibilities forgone, or "market penetration").

■ *Principle:* The board can best control organizational means not by prescribing them or by participating in their formation, but by placing limits within which the means—or activities—must fall when others choose them.

Implications: This means that once the board has selected a CEO to run the institution, it should let her or him run it in whatever way accomplishes the board-stated ends. Recognizing, however, that some actions could be unacceptable, the board establishes policies defining just

> Governance as we have known it is not so good as to need little alteration; it is so bad as to defy improvement.

what would incur its disapproval. These policies, called *executive limitations,* give the optimal combination of board protection and management latitude. They state the boundary of acceptability on operations instead of prescribing how operations will be carried out. Executive limitations tell the CEO not how to do his or her job, but—curiously, yet effectively—how *not* to do it. With this unconventional approach, board committee work and meeting material that deal with the "how to" of operating the institution can be discontinued.

■ *Principle:* The board states its ends policies and its executive limitations policies in the broadest form possible, then in greater detail *one increment at a time* to the point where further definition can be delegated away.

> Once the board has selected a CEO to run the institution, it should let her or him run it in whatever way accomplishes the board-stated ends.

Implications: The board makes broad, general determinations, then checks to see if it is willing to empower its CEO to make *any reasonable interpretation* he or she wishes. If not—that is, if some reasonable interpretations would not be acceptable to the board—then the board adds a level of detail, thereby narrowing the range of possible interpretations. The board repeats this process in any given policy until it reaches the point where it is willing to delegate any remaining reasonable interpretation. As a result, policies are created in outline format, with major points followed by minor ones where they are needed to restrict the interpretive ranges.

■ *Principle:* The board delegates to its CEO the authority to make any decision that is a reasonable interpretation of the narrowest wording of the board's ends and executive limitations policies.

> **FAQ** ➡
>
> Who interprets board policies on ends and executive limitations?

Implications: This authority—the right to make any reasonable interpretation of ends and executive limitations policies—along with the attendant accountability *define the CEO job.* The board pledges never to subject the CEO to judgment on anything else and refrains from meddling in the CEO's choice of interpretations. Board policies on board-management linkage deal with the nature of delegation and the CEO's job, which is to accomplish the ends and not violate the limitations upon the means.

■ *Principle:* The board never allows its group role as governor to be confused with possible individual roles as sources of advice and help.

Implications: Advice and help to management are always under the control of managers, never under the control of the would-be advisors or helpers. Therefore, advising management can never be an official board function. Advice from trustees can always be ignored by managers without consequence; if not, then it was really illegitimate direction, not advice.

■ *Principle:* The board monitors organizational performance—thereby compiling an ongoing evaluation of CEO performance—*only* on attainment of ends and compliance with executive limitations.

> **← FAQ**
>
> How does the board assess CEO and organizational performance?

Implications: With criteria in place (found exclusively in policies on ends and executive limitations), monitoring becomes pointed and rigorous, yet fair. The board need not forage about in mountains of data, inspecting every jot and tittle of management, as is necessary when performance criteria are not known. Monitoring becomes routine enough that it requires almost no board meeting or committee time.

■ *Principle:* The board states explicitly, in policies on governance process, sufficient principles and rules for its own operation to assure strategic leadership, disciplined board behavior, management performance, and its own accountability to the ownership.

Implications: The board recognizes that its job requires discipline, for it must attend to a few critical, difficult variables without being sidetracked. It must cultivate a new level of linkage with its "moral ownership" and eliminate all mixed messages to management. Because the board is accountable for medical matters beyond its technical competence, its relationship to the medical staff is designed to permit that staff to serve in a critical advisory function. The board's policies on governance process cover topics such as the board job description, medical staff role, committee principles, committee structure (terms of reference for committees set up to help with the board's job), governance style, and agenda control.

■ *Principle:* The board delegates to its chairperson the authority to implement the board's own process, including the right to interpret language in its policies on governance process and board-management linkage.

> **← FAQ**
>
> What is the relationship between the board chair and the CEO?

Implications: The chairperson is a powerful officer with respect to board operation, but has *no* authority over the CEO. Thus, the chairperson and the CEO are colleagues. The chairperson fleshes out agendas and other governance matters. The CEO fleshes out definitions of ends and methods of operation. Board agendas and board meetings are no

---

Board meetings are for creating the future, not for hearing reports about last month.

---

longer stage-managed by administrators but are arranged by the chairperson in accordance with the board's statements about the conduct and products of its meetings. Personality congruence between the chairperson and the CEO becomes less important. Chairpersons do not become CEOs-one-step-removed, nor do CEOs pull governance strings behind the scenes.

■ *Principle:* The board must focus on its own job more than on those of subordinates, employing rigorous self-evaluation to stay on track.

Implications: The board spends most of its time on (a) meeting with the ownership and other organs of ownership (such as other boards) to forge a powerful, informed link, and (b) exploring, gathering wisdom on, debating, and resolving issues around long-term ends. No board or committee time is spent on helping or advising management, on making decisions that have been delegated to the CEO, or on hearing long reports that purport to be monitoring but address no board-established criteria.

Clearer and More Capable

These principles are simple ones, extrapolated from well-established management principles. Board policy becomes the central board product. With the board job clearly defined, attributes to be sought in recruiting or appointing trustees also become clearer.

The intention of this radical shift in the rules of governance is that management be allowed as much room to move as is prudent and ethical, so long as managers understand that the real reason for the organization to exist is not survival itself or organizational size and prestige. The reason is that human beings in need are better off, that lives are improved, that pain is lessened, that the unhappy effects of trauma and disease are minimal.

A rapidly changing health-care environment demands organizational capability far beyond what yesterday's management could provide. And the necessary improvement of management requires governance sophistication far beyond what the conventional wisdom about boards can provide. Governance must acquire the capability to lead leaders.

Board meetings are for creating the future, not for hearing reports about last month or for ritualistically approving decisions that could as well have been finalized by management. Governance is not about budget lines, benefit plans, or reacting to administrative initiatives. It is about empowering an organization toward visionary but attainable results within carefully crafted boundaries. The governance of tomorrow—the governance that will be worthy of our missions—is about values, vision, and strategic leadership.

Corporate Governance Model from an Unexpected Source—Nonprofits

Corporate Board, Number 103, Mar.-Apr. 1997

WHAT CAN CORPORATE BOARDS learn from nonprofit boards? Corporate directors have normally viewed their role as a world apart from nonbusiness governance. After more than twenty years working with governance in all settings, I am compelled to agree that the circumstances, traditions, and aims are quite different. Learning can transfer from one to the other, of course, but advances in management ordinarily start in business, then move to nonbusiness.

However, I have also seen a significant exception to the rule. Corporate directors can learn from the recent development in nonprofits of a governance model—an advance more consequential than any yet established in corporate governance.

Nonprofit boards have long had a few advantages. First, it is rare for insiders to dominate the board process; in fact, inside directors are seldom seen. Second, the knotty issue of the same person officially holding both CEO and chair positions is almost always avoided. Nonprofit CEOs are not normally members of their boards and often have no role in appointing directors. Third, in many cases board members have an almost missionary commitment to the people they represent, rather than a misplaced commitment to the CEO.

In most respects, however, directors have little to learn from nonprofit board practices. Their flaws are legion: tendencies to micromanage, to engage in trivialities, to proliferate committees, and to be careless in granting CEO authority. While directors have little to learn from *traditional* nonprofit governance, a radical nonprofit departure from governance-as-usual has potential to transform the corporate board room.

The key is a coherent model. Earlier I cited outsider-dominance, separation of CEO and chair roles, and director commitment to owners rather than management as *good* features. To rise above mere opinion, specific characteristics like these can be called advantageous only if they are desirable in a larger—and defensible—conceptual framework, that is, a model.

FAQ ➡
What is missing from corporate governance?

The missing link in corporate governance as we approach the twenty-first century is not authoritative answers to any of the high-profile, specific issues but rather a coherent model within which the specific issues can be sensibly addressed. Corporate governance today is as medicine would be if it had various trial-and-error remedies for measles, moles, and malignancies, but no frameworks of biochemistry and microbiology. A model can contribute a new way to *think about* old issues—especially important in times of rapid change.

The tide of corporate governance opinion is swinging toward active boards, boards that add value, with their hands firmly on the switch. Yet more proactive and controlling boards will, in the fashion of all pendulum swings, threaten to erode proper CEO prerogatives and managerial agility.

Germany's experience with co-determination suggests that once board involvement in management issues begins, it is hard to stop short of shop-floor issues. Closer to home, directors are already being urged to select senior managers layers below the CEO to participate in managerial planning and to pursue other intrusive involvement in the cause of "adding value."

> Corporate governance today is as medicine would be if it had various trial-and-error remedies but no frameworks of biochemistry and microbiology.

Does a stronger, more independent board recklessly threaten executive potency? The central dilemma in governance, as in management, is how to control without meddling, how to get one's arms around the organization without one's fingers in it.

Boards have traditionally feared meddling more than loss of control, so they avoid meddling, even at the expense of exercising control. Now that public pressure and legal scrutiny are rendering this approach unacceptable, it is only natural that boards now struggle anew with the old dilemma.

Personality will play a disproportionate role in this quest for appropriate governance models. For example, a meddlesome director, abetted by the new expectations, can subvert a good system and make life intolerable for a fine CEO. A controlling CEO could so deluge a board with internal issues that it will think it is governing when it is merely being kept busy.

To assume responsibility for governing, directors' first challenge is to determine just what governance is. Generic questions about the nature of governance must be answered in a conceptually whole way before specifics about communities, insider-outsider ratios, chair-CEO roles, board composition, or director compensation can be addressed adequately.

A theory of governance should resolve such questions, not one at a time but as a coherent package. It must yield internally consistent, workable definitions for otherwise disjointed concepts like policy, strategy, CEO assessment, planning, fiduciary responsibility, and even accountability itself. Conventional wisdom is not so much a theory as a collage of traditional practices—a mosaic of bits and pieces.

What should a model of corporate governance do? First, it must recognize the board's dominant role *as a group* to be shareholder representative, superseding other corporate functions and authorities.

This implies freedom from CEO dominance, being proactive, owning its own agenda, providing constancy of corporate purpose, having an authoritative rather than advising role, and exercising authority as a body, not as individuals. While a board is certainly to add value, its purpose is not to add value to the CEO, but to the exercise of shareholder prerogatives.

Second, a governance model must enable the necessary board control without enervating the CEO role. That implies clear guidance about what decisions should be hands-on and what should be hands-off. It implies the protection of CEO prerogatives by codifying just what those prerogatives should be, apart from the personal power needs of either CEOs or directors.

Third, a total governance model must offer continual evaluation of CEO performance so that incremental board responses are possible. It must give boards better choices than being either docile or disciplinary. Boards are reluctant to take action until problems become more painful than the disruption of diplomatic boardroom behavior. The time for prudent action can be long past by the time the board asserts its legal and moral powers.

Following are some facts of the Policy Governance model I first developed for the nonprofit sector, though it has been well applied in corporate boards. Because it introduces a new view of the board role, it cannot be properly understood as a set of tips, but as a *redesign of the philosophy of corporate leadership.*

Newcomers to the boardroom as well as to the executive suite are confronted with a bewildering set of facts, issues, and personalities. Directors must learn which characteristics to seize upon and which to ignore, how to distinguish the important from the unimportant.

The distinctions of greatest use to governance may be different from those best used by managers. A large source of directors' difficulty in telling their job from that of the CEO is that managers always bring issues and data to the board that meet managerial rather than governance needs. Governance and management are different, and that difference is most strikingly evident in the unique distinctions best used by each.

The Policy Governance model begins with a distinction for directors to use in classifying every decision in the company: the *ends* versus *means* distinction. This distinction replaces all other distinctions, such as goals versus objectives, strategy versus tactics, or policy versus procedure. It is not that these traditional distinctions are wrong, just that they serve the task of management more than that of governance.

The ends-means principle. The board should prescribe corporate *ends* and the board's own means, but stay out of management's *means* except to declare those that are unacceptable.

Ends decisions. These are decisions that directly answer the "why" of corporate existence: What justifies the business's existence? What performance in pursuit of that goal is acceptable? *Ends* decisions are about what the business is *for*—as distinct from what it *does*. They prescribe the intended economic performance of the corporation rather than the corporate involvements that deliver these outcomes.

Different shareholders will bring varying opinions about just what the ends should be and within what time frame. The shareholder-representative (the board) thus inherits the task of determining what shareholder value is to be pursued. This task is obviously difficult, but the board must succeed or it will have failed its central purpose. The ends define the primary standards against which CEO performance must be evaluated.

Means decisions. What is the best way to capitalize a venture? How should we be structured? Should we produce nearer to raw materials or nearer to markets? Should we own our fleet or lease? Should we make or buy this component? Should we self-insure? Whatever the desired ends, there are endless views on how to achieve them.

Means issues take up the majority of corporate time and energy. They include practices, activities, methods, situations. They address what the company *does* or is, rather than what it is for. While most activities, methods, and situations are in management's domain, some are *means* of the board itself, such as committee structure and meeting frequency and director compensation.

It is vital that the board determine its own means. Not to do so would be an abdication of its role. However, it is equally important that management be allowed to determine its own means as well—within limits. So while the board must control both ends and means, it will control management's means only in a negative or limiting manner. The benefit of limiting rather than prescribing executive means is twofold. First, setting bounds on CEO authority lets the board grant the CEO *total* authority within those bounds ("if we haven't said you can't, you can"), thereby maximizing executive prerogatives. This may sound negative, but the effect is psychologically positive and empowering.

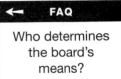

FAQ

Who determines the board's means?

Second, the board task is simplified. Describing what is unacceptable is easier than detailing how to get a job done.

Third, setting a bounded field for management power avoids the burdensome "approval syndrome," a delegation-weakening practice, common in nonprofits, that increasingly assertive boards will otherwise develop ("if you want to act, come ask us first").

The result of the ends-means principle is that corporate ends are clearer and authoritatively set by owner-representatives, while at the same time management practices are granted maximum freedom within established boundaries. The resulting three board decision categories (ends, limitations on management means, and board means) would still leave the board with uncountable decisions to make, so another principle is needed to save the board from an impossible job.

The logical containment principle. Included in each category are both large and small decisions. However, small decisions occur within larger ones, a fact that can be harnessed by directors to minimize the number of issues the board itself must resolve.

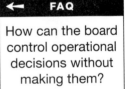

FAQ

How can the board control operational decisions without making them?

The board should address issues in each decision category in a disciplined sequence from the broadest toward the narrowest, but only to the point where it can accept any reasonable interpretation of its words.

For example, determining what business to be in limits the next lower decision about which markets within that business will be given top priority. By carefully attending to the size of decision it handles, the board defines a field within which all narrower decisions must lie. The board can indirectly control all levels of corporate decision making by dealing directly only with the larger decisions.

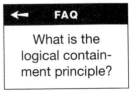

FAQ

What is the logical containment principle?

The first decision for each category, then, is a statement on the biggest issue in that category. For example, the broadest level in limiting executive means might be, "The CEO shall not cause or allow any action or practice which is imprudent or unethical." If the board is willing to let the CEO interpret this statement, then it need say no more.

If, however, this statement leaves a wider range of interpretation than the board can accept, then the board goes on to address the next lower (narrower) level, and so on until the board can accept any reasonable interpretation of the narrower language.

A number of issues would be addressed at this second level, such as treatment of personnel, financial risk, and other management means. One might be, "Don't allow assets to be unnecessarily risked or inadequately maintained." Ends would not be phrased in this peculiarly negative way.

The ends-means and logical containment principles together recognize that the board is accountable for all practices, achievements, and failures of the corporation. Yet the board's ultimate accountability does not have to draw it into meddling with management details. The principle of logical containment places only the largest levels of decisions within the board's direct, "hands-on," ambit.

Through judiciously addressing this "big picture" the board fulfills its accountability for even the smallest corporate detail. The resulting broad statements set forth the values that underlie all corporate action. Board policies thus constructed tend to be few, brief, and seamless.

Obviously, this new Policy Governance model will have implications that reach into every aspect of board work—policymaking, agenda control, planning and strategy, committees, and links with shareholders.

A few implications derived from the model include

Delegation to the chair. All decisions about how the board does its own job—after that job is defined by the board—automatically belong to the chair, unless the board delegates a portion of this authority to others. The "lead director" solution is a patchwork response to an improper chair role. The chair should see to the integrity of governance.

Delegation to the CEO. After the broadest ends have been defined by the board, all further ends decisions automatically belong to the CEO. After the broadest *limits* on means have been defined by the board, all decisions about corporate means automatically belong to the CEO.

In both cases, the CEO is only obliged to use a reasonable interpretation of the board's policy and not the interpretation favored by specific board members. Throughout, it must be clear that the CEO works for the entire board, not for the board chair.

Splitting the roles of chair and CEO. Strong yet bounded chair and CEO roles are critical. Governance works best when the board attends to the board job (with the chair's help) and the CEO attends to management's job. When the CEO is also the leader of the board's effort, the stage is set for role confusion. As long as the board defaults to its chair or to the CEO, the discrepancy may not be noticed. However, when rigor in governance becomes important, vesting CEO and chair roles in the same person is problematical if not dysfunctional.

Adding value as a CEO advisor. The CEO can find directors to be a convenient and experienced source for advice. However, the board as a unit exists not to add value to the CEO, but to shareholders. So while individual directors may advise as much as the CEO wishes, it is best for the board as a body to attend single-mindedly to its role of directing, lest it jeopardize the task for which it is responsible.

CEO evaluation. When both the ends and limits on means are clear, CEO evaluation becomes much simpler. The board just compares actual performance to board policies. Directors are unlikely to be distracted by incidental data when the criteria of actual performance take center stage.

The most useful lesson corporate directors can glean from the nonprofit governance breakthrough is that a coherent model for governance must precede resolution of the many separate issues facing directors. Because of pressures on corporate boards to perform more assertively and proactively, the need for a model will grow in the years ahead, if only so that strengthening boards does not equate to weakening CEOs.

Better board leadership lies not in directors' simply becoming more active. That path can lead to meddling at worst and, at best, merely foraging about. The solution lies in debating and determining the broadest corporate values for both the board and CEO.

A Theory of Corporate Governance: Finding a New Balance for Boards and Their CEOs

Gouvernance: Revue Internationale, Volume 1, Issue 1, Spring 2000

Peter Drucker (1974) observed that corporate boards have one thing in common: "They do not function." Others have characterized them as "largely irrelevant through most of the twentieth century" (Gillies, 1992), "pawns" rather than "potentates" (Lorsch, 1989), "ornaments" (Mace, 1971), and most picturesquely, "like ants on a log in turbulent water who think they are steering the log" (unknown source, quoted by Leighton and Thain, 1997). If boards have been ineffective for much of corporate history, they have been even more unobserved. The topic of corporate governance interested few, graduate business schools paid little attention, and books and professional articles on boards were rare.

How things have changed! Today, as we enter the twenty-first century, the world of corporate leadership is viewed with fascination. Stock exchanges and other authoritative groups issue reports and recommendations. At this writing, there are at least fifteen codes of best practice of recent vintage (Lechem, 1999), including those issued by the Toronto Stock Exchange (Canada), the Cadbury Commission (United King-

---

Note: This article was originally published in French as "Un nouveau paradigme de gouvernance: un nouvel équilibre entre le conseil d'administration et le chef de la direction" in the Canadian journal *Gouvernance: Revue Internationale*, 2000, *1*(1), 100–108. It was also published in Spanish as "Una teoria de gobierno corporativo" by the Oficina de la Presidencia para la Innovación Gubernamental, Mexico City, Mexico, 2001. The English version has been published electronically by *Corporate Board Member* (www.boardmember.com) in early 2001.

dom), the Organization for Economic Cooperation and Development (Europe), and the King Report (South Africa). Governance may have become the most arousing topic in the management spectrum, judging by the rapid increase in books and articles by distinguished experts.

The explosion of commentary deals extensively with committee structure, balancing inside and outside directors, combining the roles of CEO and chair, mergers, acquisitions, using directors as customer contacts, and countless other aspects of the board role. What is missing, however, is a theory of the governance job itself. *How* to do the job is important, of course, but the first question is to define just what the job *is*.

Is it even possible to design a part-time leadership role with any hope of addressing the massive burden of accountability thrust upon it? How can a board do more than rubber-stamp the rapid flow of modern corporate choices when there is no time for relaxed deliberation? How can boards fully exercise their authority without intruding into CEO prerogatives, thereby damaging the executive force crucial to corporate success? How can a board know what it needs to know without being overwhelmed with data? How can boards enhance shareholder value while protecting the interests of society as well? Harold Geneen (1984) claimed they have no capacity for increasing shareholder value, and critics carp that they have scant interest in benefiting society. How can boards consistently exercise real authority prior to the need to do so cataclysmically—as in firing the CEO?

> *How* to do the job is important, of course, but the first question is to define just what the job *is*.

There is nothing new about the challenge of getting one's arms around the company while keeping one's fingers out, but the pressures of this new age make that task both more necessary and more difficult. The problem is greater than that traditional *practices* are inadequate—existing *concepts* of governance are not up to the task. We need new paradigms that reexamine and redesign the fundamental task of governing boards.

Preparing for a New Governance Paradigm

For twenty years I have been concerned with a theory of governance. My work yielded the Policy Governance model, a rational paradigm for directors. The model does not prescribe a certain structure but rather a set of principles. These principles are universally applicable and sufficiently integrated to be called a model or, indeed, a *theory* of governance.

To my knowledge, no other complete or conceptually coherent model exists. Mueller (1996) claimed "that there is no accepted theory of governance" (p. 11). Indeed,

> The board is the owner-representative, and as such, it has no responsible alternative but to exercise the authority of that role, lest shareholders lose their voice.

not everyone agrees that such a framework is possible. Leighton and Thain (1997), for example, observe not only that "there is no existing generally agreed description, theory, or model of the board system" (p. 29) but express a belief that it is "impossible to frame a statement of board system rules that would be universally valid" (p. 64). I have challenged this position (Carver, 1997, 1998, 1999a) and proposed the Policy Governance model as one candidate for the thus-far missing theory.

Put simply, the Policy Governance model as applied in business answers one question: *How can a group of peers, on behalf of shareholders, see to it that a business achieves what it should (normally in terms of shareholder value) and avoids unacceptable situations and actions?*

The model begins by accepting several assumptions at face value. The board is the owner-representative in fact, not merely in rhetoric. As such, it has no responsible alternative but to exercise the authority of that role, lest shareholders lose their voice. Nor can it abdicate its prerogatives or even allow them to be defined by its employees, including the CEO. Further, the board cannot allow its prerogatives to be assumed

> Both the chair and the CEO work for the board; the integrity of governance is destroyed if in either case that relationship is reversed.

or even defined by any subcomponent of the board, including the chair. These assertions are inescapable—no authority can be exercised within the company that does not flow initially from the board, even if by default. As the supreme authority (after shareholders), the board must be in full control of its own job before presuming to control anything else. This requires that the board *as a group* be responsible for its own actions, its omissions, its agendas, and the delegations it makes.

Beyond devising and controlling its own job, the board must decide what authority and accountability to give others. Chief among those others are the chair and the CEO—separate roles whether or not they are filled by the same person. It is important to reiterate that both the chair and the CEO work for the board; the integrity of governance is destroyed if in either case the superior-subordinate relationship is reversed. Similarly, the board creates and controls whatever committees it deems helpful to its job; the board cannot be beholden to any committee, including the optional executive committee.

A board exists to govern. Though no one disputes this, widespread practice suggests that the board exists primarily to advise. CEOs often use their boards for advice, so much so that directors can begin to see their jobs as more advisory than supervisory. Without denying that individual directors have advice to give and without in any way making that advice unavailable to CEOs, it must be recognized that the board—*as a governing body*—does not exist to advise the CEO but rather to form the accountability link between owners and operators. As that link, the board's job is fulfilled only if it properly defines expectations and demands achievement. Its job is not fulfilled by even sterling advice in the absence of defining and demanding. Conversely, if defining and demanding are successful, the fact that a board refrained from advising doesn't matter. The board cannot allow its natural desire to advise to obscure the central challenge: How can a board *command* in such a way that management is optimally empowered and challenged at the same time?

> The board does not exist to advise the CEO but rather to form the accountability link between owners and operators.

I realize that so strong a word as *command* may seem outdated and may not be welcomed by either directors or CEOs. But the accountability chain is weakened if the board fails to recognize that it has not only the authority but the obligation to demand. After all, the company belongs to the shareholders, not to the CEO or the board. The board has no right *not* to exercise authoritative ownership prerogatives. Of course, I mean *command* in the same way that the CEO has the right to command in management; it does not imply a dictatorial style.

It is important that the board be painstakingly explicit in describing the nature of any delegation; clarity of roles is crucial at so powerful a level in the organization. What is the chair for? What is the CEO for? What is the audit committee for? What are other officers and committees for? These may seem simplistic questions, but slight variations can be the source of great differences in the governance process and the certainty of delegated performance.

> The company belongs to the shareholders, not to the CEO or the board. The board has no right *not* to exercise authoritative ownership prerogatives.

A board needs a CEO so that the *business* proceeds successfully. A board needs a chair so that the *board itself* proceeds successfully. Inasmuch as the chief role of the board, as owner-representative, is to speak for shareholders in defining and demanding operational success, the chair and CEO roles are important ingredients in a board's obligation to shareholders. In that light, let me summarize each of these roles (whether or not chair and CEO roles are filled by the same person).

1. *The board is accountable to the shareholders* for the company's achieving what it should (return on equity, long-term investment value, and the like) and avoiding what is unacceptable (such as excessive risk, illegality, and unethical conduct). The board must, then, connect with shareholders sufficiently to be able to speak on their behalf, define success and failure for the CEO, and ascertain and assure CEO performance.

2. *The chair is accountable to the board* for chairing the process so that directors fulfill their commitment to the discipline they have accepted in doing the job. The chair is not, therefore, the "boss" of the board but its specially empowered servant whose task is tied to board, not CEO, performance. (If the chair is accountable for CEO performance, the chair becomes the de facto CEO.)

> The chair is not the "boss" of the board but its specially empowered servant.

3. *The CEO is accountable to the board* for fulfilling the board's definition of business achievement and avoiding the board's prohibitions. The CEO is not accountable for board performance, nor is the CEO accountable to the chair.

These three points are merely logical extensions of the paramount shareholder-board relationship, which is a principal-agent relationship. Though it may seem counterintuitive, this relationship requires that the CEO and chair, in their respective roles, are not accountable to the shareholders (despite the frequent assumption of such accountability in corporate writing) but in fact to the intermediary, the board of directors. Obviously, the owner-representative role requires that the board take on that role in a real rather than a rhetorical way, allowing no intervening decision maker between principal and agent.

These assertions are not enough to constitute a model of governance. They speak merely to integrity in the chain of command. Even with clarity in the chain, it would still be unclear how the board translates shareholder interests and social conscience into decisions that truly govern the institution yet avoids intruding into management. To introduce this topic, we must focus on the board-CEO relationship.

The fundamental dilemma is this: On the one hand, a responsible board must maintain control over the CEO. On the other hand, a responsible board wants the CEO to have all the managerial power and latitude possible—short of giving away the shop. So the format for board expressions to the CEO must somehow achieve optimum board control while granting optimal CEO freedom. Although historically, critics of corporate boards have contended that boards tend to exercise too little authority, growing social and legal factors currently press boards in the other direction, toward micromanagment and "meddling." Leighton and Thain (1997) lament that pressures of accountability are driving directors into management's job but find—with, I believe, unnecessary pessimism—that "this trend can probably not be reversed and the confusion and problems involved cannot be avoided." They call for directors to find "a new balance between unavoidable participation in and necessary detachment from management" (p. 101).

> The format for board expressions to the CEO must somehow achieve optimum board control while granting optimal CEO freedom.

Distinguishing Ends from Means

So how can a board be powerful in its role yet grant the CEO as much authority as possible but not too much? In short, how can directors find that "new balance"? Using the Policy Governance paradigm, they can do so by controlling corporate *ends* in an affirmative, prescriptive way and by controlling corporate *means* in a limiting, proscriptive way. Let me explain.

I define *corporate ends* as the intended results for various shareholder classes, along with their relative priority—that is, the outcomes for which the corporation exists. Ends describe, in the words of Argenti

> Ends describe what the company is *for* rather than what it *does*.

(1993), what the company is *for* rather than what it *does*. For example, a company might be in business so that shareholders have a long-term return above market. It does not exist to have a particular plant or distribution system—these are means. I define *corporate means* as any decisions or realities that are not ends; it is therefore a definition through exclusion. Means include activities, practices, methods, technologies, conduct, systems, and a host of operational decision areas. Notice that the categories of ends issues and means issues are defined so as to cover all corporate issues. Notice also that I am avoiding such terms as *goals, objectives,* and *strategies* because these words commonly refer to both means and ends, thereby obscuring the distinction between them.

To control ends in an affirmative and prescriptive way, the board expresses to the CEO its performance expectations with respect to return, share price in relation to market, or whatever in the board's judgment are appropriate benchmarks of corporate success *from the shareholders' perspective.* In other words, an organization is *for* whatever its owners want it to be for.

To control means in a limiting and proscriptive way, the board expresses to the CEO boundaries around acceptable managerial decisions. This admittedly unnatural

---

The board tells the CEO not how to do the job but how *not* to do it.

---

approach preserves a broad range of managerial prerogatives yet keeps that range within the board's limits of acceptability. So rather than enter into the management arena to tell the CEO how to run the business, the board constructs a fence around that arena, directing the CEO to stay inside it. The board, then, tells the CEO not how to do the job but how *not* to do it. In other words, short of imprudent and unethical practices, what an organization *does* (the choice of the CEO) is allowed to be whatever will best serve what it is *for* (the choice of the board).

Let me reiterate that the board *as a body* tells the CEO what to achieve (ends) and what to avoid (unacceptable means). What any given director has to say on these topics is of interest to other directors but need not be to the CEO. No director, including the chair, has any authority over the CEO. The board jealously guards its wholeness and its authoritative single voice as a group. The CEO is not confronted with a laundry list of directors' individual wishes, only with the will of the group. Getting to that point, of course, calls for maximum diversity and dialogue within the board and will on many issues require extensive input from others (management, auditors, shareholders, investment bankers, and so on). Management is included in this rich dialogue but should not steer it or be responsible for it.

So the board as a body controls corporate ends *and* means—that is to say, everything. It must do so because it is accountable for everything. But the enlightened method of control is to prescribe the ends while only proscribing the means. Corporate ends are relatively straightforward, brief statements of achievement normally in terms of shareholder value; they are not the company's strategic plan and perhaps not even its long-term goals, except for portions of those documents that reproduce the board's decisions. In short, the planning process is left to management; the board produces the ends toward which plans plan. But if the prescription of ends is relatively straightforward, the proscription of means is ordinarily a little harder to understand, though not difficult to translate into action.

Means control is best thought of this way: What situations, activities, or decisions by management would not be acceptable to the board *even if they worked?* That is, even if ends are being achieved, there are certain risks, ethical violations, and improprieties that would still be off-limits. Proactive expression of these unacceptables fulfills the task.

Nested Corporate Decisions

Decisions about ends and unacceptable means can be stated in language that is broad and comprehensive or narrow and specific. For example, the board might call for "return on equity greater than market" or "ROE greater than similarly capitalized construction firms." Similarly, the board might demand that the CEO avoid "fiscal jeopardy" or "a current ratio less than 1.7:1." In each case, the former statement is open to more interpretation than the latter. Since the board is establishing criteria for CEO performance, it must take into account the *interpretive range* of the words it will use.

To be sure that the board covers everything in its overview of the business, it has no choice but to use very broad statements. ("Fiscal jeopardy" covers far more potential danger than "a current ratio less than 1.7:1.") However, a board must be sure it has not been so broad in its pronouncements that it has in effect said little. But addressing narrower issues, the board takes a greater risk of missing something important, of leaving gaps in its expectations. (Avoiding a current ratio less than 1.7:1 leaves other fiscal jeopardies unaddressed.) Consequently, broad decisions by the board have the advantage of not omitting issues; narrow or more specific decisions have the advantage of being more pointedly instructive to the CEO. *Completeness is mandatory;* the board's accountability to shareholders for everything requires that the board blanket everything with its oversight—otherwise portions of corporate activity are not under board control. *Specificity is discretionary;* how tightly or specifically the board needs to exercise that control is a matter of board judgment. Different circumstances and different topics call for different degrees of control.

> The planning process is left to management; the board produces the ends toward which plans plan.

A simple three-part principle of board decision making can enable a board to deal with this dilemma and at the same time avoid unnecessary intrusion into managerial prerogatives. First, the board makes decisions at the absolute broadest level in each category (ends and unacceptable means). The board then proceeds step by step into lower levels, making increasingly narrower and more specific decisions. The board stops this progression into detail at the point where it is willing to accept *any reasonable interpretation* of the words used to that point. Since the CEO begins where the board stops, this actually means that *any interpretation the CEO chooses* will pass as acceptable performance if it can be demonstrated to the board's satisfaction to be a reasonable interpretation.

The board simply manages the amount of interpretation to which its words are open. This has the effect of leaving the CEO room to use independent judgment, depending on how detailed the board chooses to be. It is as if you were to pick up a nested set of boxes by touching only the outside box while the other, smaller ones are allowed to move about inside. A board, of course, can decide to control the next biggest box as well, but under Policy Governance, it must stop at some point and allow the CEO to control the rest.

This approach yields board documents in categories of ends and means limitations that address the broadest levels of these topics, successfully embracing but not micromanaging the smaller levels. The documents constitute the board's only authoritative instruction to the CEO. So in the place of rubber-stamping and predictable approvals, there is extensive delegation disciplined by explicit standards of performance. It is possible in this way for the board to control what it must (not all it can), fulfilling its accountability to the shareholders while empowering management extensively. Define-and-demand as a governance approach beats not only the stultifying, intrusive effects of poke-and-probe but the fecklessness of react-and-rubber-stamp as well.

Rigor and Justice in CEO Evaluation

CEO evaluation, to be as meaningful as evaluation in other contexts, must be an ongoing, criterion-focused process. Minimal, clear criteria established by the board as just explained enables a define-and-demand approach by the board, as opposed to the more typical poke-and-probe method. The latter appears diligent (directors are constantly advised to "ask good questions") but is spotty and weak as a control device. It is like a manager who, rather than establish objectives for his or her subordinates, skips that step and simply "asks good questions" as performance goes along. With criteria in place at the front end, the most useful evaluation of the CEO's performance is found in the systematic monitoring of company performance against those criteria.

> CEO evaluation, to be as meaningful as evaluation in other contexts, must be an ongoing, criterion-focused process.

Of course, as rigorous and uncompromising as this comparison of reality to expectations is, it must be fair as well. Directors must forgo any tendency to make judgments of CEO performance on criteria the board has never stated. In other words, if expectations have not been settled by the board as a body and incorporated into its ends or means limitations policies, they cannot be admitted into the evaluative monitoring. Further, "*any* reasonable interpretation" must mean just that. If allowed to mean the interpretation of the most influential board member or what the board had in mind but didn't say, the CEO learns that the board cannot be taken at its word.

Proper CEO evaluation, then, is a seamless process through time, not a sporadic event. It avoids the phenomenon described by Lorsch (1989) wherein an agreeable club atmosphere is maintained until performance gets so bad the "social fabric" of the board room is rent asunder. Board control is a myth if achieving or retrieving it exacts a calamitous price.

Board Control of Its Meetings and Its Relationships

It may seem unnecessary to say that effective governance requires the board to be in charge of its own job, but boards are typically not in control of governance. They act as if their CEOs are responsible that they be responsible. CEOs rise to the occasion so that consequently, board meetings are not so much *the board's* meetings as they are management's meetings for the board!

It is important that a board codify its role in terms of values added, the process to fulfill that role, the discipline necessary to stick to that process, and its relationships to various other entities. If it does not, management will supply the board with whatever management wishes the board to deal with—hardly the mark of a body that truly governs. Part of the board's getting in control of its own role is taking the lead in defining its relationships with others. It is important that the board define the relationship with each of its "significant others" so as to preserve the wholeness of the board as the single, authoritative position of owner-representative.

> The chair is an instrumentality of the board, and great care must be taken to prevent the board from becoming the instrumentality of the chair.

Shareholders. Directors using the Policy Governance model put most of their attention on shareholders—avoiding what Monks and Minow (1996) decry as "a failure to link ownership and control" (p. 93). After all, if directors represent shareholders, does it not follow that directors must be in frequent contact with shareholder concerns and wishes? Even if, as argued by Broncato (1997), the very identity of shareholders can and should be determined by board action, it is these owners for whom the board is the agent. Contrary to the antiquated, imprecise language of corporate law, directors' *moral* duty is to the shareholders, *not* to the company—particularly since "the company" so easily comes to mean current company management and in any event can actually conflict with one's obligation to shareholders.

Chair. The model requires that the board as a body accept *group* responsibility for governing the corporation. That is easier said than done, inasmuch as directors are chosen on the basis of their history of *individual* responsibility. The role of chair is a group's device to help it assume its group responsibility well (Carver, 1999b). The chair is an instrumentality of the board, and great care must be

← FAQ

What are the proper chair and CEO roles in business?

taken to prevent the board from becoming the instrumentality of the chair. The chair exists to aid the board in being true to its accountability, not to supervise the CEO.

CEO. The relationship of the board as a body to its CEO is unambiguously as the CEO's superior, not as an advisor or social partner. The CEO reports to the board, not to

The CEO reports to the board, not to the chair; consequently, the CEO is not supervised or instructed by the chair.

the chair; consequently, the CEO is not supervised or instructed by the chair. (Directors may interact individually with the CEO and his or her subordinates in whatever ways they deem mutually acceptable.)

CoCEO-Chair. When CEO and chair roles are combined, governance integrity is much harder and perhaps even impossible to achieve. There is no more certain route to management dominance than combining these distinct roles. Unfortunately, the independent voice of ownership seems to have as little importance as it did nearly seventy years ago when Berle and Means ([1932] 1970) noted the breakdown in corporate accountability caused when the board is co-opted by management.

Committees. Committees are creations of the board, always under board control. To preserve the board-CEO relationship, they cannot be given authority over the CEO and should not be allowed to fragment directors' sense of whole board responsibility.

When a board committee is assigned to help or advise management on some topic, it is interfering with management.

Board committees might legitimately be given the task of helping the board with some aspect of its job, but when a board committee is assigned to help or advise management on some topic, it is interfering with management. A committee's charge, then, can only be derived from some decision area that the board has retained for itself. For example, shareholder relations, audit, and CEO compensation are such topics; human resources would not be.

Inside (Executive) Directors. There is an inherent conflict in being, at the same time, a director and an executive working for the CEO, who works for the directors. It is hard to imagine how such an obvious structural conflict could have become accepted practice if boards of outside (nonexecutive) directors had been capable and willing to fulfill their owner-representative role. Board access to the wisdom and knowledge of upper management does not require their being directors. The inside-outside composition of boards has led to such jury-rigged solutions as "lead director."

Lead Director. The unofficial role of "lead director" (described well by Ward, 1997) is a patchwork solution to the board leadership dilemma inherent in the combined CEO-chair role. When a board needs its independence and effective chairing most, the chair position fails to suffice and must be supplemented by an unofficial role. It is hard to devise a suitable board relationship for this role, since it would not exist where governance integrity is paramount.

Conclusion

Mueller (1996) complains of companies "where the leadership clings to the obsolete concept of a board dominated by the chairman and/or CEO." He calls for "a board free from domination by inside directors, the CEO or chairman, with informed and qualified independent directors acting in an independent, unaffiliated, disinterested manner" (p. xiii). Corporate practice, however, and even a great deal of corporate governance literature suggest that attaining the degree of governance integrity that shareholders deserve is a long, hard road.

> There is an inherent conflict in being, at the same time, a director and an executive working for the CEO, who works for the directors.

Major advances in the practice of corporate governance, long overdue, are possible only with a fresh paradigm, one comprehensive enough to be a true theory of governance rather than merely a collection of practices guided largely by historical happenstance. Policy Governance is such a model. Its widespread use requires only that institutional investors and directors be committed to excellence in the boardroom.

The Opportunity for Reinventing Corporate Governance in Joint Venture Companies

Corporate Governance, Volume 8, Issue 1, Jan. 2000

Boards of companies totally or largely owned by two or more distinct parent companies present unique opportunities for significant governance improvement. The motivations of shareholders and directors in joint venture companies are unusually amenable to a governance style designed to enable stronger boards and powerful chief executives at the same time. This article highlights the fortuitous setting that joint venture boards provide for successful implementation of an emerging theory of corporate governance. Although the perspective is based on corporate experience in the United States, the governance realities are by no means uniquely American.

Pawns or Potentates

The dilemma that corporate directors face is aptly captured by the title of Jay Lorsch's book *Pawns or Potentates* (1989). Directors are theoretically and legally powerful yet are in practice often merely the politically and socially acceptable front for a chief executive who is really in charge.

In theory, the line of corporate authority is unambiguous: shareholders delegate most of their powers to a board of directors, the board delegates to a chief executive officer, and the CEO divides labor still further through executives and others in the management structure. Accountability is unbroken from the lowliest clerk, lineman, or technician all the way to shareholders. But while this theoretical simplicity is normally true *within* company management, it is just as normal for theory and reality to separate in the boardroom.

CEOs formally work for the board. But in the curious CEO-centric development of corporate history, it is frequently the directors who are chosen by and often chaired by the CEO. Often, until there is a crisis of confidence in the CEO, the board in many practical respects works for the CEO. When a crisis of confidence arises, however, the board is likely to assert itself in an extreme manner. If the CEO is also the chair, nonexecutive directors may be forced into intrigue as they scramble to regain control. (A so-called lead director is often the de facto chair of such a desperate effort.) Shareholders could well complain that the one organ that protects their interest is normally ineffectual and takes action impulsively when it is almost too late. Corporate governance—thus dominated by management and beset with a tradition of cloudy governing authority—largely fails to govern. In fact, directors are as likely to see themselves as the CEO's advisors as the CEO's superiors.

In the burgeoning literature on corporate governance spawned in recent years, the trend has been increasingly to recognize boards as sources of value added and wielders of growing influence in corporate affairs. But there is a downside to greater board involvement. Management prerog-

> Driven by the pressure of institutional investors or the press, boards are less likely in the future to accept traditional conditions of service.

atives are a precious commodity in the modern corporation, prerogatives that it is in the board's best interest to protect. They are sacrificed at great peril. Some authors have expressed fear that increased involvement might well mean increased meddling in management. Certainly the balancing act of controlling without meddling—getting the board's arms around the company without its fingers in it—is not one that boards have typically been good at. Some boards have a history of straying back and forth from rubber-stamping to meddling, as if striking the balance is an almost unattainable goal.

Corporations worldwide have dealt with this dilemma by making sure the board is under the watchful control of management. Keeping the tiger in the cage is the safest route for corporate management. Of course, CEOs generally exercise control over their bosses in a very gentle and palatable way—through setting fees for directorship, holding meetings in pleasant sites, making dazzling presentations, and entertaining well. Management-authored agendas have been a useful tool, for one who establishes what a board talks about can stage-manage even intelligent, assertive directors.

But changes in the environment and in the expectations of shareholders and public render this time-honored practice less and less acceptable. Driven by the pressure of institutional investors or the press, boards are less likely in the future to accept the same conditions of service. "Where was the board?" has been asked enough recently that its message is beginning to stick. But despite these evolutionary shifts, on a meeting-to-meeting basis, there is little to cause a board to discard traditional board behaviors. It isn't as if all shareholders are keeping an eye on each board meeting. A large proportion of owners of a large, publicly traded company are sufficiently dispersed, anonymous, apathetic, and capable of divesting that their expectations are not immediately or authoritatively felt.

FAQ ➡

Are certain corporate circumstances particularly conducive to Policy Governance acceptance?

Except in a joint venture company. When two or more existing companies create another company to serve their interests, the dynamics of ownership change entirely. The parent companies have a great interest that the new company succeed. Their only direct, legal connection to the new company is their representation on the board of directors. They could seek to control the CEO, but if they do so, they cannot realistically expect the new board to work. Once the joint venture board is circumvented by parent companies, its authority over its own CEO is broken. So in the joint venture setting there are identifiable, forceful owners with an investment in strong governance—strong governance that cannot tolerate domination by its employed CEO. There is no room in this scheme for a CEO who governs the board.

Under joint ownership, the opportunity for the development of a new level of excellence in governance stands out from all other corporate settings.

But the prospect of a board that authoritatively governs may be a mixed blessing. A strong board stands independent from the CEO—good for the parent companies in that directors can guard their interests. But a powerful board might weaken executive leadership—*not* good for the parent companies in that managerial impotence bodes ill for corporate performance. As mentioned earlier, boards have not had good tools for making both the board *and* the CEO strong. The art of governance has not had the kind of model development that such an important, high-level balancing act demands.

Under the conditions engendered by joint ownership, the opportunity for the development of a new level of excellence in governance stands out from all other corporate settings. Owners have the motivation for a strong board. And yet, wise to the ways of corporate leadership and market discipline, owners are equally certain that whatever the approach to governance, the new board must be able to attract and keep a really strong CEO.

Such a board would control all it must, not all it can. Such a board would jealously guard its prerogatives yet pass on to the CEO as much authority and freedom of action as it possibly can—without giving away the shop. Such a board, in short, will attend powerfully to governance and

> Such a board will attend powerfully to governance and expect its CEO to attend no less powerfully to management.

expect its CEO to attend no less powerfully to management. But that distinction requires much more sophistication about how to tell the difference than traditional corporate governance thinkers have supplied. Let's briefly examine a new level of sophistication in corporate governance.

Reinventing Corporate Governance

Reference to reinventing may seem a little dramatic, but I use the word quite intentionally because I believe that the boardroom is the most fitting site for the next significant management revolution. Every other aspect of enterprise has received more study, seen more model building, and undergone more painful self-examination than the most powerful function of all.

In what may herald an end to that inattention, the past several years have seen an explosion of books, professional articles, and authoritative reports on what was for so long a quiet topic. Boards that do not lead and, indeed, often seem not

> The boardroom is the most fitting site for the next significant management revolution.

even to understand the need to lead have become fodder for shareholders' rights groups and for the press. Some observers go so far as to decry the board of directors as an obsolescent and irrelevant institution. More frightening, the inability of boards to govern invites people to propose greater government intrusion into the boardroom (as if governments know how the job can be done better!). In any event, there is widespread conjecture that boards of corporations are overdue for an overhaul.

Most observers propose that the board of directors will become more relevant and its job more executable if only a few familiar issues can be resolved. Should there be more nonexecutive directors, and if so, in what proportion? Should the CEO also be the chair? If the corporation is seen to be owned not just by shareholders but by a wider group of stakeholders, does that mean that every board should have an environmentalist, a minority rights activist, and a member of the local community? There are advocates for all points of view on these and other questions. I believe that solving these

---

> There is widespread conjecture that boards of corporations are overdue for an overhaul.

issues, though important, amounts to nipping around the edges of the real issue facing corporate governance. Doing so is like focusing on the well-intentioned repair of an old typewriter instead of acquiring a word processor.

By and large, cures offered for the ills of the boardroom suffer from a similar flaw—*the complete lack of a coherent and overarching conceptual framework for governance.* Learned commentary on this crucial leadership role consists of anecdotal wisdom by persons with formidable experience and intelligent analyses but without a full conceptual paradigm (or theory of governance) to give compelling logic to their solutions. Thain, Leighton, Lorsch, Demb, and Neubauer among the moderns—and Koontz, Juran, Louden, and even Geneen among earlier commentators—attempt to meet the challenge with an approach based on minor adjustments to existing roles and structures—as if physicians were still trying to devise cures with no foundation in the paradigms of biochemistry, microbiology, or genetics.

Some propose greater CEO accountability by adding to the role of the chair, often simply exhorting the chair to "take control." But when there is scant conceptual help about *what* to control, the chair simply becomes the new, untitled CEO. The shift—

> What is needed above all is a sound conceptual framework, a governance technology, a new paradigm for governance.

having changed nothing but where the de facto CEO role resides—leaves the accountability relationship between the chair and the board as undefined as the relationship between the CEO and the board was earlier. Others focus on more effective use of committees and more conscientious reading of reports. Some are given to devising lists of duties of the board and of the chair. Everyone wants to redesign the tanks and airplanes, but few seem interested in the strategy of war. Current literature, unfortunately, does not assist in the development of a model of governance theory, and it is exactly the lack of such a model or theory that renders the otherwise intelligent work done to date piecemeal and incomplete.

A breakthrough will emerge not from arguing the several popular points but from a *metasolution:* organizing the way in which we think of the job of governing a corporation. What is needed above all is a sound conceptual framework, a governance technology, a new paradigm for governance. It is *within* that more powerful, higher-integrity framework that the answers to all the single-issue questions are to be derived. The new conceptual picture is the critical factor and is my peculiar contribution to the debate. Because my Policy Governance model is a complete reordering of governance thought, it cannot be adequately conveyed in brief form. Enumerating some of its tenets, however, may give the flavor of this approach. The following points are not peculiar to joint venture boards—they are applicable to corporate governance in any setting—but the motivations of joint venture shareholders and directors provide a more fertile ground for their taking root.

1. *The accountability chain must be unbroken and rigorously observed.* Initial ownership resides in shareholders who (with the exception of a few reserved powers) are represented by directors. Directors carry the ownership authority and must be beholden to the owners, *never* to management *about anything.* Accordingly, directors' primary relationship should be with shareholders, not with management. *All* directors have this accountability and cannot therefore be subservient to the chair. Because directors *as a group* are higher on the accountability chain, neither the chair nor the CEO has any authority except as the board grants it—not just on paper, but in reality.

> Directors carry the ownership authority and must be beholden to the owners, *never* to management *about anything.*

2. *Directors' group responsibility must be preserved.* Fulfilling its place in the accountability chain requires that a board decide its own values added, its discipline, and its agenda, at least in broad terms. Defaulting to chair or CEO hegemony occurs when directors fail in this group responsibility. Establishing expectations (performance criteria) for the CEO (which is to say, for the corporation as a whole) is a product of this group decision process, not of the chair. The CEO works for the board, not for the chair. If the board designates the chair to be CEO, then the CEO-chair must work for the board in all respects.

> Establishing expectations (performance criteria) for the CEO is a product of the board's group decision process, not of the chair.

3. *Delegated authority to the chair and CEO must be controlled by the board—specific and totally.* The CEO should be delegated expansive authority to manage the company. The chair will be delegated authority to see that the board gets its own job done (the board's "point person" for its own discipline). The first deserves clarity due to the massive nature of the delegation. The second deserves clarity due to the seductive ease with which the elected board leader can become the board's boss instead of its specially-empowered servant-leader.

4. *Chair and CEO are separate jobs, even if held by the same person.* The job of seeing to it that the board functions well and the job of managing the company are two distinct functions. Different principles apply to each task, and different personalities provide the best fit for them. If a board chooses to combine the roles (against what I would argue is best), it must carefully delineate the two roles so that one does not get short shrift.

5. *Committees cannot relieve the board of its role.* Just as the primal role of directors cannot be relieved by defaulting to the chair or the CEO, it cannot be lessened by committees. Giving free rein to an audit or executive compensation committee, for example, does not take the board off the hook for its group accountability. Whatever board committees exist work for the full board, and consequently, the full board is accountable for their actions.

> The job of seeing to it that the board functions well and the job of managing the company are two distinct functions.

6. *Board leadership is best expressed in succinct written documents that codify broad values.* These documents need not be voluminous, but the exercise of putting them into print focuses board discussion on resolving the diversity of director opinion and wisdom. In keeping with the proactive leadership role already mentioned, however, these documents arise from the exercise of *board leadership,* not executive leadership. About whatever topic it addresses, the board would debate and decide on the broadest value and then on successively more detailed ones until it reaches the point where *any* reasonable interpretation of its words would be satisfactory. For example, the board would address general prudence prior to delineating proper liquidity. This effort yields a few succinct documents that, using simple outline form, illustrate an unbroken "cascading" of board values from broad (open to much interpretation) to more defined (open to less interpretation). It is when the board feels that the interpretation range remaining is acceptable that it stops going into detail.

7. *Board documents are best configured along lines of corporate "ends," management "means," and board "means."* Because the technology of governance has lagged technologies of management, boards have traditionally used formats, concepts, and metrics developed for management, further confounding board and management roles. These three new categories of board decisions—embracing all possible legitimate board decisions—are designed for the special needs of governance, not for management. All other terms—such as *strategy, plan, goal,* and *objective*—are overridden

by these three master categories of governance decision making.

> Carefully crafted ends constitute the board's primary expectations for corporate achievement.

8. *Corporate "ends" are decisions that summarize at the board's broad level of concern what the corporation is for, as opposed to what it does.* Ends issues include the specification of what results are to be achieved for whom and at what relative worth or cost—typically expressed in terms of shareholder value. Carefully crafted ends, then, constitute the board's primary expectations for corporate achievement. This category of board decision drives the entire corporate enterprise.

9. *Management "means" are decisions that cover all management activities, conduct, and situations.* The most reliable definition of means in the Policy Governance model is an exclusionary one: if an issue is not an ends issue, it is a means issue. Thus, management, practices, situations, methods, activities, conduct, style, programs, and all other non-ends aspects of organization are means. The board will get the most from managerial talent if it leaves means to management, as long as management stays within the limits of acceptability. These limits are set proactively by the board and would typically limit the CEO regarding treatment of employees, com-

> If an issue is not an ends issue, it is a means issue.

pensation systems, financial situations, asset protection, and other areas in which the board does not wish to leave decisions entirely to CEO prerogative. These pronouncements are proscriptive, not prescriptive; they enable the board to give the CEO massive amounts of (bounded) freedom. They do not enable the board to tell the CEO how to management but do allow the board to say that certain situations and activities are unacceptable even if they work. In summary, then, the board's message to its CEO is to accomplish the board-prescribed ends while avoiding the board-prohibited means.

10. *Board "means" are decisions that guide the board's specification of its own job and process.* This includes its method of governing and delegating, use of committees, relationship to shareholders, and other aspects of board practices, methods, and job design. The board's values added are described in this category, as well as the board's method of passing authority to the CEO and codifying his or her accountability. The role of the chair as guarantor of board process is defined in this section. Because the board must take control of its own authority and accountability, it is doubly important

> The board's message to its CEO is to accomplish the board-prescribed ends while avoiding the board-prohibited means.

for the board to codify its job and the principles it is committed to live by.

11. *CEO evaluation consists of comparing actual performance to board expectations as stated in board decisions that prescribe ends and decisions that limit management means.* Assessment of CEO performance is continual, not sporadic, and performance is always measured against what the entire board has determined the criteria to be, not what particularly assertive directors have decided. (The CEO works for the board as a group, not for individual directors, so the board is obligated as a body to protect its CEO from directors as individuals, should that become necessary.) Every board decision on ends and every board decision limiting management means is assigned a frequency and method of monitoring. Methods are not limited to reports under management's control but may include, say, reports by outside auditors or from an audit committee. These data are the only source of CEO evaluation, for it is never acceptable for the board to judge the CEO on criteria it has not set out. It follows, then, that the CEO must satisfy criteria adopted by the board as a body but must *never* be held accountable for pleasing individual directors or for merely implied board expectations.

> CEO performance is always measured against what the entire board has determined the criteria to be, not what particularly assertive directors have decided.

Although this is but a thumbnail sketch of the Policy Governance model, implications for the more frequent questions about board composition and structure can be drawn.

■ *Board composition.* Directors represent owners, not management; therefore, nonexecutive directors should predominate or even be the sole directors. For dominance of nonexecutive directors to work, of course, calls for particularly able persons who can faithfully represent shareholder interests without resorting to amateurish nor nonassertive leadership. Directors represent shareholders rather than the broader category called stakeholders; therefore, token environmentalists and others with a competing primary allegiance have no place as directors.

■ *Directors' role.* Although individual directors may advise managers on an invited and informal basis, to construe directors *as directors* to be advisors to management is a corruption of their governing role. Directors do not occupy their seats to help management manage but rather to own the business on behalf of shareholders.

■ *Chair's role.* The chair's job is to see that the board gets its job done, not to supervise the CEO. Proper governance by a group is difficult and calls for all the group dynamics skills and group responsibility that a capable chair can muster. If the board does its job, there is no need for the

> Directors do not occupy their seats to help management manage but rather to own the business on behalf of shareholders.

chair to play a board-to-CEO communication or supervisory role. The chair must be a skilled group leader who has mastered the servant-leadership concept.

■ *CEO's role.* The CEO is not to stage-manage the board and its meetings but rather to be the operational leader. The CEO works for the board as a whole, not for board officers, board committees, or insistent individual directors. The CEO should be left to manage the corporation in any way he or she sees fit, so long as the board's ends are being achieved and means that the board has placed off limits do not occur.

■ *Combined chair-CEO role.* This tradition-honored conflict of interest and confounding of roles has become an extensive practice only because of the failure of boards to develop the group responsibility appropriate to their heavy group bur-

> The chair's job is to see that the board gets its job done, not to supervise the CEO.

den. With proper board job design, the combined role would disappear. Moreover, with a proper chair free of the conflict, the recently emerging patchwork role of "lead director" is not needed.

■ *Board meetings.* Meetings are not a management show-and-tell but forums in which the board weighs competing viewpoints and considers relevant business environmental factors in order to formulate wise decisions with a long-term perspective. Board meetings are the board's meetings, not management's meetings for the board.

The Policy Governance model is designed not only to correct the situation in which boards are led by their CEOs but also to prevent boards—in their enthusiasm to control—from intruding on prerogatives more properly left to management. The intention is not that boards become group CEOs but that they not default on their appropriate role in the accountability chain. The model is designed around the obligation of the board to add value to shareholders (as opposed to currently popular advice that the board is to add value *to the CEO*), while supporting optimal CEO independence. It supports a very

> The CEO works for the board as a whole, not for board officers, board committees, or insistent individual directors.

strong CEO role, but within a framework where ownership has the dominant voice.

What use can companies appointing directors to joint venture boards make of this redesign of the governance process? They can charge directors to exercise their governance authority fully, but with the discipline supplied by the model in order not to enfeeble the chief executive. They can insist that directors neither take a backseat to their chief executives nor reduce rightful CEO prerogatives. They can appoint directors who are bold enough to pioneer in making corporate governance what it should be—a powerful voice of ownership rather than a pale reflection of management. Since the job of the board is to govern the company, not to manage it, directors are needed who can scrupulously distinguish governing from managing. This is easier said than done because the history of corporate governance is not given to such a clean distinction.

> The intention is not that boards become group CEOs but that they not default on their appropriate role in the accountability chain.

The distinction is even more fraught with difficulty when directors are personally engaged in both managing and governing. When senior managers of the joint venture company are appointed as directors, appointing companies must demand that their thinking and acting as directors be at a governance level rather than that of management. Proper governance questions and decisions are different from proper management questions and decisions. Perseverating from what is appropriate in management to behavior in the boardroom is tolerated and even expected in traditional governance, but not under a more sophisticated role distinction. Moreover, board and management allegiances differ; directors' allegiance is to shareholders, while executives' allegiance is to the board. Executive directors who are not the CEO can find their governance obligation to be in conflict with their subordinate relationship to the CEO.

The role of executive directors will present great difficulty for boards adopting a governance model in which role conflicts stand out so boldly. Whatever the argument for the necessity of executive directors in widely held companies, it is hard to make a case that parent companies of joint ventures are unable to appoint nonexecutives fully capable of governing. At any rate, the joint venture company presents an unparalleled opportunity for the practical implementation of a new paradigm of corporate governance.

What Use Is Business Experience on a Nonprofit or Governmental Board?

BOARD LEADERSHIP, NUMBER 58, NOV.-DEC. 2001

IT IS COMMON for nonprofit and governmental boards to place a premium on members' business experience. The reputed rough and tumble of corporate life and the rigors of the market are thought to be fitting background for maximum contribution. Business acumen brought by board members is believed to strengthen what are assumed to be inherent weaknesses in finance, purchasing, personnel, productivity, compensation systems, information systems—in short, all areas of nonbusiness life but the strictly programmatic.

Like all conventional wisdom, these ideas contain some truth. But like much of common wisdom, closer inspection reveals a few problems. In this article I want to demonstrate that business experience can contribute to being a valuable board member and can at the same time detract from board competence. The solution lies in using certain aspects of business experience in specific ways, while avoiding it in other ways. Unfortunately, the state of the art in governance is not well-equipped to distinguish good contributions from bad.

In scores of other publications (for example, *Boards That Make a Difference,* Jossey-Bass, 1997), I have explained a radical redesign of the governing board's job. This conceptually coherent, complete, universally applicable paradigm for governance is called the Policy Governance model. The concepts of Policy Governance have become increasingly influential in North America—arguably the only widely known, identifiable theory of governance.

While there is not space to explain the model here, it may suffice to say it clearly distinguishes governance from management, crafts a policy-based mechanism for the expression of board leadership, establishes a powerful chief executive role in a way that safeguards board prerogatives, and optimizes visionary leadership, accountability, and staff empowerment. The board can be in control without "meddling" because it proactively sets expectations about ends (designations of desired organizational results, recipients of the results, and worth of the results) while authorizing the CEO to use whatever means he or she wishes except those expressly prohibited by the board.

Moreover, the board's authority is only expressed as a group, never as individuals, so the CEO is not constrained to treat individual board member's opinions as any more than advisory. CEO evaluation, then, is only against the expectations stated by the board as a body—expectations in the form of ends to be achieved and means to be avoided.

So what does business experience bring to the board's job under these conditions? First, let's recognize that "business" skills and insights cover a wide swath. Accounting, planning, purchasing, inventory control, marketing, interviewing, financing, budgeting, motivating, compensating, measuring, press relations, and a host of other topics are included. These are important matters, unarguably ones with utility within the management of a nonprofit or governmental organization. But when there is a CEO, the role of the board includes none of these things, for they are managerial "means" intentionally placed under the control of the CEO.

> The board proactively sets expectations about ends while authorizing the CEO to use any means except those expressly prohibited by the board.

Of course, nothing prevents the CEO and his or her staff from tapping any source of useful advice. Board members with advanced abilities of the sort needed in the staff organization can certainly offer that advice with no harm done to accountability, so long as the CEO is still accountable for the outcome. But as already implied, preserving CEO accountability requires that the CEO not be forced to take or even hear board members' advice. Advice from a board member is on the same footing as advice from a non-board member—to be dealt with due to its merits rather than its source. In other words, while advice from board members with business experience may add value to the organization, it has nothing to do directly with their board membership. *As board members,* the foregoing contributions simply don't count. Thus, at this stage of discussion, there is *no benefit to governance* in having board members with such experience.

But there are two ways in which business experience can be quite useful to a board using the Policy Governance model. These are ways in which the business setting provides insights and even ways of thinking that should be incorporated into every board's mentality. In both cases, the board seeks to use specialist knowledge to enhance the board's capability as a good generalist.

Bottom-Line Thinking

Bottom line is a common phrase that typically means the final outcome, as opposed to steps in the process or interim results. In financial management, it may refer to profit-loss or to surplus-deficit. Often it implies "cut to the chase" or "give me the score, don't tell me about the game." It isn't that business experience teaches people that process and method are unimportant, but that their chief importance lies not in themselves but in their effects on results.

In a business, bottom-line thinking ordinarily takes us directly to profitability, return on equity, or other such summative measure of economic performance. Because successes are, in the end, *defined* by market performance, the outside, evaluative function of a market is indispensable to assessing business success. For business in a classical marketplace, potential buyers decide the relative worth of a firm's product or service against other uses of their resources. That is, they compare the value of the product or service, compared with other competing sources of satisfaction. If, at a price sufficient to cover all costs of production, enough buyers choose to buy, the company stays in business. (I use *costs of production* here in a broad economic way rather than in a strictly accounting way, that is, it includes a market return on capital.) However, the normal situation for nonprofits is that recipients do not bear the full cost of production (even in the narrower accounting sense), and therefore cannot by their choices discharge the crucial market test.

Consequently, while the sales figure in a company's income statement summarizes consumer choice, the market judgment to be found in the income statement of a nonprofit or government is insignificant. That clients, patients, students, or other consumers choose to avail themselves of a service only demonstrates that the benefit is worth more to them than what they actually pay for it, not more than what they would have paid were it not subsidized. For a business person accustomed to relying on sales to express whether consumers think the product or service is worth its price, this should be disconcerting. But because most business persons on nonprofit boards seem to be unaware of this illusion, they continue to act as if there is a "bottom line" to be found in financial statements—at least a bottom line significant to whether the organization is producing anything worth its cost. Experienced business persons, therefore, are to be found looking for worth in all the wrong places. So it is that the central difficulty in assessing nonbusiness success is not due to the "human service" nature of the undertaking but due to the nature of the market.

It is for this reason that nonprofit and governmental boards must assume a role that business boards mercifully escape: the

FAQ ➡

What is the difference between nonprofit or public boards and business boards?

role of *market surrogate*. They must speak for a market that is unable to speak for itself. Simply put, boards in this "muted" market must decide what outputs are worth what costs. Association boards must decide how much members' legislative awareness is worth. School boards must decide what it is worth to be literate at the tenth grade level. Hospital boards must decide the differential worth of producing results for psychiatric patients versus obstetrics patients. It is not that market considerations are not taking into account these decisions, it is that the market cannot provide a definitive, automatic judgment of relative worth the way it can when consumers pay the full costs of production in the way they do for automobiles, toasters, and footwear.

But this circumstance does not diminish the utility of bottom-line thinking outside business settings. To the contrary, due to the

FAQ ➡

What does *bottom line* mean in a government or nonprofit organization?

inherent difficulty, there is even more need to focus on the same kind of summative mentality so common in business. But if not in financial summaries, where might one look for an appropriate bottom line? An archaic economics term provides a clue. *Surplus value* referred to new value created in greater quantity than that consumed to produce it—in a word, profit. Nonprofits and government by definition have no profit, but it is possible to derive a useful fiction of profitability. After all, the function of any organization is to make a difference and to do so at an acceptable cost. For a school system, that difference might be skills and insights; for a board of realtors, it might be realty market information and a favorable legislative climate for commerce in real property. In other words, the equivalent of return on equity, profitability, or other useful version of bottom lines in business is simply whether the nonprofit or governmental organization brings about the right results for the right recipients at the right cost. Doing so justifies the organization's existence; what better definition can there be for *bottom line*?

Unfortunately, few nonprofit or governmental boards focus on this kind of bottom line at all. Ironically, business persons on such boards have not been a force for such a focus. The main reason, in my experience, is that business persons, like others, become caught up in what I'll call the "righteous busyness" of their organizations. That is, descriptions and examination of methods and practices get far more attention than the results and costs of results for which those methods and practices ostensibly exist. This can take the form of being bedazzled by staff professionalism and technology or being seduced into "helping" staff with inadequacies in marketing, budgeting, or other business skills. Business persons, with no less frequency than non-business persons, are drawn into the "how" of organization when they should be leading about the "why."

Realizing this can refocus board meetings upon carefully defining success. Typically, board meetings are an endless stream of internal, managerial material that drowns the board in the interminable "how" of operations. In a misguided, albeit tradition-blessed, practice, boards review and approve management plans and dutifully listen to or read lengthy reports of managerial activities. The cluttering of leadership time is to fulfill some unquestioned expectation that it is more important for board members to "know what is going on" than it is for them to define and demand successful production.

← **FAQ**

Shouldn't a board be involved in an organization? Isn't it the board's job to know what's going on?

School boards, for example, are heavily involved in internal matters, yet rarely work out just how much of which skills and understandings twelve or more years of public investment should buy. Both they and the public seem to think that amateurish "involvement" is a good thing, that meticulously going over budget lines serves the public interest, and that their individual and collective intrusions into the system demonstrates vigilance. All the while engaged enthusiastically in these superficial actions, board members would not even recognize the central question they should be answering and imposing on management: How much of what skills and understandings should students get per dollar?

And that's the bottom line. To be sure, measuring such a bottom line presents a challenge. Accountability is best evidenced through data, not fuzzy and rhetorical assurances. But this dilemma need not be the impediment that we've allowed it to be.

First, measurement of performance fulfills its greatest contribution, not in producing a report card for management, but when it causes the future to be better than it would have been. In other words, even though evaluation inspects the past, its highest calling is to affect the future. To affect the future, that is, to influence the organization in the desired direction, the accuracy of measurement isn't so important as its referent. That is, a crude measure of the right thing beats a precise measure of the wrong thing.

← **FAQ**

How does a board cope with the inherent imprecision of measuring certain ends?

Precision in measuring management *activities* (for example, numbers of persons in a training program) can never have the same influence on organizational achievement

> Measurement of performance fulfills its greatest contribution when it causes the future to be better than it would have been.

as imprecisely measuring the *outcome* that is desired (for example, subsequent level of skill or knowledge in trainees). The U.S. Occupational Safety and Health Administration at one time grouped inspectors by functional expertise. OSHA measured their success by the number of inspections and amount of fines collected. Safety in the workplace, the "end" for which OSHA existed, was frequently lost in the means. For business persons accustomed to the mathematical accuracy of, say, sales figures or return on investment, the inherent albeit inconsequential inaccuracy takes some getting used to. But it is greatly to be preferred over retreating into the illusory comfort of the activity trap so well described by Odiorne four decades ago (1974).

Second, an authoritative, repetitive, insistent emphasis by the board on the expected results per dollar has a powerful effect. Management does, after all, try to please a board's expectations—though it usually has difficulty finding out just what those expectations are. When a board obsesses on results, recipients, and costs of those results, management follows. *Obsesses* may seem a strong term, but that is exactly what these definitive, summative criteria deserve and demand—unrelenting conversation, inspection, inquiry, and speculation about organizational ends as opposed to *means.* While intending no denigration of either the obligation or the substantial effects of measurement, it can be said that such consistent, unyielding, board concentration on ends raises the probability of their attainment far beyond what it would have been without such emphasis—whether they are ever measured or not.

In summary, the bottom-line mentality, so revered in business, has just as much utility in nonprofit and government. The problem has been that business people on nonbusiness boards have directed their propensity for summative, performance thinking at the wrong aspects of nonbusiness operation. Bottom-line thinking for nonprofit and governmental boards is no less relevant just because it can be particularly vexing.

Informed Worry

FAQ ➡
Can businesspeople bring special skills to nonprofit and governmental boards?

There is another area in which business expertise on nonprofit and governmental boards can make a substantial contribution. Quite apart from whether an organization is achieving the purpose that justifies its existence is the whole question of probity. Even if an organization successfully creates the right results for the right people at the right cost, it might still engage in imprudent and unethical behaviors. It might, for example, unnecessarily expose itself to liability, allow liquidity to drop to dangerous levels, mistreat employees, or allow conflicts of interest in purchasing.

Most of a board's worries about the *way* an organization functions can be dismissed if the organization is successful in achieving what it should. Most means are, in fact, justified by the ends . . . except those that are not. The board's concern about means that are unjustified even if they work can be economically discharged using a simple guideline: Rather than tell management how to do its job (achievement of results per dollar will judge that anyway), the board need only tell management *how not to do its job*. This counterintuitive approach engages the board not in management one-step-removed (as so much board micromanagement does), but in *proscribing* certain unacceptable situations, decisions, and conduct. Management is then authorized by the board to use whatever means it wishes, as long as the ends are achieved and as long as the prohibited means do not occur. Subsequently, data gathered on these two aspects of performance form the *only* evaluation of CEO performance.

← **FAQ**

Under Policy Governance, do ends always justify means?

The creation of proactively stated, bounded freedom for the CEO requires the board to explicitly prohibit all the unacceptables. In practice, this is not nearly as difficult as it appears. Beginning with a broad, inclusive proscription, the board expands its prohibitions into more detail, topic by topic, until reaching a comfortable stopping place. That place is the level of definitional detail at which the board is willing to let the CEO use *any reasonable interpretation* of its words. For example, if the board's global proscription is "don't allow anything unethical or imprudent," its next level might prohibit "inadequately maintained, unnecessarily risked, or inappropriately maintained assets" or "compensation materially deviating from market." Instructions at this "second level" can be further defined, of course, and then even further defined until the terms are narrow enough for a majority of board members to reach a comfort level—comfortable with *any* reasonable interpretation of the final words.

> Management is authorized by the board to use whatever means it wishes, as long as the ends are achieved and as long as the prohibited means do not occur.

This kind of governing by setting boundaries does not require directors to be skilled in the various management jobs. But it does call for studied consideration of what aspects of organization are deserving of worry. The board will benefit from giving managers as much room as possible to innovate, to change course, to be creative with the *means*. But giving away the shop is a real danger, so that granting unfettered authority would be imprudent. Consequently, the economical use of board time as well as the optimization of management latitude can be attained by the boundary approach. But the board must take on an unfamiliar task: determining which circumstances and activities cannot be allowed. To be so comprehensive and to balance the factors of control and restraint so handily, documents reflecting the board's proscriptions surprisingly consume fewer than ten pages in total.

For the task of establishing prudent boundaries on managerial latitude about means, business experience is invaluable. Remember that this task does not engage board members in telling staff how best to budget, devise personnel practices, or perform any other function. The task is to establish the boundaries of propriety and probity. The topics for which limits need to be set ordinarily include asset protection, staff compensation and benefits, budgeting, fiscal conditions, mistreatment of staff, protection against emergency events, and other dangers. If a CEO is told by the board, for example, to avoid conditions of illiquidity or, in greater detail, to avoid current ratios below 1.5:1, how does the board arrive at those values? It does so because it has gathered the appropriate wisdom to enable it to say to the CEO that certain means are not acceptable even if ends are being satisfactorily achieved. Business expertise on the board (or "borrowed" through advisory linkages) is important in forming that wisdom.

Business Person as Generalist

Surely persons experienced in business have unique gifts to offer a nonprofit or governmental board. I have discussed two specific ways in which those contributions can be made from the position of board membership. I remind the reader that *individual* board members can assist staff in any way that they mutually agree, but that the *board role* and, therefore, the role of any individual when acting as a board member, is to govern, not to help. In the board role, one brings life experiences, part of which is the occupational background and special wisdom it provides. But despite the unique offerings business persons might bring, their major role is the same as all other board members—leadership as a generalist.

The board exists as a group owner-representative wherein members have no authority except when acting as a group. Its moral obligation is best summarized in the late Robert Greenleaf's "servant-leader" concept. The board is a leader, to be sure, but is first the servant of some body of persons who own the organization. Whether in a moral or legal sense, these owners stand in relation to the board as shareholders do in an equity corporation. For example, the board of a trade association stands in for the members, the real owners. A public school board operates on behalf of the general public, the real owners. Sometimes determining who the owners are is more difficult (for example, in the case of a public radio station or a national health organization), but the concept still has utility for a board seeking its source of legitimacy and, consequently, for its primary accountability.

It is, therefore, a *corporate* body (only meaningful as a total group) that one joins when accepting board membership. Each board member comes from some walk of life and, while that life experience is neither to be denied nor ignored, it is not the determinate of one's role. The role is determined by the owner-representative obligation of the body one has joined. There is serious danger to governance integrity when an accountant board member, for example, is automatically assigned to be treasurer. It is the same, of course, when any board member is given oversight responsibility over some aspect of organization in which he or she has specific skills. The integrity of group responsibility and the utility of a CEO role answering only to the full body will have been severely compromised.

Persons with business experience have much to offer a nonprofit or governmental board. But their contribution must be one of transferring the *underlying mentality* of business rather than its *external form* into the muted market domain.

Seizing the Governance Opportunity for Central European NGOs

Presented to the National Forum of Bulgarian Foundations, Sofia, Bulgaria, Feb. 1992

Two essential ingredients of a vigorous democracy are (1) a safe and encouraging sociopolitical environment for pluralism and (2) a widespread inclination and capability for participation and leadership.

As to the first, many private citizens and elected officials in post-communist Europe are struggling to create a legal and civic setting where a diversity of viewpoints can survive and where public debate is open. The remarks that follow will focus on the second point: As free citizens increasingly form nongovernmental organizations (NGOs), it is necessary to build understanding and opportunity for broad-based and sustainable leadership. These comments are addressed to leaders of the emerging "Third Sector."

<table>
<tr><td>FAQ →

What does non-profit governance have to do with democracy?</td></tr>
</table>

A pluralistic society allows individuals unrestricted freedom of thought, almost unlimited freedom of speech, and extensive freedom of action. When like-minded individuals become groups, the groups enjoy these same freedoms. A group may wish to conduct activity as a legal entity, but *not* as a business corporation subject to business taxation. The state can recognize such a "legal person" under special laws for foundations or nonprofit corporations. In countries where the legal framework for nonprofit organizations is nonexistent, it will surely develop over the next few years.

When an organization has enough resources, it employs staff. The staff exists to do the direct work that will fulfill whatever dream compelled the organization to be formed in the first place. If the resources continued to expand, the staff might also grow to many people working toward that dream.

But whose dream is it? Was it the dream of a founder who inspired others enough for them to become a board? Did the founder remain at center stage, becoming the chief executive or managing director? Is the board now following the dream of the chief executive? Or is the chief executive leading staff to achieve the dream of the board? And what happens when the chief executive retires, dies, or leaves for other opportunities? Who deals with a chief executive who fails to manage responsibly, is dishonest, or is for any reason ineffective in achieving the dream? Where is the *board leadership* through all these potential turns in the road?

> To fulfill their promise, boards must be more than dedicated followers of some individual leader-founder, no matter how inspiring or competent that leader might be.

On one hand, boards that dabble in staff details and interfere in staff work will not be able to create and sustain vision. On the other hand, boards that simply follow their founders will be vulnerable to loss of their chief executives and blind when situations arise that should be corrected.

To fulfill their promise, boards must be more than dedicated followers of some individual leader-founder, no matter how inspiring or competent that leader might be. They must be more than overseers, helpers, and cheerleaders. They must see themselves as trustees for some community of interest, as a type of civic trustee.

← FAQ

Who is responsible for the board getting its job done?

And they must learn to fulfill their responsibility and leadership as groups, not just as collections of individuals. A responsible board must learn to exercise its own leadership.

- From the perspective of *each organization's efficiency,* strong boards will assure better management of resources and more effective achievement of goals in each Third Sector organization.

- From the perspective of *each organization's legitimacy,* strong boards constitute a forum of diversity upon which strategic goals are more firmly based and compellingly argued.

- From the perspective of *each organization's moral obligation,* strong boards can better fulfill the civic responsibility of being legally accountable for their organizations.

- From the perspective of *each organization's continuity,* strong boards are in the best position to maintain the organizational dream through changes in staff over the years.

- From the perspective of the *entire Third Sector's long-term sustainability,* strong boards can be a stabilizing foundation for sustaining the sector through shifting economic conditions and evolving management fashions.

- From the perspective of *national democracy,* strong boards teach participation and civic leadership. They give emerging leaders many channels of practice and expression.

FAQ ➡

What does non-profit governance have to do with democracy?

Therefore, *creating and nurturing strong boards is a critical factor for any society wishing to build a vibrant, visionary, effective Third Sector.* W. Edwards Deming, partially responsible for the Japanese production miracle, has said that "quality begins in the board room."

Yet Third Sector boards do not become strong just by having good intentions and working hard. They need a pattern or paradigm to give effective definition to their jobs. Just as we need technologies of health care, education, and any other endeavor, we need a *technology of governance*—a coherent blueprint to enable a group to lead leaders.

FAQ ➡

What does a nonprofit have to do with the civil society?

In Canada and the United States, nongovernmental organizations (there called *nonprofits)* are pervasive and have a long history. Approximately a hundred million citizens are involved as volunteers, over twelve million of those on governing boards. These boards spend more than U.S. $1 billion *every day.* Peter Drucker, a prominent management thinker, has said that "virtually every success we have scored [in solving social problems] has been achieved by nonprofits," not by government.

Yet despite vast experience and impressive contributions, governance of North American NGOs is in bad condition. Boards constantly struggle with board-staff relationships and with unclear or nonexistent policy. They typically have no long-term planning, and have underdeveloped vision and inadequate linkage with the very people they claim to represent. These problems are not due to uncaring or incompetent board members, but to decades of an inadequate governance process.

Recently thousands of boards in North America have been trying hard to bring profound change to the way they operate. But adopting a new paradigm is not easy, particularly when formats for agendas and reporting, rituals and symbols of responsibility, and tradition-derived public expectations all support the old ways.

Essentially all existing literature and consulting advice is aligned with old paradigms. The undeveloped condition of the Third Sector in post-communist Europe, in at least one way, is an advantage: If boards are designed well from the beginning, the bad habits and dysfunctions of North American Third Sector boards can be avoided. That is, *Third Sector governance in post-communist Europe need not "catch up" with North America, but has the opportunity just as easily to leap ahead of it.*

> Strong boards constitute a forum of diversity upon which strategic goals are more firmly based and compellingly argued.

Exceeding North American NGO board standards is within reach simply by designing boards' jobs according to a few simple principles. For example, by treating organizational *ends* different from operational *means* and by allowing large board decisions to "enclose" smaller ones by staff, boards can practice a new, more advanced form of policymaking and strategic leadership that empowers board and staff alike.

For a limited time, I am available without fee to contribute whatever I can to building a tradition of vigorous, visionary governance in central Europe's emerging Third Sector.

Building an Infrastructure of Governance in Eastern Europe

SUBMITTED TO THE GOVERNMENTS OF CZECHOSLOVAKIA AND HUNGARY IN 1990.

T HE COUNTRIES of Eastern Europe are engaged in a heroic struggle to reorient their political and economic structure after half a century of oligarchy. The "dictatorship of the proletariat" phase of Marxism called for central planning, bureaucratic statism *in extremis,* and official suspicion of pluralism. Disengaging from decades of the economic deterioration caused by such a conceptual framework is fraught not only with the normal difficulty of changing any system, but with the particularly frustrating likelihood that artificially supported consumer conditions must worsen before they can improve. Free markets, with all their long-term strength, are not without costs. Bread in Poland must cost more before meat becomes more available. Inefficient plants close. Unemployment occurs. Success in ventures is not assured. Risk brings failure as well as reward.

Similarly, decades of political deterioration caused by centralized decision making yields a people not accustomed to making political choices and bereft of traditions, mechanisms, and models for melding diversity into democratic compromises. The challenge of pluralism is not only to transform the central government into one that tolerates multiple parties and points of view, but to *transform the myriad, virtually uncountable lesser decision processes into responsible microcosms of democratic pluralism.*

Democratic pluralism means not only the toleration and incorporation of diverse viewpoints, but the effective translation of this diversity into effective action. That is, it is not enough to open the system to plural views; it is also necessary to resolve the diversity into specific action. Decision forums must honestly incorporate diversity, but they must also *make decisions.*

> ← **FAQ**
>
> What does non-profit governance have to do with democracy?

The dictatorship of the proletariat suggests a belief in well-developed decision processes for the people. But in fact, the reality was a dictatorship of the party that purported to speak for the proletariat. And even within the Communist party existed a centrally controlled process, thereby creating an autocracy within an autocracy. Instead of a dictatorship of the proletariat, there existed a dictatorship of the party's hierarchy. Clearly, such a centrally concentrated control could admit of no toleration of the unpredictable variation inherent in pluralistic decision processes.

Consequently, in Eastern European nations, the *infrastructures of making choices* are either nonexistent or inadequately developed. The long road of building such structures will include not only new forms and procedures, but conceptual frameworks, models, and—in short—changes in the general view of making public decisions.

The most apparent course is for Eastern European countries to mimic those peoples whose history has afforded a testing period and development opportunities for such models and systems. But even the Western democracies are beset with institutional inertia, deterioration of processes, and other factors that impede continued learning and improvement. Once set upon a path of democratic pluralism by fortunate founding circumstances, the United States, for example, has arguably made only incremental improvements to the fundamental paradigm. Suffrage and one-person-one-vote, for instance, have been areas of improvement contributed after initiation of the system. But these were incremental improvements to the existing concepts. Conceptual leaps have simply not occurred, for it has proven too easy to coast on the conceptual work of our founding fathers. As might be expected in any system, calcification and the compelling strength of orthodoxy have impeded further development.

> It is not enough to open the system to plural views; it is also necessary to resolve the diversity into specific action.

Still, democracy has been alive and largely well in the United States throughout Eastern Europe's dark night. There is much Eastern Europe can learn from all the Western democracies. But Eastern Europe can do better than merely create its own copy of Western democracy. Its most engaging opportunity is not to "catch up," but to

learn from the democracies in such a way as to *jump ahead* of them. Social better-
ment occurs most strikingly when peoples learn vicariously, using borrowed experience as a springboard purchased by the toil and pain of others. To go through the
same process would be to have learned little from history.

The leapfrog mentality is the major point of this paper. Eastern Europeans need
not be content to import the state-of-the-art political decision structures. Perhaps
babies truly must learn to crawl before they can walk, but this maxim may be misplaced wisdom for the body politic. More importantly, that attitude can cruelly cheat
the visionary opportunity that history has thrust into Eastern Europe's hands. Their
sterling challenge is not to match Western democracies, but—free during this window
of time from the calcification and institutional inertia that must surely come—to
bound beyond their foreign friends, creating a fresh template for others to emulate.

There is historical precedent for a suppressed people to forge ahead of their would-
be role models. The experience of Japanese manufacturing provides a perfect and
recent example. Just following the end of World War II, as Japan lay in ruins, American consultant W. Edwards Deming brought the Japanese not only a new management philosophy but the vision that they need not be satisfied with rebuilding their
manufacturing capacity to catch up with American might. Utilizing new learning that
American manufacturers' inertia made them blind to, the Japanese could leap beyond
those whose military might had destroyed them. Had the Japanese been content
merely to ape the admittedly impressive American state of the art, it is likely that the
greatest economic miracle of the postwar era would not have unfolded as it has.

Surely there are numerous fields in which this principle can be profitably applied.
The focus in this essay is on the building of an infrastructure of pluralistic decision
making within Eastern European countries as they throw off the burden of centralized control. Simply being free to make decisions does not itself assure that decisions
can be made. Systems based on power relationships can reemerge where systems
based on protecting diversity are not deliberately debated and installed. The aim of
Eastern Europeans is neither to trade central statism for anarchy, nor to swap dictatorial edicts for indecision. The aim is to develop philosophies, structures, and
processes that allow people to value their diversity without their ability to take action
being held hostage by it.

That challenge is no easy matter. In microcosm, this happens in literally millions
of empowered groups such as boards, councils, and commissions. The United States,
with its lack of monolithic government, is a fertile ground for developing this capability, yet we have deep flaws in what we have developed. Our quiltwork of single-issue
jurisdictions, for example, and our vast network of not-for-profit corporations compose a complex array of informal jurisdictions so familiar to us that we forget how inte-

gral it is to our pluralism. In fact, we have been so unable to coordinate these endeavors or even to have them aware of each other that the term *hyper-pluralism* has emerged. (The term was coined by Theodore J. Lowi in *The End of Liberalism,* 1979.)

The decision bodies that influence a great proportion of American life are numerous and, taken in the aggregate, quite powerful. Nonprofit boards in the United States, for example, have annual budgets that exceed the gross national products of all but eight nations! Twelve to fifteen million U.S. nonprofit board members govern the daily expenditure of over $1 billion (*Board Member,* Jan.-Feb. 1992). It should be noticed that these vessels for public decision making are not functions of government at all, but private undertakings of citizens who wish to make a difference, who wish to participate in creating the kind of neighborhood, town, state, or nation in which they and their children will live. Taken together, they constitute the antithesis of central control.

> ← **FAQ**
>
> What does a nonprofit have to do with the civil society?

Although the systems yet to emerge in Eastern Europe may look very different than American hyper-pluralism, it is still likely that any society that would protect its pluralism without being stymied by it must provide for these uncountable mini-jurisdictions in some way. In other words, it is not simply the macrogovernmental decision structures of parliaments and ministries that yield a stable framework for pluralism. The innumerable microcomponents of an extensive grassroots outlet for meaningful participation almost invisibly provides the glue not only to support the larger system but to keep it honest.

Yet in Western nations with extensive microsystems, the governance practices to be found within boards, councils, and commissions is depressingly ineffective. No element in enterprise is as understudied and conceptually undeveloped as the board process. Public education in the United States, for example, is governed by thousands of separate school boards that are, with extremely rare exceptions, hopelessly ineffective, mired in trivia, out of touch with their own educational products, and unable to lead. Hospitals, health clinics, counseling services, community colleges, and a host of other activities that, taken together, virtually define what and how a community is to be, are governed by boards with similarly primitive methods. Political jurisdictions such as county and city government are governed by boards or councils whose methods are a travesty of what, by this point in our history, should be expectations for the integrity to be found in public policymaking.

With all our opportunity in two hundred years to develop and hone the process of democratic decision making, we have largely failed to do so. It is as if this nation were handed a precious gift by its founding fathers and has conceptually coasted on that precious work ever since. Only the mantle of power and dignity keeps the antics of Congress, state legislatures, city councils, and boards of county commissioners-super-

---

In Western nations with extensive microsystems, the governance practices to be found within boards, councils, and commissions is depressingly ineffective.

---

visors from being seen as ridiculous perversions of governance. Micromanagement, demagoguery, and trivial pursuits undermine the ability of such bodies to fulfill their charge. Though voters surely have the opportunity to "throw the rascals out," we seldom see that the fundamental problem is in the process. We are as blind to the need for conceptual change as the Soviets, who could only see sluggish workers, alcoholism, and absenteeism—never the incentive-crushing system—as the cause of economic disaster.

Let me point out that the radical message here is fully in tune with free markets, with democratic decisions, and with minimal government. The message is that Western democracies have been committed largely to the right things, but that they have not pressed themselves to continue getting better at their ability to perform upon those beliefs. Watching any city council or school board for only a few meetings is enough to question how our system works at all. But it does, a happy comment on the basic workability of pluralism, though a less happy comment on how carefully we have tended it. The inertia of our ingrained systems hampers the revival of integrity in these little microcosms of democracy. It will undoubtedly occur, in the same way Deming's advice to the Japanese will eventually be followed in North American management. But we fight it every step of the way. Comfortable systems are only begrudgingly dragged into the future.

Much to the contrary, Eastern Europe is in a different phase, an excitingly pregnant phase in terms of openness to new ideas and malleability of current systems. Now is the time to make not only just enough change to draw even but to make better use of America's experience than even America itself. The potential Eastern European infrastructure of governance can in fact become a model toward which we can aim, just as Japanese management is now regarded so admiringly.

What are the characteristics of the decision infrastructure that would constitute such a breakthrough? Let us look at a few of the goals for such a system. An effective model or approach must

- Be replicable across a wide variety of enterprise. Consequently, it must be a generic model, capable of application in virtually any setting.
- Encourage diversity in points of view within the same body, being robust enough to be enriched by differences rather than shaken by them.
- Allow for group resolution of differences insofar as taking action. That is, it must provide a mechanism by which diversity is valued and protected, yet through which decisive resolution can emerge to guide public or organizational activity.

- Enable a focusing of member intelligence, debate, and involvement so that energy is expended on the "right" issues, ones most likely to empower the governing group and those who carry out the group's will.

- Provide groups a way to assure that (1) staff organizations are sufficiently empowered (maximizing staff freedom) yet (2) uncontrolled officiousness and disproportionate administrative authority cannot become the real power. Technocracies, staff-dominated organizations, and a military not adequately under civilian control illustrate an awkward, confused, or emasculated governance that fails to govern. Functionaries, wielding undue influence, come to be the masters.

> How can a small group of individuals—all of whom disagree—make value decisions on behalf of some larger population?

- Emphasize the primacy of the link between governance and the population for whom the governing body acts in trust. The governing group must be more closely tied to its public than to its staff in order to preserve this civic trusteeship.

To the extent the pluralistic infrastructure is disconnected from the people, overcontrolling, or indecisive, it will not be as powerful a supportive network for democratic institutions of a more sweeping scope, such as national institutions. To the extent that central government must fill the vacuum allowed by insufficient or inadequate microdecision processes, the resulting statism will stifle political development, gravely damage the development of potential individual leaders, increase further dependence on central decisions, and ultimately render democratic pluralism an illusive dream.

The Policy Governance model for decision making and governing by empowered boards may be the only newly conceptualized reframing of the single organization governance process to emerge from American hyper-pluralism. It was spawned from a managerial perspective rather than one of political science or sociology, though it can easily be related to these fields. It is compatible with American and Canadian experience in community development, "visioning," and modern management principles. Although cast in terms of single organizational governance, it represents a republican form of government in microcosm. How can a small group of individuals—all of whom disagree—make value decisions on behalf of some larger population without disservice either to the pluralism of that population or to the need for decisive action? The model is a tool for addressing this question in a new and rigorous way.

References

Anheier, H. K. "Themes in International Research on the Nonprofit Sector." *Nonprofit and Voluntary Sector Quarterly*, 1990, *19*(4), 371–391.

Argenti, J. *Your Organization: What Is It For?* London: McGraw-Hill, 1993.

Armstrong, R. "The 'No' Response." In R. Armstrong and P. Shay, "Does the Carver Policy Governance Model Really Work?" *Front and Centre*, May 1998a, pp. 13–14.

Armstrong, R. "A Study in Paradoxes." *Association*, 1998b, *15*(4), 13–14.

Bader, B. S. "Keys to Better Hospital Governance Through Better Information." In R. D. Herman and J. Van Til (eds.), *Nonprofit Boards of Directors*. New Brunswick, N.J.: Transaction, 1989.

Bellah, R. N., Madsen, R., Sullivan, W. M., Swidler, A., and Tipton, S. M. *Habits of the Heart: Individualism and Commitment in American Life*. New York: HarperCollins, 1985.

Berle, A. A., and Means, G. C. *The Modern Corporation and Private Property*. (Rev. ed.) Orlando, Fla.: Harcourt Brace, 1970. (Originally published 1932)

Bozeman, B., and Straussman, J. D. *Public Management Strategies: Guidelines for Managerial Effectiveness*. San Francisco: Jossey-Bass, 1990.

Broncato, C. K. *Institutional Investors and Corporate Governance: Best Practices for Increasing Corporate Value.* Burr Ridge, Ill.: Irwin, 1997.

Carver, J. "The Director's Employment Contract as a Tool for Improved Governance." *Journal of Mental Health Administration,* 1979, *6,* 14–25.

Carver, J. *Business Leadership on Nonprofit Boards.* Board Monograph Series, no. 12. Washington, D.C.: National Association of Corporate Directors, 1980.

Carver, J. "The Market Surrogate Obligation of Public Sector Boards." *Journal of Mental Health Administration,* 1981a, *8,* 42–45.

Carver, J. "Toward More Effective Library Boards." *Focus on Indiana Libraries,* 1981b, *5*(7–8), 8–11.

Carver, J. "Redesigning Governance in the Cities." *Florida Municipal Record,* 1984, *58,* 2–4.

Carver, J. "Women on Governing Boards." Unpublished manuscript, 1985.

Carver, J. "Vision, Values, and the Trivia Trap: Moving Private Industry Councils Toward Strategic Leadership." *Florida Focus,* 1988, *1*(2), 1–5.

Carver, J. "A Model for Strategic Leadership." *Hospital Trustee,* 1989a, *13*(4), 10–12.

Carver, J. "Re-Inventing the Governing Board." *Access,* 1989b, *1*(1), 4–8.

Carver, J. *Boards That Make a Difference: A New Design for Leadership in Nonprofit and Public Organizations.* San Francisco: Jossey-Bass, 1990a.

Carver, J. "Economic Development and Inter-Board Leadership." *Economic Development Review,* 1990b, *8*(3), 24–28.

Carver, J. "Governing Boards Cost Money Too." *Nonprofit Times,* 1990c, *4*(3), 31, 37–38.

Carver, J. "Governing Parks and Recreation: A New Approach." *Parks and Recreation,* 1990d, *25*(11), 54–56.

Carver, J. "The CEO and the Renegade Board Member." *Nonprofit World,* 1991a, *9*(6), 14–17.

Carver, J. "Monitoring Executive Performance." Unpublished manuscript, 1991b.

Carver, J. "Toward a Theory of Corporate Governance: Reinventing the Board of Directors." Unpublished manuscript, 1991c.

Carver, J. "The Founding Parent Syndrome: Governing in the CEO's Shadow." *Nonprofit World,* 1992, *10*(5), 14–16.

Carver, J. *Boards That Make a Difference: A New Design for Leadership in Nonprofit and Public Organizations.* (2nd ed.). San Francisco: Jossey-Bass, 1997.

Carver, J. "Are Boards Searching for the Holy Grail?" *Association,* 1998, *16*(1), 27–29.

Carver, J. "Foreword." In C. Oliver (ed.) *The Policy Governance Fieldbook.* San Francisco: Jossey-Bass, 1999a.

Carver, J. *The Unique Double Servant-Leadership Role of the Board Chairperson.* Voices of Servant-Leadership series, no. 2. Indianapolis, Ind.: Greenleaf Center for Servant-Leadership, 1999b.

Carver, J., and Carver, M. M. *The CarverGuide Series on Effective Board Governance,* nos. 1—12. San Francisco: Jossey-Bass, 1996–1997.

Carver, J., and Carver, M. M. *Basic Principles of Policy Governance.* The CarverGuide Series on Effective Board Governance, no. 1. San Francisco: Jossey-Bass, 1997a.

Carver, J., and Carver, M. M. *Reinventing Your Board: A Step-by-Step Guide to Implementing Policy Governance.* San Francisco: Jossey-Bass, 1997b.

Carver, J., and Clemow, T. "Redeeming the Church Board." Unpublished manuscript, 1990.

Carver, J., and Mayhew, M. *A New Vision of Board Leadership: Governing the Community College.* Washington, D.C.: Association of Community College Trustees, 1994.

Chait, R. P., and Taylor, B. E. "Charting the Territory of Nonprofit Boards." *Harvard Business Review,* 1989, *89,* 44–54.

Chait, R. P., Holland, T. P., and Taylor, B. E. *Improving the Performance of Governing Boards.* Phoenix, Ariz.: American Council on Education/Oryx Press, 1996.

Collins, L. "The Carver Model: A Brief Analysis." *Senate Rostrum,* Jan. 1997, pp. 1, 6–11, 13.

Danzberger, J. F., Carol, L. N., Cunningham, L. L., Kirst, M. W., McCloud, B. A., and Usdan, M. D. "School Boards: The Forgotten Players on the Education Team." *Phi Delta Kappan,* 1987, *69*(1), 53–59.

Dayton, K. N. "Governance Is Governance." In *Proceedings: Professional Forum II.* Washington, D.C.: INDEPENDENT SECTOR, 1987.

Donnelly, P. R. "The Trustee as Steward for the Community and the Sponsor." *Hospital Progress,* 1979, *60*(7), 62–80.

Drucker, P. F. *Management: Tasks, Responsibilities, Practices.* New York: Harper-Collins, 1974.

Drucker, P. F. "Lessons for Successful Nonprofit Governance." *Nonprofit Management and Leadership,* 1990, *1*(1), 7–14.

Duca, D. J. *Nonprofit Boards: A Practical Guide to Roles, Responsibilities, and Performance.* Phoenix, Ariz.: Oryx Press, 1986.

Fenn, D. H., Jr. "Executives as Community Volunteers." *Harvard Business Review,* 1971, *49*(2), 4ff.

Fink, J. "Community Agency Boards of Directors: Viability and Vestigiality, Substance and Symbol." In R. D. Herman and J. Van Til (eds.), *Nonprofit Boards of Directors.* New Brunswick, N.J.: Transaction, 1989.

Gelman, S. R. "The Board of Directors and Agency Accountability." *Social Casework,* 1983, *64*(2), 83–91.

Geneen, H. S. "Why Directors Can't Protect the Shareholders." *Fortune,* 1984, *110,* 28–29.

Gillies, J. *Boardroom Renaissance.* Toronto: McGraw-Hill Ryerson/National Centre for Management Research and Development, 1992.

Greenleaf, R. K. "The Trustee: The Buck Starts Here." *Foundation News,* 1973, *14*(4), 30–35.

Greenleaf, R. K. *Servant-Leadership: A Journey into the Nature of Legitimate Power and Greatness.* New York: Paulist Press, 1977.

Greenleaf, R. K. *Trustees as Servants.* Indianapolis, Ind.: Greenleaf Center for Servant-Leadership, 1991.

Hall, P. D. *Cultures of Trusteeship in the United States.* Working Paper no. 153, Program on Non-Profit Organizations. New Haven, Conn.: Institution for Social and Policy Studies, Yale University, 1990.

Hange, J. E., and Leary, P. H. "An Analysis of the Actions and Decisions Made in West Virginia Local School Board Meetings Between 1985 and 1990." Unpublished manuscript, 1990.

Heimovics, R. D., and Herman, R. D. "Responsibility for Critical Events in Nonprofit Organizations." *Nonprofit and Voluntary Sector Quarterly,* 1990, *19*(1), 59–72.

Herman, R. D. "Board Functions and Board-Staff Relations in Nonprofit Organizations: An Introduction." In R. D. Herman and J. Van Til (eds.), *Nonprofit Boards of Directors.* New Brunswick, N.J.: Transaction, 1989a.

Herman, R. D. "Concluding Thoughts on Closing the Board Gap." In R. D. Herman and J. Van Til (eds.), *Nonprofit Boards of Directors.* New Brunswick, N.J.: Transaction, 1989b.

Herman, R. D., and Heimovics, R. D. "The Effective Nonprofit Executive: Leader of the Board." *Nonprofit Management and Leadership,* 1990, *1*(2), 167–180.

Herman, R. D., and Heimovics, R. D. *Executive Leadership in Nonprofit Organizations: New Strategies for Shaping Executive-Board Dynamics.* San Francisco: Jossey-Bass, 1991.

Holland, T. P. "Self-Assessment by Nonprofit Boards." *Nonprofit Management and Leadership,* 1991, *2*(1), 25–36.

Hospers, J. *Human Conduct: An Introduction to the Problems of Ethics.* London: Harcourt Brace, 1970.

Hume, D. *Philosophical Essays on Morals, Literature, and Politics.* Washington, D.C.: Duffy, 1817.

Juran, J. M., and Louden, J. K. *The Corporate Director.* New York: AMACOM, 1966.

Kaplan, R. S., and Norton, D. P. *The Balanced Scorecard: Translating Strategy into Action.* Cambridge, Mass.: Harvard Business School, 1996.

Kerr, N. D. "The School Board as an Agency of Legitimation." *Sociology of Education,* 1964, *38*(1), 34–59.

Kirk, W. A. *Nonprofit Organization Governance: A Challenge in Turbulent Times.* New York: Carlton Press, 1986.

Koontz, H. *The Board of Directors and Effective Management.* New York: McGraw-Hill, 1967.

Kramer, R. M. "Voluntary Agencies and the Personal Social Services." In W. W. Powell (ed.), *The Nonprofit Sector: A Research Handbook.* New Haven, Conn.: Yale University Press, 1987.

Kuhn, T. S. *The Structure of Scientific Revolutions.* (3rd ed.) Chicago: University of Chicago Press, 1996.

Larkin, R. F. "Effective Budgeting." *American Arts,* 1983, *14*(1), 27.

Lechem, B. "OECD Gets into the Act—New Governance Guidelines." *Boardroom,* 1999, *7*(2), 1, 6.

Leighton, D.S.R., and Thain, D. H. *Making Boards Work: What Directors Must Do to Make Canadian Boards Effective.* Toronto: McGraw-Hill Ryerson, 1997.

Lilly Endowment. *Trustee Education Manual.* Indianapolis, Ind.: Lilly Endowment, 1990.

Lorsch, J. W. *Pawns or Potentates: The Reality of America's Corporate Boards.* Boston: Harvard Business School Press, 1989.

Louden, J. K. *The Effective Director in Action.* New York: AMACOM, 1975.

Lowi, T. J. *The End of Liberalism: The Second Republic of the United States.* New York: Norton, 1979.

Mace, M. *Directors: Myth and Reality.* Boston: Division of Research, Harvard Business School, 1971.

Mascotte, J. P. "The Importance of Board Effectiveness in Not-for-Profit Organizations." In R. D. Herman and J. Van Til (eds.), *Nonprofit Boards of Directors.* New Brunswick, N.J.: Transaction, 1989.

McAdam, T. W., and Gies, D. L. "Managing Expectations: What Effective Board Members Ought to Expect from Nonprofit Organizations." In R. D. Herman and J. Van Til (eds.), *Nonprofit Boards of Directors.* New Brunswick, N.J.: Transaction, 1989.

Middleton, M. *The Place and Power of Non-Profit Boards of Directors.* Working Paper no. 78, Program on Non-Profit Organizations. New Haven, Conn.: Institution for Social and Policy Studies, Yale University, 1983.

Middleton, M. "Nonprofit Boards of Directors: Beyond the Governance Function." In W. W. Powell (ed.), *The Nonprofit Sector: A Research Handbook.* New Haven, Conn.: Yale University Press, 1987.

Mill, J. S. *Considerations on Representative Government.* New York: Harper, 1867.

Monks, R.A.G., and Minow, N. *Watching the Watchers: Corporate Governance in the 21st Century.* Malden, Mass.: Blackwell, 1996.

Mueller, R. K. *Anchoring Points for Corporate Directors: Obeying the Unenforceable.* Westport, Conn.: Quorum Books, 1996.

Murray, V., and Brudney, J. "Improving Nonprofit Boards: What Works and What Doesn't?" *Nonprofit World,* 1997, *15*(3), 11–16.

Murray, V., and Brudney, J. "Do Intentional Efforts to Improve Boards Really Work?" *Nonprofit Management and Leadership,* 1998a, *8*(4), 333–348.

Murray, V., and Brudney, J. Letter to the editor. *Nonprofit World,* 1998b, *16*(1), 4–5.

National Association for Community Leadership. "Preparing 'Civic Trustees': What Is the Role of Community Leadership Programs?" Indianapolis, Ind.: National Association for Community Leadership, 1989.

Nelson, C. A. "Managing Resources." In R. T. Ingram (ed.), *Handbook of College and University Trusteeship: A Practical Guide for Trustees, Chief Executives, and Other*

Leaders Responsible for Developing Effective Governing Boards. San Francisco: Jossey-Bass, 1980.

Neu, C. H., Jr., and Sumek, L. J. "Municipal Governance Challenge of the 1980s." *Florida Municipal Record,* 1983, *56,* 11–22.

Odiorne, G. S. *Management and the Activity Trap.* New York: HarperCollins, 1974.

Oliver, C. (ed.). *The Policy Governance Fieldbook.* San Francisco: Jossey-Bass, 1999.

Price, J. L. "The Impact of Governing Boards on Organizational Effectiveness and Morale." *Administrative Science Quarterly,* 1963, *8*(3), 361–378.

Reecer, M. "Yes, Boards Are Under Fire, but Reports of Your Death Are Greatly Exaggerated." *American School Board Journal,* 1989, *176*(3), 31–34.

Riesman, D. "Foreword." In M. M. Wood, *Trusteeship in the Private College.* Baltimore: Johns Hopkins University Press, 1985.

Robins, A. J., and Blackburn, C. "Governing Boards in Mental Health: Roles and Training Needs." In S. Slavin (ed.), *Social Administration.* New York: Haworth Press, 1978.

Rousseau, J. J. "Discourse on Political Economy." In *Jean-Jacques Rousseau: The Social Contract.* Trans. C. Betts. Oxford: Oxford University Press, 1999a. (Originally published in 1758)

Rousseau, J. J. "The Social Contract." In *Jean-Jacques Rousseau: The Social Contract.* Trans. C. Betts. Oxford: Oxford University Press, 1999b. (Originally published in 1762)

Royer, G. *School Board Leadership, 2000: The Things Staff Didn't Tell You at Orientation.* Houston: Brockton, 1996.

Savage, T. J. "Not-for-Profit Trusteeship: Salvaging the Myth." Paper presented at the Conference on Research on Volunteerism and Nonprofit Organizations, Blacksburg, Va., 1984.

Smith, E. E. "Management's Least Used Asset: The Board of Directors." In *The Dynamics of Management.* AMA Management Report no. 14. New York: AMACOM, 1958.

Tocqueville, A. de. *Democracy in America.* Trans. G. Lawrence. New York: HarperCollins, 1966. (Originally published in 1835)

United Way of America. *Boardwalk: Working at Leadership Knowledge.* Unnumbered vol.: *Financial Decision Making.* Alexandria, Va.: United Way of America, 1985.

Walker, J. M. "Limits of Strategic Management in Voluntary Organizations." *Journal of Voluntary Action Research,* 1983, *12*(3), 39–55.

Ward, R. D. *Twenty-First-Century Corporate Board.* New York: Wiley, 1997.

Wilson, E. O. *Consilience: The Unity of Knowledge.* New York: Vintage Books, 1998.

Witt, J. A. *Building a Better Hospital Board.* Ann Arbor, Mich.: Health Administration Press, 1987.

Wolfe, J. *An Introduction to Political Philosophy.* Oxford: Oxford University Press, 1996.

Wood, M. *The Governing Board's Existential Quandary: An Empirical Analysis of Board Behavior in the Charitable Sector.* Working Paper no. 143, Program on Non-Profit Organizations. New Haven, Conn.: Institution for Social and Policy Studies, Yale University, 1989.

Index

A

Abstracting up: and broader concerns, 358–359; and executive limitations policies, 357–360; and pinning down details, 359–360

Accountability, board, 29, 33, 58; for staff behavior, 399–404

Accreditors, protection of governance from, 504–508

Actual fiscal condition, 311–313, 413–414

Administrative cost: as CEO's prerogative, 410–412; definition of, 408–410

Advice: and advisory role of board members, 23; asking for, 304; *versus* instruction, 518; mechanisms of, 513–514; putting in perspective, 517–518; and tips for creating advisory boards, 516–518

Advocacy, 270

Agenda: board ownership of, 387–389; CEO role in putting together, 387; chairperson role in putting together, 388, 389; control of, 22–23, 385; and governance implementation, 476–477; perpetual, 388–389. *See also* Consent agenda

American Assembly of Collegiate Schools of Business (AACSB), 272

American Hospital Association, 123

American Institute of Architects (AIA), 323–325

American Red Cross, 65

American School Board Journal (ASBJ), 531, 536, 539

Anheier, H. K., 335

Any reasonable interpretation rule, 235, 303; logic of, 347–348; philosophy of, 348–349; practice of, 349–352; and staff assistance, 425; and too much confidence in CEO, 350. *See also* Interpretation

Appalachia Educational Laboratory, 566

Approval process, 20–21, 302, 316–318, 328, 330–333. *See also* Approval syndrome; Consent agenda

Approval syndrome, criterion-based evidence *versus*, 419–423. *See also* Approval process

Aramony, W., 399–400, 402

Argenti, J., 14, 607

Armstrong, R., 36

Association, 42

Association Management, 579

Association of Community College Trustees (ACCT), 65

Associations: and essential characteristics of boards, 43; expectations of, for governance model, 46; and member associations, 363–366; and need for universal model for governance, 42–46; and nonmember associations, 366–367; ownership in, 61; and problem of process, 580–581; and trade associations, 274–280. *See also* Federations; Trade association

Attendance, 482. *See also* Quorums

Authority: acting as final, 354–356; acting as initial, 356; and acting as initial, *versus* final authority, 355; and board-ownership relationship, 58–59; confusing chain of, 361–367; delegation of, to CEO, 238; and membership association, 363–366; and non-member associations, 366–367; source of board, 63–64

B

Bader, B. S., 340

Balance sheets, 406

Belief statement, integration of, 193

Bellah, R. N., 339

Berle, A. A., 612

Best practices, 41, 44

Blackburn, C., 336

Board: and board-CEO relationship, 512; and board-executive relationship policies, 475; and concerns about CEO competence, 242; cost of operating, 390–392; culpability, 399–404; governor role of, 7–9; interaction,

23, 74–75; owner-representative role of, 5–7, 32; self-evaluation of, 434–436. *See also* Board families; Board members; Board-ownership relationship

Board approval. *See* Approval process; Approval syndrome; Consent agendas

Board documents. *See* Documents

Board families: and federations, 104–112; and holding companies, 113–120. *See also* Federations; Holding companies

Board members: advisory role of, 23; CEOs as, 169–171; and constituency expectations, 76–78, 538; direct inspection by, 432–433; and governing-managing distinction, 526–528; recruitment of, 72, 164–168. *See also* Governing *versus* managing distinction; Recruitment; Single voice principle

Board-ownership relationship: and authority of board, 57–58; and consumer confusion, 61–65; formalizing, 68–69; and identification of ownership, 58–59; and stakeholder confusion, 59–61; understanding, 57–65

Boards That Make a Difference (Carver), 275, 338, 541, 625

Bottom-line thinking, 627–630

Boundary setting, 303–304

Bozeman, B., 330–331

Broadcast communication, 73

Broncato, C. K., 611

Brudney, J., 35, 36

Budgeting: actual fiscal condition *versus,* 312–313; appropriate control of, based on governance significance, 320–322; beyond numbers to governance values in, 322–323; board's role in, 414; and budget approval, 316–318; and budget as governance document, 487–488; and building budget policy, 323–326; and levels of detail, 318–320

Burton City Council, 289–292

Business experience, 625–633

Bylaws, 140, 289; and medical staff, 489; relationship between policies and, 479–480; and tips for creating bylaw provisions, 480–485; updating existing, 485

C

Cadbury Commission (United Kingdom), 602–603

Capital budgets, 488

Carter, J., 527

Carver, J., 4, 6, 16, 17, 35, 36, 123, 127, 234, 338–340, 586, 604, 611

Carver, M. M., 16, 17

Carver user, definition of, 36–37

CEO (Chief executive officer): administrative cost as prerogative of, 410–412; advantages of having, 240–242; board delegation to, 19, 238; and board membership, 169–171; checklist for self-evaluation of, 462–463; delegating administration of discipline to, 218–223; evaluation of, 448–449; and executive committees, 153–154; executive director *versus*, 206–208; guidance of, toward Policy Governance, 496–499; and illusion of personal objectives, 233; and issue of trust in relationship to board, 444–447; job description for, 237–239; putting evaluation of in perspective, 450–459; relationship of chairperson to, 177–180, 241; role of, in support of board unity, 134

Chairperson: board delegation to, 19–20; and bylaw, 483; and lack of leadership, 188–190; relationship of, to CEO, 177–180, 241; role of, in putting together agenda, 388–389; and tips for effective chairing, 185–187

Chait, R. P., 338

Chamberlaine, M., 92

"Changing the Entitlement Culture" (McGowen and Miller), 539

Chief administrative officer. *See* CEO

Citizen input, 69–71

City council, ends policies for, 288–292

City manager, delegating to, 207

Clemow, T., 338

Colorado Springs, Colorado, 198

Commitment, 40–41, 438–439, 474

Committees: and advisory, 516–518; and bylaws, 483–484; and committee confusion, 512–513; and conceptual wholeness, 22; and direct inspection, 431–432; executive, 150–155; school superintendent and, 546; and wholeness, 22. *See also* Executive committees; Finance committees

Communication: broadcast, 73; CEO, to board, of operational decisions, 211–213; inter-board, 470–471; of operational decisions, 211–213

Community College League of California (CCLC), 271

Compensation plan, 487

Compromise, 40

Conceptual wholeness: and committees, 22; difficulty of, 38–41; mechanics to realize, 133–134; most common obstacles to, 40–41; unfamiliarity with, 41

Conduct, board: and designing discipline for the board, 203–206; and governing approach, 204; planning, 202–208; and setting expectations for relations with staff, 206–208

Conduct, organizational, and staff means, 301–302

Confederation Life (Toronto), 371–372

Consensus, 19

Consent agenda, 140; modified, 505–506; and responsible rubber-stamping, 393–395

Constituency expectations, 76–78, 99, 538

Consumers: as board members, 76–78; input of, 69–71; owners *versus*, 61–65

Continental Illinois (Chicago), 371–372, 400–401

Control: appropriate, over budget, 320–322; and Policy Governance model, 427–428; staff, over advisory arrangements, 513–514

Corporate Board, 595

Corporate governance: board control of meetings and relationships in, 611–612; CEO evaluation in, 610; and corporate ends, 607–608; in joint venture companies, 611–612; and nested corporate decisions, 608–610; new paradigm for, 603–607; nonprofit model for, 595–601; reinventing, 617–624

Corporate Governance, 614

Corporate membership, 480–481

Cost: administrative, 408–412; and cost accounting, 275; of desired outcomes, 255–259; ineffectual governance, 391–392; of meetings, 391; of operating board, 390–392; of staff time, 391; of time and energy, 390; and worth of results, 95–97

Council-City manager relationship, policy type, 207

Covenant House, 400–401

Criteria: and CEO evaluation, 453–454; in self-evaluation, 435–436; setting and checking, 420

Curricula, transparency of, 251–254

Customer focus, 61–64, 122

Customer-owner distinction: confusion about, 106–107; and customer-owner overlap, 121–123; maintaining, 124–126; systematic support for, 126–128

Czechoslovakia, 638

D

Danzberger, J. F., 335–336

Dayton, K. N., 338

Delegation: to CEO, 19, 218–223, 238; to chairperson, 19–20; to city manager, 207; of discipline to CEO, 218–223; and monitoring, 405–407; overlap in lines of, 115–116; pathways, 119; and reverse delegation, 545

Demb, A., 618

Deming, W. E., 636

Democracy, nonprofit governance and, 634–635, 639

Detail, levels of, 284, 297, 318–320

Direct inspection: by assigned member, 432–433; by committee, 431–432; method of monitoring, 429–433; turning approval into, 506–507; by whole board, 430–431

Discipline: delegation of, to CEO, 219–223; designing, for board, 203–206; and direct inspection monitoring, 429–433; ends policy for, 221

Dissent, 82–83

Diversity: achieving, 79–84; and obligation to ownership, 79–80; positive steps for, 81–84; and representation, 80–81

Documents: conversion process for, 490; converting old to new, 487–489; hierarchy of board, 480; and Policy Governance, 487–489

Donnelly, P. R., 343

Drucker, P. F., 336, 337, 580, 589, 602, 636

Duca, D. J., 331

E

East Allen County Schools (EACS), 273

Eastern Europe, 638–643

Eclecticism, allure of, 40

Education, 73, 270, 469, 531–539. *See also* Public education

Einstein, A., 34, 44, 45, 551

Elected boards: commonality among, 288–289; difference of, from nonprofit boards, 90–91; and raising expectations of governance, 92–93; and resistance to change, 91; and responsibilities of electorate, 91–92; similarities of fundamental tasks of, with nonprofit governance, 89–90; special governance challenge of, 89–93

Elvedon Community College, 69

Embroiderer's Guild of America, 123

Ends: authoritative prescription of, 534–535; brief refresher on, 275; corporate, 607–608; of federations, 109–111; issues in flux, 467–468; judicious choice of, 101–102; and mega-ends, 256, 269–272, 276; and presence of founder parent, 216–217; relationship of, to budget, 323–326; separation of, from means, 252–253, 270, 551–552; stability of organizational, 467–468

Ends policies: amount of information needed for, 287; for board of trade association, 274–280; CEO interpretation of, 234–236; and CEO organizational objectives, 231–233; for city council, 288–292; detail in, 284, 297; for hospital board, 293–297; and low confidence ends, 231–233; for ministry, 554–555; for public school board, 281–287; and revitalization of mission, 264–267; and single temporary, 475–476; in social services, 551–552

Ends-means distinction, 13–15, 252–253, 270, 551–552

Environmental changes, 468

Evaluation, CEO: assessing, 457–459; in corporate governance, 610; importance of, 448–449; and meeting of criteria, 453–454; and monitoring, 469–470; necessity of, for organizational success, 450–459; pitfalls for, 460–461; purpose of, 456–457; putting in perspective, 450–459; self-assessment of board readiness for, 454–455; and self-evaluation by CEO, 462–463; staff, client, or public input for, 461; steps for, 452–453

Evangelical Lutheran Church in America, 269

Executive committees: and bylaws, 484–485; and CEO, 153–154; overuse of, 150–155; reasons for authorization of, 151–153; rethinking, 154–155

Executive limitations policies: and abstracting up, 358; and avoidance of policing function, 310; CEO interpretation of, 234–236; and implementation, 474–475; as set of minimal requirements, 308–309; and staff means, 301–304

Expertise, use of individual, 306–307

F

Family Service Ontario (FSO), 313–315, 417

Federations: definition of, 105–106; ends appropriate to, 109–111; ends relationships in, 111; as families of boards, 104–112; and fidelity to entire memberships, 107–108; and interface between owners and operators, 109; members of, as responsible owners, 111–112; owner-customer relationship in, 106–107; structural configuration of, 105. See also Associations

Fenn, D. H., Jr., 338

Fiduciary responsibility, 330–343

Finance committees, need for, 173–174, 320, 328

Financial condition policy, 313–315. See also Actual fiscal condition

Financial management: board leadership in, 329; ends development in, 323–326; and fiduciary responsibility, 327–329; and financial planning policy of American Institute of Architects, 324; monitoring, 413–418; and traditional financial approval practices, 328

Fink, J., 337, 338

Fiscal planning: and building a budget policy, 340–342; and conceptual coherence, 335–337; and governance value of budget numbers, 333–335; making informed fiscal policy, 305–307; and policy governance model, 337–340; redefining board's role in, 330–343; and traditional board approval, 330–333; at various levels of detail, 319

Focus groups, 73, 100

Fort Wayne, Indiana, 273

Founder-members: and abuse of personality-based power, 216; and founder vision, 217; and founding parent syndrome, 149; and governing in shadow of founder-CEO, 214–217; presence of, on board, 146–149

Fundraising, 469; board's role in, 520; building into board activity, 521–522; and funding sources, 82; and organization worth, 521; and protection of governance from funders, 504–508; and responsibilities of governing, 519–522

Futurists, 381

G

Gelman, S. R., 336, 338

Geneen, H. S., 336, 603, 618

General Motors, 148

General will, 5–6

Germany, 596

Gies, D. L., 340

Gillies, J., 602

Girl Scouts, 65, 523–525

Goals, use of, in Policy Governance, 15

Gouvernance: Revue Internationale, 602

Governance: central questions for a theory of, 9; corporate, 595–601; flaws of, 335–337; hands-on *versus* hands-off, 371–375; as inductive, 157–159; *versus* management, 8, 156–159, 526–528; myths that impede good, 581–584; and policy governance model, 9–23; practice *versus* concepts in, 3–4; process policies, 475; protection of, from law, funders, accreditors, 504–508; remaking, 531–539

Governance, effectiveness of: elements of, 33; and purpose of governance, 31; and rela-tionship to organizational effectiveness, 29–34

Governance model: flexibility of, 25–28; function of, 26; universality of, 42–46

Governance research: misleading interpreta-tions of, 35–37; rethinking, 29–34

Governing *versus* management distinction, 8, 156–159, 526–528

Grant applications, 488–489

Great Britain, 576–578

Greenleaf, R. K., 6, 10, 19, 22–23, 34, 187, 336, 337, 526, 532, 581, 632

Group wisdom, 385

H

Hall, P. D., 334, 335, 337–338

Halton Region Board of Education, 65

Hange, J. E., 340–341, 566, 567, 569, 570

Health Management Quarterly, 589

Heimovics, R. D., 336, 337

Herman, R. D., 334, 336–338

Hierarchy: appropriate use of, 87–88; and board authority, 84–88; and horizontal organiza-tions, 84–85; and ownership, 85–86; recog-nizing, *versus* accepting, 86

Holding companies: and confounding of federa-tion and parent-subsidiary forms, 114; and empowerment within boundaries, 117–118; and establishing a stockholder representa-tive, 118–120; as families of boards, 113–120; line of authority in, 116–117; and overlap in lines of delegation, 115–116; ownership in, 115; structural configuration of, 105

Holism, board, 21–22

Hospers, J., 9, 15

Hospice of North Iowa (HNI), 271–272

Hospital board, ends policies for, 293–297

House of Commons, 20

Hume, D., 6

Hungary, 638

I

Imai, M., 337

Income statements, 406

Indiana Association of Realtors (IAR), 272–273

Information, asking for, 172–176; avoiding micromanagement in asking for, 175

Informed worry, 630–632

Input: distinguishing between owner and consumer, 69–71; diversity, 83; gathering of, from ownership, 71–74, 83, 468–469; from nonowners, 71

Interest groups, *versus* general will, 7

Interpretation, 234–236; and any reasonable interpretation rule, 235, 303, 347–352; board role in limiting, 351; CEO, of executive limitations policies, 234–236

J

Job description, board: and CEO job description, 237–239; crafting of, 196–201; and defining achievement, 198–201; expression of, in outcomes, 388–389; and focus on outputs, 197; as perpetual agenda, 388

Joint venture companies, 614–624; corporate governance in, 611–612

Juran, J. M., 335, 618

K

Kaizen, 337

Kerr, N. D., 340–341

King Report (South Africa), 602–603

Kirk, W. A., 339

Koontz, H., 335, 618

KQED (San Francisco), 65

Kramer, R. M., 338

L

Larkin, R. F., 331, 335

Law, protection of governance from, 504–508

Leadership: corporate, 597; creating single voice as prerequisite for, 131; and piecemeal application of Policy Governance, 492–495; proactive nature of, 353–356; in public institutions, 559; voice of unity and, 133–134

Leary, P. H., 340–341, 566, 567, 569, 570

Lechem, B., 602, 602–603

Legislature: and focus on results, 571; and oversight of public education, 565–575; and roles of State Board of Education and Department of Education, 572; for Rousseau, 5

Legitimacy: initial base of, 55, 60; source of, 58, 63–64

Leighton, D.S.R., 4, 602, 604, 606–607, 618

Lewin, K., 41, 44

Lilly Endowment, 337

Linkage responsibility, 72–73

Listening, attentive, 100–101

Local governance, integrity of, 552–553

Logical containment principle, 17, 599–560

Lorsch, J. W., 335–336, 337, 338, 602, 610, 614, 618

Louden, J. K., 335, 618

Lutheran Social Services of Illinois (LSSI), 269

M

Mace, M., 602

Madonna, 96

Madsen, R., 339

Management: board accountability for, 400–401; as deductive, 156–157; focus on, in public management, 3; *versus* governance, 8, 156–159, 526–528

Market surrogate obligation: as difference between nonprofit and profit governance, 94–98; and market voice, 96

Marxism, 638

Mascotte, J. P., 338

McAdam, T. W., 340

McGowen, P., 539

Means. *See* Ends-means distinction; Staff means

Means, G. C., 612

Measurement: anxiety, 49; necessity for, 426; in Policy Governance, 424–427

Meddling, 404, 527, 562, 626

Medical staff bylaws, 489

Meetings: cost of, 391; energizing, 379–381; establishing quorum for, 382–386; school board, 537–539; and what-if sessions, 380, 471

Mega-ends, 256, 269–272, 276, 289–290. *See also* Ends; Ends policies

Mental laziness, 41

Metropolitan Indianapolis Board of Realtors (MIBOR), 65

Micromanagement: and executive limitations, 301–304; and fiscal condition policy, 311–315; and informed fiscal policy, 305–307

Middleton, M., 334–337

Mill, J. S., 6–8, 11, 12, 20

Miller, J., 539

Ministry: ends challenge in, 554–555; governance challenge in, 556–557; internal challenge of, 557–558

Minow, N., 611

Mission statement: checklist for, 270–271; evaluating, 268–273; integration of, 192; revitalization of, 264–267

Model, concept of, 44

Monitoring: and CEO evaluation, 469–470; as comparison, 405–407; and delegation, 405–407; direct inspection method of, 429–433; fiscal management, 413–418; frequency of, 50–51; and gathering performance data, 416–418; in Policy Governance, 405–407, 420; questions, 406; and understanding monitoring data, 417; and what constitutes monitoring information, 416. *See also* Performance, monitoring

Monks, R.A.G., 611

Moral ownership, 59

Mueller, R. K., 4, 603, 613

Murray, V., 35, 36

N

NAACP, 371–372

National Association for Community Leadership, 337

National Association of State Boards of Education, 566

National Ballet of Canada, 203, 205

National Council of Car Care Companies (NCCCC; hypothetical), 274–279

National Endowment for the Arts, 65

National Forum of Bulgarian Foundations, 634

National School Boards Association (NSBA), 105, 111, 541, 570

Natural hierarchy, 85. *See also* Hierarchy

Nelson, C. A., 334

Neu, C. H., Jr., 336

Neubauer, F., 618

Newton, I., 44, 45

Nonprofit boards: difference of, from elected boards, 90–91; market surrogate obligation of, 94–98; as model for corporate governance, 595–601

Nonprofit World, 121

No-staff organization: and policy governance, 227; three peculiarities of, 228–230

O

Odiorne, G. S., 339, 630

Officers, 482–483

Oliver, C., 17

Ontario, 548–549, 558

Ontario Ministry of Community and Social Services, 548

Opportunity cost, 96

Ordinances, 289

Organization for Economic Cooperation and Development (Europe), 602–603

Organizational objectives: illusion of, 232–233; and illusion of CEO personal objectives, 233. *See also* Ends

Organizational performance: decision pathway for, 236; and failure to create organizational policy, 403; relationship between governance and, 29–34

Outcome, intended: cost of, 255–259; reflection of, in mission statement, 270

Outputs: focus on, 197; and hands-on responsibilities, 373–375

Oversight Commission on Education Accountability (West Virginia Legislature), 565

Owner-representative role: and active listening, 100–101; as chief function of boards, 5–7; of federations, 108; primacy of, 532–533; and sound judgment, 102–103; and studious learning, 101–102

Owners: *versus* consumers, 61–65, 274; identification of, 58–59, 66–67; input of, 69–71; members as, in federations, 109; *versus* stakeholders, 59–61

Ownership: *versus* advisor role, 23; concept of, 55–56; connecting with, 68–75, 477; definition of, 5; determination of, 66–67; diversity of, 79–80; and governance effectiveness,

31–32; measures toward connecting with full, 71–74; of public enterprise, 5–7

P

P&R magazine, 560

Parent-subsidiary families, 114. *See also* Board families; Holding companies

Partnership: intention of, 548; for public service, 548–559

Pawns or Potentates (Lorsch), 614

Performance, monitoring, 21; and board self-evaluation, 435; and clear set of evaluative criteria, 403; *versus* consent agenda, 394–395; frequency of, 50–51

Performance objectives and perpetual agenda, 389

Perpetual agenda, 388–389. *See also* Agenda

Personal objectives, illusion of, 233

Personality-based power: and ends, 216–217; and executive limitations, 216

Personnel policies, 420, 487

Peters, T., 41

Philosophy, integration of, 193

Planned Parenthood Federation of America, 110

Plano, Texas: City Council, 206–207; city government of, 65

Plato, 9

Poland, 638

Policies: budget, 323–326; and bylaws, 479–480; and confusion of board and staff values, 162–163; four categories of, 160–161; philosophical values as central to, 161–162; and Policy Governance solution, 163

Policy Governance: after policies are in place, 467–471; and associations, 579–588; and British further education, 576–578; and Central European nongovernmental organizations (NGOs), 634–637; in Eastern Europe, 638–643; and hospitals, 589–594; and joint venture companies, 614–624; and nonprofits, 595–601; and non-staff board, 227–230; in park and recreation boards, 560–564; and public education, 540–547; and school boards, 531–537

Policy Governance model: and amount of authority delegated to CEO, 243–247, 427–428; and board approvals, 422; common reservations about, 500–503; and control, 427–428; and customizing distinctions for governance, 11–12; and distinguishing values of different sizes, 15–17; and failure to create organizational policy, 403; flexibility of, 368–370; and governing by values, 12–13; implications of, 17–23; and leadership in fiscal planning, 337–340; nine steps to implementing, 472–478; ownership *versus* management in, 9–10; philosophical basis for, 10–11; policy making in, 20; and values about organizational ends, 13–14; and values about organizational means, 14–15

Political science, as job of public board, 24

Press, 74

Price, J. L., 336

Products: determining board's, 373–375; results as, 97; worth of, 95–97

Programs, 270; targeting specific, 253–254; transparency of, 251–254

Proxy members, 482

Public: board connection to, 18; input, 18–19

Public education: legislative oversight of, 565–575; and staff autonomy, 573–574; theory *versus* data for, 566–567; toward coherent governance in, 540–547; weakest link in, 565–567

Public management: focus on management in, 3–4; leadership in, 559; and social contract philosophy, 4–9

Public school board, ends policies for, 281–287

Public service: economic context of, 549; emphasis on ends rather than means in, 551–552; ends challenge in, 554–555; governance challenge in, 556–557; governance criteria for, 556–557; internal challenge of, 557–558; and local latitude, 552–553; meaning of public organization, 4–5; partnership for, 548–559; philosophic dilemma in, 550

Q

Quality, 260–262

Quorums, 382–386, 481–482

R

Recruitment, 72, 470; and codification of desired characteristics, 168; and desired board member characteristics, 167–168; and job requirements, 165; obstacles to, 181–184

Reecer, M., 335

Reflection, 469

Relationships,: organizational chain of, 108

Renegade member, 142–145

Representational governance, 60, 77, 80–81

Research inquiries, 29–34

Results: as base for CEO job description, 237–239; and costing desired outcomes, 255–259; ignoring, 309; worth of, 95–97

Riesman, D., 337

Robins, A. J., 336

Roles, clarifying, 514–515

Rousseau, J. J., 4–8, 11, 13, 18, 19, 532

Royer, G., 17

Rubber stamping, 162–163. *See also* Consent agenda

S

Savage, T. J., 338

Schedule, 389

School Administrator, The, 540

School boards: and constituency expectations, 538; meetings, 537–539; new governance model for, 531–537; and role of education, 539

School superintendent: accountability to board *versus* public, 543–544; culpability of, 533; and define-and-demand control, 544–545; engagement of, with long-term future of education, 546–547; expectations of, under Policy Governance, 543–544; and responsibility for governance, 543; system-focused evaluation of, 536, 546, 574; as true CEO, 534, 545–546, 574

Select Seminar, 566, 568, 569

Self-affirmation, 40, 41

Self-evaluation, board: assigning responsibility for, 440–441; commitment to constant, 438–439; criteria for, 435–436; exploratory worksheet for, 442; frequency of, 436; guidelines for, 438–443; Policy Governance approach *versus* traditional approach to, 438; policy-driven method for, 441; and preestablished criteria, 439–440; and prefabricated forms, 440; redefining, 434–436

Servant-leadership: and chairperson, 187; and governance effectiveness, 34; heart of, 32; and owner-representative role of board, 6, 632

Service: providers, 553–554; and quality fetish, 260–262; transparency of, 251–254; as type of means, 270

Short-term thinking, 48–49

Single voice principle: and approving or accepting staff performance reports, 138–139; and approving staff plans, 137–138; and deciding issues below proper board level, 139–140; finding, 136–141; and leadership, 131–135; and plural trustees, 533–534; protecting from renegade member, 142–145; singleness of, from plural trustees, 533–534; and staff end runs, 227–228; and subjects board should officially speak on, 140–141; and trust, 446

Sloan, A. P., 148

Smith, E. E., 335

Social contract philosophy, 4–9, 10, 15, 532

Social services: economic context of, 549; and integrity of local governance, 552–553; and local determination, 550; and need

for emphasis on ends rather than means, 551–552

Sound judgment, 102–103

Sovereign, 4–5

Staff: complaints of, directed to board members, 224–227; and cost of staff time, 391; giving control to, 513–514; ministry relation to, as governance criteria, 557

Staff means, 50; and boundary setting, 303–304; bounded freedom for, 535; and organizational conduct, 302; policing of, 308–310; prescription of, 302–303; separation of, from ends, 13–15, 252–253, 270, 551–552

Stakeholders: concept of, 57; owners *versus*, 59–61, 79–80

Stanford University, 400–401

Strategic leadership, 556–557

Strategic plan, 488

Straussman, J. D., 330–331

Substitute members, 482

Sullivan, W. M., 339

Sumek, L. J., 336

Surveys, 73

Swidler, A., 339

T

Taylor, B. E., 338

Teamness, 158

Thain, D. H., 4, 602, 604, 606–607, 618

Third Sector governance, 634–637

Times Educational Supplement, 576

Tipton, S. M., 339

Tokenism, 77, 122

Toqueville, A. de, 339

Toronto, 203, 205

Toronto Stock Exchange, 602–603

Totality, expectation of, 383, 385

Trade association, board of, 274–280

Trust: in board-CEO relationship, 444–447; as ever-present issue, 444–445; moving toward, 445–447

Trusteeship, 56, 78, 82, 544, 556

Turnover, 48–49

U

United Kingdom, 42, 113

United States Cycling Federation (USCF), 198, 200, 201

United States Occupational Safety and Health Administration (OSHA), 630

United States Postal Service, 113

United Way of America (UWA), 330–331, 335, 371–372, 399–404

Unity: and CEO's role in support of board unity, 134; and creating single voice, 133–134; and leadership, 133; threats to, 131–132

Universality, in governance model, 42–46

University of Georgia, Athens, 29; Institute of Nonprofit Organizations, 29

University of Minnesota, 400–401

USCF. *See* United States Cycling Federation

V

Value-added, 271

Values: and board's role in budgeting, 414; clarification of, and reinventing government, 402; integration of, 194–195

Vision: as board's primary function, 263–264, 301; narrow, 49–50; statement of, 194

Volunteers: and meeting attendance, 386; proper role for, 361–367; and working *versus* governing, 524–525

W

Walker, J. M., 336, 337

Ward, R. D., 612

West Virginia, 565–575

West Virginia Legislature, 565, 566

West Virginia University College of Graduate Studies, 566

West York School Board (hypothetical), 282–287, 292

What-if sessions, 380, 471

Wholeness. *See* Conceptual wholeness

Wilson, E. O., 34, 45

Witt, J. A., 336

Wolfe, J., 5, 7, 19, 22–23

Wood, M., 334, 337–338

Worth, 95–97. *See also* Cost

Y

Yale University, 335; Program on Non-Profit Organizations, 335

YMCA, 357

YWCA, Vancouver, British Columbia (YWCAV), 273

Board Leadership

Policy Governance® in Action

John Carver, Executive Editor

Find out what it takes to exercise genuine leadership. Subscribe to *Board Leadership*, the only newsletter devoted to coaching boards in the implementation of John Carver's Policy Governance model.

Every other month, your board will receive a package of essential information personally selected by John Carver—presented in a concise 8-page format for busy board members—that will truly help them see how to make real change happen in the board room.

If your board has decided to adopt Carver's revolutionary approach to governance, *Board Leadership* is the essential resource you need. It can help you stay on course, move around road blocks, and achieve the full potential of Policy Governance in eliminating unsatisfying board and committee work, board interference in administration, staff manipulation of the board, unclear evaluation criteria, and role confusion. If your board has yet to decide whether Policy Governance is right for your organization, *Board Leadership* will let all board members sample for themselves how it works in practice and learn from the experiences of real boards who are using it day by day. Either way, *Board Leadership* represents a modest investment that will pay large rewards.

"Our board members are enthusiastic disciples of the Policy Governance model and use *Board Leadership* to deepen our understanding of its principles."
 —*Dorothy L. Mitstifer, Executive Director and CEO, Kappa Omicron Nu Honor Society*

"John Carver's conceptual approach to leadership and decision making allows board members and management alike to focus on mutually supportive but separate roles within the organization."
 —*James T. Lussier, Chief Executive Officer, St. Charles Medical Center, Bend, Oregon*

Published bimonthly

Individual subscriptions to *Board Leadership* are $105

Board subscriptions: (6 copies) are $139.50

(12 copies) are $210.00

(18 copies) are $279.00

ISSN 1061-4249
Please use promotion code BLBK when ordering a subscription.
Prices subject to change without notice.

FAX	CALL	MAIL	WEB
Toll Free	Toll Free	Jossey-Bass,	Secure ordering at
24 hours a day	6am to 5pm PST	A Wiley Company	www.josseybass.com
800-605-2665	888-378-2537	989 Market Street	
		San Francisco, CA	
		94103-1741	

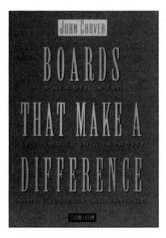

Boards That Make a Difference

A New Design for Leadership in Nonprofit and Public Organizations, Second Edition

John Carver

John Carver's groundbreaking Policy Governance model has influenced the way public and nonprofit boards operate around the world. Now, as widespread experience with the model accumulates, Carver enriches his definitive exposition with updated policy samples, a new chapter on the process of policy development, and additional resources for various types of boards. Carver debunks the entrenched beliefs about board roles and functions that hamper dedicated board members. With creative insight and commonsense practicality, he presents a bold new approach to board job design, board-staff relationships, the chief executive role, performance monitoring, and virtually every aspect of the board-management relationship. In their stead, he offers a board model designed to produce policies that make a difference, missions that are clearly articulated, standards that are ethical and prudent, meetings, officers, and committees that work, and leadership that supports the fulfillment of long-term goals.

"This book should be in the library of everyone who serves—or aspires to serve—on the governing board of any organization, large or small, nonprofit or corporate. Better than any other available resource, it tells what the roles of board members are and what they must and shouldn't do. An indispensable guidebook to leadership excellence."
  —*George Weber, secretary general, International Federation of Red Cross and Red Crescent Societies, Geneva*

 "John Carver's book is important reading for chief executives and directors alike. This book's sound premises regarding proper role delineation and its practical advice about how to affect due diligence combine to provide an invaluable resource to any board dedicated to efficiency and high-quality performance."
  —*John R. Seffrin, CEO, American Cancer Society*

| Hardcover | 272 pages | ISBN 0-7879-0811-8 | $32.00 |

Price subject to change without notice.

FAX	CALL	MAIL	WEB
Toll Free	Toll Free	Jossey-Bass,	Secure ordering at
24 hours a day	6am to 5pm PST	A Wiley Company	www.josseybass.com
800-605-2665	888-378-2537	989 Market Street	
		San Francisco, CA	
		94103-1741	

Reinventing Your Board

A Step-by-Step Guide to Implementing Policy Governance

John Carver and Miriam Mayhew Carver

*J*ohn Carver's revolutionary Policy Governance Model, introduced in his best-selling book, *Boards That Make a Difference,* is recognized as a highly effective, results-oriented approach to nonprofit board governance. With *Reinventing Your Board,* John Carver and Miriam Mayhew Carver show how to put the model in motion and take organizations to new levels of achievement.

This hands-on, step-by-step guide serves as a practical manual for implementing the Policy Governance model and provides guidelines for staying on track. The authors illustrate effective board decision making, show how to craft useful policies, and offer practical advice on such matters as setting the agenda, monitoring CEO performance, defining the board role, and more. Step-by-step instructions, sample policies, illustrations, exercises, and other practical materials make this a valuable resource for boards wanting to improve the performance of organizations in the public and nonprofit sectors through effective board leadership.

"After reading *Boards That Make a Difference* and studying the theory behind John Carver's approach to improving the functioning of boards and their linkage with the chief executive officer, this book is a natural next stage for a board committed to improving its capacity. *Reinventing Your Board* is a must."
  —*Mike Whitlam, director general, British Red Cross Society*

"This 'how-to' navigational tool will help boards get policy governance right the first time. It is a must for anyone looking to make their board effective into the next century."
  —*Susan Elliot, president, The Law Society of Upper Canada*

| Hardcover | 256 pages | ISBN 0–7879–0911–4 | $32.00 |

Price subject to change without notice.

FAX	CALL	MAIL	WEB
Toll Free	Toll Free	Jossey-Bass,	Secure ordering at
24 hours a day	6am to 5pm PST	A Wiley Company	www.josseybass.com
800-605-2665	888-378-2537	989 Market Street	
		San Francisco, CA	
		94103-1741	

The Policy Governance Fieldbook

Practical Lessons, Tips, and Tools from the Experiences of Real-World Boards

Caroline Oliver, General Editor

With Mike Conduff, Susan Edsall, Carol Gabanna, Randee Loucks, Denise Paszkiewicz, Catherine Raso, and Linda Stier

This practical, unflinching resource closely examines eleven diverse organizations that have implemented Policy Governance. Each chapter is built around a hands-on framework—first introducing a specific Policy Governance activity, exploring the experiences of boards that met this challenge, and then drawing key lessons from those experiences. Filled with tips and tools, *The Policy Governance Fieldbook* is an ideal guide for boards ready to lead their organizations to success.

"Local elected officials and professional staff will find Carver's model provocative and intriguing. This practical guide is one of the best I have encountered. The useful tips at the end of each chapter are worth the price of the book."
—*John Nalbandian, professor of public administration, University of Kansas*

"*The Policy Governance Fieldbook* is not a theoretical treatise, but a practical study. Its authors are concerned with real people in real organizations with real challenges. . . .It is the first book to start down what is surely to be a very long road. For that boldness, I am in its authors' debt. But more importantly, boards everywhere and those who rely on the integrity of governance—that means all of us—are in their debt as well."
—*from the Foreword by John Carver*

CAROLINE OLIVER, the general editor, is a founding partner of The Leadership Team, a Canadian organization that focuses on board leadership issues. She has consulted with organizations in Canada and the United States, and has served on national and European government committees.

Paper	272 pages	ISBN 0-7879-4366-5	$32.00

Price subject to change without notice.

FAX	CALL	MAIL	WEB
Toll Free	Toll Free	Jossey-Bass,	Secure ordering at
24 hours a day	6am to 5pm PST	A Wiley Company	www.josseybass.com
800-605-2665	888-378-2537	989 Market Street	
		San Francisco, CA	
		94103-1741	